DATE DUE

DE2 0 00			
MY 22 06			

DEMCO 38-296

GREATNESS
Who Makes History and Why

GREATNESS
WHO MAKES HISTORY AND WHY

DEAN KEITH SIMONTON
University of California at Davis

THE GUILFORD PRESS
New York   London

© 1994 The Guilford Press
A Division of Guilford Publications, Inc.
72 Spring Street, New York, NY 10012

Printed in the United States of America

This book is printed on acid-free paper.

Last digit is print number: 9   8   7   6   5   4   3   2

Library of Congress Cataloging-in-Publication Data

Simonton, Dean Keith.
    Greatness: who makes history and why / Dean Keith Simonton.
        p.   cm.
    Includes bibliographical references and index.
    ISBN 0-89862-370-7 — ISBN 0-89862-201-8 (pbk.)
    1. Genius—History.   2. Genius—Philosophy.   3. History—
Philosophy.   4. History—Psychological aspects.   I. Title.
    BF412.S56 1994
    153.9'8—dc20   93-48127
                                                                   CIP

Per festeggiare il sovvenire
di un grand Uomo *

*°"To celebrate the memory of a great man"—If I may borrow Beethoven's dedication to his *Sinfonia Eroica* (1804). The "great man" referred to was Napoleon, but could here point to all men and women who have attained greatness, including Beethoven himself.

PREFACE

I have aimed this book at two audiences. First, I have tried to write a book
that would appeal to my fellow psychologists. In this group I would place
not only teachers and professors of psychology, but also students who are
entering the field. For these present and future psychologists, I have reviewed
what we have so far learned in a unique subdiscipline of the behavioral sciences.
Indeed, through this scholarly synthesis, I hope to define the nature of a field
that I call the "psychology of history." To this end, I have provided the complete documentation for all reported findings. Those wishing to pursue a particular remark can turn to the notes and references at the book's close. From
there they can go directly to the primary sources.

Yet I have also tried to produce a volume accessible to a wide readership.
This would include anyone who wants to know something about the psychology of greatness. Besides the ubiquitous educated layperson, potential readers
might include journalists and broadcasters, politicians and soldiers, entrepreneurs and reformers, scientists and artists, athletes and celebrities. With this
audience in mind, I have avoided the reference format favored in scientific
journals. The public usually finds this scholastic apparatus distracting, cumber-
some, and even superfluous. Moreover, I have kept the technical details to the
absolute minimum. When technical concepts must be introduced, I have made
every effort to make them intelligible to the general reader. Finally, I have
sought an informal writing style that shuns the pedantic and convoluted.

Thus, I have tried to create a volume that is both erudite and readable.
This double goal reflects my belief that the subject matter should have immense
intrinsic interest to many people, both within and outside of psychology. For
readers to enjoy this book, they must fulfill only one requirement: They must
be curious about how psychology can help us understand the important personalities and big events that have helped shape the past and present.

Some acknowledgments are in order. My wife, Melody, and my stepdaugh-
ter, Mandy, helped me find examples of celebrities to illustrate certain points.
A few students did some useful research as well. In particular, I thank Molly
Cash, Gonzalo Calderón, Heather Davids, Lisa Lawrance, Apollo Madayag, José
Ortega, and Thomas Sanchez. Beyond this assistance, this book has been the

usual product of many solitary hours. But the hours were not lonely: Besides constantly dipping into the minds that grace histories and almanacs, I have taken much sustenance from the downstairs voices. Even when my family gave up on me and escaped to less boring locales, the household pets were always here to comfort me. I thank our obnoxious cat, T. G.; our vociferous parakeets, Sushi and Tiki; the laid-back Algae Buster (who outlived many of his fishy companions); and, as I entered the final stretch, our jovial bunny, Buff.

DEAN KEITH SIMONTON

CONTENTS

PROLOGUE: THE PSYCHOLOGIST CONFRONTS GREATNESS

What does it take to go down in history as a great president or prime minister? Why do revolutions occur, riots break out, or lynch mobs assemble? What decides military success on the battlefield? What affects the success of entrepreneurs or the prosperity of nations? Why do actors make so much more money than actresses do? Will a computer ever become the chess champion of the world? Can we predict which baseball team will win the World Series? At what age do scientists make the discovery that earns them a Nobel Prize? What accomplishments can we expect from persons entering their "golden years"? Are illustrious artists invariably insane or notable authors always alcoholics? Can computers distinguish highly acclaimed masterpieces from mediocre works? How high must your IQ be for you to attain worldwide recognition in your chosen profession? Are celebrities born great, or must they achieve greatness? If the latter is true, are there any shortcuts to fame? Do child prodigies grow up to become renowned geniuses? Why are so few women inscribed in the annals of history? What is the impact of race and racism on the flow of human affairs? Are first-born children more likely than later-born children to make a name for themselves? What are the pros of being orphaned early in life? Should high school valedictorians be routinely voted the most likely to succeed? Are prominent politicians driven by a hunger for power? Is high moral caliber helpful or detrimental to winning fame and fortune? Why are some happenings or people so memorable? Do some current events goad us to commit murder, or succumb to suicide? How are our perceptions of historic occasions or personalities clouded by our personal values or failings?

These are just an armful of the many questions I address in the following chapters. In building an inventory of replies, I will, in effect, define a distinct subdiscipline: the "psychology of history." In this chapter, I first outline the features of psychology and history separately; I then delineate the aims and methods of a genuine psychology of history.

What Is Psychology?

When psychology first emerged as a discipline over a hundred years ago, its definition was faithful to its etymology. The word came from two Greek words: *psyche* for "mind," and *logos* for "discourse." Psychology was the study of the mind, plain and simple. Thus, William James could open his classic 1890 textbook by describing the field as "the science of mental life, both of its phenomena and of their conditions. The phenomena are such things as we call feelings, desires, cognitions, reasonings, decisions, and the like." With behaviorism's arrival in America, this notion yielded to the concept of psychology as the scientific analysis of behavior. In the heyday of the behaviorist school, especially as propagated by B. F. Skinner, the discipline strove to erase consciousness from its subject matter. Nevertheless, with the coming of cognitive science, psychology has returned to its roots. The sole proviso in this resurrection is that many psychologists find overt behavior worth investigating as well. Hence, most psychologists today would feel comfortable describing psychology as both a mental and behavioral science.

I must emphasize the term "science." Philosophers ever since the days of Confucius, Buddha, and Socrates have often contemplated psychological questions. These perennial issues include the attributes of human nature, the motives that underlie human action, the sources of human happiness, and the similarities and differences between human and beast. What distinguishes psychology from these philosophical discussions is the conviction that the scientific method can help resolve certain debates. Science involves the collection of data to test hypotheses, along with the construction of theories or models that are logical, precise, and comprehensive. As in many natural sciences, psychologists most often conduct laboratory experiments in the quest to expand the discipline's base of scientific knowledge. However, psychologists also study mental and behavioral phenomena in the real world. They search newspapers, census data, survey results, and historical archives for useful information. It is precisely these "correlational" inquiries that are most likely to promote the psychology of history.

Of course, sociologists, political scientists, and anthropologists also study human activities, and usually do so scientifically. Yet, most often, their focus differs from that of psychologists. Sociologists concentrate on societies, political scientists on government institutions, and anthropologists on cultures. Yet psychologists remain obsessed with individuals. Even so, we should acknowledge that researchers in these and other disciplines may sometimes favor the same emphasis as psychologists. Accordingly, we must always remain receptive to contributions from outside psychology proper. For example, the field of "political psychology" enlists the efforts of both political scientists and psychologists, as well as psychiatrists and historians. Likewise, some of the most provocative work in cognitive science comes from the hands of computer scientists rather than certified psychologists. Hence, in the following pages, I by no means use a Ph.D. in psychology as the touchstone for citation. The psychology of history is inherently interdisciplinary.

What Is History?

"History is more or less bunk," Henry Ford once said. This comment may evoke an involuntary nod from readers who remember boring lectures and homework in mandatory high school history classes. The subject too often reminds us of having to memorize countless names, dates, and places. Who was Crispus Attucks? Why do the French celebrate Bastille Day on July 14? What was the big deal at Marathon? Committing a bunch of such minutiae to rote memory is not the best way of inspiring enthusiasm for a subject. What possible utility do such facts have except winning a game of Trivial Pursuit?

Yet, as Abraham Lincoln once said, "We cannot escape history." One reason is plain: Only the most puny passage of time separates what counts as a current event or contemporary celebrity from a historical name, date, and place. "The newspaper is the second hand in the clock of history," noted Schopenhauer. As soon as an occasion or person appears in a newspaper or magazine, the "right now" is converted irrevocably to a "back then." This truth is manifest to anyone thumbing through the dated news weeklies that commonly decorate the waiting rooms of doctors' offices. Hence, modern history can be nothing more than our own personal memory supplemented by printed records.

Yet we cannot avoid even more remote history. We live inescapably in a world shaped by the ambitions, decisions, and creations of individuals who died centuries ago. At this very moment you are reading a book printed on paper, most likely by the light cast by an incandescent bulb as it consumes alternating current. These activities alone presuppose the contributions of Cai Lun, Gutenberg, Volta, Ohm, Faraday, Westinghouse, Edison, Tesla, Steinmetz, Coolidge, and a myriad other lesser lights of the past.

For a good lesson on our debts to long-dead personalities, we can read the book *The 100: A Ranking of the Most Influential Persons in History*. Even if we may quibble with the rankings and the choices, there can be no doubt about those individuals who made the final cut. All diverted the course of history, even as events have meandered down to our own day. Ranked are the names of military figures (Genghis Khan and Napoleon), revolutionaries (Jefferson and Mao Zedong), politicians (Aśoka and Hitler), religious leaders (St. Paul and Muḥammad), scientists (Newton and Darwin), philosophers (Confucius and Karl Marx), writers (Homer and Voltaire), artists (Michelangelo and Picasso), and composers (Bach and Beethoven). Although it is not immediately obvious, the world we live in today bears the indelible stamp of the actions and thoughts of these figures who are now long dead. This impact is implicit in the national boundaries we defend, the laws we live by, the religious beliefs we practice, the languages we use, and the recreations we seek. This lasting influence even holds for names that are obscure to the average person on the street. It was Cai Lun, a Chinese eunuch, who invented paper nearly two millennia ago. It was Gregory Pincus who devised the oral contraceptive ("the Pill") held accountable for the sexual revolution.

Naturally, it is far easier to discern why we must acknowledge the contributions of religious, political, and technological innovators than it is to understand why we owe any debt to the artistic types on such lists. The workings of such creators can be far more surreptitious, but no less consequential. For instance, the ratings above included William Shakespeare, who was ranked, for what it's worth, 36th. Why even that high? For a partial answer, take a peek at another enjoyable book, *Brush Up Your Shakespeare!* Here we have a quick demonstration of how easy it is for a speaker of the English language to quote the Bard: "All the world's a stage," "caviar to the general," "the dogs of war," "eaten me out of house and home," "household words," "a lean and hungry look," "the milk of human kindness," "one fell swoop," "the primrose path," "strange bedfellows," and "wild-goose chase," to offer a handful of phrases. So common are these expressions that most grammar checkers in word-processing software will tag many of these quotes as cliches.

Better yet, imagine speaking or writing without using such words as "assassination," "birthplace," "critical," "droplet," "equivocal," "fashionable," "go-between," "hostile," "invitation," "lament," "majestic," "ode," "pious," "quarrelsome," "retirement," "shooting star," "transcendence," "useless," "vulnerable," "watchdog," and "zany." Yet this is a mere smattering of the hundreds of common words first coined by this long-dead poet. Nor is it only English that shows this imprint of Shakespeare's literary genius. Translated into every major language of the world, his metaphors and images have become the common stock of the human race as well. His contemporary Ben Jonson claimed that Shakespeare "was not of an age, but for all time." Indeed, "Three hundred years have passed 'twixt then and now," said the modern Chinese poet Liu Bo-duan in his "Ode to Shakespeare," "Yet all the world looks to that mountain's brow!"

Shakespeare's example suggests that history often sneaks itself into our present by enriching our language. An obvious path by which this infusion takes place is the conversion of a person's proper name into a place name, a term, or an expression. Because such eponyms often lose the capitalization of proper nouns, we frequently overlook how much of our vocabulary pays homage to notables born ages ago. Instances of eponyms in English alone number in the thousands, and so a complete inventory is impossible here. Table 1.1 does provide a sampling, however. Those that refer to geographical locations are perhaps the most straightforward. Others concern technical subjects, and accordingly may only be known to specialists. Scientists are particularly fond of naming laws, techniques, laboratory apparatus, units of measurement, plants, elements,

TABLE 1.1. Eponyms: Some Names That Have Become Words

algorithm; America; Amish; ampere (amp); Archimedean screw; Aristotelian; August; Baltimore, Maryland; beef Stroganoff; Bessemer converter; John Bircher; bloomers; bogus; Bolivia; bowdlerize; Bowie knife; boycott; braille; Bright's disease; Buddhism; Browning rifle; Bunsen burner; Byronic; Caesarean section; Calvinist; cardigan; Casanova; degrees Celsius; chauvinist; Chippendale furniture; Chisholm Trail; Colt; Colombia, Columbus; Confucian; Copernican revolution; curie, curium, Curie point; Cyrillic script; czar; daguerreotype; Darwinian; Davis Cup; decibel; derby; derringer; Dewey Decimal System; diesel engine; Doberman pinscher; Donner Pass; Doppler effect; doubting Thomas; Draconian; dunce; Eiffel Tower; Eisenhower jacket; Elizabethan Age; Erlenmeyer flask; Euclidian geometry; Eustachian tube; degrees Fahrenheit; Fallopian tube; Fechner's law; Fourier analysis; Franklin stove; Freudian slip; Galilean telescope; galvanic, galvanize; Gatling gun; Gaussian curve; Geiger counter; Geronimo!; gerrymander; gimlet; graham crackers; Gregorian chant, Gregorian calendar; guillotine; guy; Halley's comet; Hillel Foundation; Hindenberg line; Hippocratic oath; Hodgkin's disease; according to Hoyle; jackknife; Jacksonian democracy; John Hancock; Julian calendar, July; kaiser; degrees Kelvin; Keynesian economics; lawrencium; Leningrad, Leninism; leotards; lesbian; Levis; Lincoln, Nebraska; Linnaean system; Listerine; loganberry; Louisiana; Lutheran; lynch; macabre; macadam; Mach number; Machiavellianism; Macintosh apple; mackintosh; magnolia; mansard roof; Maoism; Marshall Plan; martinet; Marxism; masochism; Mason–Dixon Line; mason jar; mausoleum; maverick; melba toast; Mendelian; Mercator's projection; mesmerize; Möbius strip; Moho discontinuity; Molotov cocktail; Monroe Doctrine and Monrovia, Liberia; Montessori system; Moog synthesizer; Morse code; Nehru jacket; Newtonian mechanics; nicotine; Nobel Prize, nobelium; Occam's razor; Ohm's law, ohm; ottoman; pamphlet; Pap test; pasteurize; Pavlovian; Pennsylvania; Peronist; Petri dish; philippic; Philippines; Pike's Peak; Platonic love, Platonism; poinsettia; pompadour; Ptolomaic system; Pulitzer Prize; Pyrrhic victory; Pythagorean theorem; Queensberry rules; quisling; Remington rifle; ritzy; Robert's rules of order; Rorschach test; Rube Goldberg; sadism; Salisbury steak; Salk vaccine; salmonella; sandwich; saxophone; Seattle; sequoia; Shakespearean sonnet; sherry; shrapnel; sideburns; silhouette; Skinner box; Smithsonian Institution; Socratic irony, method; Sorbonne; sousaphone; spinet; Stalinism; Stetson hat; Stradivarius; tabby cat; tawdry; teddy bear; thespian; Tiffany; tommygun; Tony Award; Trotskyism; valentine; Vancouver; Victorian; Virginia; volts, voltage; Wagnerian; Washington (city and state); Wasserman test; watt, wattage, kilowatts; Weber's law; Wedgwood; Winchester rifle; wisteria; Yale lock; zeppelin; Zoroastrian.

and other discoveries or inventions after their originators. Whatever the details of source or purpose, these eponyms and thousands more document how inextricably history has implanted itself in modern life.

Let me not be misconstrued. I am not arguing that history is nothing more than a chronicle of decisive events and influential personalities. It comprises much, much more. There are mass movements, economic trends, demographic shifts, and many other temporal changes. These transformations clearly provide the substrate of human civilization. The main point is that history is not merely of historical interest. History is a record of the process by which men and women became what they are in today's world.

What Is a Psychology of History?

We can now put together the two pieces of the puzzle. The discipline presented in this book entails the application of psychological science to historic phenomena. These phenomena define the milestones in the development of politics, culture, society, economics, and entertainment. There are no restrictions on the domain, so long as the happenings and personalities are of historic significance. Significant events and people are those that later generations think worthy of entering the permanent record of human acts. This repository of the past may consist of encyclopedias, biographical dictionaries, almanacs, record books, lists of international prizes and awards, chronologies of celebrated events, anthologies of classic compositions, museum catalogs, plaques in halls of fame, stars along Hollywood Boulevard, and so on *ad infinitum*. Furthermore, this record has no geographical boundaries; the psychology of history embraces all peoples who have produced an enduring trace of their achievements.

Whatever the nature or contents of the archival record, the psychology of history is at bottom a psychological rather than a historical enterprise. Psychologists who dip into this activity are not infatuated with the secrets and niceties of history. Instead, history merely provides a collection of information that permits the psychologist to examine certain hypothesized principles of human cognition, emotion, and conduct. Hence, a luminary of the past enjoys a status by no means superior to that of the more commonplace subjects in experimental and correlational studies. This emphasis separates the psychology of history from another discipline known as "psychohistory." Most psychohistorians are enthralled by history. Their goal is to explicate the inner workings of some important incident or influential person. Reflecting this divergence of purpose, psychohistory is now more popular among historians than among psychologists.

The contrast between the psychology of history and psychohistory can be seen in their divergent methods. In the main, the psychohistorian adapts procedures of the clinical interview to historical materials. Sometimes this adaptation is rather direct, as when Freud applied dream analysis to an episode in the life of Leonardo da Vinci. At other times the application of clinical methods entails rather more precarious extrapolations. In contrast, the psychology of history employs a collection of techniques that stress scientific rigor. Four methods stand out:

1. Some researchers recruit illustrious figures of their day to participate in psychological *assessment*. For example, Anne Roe traveled around the country to interview 64 scientists. These subjects were already acclaimed by their contemporaries as having made lasting contributions to science. Now and then we can make this process more convenient by having the mountain come to Muḥammad, so to speak; this has happened often at the Institute for Personality Assessment and Research at the Berkeley campus of the University of California. Here famous architects, writers, and mathematicians have spent long weekends in extensive examination. Whatever the logistics, these current celebrities become the objects of a wide array of assessment approaches. They are bombarded by everything from unstructured interviews to standard tests of intelligence, motivation, values, and attitudes.

    2. Whereas the preceding approach concentrates on the agents of history, *survey* methods examine the victims or beneficiaries of historic events. For instance, in Chapter 12 I scrutinize how a president's popularity with the American people varies according to specific events. How the populace rates the incumbent's performance then affects how well he can impose his vision on the course of political events.

    3. A bit more remote from the real world is the experimental *simulation*. There are two main types of simulations. One is the laboratory experiment designed to duplicate a process operating in history. Thus, changes in literary styles that normally took place over generations have been successfully simulated in the laboratory over far less time. The other type is the computer simulation in which a software program replicates events of historic merit. In Chapter 4, I review the "discovery programs" that may some day make history by generating a product worthy of a Nobel Prize.

    4. Perhaps the most direct route to the psychology of history is to draw upon the *archive*. Historical records contain a diversity of raw information that psychologists may use for their own scientific purposes. There are secondary sources, such as encyclopedias, dictionaries, histories, and biographies, and chronologies. And there are many primary sources, such as autobiographies, letters, diaries, novels, poems, paintings, musical scores, monuments, ceramics, sketch books, magazines, newspapers, and various other artifacts of civilization. Appropriately enough, of all techniques used in the psychology of history, archival methods are by far the oldest. Back in 1835, Adolphe Quetelet first applied this strategy to the study of the relation between personal age and creative achievement. In 1869, Francis Galton took this approach when he investigated the inheritance of genius.

    These four lines of attack—assessment, survey, simulation, and archive—are critical to any psychology of history. We have learned so much from these methods that it would be easy to write a big book on the central results. In fact, I have had to impose a restriction on the present book's contents.

    Many psychologists have conducted inquiries that are inspired by history and clearly applicable to history, and yet that do not directly *use* history. A case is Stanley Milgram's laboratory experiments on obedience. Milgram's inquiry was motivated in part by the stark historical truth that Hitler found it too easy to find officers willing to commit horrible atrocities, not excluding systematic genocide. Yet Milgram got laboratory results suggesting that Adolf Eichmann and other Nazis of his stripe were not the moral monsters we might imagine them to be. Moreover, Milgram's thought-provoking findings provided ready ammunition for interpreting later acts of cruelty. For instance, his results have contributed to understanding the massacre of innocent Vietnamese by Lieutenant Calley and his troops at My Lai. Even so, none of these noteworthy implications can undo this rudimentary fact: Historical materials are missing from Milgram's actual experiment. Therefore, in the following pages I discuss neither Milgram's classic experiments nor any other psychological investigations failing to satisfy the same criterion. At most, such inquiries can provide the context for describing studies more intimately tied to landmark events and persons.

Despite this Draconian truncation of the subject matter, I think most readers will be astounded by the diversity of the landscape we shall tour in this book. We will scrutinize events as disparate as battles, revolutions, elections, rumors, scientific discoveries, literary masterpieces, swan songs, sports championships, and celebrity suicides. And we will examine personalities as varied as presidents, religious leaders, philosophers, entrepreneurs, chess grand masters, child prodigies, and stars of the silver screen. Permeating all this diversity is a secure source of coherence: We will consistently focus on the role of the individual human being in major historic events, whether as an agent or as a recipient. Indeed, without the psychological processes discussed throughout this book, history now would no longer be made.

CHAPTER 2

BIRTHRIGHTS AND BIRTHMARKS: PSYCHOBIOLOGICAL EXPLANATIONS

Psychology's roots were biological. Pioneers such as Hermann von Helmholtz, Jean-Martin Charcot, Wilhelm Wundt, William James, and Sigmund Freud all had medical degrees. Moreover, whenever a notable outside the discipline earned acclamation as a psychologist, that person usually hailed from the biological sciences. Ivan Pavlov was a physiologist, Konrad Lorenz a zoologist, and Jean Piaget a biologist. Psychology's willingness to appropriate these figures may reveal some defensiveness about its status as a natural science. Alfred Nobel's testament did not list psychology among the categories for receiving his annual prize. So when Pavlov received a Nobel medal in 1904 and Lorenz shared one in 1973, psychology enhanced its prestige by making these laureates honorary psychologists.

Nevertheless, psychology's standing as a biological science may not be an asset in the psychology of history. The gap between organism and historic affairs may simply be too vast. Even so, on certain points psychobiological explanations do touch upon the realm of fame and infamy. In this chapter I weigh the impact of genetics, psychoneurology, gender and race, and evolution. I conclude by discussing the prospects for a "psychobiological psychobiography."

Genes and Genius

There is no doubt that genetic influences participate in the making of history. The excessive inbreeding of the royal Habsburg line supposedly produced not just the famed lower lip, but a good many infertile and dull monarchs besides. We may even consider a genetic disorder the distal cause of the Russian Revolution: Had not the imperial heir inherited hemophilia, the royal family would not have needed the services of the notorious Rasputin, who helped discredit the Romanov line. Naturally, genes may bring good tidings as well. British poet John Dryden praised his protégé William Congreve with these lines: "Time, place, and action may with pains be wrought,/But genius must be born, and never can be taught." This idea that genius may be in one's genes is among the oldest and most widespread notions in the world. But is there any truth to this concept?

Galton's Eugenics

Francis Galton was one of the most versatile men who ever lived. After first making his mark as an African explorer, Galton invented the dog whistle, devised the fingerprinting methods used by Scotland Yard to identify criminals, developed the basic principles of weather forecasting, introduced such statistics as correlation and regression, conducted one of the earliest surveys, and created some of the first psychological tests—to cite just a few contributions. In addition, Galton published the first systematic examination of distinguished people in 1869: *Hereditary Genius*, in fact, is a landmark book in both the history of psychology and the psychology of history.

Galton wanted to present a three-part thesis. First, people vary tremendously in what he called "natural ability." At the low end we see the ill-fated moron, and at the high end the undoubted genius. The highest-grade geniuses have intellects equaled by maybe one out of several thousand people. Second, this immense variation in natural ability is inherited biologically: Like parent, like child, on down through the generations. Third, those persons endowed with superior levels of natural ability will almost invariably make names for themselves. In other words, genius-caliber ability enables a person to attain an enduring reputation. This Galton defined as "the opinion of contemporaries, revised by posterity . . . the reputation of a leader of opinion, of an originator, of a man to whom the world deliberately acknowledges itself largely indebted." Now if we grant Galton these three suppositions, an important deduction follows: Renown should run in family lines. By inheriting exceptional natural ability from an illustrious parent, a child should get a head start in the quest for fame and glory.

To prove this thesis, Galton collected data showing how genius clusters into distinguished families. Indeed, his chapter headings read like a list of the ways one can attain a durable reputation: "Statesmen," "Judges," "Commanders," "Divines," "Men of Science," "Literary Men," "Poets," "Musicians," and "Painters." He even threw in a few odds and ends, such as "English Peerages," "Senior Classics of Cambridge," "Oarsmen," and "Wrestlers of the North Country"! Galton filled each chapter with alphabetical listings of family lineages whose members graced the world with notable achievements. For example, Table 2.1 presents just a handful of the family lines that have staked out a claim to scientific eminence. Here I have brought Galton's original table up to date; Galton did not list himself as a member of the distinguished Darwin family. His modesty only allowed him to say that he "could add the names of others of the family who, in a lesser but yet decided degree, have shown a taste for sub-

TABLE 2.1. Some Notable Family Lines in Science, According to
Francis Galton

Bernoulli: Jakob (Jacques) B. I (1654–1705), mathematician; Johann (Jean) B. I
(1667–1748), mathematician; Nikolaus B. I (1687–1759), mathematician; Nikolaus
B. II (1695–1726), mathematician; Daniel B. (1700–1782), mathematician; Johann
(Jean) B. II (1710–1770), mathematician; Johann (Jean) B. III (1744–1807),
mathematician and astronomer; Jakob (Jacques) B. II (1759–1789), mathematician.

Cassini: Giovanni Domenico C. (1625–1712), astronomer; Jacques C. (1677–1756),
astronomer; César-François C. de Thury (1714–1784), astronomer and geographer;
Jean–Dominique de C. (1748–1845), mathematician and geographer; Alexandre
Henri Gabriel C. (1784–1832), botanist.

Darwin: Erasmus D. (1731–1802), naturalist; Charles D. (1809–1882), naturalist,
geologist; Francis D. (1848–1925), botanist; George Howard D. (1845–1912),
mathematician and astronomer; Charles Galton D. (1887–1962), mathematician
and physicist. Additional blood relations: Josiah Wedgwood (1730–1795), chemist
and ceramic technologist; Thomas Wedgwood (1771–1805), physicist and inventor;
Francis Galton (1822–1911), statistician, psychologist, and anthropologist.

Herschel: William H. (1738–1822), astronomer; Caroline Lucretia H. (1750–1848),
astronomer; John Frederick William H. (1792–1871), astronomer, physicist, and
chemist.

Jussieu: Antoine de J. (1686–1758), botanist and paleontologist; Bernard de J.
(1699–1777), botanist; Joseph de J. (1704–1779), naturalist; Antoine-Laurent de J.
(1748–1836), botanist; Adrien Henri Laurent de J. (1797–1853), botanist.

---

jects of natural history." Galton was a second cousin of Charles Darwin, and
both were descended from Erasmus Darwin.

For those family pedigrees that were especially extensive and rich, Galton
would often present the lineages in the form of the family tree. Figure 2.1 shows
one surely remarkable lineage, that of the Bach family. Galton observed: "There
are far more than twenty *eminent* musicians among the Bachs; the biographical collections of musicians give the lives of no less than fifty-seven of them."
For a while in some parts of Germany, the name became virtually synonymous
with "musician." To be sure, the supply of distinguished *composers* in the family line is smaller; few of their compositions are heard today. Even so, we still
hear the works of Karl Philipp Emmanuel, Johann Christian, and Wilhelm
Friedemann on concerts and radio programs. And we cannot overlook the greatest Bach of them all, Johann Sebastian.

Because Galton had a penchant for mathematical calculations, he did more
than just present lists and trees. He performed detailed estimates of the odds
of eminent people's having eminent relatives, considering the closeness of biological relationship and the magnitude of achievement. Thus, Galton claimed
that the more famous a person, and hence the higher the presumed amount of
natural ability, the higher the likelihood that the person had illustrious rela-

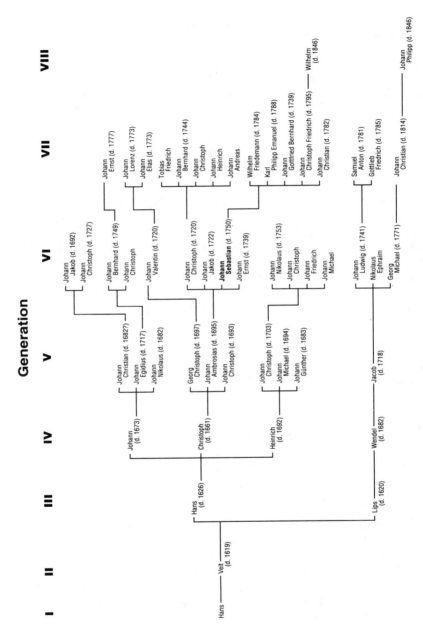

FIGURE 2.1. The Bach family tree of musicians.

12

tives in the family line. Furthermore, the closer the blood connection, the bigger the odds that family greatness would continue. For example, 26% of the famous judges had famous fathers, but the odds declined to 7.5% for grandfathers and 0.5% for great-grandfathers. Yet the most important calculation is this: The likelihood of genius appearing randomly in family pedigrees is so infinitesimal that these familial clusters cannot be credited to mere chance. A person who comes from a notable lineage enjoys a ponderable edge over those of the same generation whose ancestors were nonentities.

Given Galton's prior activities in practical affairs, he quickly contrived social policies from his theory. He argued eloquently for the need to practice "eugenics." In other words, men and women owning the best genetic endowment have the responsibility to their nation to pass their "good genes" down to the next generation. Galton was, in fact, the primary father of the eugenics movement. In the early part of this century, he established the Eugenics Laboratory at University College, London, and helped found the Eugenics Education Society, which published the journal *Eugenics Review*. Ironically, Galton did not practice what he preached: He fathered no children!

A Sequel?

Later psychological research complemented, even extended, Galton's *Hereditary Genius*. A 1948 article in *Eugenics Review* continued Galton's 1869 family trees for three further generations. For judges in particular, the advantage of birth in eminent pedigrees of jurisprudence was unmistakable. The wisdom of choosing one's parents carefully was also evident (although often not so pronounced) for statesmen, commanders, scientists, and classical scholars. This follow-up even explored domains of achievement not specifically treated by Galton, and identified new family lines of distinction in areas he had treated. For example, such novelists as Robert Louis Stevenson, Aldous Huxley, and Virginia Woolf all had "relatives of distinction on both sides of their family."

Another inquiry took off in a rather different direction, studying a realm of eminence that Galton quite ignored—royalty. The goal was to confirm the aristocratic hypothesis that qualities of both intellect and virtue were subject to genetic inheritance. This finding might offer a partial justification for hereditary monarchy as a political system. If the sovereign's genes are the best, why not make sure his or her successor's genes are also the best, by making governance part of the inheritance? Hence, we can defend the long dominance of the Bourbon, Habsburg, Romanov, Mogul, Ming, and Tokugawa family lines. Aside from moral qualms, however, a stumbling block confronts this justification. Scrutiny of these data reveals that only intellect appears to be transferred by genetic means. Other qualities equally essential to rulers' success, such as morality and leadership, seem to be passed from one generation to the next by rather different mechanisms. So maybe hereditary leadership is not such a good idea after all.

Many examples of family pedigrees appear in recent times as well. In politics, for instance, we can cite the prominence of the three Kennedy brothers—John, Robert, and Edward—in the White House and on Capitol Hill. The chip-off-the-old-block effect also occurs. When Jerry Brown became governor of California, his portrait could join that of his father, Pat Brown, in the state capitol. Kathleen Brown, whom Pat considers the most talented of his offspring, is now state treasurer and a current aspirant to the governorship. Psychology and kindred professions have their own examples. Sigmund and Anna Freud illustrate the parent–child link, while Gordon and Floyd Allport exemplify the sibling connection. And, of course, the famed Menninger Clinic, founded by Karl, is well staffed with psychiatrists who have the same surname. In the arts, finally, we can cite dancer Vaslav Nijinsky and choreographer Bronislava Nijinska, brother and sister; concert pianists Rudolf and Peter Serkin, father and son; Marian Anderson, the singer, and her nephew James DePreist, the conductor.

Nor must we confine ourselves to what the Germans style the *Hochkultur* ("high culture"). Popular culture is especially rich in examples, as is seen in Table 2.2. This listing makes no claims at comprehensiveness. With the omnipresence of stage names and *noms de plume*, it is easy to overlook blood connections.

Given all these exemplars, Galton's argument looks even better. Perhaps eugenics can help breed a race of superstars in any domain a nation so chooses. Perhaps Galton's study and its sequels justify the proliferation of the "sperm banks" in which (male) intellectual celebrities make their deposits for the benefit of posterity. Already we have over 100 "Nobel sperm kids" just waiting to enter adulthood. How much should we expect from the eugenically engineered children so spawned?

A Critique?

It is not hard to poke holes in Galton's argument and evidence, however. For now, let's just look at three difficulties:

1. Galton probably underestimated the impact of the environment in deciding a person's fate in the annals of fame. Coming from a distinguished family means more than getting a high-quality set of genes. Such origins also imply other riches, such as solid training or education in a special domain. It certainly helped the little Mozart that his father, Leopold, was not only an exceptional musician but an outstanding music educator. Later I will discuss the importance of models and mentors, including parents, whose influence is social rather than biological (see Chapter 13).

TABLE 2.2. Representative Blood Relations in Popular Culture

Parent(s) and child: Edgar and Candice Bergen; Ingrid Bergman, Roberto Rossellini, and Isabella Rossellini; Barry and Bobby Bonds; Pat and Debby Boone; Johnny and Rosanne Cash; Lon Chaney Sr. and Jr.; Tommy and Rae Dawn Chong; Nat King Cole and Natalie Cole; Janet Leigh, Tony Curtis, and Jamie Lee Curtis; Bruce Dern, Diane Ladd, and Laura Dern; Kirk and Michael Douglas; Douglas Fairbanks Sr. and Jr.; Judy Garland, Vincente Minnelli, and Liza Minnelli; Woody and Arlo Guthrie; Tippi Hedren and Melanie Griffith; Hugh and Christie Hefner; Bobby and Brett Hull; the Judds (Naomi and Wynonna); John and Julian Lennon; Mary Martin and Larry Hagman; "Old Tom" and "Young Tom" Morris; Ryan and Tatum O'Neal; Maureen O'Sullivan and Mia Farrow; John and Bonnie Raitt; Carl and Rob Reiner; Eddie Fisher, Debbie Reynolds, and Carrie Fisher; Donald and Kiefer Sutherland; Danny and Marlo Thomas; Hank Williams Sr. and Jr.; Chic and Dean Young; Efrem Zimbalist Jr. and Stephanie Zimbalist.

Siblings: Greg and Duane Allman; the Andrews Sisters; James Arness and Peter Graves; Warren Beatty and Shirley MacLaine; John and James Belushi; Everly Brothers; Olivia De Havilland and Joan Fontaine; Zsa Zsa and Eva Gabor; Lillian and Dorothy Gish; Margeaux and Mariel Hemingway; Michael, Janet, La Toya, and Jermaine Jackson; Ann Landers and Abigail Van Buren; Gypsy Rose Lee and June Havoc; Loretta Lynn and Crystal Gayle; Audrey and Jayne Meadows; Wynton, Branford, Jason, and Delfeayo Marsalis; Marx Brothers; Eric and Julia Roberts; Maximilian and Maria Schell; the Smothers Brothers; Eddie and Alex Van Halen; Damon, Keenen Ivory, Kim, Shawn, and Marlon Wayans; CeCe and BeBe Winans.

Various family groupings: Mario, Michael, Jeff, and John Andretti; Lucille Ball, Desi Arnaz Sr. and Jr., and Lucie Arnaz; Lionel, Ethel, John, and Maurice Barrymore, and John and Georgiana Drew; Lloyd, Jeff, and Beau Bridges; John, David, and Keith Carradine; Charlie, Geraldine, and Michael Chaplin; Francis and Sofia Coppola, and Talia Shire; Henry, Jane, and Peter Fonda; Loretta Lynn, Crystal Gayle, and Patty Loveless; Maurice Hines Sr. and Jr., and Gregory Hines; Cissy and Whitney Houston, and Dionne Warwick; Walter, John, Angelica, Danny, and Tony Huston; Sir Henry, H. B., and Laurence Irving; family of Ozzie, Harriet, and Ricky Nelson merging with family of Elyse Knox and Tom and Mark Harmon to produce Tracy, Matthew, and Gunnar Nelson; the Osmond Family (including Donny and Marie); Lee, Richard, and Kyle Petty; John, Michelle, Mackenzie, and Cynna Phillips; Michael, Vanessa, Corin, and Lynn Redgrave; Jason Robards Sr. and Jr., and Sam Robards; Martin and Charlie Sheen, and Emilio Estevez; the Flying Wallendas; Brian, Carl, and Dennis Wilson, and cousin Mike Love (Brian with Marilyn producing Carnie and Wendy Wilson); Frank, Dweezil, and Moon Unit Zappa.

2. We must not overlook the purely social resource of having the right last name. What Edward Young said in his "Love of Fame" certainly applies to many: "He stands for fame on his forefathers' feet,/By heraldry proved valiant or discreet." This familial edge sometimes assumes the concrete form of career connections. Is it mere accident that judges line up in family pedigrees? When the time comes to appoint a lawyer to a judgeship, we cannot dismiss the impact of a candidate's already having a relative on the bench. In contrast, poets may be less likely to form family trees, owing to the tenuous nature of "old boy networks" in their world. Because literary magazines have terribly brief life expectancies, an aspiring poet cannot get much mileage out of having a parent who once knew the editor of a long-defunct gazette.

3. Sometimes ancestors hand down more than the training and the name. The next generation also receives the material resources as an inheritance. As an example, the Zambelli family of New Castle, Pennsylvania, has some right to proclaim itself the First Family of Fireworks. For three generations the Zambellis have dominated pyrotechnics in America. Yet each family member, besides getting training in the secret recipes for explosives, has also received a chunk of the business. These are not progeny who struck out on their own, who successfully built rival businesses from the ground up.

These three criticisms converge on a single complaint: Galton did not prove that reputation intimately reflects *natural* ability. Instead, when we graph eminent family trees, we may be delineating merely the transfer of nurtured ability—or even mere milked advantage. To make Galton's case stronger, we must show more directly how genes translate into genius.

Behavior Genetics

Although Galton's *Hereditary Genius* came out after Gregor Mendel published his classic experiments, the laws of Mendelian inheritance had no influence on Galton's thinking. Indeed, Mendel's ideas did not become part of mainstream biology until after Galton's death. So Galton's logic often looks rather naive from a modern perspective. For instance, when he found that in some achievement areas the family pedigrees were more likely to continue through the female line, he had no difficulty accepting this as still consistent with his basic hypothesis. Hence, he could say that the eminence of divines arises more from feminine than from masculine inheritance. This would represent a rather bizarre form of sex-linked transmission, in comparison to what holds for such single-gene traits as hemophilia and color blindness.

Despite Galton's conceptual naiveté, he was a pioneer in the field that has come to be known as "behavior genetics." Behavior geneticists study how individual characteristics pass from generation to generation. Galton introduced many of the techniques now current in this discipline, including the family pedigree method. And modern behavior genetics could not continue without certain statistical methods that Galton first developed. Yet of all the strategies and tactics that Galton devised, the most crucial to the behavior geneticist today is probably the twin study.

Identical versus Fraternal Twins

Identical twins have an uncanny resemblance to each other, not only physically but behaviorally. In contrast, fraternal twins seldom look more similar than other siblings of the same family. The reason, of course, is that the identical twins came from a single egg that split shortly after fertilization; being thus "monozygotic," they share precisely the same genetic material. By comparison, fraternal or "dizygotic" twins have as many genes in common, on the average, as any other two siblings. Accordingly, we can learn an immense amount about how we all inherit traits by comparing monozygotic twins against the baseline of dizygotic twins. And we can go one step further. For various reasons, when some pairs of twins are put up for adoption as infants, each twin ends up in a different home. This circumstance enables the behavior geneticist to estimate the heritability of various personality traits and behavioral dispositions.

What researchers have found in such studies is well-nigh sensational. A large and diverse array of character traits claim respectable "heritability coefficients." To some fair degree, people inherit from parents not just intellectual ability, but also vocational interests, leisure-time activities, social attitudes, religiosity, and many other complex attributes. Even highly idiosyncratic attributes can be shared, such as offbeat hobbies, quirky habits, and weird mannerisms. Hence, two identical twins can be almost interchangeable, just like the characters in Shakespeare's *Comedy of Errors*.

If we can attribute so many traits to genetic endowment, as these twin studies suggest, Galton's original thesis would seem to be vindicated. We could credit to genetics most of the traits essential to achievement in a diversity of domains. So the twin studies may reveal the biological roots of the family pedigrees Galton so assiduously compiled.

Emergenesis and Genius

But there is an ironic glitch in all this: Monozygotic twins are frequently *too* similar. Identical twins, even with separate upbringing, will occasionally be extremely similar on attributes that show no heritability in dizygotic twins. After all, on the average, we would expect fraternal twins to be about half as similar on a genetic trait as are identical twins. David Lykken has given the example of "social potency," which concerns "the self-perceived ability to influence, lead, or dominate others." Because social potency is germane to accomplishments as a leader, we might expect it to follow familial lineages, as Galton noted for his statesmen. Yet the picture gets more complicated. On the positive side, monozygotic twins, whether reared apart or together, match closely on this trait. But on the negative side, dizygotic twins are no more alike than any two randomly selected people from the population! Social potency can only yield fragmented pedigrees, and then solely when a lineage displays an unusual tendency to produce identical twins. How can this be?

The answer could be "emergenesis." We often assume that most inherited traits result from the separate contributions of many genes—that the total outcome is merely the sum of the individual effects. This is an "additive" model. For example, many factors determine a person's height, and the genes controlling each of these factors make their separate inputs without regard for the other genes. Yet other traits not only may be polygenetic, but also may require all the genes to participate if the trait is to appear at all. This is a "multiplicative" or "interactive" model. The characteristic of social potency, for instance, "probably depends on some configuration of attractiveness, self-confidence, assertiveness, dominance—whatever the ingredients are of 'charisma.'" If one component is lacking, social potency cannot emerge as a character trait. It is emergenetic.

Lykken has argued that emergenesis can help explain the emergence of geniuses who do not fit Galtonian pedigrees. He cites the example of Karl Friedrich Gauss, one of the most intimidating mathematical minds of all time. Gauss's father was a bricklayer; his mother was a peasant; and Gauss's own son came nowhere close to matching his father's mathematical skills. Apparently, to become a Gauss requires a distinctive convergence of many abilities, interests, and values. If a single attribute is missing, a Gauss is not produced. Galton was implicitly aware of this, for he failed to mention Gauss in *Hereditary Genius*. This omission is surprising, because Gauss introduced some concepts that proved important in Galton's own work.

The emergenetic model of genius is only mere speculation at this point. Nevertheless, evidence scattered here and there supports the conjecture. For instance, scores on some creativity tests may be guided by the multiplicative contributions of genes. More provocative, perhaps, are the data hiding in Galton's own *Hereditary Genius*. In the chapters on literary men and poets, we look in vain for William Shakespeare's pedigree. Galton dug up a lineage for Francis Bacon, a contemporary some have claimed to be the real author of the Bard's works, but not for Shakespeare himself. And, what does Galton have to say about Isaac Newton? He devoted nearly two pages to discussing a possible link between Newton and other relatives of far lesser distinction. The connections are speculative to the extreme. Another mysterious blank appears in Galton's treatment of Ludwig van Beethoven in the musicians' chapter. The best Galton could do was to repeat a rumor that Beethoven was the illegitimate son of Frederick the Great of Prussia! Now Frederick was a competent flute player, and even something of a composer—J. S. Bach used one of his melodies in the *Musical Offering*. Still, even if the rumor were true, Frederick's mediocre talents are not enough to account for Beethoven's transcendent powers. And, to wrap this up, what did Galton have to say about Michelangelo's lineage? Absolutely nothing.

So there we have it: Shakespeare, Newton, Beethoven, and Michelangelo—four creative minds of the highest order. We frequently put geniuses of this high caliber in a class by themselves. In doing so, we implicitly acknowledge that their configurations of traits are so distinctive that the occurrences of such personalities on this planet are few and far between. For this level of greatness, the Galtonian model may be woefully deficient, and eugenics utterly impotent. Genes may still play a role in the appearance of such genius, but solely through a multiplicative and hence singular effect. For the emergence of genius that is *sui generis*, the answer may indeed be emergenesis.

The Human Brain

The "natural ability" that so preoccupied Francis Galton must be located in the central nervous system. Below I survey two aspects of the brain that might determine greatness—its organization and its functioning.

Right and Left

Any history of psychoneurology must include the name of Franz Joseph Gall, a Viennese anatomist. Among his contributions was the distinction between the gray and white matter of the cerebral cortex. Moreover, Gall fully appreciated that the cortex of the human brain contains the faculties that define intellectual and motivational differences among individuals. But Gall's career eventually veered off the path of science, making him the founder of a once-popular pseudoscience. Gall began with the hypothesis that the diverse mental functions are *localized* in specific regions of the cortex. He further speculated that when a particular function is unusually well developed in an individual, the cortical area responsible for that function is enlarged. Undeveloped functions, in contrast, correspond to cortical regions that have atrophied. Finally, Gall made the big assumption that the expanded regions of the brain press upon the skull, leaving bumps and depressions. By inspecting the skull, an expert should thus be able to read a client's entire intellectual and motivational constitution. Gall's ideas eventually became known as "phrenology," and attracted many practitioners.

Scientists attacked the practice as mere quackery. It certainly did not help that Gall's followers would make pronouncements that sounded plain silly:

> When a cast of the right side of Napoleon's skull indicated a phrenological analysis markedly at variance with the emperor's known characteristics, the phrenologists unhesitatingly replied that his true personality was reflected on the left side—

a cast of which was conveniently missing. When Descartes's skull was examined, it was found to be exceptionally small in the parts associated by phrenology with the rational faculties. The phrenologists retorted that Descartes's rationality had always been overrated.

One ill-fated phrenologist was given the brain of an imbecile, but was told that it was that of the great mathematician Laplace. The charlatan was not at a loss for words when it came to praising the specimen's mental powers. No wonder, then, that the story circulated widely among scientists that "Gall's own skull, which was preserved following his death and placed on exhibition at the Musée de l'Homme in Paris, was twice as thick as the average."

Although phrenology was thus thoroughly discredited, echoes of Gall's ideas can still be found in current research on genius. Many illustrious figures of modern times have had their brains preserved in formaldehyde for the future examination of curious scientists. For example, judging from the remnants of Albert Einstein's cortex that float around in jars, an investigator claimed in 1985 that this brain was indeed distinctive. The receptive layer of a particular region of his left hemisphere was twice as big as normal, with about 73% more glial cells to back up the hard thinking of the neurons crammed there. However, because none of this work appeared in respectable scientific journals, Gall must wait still longer for vindication.

However, another of Gall's discoveries has had better luck. Gall observed that the two halves of the brain—the right and left hemispheres—are interconnected by commissures. The largest and most important of these links is the corpus callosum. For a considerable time brain scientists were at a loss to explain what this structure did. Animals who suffered commissurotomies, and thus had their two hemispheres disconnected, did not seem to behave any differently. In fact, "The apparent absence of any noticeable changes following commissurotomy led some scientists to suggest facetiously that the corpus callosum's only function was to hold the halves of the brain together to keep them from sagging." Only when the surgeon's scalpel was applied to the corpus callosum of a living human being did perceptions radically change. Some scientists even speculate that this organ, secluded in the middle of the brain, may hold the secret to genius.

One Brain or Two?

The commissurotomies are surgical interventions for medical conditions in which nothing less drastic will work, such as severe cases of epilepsy. There are enough of these split-brain patients, however, to enable us to learn an immense amount about how the two hemispheres are organized. Apparently, many important higher mental functions are lateralized: Some faculties are located on the right, others on the left. Accordingly, once the commissures are cut, the two halves of the brain go their separate ways. It is almost as if the patient gets two personalities for the price of one. In a manner unexpected by Gall, mental functions are indeed subject to dramatic localization, but with the division separating the right from the left cortex. For the right-handed, this differentiation goes as follows.

The left hemisphere, besides controlling the right hand, usually handles the production and perception of speech, as well as all activities closely linked with language. Thus, the left hemisphere concentrates on logic, analysis, reason, mathematics, and science. In line with this focus, the left side is more proficient at sequential or temporal processing of information, and specializes in input that is more abstract and digital in nature. In contrast, the right hemisphere controls the left hand, and has rather minimal competence in the generation and reception of language. In fact, the right side has a small vocabulary and little grammar—but a passable collection of swear words! In lieu of verbal skills, the right hemisphere apparently accentuates visual and spatial reasoning. Information processing is also largely holistic and simultaneous rather than analytical and sequential. It is on the right side of the cortex, too, where such creative activities as fantasy, intuition, and aesthetic appreciation supposedly dwell.

Many of these findings remain controversial. Not everyone agrees that the localization of function is nearly as pronounced as it is commonly depicted. Moreover, the results are perhaps too provocative. They have inspired many scholars to embark on rhapsodic speculations that may be ill advised from a scientific (left-hemisphere) perspective. Examples abound in Jan Ehrenwald's book *The Anatomy of Genius: Split Brains and Global Minds*. Ehrenwald begins by expanding the hemispheric differentiation to include faculties of a far more global character. For example, the left hemisphere is linked to Aristotle, Marx, Freud, and the Apollonian mode of thought and art, while the right lines up with Plato, Nietzsche, Jung, and the Dionysian mode. The rest of Ehrenwald's book then documents these distinctions in the lives and works of many notable figures. Beethoven, Nietzsche, Leonardo da Vinci, Freud, Jung, Mozart, Einstein, Picasso, Kafka, and the psychic Eileen Garrett each get one chapter. Then the chapters that follow touch upon leaders as diverse as Hernando Cortés and Montezuma, Julius Caesar, Napoleon, Churchill, Hitler, Stalin, and the Reverend Jim Jones, with a final glance at Jesus and Plato. In each instance, the personality and achievements of a given luminary are elucidated in light of the right–left dichotomy. For example, Ehrenwald holds Beethoven's dominant left brain accountable for the odd-numbered symphonies, such as the Third, Fifth, and Ninth. The master's subdominant right brain supposedly produced the more melodious and romantic even-numbered symphonies, such as the Pastoral (Sixth) Symphony. Even the author of the book's foreword has gotten into the act, assigning single movements of Beethoven's Third Rasumovsky Quartet to either the right or the left side of the neurological division. The upshot is a fantastic (right-hemisphere) odyssey.

The split-brain research has stimulated not just theorizing, but practice. Books of all sorts, including those of the "self-help" variety, purport to get us closer to the normally repressed right hemisphere. All we need to do to rise above mediocrity is to lug our right hemispheres back in, and we will leave our marks on posterity. Ir we were phrenologists, we would expect that our heads all tilt to the left, because of the serious atrophy of the right hemisphere! Still, we should not dismiss this thinking in its entirety. There is certainly a grain of truth in Ehrenwald's thesis that accomplishments require the coordinated efforts of *both* right and left brains. For example, experimental studies with split-brain patients show them to be incapable of the complex fantasizing, dreaming, and metaphorical thinking so essential to creative expression and appreciation. The patients' right hemispheres are functioning just fine, but they have lost their mental partners.

So instead of speaking of right versus left, we should perhaps talk of a "magic synthesis" of the two. We must not forget that both hemispheres emerged from a long evolutionary process. Presumably, cortex on both right and left grew over the millennia, because the mental functions localized on each half were both essential to survival. And since genius of the highest magnitude probably requires the fullest powers of the human mind, both hemispheres must be indispensable. Carl Sagan, the planetary scientist, has expressed it well:

> I think the most significant creative activities of our or any other human culture—legal and ethical systems, art and music, science and technology—were made possible only through the collaborative work of the left and right cerebral hemispheres. These creative acts, even if engaged in rarely or only by a few, have changed us and the world. We might say that human culture is the function of the corpus callosum.

Yet if the whole brain must work in harmony as an integrative sum of neurons in both hemispheres, why bother talking about right and left at all? Isn't the psychoneurology taken out of the phenomenon? So what if we need intact commissures to think like a human and like a genius? We need other parts of the brain too. Even so, the psychobiologist has an argument to pose against attempts at discrediting the split-brain literature. Some of you may be holding a cup of coffee in your right hand; others may imbibe courtesy of your left. That tiny fact may salvage the psychoneurology.

One Hand or Two?

Hemispheric lateralization of function is intimately related to that of handedness. In the Library of Congress Catalog System, books on both subjects are located together under the label "QP385." Hand preference has a neurological basis, and it also correlates with how the hemispheres are organized. For example, many left-handed people have brains that are mirror images of the typical right-handed brain. Therefore, we may find the evidence more telling here than elsewhere. Any such discussion must begin with this fundamental fact: Left-handed people are in the minority, everywhere and for all time. Among the earliest historical references is in the Bible (Judges 20:15–16): "And the Benjaminites mustered out of their cities on that day twenty-six thousand men that drew the sword . . . Among all these were seven hundred picked men who were left-handed." That converts to a percentage of 3% southpaw warriors. Yet the most extensive data on the disparity can be found in the art that has passed down through the centuries.

One early study looked at the murals in the Egyptian tombs of Beni Hasan. Dated to about 2500 B.C., these depict people in diverse activities, from which the investigator could determine hand preference. Of 120 pictures presenting the proper evidence, 105 show the tool or other object held in the right hand. Hence, among ancient Egyptians, lefties accounted for only around 13% of the population. This inquiry was extended with superb flair when two investigators scrutinized 1,180 works of art from all over the globe. These works dated from before 3000 B.C. to A.D. 1950. The percentage of lefties ranged from a high of 12% to a low of 2%, with an average of 7%. The only crucial exception to this right-hand preference occurs in paintings of the Madonna and Child. Mary usually holds Jesus on her left, as we witness in, say, *The Madonna of the Long Neck* of Parmigianino. Yet this may only reflect the need to keep the right hand free for more critical matters.

Hence, it is unmistakable that human populations are preponderantly right-handed. The next question is whether those who are not so endowed suffer the fate of many other minorities in history—obscurity. If you ask almost any lefty, you surely will hear an onslaught of notables. Table 2.3 shows some of the names available. This list includes both sinistrals and ambidextrals, although the bulk were or are purely sinistral. Also, not all of them retained their sinister habits. Many trained their right to replace their left, whether by voluntary decision or by parental compulsion.

Unfortunately, Table 2.3 itself cannot tell us anything conclusive. Thousands of people have made a name for themselves, so by chance alone some must have used their left rather than their right hands. Hence, do we have any reason to believe that lefties grasp fame at a higher rate than righties? The answer is no. For instance, Table 2.3 has quite a few visual artists, including some of great importance. Yet, despite some tendency for lefties to be slightly overrepresented among art students, we cannot conclude that notable artists reflect the same disproportion. The table also lists several athletes; even so, careful analysis of major sports figures of Olympic, professional, and international standing reveals no broad and secure pattern. If lefties enjoy any universal asset or deficit, it is not apparent in baseball, football, basketball, soccer, ice and field hockey, volleyball, bowling, boxing, figure skating, gymnastics, racquet sports, rifle and pistol shooting, archery, swimming, or track and field. What's left? Frisbee?

TABLE 2.3. Notables among Reputed Sinestrals and Ambidextrals

Alexander the Great, Hans Christian Andersen, Aristotle, Dan Aykroyd, F. Lee Bailey, Ludwig van Beethoven, Leonard Bernstein, Carol Burnett, George Bush, Julius Caesar, Sid Caesar, Gerolamo Cardano, Vikki Carr, Lewis Carroll, Cato, Charlie Chaplin, Charlemagne, Prince Charles, Cicero, Bill Clinton, Chuck Connors, Jimmy Connors, Clarence Darrow, Albert Desalvo (the Boston Strangler), Richard Dreyfuss, Bob Dylan, Albert Einstein, Queen Elizabeth the Queen Mother, W. C. Fields, Peter Fonda, Gerald Ford, Greta Garbo, James A. Garfield, Judy Garland, Lou Gehrig, Uri Geller, King George VI, Lefty Gomez, Betty Grable, Dorothy Hamill, Rex Harrison, Goldie Hawn, Jimi Hendrix, Ben Hogan, Hans Holbein, Herbert Hoover, Rock Hudson, Danny Kaye, Caroline Kennedy, Paul Klee, Michael Landon, Rod Laver, Cloris Leachman, Leonardo da Vinci, Livy, Louis XVI, Marcel Marceau, Harpo Marx, Bill Mauldin, Paul McCartney, John McEnroe, Robert S. McNamara, Johnny Miller, James Michener, Marilyn Monroe, Wolfgang Amadeus Mozart, Edward R. Murrow, Ryan O'Neal, Arnold Palmer, Jackie Patterson, Edson Pelé, Ross Perot, Pablo Picasso, Cole Porter, Richard Pryor, Raphael, Robert Redford, Don Rickles, Jack the Ripper, Nelson Rockefeller, Dean Rusk, Babe Ruth, Wally Schirra, Warren Spahn, Mark Spitz, Ken Stabler, Ringo Starr, Rod Steiger, Casey Stengel, Emperor Tiberius, Tōjō Hideki, Harry S Truman, Dick Van Dyke, Queen Victoria, James Whitmore, Ted Williams, Joanne Woodward.

Perhaps the only reliable contrast between lefties and righties concerns youths who are mathematically precocious. Those who score extremely high on the mathematics segment of the Scholastic Aptitude Test include a proportion of sinistrals much larger than any comparison group. Hormonal theories have even been proposed to account for this phenomenon. Still, we have to wait awhile for these math-whiz lefties to grow up before we learn whether there is any Newton, Euler, or Gauss among them. That prospect does not look good. Cardano is the sole southpaw mathematician among those honored in Table 2.3.

And so we stand pretty much where we were at the beginning of this section: If we want to identify those personalities who are most likely to move and shake the world, we have no strong rationale for using hand preference as a marker. Furthermore, given the conceptual overlap between handedness and hemispheric lateralization, we have not reinforced the case for the right–left brain dichotomy either. Until new data prove otherwise, the Fates are best described as whole-brained and ambidextrous.

Supernormal and Abnormal

If we can draw any conclusion whatsoever from the discussion above, it is that greatness probably requires a normally functioning brain. Let us now explore this inference further by looking at drugs, sleep, and organic disorders.

Drugged Success?

The brain is at the mercy of whatever may circulate in the blood. This opens up the possibility that certain chemicals could improve mental functioning. Creativity, in particular, may be bettered through chemistry. An oft-cited example is alcohol. The wonders of this liquid drug are praised by poets near and far, from the Li Bo of China to Omar Khayyam of Persia. The short-story writer O. Henry was more specific: "Combining a little orange juice with a little scotch, the author drinks the health of all magazine editors, sharpens his pencil and begins to write. When the oranges are empty and the flask is dry, a saleable piece of fiction is ready for mailing." Here is one "mind-altering drug" that may have served history well.

Still, we have no strong scientific evidence that alcohol in any concentration enhances creativity of any value. This point is well documented by the psychiatrist Albert Rothenberg. Besides studying the lives of deceased creators, Rothenberg interviewed several contemporary creators at some length. Some of those interviewed had severe problems with alcohol, such as Pulitzer-winning John Cheever, the author of the novel *Falconer*. Even so, intoxication was more likely to interfere with creativity than to facilitate it. Those with a weakness for alcohol were rather unlikely to compose their best works under its influence. As one chaplain of the Tudor era aptly cautioned, "when the wine is in, the wit is out." And far too many master minds have succeeded without showing an inclination to abuse drink. If we are looking for a chemical panacea for creative mediocrity, we have to look somewhere else.

What about more potent mind-altering drugs? In his prefatory note to "Kubla Khan," Samuel Taylor Coleridge claimed to have conceived a few hundred lines of the poem while in a stupor induced by opium. The obstacle to accepting this account is that earlier drafts of "Kubla Khan" gainsay Coleridge's narrative. The poet was simply telling a creation myth that was compatible with ideas then fashionable. During the first few decades of the 19th century, marvelous powers were attributed to opium. This is the same era that produced Thomas De Quincey's *Confessions of an English Opium-Eater*, a work that inspired the *Symphonie Fantastique*, Hector Berlioz's musical illustration of an opium dream. Later generations saw through the myth, and opium ceased to be the elixir of choice for realizing creative genius.

The 1960s offered Americans and the world a new choice, the notorious psychedelics. By playing havoc with the brain's neurotransmitters, these chemicals supposedly served as "mind-expanding drugs." Despite the obvious impact of these mind-altering chemicals on the counterculture, and especially their place in creating acid rock and psychedelic art, empirical data supporting their general utility are in short supply. Perhaps the sole domain where these chemical agents might confer some advantage is in religious mysticism. Reading the book of Revelation, which closes the Bible, is very much like having a vicarious psychedelic experience. Psychedelic art might decorate the Temples of Tibet with minimal incongruity. Many of the practices of the mystics certainly would contribute to mind-altering experiences of some kind. Several varieties of hallucinogens have been integrated into the rituals of some established religions and cults. In these instances, we cannot deny the impact of "altered states" on world culture and history.

Whether these alterations can produce personal insights of true worth is another matter. In his classic work *The Varieties of Religious Experience*, William James discussed the paradoxical effects of laughing gas:

> Nitrous oxide and ether, especially nitrous oxide, when sufficiently diluted with air, stimulate the mystical consciousness in an extraordinary degree. Depth beyond depth of truth seems revealed to the inhaler. This truth fades out, however, or escapes, at the moment of coming to; and if any words remain over in which it seemed to clothe itself, they prove to be the veriest nonsense. Nevertheless, the sense of a profound meaning having been there persists; and I know more than one person who is persuaded that in the nitrous oxide trance we have a genuine metaphysical revelation.

This sketch can be applied with only minor adjustments to the typical experiences of those who believed they reached mystical domains via LSD, mescaline, and other psychedelics.

Hence, perhaps it is better to maintain a healthy dose of scientific skepticism about all this. People are often searching for the "quick fix" to enlightenment, and drugs are frequently the solution chosen. This makes many otherwise intelligent human beings vulnerable to the latest chemical shortcut to success. In 1991, for example, the craze became "smart drugs," which were said to heighten IQs. Within a decade or so, this fad will probably be forgotten. Yet the claims of chemical miracles will continue to be made as long as there exist persons whose attainments fall short of their ambitions.

Sleepless Ambitions?

Of all the basic behaviors on which people may vary, one of the most mysterious is how much each person sleeps. Some are long sleepers, relegating nearly half their lives to slumber and dreams. Others have the enviable capacity to get by on just a few hours of sleep each night. As far as we know, the amount of sleep each of us requires is wired into our brains. Yet the issue that is really of interest here is whether individual variation in sleeping habits translates into contrasts in success.

One sleep researcher, Ernest Hartman, has offered an intriguing speculation. He began by reviewing the personality differences between long and short sleepers. The long sleepers, who averaged 9.7 hours per night, tended to be introverted, anxious, unconventional, unsettled, and creative. The short sleepers, who averaged 5.6 hours per night, were more likely to be extroverted, energetic, efficient, and ambitious. Hartman has thus speculated that

> great men and geniuses are often reported to be either very long or very short sleepers. Edison and Napoleon are examples of persons who were reputed to get along on 4–6 hours of sleep per day regularly. Einstein was reported to be a very long sleeper. From a number of interviews, aside from the main study, I have gotten the impression that certain very creative, concerned persons both in art and in science often are long sleepers. One might suggest very roughly that great men in the sense of "tortured geniuses" might be more likely to be long sleepers, while great men in the sense of extremely effective practical persons—administrators, applied scientists, political leaders perhaps—may tend to be short sleepers.

No one has yet subjected the Hartman hypothesis to a systematic test. If the conjecture fits the facts, further inquiries must resolve the basis for the connection. Does innate sleep needs determine the domain of achievement? Or does the domain decide how much one can sleep? Hartman admits that the latter may be the case. Political leadership, for example, may attract hard-driving personalities who train themselves to do with less. Political leaders may go so far as to extol the wonders of self-disciplined insomnia. In *Six Crises*, we find Richard M. Nixon saying: "Many times I have found that my best ideas have come when I thought I could not work for another minute and when I literally had to drive myself to finish the task before a deadline. Sleepless nights, to the extent that the body can take them, can stimulate creative mental activity." Whether the products of these occasions are of historic merit is another question altogether. For instance, I wonder how much sleep Napoleon got June 18, 1815, on the field before Waterloo. Do zombies more often lose?

Organic Failures?

If the brain is the seat of all thought, feeling, and action, then disorders that affect the brain must have adverse reactions. These pathological conditions may produce surprising, even tragic, events. On August 1, 1966, a scout-master named Charles Whitman Jr. killed his mother and his wife. He next climbed the tower overlooking the University of Texas at Austin, and from that vantage point pumped rifle bullets into 14 students below. After he was killed by a SWAT team, an autopsy revealed a malignant tumor in the region of the midbrain responsible for aggressive behavior. Ironically, he had earlier written in his journal this request: "After my death, I wish that an autopsy could be performed on me to see if there's any visible disorder." He had been seeing a psychiatrist because he had severe headaches, along with irrational urges to hurt others.

Another illustration concerns a historic personality—the conductor Arturo Toscanini. Maybe the most bizarre episode in his entire career was what one physician called "Toscanini's fumble." In 1954, in the middle of a radio broad-cast of the NBC Symphony, the orchestra suddenly ground to a halt. A recorded piece of music was briefly substituted, after which the maestro finished the con-cert as originally planned. It was Toscanini's last performance. A "transient ischemic attack" probably cut off the supply of blood to his brain, producing a curious lapse for all to hear.

For a couple of reasons, the preceding two cases may be trivial. First, neither required superlative medical detective work. Second, the two occasions did not change the course of history. Therefore, let us switch to a more pro-found question—that of President Woodrow Wilson's disastrous rigidity in late 1919 and early 1920. Wilson was then striving to win Senate consent to the Versailles Treaty. Wilson's primary stumbling blocks were those Republicans, led by Senator Henry Cabot Lodge, who wanted some reservations attached. America's allies were willing to accept the amendments. Wilson's supporters in the Senate were open to compromise, but Wilson stood inflexibly on prin-ciple. So when his enemies tacked on the additions, Wilson demanded that his proponents vote against the treaty. Lodge won the fight by default. Why did Wilson fail?

The answer has been hotly debated in psychobiography. On one side is Alexander and Juliette George's *Woodrow Wilson and Colonel House: A Per-sonality Study*, one of the classics in political psychobiography. Like most psychodynamic studies, the Georges locate the roots of Wilson's problems in early childhood, especially in his hostility toward his father. They contend that as an adult, Wilson repeated a "self-defeating pattern" whenever he encoun-tered opposition from a rival male, a father surrogate. The conflict with Sena-tor Lodge was just one of several such sad episodes. On the other side, some scholars claim that the secret lay in a series of strokes that impaired his brain. The stroke that occurred on October 2, 1919, was the most catastrophic of these. An invalid for seven months, Wilson was isolated from the world during a criti-cal period in history. The crux of the whole debate is that we cannot conduct a medical examination on Wilson to adjudicate the matter.

Or can we? We all may have read of attempts to diagnosis deceased fig-ures of history through hair and blood samples. Recently, for example, chemi-cal analysis showed that Abraham Lincoln had Marfan disease, while another analysis indicated that Zachary Taylor did not fall victim to arsenic poisoning. Yet even more subtle tools are available, methods that do not require even the individual's remains. This is demonstrated in a study using the Cognitive Impairment Scale, a diagnostic device that gauges incoherence of thought from samples of spontaneous speech. Poor performance on this instrument usually corresponds to various organic cerebral dysfunctions. The investigators applied this technique to the extemporaneous speeches of Jimmy Carter, Ronald Reagan, and Walter Mondale during the televised debates of the 1980 and 1984 election years. They discovered that "President Reagan had significantly higher levels of cognitive impairment scores than President Carter, Vice-President

Mondale, or the non-candidate participants in the three debates studied." Worse still, Reagan's cognitive impairment showed a significant increase over the years between 1980 and 1984. Could this progressive decline explicate Reagan's fateful decision to negotiate with Iran for the exchange of arms for hostages?

The investigators have explicitly suggested that the same technique might achieve the posthumous diagnosis of brain disorders. They cite the cognitive impairment evident in Franklin D. Roosevelt when he addressed Congress on the Yalta conference. They also specifically mention Woodrow Wilson's cognitive deficiencies in his last year of office. Of course, one drawback of this device is the requirement that we have spontaneous verbal productions in hand; prepared and rehearsed speeches will not do. Nevertheless, insofar as we can access word-for-word transcripts of conversations, impromptu addresses, and similar verbal samples, the potential of this scale for our comprehension of historic figures remains immense. By this unique procedure, we can monitor the condition of a luminary's brain long after the tissue has passed into dust.

Ethnicity and Gender

If we are not careful, the ideas of Galton and Gall can easily lead us astray. Perhaps the most serious error is to derive from their theories implications that are patently sexist or racist. This offense is most easily committed in Galton's case. Brilliant though *Hereditary Genius* may be as a landmark treatise in psychology, most of us moderns cannot read it from cover to cover without wincing more than once. Galton undoubtedly saw women as the inferior sex and whites as the superior race. Indeed, this inference follows almost as a reflex from his supposition that natural ability leads to an enduring reputation. If there are fewer women in the history books, then they must have less natural ability; the parallel syllogism holds for people of color.

Gall's contribution to sexist and racist judgments is less direct, but nonetheless potent in its own way. By advocating the sheer mass of cortical tissue as a secure index of advancement in cognition and character, Gall opened the gates for gender and ethnic comparisons of brain size. In the 19th century, physical anthropologists were fond of filling skulls with pellets to determine the comparative cranial capacity of the world's races. And the same operation was applied to the crania of men versus women. Any gender or ethnic contrasts in average cubic centimeters then became the basis for setting up hierarchies of intellect. Happily for the white males who conducted this research, it always appeared that the women and the nonwhites were those with lamentably tiny brains. There were even phrenological analyses that tried to pinpoint those domains where the "lower orders" might display some redeeming powers. Miraculously, the phrenological portraits always fell right in line with Victorian males' preconceptions about women's place in society and with European prejudices about the justice of slavery or imperialism.

Given these offshoots of Galton and Gall, we must address head-on the standing of ethnicity and gender in the making of history.

Race and Racism

Galton allocated a complete chapter in *Hereditary Genius* to assessing "The Comparative Worth of Different Races." There he argued that "the average intellectual standard of the negro race is some two grades below our own." On the other hand, Galton ventured the idea that his own British stock need not represent the acme. Judging from the Golden Age that graced Attica in ancient times, Galton inferred that "the average ability of the Athenian race is, on the lowest possible estimate, very nearly two grades higher than our own—that is, about as much as our race is above that of the African Negro."

Galton did not identify any contemporary race as superior to his own. Yet some of his day would have given that distinction to the Jews. Mark Twain, Galton's younger contemporary, was of this persuasion: "The Jews have the best average brain of any people in the world. The Jews are the only race who work wholly with their brains and never with their hands . . . They are peculiarly and conspicuously the world's intellectual aristocracy." Indeed, Galton missed a golden opportunity to use the Jews to prove the efficacy of eugenics. Norbert Wiener, the famous mathematician, offered this hypothesis:

> At all times, the young learned man, and especially the rabbi, whether or not he had an ounce of practical judgement and was able to make a good career for himself in life, was always a match for the daughter of the rich merchant. Biologically this led to a situation in sharp contrast to that of the Christians of earlier times. The Western Christian learned man was absorbed in the church, and whether he had children or not, he was certainly not supposed to have them, and actually tended to be less fertile than the community around him. On the other hand, the Jewish scholar was very often in a position to have a large family. Thus the biological habits of the Christians tended to breed out of the race whatever hereditary qualities make for learning, whereas the biological habits of the Jew tended to breed these qualities in.

Sorry speculations like these are not yet passé in the behavioral sciences. Recently, a (white) psychologist put forward another ranking of races, this time putting the "Mongoloids" on top. He tried to show that this racial hierarchy ensued from the selection pressures operating on the principal races during human evolution. Nor is this the only case of racial thinking in contemporary thought. A "blacklash" may partly motivate the Afrocentrist movement among African-American scholars. Here the "melanin scholars" turn the tables on the white supremists by making Africa and Africans the center of civilization. One manner of accomplishing this task is to point out the black ancestry of so many notable "whites" of European culture. The Russian poet Alexander Pushkin and the French novelist Alexandre Dumas *père* are prime examples. Afrocentrists may go even further by (1) making Egypt into a black civilization and then (2) tracing the powerful influences that Egyptian culture had on the ancient world, classical Greece not excepted.

Afrocentrism may be a necessary antidote to the still-prevalent Eurocentrism and white racism of American culture. Yet it often suffers from the same fallacies that have plagued racial theories ever since the first human being used physical attributes to assess mental capacities. The problems with any racial theory are fourfold:

1. "Race" is an extremely slippery concept. Superficially, it is a biological classification associated with such physical traits as skin pigmentation, hair color and form, facial shape, body type, and so on. But upon closer examination, these physical attributes become fused with other characteristics, such as language, culture, and historical heritage. The Aryans are defined by their presence in the Indo-European linguistic group, but include peoples as physically varied as the Scandinavians and the Hindus. Even a more narrow category like the Jews includes a rather heterogeneous group of people. By contrast, the Croats and Serbs are physically indistinguishable and even speak mutually intelligible tongues. Yet they split themselves according to their different historical relations to previous Balkan empires—the Roman, Byzantine, Venetian, Habsburg, and Ottoman. The very concept of "race" lacks enough precision to have much scientific utility.

2. Suppose that we can identify a human group homogeneous enough to count as a biological subpopulation of the human race. Invariably, the variation among persons within the group amply exceeds the differences between that population and other human populations. Take the much-debated IQ difference between blacks and whites in the United States. The *average* performance of African-Americans may fall below that of Americans of European ancestry; even so, the range in IQ scores within each subpopulation is so wide that millions of whites will be intellectually inferior to millions of blacks. To offer an extreme case, the mean difference did not prevent the emergence in the 1930s of a nine-year-old girl of purely African ancestry with an IQ of 200. That was better than more than 99% of the white children of her generation. And she achieved this score notwithstanding the intimidating handicaps that black Americans had to face when she was growing up.

3. As implied by the last remark, it is always difficult to prove beyond the shadow of a doubt that a particular group contrast has biological origins. The environments in which members of different ethnic groups develop are seldom equal. Furthermore, as the opportunities become more equitable, racial gaps narrow or even vanish. For instance, the IQ differences in American subgroups have been progressively declining, and further declines may result from improved nutrition alone. More generally, as populations migrate or as economies sway and surge, different subgroups of the human race are afforded new opportunities to display their inherent talents. For example, the Arabs lived for

ages in a cultural backwater of the Fertile Crescent, and only their poetry showed any mark of distinction. Within centuries of their conversion to the Islamic faith, the Arabs were producing landmarks in science, philosophy, literature, art, and music. As one scholar concluded, "What history and ethnology seem to teach is that the fundamental traits are the same in all races, and that the adaptability of individuals of one race to social and cultural conditions created by other races is not limited by inherited qualities."

4. Even if some contrasts should survive, we must always be wary of imposing ethnocentric judgments upon any residual differences. For instance, the Jews and the Japanese are two peoples with rather distinct cognitive constitutions. The Jews perform at superior levels on tests stressing logical, mathematical, and linguistic skills, whereas the Japanese do best at spatial and structural thinking. This contrast reflects different child-rearing strategies, and it is reflected in their respective cultural achievements. The Jews have produced some of the greatest minds in philosophy, science, and music, such as Maimonides, Spinoza, Einstein, and Schoenberg. In contrast, the Japanese have produced some of the greatest names in the visual arts, such as the ceramicist Chōjiro, the painter Sesshū, and the printmaker Hokusai. And although Jewish and Japanese literatures are both world-class, the tendencies are for Jews to concentrate on ideas while the Japanese focus on images. Now even when these differences are acknowledged, a proponent of racial hierarchies is in danger of falling into two traps:

a. Which group comes out on top depends on the comparative weights people assign to various modes of achievement. For people who love the visual arts, the Japanese may rise highest. No era of Jewish culture can match that of the Ukiyo-e period in Japan. But for people whose passion is for abstract and rigorous thought, the Jews may rise supreme. Neither Spinoza nor Einstein has an exact counterpart in Japan. Yet, obviously, no *a priori* basis exists for ranking the myriad ways of making an imprint upon posterity. If people think there is one, it is probably because they take their ethnic group's own virtues as marking the most critical attainments of *Homo sapiens*.

b. All too often, racial caricatures provide the impetus for prejudiced evaluations of individuals who contradict our rules. Bernard Berenson was a great art critic, but he also had the fixed idea that the visual arts and Jewish culture don't mix. And so we find him saying that

> even in recent years when Jews emancipated from the ghetto have taken in painting and sculpture and architecture, they have proved neither original nor in the least Jewish. I defy anyone to point out in the work of Liebermann, Pissarro, Rothenstein, Modigliani, Messel, Antokolskij, Epstein, Chagall, or Soutine, anything except subject matter that is specifically Jewish.

Even allowing for the unequal worth of the artists named, we certainly cannot dismiss them all in so cavalier a fashion. The lack of a centuries-old tradition of great Jewish art does not preclude a Jew from creating great art.

So a psychology of history is probably better off without the race concept. It only interferes with an unbiased appreciation of greatness. Too often, racial theories degenerate into crazy affirmations of superiority and inferiority. We see the anti-Semitic composer Wagner deriding the Jewish involvement in German music (Mendelssohn), or the pro-Nazi physicist Stark attacking the corrupting impact of Jewish physics (Einstein). All too often, racial theorists insult the dignity of other ethnicities by contriving pseudogenealogies that are quite irrelevant. Would we appreciate Goethe's masterworks any more or less if he had a Jewish ancestor? Would Beethoven's compositions suddenly become any better or worse if he were found to be the descendant of an African? Must we prove that the ancient Egyptians were whites to apprehend the grandeur and beauty of their art? To answer "yes" is to take one step toward the reasoning that justifies genocide, the *reductio ad absurdum* of Galton's eugenics. It is not race that leaves its mark on history; it is racism. And the mark is a scar.

Women and Sexism

As a concept, gender has a rather different status than does race. Certainly, we cannot deny that the distinction between males and females is biological. The contrasts reside in the chromosomes. These chromosomal contrasts translate into differences in sex hormones; such chemicals then yield the two sexes with contrasting distributions of body hair and fat, distinctive musculature, and identifiable sex organs. Thus, the physical differences between men and women are far greater than those supposedly separating many races. At the same time, these biological dissimilarities are not nearly as confounded with other differences as in the case of different races. Men and women in the same society live in the same climate and economic circumstances. They speak nearly the same language, and (at least potentially) have access to the same cultural and historical heritage. As a result, a psychobiologist can argue that gender offers a critical research site for examining the biological determination of achievement. If the annals of genius, creativity, and leadership portray women differently from men, those discrepancies could reflect contrasts inevitable from birth. And what do the annals say?

In the diverse histories of cultural attainments, the names are overwhelmingly male. In Western civilization, for example, women make up only about 3% of the most illustrious figures of history. And many of these females, some might argue, entered the records in part by lucky birthright or marriage. Elizabeth I of England, Christina of Sweden, Catherine the Great of Russia, and Maria Theresa of Austria are prime examples. Furthermore, in specific areas the female presence may sink to one-third of that percentage. In the annals of science, fewer than 1% of all notables are female. Names like Hypatia, Caroline Herschel, Marie Curie, and Barbara McClintock are but drops in a sea of male scientists. Indeed, in classical music, the proportion of female luminaries may shrink to near zero. For every Fanny Mendelssohn, Clara Schumann, Amy Beech, and Nadia Boulanger, there are hundreds of more famous male composers. Until recently, creative writing was the only area where women could really shine: Among the giants of world literature, about 1 out of 10 are female. Even so, only in Japanese literature can we say that female authors have won reputations right at the top. In Japan, Lady Murasaki wrote the world's first novel, *The Tale of Genji*, securing herself a status that compares favorably with that of William Shakespeare in England.

What do these differential representations tell us?

Chromosomes and Hormones

One solution is to apply a simple extension of Galton's theory: We could just claim that the average level of natural ability for women is a grade or so below that for men. Men inherit more brain as well as more brawn. One drawback to this interpretation is that we have no particular justification for holding that women are intellectually inferior to men. Since the two sexes naturally must come from the same gene pool, the safest bet is to assume that men and women are the same unless we have empirical or theoretical reason to think otherwise. To be sure, men and women have often performed differently on various measures of cognitive skills. Yet these gaps, like those that separate racial groups, are closing. At present, it may not be wise to wager on innate gender contrasts in cognitive capacities to explain the impoverished representation of women in history.

An alternative account is more subtle. Charles Darwin and Francis Galton provided the inspiration for a whole school of psychology that sought to tie individual differences to evolutionary theory. Some of these "functional psychologists" proposed that the contrast between men and women is not captured by differences in average competence, but by differences in individual variability. These theorists claimed that men are more variable than women in cognitive abilities, exhibiting far bigger departures from the average *in both directions*. One implication of this position is that more geniuses will be male than female; another implication is that men will be better represented among the mentally deficient. Women may not win the big honors that we accord our most impressive intellects, but at least they get the consolation prize of not having to be so frequently institutionalized!

Although enthusiasm for this variability hypothesis waned somewhat in the middle of this century, the notion resurfaced in a new form. In 1987, Norman Geschwind proposed that the level of testosterone in the early fetal environment alters the development of lateralization in the two cerebral hemispheres. This prenatal influence supposedly explains a host of otherwise disconnected findings: (1) why males are more likely to be left-handed than females; (2) why men are more prone to exhibit speech disorders such as stuttering, dyslexia, and autism; (3) why female superiority on tests of verbal ability is counterbalanced by male superiority on tests of spatial ability; (4) why childhood developmental disorders are so often found among sinistrals and ambidextrals; (5) why lefties of either gender, and especially those with learning disabilities, often demonstrate exceptional right-hemisphere functioning; and, finally, (6) why certain syndromes, such as the immune disorders responsible for allergies, are more common among sinistrals and ambidextrals. If Geschwind's hypothesis is true, much more might be explained as well, including the male dominance of science and the conspicuous female presence in literature. Yet the empirical standing of the hypothesis remains controversial.

Cultures and Societies

We probably should treat all psychobiological theories with skepticism. As later chapters will show, success is not merely a matter of innate personal capacities; rather, countless sociocultural forces calibrate the tools by which an individual attains distinction. Only if these external agents were equal for men and women could we be sure that disparities emanate from inherent gender differences. Yet there are at least four ways in which men and women compete on an uneven playing field:

1. Parents raise children differently according to gender. In most literate societies across the globe, boys are socialized toward independence and achievement, whereas girls are trained to center their lives around family and relationships. Therefore, many women of enormous talent do not even consider the prospect of life goals outside the home. The problem is notably acute when a family has both boys and girls, in which case the parents will usually channel limited resources toward their sons. The daughters, the culture says, can always rely on catching prosperous mates. A longitudinal study of Mills College graduates showed this bias: Those women "who were successful in careers at age 43 were, with few exceptions, those who did *not* have brothers." Similar results held for eminent female mathematicians.

2. We must be ever aware of the terrific costs of marriage and family in the pursuit of excellence. Francis Bacon warned:

> He that hath wife and children hath given hostages to fortune; for they are impediments to great enterprises, either of virtue or mischief. Certainly the best works, and of greatest merit for the public, have proceeded from the unmarried or childless men, which, both in affection and means, have married and endowed the public.

If Bacon advised ambitious men to shy away from domestic commitments, how much more this advice applies to women! Females are socialized to take family matters far more seriously. Accordingly, women who manage to win an entry in *Who's Who* are four times more likely than equally distinguished men to be unmarried. Furthermore, those successful women who somehow fit marriage into their lives are three times more likely to be childless than are equally successful married men. Hence, a woman with a husband and children suffers a handicap not experienced by an equally capable man with a wife and children. A woman can only combine a career and family if she has a supportive husband and financial means. As this book goes to press, Danielle Steel is the author of more than two dozen popular romance novels, and has nine children to boot. But she has the spousal encouragement and monetary resources that most women can only envy.

3. If the preceding two factors have not diverted an aspiring woman from her quest, active sex discrimination may obstruct her path to success. Sometimes discrimination takes the form of subtle but prejudiced judgments: The assets of women may be undervalued in comparison to those of equally capable men. At other times the discrimination is blatant: Men who control the gateways to success often deny women access quite deliberately. Marie Curie was not elected to the French Academy of Sciences notwithstanding two Nobel Prizes, and lacked a regular academic position until she was allowed to succeed her husband, Pierre, at the Sorbonne after his death. This male dominance of resources alone could explain why women have the best prospects of success in literature. It doesn't require a well-equipped laboratory, a full orchestra, or a large block of marble to write a masterpiece of fiction or poetry. A writing desk and a brain will do. Anne Sexton, for one, wrote prize-winning poetry in the corner of her dining room, taking advantage of whatever moments she could steal from raising two children and housekeeping. Moreover, female authors can bypass prejudices by adopting a male *nom de plume*, like the incognito women George Sand and George Eliot. As a last resort, pieces can always appear anonymously. In *A Room of One's Own*, Virginia Woolf said, "I would venture to guess that Anon, who wrote so many poems without signing them, was often a woman."

4. The most widespread and insidious factor may be the gender ambience of a particular civilization at a given time. For instance, some religious and philosophical systems are not very sympathetic to female attainments. Whenever one of these systems monopolizes the *Zeitgeist*, women suffer accordingly. Confucianism advocates extremely hierarchical views about sex roles, with the woman placed irrevocably subordinate to the man. In line with this bias, the ups and downs in the achievements of women in Japanese history correspond roughly to the fluctuations in the prevalence of this ideology. At other times the milieu does not disfavor female attainments directly, but rather discourages women by emphasizing those activities where women have fewer opportunities to enter the competition. Again taking Japan for an illustration, we find that those periods in which the machismo cult of the warrior flourished tended to be the periods in which literary creativity languished. This inverse relation harmed women more than men, for the latter had many alternative routes to making a name for themselves. Women could not become samurai.

A sexist *Zeitgeist* can dishearten women in ways that are still more surreptitious. Women often live in a visual world in which the image of their gender contrasts starkly with that of men. Women are depicted as unimportant, inconspicuous, even irrelevant to human affairs. One investigation looked at the pictures of men and women in periodicals all over the globe. Analysis of the photographs revealed a bias beyond mere discrepancies in the proportions of men and women. The investigators styled this bias "face-ism." Here a man's face tends to be a more prominent feature than a woman's, whereas the woman's body is usually featured more than the man's. Of the magazines examined in this study, only *Ms.* selects its illustrations to underscore that females do indeed have something more than legs, hips, and breasts to their credit. Significantly, this "face-ist" slant goes beyond the confines of popular culture. The same bias riddles 920 portraits by painters as celebrated as Leonardo, Raphael, Rembrandt, Velasquez, Renoir, Cézanne, Modigliani, and Matisse.

Another study also scrutinized art, only this time concentrating on 468 masterpieces of modern painting and sculpture. Men again far outnumbered the women, in contradiction to their proportions in the human population. The men were also more often shown doing something significant outside the home, while the women were more frequently depicted performing household and child-rearing tasks. Furthermore, the odds of women's being nude were several times those of men, in line with the commonplace view of them as mere sex objects. In addition, the artists were far more likely to portray women as "doing nothing," as if they had no rationale for being on this planet. But the final shocker comes from inspecting the representation of women by the separate schools of modern art. Despite the predominance of male subjects for most movements and styles, cubism and abstraction are noticeably different. There alone do women subjects make up nearly two-thirds of those represented. Yet these two styles are well known for distorting the human figure almost beyond recognition! Moreover, even when a man appears in one of these styles, the male suffers less drastic contortions than does the female. What self-image does a woman pick up from just walking through a museum of modern art?

I certainly have not offered a complete inventory of external factors here. Even so, a consideration of what I have listed forces the conclusion that the cards have always been stacked against female acclaim. Even today, women live in a man's world. Women are less likely to have their faces on the cover of *Time* magazine, and they are more likely to receive only passing treatment in obituary columns. The lesser status of the "weaker sex" is pounded into their brains everywhere they turn. Given these chronic and omnipresent forces, it is unwise to blame the chromosomes or the hormones for the dearth of heroines in the annals of triumphs. "One is not born, but rather becomes, a women," said Simone de Beauvoir. "No biological, psychological, or economic fate determines the figure that the human female presents in society; it is civilization as a whole that produces this creature, intermediate between male and eunuch, which is described as feminine."

Sociobiology

Sociobiologists believe that natural selection has shaped the evolution of more than just personal adaptations to the environment. For social animals such as ourselves, the patterns of interactions, even societal structures, are the products of the evolutionary process. The patterns and structures that endure are those that have enabled the participants to thrive and reproduce their kind. In many primates, such as baboons or chimpanzees, these social habits often closely parallel those seen in our species. So can sociobiologists enlighten us on the evolutionary roots of history-making persons and events? There are two areas of latent relevance: interpersonal relations and sociopolitical systems.

The Knight and the Damsel: Interpersonal Relations

Social relationships in our nearest animal relatives rotate around two biological realities. First, the higher primates exhibit strong dominance hierarchies; usually a male or a cohort of males rules the roost. Second, primate societies revolve around reproduction. Indeed, often one of the functions of dominance hierarchies is to determine who has access to the most desirable females in the troop. These two facets of primate interactions have obvious counterparts in two types of historic behaviors: those related to power and love.

Power

Comparative psychologists sometimes call the most powerful male in a primate troop the "alpha male." He is the leader of the group. He gets first claim on food and sex, if he chooses to assert his rights. And in return, this highest-status male often must take the lead in defending the troop against predators and invaders. On occasion, this responsibility may bring about painful defeat, even death. Consequently, the typical alpha male is mature, muscular, and experienced. He has usually fought his way to the top, and must repeatedly defend his privileges against challenges from those below him in the hierarchy. He may, therefore, be battle-scarred and war-weary.

Possibly the eminent leaders of history, the celebrated heroes of the past, are merely *our* alpha males. One study examined charismatic leadership in 34 heads of state throughout the modern world. Included were the dictators Hitler and Mussolini, the presidents Franklin D. Roosevelt and John F. Kennedy, the revolutionaries Lenin and Mao, and the Third World leaders Kenyatta and Sukarno. Across this diversity, charisma was associated with (1) women's making sacrifices for the leader and (2) the leader's getting a reputation for sexual prowess. Kennedy illustrated this second feature perhaps too well. In the harems of the Ottoman sultans and Chinese emperors, this exertion of sexual prerogatives was even institutionalized. The link between sexual and social power may underlie the surprising paucity of homosexuals among the world's great leaders. Cases such as Emperor Hadrian, Richard I (the Lion-Hearted), and Shaka are rare. It is harder for gay men to prove their virility when they are disinclined to spawn countless offspring.

More significant, perhaps, is the research showing that a leader's physical height is an important antecedent of success. In democratic systems, for instance, the taller of two candidates is more likely to win the election. For example, in New York City's 1969 mayoral election, the two leading candidates were John Lindsay and Mario Procaccino. These opponents exhibited a striking nine-inch contrast in height. Despite some tendency to prefer the candidate with whom they could stand eye to eye, the shorter voters defected to the taller candidate far more than the taller voters defected to the shorter candidate. Lindsay won.

At a higher level, the taller of the two main U.S. presidential candidates, with few exceptions, wins in November. In recent elections, Bush towered over Dukakis, Reagan over Mondale and Carter. Carter was shorter than Ford, but reportedly in the televised debates wore shoes with extra-high heels to cover up this defect! Also, taller incumbents have higher odds of getting re-elected to the Oval Office. Among the six tallest presidents, only Arthur was denied a second term, whereas of the six shortest presidents only Madison and McKinley were re-elected. Better yet, a president's height is highly associated with whether he goes down in history as a great president. By scholarly consensus, the greatest presidents are Lincoln (6'4"), Washington, Jefferson, and Franklin Roosevelt (all around 6'2"), and Jackson (6'1").

Lastly, acclaim as a political leader goes along with participation in aggressive activities. As an example, another effective predictor of a president's performance rating is whether or not he was a national war hero before entering office. Washington and Jackson are two prime examples. Moreover, serving as the nation's wartime leader is a crucial antecedent of acclaim not just for American presidents, but for absolute monarchs. And modern exemplars of charismatic leadership are often seen as leading their respective nations to military victory. Also, a leader's stature with both contemporaries and posterity is often heightened when he is a victim of violence. Julius Caesar, Gustavus Adolphus, Lord Nelson, and Abraham Lincoln exemplify this tendency. Assassination may reflect the attempts of males in the basement of the hierarchy to challenge the leader's primacy; war death may mirror the leader's role as defender of the nation's rights and wishes.

So, all told, alpha males in human societies are virile, tall, and violent. It is conceivable, then, that social behaviors innate to the human species are merely magnified to historic proportions in leaders. Through the course of evolution, natural selection has favored both the emergence of the high-status male profile and our affective response to that biological leader's actions. Both the leader and the followers are behaving in an individually adaptive fashion. By assuming the topmost position in the hierarchy, the alpha male gains access to females, and thereby upgrades his reproductive success. This is an adequate payoff for putting his safety at risk. Concomitantly, subordinate males know to bide their time until the opportunity arises to win a higher spot in the hierarchy. Meanwhile, the females wait on the sideline, ready to exclaim, "My hero!" By choosing the hero of the hour to father their offspring, women assure the survival of their own genes.

We really should weigh some facts that cannot be fitted so comfortably into this sociobiological account. For one thing, the supreme males of human history are not always physically impressive individuals. Among notable conquerors, Julius Caesar and Genghis Khan were small or even frail. Of the greats of the Napoleonic Wars, Wellington was 5'5", Nelson 5'4", and Napoleon just shy of 5'2". One reason for this discrepancy is that human warfare and violence depart in one consequential manner from that found in other primates: Death or defeat need not occur in hand-to-hand combat. Rather, human beings have designed ingenious means to kill at a distance: arrows, spears, bullets, cannon balls. Many of the fallen heroes of history were struck down by a lucky shot: Harold II at Hastings, Gustavus Adolphus at Lützen, Charles XII at Fredrikshald, Lord Nelson at Trafalgar, and Stonewall Jackson at Chancellorsville. In *Hereditary Genius*, Galton actually took note of this reality, and calculated the odds of getting hit as a function of body size. He concluded that the risk faced by big men is substantial enough to confer an edge on the short and thin. The Mongol hordes that swept over Eurasia were manned by soldiers of diminutive stature—who also rode on small horses.

In modern warfare as well, military prowess does not always translate into abundant progeny. Ever since the campaigns of Alexander the Great, wars can assume such a global scale that a military hero may have little opportunity for conjugal and familial joys. Galton also noted this surprising infertility of great soldiers in his chapter on commanders. Nor is it clear that a mistress in every port or city can remedy this logistic reality. Napoleon had many sexual escapades and few offspring—perhaps fewer progeny than the typical French peasant hoeing the fields back home. The sexual part of the victor's "rape and pillage" may not make up the deficiency either.

Lastly, unlike primate societies, human social entities sometimes have female "alpha males." Queen Isabella of Castile, Elizabeth I of England, Catherine the Great of Russia, Maria Theresa of Austria, and the Empress Dowager Ci Xi ("The Old Buddha") of China all occupied the utmost power positions of their respective nations. All executed their powers to the fullest. Even among heroes of the battlefield, we must not overlook Queen Boudicca, leader of the British revolt against Roman rule, and Joan of Arc, the heroine of Orleans during the Hundred Years' War. Moreover, at least one empirical study found that the leadership performance of women cannot be distinguished from that of men occupying the same positions. Many of the peripheral activities of the alpha male can even be displayed with equal nerve by the alpha female. Catherine the Great earned a reputation for an insatiable sexual appetite rivaling that of any male leader before or since. Thus, whatever the in-built predilections of human social systems, we cannot assign a specific gender to the role of the alpha male. The possession and exploitation of power are potentially androgynous honors.

Love

According to evolutionary theories of interpersonal attraction, men are "success objects" and women are "sex objects." The males exchange power for sex; females trade sex for power. Inspect the "lonely hearts" advertisements in the personal section of the newspaper: Women offer looks, men offer money. Accordingly, a woman's sexual attractiveness is her number one resource. This is especially the case in societies where men control the means to economic and political power. In such circumstances, only women of unparalleled beauty can grasp a power that moves mountains. History is replete with women of surpassing beauty who have ensnared men of unrivaled power, and have thereby left a durable impression upon posterity. In China there was the case of Yang Gui-fei, whose beauty destroyed the Tang Dynasty. In India there was Mumtāz Maḥal, whose death in childbirth was the impetus for the Tāj Mahal. In the West there was Cleopatra, of whose nose Blaise Pascal said that "had it been shorter, the whole aspect of the world would have been altered." For each of these women we can echo Dante Gabriel Rossetti's line, "Beauty like hers is genius."

What is the basis of this sexual genius? Here evolutionary biology supplies some answers. The powerful male is supposedly looking for the best mate in whom to deposit his superior sperm. Therefore, she should not have any physical features that suggest abnormalities. Hence, unlike men, women should not have any physical features that depart too far from the population average. For example, following up some pioneer research by Francis Galton back in 1883, researchers have computed the "typical" female face by taking a statistical average of the facial features of many normal women. The resulting image is more attractive than most of the faces that went into the composite. This helps explain why female models and actresses so often look alike. Researchers have even gotten down to the brass tacks of beauty. For instance, one study calibrated the facial measurements of such beauties as Miss Universe contestants to arrive at a formula for female facial success. The eye width should be about 0.3 times the facial width, the chin length about 0.2 times the facial height, and the nose area less than 0.05 times the facial area! Apply a pair of calipers to an issue of *Cosmopolitan* to verify these specifications.

We can more easily gauge another physical attribute of female beauty. In Shakespeare's *Antony and Cleopatra*, we find this tribute to Cleopatra:

Age cannot wither her, nor custom stale
Her infinite variety. Other women cloy
The appetites they feed, but she makes hungry
Where most she satisfies.

Evolutionary biologists would question this assertion. A primary basis for female attractiveness is age. Age defines a woman's fertility. A female's capacity for producing offspring begins after the menarche and ceases at menopause. Hence, at the minimum we would expect a woman's beauty to commence in her early teens and to decline sometime in her late 40s. However, the maximum capacity for bearing children falls into an interval much shorter and younger than this—somewhere between the late teens and 20s. The peak age for feminine charms should correspond to this brief period. In contrast, a man can be virile from puberty to death, enabling him to sustain his sexual attractiveness. Indeed, because increased age can mean increased power, and because signs of age signify a male who is adept at survival, a man can be considered handsome until quite late in the game.

In the 1940s, Harvey Lehman collected data applicable to this prediction. His sample consisted of actors and actresses of the silver screen; his primary source of information was the *Motion Picture Herald*. For each year he identified those who made the most money according to box-office draw. Actresses made big money sooner than actors, and made their biggest bucks in their late 20s. Thereafter, their monetary rewards dropped swiftly. Few actresses continued as major box-office attractions after age 35; a Katherine Hepburn was and still is a rarity. Actors, in contrast, usually did not become impressive attractions until their early 30s. Moreover, the decline after becoming a superstar was gradual for men, unlike for women. Actors in their late 40s still had excellent money-making powers, and it was not until the 70s that they declined to the same level as the actresses. Even today, actors like Sean Connery, Clint Eastwood, and Burt Reynolds are typical. Hence, actors earn far more over a lifetime than do actresses, aggravating the injustice that they also tend to receive more per picture as well.

Even worse, the age-determined sex appeal contaminates ratings of acting abilities. Lehman consulted *Photoplay Magazine* to examine who on film in a given year were judged to have delivered "best performances." The actresses peaked in the early 20s and then suddenly vanished from view. The actors peaked a decade later and exhibited more staying power. A woman past her prime could not be a great actress. Despite the invention of face lifts and tummy tucks, this reality has not changed much over the years. For instance, in the 1992 Oscar nominations, nominees for best actor were 13 years older on the average than nominees for best actress. Warren Beatty was 54, Nick Nolte 50, and Robert De Niro 48; Robin Williams, the youngest male, was 39. In contrast, the oldest woman up for best actress in 1992 was Bette Midler, age 46.

These results do not contradict what Shakespeare said of Cleopatra, whose career actually paralleled that of female movie stars. She was probably a 21-year-old beauty when, according to legend, she had a servant deliver her wrapped in a rug to Julius Caesar. She was his lover until her 25th year. She was about 27, and still stunning, when she met Marcus Antonius. Judging by military prowess, he was not nearly the catch that Julius was; nonetheless, this meeting still launched one of the world's famous love affairs. *This* was the Cleopatra praised in Shakespeare's play, a woman yet in her prime. But the affair lasted a dozen years. So when Marcus Antonius committed suicide after losing the battle of Actium to Octavius, Cleopatra was about 40 years old. In a manner that would cause sociobiologists to smile, Cleopatra then made a big play for the winner of the battle, now the mightiest leader in the Western world—Octavius (later Caesar Augustus). Yet this new alpha male *par excellence* rejected her advances. She had lost her sexual genius. Rather than be paraded through Rome as a trophy of war, Cleopatra held a poisonous asp to her breast.

If beauty is based on reproductive capacity, other aspects of sexual attraction fall neatly into place. For example, we can explicate contrast effects according to this principle. In one study, college males were asked to judge the physical attractiveness of unknown women pictured in photographs. Some of the men did this task immediately after watching *Charlie's Angels*, a popular TV program featuring the sexy actresses Farrah Fawcett, Kate Jackson, and Jaclyn Smith. Under these conditions, the anonymous women were deemed less fair. If we view men as constantly engaged in maximizing their adaptive fitness, beauty should be largely a relative rather than an absolute standard. The most comely is the best that a man can get at a particular moment.

Yet this principle can only take us so far. Certain phenomena of interpersonal attraction must have cultural rather than biological roots. Take the female figure as a test case. One would think that a particular body type is most indicative of fertility—say, large and firm breasts, wide hips, and enough body fat to round out the woman's form with voluptuousness. Judging from the dimensions of women who attain distinction as stripteasers or who expose themselves in *Playboy* centerfolds, the traditional 36-24-36 bust–waist–hip physique may set the benchmark against which all women are judged, everywhere and for all time. Yet the reality differs: Standards of feminine sexiness change according to time and place. On the one hand, the Venus de Milo and the nudes of Rubens appear a bit more matronly than the biological ideal. On the other hand, the current emphasis on female thinness looks excessively unhealthy. The anorexia nervosa that killed singer Karen Carpenter is a syndrome that makes no sense if young women are trying to project the image of fertility. By studying nudes in *Playboy* centerfolds, winners of Miss America contests, and even models in such women's magazines as *Vogue* and *Ladies' Home Journal*, investigators have actually traced dramatic fluctuations in female body size and "curvaciousness." Human culture can apparently override the supposed mandates of evolutionary principles.

And societal norms are not the only nullifying forces. Personal history can also void the presumed biological imperatives. This fact is well known to those who still find themselves in lust with lovers past their prime. In *The Tale of Genji*, Lady Murasaki included a sublime scene that expresses this emotional truth. The title character at this stage in the novel is an aging prince who has always been a Don Juan with a heart. The light falls on the face of a lady whom he has not seen for some time, but who was an old flame of his. Sadly, Genji realizes that to others she is merely a middle-aged woman. But she does not appear so to him. This probably spotlights the contrast between the way Marcus Antonius and Octavius saw Cleopatra in August of 30 B.C.

The Conquistador and the Tyrant: Sociopolitical Systems

In many birds and mammals, aggression is more overtly manifested by males than by females. Aggressive behavior may be a direct consequence of having excess testosterone circulating in the bloodstream. Furthermore, there is ample cause for believing that physical aggressiveness is perhaps the sole dispositional trait that universally distinguishes women and men. According to one cross-cultural survey of children aged 3 through 11, boys exhibit more aggressiveness than girls throughout the world. Although by many criteria women can be just as aggressive as men, masculine aggressiveness is distinctive in one crucial manner: Men are more enthusiastic about doing physical harm to a fellow human being. This contrast is reflected in the typical FBI crime statistics for any given year. Normally, about 90% of all homicides, robberies, aggravated assaults, and other violent crimes are perpetrated by men. This difference is also manifested in the male preoccupation with instruments of destruction. In virtually every society on this planet, if animals are hunted, it is the males who do the killing. More importantly, men monopolize both weapons manufacture and warfare. The Greek legend about the Amazons notwithstanding, a human culture has never existed in which the men huddled in the hut while the women fought battles miles away.

The male predilection for aggression has obvious adverse results. The principle that the strong can enslave the weak too often leads to oppression at home. Not only does this creed justify one race to subordinate another, putatively weaker race; it also rationalizes the subjection of the "weaker sex" by the "stronger sex." Women are putatively helpless without men to protect them (from other men, no less). In addition, the doctrine that "might makes right" excuses the ambitions of the conqueror. The masculine instinct for aggression can only be fully satisfied by conquests of neighboring nations. Einstein, the pacifist, pondered whether "man has within him a lust for hatred and destruction." What is within may simply be excessive amounts of testosterone in the human male. That hormone may be the cause behind all dominance and violence of human society.

This linkage is apparent in the history of politics and culture. Genghis Khan said that the greatest pleasure was to kill an enemy and then rape his wife. In pursuit of this happiness, he massacred and enslaved millions of people. It is no accident that Don Juan, the prototype of all sexual conquerors, was said to be descended from a line of Spanish conquistadors. In the *Ring* cycle of Richard Wagner, a hero cannot win the hand of a woman without killing some adversary. Nor are we more enlightened today, as witnessed in the popular movies of our time, such as the James Bond series. No hero wins the women's love without first exterminating a quota of rivals or villains. And as psychoanalysts can point out, the choice weapons of death—knives, swords, arrows, spears, pistols, and rifles—have a decidedly phallic appearance. Indeed, in both primate and human societies, the erect phallus is often a sign of hostility, as when we "give someone the finger." Sex and death seem intimately bundled up in the masculine self-image.

When some thinkers consider facts like these, the temptation is to propound a biological determinism: Human evolution has produced a characteristic set of instincts, and especially a male disposition, that exerts itself in an injurious style of behavior. Aggression is inevitable. Male dominance is preordained. Oppression of the weak by the strong is unavoidable. These are the repercussions of human nature working itself out in the collective enterprises of our race. Accordingly, there are no shortage of theorists willing to reduce historic events and personalities to some biological scheme.

Typical is Paul Colinvaux's *The Fates of Nations: A Biological Theory of History*. "The fates of whole peoples may be understood, and even predicted in outline, from a knowledge of the ecological nature of our kind." As an ecologist, Colinvaux argues that a "niche theory" explains many big events that shape history. Human groups must constantly compete with one another for limited space and resources, and population pressure inflames this incessant struggle. From this assumption, Colinvaux has derived two social laws of ecology: (1) "Social oppression is an inevitable consequence of the continued rise of population," and (2) "Aggressive war is caused by the continued growth of population in a relatively rich society." Colinvaux then applies his theory to the wars of classical times; the Mongolian invasions under Genghis Khan; the American Revolution; and the political and military history of Sweden, France, Germany, Japan, and England. One chapter's title encapsulates the thrust of his argument: "Human Lemmings: The Army That Genghis Led."

It may be fun to play around with such ideas, but in the end it is a pessimistic game. If we take such biological theories seriously, not only will poverty always be with us, as Jesus said, but also sexism, racism, violence, and conquest. Such pessimism can easily suggest that any effort to change things is useless. Men will always be men, and everyone must endure the ramifications with resignation. Before we succumb to this temptation, we should deliberate the alternative.

Although *Homo sapiens* has probably acquired, through the course of evolution, certain species-specific behavior patterns, these patterns are more inclinations than instincts. The instincts have been reduced to inclinations because human culture has also evolved into a potent force. This force conditions whatever part of our character is inherent. The power of culture is evident in the infinite diversity of human societies. For instance, except for a handful of constraints (such as warfare), sex roles display an amazing variety of alternatives. Marriages can be monogamous, polygamous, or polyandrous; lineages can be matrilineal or patrilineal; and the very gods can vary their gender. Western conceptions of masculinity and femininity may be turned completely topsy-turvy. In our own society, virtually all differences between men and women may be safely ascribed to how we have chosen to define the male and female roles. Even aggression may be more subject to cultural indoctrination than to biological manifestation. For example, men and women need not differ on a wide array of ways of expressing aggressiveness, including the need to dominate others. The historical record even endorses this egalitarianism of human potential. The famous queens of history were far from submissive souls. In our own time, several women have stood as tall as any statesman: Golda Meir, Indira Gandhi, Sirimavo Bandaranaike, Margaret Thatcher, Benazir Bhutto, Corazon Aquino, and Aung San Suu Kyi.

Human nature is more than what has nature has put into us. Part of our nature—and the portion that is especially human—is our natural capacity for devising artificial cultures. That cultural heritage then instills in each of us the ability to transcend the limitations of our biological past. To be sure, in *Civilization and Its Discontents* Freud warned us that the disruptive impulses always lurk beneath the surface, ready to erupt the moment we relax our vigilance. In recent times, we have seen this happen in atrocities committed at My Lai or in the killing fields of Cambodia. We continue to witness this in lynch mobs and urban riots. Even so, neither men nor women are fated to be mere animals. As Katherine Hepburn (playing the missionary Rose Sayer) reprimanded Humphrey Bogart (playing the boozy boat captain Charlie Allnutt) in the film *The African Queen*: "Nature, Mr. Allnutt, is what we are put in this world to rise above."

Psychobiological Psychobiography?

Sigmund Freud began his career as a biological scientist. His interests in the natural sciences were inspired, in part, by reading Charles Darwin. As a medical student at the University of Vienna, he was heavily involved in laboratory research. He did his early work under the famed physiologist Ernst Brücke, after whom Freud named one of his own sons. In his first independent project, Freud investigated the structure of the testes in eels, presaging his later preoccupation with sex. Even when Freud made his first steps toward creating psychoanalysis, his thoughts were deeply embedded in the biology of his day. For example, in his "Project for a Scientific Psychology," an unpublished treatise written about 1895, Freud tried to provide a neurological theory for libido, repression, and other psychological concepts.

As the psychoanalytic movement gained ever more adherents, the biological roots became obscured. Freud himself emphasized that his ideas emerged from the raw data of the clinical session, such as his patients' dreams and free associations. He began to downplay the extent which his thoughts were speculative extrapolations from then-current biological theories. Accordingly, when Freud and his colleagues began to develop psychobiography and other forms of psychohistory, biology played a minimal role, if any, in the psychoanalytic interpretations. Freud's analysis of Leonardo da Vinci set the tone: If you wish to comprehend what makes someone tick, search into the figure's childhood for the critical experiences. Freud wrote:

> In Leonardo's case, we have had to maintain the view that the accident of his illegitimate birth and the excessive tenderness of his mother had the most decisive influence on the formation of his character and on his later fortune, since the sexual repression which set in after this phase of childhood caused him to sublimate his libido into the urge to know, and established his sexual inactivity for the whole of his later life.

This same emphasis reigns in other classic psychobiographies. Besides the analysis of Woodrow Wilson by the Georges, this path has been followed by Erik Erikson in his influential *Young Man Luther: A Study in Psychoanalysis and History*. Yet, by interpreting adulthood personality via childhood relationships, the psychobiographers seem to throw biology out the window. Child–parent interactions are treated as shapers of personality development, and any biological substrate is ignored. In most psychobiographies, the conversion of psychoanalysis from a biology to a psychology is complete.

To be sure, exceptions do exist. I have already noted the rival explanation of Wilson's rigidity. And a sizable literature has accumulated around King George III of Great Britain, in which his spells of insanity are diagnosed as attacks of a rare metabolic disorder known as porphyria. Nonetheless, exceptions like these are rare. Certainly psychobiology is seldom called upon to explicate a luminary's personality development. For example, I have yet to come across a psychobiography that uses the latest findings in behavior genetics. But what if it is true that anyone's basic personality results more from biological inheritance than from environmental effects? Then certainly it would be incumbent on any psychobiographer to determine whether the subject's personality profile can be ascribed to genetic dispositions. This would require assessment of parental and sibling characteristics, compelling the psychobiographer to construct family pedigrees *à la* Galton. Take Freud himself. Ernest Jones, Freud's foremost biographer, observed:

> From his father Freud inherited his sense of humor, his shrewd skepticism about the uncertain vicissitudes of life, his custom of pointing a moral by quoting a Jew-

ish anecdote, his liberalism and free thinking, and perhaps his uxoriousness. From his mother came, according to him, his "sentimentality" . . . [which] should probably be taken to mean his temperament, with the passionate emotions of which he was capable. His intellect was his own.

Granted, not all of the suggested transmissions are necessarily genetic. Yet if Freud had an identical twin raised in a separate family from his, behavior genetics would predict that the same basic sketch might still apply (although the favorite type of anecdote might not be Jewish). Furthermore, the final sentence in the quotation hints at the operation of another crucial genetic process. Freud's intellect was truly his own. It is clear from Freud's childhood that he was extremely precocious. He would do such things as teach himself Spanish so that he could read Cervantes's *Don Quixote* in the original. His prodigious powers exceeded by far what we would expect from his parents' genetic contributions alone. Moreover, none of his siblings exhibited anything like Freud's capacity. Only his daughter Anna has a claim to fame. From a Galtonian standpoint, Freud juts out from familial obscurity almost as much as Gauss, Newton, Shakespeare, Beethoven, and Michelangelo. Freud's unique genius may illustrate the impact of emergenesis.

Behavior genetics is not the only psychobiological discipline that might be brought to bear on psychobiography. Another possibility would be to exploit the scientist's alternative to the astrologer's horoscopes. Since time immemorial, astrologers have forecast a client's personality constitution according to his or her date of birth. Although the scientific case for astrology is dismal indeed, the pseudoscience captures a grain of truth. For instance, researchers have found that the season of a person's birth affects the odds that the person may succumb to schizophrenia or other mental disorders. Better yet, several investigators have shown that the proper timing of an infant's birth may predispose the offspring toward greatness. Famous personalities are most likely to be conceived in the summer and born sometime in the later winter and early spring. Birth under the sign of Aquarius is particularly auspicious.

Evidently, these season-of-birth effects are not mere artifacts of summer romances causing increased birth rates nine months later. Besides exceeding the baselines for the general population, the more famous the historical figure, the higher the odds of a birth in the first three months of the year. Inductees into the Hall of Fame for Great Americans, for instance, show this preponderance far more than a matched group of fellow Americans. In addition, the optimal months may depend on the specific domain of achievement. Hence, the effects may reflect some combination of prenatal and early postnatal factors. These factors apparently operate by their effects on intellectual and personality development. Research has found enough of these effects to inspire Hans Eysenck to name this whole discipline "cosmobiology." After a hefty inventory of season-of-birth effects has been built up, cosmobiology might someday be used to devise rough personality sketches. These outlines would enlarge upon whatever we can surmise from a person's genetic endowment alone. These "scientific horoscopes" might then contribute, however modestly, to a well-rounded psychobiological psychobiography.

Whatever the fate of this cosmobiological application, my main point remains: At least a part of what makes a person pre-eminent may be governed by events occurring before his or her birth. Psychobiographers must document this birthright if they wish to explain an individual's greatness. Some important personalities are indeed "born great."

ACTS, AFFECTS, AND THOUGHTS: LEARNING-BASED AND COGNITIVE THEORIES

Recent years have seen the emergence of cognitive science as a distinct enterprise. This discipline includes researchers in cognitive psychology, linguistics, artificial intelligence, neuroscience, philosophy, and even anthropology. These assorted scholars all share a fascination with the inner workings of the human mind. They seek knowledge about how the intellect acquires, transforms, and applies mental representations of our external world. At first glance, cognitive science might appear to offer little to a psychology of history. Almost as a matter of principle, cognitive scientists mostly ignore "the influence of affective factors or emotions, the contribution of historical and cultural factors, and the role of background context in which particular actions or thoughts occur." Researchers believe that disregarding such factors marks the optimal route to raising the study of the mind to the status of a true natural science. Even so, the corollary is often the publication of results irrelevant to comprehending the full range of human thought, feeling, and action in the practical world.

Still, enough investigators have veered from the mainstream to make a whole chapter on the mind in history possible. Here, I specifically survey perception, memory, and thinking. But before turning to these topics, I must discuss two more basic processes, both having to do with learning.

Adjusting to the World: Modes of Learning

The study of learning has long been a subject most strongly associated with behaviorism, the very school of psychology that the cognitive revolution strove to overthrow. By studying learning, many behaviorists sought to bypass discussion of the mind. Thus Ivan Pavlov, who despised the introspective methods of early psychological science, viewed conditioned reflexes as a far more objective foundation for understanding human behavior. Even more vociferous was B. F. Skinner, whose concept of operant conditioning supposedly allowed psychology to circumvent the examination of consciousness. Moreover, Pavlovian conditioning focused on the learning of stimulus associations, while Skinnerian conditioning focused on the learning of behavioral adaptations. Accordingly, neither mode of learning considers cognition directly. Even so, these processes may participate in the making of significant human events.

Pavlovian Conditioning

Pavlov won his Nobel Prize for his pioneer research on digestive processes. As part of this work, he devised new techniques for gauging salivation in a dog when it consumes food. Being a meticulous experimenter, he noticed that the salivary glands responded to other stimuli in the laboratory that happened to be associated with the food. By pursuing this serendipitous finding further, Pavlov established a new fame for himself in the psychology of learning. In particular, he investigated many of the critical circumstances by which organisms learn "conditioned reflexes." If an experimenter rings a bell whenever a dog receives meat, the ringing sound will come to be associated with, or "conditioned to," the food. Accordingly, the canine will eventually salivate to the bell as well as the meat. The bell-inspired salivating has become a "conditioned response."

On first blush, Pavlov's discoveries may seem remote from the realm of history making. Yet others extended his research paradigm to other questions far more applicable to our current concerns. In the United States, many of these extensions were carried out by John B. Watson, the founder of the behaviorist school of psychology. Watson conducted a classic demonstration with a one-year-old boy, "little Albert," to show how "aversive conditioning" could explain the learning of emotional reactions in human beings. When Watson's study began, Albert showed no fear of white rats. But the child did have an instinctive terror of a loud clanging sound produced by suddenly striking a long steel bar with a hammer. So whenever Albert approached the rat, the experimenter would strike the bar, and thus Albert rapidly learned to hate white rats. Furthermore, the fear generalized to other white furry objects, even Santa Claus beards! Little Albert had picked up a "phobia" to such stimuli. Unfortunately for the innocent subject of these manipulations, Watson had to end the study before Albert's negative affective response could be extinguished. In a rather callous conjecture, Watson suggested that years later Albert might have to see a psychoanalyst about his irrational fears.

This very process operates in the domain of history. One instance is the attitude that European Jews developed toward the music of Richard Wagner. During the rise of the Nazis in Germany, an emotional association was built between this anti-Semitic ideology and Wagner's music. Wagner's operas had a special appeal to Adolf Hitler and his party because the librettos were inspired by Nordic legends, the mythologies of those whom the Nazis viewed as the master race. Few Jews of that time and place could forget the pilgrimage that Hitler made to Bayreuth, where Wagner had built a theater to perform his operas in the proper style. There Der Führer was welcomed by the theater director, Wagner's own son Siegfried. Years later, when the survivors of the holocaust emigrated to Israel, the antipathy remained. The Israeli Philharmonic, though a world-class orchestra, refused to play any Wagner piece. Almost half a century after Hitler's Bayreuth tribute, when Zubin Mehta ended his valedictory concert with the orchestra by using a Wagner encore, members of both the audience and the orchestra walked out!

We can even go beyond anecdotal evidence. Below I discuss two applications. The first regards the learning of negative affect, the second the learning of positive affect.

The Black Hat: Learning Negative Affect

The villains hissed in melodramas are by custom decked from head to toe in black. As a rule, the outlaws in classic movie Westerns wore black hats. In the *Star Wars* movies, the modern science fiction trilogy, Darth Vader, or the "Dark Father," robes himself in black helmet, cape, and gear. The symbolism is obvious: Black represents evil. Nor is this negative connotation confined to film and television. Table 3.1 offers instances from several domains. The badness of black permeates common words and expressions, literary quotations, implicit contrasts, and many historic events.

This connotation is not even unique to white European civilization. The same negative associations are found in cultures all over the globe. Similar examples are even found among the peoples of black Africa. The negative connotations are so universal that they could have ancestral roots in primates' fears of darkness, when danger approached the unwary. Yet, whatever the source of the sense, we have all experienced this meaning so many times that black may lend itself to classical conditioning. Any event or person associated with blackness may take on a negative affective tone. In addition, when we associate a person with blackness, we may inadvertently produce a "self-fulfilling prophecy." That is, we may change our expectations about their behavior, and by doing so may end up encouraging bad or even evil behaviors in the individuals who are the objects of our expectations. This influence may be reinforced by the actors' own conceptions of blackness as well. Let us examine a concrete example from an actual empirical investigation.

North American football and ice hockey are among the most violent of team sports. Players are frequently penalized for "unnecessary roughness" and other aggressive behaviors. Some professional teams in each sport also wear black uniforms, or at least uniforms that look black in the vast distances of the stadium. The Los Angeles Raiders in the National Football League (NFL) and

TABLE 3.1. Examples of "Black" Having Negative, Evil, or Aggressive Connotations

Words and expressions: blackball, black art, black beetle, blacken, black flag, blackguard, black hat, black-hearted, black humor, blackjack, blackleg, blacklist, black looks, black magic, blackmail, Black Maria, black mark, black market, black mass, black outlook, black sheep, black spot, black words.

Literary quotations: "I am black, but comely" (Song of Solomon); "The devil damn thee black" (William Shakespeare); "But I am black, as if bereav'd of light" (William Blake); "As black as a tar-barrel" (Lewis Carroll); "From a cheap and chippy chopper on a big black block" (William Gilbert).

Implicit contrasts: snow white versus pitch black; angel's food versus devil's food cake[a]; Eve White versus Eve Black.[b]

Historic instances: Black Bartholomew (England, 1662); Black Death (Europe, 1347–1351); *Black Diaries* (Roger Casement, 1959); Black Flag Army (Southeast Asia, 1883–1885); Black Friday (United States, 1869 and 1873; Germany, 1927); Black Hand (Spain, up to 1883, and Serbia, before World War I); Black Hole of Calcutta (India, 1756); Black Hundreds (Russia, 1905); Black Legend (about the Spanish Inquisition); Blackshirts (Mussolini's fascists and Hitler's SS); Black Sox scandal (actually Chicago White Sox, 1919); Black Week (Boer War, 1899).

Note. Most of these examples come from a diversity of sources—dictionaries, encyclopedias, and histories—simply by looking up entries or indexed items under "black."
[a]This example courtesy of Muhammad Ali, the former boxing champion.
[b]From *The Three Faces of Eve*.

the Philadelphia Flyers of the National Hockey League (NHL) are examples. Hence, do the black-uniformed teams seem meaner? The answer is yes. For instance, investigators found that between 1970 and 1986, the Raiders led the NFL in the number of yards penalized. In contrast, over the same period the brightly colored Miami Dolphins suffered the fewest penalty yards. Likewise, in the NHL between 1970 and 1986, the Philadelphia Flyers exceeded all other teams in the number of minutes they were penalized. Judging from a simulation study the researchers conducted, part of such unsportsmanlike behavior may be in the eyes of the beholder. The same action looks different according to whether the actor is black or white. But a portion of this difference is also the result of the athletes' rising (or lowering) to the occasion. There is something about being dressed in black that inspires a little extra meanness in a soul that is already pretty fierce. In line with this are the histories of two professional hockey teams, the Vancouver Canucks and the Pittsburgh Penguins, that switched from nonblack to black uniforms. The altered appearance became reflected in the penalty minutes the two teams chalked up! Black acts bad.

The study above helps us comprehend stories on the sports pages such as this one:

It was aptly billed as a kind of turf battle between the NFL's two most notorious black-clad bullies, and in that sense it didn't disappoint. The Raiders and Atlanta Falcons combined for six personal fouls (evenly distributed), 18 penalties and numerous scrapes, skirmishes and shouting matches.

More importantly, we also have a useful model for understanding historic events outside the sports arena. Sometimes commentators apply the term "black" retrospectively, as in the Black Sox baseball scandal. Yet other times individuals or groups may shrewdly select blackness to implant terror in the hearts of their enemies. When the Abbasids raised the flag of revolt against the Umayyad Caliphate of Damascus, blackness and darkness were among their weapons. Not only did the rebels unfurl a black flag, but they dressed in black uniforms to face their enemy. They even fought under banners bearing such names as "the Shadow." The terrifying image may have had the desired effect. The rebel soldiers were probably more ferocious, and their opponents more afraid. The black act was victorious.

The Insidious Smile: Learning Positive Affect

The next example of emotional conditioning concentrates on how we may develop a more positive attitude toward some person. In particular, to what extent are our feelings about politicians shaped by the electronic media? Most Americans learn the bulk of what they know about a politician's policies from watching the news on television. Even if the network newscasters seem to be nonpartisan and unbiased in their reports, rather subtle processes may be going on while we gaze at the flickering screen. David Brinkley, a face familiar to many viewers of network news, once admitted:

> A person presumably is expected to go on the air and be objective, which is to say that he is to have no likes, no dislikes, no feelings, no views, no values, no standards; to be a machine. . . . I'm not objective, make no pretense of being objective. There are a great many things I like and dislike, and it may be that at times some indication of this appears in my facial expression.

An obvious facial expression at a newscaster's disposal is the smile. Anyone can convey personal feelings about a politician by smiling to express positive affect, such as liking. So suppose that two candidates are running for president, and one elicits more newscaster smiles on the evening news. Can the viewer undergo conditioning, and thus pick up the same emotional response?

According to a recent investigation, this conditioning of liking may indeed happen during the presidential election season. In the eight days leading up to the 1984 presidential election, the investigators videotaped the nightly news programs for all three national networks. They then carefully examined the facial expressions displayed when the newscasters spoke of Ronald Reagan and Walter

Mondale. The faces they scrutinized were those of Peter Jennings (ABC), Dan Rather (CBS), and Tom Brokaw (NBC). Whereas Rather and Brokaw revealed no smiling biases favoring one candidate or the other, the smiling behavior of Jennings was strongly pro-Reagan. The next step in this study was to conduct a telephone survey of television viewers. The researchers found out which newscaster viewers watched and which presidential candidate they voted for. Those respondents who turned to Peter Jennings for their nightly news were far more likely to cast their ballot for Reagan than were those who favored the rival newscasters. Moreover, the investigators analyzed the content of the news programs to make sure that no bias was present in the factual coverage. No bias was evident. The sole difference in the message was the quantity of smiling the newscasters allotted each candidate.

Naturally, alternative explanations might still apply to these findings. Yet the results at least suggest some of the potential power of emotional conditioning. People often see the media as presenting a biased image of the news. Yet, by objective standards, the reporting may not be all that distorted. The facts may not conflict if the secret is hidden in the smile.

Skinnerian Conditioning

In later chapters I will have more to say about emotional conditioning. The cognitive revolution notwithstanding, it continues to be important to our comprehension of how people assign emotional meaning to events and persons. Nonetheless, even within the behaviorist tradition, this type of learning cannot tell the whole story. In rough terms, the focus is on how old responses are assigned to new stimuli. When a dog salivates to a bell, the canine's new trick is responding to the bell, not salivating. Yet much learning entails the acquisition of altogether novel behaviors. Hence, a different process must be responsible. We call this alternative mechanism "operant conditioning," because the organism learns new ways to operate on its environment. And the psychologist who did more than anyone else to demonstrate the explanatory power of operant conditioning was B. F. Skinner.

Until his death in 1990, Skinner was the most famous psychologist alive. In 1970, Skinner was declared one of the "100 most important people in the world today." This is an enviable claim to fame for a mere academic researcher. At first, Skinner's celebrity status is hard to comprehend. After all, he devoted most of his career to measuring how often rats pressed down levers or pigeons pecked at disks. If Pavlov's research is characterized by a dog attached to laboratory apparatus, Skinner's work is defined by his famous "Skinner box." There a single animal would earn food pellets, or "reinforcement," upon performing a particular act, or "operant." Graphs would roll out of the laboratory equipment, recording precisely when the organism performed the operant and when the reinforcements were dispensed. The elementary tenets of all Skinner's research are straightforward: Organisms do what they have been reinforced to do, and they avoid doing what they have been punished to do. Skinner systematically studied various schedules of reinforcement, compared the comparative efficacy of punishment versus rewards, and generally worked out the details about how operants are acquired.

Skinner's efforts might not have attracted nearly so much attention were it not for his boldness. He was always willing and able to extrapolate well beyond the "cumulative records" generated in his lab. Based on the principles of operant conditioning, for example, he devised teaching machines for use in schools. His behaviorist principles became the foundation for the innovative methods of behavior therapy. And in his novel *Walden Two*, Skinner went so far as to design a society superseding Thomas More's *Utopia*—a perfect community guided by the laws of behavior analysis. Finally, Skinner fought hard battles against what he considered to be outmoded ideas about human nature, expressing his radical notions in books with deliberately provocative titles such as *Beyond Freedom and Dignity*. Skinner's primary goal was to remove all mental concepts from psychology, to make the discipline a science of behavior rather than an inquiry into the mind. Owing to the controversial quality of his claims, Skinner was probably as infamous as famous. Rumors abounded about a supposedly heartless man who raised his own daughter in a Skinner box.

When the cognitive revolution took place, Skinner became the designated archenemy, and he responded in kind. Although the dust is still settling after this debate, one truth remains: Skinnerian learning represents a central process in both animal and human behavior. As such, operant conditioning may participate in the making of history. I give two rather divergent examples below, the first concerning campaign speeches and the second creative productivity.

Campaign Rhetoric

To illustrate the effectiveness of operant conditioning, many an instructor in introductory psychology has told the anecdote about a lecturer who was the secret target of Skinnerian learning. As the story goes, his students had conspired to pay attention to him only when he approached one specific side of the lecture hall. If he ventured to the center or the opposite side, the students diverted their gazes and began to fidget and doodle. By the hour's end, the human guinea pig found himself delivering his concluding words huddled in one corner of the room. This anecdote may be apocryphal, but it does show how operant conditioning applies to the shaping of human behavior. Moreover, psychologists have conducted experiments proving that we can manipulate human beings in this fashion. Using social rewards as innocuous as saying "uh-huh" in a conversation, anyone can influence what a naive person says during an exchange.

The relevance of this mechanism to the political arena is obvious. When candidates for office deliver their "stump speeches" before audiences, they are opening themselves up for operant conditioning. When they express some opinions, cheers resound throughout the audience; other remarks elicit silence, if not jeers. Little by little a shrewd politician learns what wins and what alienates voters. One researcher studied this very phenomenon by examining audience reactions to candidates' speeches during the 1980 presidential campaign. He actually counted the applause, cheers, laughter, and boos that audiences gave to statements by the various presidential candidates. He found evidence that the more successful aspirants learned to adjust their speeches according to the feedback. Evidence also suggests that an experienced campaigner learns to avoid complicated policy statements or stands on controversial issues. Instead, audiences reinforce harmless references to general goals and broad visions. Voters may have become cynical about the sincerity or courage of their political leaders, but given the way they dispense rewards and punishments, should they expect otherwise?

Admittedly, other factors besides policy statements affect voter responses, such as the visual image a candidate conveys. Even so, from the perspective of the politician, the impact of cheers and jeers upon speechmaking cannot be denied. Hence, the conditioning of verbal operants may be a potent force in politics. Yet we must also confess that this phenomenon may be more cognitive than the behaviorist might like. When experimenters expose human subjects to Skinnerian schedules of reinforcement, the subjects often notice the contingencies that shape their behavior. By the same token, the political candidates' heads contain cortical matter, which they certainly can use to determine consciously what rhetoric works and what doesn't. So revisions of their favorite addresses may be conscious and deliberate. Nevertheless, it remains curious that the candidates exhibit the same learning curves as those found for the pigeons in a Skinner box.

Creative Output

It may be common sense to conclude that political candidates conform to audience feedback. After all, in a democracy they cannot expect to win without the votes. Yet when we turn from political leadership to the contrary world of creative genius, our expectations switch dramatically. "The true artist," said Shaw, "will let his wife starve, his children go barefoot, his mother drudge for his living at seventy, sooner than work at anything but his art." Material rewards mean nothing, and even the approbations or condemnations of critics are meaningless. Indeed, many men and women of genius fear the corrupting or distracting influences of fame and fortune. T. S. Eliot got depressed when he won the Nobel Prize for literature: "The Nobel is a ticket to one's own funeral. No one has ever done anything after he got it." And Dostoevsky, after receiving a handsome advance from a publisher, said to a fellow writer of his horror: "I believe that you have never written to order, by the yard, and have never experienced that hellish torture." Oscar Wilde put it succinctly: "Genius is born, not paid."

In support of these testimonials, psychologist Teresa Amabile has staked her reputation on a single principle: "Intrinsic motivation is conducive to creativity, but extrinsic motivation is detrimental." Persons are intrinsically motivated when they are driven "to do some creative activity by their own interest in and enjoyment of that activity." They are extrinsically motivated when the impetus comes from "some goal imposed on them by others," whether by rewards or by evaluation. To prove her hypothesis, Amabile has conducted ingenious laboratory simulations. In one experiment she assigned self-identified creative writers to two groups. She asked the writers in one group to fill out a questionnaire about the inherent joys of composition, such as liking to play around with words. Those in the other group filled out a different questionnaire on the more external benefits of writing, such as winning financial security by publishing a bestseller. Writers in both groups then wrote short, haiku-style poems. A panel of judges, themselves poets, rated the products. Amazingly, those writers who were tricked into contemplating extraneous rewards composed inferior pieces. Amabile's intrinsic-motivation principle of creativity was confirmed.

Even so, this research was not done on illustrious creators. Most often, college students or even children served as subjects. When we turn to creative behavior of more profound significance, the case against extrinsic reinforcements is not nearly so clear. In fact, often creative individuals operate precisely as if they were in the equivalent of a Skinner box. For example, several sociologists have proposed models that explain the productivity of scientists according to the "reward structures" of science. A few economists have similarly accounted for changes in creativity across the life span according to expected benefits, or "utility functions." Several psychologists have even gotten into the act, proposing investment and psychoeconomic theories to explicate output. These models are too formal to sketch here. Yet we can envision a little *Gedanken* (thought) experiment that illustrates one way reinforcements and punishments may operate.

Imagine this scenario: There are 100 aspiring young creators all wanting to make a name for themselves as short-story writers. All 100 have equal talent, and all graduated from a creative writing program in the same year. All send off their first creative gems to the most prestigious magazines and periodicals. Alas! Editors cannot accept all manuscripts. The space available in literary journals is limited. Let us say that the editors can only accept 10%, and they mail rejection slips to the remaining 90% of the authors. In effect, the editors have reinforced story-writing behavior in the lucky few, and punished the same operants in the unlucky many. According to the principles of operant conditioning, the probability of submitting another story will be enhanced for the 10% and weakened for the 90%. Now imagine that this process is repeated over and over. Ever more would-be authors will become disheartened and drop out of the competition, becoming taxicab drivers and the like. Ever fewer survivors will dominate the output of short stories, becoming the literary giants of their generation. The latter soon receive prizes and honors, which in turn encourage them to take on bigger and better projects, such as the next great American novel.

What I have just described is the scheme by which the rich get richer and the poor get poorer. The recipe operates in all creative domains, not just in short-story writing. Sociologists of science often term this reinforcement process "cumulative advantage," but the essential idea is the same. This process is related to the general phenomenon known as the "Matthew effect," which has been defined as follows: "The Matthew effect consists in the accruing of greater increments of recognition for particular scientific contributions to scientists of considerable repute and the withholding of such recognition from scientists who have not yet made their mark." The inspiration for this term is a passage in the Gospel: "For to every one who has will more be given, and he will have abundance; but from him who has not, even what he has will be taken away" (Matthew 25:29). Significantly, mathematical models based on the doctrine of cumulative advantage correctly predict how elitist the population of successful scientists will eventually become.

Besides predicting the contrasts between the prolific and the nearly silent, reinforcement models have been extended to the nitty-gritty details of the creative process. Skinner himself applied his mode of analysis to the operations involved in writing poetry, to Gertrude Stein's method of composition, and to the use of alliteration in Shakespeare's sonnets and Swinburne's "Atalanta in Calydon." More recently, one of Skinner's star disciples, Robert Epstein, has built a brilliant theory of creative insight upon the principles of operant conditioning. In testing his theory, Epstein has simulated moments of insight behavior in pigeons! We can even exploit Skinnerian theory to explicate the directions taken in the life of the theory's maker.

B. F. Skinner's original ambition was to become a creative writer. Only after a miserable struggle to make his mark in Paris and New York did he realize that the literary world was not going to reward his offerings. As Samuel Johnson once said, "No man but a blockhead ever wrote, except for money." So Skinner became a psychologist. As such, Skinner earned praise and promotions, and hence more reinforcement, for emitting that peculiar operant known as the scientific journal article. In line with the doctrine of cumulative advantage, Skinner eventually became extremely prolific, and many honors and awards came his way. Operant conditioning, in the guise of cumulative advantage, shaped Skinner's life toward success.

Skinner would not look unkindly on this application of his theory to his life. In his own autobiography, Skinner describes his personal history from the outside, as if he were an organism genuinely at the mercy of reinforcement contingencies. Skinner even spent much of his life in a glorified Skinner box. An inventor of ingenious gadgetry his entire life, Skinner invented a contraption to keep track of the amount of time he spent at his desk. When he accumulated enough credit, he allowed himself the luxury of sitting at the keyboard to play music. Hence, operant conditioning, whatever its value in explaining creative output in people at large, may provide a reasonable interpretation for the behavior of one particular creative genius.

Perceiving People

We come now to a topic easily within the domain of cognitive psychology. When empiricist philosophers such as Locke and Hume asserted that all human knowledge comes via the sense organs, they were assigning primacy to perception. Perceptual processes provide the basic substance for all cognitive operations that follow. However, perception may be too basic a process for someone interested in the psychology of history. Most of the connections often look quite lame. For example, the psychologist can apply the laws of perception to great works of art, offering insights into how our experiences fit the aesthetic stimulus. Thus, psychologists can analyze the distinctive use of additive rather than subtractive pigments in the pointillist paintings of Seurat. Or psychologists can scrutinize the distorted laws of perspective in the surrealistic compositions of de Chirico.

Yet such applications of psychology are seldom superior to what the art critic can offer the connoisseur. At best, psychologists can merely correct the errors of those who make false assumptions about perceptual processes. For instance, people have often speculated that the vertically elongated figures in the paintings of El Greco resulted from astigmatism. Yet back in 1914 David Katz pointed out the absurdity of this explanation. If El Greco saw real people stretched out, he would have seen figures drawn with normal proportions in the same way. Otherwise, the reclining figures in his paintings would have been unduly fat!

More profound are the effects of more complex perceptual processes. How we perceive our social world, particularly in the political arena, can shape the course of human affairs. Our very notions about the "lessons of history" may distort our perceptions of international politics. A laboratory simulation has shown how this distortion can occur. The experimenter exposed subjects to the same political scenario, but by subtle cues manipulated the historical analogies that might apply to the facts. Was this another situation like the 1938 Munich agreement, in which appeasement of Hitler failed miserably to guarantee "peace in our time"? Or would the proper analogy be Vietnam, where a nation became mired in a war in which it could not easily attain "peace with honor"? Not only were the facts of the case perceived differently according to the lesson applied, but the recommended judgments varied too. The subjects were much more likely to advise armed intervention if the hypothetical crisis represented "another Munich." But if the circumstances defined "another Vietnam," the advice leaned toward restraint.

Hence, it is in the domain of political perception that cognitive psychology may offer most to a psychology of history. Below I review two additional examples of perceptual distortions with political outcomes.

Good versus Bad

In Aristotle's *Poetics*, we find the first mention of the "tragic flaw." The plot of many Athenian tragedies pivots around this dramatic device. The hero or heroine of the play may be replete with strengths and virtues, but a single weakness or vice brings about the lead character's destruction and doom. Shakespeare, too, adopted this technique. We discern its workings in the irresolution of Hamlet, the ambition of Macbeth, the jealousy of Othello, the pride of Coriolanus, and the vanity of Lear. Yet the spectacle of the tragic flaw may also befall real and important people. The history of Christianity in the United States is riddled with fallen ministers who succumbed to sexual temptations: Henry Ward Beecher, Aimee Semple McPherson, and, more recently, the televangelists Jim Bakker and Jimmy Swaggart.

Of more significance, perhaps, the tragic flaw may strike down candidates in the midst of political campaigns, and therein alter the course of history. James Blaine would have become president in 1884 were it not for his failure to repudiate at once the catchy but anti-Catholic and anti-Irish slogan "Rum, Romanism, and Rebellion." More recently, Edmund Muskie's quest for the presidency in 1972 was derailed by one episode in which he broke down in tears. Gary Hart threw away his chance at the White House in 1988 when reporters caught him having a midnight rendezvous with an attractive model.

Psychologists who study person perception have often observed the disproportionate impact of negative information on impression formation. A negative item about a person carries far more weight in our judgments than does a positive item that objectively should have equal importance. This asymmetrical effect equally operates in the perception of politicians. Whether we look at congressional races or presidential campaigns, voters are more swayed by what is wrong about a candidate than by what is right. For instance, in the 1984 presidential election, American voters viewed Mondale as weak on leadership, whereas they perceived as Reagan as lacking compassion. These flaws carried far more weight in voter judgments than did the apparent assets of the two candidates. Luckily for Reagan, leadership is a more essential part of the White House job description than is compassion. Why does the negativity effect happen? There are two main explanations.

First, voters may be "risk-adverse." They would prefer to minimize costs than to maximize benefits. In the 1964 presidential election, the chance that

Barry Goldwater might be more apt than Lyndon Johnson to use the atomic bomb was a risk that far outweighed any conceivable advantage of a Goldwater presidency. Similarly, whatever virtues Muskie or Hart may have had, few voters wished the potential embarrassment of having their chief executive crying in the Oval Office or sneaking sex in White House broom closets.

Second, the negativity effect may be an offshoot of a "positivity bias." People have positive attitudes toward most people, as if everyone agreed with Will Rogers's upbeat "I never met a man I didn't like." Indeed, this bias is irrational. Garrison Keillor, in his popular *A Prairie Home Companion* radio broadcasts, described Lake Wobegon as the small town where all the children are above average. In fact, students rate their teachers, on the average, as above average, and voters do the same for their representatives in Congress and the candidates running for the White House. This positivity bias sets a high baseline for comparison when a person's actions or words reveal a failing. The result is that more weight is assigned to negative than to positive information. We get a figure–ground phenomenon: When goodness is background, badness becomes foreground.

Because experiments support both explanations, they probably operate in tandem. Yet of the two, the second account has the more curious implication. What happens if we are antagonistic toward a particular figure, such as Adolf Hitler or Saddam Hussein? If we then come across positive information about the despised personality, would it have an exaggerated influence on our impression? Or would we distort the information to fit our initial notions? The next topic suggests that the second alternative may actually occur.

Them versus Us

A famous person once said, "I hold that a little rebellion, now and then, is a good thing, and as necessary in the political world as storms are in the physical." What's your own opinion? If I told you that this remark came from the pen of Vladimir Lenin, what would you think? Would your interpretation change if I told you that the passage was Thomas Jefferson's instead? This quotation has actually been the stimulus in studies of "prestige suggestion." The core idea behind this research is that people's readings of a statement depend on the prestige of its alleged author. Indeed, the same concatenation of words can assume rather contrary meanings, according to the attribution of authorship. Solomon Asch demonstrated this effect using American college students as subjects. When subjects thought Lenin was responsible for the quote, they concluded that he "was probably vindicating the Russian Revolution. He meant that a Revolution is not bad but good and necessary. It is necessary as it removes evils and cleanses as a storm does the physical world." But with Jefferson's name attached to the remark, subjects reinterpreted the passage to render it less revolutionary. "By 'little rebellion' Jefferson might have meant what we would now call third parties," said one student. "By rebellion he means alertness and the exercise of political rights," said another. It was as if the two groups of students read different words!

Jefferson was the true author of this subversive preference. Because the subjects were Americans, Jefferson was a founder of their republic, and thus a member of the "ingroup." They therefore felt the need to soften the inherent violence of the assertion. In contrast, Lenin belonged to the "outgroup." After all, he was the founder of the Soviet Union, which at the time of the experiment was headlocked with the United States in the Cold War. Therefore, we might subsume this distortion under the more extensive process of ingroup–outgroup misperceptions. Two groups of people at opposing ends of some hot political debate will not see the world in the same way. An example is the "hostile-media phenomenon." In 1982 Israeli forces in Lebanon entered the Sabra and Chatilla refugee camps, and many Palestinian civilians were killed. When subjects watched news coverage of this event on U.S. network television, what they saw hinged on their stand in the Arab–Israeli conflict. Pro-Arab viewers thought the broadcasts were blatantly pro-Israeli, while the pro-Israeli viewers believed the coverage to be unquestionably pro-Arab. Since the same news segments were seen by both sets of viewers, the newscasters' attempts at objectivity went for naught, at least with this audience. Objectivity must appear biased to those who have polarized stands on an issue.

Of course, the media themselves are not always objective. Newspapers, in particular, will often join the fray, and thus accentuate ingroup–outgroup antagonisms. For instance, in two studies, David Winter examined how newspapers of different political persuasions reported the speeches of American politicians. In the first study he looked at the newspaper reportage of the presidential debates in 1960 between Nixon and Kennedy, as well as the 1980 New Hampshire primary debate among the Republican candidates. In the second study, Winter scrutinized media reports of the speeches of Jefferson Davis and Abraham Lincoln on the eve and onset of the Civil War. In both studies, the newspapers favorable to one political figure distorted the image of the opposing figure through selective quotation. Specifically, the reporters and editors culled material from the opponent's speeches that made him appear to be far more power-driven than could be justified by an unbiased perusal of the entire speech. In contrast, the media underemphasized the power orientation of the favored politician, again by the same means.

Now it could be that these biased quotes were quite deliberately chosen to defame the enemy. But it could be true as well that the distortion occurred at the very beginning, when the words were first read. Whichever cause holds, the outcome may be equally serious. The warped images of Lincoln and Davis certainly did not do anything to dampen the hostility then inflaming both North and South. In fact, Winter has speculated that this "mirror-image distortion" may function to escalate conflicts until they take violent form.

Psychologists who study international relations would concur. Urie Bronfenbrenner observed during the height of the Cold War that citizens of the world's two biggest powers held mirror images of each other's governments. Soviet citizens saw the United States as the aggressor in world politics, while Americans held the same view of the Soviet Union. Each side viewed the policy makers of the opposing side as pursuing policies that failed to represent the genuine opinions of the masses. Although these mirror-image perceptions did not provoke the two superpowers into overt war, other areas of the world have not been so fortunate. Ralph White has documented the pernicious effects of this process in several bloody confrontations, including the Vietnam War and the Arab–Israeli conflict. For example, Arabs and Israelis see each other in the same ingroup–outgroup terms: *"We* have both right and might on our side, while *they* are inhuman and inhumane." After inspecting the circumstances behind 37 wars fought between 1913 and 1968, White decided that at least 21 were patent cases of mirror-image conflicts. Hence, ingroup–outgroup bias does more than merely twist our perceptions of the political world. Our misperceptions also contribute, often horribly, to its unmaking.

Remembering Things and Happenings

History is often called the collective memory of a people. If this is true, research on memory might have something to say about historic events. Yet much memory research concerns phenomena leagues distant from practical affairs. The precedent was set by Hermann Ebbinghaus, whose 1885 *On Memory* became the first classic in this area. Ebbinghaus devised "nonsense syllables" that he could then commit to memory without any semantic connotations. To be sure, he also memorized genuine literature, such as Lord Byron's *Don Juan*, just for comparison purposes. Even so, it was his more scientifically refined approach that inspired most later researchers.

Yet in recent years, more psychologists have turned to the study of everyday memory. From our standpoint, the most provocative results concern the acquisition of expertise and the distortion of recollections.

Memory as Expertise

Every so often, nature conjures up a human intellect with intimidating powers of memory. These "mnemonists" may forget nothing that they have ever attended to. Many of these prodigal memorizers lead obscure lives, their phenomenal ability to recollect merely assuming the status of a private eccentricity. Sometimes, too, the remarkable skill belongs to a notable person, and yet the asset fails to figure prominently in the individual's expertise. For example, although Alexander Craig Aitken was an exceptional mathematician with a rare memory, his memorizing ability was mostly a sideshow in his professional achievements.

Even so, it also happens that an eminent figure not only enjoys an extravagant memory, but also manages to exploit this capacity in a domain of achievement. Arturo Toscanini, the famous orchestral conductor, provided a convincing example. He could remember virtually every note of every score he had ever studied in his entire life. Once when he wished to perform an old and obscure piece, the score could not be found. So he simply wrote the piece down from memory, dynamic markings and all. Later, when the music was finally dug up, he was found to have made only a single error. In another emergency, the orchestra's second bassoonist told Toscanini, just before a concert, that one key on his instrument was broken and thus unusable. After sinking into thought a moment, the conductor responded: "It is all right—that note does not occur in tonight's concert." Because late in life his eyesight failed him, Toscanini had no choice but to conduct all concerts from memory, and did so with aplomb. Toscanini had an extraordinary ability that served him well in his path toward greatness.

What about yet another alternative? Can anyone attain distinction in a field without displaying special skills at memorization? How big must an aspirant's storage capacity be for him or her to expect a reasonable chance of success?

Capacity Needed: 50,000 Chunks

For psychologists desiring to canvass the scope of expert memory, master chess players provide a prime starting place. Chess champions often show off their powers by playing blindfolded games against eight or more strong opponents simultaneously. Some champions, such as Paul Morphy, could even recall from memory all the moves from hundreds of prior matches. More important than these demonstrations is the well-defined and discrete nature of chess. Because chess has much the same character as a mathematical competition, psychologists can analyze the capacities of master players in an unusually precise fashion.

Research on chess memory has arrived at a startling conclusion: Master chess players cannot boast any special cognitive ability that sets them apart from lesser players. In particular, their general powers of memory are not necessarily outstanding. A classic demonstration of this surprising fact is a study conducted by William Chase and Herbert Simon. They compared the skills of a Class A player and a beginner with those of a master. The latter was Hans Berliner, one of the top 25 masters in the United States and once the correspondence chess champion of the world. The experimenters briefly exposed the subjects to pieces placed on a chessboard. Chase and Simon then asked the subjects to reconstruct the positions seen on another chessboard after a partition denied vision of the original. Sometimes the positions were genuine samples of actual middlegames or endgames, whereas in other test conditions the pieces were placed randomly on the board.

The results were striking. When the observed positions came from actual play, the chess master showed a pronounced superiority to the Class A player, who in turn performed far better than the beginner. This differential expertise was especially powerful for middlegames, with more pieces in more complex relationships. In stark contrast, the chess master was not any better at remembering the positions of the randomly placed pieces. Indeed, for both middlegames and endgames, the master did slightly more poorly (even if not substantially so) than the beginner! Evidently, Hans Berliner's recall supremacy was rather narrowly restricted to configurations of chess pieces that were likely to be encountered in actual games. Beyond that, his memory was no better than those of the two other players.

This outcome is not a freakish facet of chess mastery. Parallel results appear for other kinds of expertise, even in such sports as basketball. So why the effect? Chase and Simon surmised that the master's advantage came from the ability to "chunk" the complexity of chess configurations into far more manageable form. What is a chunk? Because the exact nature of a chunk varies according to the domain of expertise, here is an illustration that anyone can relate to. If someone gave you the number 289-468-7883 over the phone, you would have a tough time remembering it without writing it down. The number of digits anyone can store in short-term memory is about seven, so the area code is the last straw. But if you were given the same phone number in the corresponding letters, your difficulties would instantly vanish: BUY-HOT-STUF. Now instead of nine integers you have three words (albeit the third is misspelled). The amount of information is unaltered; yet when nine numbers are chunked into three words, the task will not exceed storage capacity.

This chunking process enables some experts to acquire seemingly impossible intellectual skills. Shakuntala Devi, a contemporary calculating prodigy, makes a living performing unbelievable feats of calculation. For instance, she made it into the *Guinness Book of World Records* when she multiplied two randomly picked, 13-digit numbers. In just 28 seconds, she found that $7,686,369,774,870 \times 2,465,099,745,779 = 18,947,668,177,995,426,462,773,730$. Arthur Jensen scrutinized Devi's speed of information processing at his chronometric laboratory, and found her to be unremarkable in any way. What *was* astonishing was Devi's ability to chunk lengthy series of digits into comfortable bits. When she saw the number 720 on a license plate, she immediately read it as $6 \times 5 \times 4 \times 3 \times 2 \times 1 = 6!$, or 6 factorial.

Nor is Devi unique, at least judging from a story told of another Indian, Srinivasa Ramanujan. When Ramanujan lay dying in a hospital, he was visited by G. H. Hardy, a notable British mathematician with whom he had collaborated. Hardy opened the conversation with the inept comment, "I thought the number of my taxicab was 1729. It seemed to me rather a dull number." Ramanujan contradicted Hardy at once: "No, Hardy! No, Hardy! It is a very interesting number. It is the smallest number expressible as the sum of two cubes in two different ways." Because Devi can and Ramanujan could so fluently chunk numbers, they could see hidden relationships among large quantities. This capacity has made Devi into a calculating prodigy, and it made Ramanujan into one of the all-time great contributors to number theory.

How many chunks must a person have available to exhibit such mind-boggling expertise? In studying chess, Chase and Simon concluded that the chess master's head was crammed with between 10,000 and 100,000 different chunking patterns. On the basis of other considerations, Simon and Chase has estimated that most experts gain about 50,000 chunks or patterns as the foundations for their expertise. This is not as monstrous a figure as it might first look. A well-educated person has a passive vocabulary approaching this size. Hence, if exceptional achievement requires only this much stored information, then most people have the potential for greatness. The only drawback is that it takes time to acquire all those chunks. Notwithstanding the claims of mail order catalogs selling batches of cassette tapes, we cannot learn foreign languages in weeks or months. Hence, before we get our hopes up, we should ask: How long does it take to assimilate 50,000 chunks?

Time Needed: 10 Years

It is rare for anyone to become a chess grandmaster, much less a world champion, without a considerable amount of experience at the game. Typically, the finest players have been staring at chess positions 3–13 hours per day for a full decade. Those masters who have taken shortcuts to fame by practicing less often find themselves making inexcusable blunders in international competition. Does the same time for apprenticeship apply to other domains of achievement? What about the precocity achievement of Mozart? When Mozart was only 14 years old, he attended a service in the Sistine Chapel during which he heard Allegri's *Miserere*. This was an elaborate work in four and five parts, with a finale in nine. Because the piece was a state secret of the Pontiff, no scores were available outside the Vatican. Mozart therefore wrote down the composition from memory. Obviously, the teenager had already gained an impressive ability to chunk compositional information. Even more critically, the young musician was already an accomplished composer by then. His name was attached to operas, masses, symphonies, sonatas, and dozens of lesser compositions. Does Mozart disprove the 10-year rule?

One psychologist thought not, and conducted a study to prove it. He began by noting that Mozart began training at an exceptionally precocious age—about age four. At the hands of his father, Leopold, a distinguished musician in his own right, Mozart thus commenced the crucial process of acquiring expertise. Moreover, Mozart's early compositions were not masterworks. By consulting a standard guide to records and tapes, the investigator defined a masterpiece as a composition for which there were five distinct recordings. Given this criterion, Mozart was 12 years into his career before he penned his first masterwork. Hence, if anything, Mozart's artistic development was slightly retarded when weighed against the 10-year rule of thumb.

The investigator next extended his study to 76 eminent composers of the classical repertoire. For each he determined the age at which they began intensive music studies, and defined that as the onset of the composer's career. As in Mozart's case, few composers produced masterpieces with fewer than 10 years of musical preparation. In fact, he identified only 3 exceptions out of 76 composers: Paganini wrote his *Caprices* and Shostakovich wrote his First Symphony only nine years into their respective careers, and Satie composed his *Trois Gymnopédies* only eight years into his career. A far greater number of composers waited longer before getting around to their first masterpiece. For example, Albéniz delayed until the last few years of his life, during which he penned *Iberia* for piano. Moreover, those who launched their careers earlier tended to conceive a masterpiece earlier; those who started later produced a masterpiece correspondingly later. Hence, it is not a simple matter of chronological age or life experience that is the crucial factor. A future musical genius needs the decade to acquire the 50,000 chunks requisite for truly original and effective creativity.

We will see later that there are interesting contrasts among creators concerning how much time they need to master the necessary knowledge and skills. Yet one declaration stands: There are no shortcuts to greatness. A person who aims to achieve anything of worth must learn, study, and practice.

Memory as Recollection

We have seen how memory, in the guise of expertise, underlies success. Yet the creation of big events also has an impact on people's memories. We often call important happenings "memorable." Thus, we must turn from memory as a maker of history to memory as the personal repository of history. Below I examine "flashbulbs," autobiographies, and hindsights. All three phenomena suggest that the mark left by the onrush of history is often poorly made.

Flashbulbs

Probably every American born sometime in the first decade after World War II has a memory comparable to this:

> I was seated in a sixth-grade music class, and over the intercom I was told that the president had been shot. At first, everyone just looked at each other. Then the class started yelling, and the music teacher tried to calm everyone down. About ten minutes later I heard over the intercom that Kennedy had died and that everyone should return to their homeroom. I remember that when I got to my

homeroom my teacher was crying and everyone was standing in a state of shock. They told us to go home.

If you were born a century or so earlier, you might have had a recollection running like this:

My father and I were on the road to A— in the State of Maine to purchase the "fixings" needed for my graduation. When we were driving down a steep hill into the city we felt that something was wrong. Everybody looked so sad, and there was such terrible excitement that my father stopped his horse, and leaning from the carriage called: "What is it, my friends? What has happened?" "Haven't you heard?" was the reply—"Lincoln has been assassinated." The lines fell from my father's limp hands, and with tears streaming from his eyes he sat as one bereft of motion. We were far from home, and much must be done, so he rallied after a time, and we finished our work as well as our heavy hearts would allow.

These striking personal records of historic occasions are so vivid, detailed, and apparently precise that they have been christened "flashbulb" memories. They are like mental photographs of the events they record. A large literature has now accumulated on these cognitive engravings of history. Table 3.2 lists some of the flashbulb memories studied so far. In general, three main conclusions can be drawn about the nature of this phenomenon:

1. Some events are more prone to produce flashbulbs than are other events. Assassinations are especially potent. The assassination of John F. Kennedy was about as likely to produce a flashbulb as shocking events in someone's personal life.

TABLE 3.2. Some Events Producing Flashbulb Memories Studied by Psychologists

Date	Event
1865 (Apr. 14)	Assassination of Abraham Lincoln
1941 (Dec. 7)	Attack of Japanese forces against Pearl Harbor
1963 (June 12)	Assassination of Medgar Evers
1963 (Nov. 22)	Assassination of John F. Kennedy
1965 (Feb. 21)	Assassination of Malcolm X
1968 (Apr. 4)	Assassination of Martin Luther King
1968 (June 5)	Assassination of Robert F. Kennedy (died June 6)
1969 (July 19)	Edward Kennedy's accident at Chappaquiddick
1969 (July 20)	NASA astronauts land on the moon
1972 (May 15)	Assassination attempt on life of George C. Wallace
1974 (Aug. 8)	Televised resignation speech of Richard M. Nixon
1975 (Sept. 5)	First assassination attempt on life of Gerald Ford
1975 (Nov. 20)	Death of General Francisco Franco by natural causes
1981 (Mar. 30)	Assassination attempt on life of Ronald Reagan
1986 (Jan. 28)	Explosion of the space shuttle *Challenger*

Note. These events are not identical in their capacity to generate flashbulbs.

2. Just as beauty is in the eyes of the perceiver, so does the occurrence of flashbulb memories depend on the observer. Thus, in comparison to European-Americans, Americans of African ancestry are far more likely to have such recollections about the assassinations of Evers, Malcolm X, and King. Even the assassination attempt on George Wallace was more productive of such memories among blacks than among whites.

3. Contrary to what the term "flashbulb" implies, the recollections are far from photographic. Rather than representing perfect records of a big event, the memories may undergo modest distortions over time. For instance, one person vividly remembered the circumstances surrounding the JFK assassination, even the messenger of the tragic news. But the supposed informant was not in the same place at the time, as verified by consulting suitable records.

Despite the consensus about the key features of flashbulbs, agreement is lacking on the psychological mechanism involved. The original investigators hypothesized a neurological "Now print!" process, motivated by the surprise and consequence of an event. Yet this account looks improbable, given the more current findings. Other researchers have highlighted the importance of an event's emotional impact on the observer, converting the cognitive "flashbulb" to an affective "flashback" phenomenon. This process may work along with another explanation put forward by Ulric Neisser, which is the most provocative in regard to the central theme of this book.

Neisser's account is as follows: Normally, we live in a world of two pasts—the thin string of events in our personal lives and that more grand succession of events that defines the course of human affairs. Certain dramatic but relatively rare events fuse these two segregated sequences into a single stream of remembrances. Hence, "we remember the details of a flashbulb occasion because those details are the links between our own history and 'History.'" It does not matter, therefore, how accurate these recollections are, as long as we possess them in the first place as special milestones of our lives. Accordingly, Neisser has concluded that "the term 'flashbulb' is really misleading: such memories are not so much momentary snapshots as enduring benchmarks. They are the places where we line up our own lives with the course of history itself and say 'I was there.'"

Autobiographies

Whether they are called "flashbulbs" or "benchmarks," the memories just discussed deal with the hand-me-down cloth of history. These memories are mere recollections of the circumstances when people heard about critical events. Yet we might suppose that the individuals so busy thus making their marks may also have flashbulb recollections of the personal events that expand to heroic proportions in world history. Such turning points are dutifully recorded in the agents' autobiographies or memoirs. A common example are creators' recollections of the great moments of insight that marked the advent of a revolutionary idea in art, philosophy, or science. In the *Autobiography* of Charles Darwin, we find this passage: "I can remember the very spot on the road, whilst in my carriage, when to my joy the solution occurred to me." The solution was nothing less than the keystone to his theory of evolution by natural selection. Darwin's flashbulb memory was of the idea's origins, rather than a more vicarious recollection of its impact.

Obviously an autobiography consists of much more than the listing of these moments. The bulk of most memoirs is devoted to narrating historic events from the standpoint of one particular maker of those events. Since even flashbulb memories are fallible, we must ask how much faith we can put in a luminary's narration of history. Comedian Will Rogers warned in his own autobiography that "when you put down the good things you ought to have done, and leave out the bad ones you did do—well, that's Memoirs." Although psychologists have conducted little research that bears directly on Rogers's skepticism, one case study does suggest precaution when reading the autobiographies of historical figures.

Most Americans born shortly after World War II will also probably have exciting recollections concerning the Senate hearings on the Watergate break-in. The biggest attention-getter in the earliest phases of the televised hearings was probably the testimony of John Dean, the former presidential counsel. In contradicting President Nixon's claims of innocence, Dean amazed his interrogators with his detailed memory of the shenanigans in the Oval Office. He repeated whole conversations virtually verbatim, and provided the precise dates for a host of important decisions. Only after Dean had completed his testimony did the investigating committee learn that Nixon had been secretly tape-recording all conversations. After much legal wrangling, the tapes were eventually released, and the transcripts of key meetings were made public. This unique circumstance provided an ideal opportunity for a direct comparison of John Dean's narration against the indubitably accurate record of the same events. Moreover, because Dean was relating events that had only occurred months before, any discrepancies between his testimony and the tapes would in all likelihood be smaller than similar discrepancies in genuine memoirs. After all, memoirs are typically the fruit of quiet retirement, years after the events.

Taking advantage of this test case, Neisser obtained some interesting results. On the one hand, John Dean's memory was demonstrably in error. He definitely did not deserve the nickname of the "human tape recorder." He frequently assigned conversations to the wrong days. He crudely paraphrased statements and remarks, and he often substituted words with wide alterations in meaning. Whereas Dean could often remember accurately exchanges with Nixon when he was one-on-one with the president, his recall would become lamentably incomplete once the conversations involved others as well. On the other hand, Dean's memory did manage to capture the essence of the whole series of conversations. The tactics adopted by the various key players, such as Nixon and Haldemann, were fairly (even if not precisely) portrayed. Those attitudes most consistently maintained throughout the period of the Watergate cover-up were those that Dean found the easiest to recollect. An abstract of Dean's testimony would closely parallel an abstract of the tape recordings.

Yet a curious and consistent distortion was also present in Dean's recollections: He overemphasized his own role during the deliberations in the Oval Office. The exchanges he recalled in the most impressive detail were those in which he was the most active participant. This exaggeration made him into a more central figure in the whole episode than he really was. Even so, we should not blame John Dean for this slant; the same egocentrism probably operates universally in memories for events in which one participates. For example, we find a kindred phenomenon in competitive team sports. When college basketball players, after a game, are asked to identify the game's turning point, 80% of the players refer to plays made by their own teammates. Human actors cannot help seeing themselves as the center of the universe, with other events and people hanging upon their actions. Even so, this tendency means that we cannot compile history from a single memoir. We must infer the facts of any episode, insofar as they exist at all, by forming a composite of the separate memoirs of all the event's participants. Historians are like the viewers of Kurosawa's film classic *Rashomon*: one rape and murder, four different stories. The true story presumably stands at the apex of various autobiographical egocentrisms.

Hindsights

When John Dean's sworn testimony was compared with the White House tapes, another provocative discrepancy appeared: Dean looked wiser and more prescient when recounting events before the Senate than he actually was in the Oval Office. For example, according to his testimony, Dean personally and explicitly warned Nixon about the repercussions of the cover-up:

> I began by telling the President there was a cancer growing on the presidency and that if the cancer was not removed the President would be killed by it. I also told him that it was important that this cancer be removed immediately because it was growing more deadly every day.

This admonition supposedly took place on March 21, 1973. The transcripts revealed otherwise. Even if Dean used the cancer metaphor more than once, he failed to caution that the cancer was terminal for the chief executive. On the contrary, Dean's emphasis was on the need for surgical measures to contain the growth. In his testimony before the Senate, Dean was displaying a "hindsight bias." It is easier to be a prophet when one already knows how the events worked themselves out.

Empirical studies have documented this bias. For example, one inquiry had college students predict the outcome of President Nixon's then-upcoming visits to the Soviet Union and China. Specifically, the students estimated the probabilities of particular events taking place (e.g., a face-to-face meeting between Nixon and Mao). After the visits became history, the students had to reconstruct the odds that they allotted the various consequences. Showing hindsight, the students assigned those events that actually happened higher *a priori* probabilities. Hindsight biases have also been demonstrated for presidential and gubernatorial elections. For instance, in the 1980 presidential election, students were superior predictors of the victor after the balloting than before. Judging from the evidence, the victims of hindsight bias are sincerely duping themselves, reconstructing their recollections to comply with actual events. To a large extent, hindsight bias is a memory distortion. Even so, we can only wonder how many so-called "political pundits" have claimed merits according to the deceptive operation of this process. Whether it be Saddam Hussein's invasion of Kuwait or the disintegration of the Soviet empire in Eastern Europe, it is always curious how many such experts can say "I told you so" or "I knew it all along."

Hindsight errors probably occur in many domains besides politics. The supposed clairvoyance of a psychic like Jeanne Dixon, for example, depends on retrospective interpretations of remarks that are hardly less ambiguous than the famed prophecies of Nostradamus. Similar specious prophecies occur in marginal science. Recently, Dr. Iben Browning received considerable attention in the press, owing to his apparent prowess at earthquake prediction. According to respected newspapers such as *The New York Times* and *The San Francisco Chronicle*, Browning was "known to have predicted the 1989 San Francisco earthquake a week in advance" or had "missed by just 6 hours hitting the Oct. 17 San Francisco quake on the nose in a forecast published in 1985 and by only 5 minutes in an update a week before the disaster." Owing to his widely publicized effectiveness, Browning terrified thousands if not millions of Midwesterners when he forecast a gigantic quake along the New Madrid fault in Missouri. Yet a close examination of his past predictions reveals no foundation for acclaim. Judging from video and transcript evidence, his supposed prophecy of the San Francisco earthquake neglected to specify even that the tremor would occur in the state of California. All that could be found was an ambiguous reference to global geological unrest. Dixon, Browning, and other prophets may be sincere, honest people. But good intentions alone cannot prevent the hindsight bias from twisting their recollections of past forecasts. Unhappily, what should be merely personal failings become magnified into prophetic events, as their revised predictions grow to become big events.

Evaluating the World

A guiding principle in cognitive psychology is that the mind processes information. To use the computer metaphor, the brain is a place where some internal program converts input to output. Below I discuss some of the difficulties that the intellect faces when trying to draw certain conclusions from received facts. I then look at how humans vary in the ability to handle information, and how this variation affects the chances of success.

Attribution: Judging People and Events

John W. Hinckley Jr. is the man convicted of trying to kill President Reagan in 1981. He is now in a mental hospital, and that is the end of the story. Yet when Lee Harvey Oswald assassinated John F. Kennedy in 1963, events unfolded quite differently. Although the Warren Commission reported a year later that Oswald acted alone, the American people, and even world opinion, are not so sure. Theories abound about conspiracies in which Oswald had only a part, sometimes even a small part. The conjectured conspiracies involved the CIA, or Fidel Castro, or the Mafia, or all of them together; theorists have pointed their fingers in diverse directions. Experts and amateurs have probed film segments and tape recordings over and over, and computers have repeatedly calculated bullet trajectories—all to no avail. To this day, a significant portion of the public still believes that a conspiracy brought Kennedy down. The year 1991 even saw a big-production movie, *JFK*, devoted to one especially popular conspiracy theory. Why all the controversy? Why can we accept Hinckley as the lone would-be assassin of Reagan, but not Oswald as the sole actual assassin of Kennedy?

Psychologists have explored this question in an instructive experiment. The inspiration behind their investigation was the hypothesis advanced by a journalist, Tom Bethell. According to this conjecture, "people have an irrational need to explain big and important events with proportionately big and important causes." Because a successful assassination is a more horrendous effect than a mere attempt, and because conspiracies involve more agents than a single crazy person, a killed president must be the victim of a conspiracy. After subjecting this possible superstition to detailed scrutiny, the researchers decided that people may not be as irrational as Bethell's hypothesis suggests. To be sure, observers are more prone to link successful assassinations with conspiracies, but the reason makes sense. People mainly believe that a group of conspirators has a higher probability of getting the job done. If Oswald had another conspirator on the notorious "grassy knoll" and perhaps a few other places, Kennedy would have been far more likely to be shot than if all depended on Oswald alone. In contrast, we may attribute Hinckley's failure to his lack of fellow conspirators ready to complete the task if he failed. Naturally, we may not be justified in the supposition that conspiracies enjoy superior odds of pulling off an assassination. Yet this would represent an error of fact rather than logic.

This inquiry marks a problem in "attribution," a topic that has attracted much research over the past few decades. Researchers seek to learn how people make inferences about the causes of events and the dispositions of actors in those events. We make these social inferences every day, mostly because they help us understand ourselves and our world. Like the study I have just described, much of the work on attribution is preoccupied with the limits of human rationality. Let me review two instances where the human race falls short when weighed against the standard of cold logic.

It's Not Their Fault!: Attributions about Others

When we make attributions about the things that other people do, we often face two major alternatives. On the one hand, we can make an "internal" attribution. That is, we can conclude that the person had some inclination, some intention, motive, or ability, that elicited the action. On the other hand, we can make "external" attributions, in which case we hypothesize that forces beyond the actor's control compelled the deed. To illustrate, Patricia Hearst, one of the heirs to the huge fortune made by William Randolph Hearst, was kidnapped in 1974 by members of the self-proclaimed Symbionese Liberation Army. Later she participated in a bank robbery with these same outlaw radicals. When she was eventually caught and tried, the jury had to make a critical choice between internal and external attributions. Was she a willing participant, someone who had sincerely converted from an heiress to a revolutionary? Or was she coerced into involvement, in fear for her life? The first was an internal attribution, the second external.

Logically, internal attributions are far more difficult to make than external attributions. In the former kind of inference, we judge what is supposedly going on inside someone's head. We cannot possibly see such covert feelings and thoughts directly; we can only infer these internal states from overt behaviors. Inferences about internal causes are especially problematic when we are trying to make attributions about an actor's "dispositions." Dispositional attributions entail the assignment of some stable trait, value, or attitude to a particular person. Thus, to conclude that Patricia Hearst was a revolutionary is to claim that this became an integral part of her personality. Dispositional attributions are dangerous because we commonly have so little useful information to go on, and what data we do have at hand are often quite misleading. Frequently, there are numerous situational forces that constrain a person to act one way rather than another. Therefore, as human beings, we all should be wary of making such judgments.

Yet, instead of holding off until we gather enough facts, we are quick to make dispositional attributions. Indeed, we ascribe actions to a person's enduring character even when the power of the extraneous circumstances can be crushing. We call this tendency to make dispositional attributions notwithstanding situational constraints the "fundamental attribution error." A curious example can be found in Thornton Wilder's popular novel *The Bridge of San Luis Rey*. Crossing a bridge in Peru at exactly the wrong moment, five persons plunge to their deaths when the span collapses. A Franciscan missionary, Brother Juniper, believes that the accident represents an act of God. He therefore probes the lives of the victims to decipher the secret of why these five have been singled out. Juniper's detective work only makes sense if one believes that these people were somehow responsible for this tragic mishap. Otherwise, the Franciscan should have spent more time studying civil engineering.

Probably the most interesting manifestation of this inferential mistake is how assassination affects our perception of the victim. Not long after John F. Kennedy fell to Oswald's bullet, he underwent an apotheosis on the part of many historians of the presidency. One author quickly identified Kennedy as one of the seven greatest presidents who ever lived. Nor is enhancement unique to this most recent of presidential assassinations. Systematic analyses of all U.S. presidents reveal that successful assassination is one of the best things that can happen to a chief executive's (necessarily posthumous) reputation. Getting assassinated adds about as much to a former president's greatness rating as serving five years in office or leading the nation through four years of war. And not only historians do this; casual observers make the same dispositional attribution as well. The same benefit may also accrue to other kinds of leaders, such as absolute monarchs.

Some might argue that this linkage of assassination and greatness does not represent a genuine error of judgment. Perhaps great presidents do great things, which in turn attract the unwanted attention of the insane or fanatic. Yet this argument falters before two facts. First, a lengthy series of inquiries has confirmed that assassinated chief executives do not substantially differ from their more lucky brethren on hundreds of possible characteristics, including personality, leadership style, or administration performance. Second, it is only a successful assassination, not a failed attempt, that boosts a president's reputation. Unless we are willing to defend the idea that the more competent chief executives attract the better shots, this discrepancy must contradict any attempt to credit the president for getting killed. Most likely, whether an assassin succeeds or fails is more the result of luck than of anything else. If Hinckley had aimed his handgun just a tiny fraction of a degree differently, Reagan would have had a bullet in his heart rather than his lung. It still appears that people are succumbing to the fundamental attribution error.

Admittedly, this error need not always enhance the image of a public figure. Dispositional attributions can be negative as well as positive. The assassination of Martin Luther King in 1968 illustrated this alternative. A survey of 1,337 American adults shortly after this tragic event revealed that fully 426, or almost one-third, thought that King had "brought it on himself." This tendency to "blame the victim" is actually all too common, particularly in instances of rape and murder. Even so, whether the recipient's reputation gains or loses points, the same attributional error remains operative. Dispositions are given more credit in either case than they deserve. And it is interesting that in King's case, the American people eventually turned around and created a national holiday in his honor. Two out of the three famous Americans so honored were the victims of assassination. The other, of course, was Abraham Lincoln, the first president to suffer such a tragic death.

It's Not My Fault!: Self-Serving Attributions

Why are we sometimes so quick to blame the victim? Why did so many Americans imply that King got what he deserved? Why does Brother Juniper investigate the lives of those who died at San Luis Rey? One answer is that these attributions are defensive in nature. By inferring that bad events occur only to bad people, we protect ourselves from the belief that similarly evil events might befall us as well. Defensive attributions suggest that our inferences are often designed not to get at the true causes, but rather to coddle our fragile egos. We choose between internal and external causes, dispositions or situations, according to what best maintains our self-esteem. Insofar as we do this, a "self-serving bias" hampers a rational understanding of our world.

This contamination is most likely to emerge when we are trying to explain victory or defeat. When we are successful, we wish to take all the credit, so we look for something inside of us that produced the worthy deed. But when we fail, we want to avoid any blame; we therefore look to forces outside our control as the responsible agents. For example, two investigators showed how this bias operates in the world of sports. They specifically examined the sports pages to see what attributions were made concerning 33 major sporting events. The events included the World Series in baseball, and football games at both collegiate and professional levels. The statements scrutinized came from the mouths of players, coaches, and the presumably less biased sportswriters. The results were clear. Players and coaches of winning teams made internal attributions 80% of the time: The team was just great, or some star player made the game-winning play. Players and coaches of the losing teams had a different view, favoring external attributions 53% of the time. The defeated felt that they were not personally responsible, but succumbed to bad luck. The sportswriters, in contrast, were more objective when explaining wins and losses, because their egos were less at stake.

Self-serving bias appears in other domains where victory or defeat spells elation or depression. One investigator looked at the attributions of both winning and losing candidates in each of 33 races. The races all took place in the state of Wisconsin in 1964, and included the candidates for the state senate and assembly, the U.S. House and Senate, and five statewide offices. The victors had no problem ascribing success to their own personal assets and effort. The losers, in comparison, made it clear that the voters were ignorant of the issues, or voted the straight party line, or blindly conformed to national or statewide trends—or they found some other external excuse. Winners seldom say, "I lucked out," and losers seldom admit, "I got what I deserved."

One last example will convey the ubiquitous operation of the self-serving bias. This time let us turn to the 1965 Watts riot. Besides learning how the reactions of African-Americans differed from those of other Americans in the community, we want to know how those who participated in the riot differed from those in the community who did not but were of the same race. According to one survey, the perceived causes of the riots were fairly distinct for the three groups. Those blacks arrested in the streets were most likely to attribute their actions to chronic circumstances beyond their control, such as grievances about racial injustice. Even though blacks in the community who did not get involved also favored this attribution, they were not nearly so emphatic about it. But the biggest contrast came from the whites in the community. Only a third ascribed the civil violence to stable external causes. Those causes would make the whites, as members of the empowered majority, part of the problem. So instead many white survey respondents pointed to some freakish condition, such as the hot weather. Alternatively, they suggested that the rioters were communists, criminals, or agitators, and thus they relinquished responsibility themselves. Few of those arrested relied on such unflattering internal attributions. There was only one Watts riot in August 1965. Yet insofar as attributions were concerned, the self-serving bias generated as many kinds of causal explanations as there were separate interests.

Needless to say, many athletes, candidates, or rioters could entertain private opinions that might depart from what they admit publicly. They would then be merely doing impression management. Yet for many individuals experiencing the games, elections, or riots, the self-serving bias informs what they believe in their heart of hearts. It allows them to live with themselves.

Two Sides of Every Question: Simple versus Complex Thinking

Up to this point, we have been looking at human information processing as if everyone were working with the same mental computer. Yet people may vary remarkably in the sophistication of their information processing. Some are complex thinkers, while others are simple-minded. Just as importantly, the effectiveness of cognitive functioning may fluctuate according to the circumstances. Psychologists have devised an instrument called the Paragraph Completion Test, or PCT, to assess variations and fluctuations on this factor. Subjects write three or four sentences that finish certain sentence stems—for example, "When I am in doubt . . ." and "When I am criticized . . ." Investigators can then score the responses according to an objective scheme that determines each subject's level of "integrative complexity." Someone with high complexity can process multiple perspectives and then integrate them into a coherent viewpoint. In contrast, a person with low complexity can handle only a single perspective; he or she views the world in simplistic, black-and-white terms.

Because scores on the PCT come from written protocols, it is easy to adapt the scoring method to other written materials. In fact, integrative complexity scores have been calculated from letters, speeches, interviews, and editorials. As a result, psychologists can assign scores to people who are too important or too busy to take the PCT. For example, speeches delivered in the Senate of the United States can betray the integrative complexity of U.S. senators. A sample of a statement low in complexity is the following:

> Stiff trade tariffs must be introduced to stop the flood of Japanese steel and cars into our country. Millions of American workers are in danger of losing their jobs. Failure to introduce tough tariffs will amount to economic surrender to the unfair trade practices of Japan.

This passage discloses the speaker's unwillingness to consider alternative interpretations about the trade imbalance between the United States and Japan. The outlook is clearly rigid and one-sided. Contrast this narrowness with the following paragraph:

> Saudi Arabia seeks to maximize the benefits it can gain from its massive oil reserves. It attempts to keep prices high but not so high that demand for oil drops off steeply or the Western economies are badly damaged, or alternative sources of energy become competitive. The Saudis also recognize the destabilizing effects that massive inflows of capital can have on their own economy and political system. The Saudis are performing a delicate balancing act in which they must weigh many competing economic, domestic and geopolitical objectives against each other.

Obviously, this speech reveals a greater sensitivity to the intricacies of Saudi Arabian oil policy. The senator understands that the Saudis must ponder a host of not always consistent goals before arriving at a unified pricing system. This second passage scored high in integrative complexity.

An impressive body of research has examined integrative complexity in a wide array of leaders. This research shows that we must take this factor into account in order to comprehend major events. Let me just give three examples now.

Peter Suedfeld and Dennis Rank were the first to assess historical figures on integrative complexity. They were intrigued with the aftermath of political revolutions. Some revolutionaries participate in the new regime that follows the government takeover, whereas other revolutionaries lose in the power struggle. In the French Revolution, a fair number of revolutionaries literally lost their heads; Robespierre was perhaps the most famous of these unfortunates. Suedfeld and Rank argued that complexity is a crucial factor deciding a revolutionary's fate. On the one hand, to pull off a successful revolution requires an intense single-mindedness. Revolutionary leaders must convince themselves and their followers that the old regime is all wrong and their cause all right. Hence, all revolutionaries must exhibit low complexity. After the takeover occurs, on the other hand, the situation changes dramatically. Running a country is never so simple as revolutionary rhetoric implies, and concessions must stabilize the government. Thus, the new rulers must become more complex. The catch is this: Not all revolutionaries can make the switch. Because some activists may be inherently dogmatic, they fail to stick around or do not last in the newly improvised political system.

To test this hypothesis, Suedfeld and Rank examined the careers of 19 leaders of five revolutions. Some of the successful versus unsuccessful revolutionaries they included in their study were Oliver Cromwell versus John Lilburne (English Civil War), Jefferson versus Hamilton (American Revolution), Lenin versus Trotsky (Russian Revolution), Mao Zedong versus Lin Biao (Chinese Revolution), and Fidel Castro versus "Che" Guevara (Cuban Revolution). After collecting the leaders' speeches and writings from both before and after the takeover in each revolution, the investigators scored the material on complexity. Consistent with expectation, the successful revolutionaries became noticeably more complex after the takeover, whereas the unsuccessful could not adapt to the changed conditions. Typical of this effect is Lenin, who compromised pure communism with the 1921 New Economic Policy. Trotsky, in contrast, eventually found himself *persona non grata*. Stalin finally had Trotsky assassinated while he was living in exile in Mexico.

A second inquiry looked at the career of a single leader, Robert E. Lee. The aim was to determine whether integrative complexity has had any repercussions for success on the battlefield. The researchers scored paragraphs written by Lee between 1839 and 1867. Also scored were paragraphs by Union generals who opposed Lee in six key battles of the American Civil War: George McClellan at Antietam, Ambrose Burnside at Fredericksburg, Joseph Hooker at Chancellorsville, George Meade at Gettysburg, Ulysses S. Grant at the Wilderness, and Grant again at Spotsylvania. In most of these conflicts Lee's army held their own against vastly superior forces, and Lee's complexity surpassed that of most of the opposing generals. However, Lee's superiority to Meade was smaller than his advantage over McClellan, Burnside, or Hooker, in line with Lee's loss at Gettysburg. More significant were Lee's confrontations at Wilderness and Spotsylvania. In those two battles Lee for the first time faced a general, Grant, whose integrative complexity surpassed Lee's own. No doubt a host of factors doomed the Confederacy. Yet certainly among these many factors was the reality that Lee had finally met his match.

The third and last study takes us to the voting booths of America. The previous two investigations suggest that integrative complexity aids effective leadership, an effect implied by other inquiries as well. Yet circumstances arise when the reverse holds. One such occasion is during a revolutionary struggle, as we have just seen. Another occasion is when politicians appeal for votes in a democratic election. There is evidence that voters want campaign messages to be simple rather than complex. On the other hand, once the elected politician assumes office, the rhetoric must change, as it must do for successful revolutionaries. To examine this process, Philip Tetlock scored the policy statements of American presidents from McKinley through Carter. Each president made some of his statements before election to the White House, whereas others were issued while he was serving as the incumbent chief executive. The contrast between pre- and postelection scores was striking. Moreover, the shift from low to high complexity was sudden; it occurred in the first month after inauguration. Therefore, we cannot ascribe the change to a president's making a gradual cognitive adjustment to the more complex environment in which he found himself. In addition, for those incumbents seeking a second term as president, complexity manifested a fast drop toward the end of the first term in office. The time would then have come to revert to simplistic campaign rhetoric.

These three findings can converge in the life of a single historic personality. This is evident in the career of Adolf Hitler. Instead of gauging integrative complexity, one study used the "dogmatism quotient," or DQ. Because DQ and integrative complexity assess opposing characteristics, they often yield comparable results. Hitler's DQ score was extremely high in the speeches he delivered in the years from 1923 through 1933. These were the years in which the Nazis struggled for power. After Nazis seized the government, Hitler's DQ declined at once, just as we would expect for any successful revolutionary. His speeches before the Reichstag were closer to those of an incumbent American president. This was the Hitler who outwitted the leaders of Europe. After the onset of World War II in 1939, Hitler became ever more dogmatic. By 1943, at the war's height, Hitler was every bit as rigid as he was in the period before his takeover. Unfortunately for the Third Reich, these were critical years in which Hitler was making some horrid military decisions. The disastrous German invasion of the Soviet Union, with the stupendous strategic mistakes at Stalingrad, now makes more sense. The Hitler of the 1940s was not the same leader as the Hitler of the 1930s. His proficiency as an information processor had dropped precipitously.

Mental Twists and Turns in History?

In Chapter 1 I have spoken of history as the collection of significant events and personalities from the past to the present. Yet the word has other meanings besides. For instance, we can talk of history as a subject taught in schools, colleges, and universities. Although this definition is somewhat less interesting than the one stressed in this book, cognitive psychologists may still have some interesting findings to offer. As an example, every student in America must come to grips with the fact that the United States has its presidents. Accordingly, it is intriguing that researchers have investigated how people recall the succession of chief executives and how they form impressions of individual presidents. Perhaps this work may someday see application in the development of new instructional techniques.

Another meaning of history leads to a problem far more acute: History is also a profession. If psychology is what psychologists do, then history is what historians do. We might then inquire into the psychology of the historian. Here the value of a cognitive analysis should be self-evident. Cognitive psychologists study how human beings process information. And historians are paid for processing data—data about historic events and persons. Because historians are *Homo sapiens*, the same principles that account for cognitive behavior in the human race must explicate their activities with equivalent effectiveness. For example, do historians also exhibit a negativity bias when they evaluate the political figures of history?

A survey conducted by Robert Murray and Tim Blessing implies an answer. They asked 846 professional American historians to rate the overall performance of 36 presidents of the United States from Washington through Carter. Three chief executives landed at the bottom as the certified failures: Nixon, Grant, and Harding. Now, what attribute do these three characters have in common that they do not share with a single president with superior acclaim? Despite the millions of factors on which the presidents may differ, only one response seems plausible: All had scandals that shook their administrations to the very core. When we reflect on their presidencies, we must recall such shameful episodes as Credit Mobilier, the Teapot Dome, and Watergate. Nor is this merely a judgment call. Statistical analyses show that whether or not a scandal plagued an administration is the single most powerful predictor of a president's posthumous reputation. Let's put it in numbers: A chief executive could serve two full terms in office, including four full years as commander-in-chief during a major war, and end up a below-average president, *if* he had a scandalous administration. Or more concretely, even if Nixon had been assassinated the day he resigned, his reputation would not have risen above that of Herbert Hoover! Aren't the historians displaying a negativity bias?

I offer one more example. We know that vivid or salient events, because they so readily catch the eye, inordinately influence the judgments of the typical human being. This fact may explain why American presidents who serve as wartime leaders receive higher ratings that those who presided over times of peace. Indeed, heads of state all over the globe are more likely to occupy conspicuous places in the history books if they led their nations in major wars. In *The Dynasts*, Thomas Hardy has the Sinister Spirit say: "My argument is that War makes rattling good history; but Peace is poor reading. So I back [Napoleon] Bonaparte for the reason that he will give pleasure to posterity." This cynical attitude could justly represent how historians are attracted to the raw data of their profession. New light is thus cast on a parenthetical remark made by Edward Gibbon in his *Decline and Fall of the Roman Empire*. He said that the reign of Emperor Titus Antoninus Pius was "marked by the rare advantage of furnishing very few materials of history; which is, indeed, little more than the register of the crimes, follies and misfortunes of mankind." How many historians even bother to narrate this boring reign?

Therefore, we might conceive a psychology of the historian as a branch of the psychology of history. By constructing such a specialty, we could better comprehend the fads and foibles of historiography, both classic and contemporary. This enterprise would dig deeper than merely pointing out precautions when scrutinizing memoirs, autobiographies, and other historical materials. For the analysis would focus on the historian's own mind, not the minds of those producing the raw facts. Of course, one might ask, "Who cares?" To have psychologists investigate how historians think seems like an ivory-tower exercise, in which one academic merely gazes at another academic's navel. Still, the matter has more than merely academic interest. At bottom, historians are the final arbiters of who makes it into the history books; they are the Guinness of the future records, the judges of the firsts and the bests. One cannot leave a mark on posterity without becoming thus co-opted by the historical profession. Hence, any creator, leader, or other celebrity, as a maker of history, is forever subservient to the capricious processes by which historians conceive past events. How they view the past defines the past, as recorded in the documents that only historians live to write. Lord Byron hinted at this inevitable truth when he wrote:

> And glory long has made the sages smile,
>   'Tis something, nothing, words, illusion, wind—
> Depending more upon the historian's style
>   Than on the name a person leaves behind.

THE CREATIVE QUEST

Who are the personalities who helped shape modern civilization? Many may name people like Thomas Edison, Albert Einstein, Jean-Paul Sartre, T. S. Eliot, Pablo Picasso, and Igor Stravinsky. However disparate their respective contributions, all fall under a single generic concept: creative genius. A "creative" individual is anyone who introduces some original product that changes how thousands of others think, feel, or behave. That product may be a treatise, technical paper, invention, poem, novel, painting, sculpture, composition, or any other tangible item. Whatever the specific vehicle, creative geniuses of the highest order are those whose influence extends well beyond the parochial confines of a particular area. Their novel and stimulating creations have become part of the public domain not only in their own time, but also for generations to come. The products of creative genius represent a primary route by which individuals attain greatness.

In this chapter I examine the processes that enable creative geniuses to exert so much leverage on history. I first review the research on human problem solving. From there I survey the various mental processes suggested by the introspective reports of the geniuses themselves. The final two sections deal with two principal forms that creativity can take: art and science.

Problem Solving

In 1845 Edgar Allan Poe published "The Raven." This poem accelerated his ascent to contemporary fame, eventually providing lines to be memorized by generations of American high school students. One year later, Poe published the critical essay "The Philosophy of Composition," which recounted the process by which this poem emerged. We might have expected Poe, as a poet in the Romantic age, to describe the flash of inspiration by which the entire poem appeared at once. As Poe put it, "Most writers—poets in especial—prefer having it understood that they compose by a species of fine frenzy—an ecstatic intuition." Yet Poe always prided himself on his analytical powers. As a result, Poe chose to present the origination of "The Raven" in a contrary light. "It is my design to render it manifest that no one point in its composition is refer-able either to accident or intuition—that the work proceeded, step by step, to its completion with the precision and rigid consequence of a mathematical problem." He emphasized that logic dictated every choice, from the poem's length and themes down to single words and images.

For cognitive psychologists who study problem solving, Poe's claim would not appear outlandish. On the contrary, these researchers have tried to make the case that creativity is nothing more than ordinary problem solving. No spe-cial mental processes are required; all participating processes are perfectly rational. According to this school, in fact, creative genius itself is pure myth. Anyone can become a history-making creator, once the right problem-solving techniques are mastered via the proper manuals. Although this notion may sound as far-fetched as yet another fad diet, we cannot dismiss this position easily. After all, an outspoken proponent of this idea is none other than Herbert A. Simon, psychologist, computer scientist, polymath—and Nobel laureate. So this hypothesis must be taken seriously. The case on its behalf is twofold: labo-ratory experiments and computer simulations.

Laboratory Models of Creativity

Experimental studies of problem-solving behavior began with the Gestalt psy-chologists, who focused on the process of insight. Those of this school viewed problem solving as primarily a perceptual process, one that entailed a sudden and novel reorganization of experience. A classic instance of the Gestalt ap-proach was Wolfgang Köhler's study of insight in chimpanzees. The chimp Sul-tan, by restructuring his world in an "ah-hah!" experience, managed to retrieve tasty bananas placed tantalizingly beyond his reach. Of course, many of the experiments used humans as well, but even these studies suffered from a big limitation: The experimental tasks were vastly more simple than those that face a creative genius. It is a big leap from these experiments to the ceiling frescoes of the Sistine Chapel or the theory of relativity.

When cognitive psychology later took up the question of problem solving, this restriction continued as well. The typical laboratory experiment had a sub-ject, usually a college student, grapple with abstract puzzles such as the Tower of Hanoi or the Mutilated Checkerboard. Consequently, the relevance of this work for understanding noteworthy achievements was not immediately obvi-ous. Even so, true believers affirmed that the psychological processes were no different in lab and world. For example, Herbert Simon argued that Men-deléev's discovery of the periodic law of the elements engaged nothing more advanced than what is "required to handle patterned letter sequences." That is not much of a mental prerequisite to produce something that, in the form of the periodic table, would eventually decorate every chemistry lecture hall throughout the world.

If we accept Simon's argument, cognitive psychologists have made considerable progress in divulging the means by which humans solve problems, both major and minor. Briefly put, problem solving entails the mental manipulation of symbolic representations of external reality. The person starts with a "problem space" that embodies the main features of a problem, including the current circumstances, the goal sought, and the various means (or "operators") for attaining the goal. The problem solver then searches through this problem space until he or she reaches the goal. Because a random search through the problem space seldom leads to an efficient solution, the clever mind employs "heuristics," or rules of thumb. Such heuristic tricks as "hill climbing" and "means–end analysis" restrict the range and depth of the search.

Take Sultan the chimp, for example. When he sighted a banana, the problem space consisted of the spatial layout of the cage, the objects within it, and the set of skills that he had learned over the years. Having first determined that the banana was beyond reach, Sultan could exploit his ability to use sticks in his environment to touch other objects. If this failed, he could move on to other options, perhaps guided by the heuristic that long objects are better than short ones. Eventually, Sultan fastened two sticks together and, thus, the chimp could triumphantly consume the object of his aspirations.

Because problem solving is seen as a conscious and deliberate process, researchers will often ask subjects to think aloud while they work. The recorded statements of the subjects' mental operations become the targets of "protocol analysis." Here the researchers decipher the details of the problem-solving process, including new search strategies and heuristics. Although these protocols confirm the broad theoretical framework underlying this research paradigm, we still must ask whether we have enhanced our comprehension of genuine creativity. Happily, cognitive psychologists have taken the offensive on this point. The initial sortie was a couple of informal "field experiments" in which unsuspecting subjects were presented with a problem of historical significance. The first of these clandestine tests, conducted by Simon himself, ran as follows:

> On eight occasions I have sat down at lunch with colleagues who are good applied mathematicians and said to them: "I have a problem that you can perhaps help me with. I have some very nice data that can be fitted very accurately for large values of the independent variable by an exponential function, but for small values they fit a linear function accurately. Can you suggest a smooth function that will give me a good fit through the whole range?"

Of the eight lunch companions, five found an answer in just a couple of minutes or less. None was suspicious of what Simon was up to, nor did any realize the historic nature of the problem given them. Still, those five anonymous individuals had independently arrived at Planck's formula for black body radiation. This was the discovery that launched the quantum revolution!

In the second miniexperiment, a mere graduate student in chemical engineering could derive Balmer's famous formula for the hydrogen spectrum.

Moreover, the subject's protocols revealed the same search process discerned in Balmer's surviving documents.

Research has advanced beyond these informal checks, as a recent laboratory experiment amply shows. Subjects drawn mostly from a student population studied raw data for two variables, s and q, for five cases. The specific scores were 36 and 88, 67.25 and 224.7, 93 and 365.3, 141.75 and 687, and 483.8 and 4,332.1, respectively. The subjects were told that the experimenters were "interested in how a human being discovers a scientific law." Therefore, each subject was to identify a precise functional relationship between s and q. "In order to follow your thoughts," the subjects were also instructed, "we ask that you think aloud, explaining each step as thoroughly as you can." Out of 14 subjects tested, 4 found the correct relationship. Yet, what these successful problem solvers accomplished was a rediscovery of the third law of planetary motion, first formulated by Johannes Kepler! In fact, the subjects wrestled with data that for all practical purposes were the same as those used in Kepler's monumental *Harmonies of the World* of 1619. The five sets of observations pertain to the planets Mercury, Venus, Earth, Mars, and Jupiter. Here s is the distance from the sun in millions of miles, and q is the period of revolution. Hence, the third pair of observations applies to the earth. The earth averages 93 million miles from the sun and takes 365.3 days to rotate around the sun. According to Kepler's third law, the distance cubed is proportional to the period squared, or $s^3 = kq^2$, where k is a constant.

Scrutiny of the protocols revealed that the successful subjects exploited the same heuristics found in other problem-solving experiments. For example, to find the relationship between two variables, one needs to find functions for each of the variables that produce a constant ratio. In this case, one must find a function f_1 of the distance and another function f_2 of the period, such that $f_1(s)/f_2(q)$ returns about the same quotient k across all observations. Moreover, the thought processes are so logical that a computer can be programmed to do the job. This cognitive simplicity suggests that computers, too, can rediscover Kepler's third law. They already have.

Computer Imitations of Genius

Ever since 1642, when Blaise Pascal built his calculating machine, the human race has felt threatened. The prospect then arose that a mere machine might usurp the privileged place of *Homo sapiens*. Philosophers from Aristotle to Descartes held that the capacity of reason is what separates men and women from dumb brutes. With the advent of calculators, however, the odds grew that machines could think. Human thinkers were repeatedly obliged to fight rearguard actions as calculating machines became ever more advanced. For example, when Charles Babbage conceived the first general-purpose computer, Augusta Ada (the Countess of Lovelace), his mathematical collaborator, carefully deliberated whether computers could exhibit authentic creativity. In 1842 at least, humanity could remain smug. She concluded that machines could not venture far beyond the instructions of the programmers. Yet nowadays computer science has reached the stage where people cannot be so sure; the original anxiety continues to mount. In the 1968 movie *2001: A Space Odyssey*, an inboard computer, HAL, decides to take over the mission to Jupiter, and kills almost all astronauts standing in its way. Is this a prophetic hint of bigger events to come here on earth?

The computer scientists dedicated to producing ever more intimidating machines are doing work on "artificial intelligence" (AI). The goal of AI research is to program a machine that can boast unmistakable intelligence. If successful, such a device would pass the "Turing test." By this we mean that a naive observer would find it impossible to distinguish the responses made by the machine from those generated by real persons. Because it is rather too ambitious to replicate an entire human mind, much AI research concentrates on fairly rudimentary behaviors. For instance, appreciable work has been devoted simply to getting a computer to understand simple English commands. Even so, several programmers have tried to make their machines emulate world-class chess players, human experts, and scientific geniuses.

Chess Players

Chess is among the oldest of all board games, and perhaps the most supremely intellectual besides. Chance is nothing; skill, even wisdom, is all. So it may not surprise us that AI researchers have been long engaged in writing computer programs that can play a decent game of chess. As we can grimly learn by purchasing a commercial chess player at a local computer store, these programs have already reached a capacity far exceeding that of the average recreational player. Indeed, computers can now take on and defeat chess masters. Still, the biggest test between mind and machine came on October 22, 1989—the day a computer program, DEEP THOUGHT, challenged the world chess champion, Gary Kasparov. Although Kasparov won both games played, those in the AI community believe that the days of human chess supremacy are numbered. It is just a matter of time before an updated version of DEEP THOUGHT will defeat all human challengers.* Only a few improvements in hardware and software are necessary to overcome our puny wetware.

Yet it is critical to note that DEEP THOUGHT does not *simulate* human chess playing. Instead, the program and its special computer chip employ a

---

*As this book went to press, a successor to DEEP THOUGHT named DEEP BLUE defeated the world's top-ranked woman chess player, Judit Polgar, in an informal match. DEEP BLUE won one game from Polgar and played her to a draw in the other. Unlike Kasparov, however, Polgar did not prepare by carefully studying the program's past games.

"brute force" approach that takes full advantage of the superlative speed of electronic circuitry. DEEP THOUGHT can scrutinize 700,000 moves per second; this enables the program to test every possible sequence of moves to a depth of five moves on each side. Chess masters, in contrast, operate according to a more efficient procedure, examining not all possible moves but only the superior ones. Human players, in addition, prefer long-term strategic advantages over short-term tactical gains. Unlike computers as well, humans try to fathom the strategy adopted by an opponent and to thwart it. Indeed, once a player defeated a program by duplicating move for move the victorious game of a previous master. Oblivious to the human's intentions, the computer mechanically repeated the very same moves—and went down to an exactly replicated defeat!

Nonetheless, when DEEP THOUGHT can inspect a billion moves per second, and thereby peek 25 moves ahead on every turn, the human being may be doomed. Still, our species will be defeated not by a chess-playing HAL, but by a beefed-up dumb brute. The collective ego of the human race should be no more threatened than it was by the old slide rule or the modern hand calculator. Besides, some may note that chess is just a game—one with finite dimensions, and lacking practical results. Can computers achieve anything of earthly consequence that requires indisputable expertise?

Expert Systems

Aldo Cimino is certainly not a household name. Yet within a specific domain he was almost irreplaceable. For 44 years, he was responsible for making sure that the big ovens used to sterilize soup cans kept running. If one of those ovens broke down, his employer, the Campbell Soup Company, lost the soup and lots of money. The problem was that Cimino planned to retire; no one else knew how to supervise the operation the way he did. So his company called in "knowledge engineers" to see whether a computer could carry on the task. The engineers followed him around, watched his behavior, and asked him questions, all with the aim of extracting everything he knew about his job. This "teasing" process continued until Cimino's knowledge was translated into 150 rules. The engineers then wrote a computer program called COOKER that succeeded Cimino when he retired. COOKER was an expert system.

Not long ago, the very idea that computers might replace human beings was the stuff of science fiction. HAL, we must recall, was a computer programmed to run the operations of the spaceship while most of the astronauts hibernated. Yet now, expert systems are not only with us; they have become a growth industry in applied computer science. Already hundreds of volumes have come out on the subject, and big money can be made by corporations that specialize in implementing systems for industry. Naturally, because machines are running machines in many of these applications, their existence may not appear too menacing. We may then see these devices as merely elaborate versions of the mechanical governors on old steam engines. Nevertheless, computer scientists have devised expert systems that can replicate far more sophisticated forms of human expertise. A fine example is MYCIN, which its creators hope will duplicate the acumen of the most knowledgeable physicians. MYCIN asks a series of questions, which a human answers. Then, through a complex chain of decision rules, the program arrives at a diagnosis and even suggests the most suitable treatment. Moreover, if the human attendant needs an explanation for what MYCIN decided, the program can provide one. MYCIN even contains a subprogram so that it can learn ever more medicine. And, unlike DEEP THOUGHT's sneaky end run around the human chess master, MYCIN really simulates the logical processes of the medical expert.

Even when all this is admitted, skeptics have raised many doubts about the ultimate utility of MYCIN and similar programs. For instance, the judgment of human experts still excels that of the best computer programs. In addition, we must wonder whether expertise of the kind modeled in these programs really qualifies a machine as something extraordinary in the human community. Let us suppose that MYCIN were so capable that it did not have to worry about malpractice suits. The most it could accomplish outside the hospital setting would be to write doctors' columns in local daily newspapers. We certainly could not expect MYCIN to make a revolutionary discovery in diagnosis or treatment. To be sure, some have tried to go beyond the mere simulation of human expertise, devising programs that actually show creativity. Even so, these attempts have not yet been successful. However, other computer scientists have pursued an alternative approach that may someday produce an idea deserving of a Nobel Prize in science.

Discovery Programs

The name "HAL" in *2001: A Space Odyssey* stood for "Heuristically programmed ALgorithmic computer." An "algorithm" is a set of routine commands that will, if faithfully followed, guarantee an answer. A heuristic, in contrast, as a mere rule of thumb, does not assure an answer. Instead, heuristics simply suggest the most promising places to look. Most AI programs are dominated by algorithmic rather than by heuristic thinking. This emphasis renders them more artificial than intelligent. Algorithms are handy enough for clearly defined, mundane problems, but questions that demand bona fide creativity require heuristic programming. Adopting this different approach, computers may simulate not chess skill or medical expertise, but outright creative genius.

Long ago, Herbert Simon argued that the discovery process has a definite logic, and therefore that scientific creativity might be programmed. Recently, this argument has taken form as actual "discovery programs." These software creations have several interesting features. First, the programs often receive the names of famous scientists of the past: OCCAM, BACON, GALILEO, GLAUBER, STAHL, FAHRENHEIT, BLACK, and DALTON. Furthermore, these tags are not wholly incidental. The heuristics implemented by the program often reflect those introduced by the human behind the eponym. Hence, BACON specializes in the inductive method, yielding data-driven discoveries as advocated in Francis Bacon's *Novum Organum* of 1620. In addition, the eponym chosen often suggests the domain of creativity the program pursues. GLAUBER, of Glauber's salt fame, concentrates on discoveries in chemistry.

These features would be merely cute were it not for a final attribute of these programs: They have shown an ability to rediscover scientific laws or principles that have made human scientists famous. GLAUBER can learn to distinguish acid and alkali. STAHL can identify elements as components of substances. DALTON can take the output from STAHL to generate structural formulas consistent with atomic theory. Yet it is BACON that is the powerhouse of discovery programs. BACON has discovered Kepler's third law of planetary motion, Black's law of temperature equilibrium, Ohm's law of current and resistance, Prout's hypothesis of atomic structure, the Gay–Lussac law of gaseous reaction, the Dulong-Petit law of atomic heats, and the derivation of atomic weights by Avogadro and Cannizzaro. No recipient of a Nobel Prize can boast this count and range of accomplishments. Often the programs make their rediscoveries using the same data that the scientific luminaries themselves used. Some programs even aim at duplicating the fine details of the process by which a scientist made a given discovery. For instance, KEKADA models the heuristics that Hans Krebs used to get the urea cycle. The programmers fixed this concordance by comparing the computer's output with both the notebooks and the living testimony of Krebs himself.

Few results in AI research are more provocative than these. Herbert Simon and others in this area believe that within a short time discovery programs will generate new scientific ideas, not just reproduce old ones. Others are more skeptical. The complaints are many, but three will suffice:

1. The programs do not always recreate the cognitive processes of creative scientists. For example, one critic compared the heuristics with the processes found in the extensive notebooks left by physicist Michael Faraday. Faraday's dynamic use of visual imagery and his reliance on cross-talk between separate projects have no counterpart in any of the discovery programs.

2. Computational models of discovery neglect the enormous effect of the social and cultural environment. Herbert Simon may claim that the periodicities in the elements seem obvious, but this was far from true at the time. Shortly before Mendeléev offered his solution, John Newlands presented his comparable law of octaves at a professional meeting. A distinguished scientist chairing the session waxed sarcastic, asking whether Newlands had also tried placing the elements in alphabetical order.

3. These programs may unduly emphasize problem-solving skills, whereas other talents may be more vital. For instance, one critic stressed that problem

finding may be more crucial than problem *solving*. What Albert Einstein said of Galileo may pinpoint an essential maxim of creativity:

> Galileo formulated the problem of determining the velocity of light, but did not solve it. The formulation of a problem is often more essential than its solution, which may be merely a matter of mathematical or experimental skill. To raise new questions, new problems, to regard old problems from a new angle, requires creative imagination and marks real advances in science.

These and other criticisms imply that creative genius involves more than logical problem solving. At best, Poe and Simon may have captured only a partial truth. That conclusion justifies the next section.

Originality

Donald Campbell proposed a model of creativity that differs greatly from Simon's. According to Campbell, creativity operates according to a process of "blind variation and selective retention." This process is the cognitive analogue of Darwin's mechanism for evolution by natural selection. Creativity begins with the unpredictable generation of a rich diversity of ideas. In essence, this process entails the chaotic recombination of ideas, images, words, and other basic elements of the mind. From this combinatory wealth of alternatives and conjectures, the intellect retains the best ideas for further elaboration and eventual communication.

A hint of this two-step procedure can be found in John Dryden's "Epistle Dedicatory of *The Rival Ladies*." He spoke of this play's creation as commencing "when it was only a confused mass of thoughts, tumbling over one another in the dark; when the fancy was yet in its first work, moving the sleeping images of things towards the light, there to be distinguished, and then either chosen or rejected by the judgment." Paul Valéry, the French poet, put it more succinctly: "It takes two to invent anything. The one makes up combinations; the other chooses, recognizes what he wishes and what is important to him in the mass of the things which the former has imparted to him."

Campbell's model has three interesting features. First, the initial process of ideational variation is blind. That is, the production of ideas is not completely guided by preconceived notions about the value of various possibilities. Second, the procedure of generating variations is not restricted to any particular cognitive processes. As will be seen shortly, many mental acts can produce the necessary variations. Third, Campbell's model applies to every form of creative genius. In recent years his theory has been applied to both artistic and scientific creativity. These three features set this model well apart from Simon's. In Simon's view, problem-solving search is rarely blind; the mental procedures are uniformly logical; and scientific discovery rather than artistic imagination offers the prototypical case.

Below I scout out the processes by which creative geniuses originate a profusion of ideas. I first lean heavily on what creators themselves have reported about their mental activities. Next I focus on a single attempt to work out the implications of Campbell's model.

What Creators Tell Us

Psychologists often take advantage of the insights that creators have offered about their own mental processes. Sometimes these firsthand accounts are spontaneous observations found in letters, essays, and autobiographies. Poe's essay on "The Raven" is an example. At other times investigators themselves have elicited the information; they have addressed the key questions directly to creative individuals, using either mailed questionnaires or one-on-one interviews. Here I survey just four sets of psychological mechanisms.

Imagination and Associative Richness

It is customary to think of artistic creativity as demanding enormous powers of imagination. In contrast, scientific creativity supposedly requires more pedestrian powers of pure reasoning. Yet the reports of scientists themselves do not sustain this distinction. Max Planck, the creator of quantum physics, said it clearly in his autobiography. According to this Nobel laureate, the scientist "must have a vivid intuitive imagination, for new ideas are not generated by deduction, but by an artistically creative imagination." Presumably, we cannot get the necessary abundance of variations in either art or science without this imagination. Yet in what does this imagination consist? According to Derek Price, a historian of science, "a scientist of high achievement . . . [has] a certain gift of what we may call *mavericity*, the property of making unusual associations in ideas, of doing the unexpected. The scientist tends to be the man who, in doing the word-association test, responds to 'black' not with 'white' but with 'caviar.'" William James broadened this answer to include all guises of genius in an essay that anticipates much of Campbell's theory. James described "the highest order of minds" in this way:

> Instead of thoughts of concrete things patiently following one another in a beaten track of habitual suggestion, we have the most abrupt cross-cuts and transitions from one idea to another, the most rarefied abstractions and discriminations, the most unheard-of combinations of elements, the subtlest associations of analogy; in a word, we seem suddenly introduced into a seething caldron of ideas, where everything is fizzling and bobbling about in a state of bewildering activity, where partnerships can be joined or loosened in an instant, treadmill routine is unknown, and the unexpected seems the only law.

This haphazard process tells us how memory is organized in the creative genius. In Chapter 3 I have discussed how a person needs 50,000 chunks of discipline-germane expertise to become an original problem solver. Yet evidently this mass of information must be organized in a very special manner for it to support noteworthy acts of creativity. The Austrian physicist Ernst Mach made this point quite clear. Mach began by admitting a certain utility in possessing "a powerfully developed *mechanical* memory, which recalls vividly and faithfully old situations." Even so, Mach insisted that "more is required for the development of *inventions*. More extensive chains of images are necessary here, the excitation by mutual contact of widely different trains of ideas, a more powerful, more manifold, and richer connection of the contents of memory." If the memory cannot support this associative chaos, there can be no creative imagination at all.

Intuition and Unconscious Processes

One can object that creators do not spend massive amounts of their time in chaotic associations. Even so, introspective reports suggest that this combinatory work takes place mostly below the threshold of consciousness. While core awareness concentrates on urgent tasks, variational ruminations occur in the background. For example, Jacques Hadamard argued that mathematical invention requires the discovery of unusual but fruitful combinations of ideas. To find such novelties, it is "necessary to construct the very numerous possible combinations." Yet "it cannot be avoided that this first operation take place, to a certain extent, at random, so that the role of chance is hardly doubtful in this first step of the mental process." Still, "we see that the intervention of chance occurs inside the unconscious: for most of these combinations—more exactly, all those which are useless—remain unknown to us."

Consciousness does not have to be obsessed with chaos, so long as subconsciousness is pursuing the byways and alleys of memory. Then "out of the blue" something potentially brilliant emerges, thrusting itself into central consciousness. Another French mathematician, the great Henri Poincaré, published an oft-cited anecdote that illustrates this process:

> Then I turned my attention to the study of some arithmetical questions apparently without much success and without a suspicion of any connection with my preceding researches. Disgusted with my failure, I went to spend a few days at the seaside, and thought of something else. One morning, walking on the bluff, the idea came to me, with just the same characteristics of brevity, suddenness and immediate certainty, that the arithmetic transformations of indeterminate ternary quadratic forms were identical with those of non-Euclidean geometry.

Poincaré concluded from this and other incidents that the moment of unexpected inspiration is "a manifest sign of long, unconscious prior work."

This work takes place in what Graham Wallas called the "incubation" period. On the basis of the introspections published by Hermann von Helmholtz, Wallas placed this phase between two other stages of the creative process—"preparation" and "illumination." In the preparatory stage, the associative chains are initiated by an in-depth exposure to a particular problem area. If this search fails to arrive immediately at a solution, the mind diverts to other activities. Yet the associations continue at a more subliminal level while the problem is incubating. Finally, when the associative chaos converges on a solution, the discovery thrusts itself into consciousness as an illumination. Poincaré described one such illumination in vivid terms: "Ideas rose in crowds; I felt them collide until pairs interlocked, so to speak, making a stable combination. By the next morning I had established the existence of a class of Fuchsian functions." He compared these colliding images to "the hooked atoms of Epicurus" that jiggle and bump "like the molecules of gas in the kinematic theory of gases" so that "their mutual impacts may produce new combinations." Poincaré used this metaphor to describe how the three stages work together to generate a creative synthesis:

> The rôle of the preliminary conscious work . . . is evidently to mobilize certain of these atoms, to unhook them from the wall and put them in swing. We think we have done no good, because we have moved these elements a thousand different ways in seeking to assemble them, and have found no satisfactory aggregate. But, after this shaking up imposed upon them by our will, these atoms do not return to their primitive rest. They freely continue to dance. . . . The mobilized atoms are . . . not any atoms whatsoever; they are those from which we might reasonably expect the desired solution. Then the mobilized atoms undergo impacts which make them enter into combinations among themselves or with other atoms at rest which they struck against in their course. . . . However it may be, the only combinations that have a chance of forming are those where at least one of the elements is one of those atoms freely chosen by our will. Now, it is evidently among these that is found what I called the *good combination*.

Hence, while creators are preoccupied with more mundane matters, this simmering broth of mental "atoms" continues until a new concoction emerges.

Sensory Imagery and Dreams

Psychoanalysts have emphasized the creative role of the unconsciousness ever since Freud's first preliminary essay on the subject. Ernst Kris, in particular, advanced the idea that creativity demands "regression in the service of the ego." That is, the creator must suspend conscious ego control to dip down deep into "primary-process" thinking—the processes of fantasy, daydreaming, wishes, and irrationality. Although many psychoanalysts overemphasize the pathological nature of this material, this formulation certainly captures a grain of truth. The concrete concepts and feelings that reside in these connotative layers of the mind are probably far more productive of associations than are the much more abstract and rarefied ideas that circulate in "secondary-process" thinking. The denotative qualities of words, the precision of refined constructs, and the constraints of logic tend to be too sterile to generate the requisite chaos. Albert Einstein's response to Hadamard's survey outlines the potential range in imagery.

For Einstein, "combinatory play seems to be the essential feature in productive thought." Moreover, "the psychical entities which seem to serve as elements in [this] thought are certain signs and more or less clear images which can be 'voluntarily' reproduced and combined." These mental "elements are . . . of visual and some of muscular type." Although "the desire to arrive finally at logically connected concepts is the emotional basis of this rather vague play with the above mentioned elements," the combinatory play occurs "before there is any connection with logical construction in words or other kinds of signs which can be communicated to others." "The words or the language, as they are written or spoken, do not seem to play any role in my mechanism of thought." Indeed, "Conventional words or other signs have to be sought for laboriously only in a secondary stage, when the mentioned associative play is sufficiently established and can be reproduced at will."

The adverb "laboriously" must be emphasized. Because words and logic come in late in the game, after the illumination is complete, the creative genius must often make an onerous effort to translate the images into a form accessible to others. Francis Galton expressed the frustration this way:

> It is a serious drawback to me in writing, and still more in explaining myself, that I do not so easily think in words as otherwise. It often happens that after being hard at work, and having arrived at results that are perfectly clear and satisfactory to myself, when I try to express them in language I feel that I must begin by putting myself upon quite another intellectual plane. I have to translate my thoughts into a language that does not run very evenly with them. I therefore waste a vast deal of time in seeking for appropriate words and phrases, and am conscious, when required to speak on a sudden, of being often very obscure through mere verbal maladroitness, and not through want of clearness of perception. That is one of the small annoyances of my life.

By relying on visual, auditory, kinesthetic, and even olfactory imagery, associations can pursue paths less traveled. But the price paid initially is that of ineffable realizations.

For many, thinking about sensory imagery may conjure up the place of dreams in acts of creation. No doubt this can occur. The most frequently cited example is the insight that led August Kekulé to the structure of the benzene ring. As someone who had once studied to become an architect, he was a vivid visualizer and dreamer. On a previous occasion he had already dreamed of atoms in playful recombinations, but on this evening,

I turned my chair to the fire and dozed. Again the atoms were gambolling before my eyes. This time the smaller groups kept modestly to the background. My mental eye, rendered more acute by repeated visions of the kind, could now distinguish larger structures, of manifold conformation; long rows, sometimes more closely fitted together; all twining and twisting in snake-like motion. But look! What was that? One of the snakes had seized hold of its own tail, and the form whirled mockingly before my eyes. As if by a flash of lightning I awoke.

As the last remark implies, the combinatory play produced by dreams may account for the frequent reports of insights on waking up. "One phenomenon is certain and I can vouch for its absolute certainty," said Hadamard—namely, "the sudden and immediate appearance of a solution at the very moment of sudden awakening." During sleep, dream material may lead to a solution, and the surprise of the illumination then wakes the sleeper up. Owing to the shock of the discovery, however, the dream itself may not always be remembered.

Janusian and Homospatial Thinking

In a stimulating book, *The Emerging Goddess*, Albert Rothenberg has probed the interconnections between creative thought and dreams. His investigations were partly based on more than 1,670 hours of interviews with 57 highly creative men and women of our time. These subjects represented both scientific and artistic modes of creativity. And they could boast enough genius to have won prestigious honors (the Nobel Prize, the Pulitzer Prize, the National Book Award) and/or election to learned societies (the American Academy of Arts and Letters, the National Academy of Sciences, the Royal Society of London). Sometimes Rothenberg could interview a creator at regular intervals while the subject was actively engaged in creativity. By combining these interview data with retrospective studies of the products and introspections of historic personalities, Rothenberg has identified two processes of value to the creative genius. Both of these represent "mirror images" of the dream process; that is, the two processes seem both identical to and yet at the same time opposite to what occurs in dreams.

If the last comment makes sense to you, it is because you are like those creators who repeatedly use "Janusian thinking." This entails "actively conceiving two or more opposite or antithetical ideas, images, or concepts simultaneously." The term comes from the Roman god who had two faces looking in two contrary directions at once. Rothenberg found that his distinguished creators resorted to this paradoxical maneuver quite often in the act of achieving original insights. In addition, he has found numerous illustrations of this trick in the historical record as well. For example, Rothenberg has shown how Janusian thinking helped Einstein to arrive at the general theory of relativity. Einstein realized that an observer who jumps off a house roof will not, in his or her immediate vicinity, find any evidence of a gravitational field. This apparent absence arises even though gravitation causes the observer's accelerating plunge. Rothenberg has found another illustration in Niels Bohr's conception of the principle of complementarity. The very claim that light is both a particle and a wave is inextricably Janusian. Moreover, according to one of Bohr's sons, this Nobel laureate elevated Janusian thinking to a basic technique of scientific discovery. "One of the favorite maxims of my father was the distinction between the two sorts of truths, profound truths recognized by the fact that the opposite is also a profound truth, in contrast to trivialities where opposites are obviously absurd."

The second process that mirrors dreaming is called "homospatial thinking." This involves "actively conceiving two or more discrete entities occupying the same space, a conception leading to the articulation of new identities." In other words, two or more images are superimposed in the mind's eye, and by a cognitive fusion a novel image results. Although homospatial thinking applies to images of any modality, its operation is most obvious in visual imagery. Rothenberg presents an ample number of examples drawn from the visual arts. Leonardo da Vinci, Paul Klee, Oskar Kokoschka, Henry Moore, Claes Oldenberg, and others all provide illustrations. For instance, in Klee's 1927 painting *Physiognomic Lightning*, the chief features of a man's face are delineated by a bolt of lightning; an integrated image ensues from two heterogeneous elements. Later, Klee even documented the steps by which he conceived this painting, and the procedure is patently homospatial. But beyond this archival support is Rothenberg's provocative attempt to simulate the homospatial operation in the laboratory. He demonstrated that superimposed images can indeed stimulate real artists to conceive superior creative ideas!

Janusian and homospatial thinking have many dream-like qualities. As in dreams, the logic of everyday reasoning and experience is violated. In this way, the two procedures appear like the acts of primary process. Yet, quite unlike the crazy inconsistencies and surprising juxtapositions that enliven the dream world, Rothenberg's processes are under conscious control. In this regard, Janusian and homospatial imagery are more akin to secondary process. Like true mirror images, they are both identical and opposite to dreaming.

Serendipity and Exploration

Not everyone's thoughts exhibit the processes so far described. Many lack the richness of associations, intuitions, imagery, and dream-like thinking. Sometimes people take consolation in an ostensible shortcut: Maybe Lady Luck will strike, entitling those of less copious talents to leave their impression nonetheless. Such chance discoveries are especially commonplace in science and technology. Table 4.1 lists several well-known examples drawn from various sources.

TABLE 4.1. Some Serendipitous Episodes in the History of Science and Technology

Name	Discovery or invention	Date
Columbus	New World	1492
Grimaldi	Interference of light	1663
Haüy	Geometric laws of crystallography	1781
Galvani	Animal electricity	1791
Davy	Nitrous oxide as anesthesia	1798
Oersted	Electromagnetism	1820
Schöbein	Ozone	1839
Daguerre	Photography (daguerrotype)	1839
Perkin	Synthetic coal-tar dyes	1856
Kirchhoff	D-line in the solar spectrum	1859
Nobel	Dynamite	1866
Edison	Phonograph	1877
Pasteur	Vaccination	1878
Fahlberg	Saccharin	1879
Röntgen	X-rays	1895
Becquerel	Radioactivity	1896
Richet	Induced sensitization (anaphylaxis)	1902
Pavlov	Classical conditioning	1902
Fleming	Penicillin	1928
Dam	Vitamin K	1929
Domagk	Sulfa drugs (Prontosil)	1932
Plunkett	Teflon	1938
de Maestral	Velcro	1948

Note. Several of the dates are only approximate.

Ever since Walter Cannon's early essay on this subject, the term applied to such accidental discoveries is "serendipity." Whole books on serendipitous contributions have been published. Given the abundance of primary examples and secondary accounts, we might conclude that creativity can be just another lottery—that everyone with enough patience will have a golden opportunity handed to him or her by a freakish act of fate. Nothing could be further from the truth.

As Louis Pasteur warned the overly optimistic, "Chance favors only the prepared mind." Very often, after a noteworthy discovery is announced, rival investigators come out of the woodwork to assert that they too have seen the same phenomenon. Alexander Fleming was not the first bacteriologist to have a culture spoiled by an invasion of penicillin mold. Likewise, Archimedes was not the first to see a bathtub overflow, Newton the falling of an apple, or Watt the steam screaming from a teapot. What made these observations discoveries was the special significance that these minds assigned to sometimes everyday occurrences. As Ernst Mach said in his essay "On the Part Played by Accident in Invention and Discovery," the fortuitous happenings that excited so many contributions "were *seen* numbers of times before they were *noticed*."

In fact, the same openness that enables creators to "regress in the service of the ego" is what most often facilitates their exploitation of chance encounters. Just as their internal thoughts refuse to follow a beaten path, so do their dealings with their environment allow for the unpredictable. B. F. Skinner emphasized "a first principle not formally recognized by scientific methodologists: when you run onto something interesting, drop everything else and study it." Too many fail to answer opportunity's knock at the door because they have to finish out some preconceived plan. And Skinner's advice can be improved upon. Creative geniuses do not always wait for the gifts of chance; instead, they may actively seek the accidental discovery. Francis Darwin had plenty of occasions to watch the investigative activities of his father, Charles. Francis admired his father's

> instinct for arresting exceptions: it was as though he were charged with theorizing power ready to flow into any channel on the slightest disturbance, so that no fact, however small, could avoid releasing a stream of theory, and thus the fact became magnified into importance. In this way it naturally happened that many untenable theories occurred to him; but fortunately his richness of imagination was equalled by his power of judging and condemning the thoughts that occurred to him. He was just to his theories, and did not condemn them unheard; and so it happened that he was willing to test what would seem to most people not at all worth testing. These rather wild trials he called "fool's experiments," and enjoyed extremely.

The same active quest for novelty can be seen in the arts. Surrealist artist Max Ernst described this episode in the development of *frottage*:

> I was struck by the obsession that showed to my excited gaze the floorboards upon which a thousand scrubbings had deepened the grooves. . . . I made from the boards a series of drawings by placing on them, at random, sheets of paper which I undertook to rub with black lead. In gazing attentively at the drawings thus obtained . . . I was surprised by the sudden intensification of my visionary capacities and by the hallucinatory succession of contradictory images superimposed, one upon the other.

The sculptor Henry Moore described a similar process, this time highlighting the need to have a prepared mind:

> Sometimes for several years running I have been to the same part of the seashore— but each year a new shape of pebble has caught my eye, which the year before, though it was there in hundreds, I never saw. Out of the millions of pebbles passed in walking along the shore, I choose out to see with excitement only those which fit in with my existing form-interest at the time.

Although these testimonials are anecdotal, we have experimental evidence on behalf of the creative utility of such open exploration. Students at the school of the Art Institute of Chicago were the subjects of this inquiry. Besides administering standard tests to hundreds of students, the investigators conducted a naturalistic experiment on problem finding in artistic creativity. Students were presented with a set of objects for use in drawing a still life. The objects included a trumpet, a book, a lens, a prism, a manikin, a woman's felt hat, and a bunch of grapes. The students' manipulations of these objects were scrutinized to gauge how they explored alternatives. In addition, the investigators had the final products rated by professional artists. The drawings that were superior in originality and overall aesthetic value were produced by those who (1) manipulated more objects, (2) chose more unusual objects, and (3) explored the various objects to a greater extent. Even more remarkable were the results of a seven-year longitudinal follow-up. The students who had the highest scores on these problem-finding activities were most likely to be those who later became successful artists!

One last observation is worth making. I have emphasized that the exploratory openness of creative geniuses is what allows them to take advantage of serendipitous events. This same playful sensitivity can also make then more receptive to the original ideas of others as well. Once Wolfgang Pauli, the discoverer of electron spin, was presenting a new theory of elementary particles before a professional audience. An extended discussion followed, which Niels Bohr summarized to Pauli as follows: "We are all agreed that your theory is crazy. The question which divides us is whether it is crazy enough to have a chance of being correct. My own feeling is that it is not crazy enough." A logic hides in Bohr's illogic.

The Unending Search for the New

The inventory provided above by no means lists all the processes behind historic originality. Even within science alone, the number of productive mental operations is legion. So I think it is a grievous error when a researcher tries to reduce all creative genius to a single psychological mechanism. As the Campbell model has it, *any* process will do as long as it can introduce unforeseen variations for later selection and refinement. Of course, some skeptics might argue that little of this evidence is very trustworthy. As we have seen in Chapter 3, autobiographical memories do not exemplify supreme accuracy. In addition, many psychologists contend that human beings are not especially adept at reliable introspection, either. We may simply not have faithful insights into our internal mental processes. Therefore, the whole section on introspections may have no scientific merit whatsoever. To make a strong case for certain mental processes may demand that we adopt an entirely different, more scientific approach.

Research by Colin Martindale illustrates one route around this latent impasse. Martindale's primary goal has been to construct a theory of artistic change.

Therefore, he has developed Campbell's model into an elaborate theory of aesthetic evolution. The gist of Martindale's theory is as follows.

The task of artistic creators is to make names for themselves. To accomplish this, each artist must generate original works that attract the attention of connoisseurs, critics, audiences, appreciators, and patrons. Because the pieces produced by the preceding generation of artists have become passé, the artist must offer something to stimulate now-jaded tastes. This task would be easy were it not for one constraint: The artist must work within a given aesthetic style or tradition. This stylistic restriction may narrow the subject matter, techniques, media, and other means by which the artist can grab attention. Therefore, to turn out ever more original work, the artist must resort to increasingly outlandish combinations of the given materials. This requires that the artist regress further and further into *primordial* cognition. This is a mode of primary-process imagery.

Now comes the glitch. As artists rely on ever more bizarre associations of ideas to create novelty, the received aesthetic style becomes progressively incapable of producing intelligible art. The products become incrementally more obscure and strange until the style disintegrates. The advent of a new style then saves the world of artistic creativity. Owing to the style's novelty, the first artists working in that style can make exciting creations without delving too deeply into primary-process imagery. But successive generations are not so lucky, and the descent into ever more remote associative material repeats itself until that new style is also exhausted.

Now theories of aesthetic change are practically a dime a dozen. It is one of the favorite hobbies of critics and connoisseurs to speculate on the comings and goings of styles. But Martindale's approach deviates from the pack in a material way: His theory leads to rather specific predictions. For example, he predicts that primary-process material should become ever more prominent as artists fully realize the potential of a particular artistic style. Yet when a new style replaces the old style, primary-process material becomes less necessary, and the level is reset much to the earlier level. Hence, primary-process imagery should display a cyclical pattern over the course of generations. In addition, Martindale predicts that the overall capacity of artistic creations to command attention should increase over historical time. Indeed, it is precisely because a style no longer permits this upward progression in originality that it must yield to a new style.

It is to Martindale's credit that he has done his utmost to test the predictions against empirical data. He has achieved this by four routes:

1. In his 1975 book, *The Romantic Progression: The Psychology of Literary History*, Martindale devotes two chapters to qualitative evidence. Putting on the cap of the literary critic, he scrutinizes stylistic changes in modern French poetry and English metaphysical poetry. For instance, he traces the growth of metaphoric distance from French Romanticism to symbolism and surrealism. As a baseline, he quotes André Chénier, a pre-Romantic poet: "Beneath your fair head, a white delicate neck/Inclines and would outshine the brightness of snow." Pretty straightforward stuff, but during this phase of French poetry the style dictated much literalness. By the end of a series of stylistic shifts, the rules became so relaxed that virtually anything could become a metaphor for anything else. Witness Breton's "I love you opposite the seas/Red as the egg when it's green." Underlying this progressive increase in metaphoric distance was a cyclical movement in the use of primary-process imagery to get the desired shock value. These fluctuations corresponded to style changes in French poetry. Overall, if qualitative evidence can persuade anyone, Martindale's argument looks strong.

    2. Martindale conducted a laboratory experiment that simulated the key features of literary change according to his theory. He put 10 highly creative subjects in a room and asked them to write a series of similes. Each subject was compelled to make each simile more original than the preceding one, while concomitantly obeying certain stylistic restrictions. Martindale spotted patterns that closely paralleled those in actual literature. Regression into primary-process material deepened as the subjects reached for ever more originality. And eventually a change took place in how the creators conceived the similes. The only way in which novelty could be achieved was through stylistic disintegration, the necessary precursor of a new style. Thus, 10 responses to "A pencil is like _____" proceeded from "a yellow cigarette, spreading its cancer on paper" to "God micturating upon the cosmos."

    3. Martindale conducted several inquiries in which judges evaluated aesthetic masterworks on several evaluative dimensions. These dimensions tap such attributes as a work's potential to elicit arousal, as well as the degree to which it introduces primary-process imagery. He applied this approach to Italian painting from the late Gothic to Rococo periods and to European classical music in several nations. In these studies, he found that arousal potential tended to increase over time. And primary-process imagery oscillated in synchrony with stylistic changes in the art forms.

    4. Most amazing is Martindale's final approach. The preceding methods cannot make a conclusive case for his theory. Qualitative analysis and student ratings are probably too subjective, and experimental simulation is probably too remote from historic acts of originality. So Martindale has become a pioneer in the computer analysis of literary texts. His computer software can evaluate poetry and prose on an immense range of objective attributes. For one thing, he has devised a Regressive Imagery Dictionary. This tells the computer what to look for when scoring the amount of primordial cognition evident in a composition. For instance, the lexicon includes words with strongly sexual or sensuous connotations. In addition, Martindale's programs can assess the stimulatory powers of literary text. An example is his Composite Variability Index. This taps such dimensions as word length and phrase length, the use of unique words, the presence of an associatively rich vocabulary, and striking or intense semantic usages. Martindale has even invented methods by which computers can identify stylistic shifts in literary traditions. One clue is a change in the literary vocabulary, a deviation that a computer can readily detect. Martindale thus escapes an uncomfortable dependence on the manifestos of writers or the discriminations of critics.

These utterly objective measurements have been applied to a variety of literary creations: English and French poetry, American and Hungarian short stories, and the lyrics of popular music. Martindale has even content-analyzed transformations within the Babylonian *Ishtar's Descent into the Underworld*, the descent into Hell in Book II of Homer's *Odyssey*, Book VI of Virgil's *Aeneid*, the *Tibetan Book of the Dead*, Dante's *Divine Comedy*, Melville's *Moby Dick*, Lewis Carroll's *Alice in Wonderland*, and T. S. Eliot's *The Waste Land*! By subjecting the resulting scores to detailed statistical analyses, Martindale has obtained more direct evidence for his theory. As predicted by his evolutionary model, the Composite Variability Index tends to increase steadily over historical time. Also, the index of primordial cognition, as determined by his Regressive Imagery Dictionary, tends to rise and fall in cycles. And these cycles are synchronized with the introduction of new literary styles.

Most of this exciting research is presented in Martindale's 1990 book, *The Clockwork Muse: The Predictability of Artistic Change*. Moreover, this volume includes much more. Analyses of Japanese Ukiyo-e prints, Gothic architecture, gravestones of New England, lyrics of American popular music, and other art forms further document his evolutionary theory. In addition, Martindale boldly extends his model and methods to domains outside the arts. For example, he has developed his theory to account for shifts in scientific paradigms—the scientist's analogue of a received style. He has then tested this extension through the computerized content analysis of journal articles appearing in the *American Journal of Psychology*, *Psychological Review*, and B. F. Skinner's own *Journal of the Experimental Analysis of Behavior*. The outcome falls in line behind theoretical expectation.

Martindale has saved his last punch for last. He knows that literary critics may not appreciate his introduction of mathematics into a domain hitherto dominated by humanistic insight. So he has turned his armament against the critics themselves. In particular, his computer has scrutinized the primordial content in articles appearing in the *Publications of the Modern Language Association* from 1885 to 1985. As expected, the index of primordial cognition oscillates. More importantly, the ups and downs correspond to major shifts in paradigmatic approaches—the onset of the "New Criticism" and again the inception of "structuralism." The computer has even detected the psychological antecedents of deconstructionism and poststructuralism. Hence, Martindale's "clockwork muse" is even ticking away in the brains of his potential critics!

Aesthetic Merit

If Martindale's evolutionary theory of literary change is valid, then poetry and other expressions of literary creativity appear doomed. Sooner or later, the full gamut of stylistic alternatives will have been explored. With their options all exhausted, writers will lack any further means to conceive original compositions. This fits Thomas Macaulay's remark, "As civilisation advances, poetry almost necessarily declines." Still, something seems amiss here. Even if contemporary authors find it increasingly difficult to create novel works in a given language, won't appreciators at least have the products of the vast literary heritage to fall back on? As English speakers, for example, can't we still read and enjoy Shakespeare, Milton, Austen, Dickens, Whitman, Eliot, Woolf, and even Joyce? Isn't it true that some creations become "classics" that always have some residual capacity to move us? Ezra Pound claimed, "Literature is news that STAYS news." Yet Martindale's theory implies that literature, and indeed all art, loses its edge once it is no longer at the leading edge.

This paradox compels us to alter our emphasis. Rather than learn how aesthetic styles evolve, we must ascertain why certain creative products are deemed masterpieces, while others slip into oblivion. This basic enigma of aesthetics has obvious importance for any psychology of history. Ambitious writers, artists, and composers cannot dream of achieving fame without putting their names on at least one creation that society reckons a masterwork. It is by some highly acclaimed poem, novel, painting, sculpture, symphony, or some other concrete product through which artists leave a mark on their own and later generations. Indeed, our very images of many artistic notables are inextricably wrapped up in certain accomplishments that elicit continual wonder. Imagine Shakespeare without *Hamlet*, Michelangelo without the Sistine Chapel fresco, or Beethoven without the Fifth Symphony!

According to psychological research, we can put forward two types of explanations. On the one hand, it could be that the decision to style one product a masterpiece has absolutely nothing to do with the work itself. Instead, extraneous factors may arbitrarily label one product as deserving of unending praise, while another is unjustly condemned as hackwork or even trash. On the other hand, the aesthetic merit of different products may be something inherent to the composition; that is, a masterwork contains specific attributes that set it head and shoulders above its competitors.

Great Art from the Outside

A movement is now afoot to obliterate the concept of the so-called "classics." Women and minorities, who have for a long time resided on the margins of Western civilization, often see any attempt to establish a canon of great works as a white male conspiracy to put females and people of color in their place. This claim is not without truth. There are too many instances in which the accomplishments of outsiders have not received the attention they deserve as high art. Unfairly dismissing these achievements sets the stage for denigrating the very capacity of those groups excluded from the lists of classics. Francis Galton, as we have seen in Chapter 2, judged the natural ability of various races according to who had managed to make the British race sit up and take note.

Certainly sexist and ethnic prejudices can intrude upon aesthetic judgments. Yet these are not the only possible extrinsic contaminants of such judgments. Two in particular have been the subject of inquiries: prestige suggestion and repeated exposure.

Name Dropping?

In Chapter 3, we have observed how the attribution of authorship—Jefferson versus Lenin—can determine how a passage is interpreted. Obviously, attributions can also deflect aesthetic evaluations in one direction or another, according to the status of the reputed author. This bias was demonstrated in a classic experiment by Muzafir Sherif. Subjects were first asked to rank 16 authors according to personal preference. The writers were James M. Barrie, Joseph Conrad, James Fenimore Cooper, Charles Dickens, Thomas Hardy, Nathaniel Hawthorne, Rudyard Kipling, Edgar Allan Poe, John Ruskin, Sir Walter Scott, Robert Louis Stevenson, William Makepeace Thackeray, Leo Tolstoy, Mark Twain, Walt Whitman, and Thornton Wilder. The subjects then ranked the quality of 16 prose passages corresponding to each of these authors. The two rankings tended to go together. But the judges were tricked: Not only were all passages by the same writer, but they were all carefully chosen to be equal in merit!

If prestige suggestion governs aesthetic assessments, then consensus on some inventory of classics may prove meaningless. That agreement may merely reflect the received opinion of the past. Thus, Shakespeare's name may have acquired a literary aura for reasons that have nothing to do with his genuine genius. But once the name gains this prestige, it glorifies whatever work is allotted Shakespeare's attribution. And so, regardless of a work's internal qualities, it receives the designation of "masterpiece." Moreover, some scholars have argued that Shakespeare's genius has been exaggerated well out of proportion to truth. As a consequence, works attributed to him will stand higher than pieces of equivalent quality composed by others. The whole basis for proposing a canon of great works looks flimsy in the extreme.

This argument, however, goes well beyond the evidence. First, prestige suggestion is less powerful when the literary passages are of unequal quality. The evaluators then have something solid to sink their critical teeth into. Second, individuals who feel more confident about their aesthetic tastes are less swayed by the nominal attributions; they know what they like. Third, recent studies have found that judges can reach an independent consensus on the relative merits of compositions without prestige suggestion. For instance, American college students agreed on the comparative aesthetic value of short stories, even though they had not the foggiest idea who the authors were. Because the stories were the creation of 20th-century Hungarian writers, the evaluations could be based solely on the intrinsic characteristics of each story. Fourth and last, detailed analyses of how creators' reputations change over historical time prove that the renown of a genius in one generation is not a mere carryover from his or her acclaim in preceding generations. Instead, the evidence suggests that each generation makes up its own mind, using the creative products at hand. Shakespeare's reputation survives because his plays and poetry continue to inspire new converts to his cult.

Acquired Tastes?

Another difficulty with dismissing aesthetic taste as mere prestige suggestion is that it fails to explain the variable success of compositions by the *same* genius. Not all of Shakespeare's plays are considered of equal merit. *Titus Andronicus*, *Timon of Athens*, and *Pericles* certainly lack adherents. Not enough connoisseurs thought highly enough of Michelangelo's pornographic "Leda and the Swan" to preserve it from destruction. Beethoven's *Wellington's Victory* embarrasses many devotees of his music. Hence, even the prestige of these three giants does not suffice to lift their failures to the status of masterpieces. If we still wish to ascribe aesthetic judgments to extraneous factors, we must search elsewhere.

The phenomenon of repeated exposure could provide the answer. Robert Zajonc has amply documented the falsity of the sayings "Familiarity breeds contempt" and "Absence makes the heart grow fonder." For a wide range of stimuli, the more frequently the stimulus is presented, the more it is liked. The only proviso is that the stimulus not elicit a negative response on its first presentation. Therefore, if we assume that the initial reaction to a given work of art is neutral, those compositions that are presented more often will be those that will evoke a stronger aesthetic appreciation.

There is experimental evidence that this can in fact take place. One study found frequency-of-exposure effects when college students were allowed to use a "jukebox" that could only play eight selections of *gagaku*—the court music of ancient Japan! Repeated exposure even works beyond the realm of human music appreciation. Infant rats heard music by a single composer 12 hours per day for 52 days. By this means, the rodents learned to like Mozart. Yet the same effect did not hold for Schoenberg's compositions; the first exposure was not neutral even for rats! Finally, we have secure evidence that potential audiences and appreciators are differentially exposed to various pieces by the same creator. For instance, Beethoven's Fifth Symphony is played almost thrice as much as his Second, and his Fifth Piano Concerto (the "Emperor") is performed nearly twice as much as his Fourth. Should we be amazed, then, that these differences in performance frequencies correlate with how often classical music buffs purchase recordings of the same compositions?

Naturally, this argument may have everything backwards: Exposure frequency may merely reflect contrasts in inherent merit. The Fifth Symphony may be verifiably superior to the Second, the Fifth Concerto to the Fourth. Conductors who decide to reverse the performance frequencies on their concert programs may soon find season subscriptions declining. Similarly, Shakespeare's *Hamlet* may be on the boards more often than *Timon of Athens* because it is an intrinsically better play. The Sistine Chapel may be visited more regularly than the Pauline Chapel because Michelangelo's best painting is to be found in the first. In brief, using the repeated-exposure effect as an explanation may beg the question.

Even so, its explanatory utility is not nil. Many pieces of considerable aesthetic merit may not appear in the canon of world masterpieces, owing to lack of familiarity. Hence arises the justification for digging up possible lost masterworks. For example, theaters and opera houses will occasionally try the revival of some long-forgotten piece. In some symphony concerts, the conductor will play an obscure composition twice to give the audience a better chance to appreciate its value. Such activities are especially useful in acquainting an audience with creative products that have perhaps been unfairly dropped from the repertoire. Thus, whole concerts have been devoted to the music of forgotten female composers. Yet, over the long haul, repeated exposure cannot prevent a creation from returning into the void. Revivals fail when the resuscitated work remains dead. Ultimately, an aesthetic product stands or falls according to what goes on inside the composition.

Great Art from the Inside

Extrinsic factors cannot explain all that we know about aesthetic success. Therefore, we must assume that each work of art itself contains a set of qualities that affects how it is received by potential appreciators. Can we glean these attributes from the masterworks themselves? If we can, what are the chief modes of inquiry? Traditionally, those psychologists who examine aesthetic creations have adopted a qualitative approach. A work of art is scrutinized according to some theoretical framework, and deductions are made according to the subjective impressions thus obtained. Two principal traditions illustrate such procedures.

First, psychoanalysts frequently inspect the *content* of products to fathom the latent meaning behind the manifest material. For example, Shakespeare's *Hamlet* can be analyzed via the "Oedipal conflict." This provides new and provocative perspectives on the relations among Hamlet, his father's ghost, Claudius, and, of course, Queen Gertrude. This psychoanalytic gloss even informed Laurence Olivier's film version of the play.

Second, Gestalt psychologists most often examine the *form* of artistic products. Presumably, critical qualities of effective art, like the elusive trait of beauty, are revealed in the formal organization of the elements of an expressive medium. An outstanding proponent of this approach is Rudolph Arnheim, whose 1971 *Art and Visual Perception* has become a classic Gestalt analysis of the visual arts. Arnheim has even devoted a whole volume to the genesis of a single painting, Picasso's *Guernica*. Both books offer us a wealth of visual insights.

Although these qualitative techniques have proven influential, they suffer from deficiencies as well. Most obviously, psychoanalytic or Gestalt interpretations are only as good as their theoretical underpinnings. Those underpinnings have been seriously undermined by modern psychological research. More important is the patent liability of any qualitative system of analysis. The insights are often subjective and vague. We sometimes get the impression that a psychoanalytic or Gestalt psychologist can explicate *any* aspect of form or content with the swish of a magic wand.

Let me report a personal experience. As a graduate student at Harvard, I took Arnheim's popular course on visual expression. Each lecture consisted of a slide show accompanied by a captivating Gestalt commentary. One lecture was devoted to how artists portray top and bottom, or up and down. About halfway through the hour, an abstract painting was projected on the screen. Arnheim dutifully used his pointer to indicate how the painter's color fields presented gravitational pull. But his exposition was interrupted by the agitated hand of a perplexed student: She noted that the artist's signature was oddly placed in the painting's upper left-hand corner—upside down!

Maybe we should develop a psychological aesthetics that circumvents the weaknesses of such subjective critiques. Instead of qualitative discourse, investigators should quantify the parameters of artistic products. These quantifications should be executed by unbiased observers. In fact, we should try to bypass the human mind altogether to procure measurements uncontaminated by personal preferences and theoretical prejudices. In short, we should recruit computers to do the critical analyses for us.

Can computers judge art? Yes, for we have already seen Colin Martindale's proof that computer content analysis can detect changes in aesthetic styles. Furthermore, computers have made great progress in the creation of original art. For example, long ago a computer was programmed to generate a work that mimicked Piet Mondrian's 1917 *Composition with Lines*. Not only were most human beings incapable of deciding which version was computer-made (the computer thus seemingly passed the Turing test), but the machine's creation was preferred over the human product! And, needless to say, computer-generated art has advanced immensely since this pioneer endeavor. So if computers can imitate creators, can they also ape critics and connoisseurs?

I offer an affirmative response in two examples. The music example focuses on form, the literary example on content.

Are There Musical Masterworks?

If an objective and precise analysis is what we desire, musical compositions provide the best place to start our search. Music is the most mathematical of the arts. "Music is the arithmetic of sounds as optics is the geometry of light," said Claude Debussy. This fact is apparent to anyone who has inspected a music score, and certainly obvious to all who have taken courses in harmony or counterpoint. The intimate link between math and music, indeed, dates back to Pythagoras. And mathematics defined the "music of the spheres" in cosmic theories.

Moreover, empirical studies have confirmed that mathematical analyses of music can teach us much about compositions. An excellent example is a study that programmed a computer to recognize the styles of great composers. The computer could decide whether a work was by Bach, Handel, Haydn, Mozart, Beethoven, Mendelssohn, or Brahms, using just the first four notes of the work's thematic material. A composition's thematic material probably can tell a computer more than just a composer's characteristic manner of constructing a melody. Because melodies are the building blocks of all musical compositions, they may provide a clue to the composition's final popularity with listeners. Of course, much else happens in a work than mere melody—harmony, counterpoint, orchestration, and formal structure. Yet, as Haydn noted, "melody is the main thing." Hence, if we can program a computer to measure the central qualities of the themes, the computer may go on to predict why some compositions become staples of the repertoire.

This has already been accomplished in a series of investigations. The inquiries began by feeding into a computer 15,618 melodies by 479 composers who created the repertoire of classical music. The computer then measured each theme's "melodic originality"—that is, the extent to which a theme is not predictable in the context of the way melodies are usually constructed in the classical repertoire. Are chromatic notes used (notes outside the key signature)? Are the intervals between notes commonplace, like thirds, or do successive notes jump around by oddball intervals, such as sixths?

Naturally, we have no reason to trust a computer's judgments, however precise and objective they may be. Still, the computer's melodic originality calculations corresponded with other characteristics of the composition in a sensible manner. Melodic originality was judged to be higher in compositions that are instrumental rather than vocal. Originality was found to be more prominent in chamber music, such as sonatas and quartets, than in theatrical works, such as opera or ballet. Themes in minor keys scored higher than themes in major keys, reflecting the exotic atmosphere of melodies in keys like C minor or D minor. And so forth. As a little demonstration, if you know a musical instrument, you may wish to play the stripped-down melodies in Table 4.2. Listen carefully. Would you rank the originality of the melodies roughly the same way as the computer did?

TABLE 4.2. Computer's Rankings of Representative Themes on Melodic Originality

Rank	Composer	Composition	First six notes					
1.	Haydn	Symphony No. 84, second movement	C	C	E	E	G	G
2.	Beethoven	"Waldstein" sonata, third movement	G	G	E	D	G	C
3.	Brahms	Symphony No. 1, fourth movement	G	C	B	C	A	G
4.	Mozart	"Dissonant" Quartet (introduction)	A	G	F♯	G	A	B♭
5.	Liszt	Faust Symphony, first movement	A♭	G	B	E♭	F♯	B♭
6.	Gesualdo	"Moro lasso"	G♯	G	F♯	F	F	B

Now comes the critical question: Did these computer judgments have anything to do with a composition's actual success? To address this question, aesthetic merit first has to be gauged objectively. This was done many different ways, but they all converged on a single assessment: the frequency with which a work is actually performed and recorded, which we can call "repertoire popularity." If we plot this criterion as a function of melodic originality, and fit a curve, we get the results shown in Figure 4.1.

Clearly, aficionados of classical music prefer compositions made up of melodies of moderate originality. If the theme sounds like a nursery tune, it is

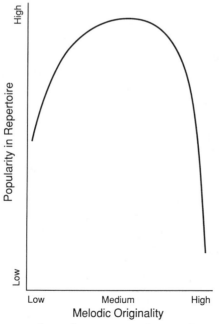

FIGURE 4.1. Curvilinear relation between a work's popularity in the classical repertoire and the melodic originality of its themes.

too predictable and hence boring. If it sounds too chaotic, it is too anxiety-producing to be appreciated. And if the choice is between the mundane and the shocking, the former wins. This summarizes the fate of much atonal and serial music. Most people would rather listen to innocuous Renaissance dances than engage in an endurance contest with the likes of Arnold Schoenberg, Alban Berg, or Anton von Webern. What is striking about this graph is its relation to the "Wundt curve" of experimental aesthetics. In this laboratory research, effective art is that which maintains an optimal level of arousal. Like Goldilocks in the house of the Three Bears, the appreciator gravitates to the range that is "just right," neither hackneyed nor aggravating.

These results represent only one of many findings the computer had to offer. Elsewhere I shall report other discoveries. For now, the important conclusion is that some pieces are played more often than other pieces for reasons inherent in the works themselves. It is not an arbitrary function of extraneous forces, at least not for the repertoire of classical music.

Do Literary Masterpieces Exist?

Psychological analyses of music concentrate on aesthetic form. Except for vocal compositions, music is a highly abstract enterprise: What is said is less crucial than how it is said. In literature, however, content becomes more central. Therefore, empirical studies of literary success have placed more weight on content factors. For example, investigators have examined the impact of thematic substance on the differential popularity of classic plays, including the works of Shakespeare. The dramas produced most often are those that treat a rich diversity of important life themes. Unfortunately, despite the accumulation of findings, drama remains an extremely complex art form. There are too many parameters on which plays may vary. Plot, characters, dialogue, themes, and structure, among other criteria, are all pertinent. Naturally, an even more expansive literary genre, such as the novel, makes matters even more difficult. So to get a better grip on what makes literature great, we have to narrow our focus.

Poetry may just offer an ideal research site. For one thing, poetry comes close to music in the use of formal rules. Although Flaubert is probably exaggerating when he claimed, "Poetry is as exact a science as geometry," the truth is not too distant. This formal constraint is especially clear in certain types of poetry, especially sonnets. For instance, the Elizabethan or Shakespearean sonnet contains just 14 lines of 10 syllables each. More technically, such sonnets consist of three quatrains and a couplet, in iambic pentameter, with the rhyme scheme *abab cdcd efef gg*. This makes the sonnet a kind of test tube for inspecting the basis of literary aesthetics. Many possible aesthetic factors are held constant. In addition, we can enhance scientific precision by considering the sonnets of just one poet. That avoids the possible contamination of any prestige suggestion. A lot of other extraneous factors would be held equal, too.

Shakespeare wrote 154 sonnets. These sonnets are very uneven in quality. Though some of these "bear the unmistakable stamp of his genius," said one critic, others "are no better than many a contemporary could have written." Some sonnets are quoted or discussed far more often than others, and some are much more frequently included in anthologies of great literature. For instance, I have yet to find a single literary anthology that includes one of the last two sonnets in the cycle (both on the Cupid theme). On the other hand, the following sonnet reappears many times:

> Let me not to the marriage of true minds
> Admit impediments. Love is not love
> Which alters when it alteration finds,
> Or bends with the remover to remove:
> O, no! it is an ever-fixed mark
> That looks on tempests and is never shaken;
> It is the star to every wand'ring bark,
> Whose worth's unknown, although his height be taken.
> Love's not Time's fool, though rosy lips and cheeks
> Within his bending sickle's compass come;
> Love alters not with his brief hours and weeks,
> But bears it out even to the edge of doom.
>   If this be error and upon me prov'd,
>   I never writ, nor no man ever lov'd.

Thus, if we measure the comparative popularity of the 154 sonnets according to an objective index, can a computer tell us why some of these poems are more successful than others? Two studies have said yes.

In the first study, a computer examined all 154 sonnets, treating each as a unit of analysis. The computer found that the more popular sonnets could be objectively discriminated according to both content and form. With respect to content, Martindale's Regressive Imagery Dictionary proved its mettle; the more highly appreciated sonnets were those more rich in primary-process imagery and more impoverished in secondary-process imagery. We want our poems to deal with the fundamental experiences of life—love, sex, sensation, feeling, dreams, fears—not with abstractions and reason. The sonnet quoted above illustrates one such preoccupation: namely, the elementary belief that true love endures the tests of time. Concerning form, the computer calculated objective indices of linguistic complexity. Among these was a measure known as the "type–token ratio." This is a straightforward gauge of the number of different words divided by the number of words. Another assessment was the proportion of words in each sonnet that Shakespeare used only once in the set of sonnets (i.e., unique words). These two aspects of form were positively related to a sonnet's final standing with connoisseurs. Great poems do more than treat central themes of human existence; they also express these themes with a lush vocabulary.

Yet something is lacking in this first study. It suggests that a poet, to achieve success, must draw from a special lexicon. Shakespeare had to find, line by line, Flaubert's *bon mot*. This implies a static conception of poetry. A poem's effectiveness should depend on more than inserting the right words; those words must also be well arranged for maximal impact on the reader. After all, Coleridge once issued this warning: "I wish our clever young poets would remember [that] . . . poetry = the best words in the best order." Consequently, to get a tighter grip on poetic merit, the computer must analyze how word usage unfolds during the course of a single poem.

Such was the purpose of the second inquiry. Now each sonnet was subdivided into its components; that is, the three quatrains and the couplet were treated as miniature poems. The computer inspected how Shakespeare's choice of words shifted in each consecutive segment. Once this baseline was fixed, the computer determined whether these trends in lexical selections differed for the most highly acclaimed products of his pen. The results were striking. In constructing the succession of quatrains, Shakespeare chose his words to build up a chain of associations in the reader's mind. He did this by dipping into an ever more rich and suggestive vocabulary. This behavior is reminiscent of what Macaulay said in his critical essay on Milton:

> The most striking characteristic of the poetry of Milton is the extreme remoteness of the associations by means of which it acts on the reader. Its effect is produced, not so much by what it expresses, as by what it suggests; not so much by the ideas which it directly conveys as by other ideas which are connected with them. He electrifies the mind through conductors.

Then comes the punch line, the concluding couplet. Suddenly Shakespeare constricted his lexicon while concomitantly optimizing the wealth of associations that the words could produce. The last two lines in the greatest sonnets were designed to tie into one tight package all the loose ends tossed about in the preceding dozen lines. Thus, a dumb computer could discern Shakespeare's aesthetic secret.

Admittedly, Shakespeare's sonnets are only a minute subset of all the poetry that comprises world literature. We also have gotten no further in comprehending drama and fiction. Even so, preliminary efforts have been made toward the analysis of more complex literary forms. Besides drama, short stories have received considerable attention. Despite the diversity, these inquiries all converge on a single conclusion: Computers can detect some of the intrinsic attributions that govern aesthetic judgments. Because computers are immune from subjective bias, these discoveries inform us that artistic merit is not a matter of pure whim. Obvious prejudices notwithstanding, there are sound aesthetic reasons why some creations attain the stature of masterpieces. And, very likely, these reasons are deeply embedded in the processes by which human beings perceive their world and give meaning to their lives.

Duplicate Discoveries

Allow me to introduce this chapter's last topic with one more story from my graduate student days. I had been admitted to the Department of Social Relations, which encompassed social anthropology and sociology along with the less behavioristic branches of psychology. Therefore, many department members were not particularly sympathetic to an individualistic perspective. Once I made the mistake of mentioning to one professor my fascination with creative genius. I was told that there was no such animal. Societies or cultural systems are creative, but not individuals. At best, so-called "creators" are mere spokespersons for their age; at worst, these erroneously acclaimed personalities are pure epiphenomena. Then the distinguished professor provided the damning evidence: The occurrence of multiples in the history of science and technology is positive proof of the perfect irrelevance of genius.

A "multiple" occurs whenever two or more individuals, working independently of one another, arrive at exactly the same idea. Table 4.3 lists several of the most celebrated examples, drawn from a diversity of disciplines. The dramatic impact of such events is often intensified when they incite priority disputes. The controversy between Newton and Leibniz over who invented calculus was notably vicious. Eventually priority was decided by a special commission of the Royal Society of London, which condemned Leibniz as a plagiarist. Only later did it emerge that the draft of the commission's report was written by the society's president, Sir Isaac himself!

A glance over the dates in the table reveals another spectacular feature of many multiples: The separate contributions are frequently simultaneous. Actually, the magnitude of simultaneity is somewhat obscured in the table, which only gives the years of conception. Sometimes discoveries or inventions take place on the same *day*! One specimen is the strange aftermath of the discovery of Hyperion, Saturn's seventh satellite, which William Bond and William Lassell observed on precisely the same evening. Two years later, Lassell discovered the dark inner "crepe" ring of Saturn. Lassell devoted the early morning hours to verifying the observation. After convincing himself that he had something to strengthen his reputation, he sat down to read the morning paper. There he read an article about how George Bond, the son of William, had just made the same discovery!

Using instances like these, sociologists and anthropologists try to prove that their disciplines, and not psychology, have more to say about scientific and technological creativity. Creative ideas are the products of the *Zeitgeist*, or spirit of the times. At a specific instant in the history of a domain, the time becomes ripe for a given idea. The idea is "in the air" for anyone to pick, making its inception absolutely inevitable. For instance, Robert K. Merton, an illustrious sociologist, claimed that "discoveries and inventions become virtually inevitable (1) as prerequisite kinds of knowledge accumulate in man's cultural store; (2) as the attention of a sufficient number of investigators is focused on a prob-

TABLE 4.3. Representative Instances of Multiple Discoveries and Inventions

Equation of the cycloid: Roberval (1640); Torricelli (1644).
Calculus: Newton (1671); Leibniz (1676).
Non-Euclidean geometry: Gauss (1799); Lobachevsky (1826); Bolyai (1832).
Quadratic reciprocity law: Euler (1772); Legendre (1785); Gauss (1796).
Sunspots: Galileo (1610); Fabricius (1611); Scheiner (1611); Harriott (1611).
Neptune (existence predicted): J. C. Adams (1845); Leverrier (1846).
Hyperion (Saturn satellite): W. C. Bond (1848); Lassell (1848).
Stellar parallax: Bessel (1838); F. Struve (1838); Henderson (1838).
Electromagnetic induction: J. Henry (1830); Faraday (1831).
Leyden jar (condenser): E. G. Kleist (1745); van Musschenbroek (1746).
Wave properties of electron: G. P. Thomson (1927); Davisson & Germer (1927).
Law of gases: Boyle (1662); Mariotte (1676).
Energy conservation: J. R. von Mayer (1843); Helmholtz (1847); Joule (1847).
Liquifaction of oxygen: Cailletet (1877); Pictet (1877).
Periodic law (elements): DeChancourtis (1862); Newlands (1864); L. Meyer (1869);
    Mendeléev (1869).
Stereochemistry of carbon: Van't Hoff (1874); Le Bel (1874).
Oxygen: Priestley (1774); Scheele (1774).
H_2O: Cavendish (1781); Watt (1781); Lavoisier & Laplace (1783); Monge 1783).
Cerium: Berzelius (1803); Klaproth (1803).
Evolution by natural selection: C. Darwin (1844); Wallace (1858).
Genetic laws: Mendel (1865); De Vries (1900); Correns (1900); Tschermak (1900).
Spinal nerve root functions: C. Bell (1811); Magendie (1822).
Plague bacillus: Yersin (1894); Kitasato (1894).
Puerperal fever contagious: O. W. Holmes (1843); Semmelweiss (1847).
Ether anesthesia in surgery: C. W. Long (1842); Morton (1846).
Photography: Daguerre (1839); Talbot (1839).
Incandescent lamp (carbon filament): Swan (1879); Edison (1878).
Telephone: A. G. Bell (1876); E. Gray (1876).
Aluminum (electrolytic production): C. M. Hall (1886); Héroult (1886).
Theory of emotions: W. James (1884); Lange (1887).

lem—by emerging social needs, or by developments internal to the particular science, or by both." Much mileage is made out of the simultaneity of so many multiples. Alfred Kroeber, a distinguished anthropologist, concluded from the simultaneous rediscovery of Mendel's genetics by DeVries, Correns, and Tschermak that "it was discovered in 1900 because it could have been discovered only then, and because it infallibly must have been discovered then."

In fact, some advocates of this sociocultural determinism have gone so far as to play down the involvement of any higher mental powers. The anthropologist Leslie White, for one, expressed these fighting words about the multiple invention of the steamboat: "Is great intelligence required to put one and one— a boat and an engine—together? An ape can do this." White went on to generalize: "A consideration of many significant inventions and discoveries does not lead to the conclusion that great ability, native or acquired, is always necessary. On the contrary, many seem to need only mediocre talents at best." To grab the ripe fruits of an age, you don't have to be the best wide receiver in the National Football League; you only need a hand.

Now if the *Zeitgeist* really determines all, the previous pages of this chapter must be radically rewritten. To start with, we can cut out the section on introspective reports. Internal thought processes such as intuition or imagination have no causal role. Serendipity looks especially suspect; it implies a greater influx of chance than allowed by sociocultural determinism. For the same reason, the section on problem solving will have to be thrown out. Genuine problem solving takes place at a higher level of analysis. Perhaps only the discussion of aesthetics and stylistic evolution can be salvaged. Indeed, it is often noted that multiples characterize scientific but not artistic creativity. One historian of science stressed

> the basic difference that exists between creative effort in the sciences and in the arts. If Michelangelo and Beethoven had not existed, their works would have been replaced by quite different contributions. If Copernicus or Fermi had never existed, essentially the same contributions would have had to come from other people.

Not only must we strip this chapter of most of its contents, but what remains must be retitled "Artistic Creativity." Scientific creativity, from this perspective, is an oxymoron!

A formidable quantity of pages has been printed on multiples. With few exceptions, all authors endorse the *Zeitgeist* as the causal agent of these events. Nevertheless, a few scholars have challenged the traditional interpretation. These dissenters have put together a strong case that the received dogma is wrong. Their objections are both logical and empirical.

Four Questions about Multiples

The *Zeitgeist* viewpoint suffers from four logical difficulties:

1. *Are multiples truly identical?* After carefully inspecting a list of nearly 150 multiples, one researcher concluded that many items listed reflect "a failure to distinguish between the genus and the individual." Two supposed duplicates are often not nearly the same; rather, an extremely generic category has been superficially imposed on quite contrary creations. As an example, nuclear magnetic resonance was independently and simultaneously spotted in 1946 by Bloch, Hansen, and Packard at Stanford and by Purcell, Torrey, and Pound at Harvard. This earned Bloch and Purcell a Nobel Prize in 1957. Still, although physicists "have come to look at the two experiments as practically identical," said Purcell, "when Hansen first showed up [at our lab] and started talking about it, it was about an hour before either of us understood how the other was trying to explain it."

Often the contributions are so different that history would have been altered if only one version or the other had been made public. One scholar, for example, has argued that we should not even credit a scientist with a contribution unless it represents a "central message" of that investigator. On this basis, we can dismiss the claims of the Polish economist Michel Kalecki and the Stockholm school of economics to have independently created what we now call "Keynesian economics." In a similar fashion, Meyer willingly admitted the pre-eminence of Mendeléev in advancing the periodic law of the elements. The Russian chemist stood alone among claimants in his willingness to advocate the controversial scheme. Only Mendeléev elaborated the details; only he risked making specific predictions that could be put to the test. The history of chemistry would have been altered had Mendeléev not made the periodic law a central message of his career.

A molecular biologist, Gunter Stent, was the first to derive a special implication from this issue. Multiples happen only in science simply because we use extremely generic categories to describe discoveries and inventions—but highly specific categories to describe paintings, plays, and other works of art. Of course, Michelangelo's Sistine Chapel ceiling was created just once. Yet how many different scientists wrote Newton's *Principia Mathematica*? How many could have? We also frequently overlook how idiosyncratic the thoughts of individual scientists are. Ludwig Boltzmann stressed how "a mathematician will recognize Cauchy, Gauss, Jacobi, or Helmholtz, after reading a few pages, just as musicians recognize, from the first few bars, Mozart, Beethoven, or Schubert." Once Newton sent off a response to a mathematical problem that had been posed as a challenge to the international community. Although the solution had been sent anonymously, the recipient at once spotted "the claw of the lion." The thoughts of true genius are not standardized like McDonald's hamburgers!

Or let's turn to the other side of the comparison. How many composers wrote a four-movement symphony in a minor key with a finale in the major key? Beethoven's Fifth is by no means the only example. Moreover, there actually have been artistic multiples in a more restricted sense. As Swinburne was astonished to learn, the notion that fame is "the last infirmity of noble minds" appears not just in Milton's *Lycidas* of 1637. It can also be found in a play attributed to John Fletcher called *Sir John van Olden Barnavelt*. The manuscript of this play was lost, not to be rediscovered until long after Milton independently conceived his duplicate!

2. *Are multiples really independent?* Zeitgeist theorists can only wish that the same independence might be claimed for multiples in science. Far too often, those cited as independent contributors were actually influenced by one or more of the other parties to the duplicate. McCormick knew about the prior reaper invented by Patrick Bell. Dollond devised his achromatic lens with knowledge of Hall's previous work. Fulton explicitly built upon the prior efforts of Jouffroy to construct a steamboat, and even was present at the first trials of Symington's ship. In creating the kinetic theory of gases, Rankine was well aware of Waterston's earlier efforts. Lavoisier was guilty of the special vice of repeating the experiments done by others, such as Cavendish or Priestley, and then passing on the discoveries as his own. Recently, Robert Gallo's claim to have independently identified the AIDS virus was challenged by the revelation that his viral sample came from Luc Montagnier's lab at the Pasteur Institute in Paris. So the examples run on and on. A large proportion of the multiples that prove the *Zeitgeist* doctrine represent the basic process of antecedence, not independence. Yet these cannot count as multiples. A football team can't get two touchdowns off one downfield lateral pass.

3. *Are multiples always simultaneous?* The separate contributions that make up a multiple are not always simultaneous. In one study of 264 multiples, only 20% were found to have taken place within a one-year interval. In contrast, fully 34% of the multiples required at least a decade to elapse before the duplications ceased. In fact, occasionally hundreds of years will divide the first and last instance of a multiple. Examples include the observation of the transit of Venus across the solar disk by al-Kindi and Horrocks; the statement of the hydrostatic principles by Archimedes and Stevinus; and the discovery of the "Eustachian" tubes by Alcmaeon and Eustachio.

This temporal hiatus raises doubts about the explanatory adequacy of sociocultural determinism. For instance, if the laws of genetics became unequivocally inevitable at a specific point in history, why were they discovered in two years separated by over a third of a century? It is begging the question to maintain that Mendel was simply "ahead of his time." The times are supposed to define what can and cannot be created. Thus, we must segregate the creative act from what grants those acts social acceptance. As William James expressed the contrast,

> social evolution is a resultant of the interaction of two wholly distinct factors: the individual, deriving his peculiar gifts from the play of psychological and infra-social forces, but bearing all the power of initiative and origination in his hands; and, second, the social environment, with its power of adopting or rejecting both him and his gifts.

The rejection is most likely to take place when, as Stent has observed, a discovery's "implications cannot be connected by a series of simple logical steps to canonical, or generally accepted, knowledge." The idea is then premature. Its dissemination must wait until the milieu has caught up with the genius. Yet the *Zeitgeist* may be powerless to prevent creators from proliferating such premature discoveries and inventions. As a result, the *Zeitgeist* cannot suppress the occurrence of rediscoveries.

4. *Are multiples genuinely inevitable?* In inferring a determinism from multiples, *Zeitgeist* theorists succumb to a fatal error. They fail to distinguish between necessary and sufficient causes. A necessary cause is one that supplies

a prerequisite for another event to happen. For example, there can be no calculus without some principle of limits. But this causal claim is too weak to support the inference of determinism. To get a stronger statement, we must argue that the milieu provides necessary and sufficient causes. Yet the evidence argues against this strong form. Very often a contribution builds upon a cultural substrate that has been around for decades, or even centuries. Martin and Synge shared the 1952 Nobel Prize for chemistry for developing paper chromatography. Yet Martin lessened the achievement by noting that "all the ideas are simple and had people's minds been directed that way the method would have flourished perhaps a century earlier." The broad applicability of this remark is proven by the many rediscoveries separated by a decade or more. If the earliest contribution is identical to the latest, then it must be the case that all the prerequisites had been satisfied years earlier. Hence, the necessary causes were not sufficient causes.

To be sure, for people who believe in the inexorable and upward push of scientific progress, the discoveries will eventually appear once the groundwork has been laid. Yet to say that something will eventually see the light of day is a far cry from claiming the inevitability of its birth at a precise point in time. Furthermore, even when we can hold that a specific discovery will happen eventually, this does not necessitate that the events will unfold in a predetermined pattern. Not just the timing, but the nature of the event may change. Stent has illustrated this point with Watson and Crick's formulation of the structure of DNA:

> If Watson and Crick had not existed, the insights they provided in one single package would have come out much more gradually over a period of many months or years. Dr. *B* might have seen that DNA is a double-strand helix, and Dr. *C* might later have recognized the hydrogen bonding between the strands. Dr. *D* later yet might have proposed a complementary purine–pyrimidine bonding, with Dr. *E* in a subsequent paper proposing the specific adenine–thymine and guanine–cytosine replication mechanism of DNA based on the complementary nature of the two strands. All the while Drs. *H, I, J, K* and *L* would have been confusing the issue by publishing incorrect structures and proposals.

It was definitely not inevitable that a single brief paper in *Nature* would preempt this messy but much more plausible scenario.

Three Characteristics of Multiples

Three characteristics of multiples contradict the *Zeitgeist* account:

1. *How many duplicates?* Glancing over Table 4.3, we see that some multiples have more participants than others do. Only two mathematicians claimed to have devised calculus, whereas four made some claim to discovering the periodic law of the elements. The calculus is a "Grade 2" multiple, the peri-

odic law "Grade 4." We might wonder whether some grades are more frequent than others. Judging from the table, the lower-grade multiples evidently outnumber the higher-grade ones. That is not a false impression; all collections of multiples gathered to date show the same tendency toward a monotonic decline. This pattern is rather suggestive to anyone familiar with probability theory. This skewed distribution is what characterizes rare events. In fact, we can fit probabilistic models to the observed frequencies of multiple grades. These models fit the data without having ever to assume that discoveries or inventions are in any sense inevitable. On the contrary, these models predict the observed frequencies by assuming that such events have extremely small odds of happening. We do not have to postulate any variety of sociocultural determinism.

2. *What is the timing?* As we have learned, the determinists make a big deal about the near-simultaneity of so many multiples. To have Alexander Graham Bell and Elisha Gray show up at the patent office on the same day looks too unlikely to warrant dismissal as mere coincidence. Yet if you think harder about these events, it is surprising that such simultaneity is not more common. What if Lassell had planned to scan Saturn's rings one day later? He would have read the morning paper and altered his observatory's schedule. In other words, if the communication system in science were perfect, multiples would have to be simultaneous to occur at all! No one deliberately reinvents the wheel. It is possible to construct probability models that incorporate this communication feature. These models predict the comparative frequencies of the multiple grades, but at the same time accurately predict how many years will lapse before duplicates can no longer appear. Again, we do not need a *Zeitgeist* theory to explain the occurrence of multiples.

3. *Who gets trapped?* We can surmise one final attribute from Table 4.3. Many who have been caught in multiples are among the "big names" of science and technology. We spot Boyle, Darwin, Edison, Faraday, Helmholtz, Leibniz, Newton, and several others on this list. Additional luminaries appear on more complete lists—names like Archimedes, Bernoulli, Cavendish, Davy, Fermat, Galileo, Halley, Huygens, Laplace, Pascal, Purkinje, and the Wright brothers. It turns out, moreover, that the more famous the individual, the more multiples he or she gets trapped in on the average. We might take this to imply that these geniuses are supremely dependent on the *Zeitgeist* as a wellspring of their creativity. Yet this appearance is deceptive.

One fact we will come across several times in this book is the extraordinary productivity of great minds. Scientific geniuses are prolific. Therefore, if they are generating so many ideas, there will be some duplications just by chance. Merton confessed that those of "great scientific genius will have been repeatedly involved in multiples . . . because [they] will have made many discoveries altogether." Indeed, those of "scientific genius are precisely those . . . whose work in the end would be eventually rediscovered. These rediscoveries would be made, not by a single scientist, but by an entire corps of scientists." That view makes the single scientific genius "the functional equivalent of a considerable array of other scientists of varying degrees of talent." The historical record adds one qualification to Merton's admission: Besides participating in so many multiples, the genius creates many ideas that will see no duplication by lesser lights. Einstein's relativity theory was his and his alone. So was Planck's quantum theory.

These logical and empirical arguments justify the contents of this chapter. Multiples do not compel us to eliminate the individual as an agent of history. Nor do they force us to believe that scientific creativity diverges from artistic creativity. We can place the introspections of Ernst Mach alongside those of Max Ernst. And, lastly, for that unnamed professor from my graduate student days, I have this to say: Despite multiples, creativity exists!

THE DRIVE TO SUCCEED

n a good murder mystery, as well as in the realm of detective work in real homicide cases, the motives of potential suspects are always central issues. To be a prime candidate for guilt, an individual must have "the means, the opportunity, and the motive." Observers of current events are often similarly preoccupied. Why didn't Richard Nixon burn the White House tapes? Why did Lee Harvey Oswald assassinate John F. Kennedy? As these questions suggest, the determination of motives often becomes a historical issue as well. Neither of these curiosities can any longer be properly called "current," both having shuttled off into the domain of history. Appropriately, one of the central issues in the writing of history is also motivation. Why did Julius Caesar cross the Rubicon? Why did Gioacchino Rossini retire from writing operas at the youthful age of 37? The grand mysteries of history could often be settled if only we could identify the motives that drove the participants in those big events.

Traditionally, psychohistory has been the discipline most strongly associated with the decipherment of what drives the personalities of the past. One definition of psychohistory calls it the "science of historical motivation—no more, no less." The psychohistorian will scrutinize the historical record for clues about the true motives behind big events and personalities. In line with psychohistory's fascination with psychoanalytic theory, these motives are almost invariably unconscious, and consequently not easily discerned. Only the full panoply of clinical skill enables the psychohistorian to tease out these subtle yet powerful forces in history.

The science of historical motivation can proceed differently, however. Psychologists have offered a scientifically more rigorous alternative.

The Motive Triad

Who in our times has not seen one of Rorschach's famous inkblots? The basic premise of the Rorschach test is that when people interpret an ambiguous stimulus, they unconsciously project the secrets of their personalities. By this means, the psychologist can unearth the motives that actually underlie a person's behavior. This is not the sole test based on this assumption, however. Another widely used instrument is the Thematic Apperception Test, or TAT. Instead of random inkblots, the TAT consists of 20 ambiguous pictures of human actors. The client or patient must write down a story about each scene. Besides describing what is happening in the present, the subject must narrate the events leading up to it as well as the future outcome. By applying coding schemes to the resulting TAT protocols, psychologists can extract scores on many traits of interest. Much of the research has concentrated on just three motives: the needs for achievement, power, and affiliation.

These motives are associated with a fascinating network of behaviors. Academic attainments, alcoholism, drunk driving, sexual assertiveness, and a host of other important actions are linked to one or more of the motives constituting this triad. But most interesting for us is the research showing how these motives intrude upon the stage of big events. I focus here on two cases: the impact of the achievement motive on economic prosperity, and that of the power motive on political leadership.

Economic Prosperity and the Need for Achievement

In *The Protestant Ethic and the Spirit of Capitalism*, the German sociologist Max Weber presented a classic thesis. Weber was trying to understand why capitalism grew most conspicuously in the European nations shaken by the Protestant Reformation. It was the followers of Martin Luther and John Calvin who apparently developed the new economic system with the most unmistakable enthusiasm and success. Because Germanic countries—especially the Netherlands, England, Sweden, and Prussia—took up the cause of the Reformation and the practice of capitalism, this historic event helped shift the balance from the Mediterranean countries to those along the North Atlantic seaboard. With economic prosperity came political power and military might. After all, "money is the sinews of battle," said Rabelais. In addition, as one economist held, "art and literature flourish in a rising economy, but they wither and perish in one that declines." Hence, the Protestant religion indirectly inspired the northern Europeans to carry the achievements of the Renaissance to new heights. Names like Shakespeare, Rembrandt, Newton, and Bach replaced those of Dante, Raphael, Galileo, and Monteverdi.

Attractive though Weber's thesis may be, as a theory it has a couple of deficiencies. First, it is rather narrow in conception: The Protestant religion is singled out. This slights the economic stimulation provided by other faiths and cultures. What about the Jains and Marwaris of India, the Gurage of Ethiopia, the Ibo tribe of Nigeria, the Jews and Quakers of Europe, or the Moslems in medieval times? All are set apart by their entrepreneurial prowess. Second, Weber did not provide an empirical test of his thesis. He was writing in the lofty style of social philosophy, in which mere insight and disquisition replace numbers and analysis. There is not one table in the treatise.

David McClelland offered an alternative in his 1961 book, *The Achieving Society*. McClelland was and is one of the most influential psychologists in human motivation research. Using the TAT in a diversity of inquiries, he has scrutinized how the motive triad guides human activities. McClelland specifically stated in *The Achieving Society* that the achievement motive, not Protestantism per se, was the proximate cause of capitalism's ascendance. A high need to achieve signifies the desire to do "something for its own sake, for the intrinsic satisfaction of doing something better." Such individuals set high standards for themselves, and try to surpass what has been done before. They are constantly working to improve things, to make things more efficient or productive. And they often endeavor to achieve something distinctive and unprecedented. According to McClelland, if the Protestant religion had any consequence for economic growth, it was only because the Reformation did something to increase achievement motivation. Yet other historic or cultural events could have attained the same end by different means. Hence, McClelland's thesis is not nearly so ethnocentric as Weber's.

But is it more testable? How can we possibly apply the TAT to historic actors long deceased? How is it possible to gauge economic property in times and places distant from our own? To be sure, we can always conduct laboratory simulations—a route McClelland and his colleagues have actively pursued. And we can always administer the TAT to contemporary subjects and weigh their scores against their economic behaviors. This approach also has not been ignored by McClelland and his colleagues. Yet these procedures remain too remote from the historical question. This is where McClelland, his students, and his collaborators have shown admirable ingenuity. In study after study, these investigators have devised direct tests of the basic thesis. Although a particular test often suffers from some flaw or limitation, the entire set of tests converges on the same answer. These archival tests can be divided into three groups: rich peoples, wealthy times, and profitable corporations.

Rich Peoples

If TAT protocols capture an individual's personality through the process of projection, perhaps other products of fantasy may be similarly analyzed. For example, the folk tales of preliterate cultures may reflect the dominant motives of a society. In fact, one study calculated the amount of achievement imagery found in the favorite stories of 45 cultures. Cultures like the Mandan, Aleut, Comanche, Yoruba, Papago, and Masai scored the highest, whereas the Chenchu, Thonga, Nauruans, and Basuto scored the lowest. The next step was to find the right index of entrepreneurial success. The best McClelland could come up with was determination of whether each society had any full-time entrepreneurs. Of those cultures highest in the achievement motive, 74% qualified by this criterion. Only 35% of those scoring lowest could boast this distinction. The technological base of these 45 tribes did not contaminate this contrast. So the achievement motive may indeed propel individuals toward economic greatness.

This admittedly crude test was bolstered by another, far more direct one. This time, McClelland studied 39 contemporary nations from all over the globe. He included modern capitalist countries, such as the United States, France, and New Zealand; Communist powers of that time, such as the Soviet Union and Bulgaria; and Third World nations, such as Mexico, Syria, and Pakistan. Instead of folk tales, the achievement motive was assessed from elementary school children's readers. These contain stories used to inculcate a culture's values into the next generation. For example, in the Portuguese version of the story of the tortoise and the hare, we find a passage that can be translated as follows: "One day the tortoise said to the hare, 'Say, Ma'am, *I bet that I can get to that bramble patch first.*' The hare replied, 'Say, mister, surely you must be off your rocker.'" The italicized passage counts as an achievement image. Turkey, India, Australia, Israel, and Spain scored the highest, and Chile, Denmark, Algeria, and Belgium the lowest. Finally, to assess economic growth, McClelland used adjusted gains in electrical power consumption. A strong relationship existed between these two measures. Those societies with the richest achievement imagery were those with the most pronounced economic expansion, on the average.

Again, McClelland's thesis received support. Admittedly, several scholars have challenged this demonstration. The issues are too technical to deserve attention here, but one matter is clear: McClelland's position does not stand or fall on just this study, as the next two tests show.

Wealthy Times

In addition to comparing economic output across nations of the world, McClelland and his associates have examined a single nation or civilization over time. The question then becomes not why some countries get richer faster than others, but rather why prosperity fluctuates in a single economy. One inquiry illustrates this complementary approach. Here the economic history of the United States was examined from 1800 to 1950. In line with the cross-national investigation, American commitment to achievement was assessed by coding imagery in those children's readers that were most widely read over that period. According to this assessment, the incidence of achievement imagery increased fairly smoothly until 1890. Thereafter a sharp decline set in. By 1950 America's achievement motive had dropped to about the same strength as that reached about a century before.

To gauge the American economy over the same interval, the investigators took the number of patents granted by the U.S. Patent Office. Concurrent census figures were used to transform this count into a per capita index. This indicator displayed a time trend very similar to that seen in the achievement motive. The per capita output of patents increased up to about the turn of the century. After continuing at a high level until the onset of the Great Depression in 1929, the index fell off dramatically. Not only was the relationship between achievement imagery and patent output quite strong, but the association was strongest when the patent index lagged the achievement measure by about 40 years. In other words, it took time for the children exposed to the achievement imagery in school to grow up and contribute to the creation of new inventions. Because these inventions usually resulted in novel products, this index should reflect the potential for economic growth in manufacturing and service sectors. And, independent of the contributions that the inventions made to national wealth, it is important that technological creativity should have been so well predicted from the achievement imagery contained in children's readers!

Of course, this test of McClelland's thesis was not all that historical. In the eyes of human civilization, 1800 is a very recent date. Nevertheless, a series of studies extended the empirical tests back further in time. This required considerable resourcefulness in conceiving measures of the two key variables. To rate achievement needs over time, the investigators often took a nation's best literature as a repository of current values. This approach was applied to the classical literatures of Greece, Spain, and England. Among the literary masterpieces tapped for achievement imagery were Aeschylus's drama *Prometheus Bound*, Sappho's poetry, and Demosthenes's oration *Second Olynthiac*; the *Poema del Mio Cid*, Cervantes's *Don Quixote*, and Quevedo's *Buscón*; *Everyman*, Marlowe's *Tamburlane*, Milton's *Samson Agonistes*, Congreve's *The Way of the World*, and Shelley's *Prometheus Unbound*—surely an impressive collection of great works!

More ingenious still was the extraction of achievement imagery from the graphic arts. Apparently, the doodles and drawings of people with a high need for achievement are distinguishable from those with minimal motives in this area. One investigator found that doodlers who produced lots of achievement imagery in their TAT protocols favored restless diagonals and S-shaped squiggles, whereas doodlers with puny amounts of achievement imagery in their protocols preferred soothing multiple-wave patterns. From this discovery, researchers created a way of objectively scoring the paintings on the vases of Minoan civilization and ancient Greece, as well as the funerary urns of pre-Incan Peru.

A tougher problem is how to calibrate economic prosperity over the same historical periods. Again, we must commend the imagination exhibited by psychologists. Indicators used in this research included the volume of public building in the Virú Valley of Peru; the rates of increase in London coal imports; the number of ships cleared from Cadiz, Spain, for the New World; and the extent of the Athenian trade area, as revealed by the distribution of the pottery jars that held wine and olive oil. Whatever the details, the results replicated what we have already witnessed: The achievement motive apparently stimulated economic growth. This connection was found to hold for pre-Incan Peru, Minoan civilization, classical Greece, medieval and early modern Spain, England going into the Industrial Revolution, and (as already noted) the United States during the first 150 years of its existence.

Profitable Corporations

One limitation of the preceding studies, whether cross-national or transhistorical surveys, is clear: The units of analysis are huge—whole nations, even civilizations. To get a better idea on how motives recruit money, it might be advisable to narrow the focus to the units that actually create wealth. In most modern economies, it is the company or corporation that generates jobs and prosperity. So what is the role of the achievement motive in making some corporations more profitable than others? This question was addressed in a study of automobile companies. One of the biggest economic events in the post-World War II era has been the rise of Japanese automobile manufacturers at the expense of once-dominant American companies. One of McClelland's students looked at the chief executive officers' (CEOs') letters to stockholders for Nissan, Honda, and Toyota versus Chrysler and General Motors. He scored these CEO communications for achievement imagery, using the standard procedures. For the period between 1952 and 1980, the achievement motive was consistently higher in the letters of the Japanese CEOs. Evidently, in order to make a car with worldwide appeal, it certainly helps if those running the business aspire to make a product better and more efficiently. The outcome is a high-quality vehicle with a low price.

If companies wish to gain a bigger market share, stockholders should insist that their CEOs be prolific in achievement imagery. This is not the only option, however. The social psychologist Kurt Lewin once said that "nothing is as practical as a good theory." Well, McClelland has certainly practiced what Lewin preached. McClelland and his colleagues have initiated a program of achievement motivation training for aspiring entrepreneurs. This practical test began with a sample of small-business owners in India, but has been extended to minority entrepreneurs in the United States. Further training sessions have been introduced in Spain and Mexico as well. The basic notion behind all of these interventions is the same: Teach courses in which businesspersons are trained to think in the proper motivational terms; then examine the impact of this training on later entrepreneurial success. The criteria include monthly sales, personal income, profits, and new jobs created. The results appear quite promising. Thus, McClelland has gone beyond merely exploring how economic history is made. He has also participated in the potential making of economic history!

Political Leadership and the Need for Power

When many of us ponder what makes politicians tick, we conjure up the word "power." We often view our political leaders as souls driven by the hunger to dominate, to influence, to control. Nor is this notion restricted to popular images; the same idea prevails among many political scientists as well. For instance, Harold Lasswell hypothesized that power motivation is central to the very personality structure of political leaders. But does this attribution represent reality? Or does an unconscious envy make us formulate derogatory stereotypes about those who reign over us?

Here the potential value of the TAT should become obvious. Power motivation is one of the primitive needs on which we can score protocols. Power images are those that stress the "concern with impact, control or influence on others; with arousing strong emotions in others; with prestige." Furthermore, we already have ample evidence that we can adapt TAT scoring procedures for use with documentary materials. Therefore, we can gauge the power motivation of political figures without having them write stories about TAT pictures. This potential has already been realized. Not surprisingly, one of David McClelland's students stands at the forefront of this extension. David Winter, both alone and in collaboration with his own students, has dedicated his career to showing how the need for power affects political leadership. In fact, his own 1973 book, *The Power Motive*, and McClelland's *The Achieving Society* enjoy roughly the same status in their respective specialties. Nonetheless, neither Winter nor his colleagues have confined their attention to the power motive alone. Repeatedly, they examine the other two parts of the triumvirate—achievement and affiliation. This yields a more profound perspective on the motives that drive political actors.

Below I review the key findings of this investigative program.

The White House

The first application of TAT-type content analysis to political personalities was carried out in 1970. The investigators used inaugural addresses of 20th-century chief executives to gauge power and achievement imagery. Several follow-up inquiries have now assessed virtually every American president between Washington and Reagan on power, achievement, and affiliation motives. The needs for power and achievement are defined as before, while the need for affiliation involves the desire for friendship, love, companionship, and nurturance. To offer some illustrations: The most power-hungry presidents were Truman and Kennedy, the least Grant and John Quincy Adams; the most achievement-driven were Carter and Hoover, the least William Harrison and Polk; and the most affiliation-oriented were Kennedy and Nixon, the least Theodore Roosevelt, Taft, and Garfield.

These scores are interesting in and of themselves, naturally. What makes these scores important as well as interesting is their relevance for understanding actual leadership performance. As we might expect, the power motive emerged as the most critical impetus behind presidential leadership. In the first place, those chief executives who scored the highest on this motive were more likely to lead the United States into a military conflict. This proclivity frequently led to territorial acquisitions that widened the sphere of American power. Yet the power motive was not always an aggressive factor. A power disposition could also permit an incumbent to put the brakes on an international crisis, preventing it from escalating into full-fledged war. A president high in power probably projected a more imposing image of national strength. On the other hand, power-driven presidents were not positively disposed toward completing arms limitation agreements with rival nations. Why should a statesman preoccupied with dominance and prestige do anything to weaken his apparent military might? Hence, in the long run, presidents hungry for power may have made this world a bit more dangerous.

The level of power motivation in an incumbent also affected his behavior in domestic affairs. For one thing, the power motive bore some relation to political affiliation: Democratic presidents scored slightly higher than Republicans. Furthermore, a power-oriented chief executive usually developed superior relations with the press. This skill might fit the association between the need for power and a president's charisma. Charismatic presidents probably knew better how to use the press to convey the image of a dynamic leadership style. Although this image of personal magnetism helped insure popularity with the masses, it was not without its costs. In particular, the higher an incumbent's power drive, the greater the likelihood that he would become the target of an assassination attempt, whether successful or not. A powerful, charismatic president undoubtedly attracted the attention of too many mentally deranged personalities. His conspicuousness was probably accentuated all the more by the tendency of such incumbents to be forceful, aggressive, radical, impulsive, and temperamental. In contrast, a below-average power motive probably yielded a leader who was far too timid, conciliatory, conservative, methodical, and moderate to provide an inviting target for a shattered ego with a gun.

Besides these attributes, power-oriented presidents made more "great decisions." That is, this motive often resulted in presidential decisions that changed the course of history. Truman's decision to send troops to defend South Korea and Kennedy's decision to quarantine Cuba are characteristic examples. This inclination might team up with the other attributes to produce a chief executive of the highest reputation. A positive relationship was found to exist between need for power and a president's performance rating according to historians. Power-motivated incumbents also attained the stature of greatness by being more charismatic and by their willingness to use military force.

Compared to all these ramifications, the effects of achievement drive were much more confined. The most remarkable aspect of this motive was its strong association with the power motive. This made our past presidents rather different from typical Americans, for whom power and achievement needs are seldom conflated. Moreover, this means that the achievement motive rarely had a repercussion besides what it could claim as a correlate of the power motive. Nevertheless, insofar as we can segregate the two motives, we can identify a few features of the presidents who were disposed toward achievement.

First, such chief executives were more prone to pursue the perverse ideals of a Machiavelli. On the average, they were sly, unscrupulous, evasive, shrewd, dishonest, insincere—and even a bit greedy. Fortunately, this wheeler-dealer personality was coupled with an actual commitment to accomplish something worthwhile as president. So achievement-driven executives scored higher on political creativity; they initiated new legislation and programs, and they adopted an innovative attitude toward their role. A difference from the power-hungry presidents was that this desire to succeed might take the form of arms limitation agreements. On the other hand, the constant emphasis on getting a job done might alienate the incumbent's advisers and assistants in the executive branch. At least those so intensely oriented toward task performance suffered a higher rate of turnover in their cabinets. Continuity and conviviality had to give way before the urge to achieve exceptional goals and satisfy extraordinary standards. Maybe this complex set of outcomes explains why high-achievement incumbents were susceptible to a neurotic style of leadership. These presidents all too often placed political success above effective policy, and adopted indirect and frequently convoluted tactics. They might even suffer health problems when confronted with difficult and critical periods in office.

Finally, there were affiliation-inclined presidents. Such chief executives were commonly more flexible in dealing with both foreign and domestic issues. In foreign policy, a need for affiliation above the norm inclined a president to negotiate compacts with other world powers to decelerate the arms race. Even so, at the domestic level such an incumbent might be less competent. Whereas presidents who scored high in achievement and power evidently made cabinet appointments according to a candidate's qualifications, chief executives who were overly obsessed with companionship and social approval were prone to select cabinet officials who made better cronies than experts. The aftermath of these choices was all too often disastrous. Highly affiliative presidents subjected themselves to the risk that a scandal would infect their administration. They surrounded themselves with chums who could not be easily fired. And they recruited officials according more to loyalty than to competence or integrity. Thus, these chief executives practically begged their less ethical pals to violate the public trust.

I have examined the three motives separately, but they actually worked together in the creation of a single president's character. The best chief executives had a distinctive profile on the triad. Specifically, the optimal profile required an intense drive toward power, a somewhat weaker but still unusual achievement motive, and a rather subdued need for affiliation. Such a configuration enjoyed the highest odds of producing what political scientist James David Barber has called the "active–positive" president. Franklin D. Roosevelt exemplified some of the assets of this style of political leadership.

The Campaign Trail

If TAT-type measures can teach us so much about incumbent presidents, they also can help us fathom those who have sought that same office. Naturally, we cannot then apply content analysis to inaugural addresses (except for that lucky minority who rose to the top). Yet we can analyze the announcement speeches by which candidates threw their hats into the ring. David Winter showed this in two separate studies.

In the first, Winter measured motivation imagery in the announcement speeches of the 1976 candidates. On the Democratic side, these included Birch Bayh, Lloyd Bentsen, Jimmy Carter, Frank Church, Fred Harris, Henry Jackson, Terry Sanford, Milton Shapp, Sargent Shriver, Morris Udall, and George Wallace. The Republican contestants were the incumbent, Gerald Ford, and his lone challenger, Ronald Reagan. The last two politicians are especially interesting because their scores on two motives were almost mirror images of each other. On power, Ford was the lowest of all candidates of either party, while Reagan was above average. But on affiliation, Reagan stood at the bottom, while Ford was second only to Shriver.

Given this baker's dozen, Winter unraveled how the motive profiles determined campaign strategies. For instance, those with a strong need to achieve were rather unlikely to remain in the competition after the odds became stacked against their candidacy. Aspirants characterized by high affiliation needs withdrew the earliest from the race, once they realized that not every voter loved them as much as they fantasized. This was a wise decision, for affiliative candidates were more likely to draw upon their own resources in financing their presidential ambitions. In contrast, candidates who were high in either power or achievement needs were more capable at fund-raising activities, although their abilities took different turns. In line with their superior charismatic appeal, the power-oriented politicians raised more contributions in amounts of $100 or less. It was the common voter who most appreciated the qualities of a potential demagogue. But the achievement-oriented types betrayed their affinities with entrepreneurs by winning more donations from party "fat cats"—amounts of $500 or more. Achievement and power also deflected candidates along distinct routes in New Hampshire, where the first primary was held. Achievement-driven aspirants allocated money more than time, trying to buy themselves a victory. The power-driven adopted the reverse path: They preferred shaking the voters' hands over the remote purchase of media time for spots.

Winter next inspected the presidential candidates in the 1988 election year. This time the Democratic aspirants were Bruce Babbitt, Joseph Biden, Michael

Dukakis, Richard Gephardt, Albert Gore Jr., Gary Hart, Jesse Jackson, and Paul Simon; the Republicans were George Bush, Robert Dole, Pete DuPont, Alexander Haig, Jack Kemp, and Pat Robertson. After gauging their motive profiles from their announcement speeches, Winter had some fun. To each candidate, he assigned a former U.S. president whose own motive profile was most similar. For example, Dukakis was average on achievement, the lowest of all 14 on power, and the highest of all 14 on affiliation. Indicative of the last distinction was this Dukakis affirmation: "From one generation to the next, America has been a covenant, a set of promises about the future which binds our people together." That distinctive profile matched him with Warren Harding. In a like vein, Dole was most like Jefferson, and Haig like Grant.

Most striking was Jesse Jackson, whose power motivation stood well above all other candidates, no matter what their allegiance. This imagery is seen in his remark that "We must defeat the merger maniacs who take our jobs, capital, tax base and hope to foreign soil!" Jackson was matched with Abraham Lincoln. Indeed, of the aspirants at the voters' disposal, Jackson's motive profile was the most compatible with that of a great president of the United States!

The International Scene

Research on the motive profile of politicians has focused on U.S. presidents. The rationale is plain to see. Because Americans conduct most of the inquiries, these researchers have more access to data about these homegrown politicians. And we cannot discount the intrinsic fascination of American psychologists with their own political leadership. Even so, this research program has gone well beyond the confines of chief executives and presidential candidates. Winter himself applied the TAT approach to interview data obtained from leaders conspicuous in the politics of southern Africa: white politicians, front-line heads of state, Zimbabwe nationalists, South African black nationalists, and South African "homeland" leaders. Again all three motives were scored. And the results were compatible with what we have already seen. For instance, those leaders who scored highest on power motivation were more prone to endorse the "initiation, continuation, or escalation of armed conflict," to invest "great energy in his leadership" and to "act when challenged [rather] than to wait."

Other investigators have scrutinized still other kinds of leaders, often relying on more direct TAT techniques. Some have studied leaders of a less history-making variety—elected county officials. The power motive frequently influenced such proclivities as whether these politicians initiated their own political activity or aspired to offices higher than the county level. A rather different inquiry looked at New Left activists among American and German students. The TAT divulged an aberrant amount of overt aggressiveness and hostility toward authority.

Perhaps the most fruitful research besides Winter's own is that pursued by Margaret Hermann, a political psychologist. In one study, Hermann probed the motives of the Soviet Politburo—men like Andropov, Brezhnev, Gromyko, and Kosygin. For the 20 members examined, scores on power and affiliation motives predicted who most favored arms reduction and détente with the United States. In a second study, Hermann examined how the personality traits of 45 heads of government affected the foreign policies of the nations they led. The leaders represent a truly international sample: Adenauer, Ben-Gurion, Bourguiba, Castro, DeGaulle, Eisenhower, Franco, Holyoake, Inönü, Jou Enlai, Kaunda, Kenyatta, Khrushchev, Marcos, Nasser, Nehru, Nkrumah, Tito, Trudeau, and Ulbricht, among others. Among the six personal attributes were two motives, power and affiliation. Once more the pattern of results followed our expectations. For example, "the greater the leaders' need for power, the more independence of action their government exhibits." But Hermann also verified another crucial conjecture: Personal attributes were more likely to affect government foreign policy when the head of state lacked experience in politics. Presumably, the better-trained politicians allowed *Realpolitik* to temper any natural inclinations to exert will and control over other political powers. It is not always wise to make international affairs a game of personal dominance over fellow leaders in the world community.

In sum, the entire body of research on the motive triad leads us to one irrefutable conclusion: Human motives do shape history, today.

Psychohistory Revisited

I have opened this chapter by noting how motivation defines the essential subject matter of psychohistory. Yet I have also insinuated that the traditional methods of psychohistory may lack enough rigor to qualify as a psychological science. Hence, does the research inspired by the TAT give us the desired methodology? To answer this properly, we must distinguish between two main types of psychohistory: group fantasy analysis and psychobiography.

Group Fantasy Analysis

Freud himself introduced the provocative idea that psychoanalysis might apply to the whole society. He first presented this theoretical extension in *Group Psychology and the Analysis of the Ego* and *Totem and Taboo*. "Freud postulated that groups tend to act through libidinal ties to their leaders because groups undergo collective regressions to an earlier mental stage dominated by a tyrannical father. Through identification, groups thus substitute for the lost father a leader." Of course, this extrapolation from individual to group processes has drawn a hefty amount of criticism. Even so, the difficulties inherent in this

enterprise have not prevented the adventurous from speculating on the unconscious motives of the group mind. The most vociferous modern proponent of
this approach is Lloyd deMause, director of the Institute for Psychohistory and
founder of the *Journal of Psychohistory*. In his book *The History of Childhood*,
and elsewhere, deMause has argued that all historic events derive ultimately
from child care. Even such matters as the infliction of infant enemas have monumental repercussions on human affairs!

Rather than critique the various brands of group fantasy analysis, let me
insist that a more rigorous alternative exists. The research conducted by
McClelland on the achievement motive reveals the power of the TAT-inspired
methods. Indeed, if anything, the account given in this chapter understates what
we can accomplish with objective measures of societal motives. In numerous
inquiries, McClelland and his colleagues have tapped all three motives—power,
achievement, and affiliation—at the group level. Moreover, with a little ingenuity, we can discern the motivational constitution of an entire nation from cultural indicators. We can thereby avoid the labors attending the analysis of documents and artifacts. A study reported in Winter's *The Power Motive* illustrates
this complementary approach.

For investigators who wish to study a society's infatuation with the power
motive, the Don Juan legend offers a terrific focal point. The central character
comes from an ancient line of conquerors, but decides to substitute sexual conquest for military prowess. Though the Don Juan legend has roots in popular
culture, the character first appeared on the Spanish stage in 1630, in a drama
attributed to Tirso de Molina. Since then he has populated the poetry, plays,
and novels of literatures throughout Europe. Mozart's *Don Giovanni* and Lord
Byron's *Don Juan* represent two of many such versions, famous or obscure.
Winter took advantage of an extensive bibliography that lists all renditions of
the Don Juan story in the histories of over a dozen European nations. He showed
that after one of these nations participated in a major military conflict, the Don
Juan story increased in popularity. The average delay between political milieu
and cultural reaction was about one decade. In fact, Tirso's original play came
about 10 years after two such occasions: Spain's ill-advised entry into the Thirty
Years' War in Germany, and the equally misguided reopening of the conflict
with the Netherlands. Apparently, imperialistic militarism nursed the power
motive symbolized by the libertine and charismatic Don Juan. He thus became
the manifestation of a group fantasy.

Clearly, this approach to the psychology of history may offer a more scientific substitute for traditional group fantasy analysis.

Psychobiography

Group fantasy analysis is only a side act in the psychohistorical circus. In the
main tent is the big show, the psychoanalysis of famous personalities. Freud's

analysis of Leonardo da Vinci was not his sole endeavor to explicate historical figures. After Freud's death, William C. Bullitt published *Thomas Woodrow Wilson: A Psychological Study*. This was reputedly the result of a collaborative effort between the aging master of psychoanalysis and a younger colleague. Although we can debate how much of the volume represents Freud's contributions and how much Bullitt's, the central thrust of the analysis is plain: President Wilson was a pathological personality. The former president was posthumously crucified on a psychoanalyst's couch.

Unfortunately, such crucifixions are all too common. Historic leaders are especially likely to become recipients of this type of psychoanalytic punishment. Adolf Hitler alone has inspired a sizable "Hitlerature." Maybe his policies were so odious that he deserves this treatment, and worse. But what about those politicians whom we can't exactly tag as "evil geniuses"? For instance, Richard M. Nixon has also attracted a respectable number of psychoanalyses at a distance— while the man is still alive to feel the psychoanalytic condemnation! Thus, in Mazlish's *In Search of Nixon*, we find the then-incumbent president labeled with a host of symptoms: anality, compulsiveness, denial, low self-esteem, suspiciousness, repressed hostility, depression, death wishes toward authority figures, the need to be surrounded by weak subordinates, the tendency to use crises as a way of dealing with his fears of death—well, it goes on and on. No wonder these pieces are so often dismissed as mere "psychopathographies"!

Once more, psychologists have provided a rival option. The research by Winter, Hermann, and others shows how the motives of historic individuals can be studied in an impartial fashion. Furthermore, we can scrutinize even contemporary politicians without injecting any political partisanship into the analysis. Nor must we fear the contamination of what psychoanalysts call "negative transference." Materials are scored in a manner so neutral that the investigator has no opportunity to project pent-up hostility about a parent upon the hapless historical figure. Hence, psychobiography and not merely group fantasy analysis can become a scientific activity.

To be sure, traditional psychobiographers may object that these methods are all designed for the analyses of many individuals, whereas they are intrigued by the complexities of a single personality. True, but the TAT-style techniques can be applied to more individualistic ends. Let me illustrate with a study conducted by David Winter in collaboration with Leslie Carlson. Winter and Carlson wanted to tease out the secret of Nixon's paradoxical personality. They began by listing five cases in which Nixon exhibited apparently contradictory behavior:

1. He proclaimed to his mother that he wanted to become an "honest lawyer," one who wouldn't sell his soul to crooks. And yet, years later, he had to protest "I am not a crook" when charged with committing criminal offenses as White House resident.

2. Early on, Nixon switched from being an almost populist liberal to a steadfast anti-Communist. Later, he found himself in Red China, toasting Mao Zedong in the Great Hall of the People.

3. After becoming a two-time loser—to Kennedy for the presidency in 1960, and to Pat Brown for the California governorship in 1962—Nixon bitterly told reporters that they "won't have Nixon to kick around anymore." And yet, in 1968 he was recast as the "new Nixon." Thus metamorphosed, Nixon became the first candidate in this century to enter the presidency after failing earlier to attain the office.

4. Nixon tape-recorded all conversations in the Oval Office. He then refused to destroy the tapes after it became clear that they would destroy his presidency.

5. Perhaps most bizarre of all was the sequence of events that occurred during the height of the conflict in Southeast Asia:

> In May 1970 he widened the Vietnam War by ordering an invasion of Cambodia. In response, thousands of college students gathered in Washington, DC, to protest. On the night of May 8–9, after a press conference in which he strongly defended his actions, Nixon made 51 telephone calls over 7 hours, and then drove to the Lincoln Memorial at 4:35 A.M. to visit with the protesting students. After telling them that "I want you to know that I understand just how you feel," he went on to discuss not the war, but rather travel, architecture, American Indians, and college football . . .

Can research generated by the TAT enable us to explain such a convoluted personality as Richard Milhous Nixon apparently possessed (and possesses)? To answer, Winter and Carlson first examined Nixon's motive profile, as revealed in his two inaugural addresses. Contrasting his scores with those of other U.S. presidents, they identified Nixon as a person more obsessed with achievement and affiliation than with power. The next step was to show that this motive profile fit well with other facts about Nixon's life and personality. Here Winter and Carlson drew upon the rich literature on the three motives based on both contemporary and historic subjects. They abstracted 28 characteristics of persons with high achievement motivation, 14 traits of those with high affiliation motivation, and 21 attributes usually descriptive of persons with high power motivation. Among these criteria were specific tell-tale behaviors, family background, personal style, interpersonal relationships, task performance, select personality traits, and life outcomes. Then the investigators simply tallied the number of traits in each motivation cluster that Nixon displayed. Nixon showed 88% of the achievement traits and 100% of the affiliation traits, but only 44% of the power traits. So the biographical data endorsed the TAT profile.

Armed with this confirmed profile, the researchers returned to the five paradoxes that inspired the inquiry. In each case, Nixon's behavior became more plausible once his underlying motives were clarified. Like any entrepreneur aiming at success, Nixon would constantly change his tactics to maximize his real or apparent achievements. Nixon was also inordinately obsessed with how others perceived him, as well as how he would stand in the eyes of posterity. At the same time, he did not feel comfortable with the exercise of power. His attempts at charisma came off as stiff and insincere. Even the bombing missions were something he almost felt he had to apologize for, as if he were being a naughty person. In this paragraph I cannot do justice to the niceties of the argument. I can only recommend that the interested reader peruse Winter and Carlson's 1988 paper for further insights.

Admittedly, Nixon's personality contains many intricacies that cannot be reduced to three scores on a motivational profile. We may need additional qualities of character to explain all the big events associated with a given historic actor, whether Nixon or anyone else. After all, with only three dimensions, we can specify only a few profile types. Yet nothing says that psychobiographers must confine their attention to motives alone. Instead, we may apply the full panoply of psychological assessment devices to the personality under view.

For example, in one study David Winter and Margaret Hermann collaborated with other researchers to produce a comprehensive picture of George Bush and Mikhail Gorbachev. Curiously, their motive profiles were rather similar to Nixon's—high in achievement and affiliation, but average in power. Hence, we could call Bush a "preppy Nixon," Gorbachev a "socialist Nixon." But the full story is richer than this. The two world leaders were differentiated on other psychological traits—conceptual complexity, self-confidence, distrust, optimism versus pessimism, beliefs about the controllability of events, methods used to reach goals, nationalism, verbal style, and more. Using this configuration of information, the investigators had a strong basis for understanding Bush's behavior in the Persian Gulf crisis and Gorbachev's behavior in the Baltic Republics crisis.

Such scientific psychobiographies could mark the wave of the future. The traditional approaches, with their qualitative and subjective evaluations, may become dinosaurs in the annals of the psychology of history.

The Ultimate Motive for Greatness?

Our preoccupation with the motive triad should not blind us to one rudimentary reality: Success in any walk of life demands that an individual display motivation of the highest possible magnitude. Extraordinary achievement does not arise from those with lackadaisical minds. In his *Discourses on Art*, Sir Joshua Reynolds warned the gifted but lazy student:

> You must have no dependence on your own genius. If you have great talents, industry will improve them; if you have but moderate abilities, industry will supply their deficiency. Nothing is denied to well directed labour: nothing is to be obtained without it. Not to enter into metaphysical discussions on the nature or essence of genius, I will venture to assert, that assiduity unabated by difficulty, and a disposition eagerly directed to the object of its pursuit, will produce effects similar to those which some call the result of *natural powers*.

In Chapter 3 we have seen that it may require a full decade of arduous labor to acquire the expertise essential to distinction in any domain. Otherwise, one cannot claim the "50,000 chunks" of discipline-relevant knowledge and skills.

Nor does life become more relaxed once the preparatory phase is over and the career is launched. On the contrary, Anna Pavlova, the world-famous prima ballerina, advised: "As is the case in all branches of art, success depends in a very large measure upon individual initiative and exertion, and cannot be achieved except by dint of hard work. Even after having reached perfection, a ballerina may never indulge in idleness." Only clock watchers and time-card punchers put in just 40-hour weeks.

Creative output in the sciences, for example, correlates positively with the number of hours devoted to scientific research. Hence, one study found that distinguished researchers in the physical and social sciences worked 60–70 hours per week for virtually the entire year. Anne Roe concluded from her intensive interviews with 64 illustrious scientists that all exhibited a "driving absorption in their work." "They have worked long hours for many years, frequently with no vacations to speak of, because they would rather be doing their work than anything else." Herbert Simon once admitted that he spent 100 hours per week doing the things that eventually earned him a Nobel Prize. No wonder Thomas Edison held that "genius is one per cent. [sic] inspiration and ninety-nine per cent. perspiration." Or, as hair stylist Vidal Sassoon put it, "The only place where success comes before work is a dictionary."

The procrastinators among you may discount these claims. After all, can we really trust mere reports without some hard data to back them up? Maybe geniuses exaggerate their labors to scare away potential competitors with more fluent talents. No such luck! These boasts (or complaints) about industry are substantiated in overt behaviors for all to see. The material evidence is implied in Michael Faraday's motto, "Work, Finish, Publish." Ultimately, the true geniuses produce publication after publication at a nearly breakneck pace. Or, if their achievements are in a nonverbal domain, these assiduous souls generate painting after painting, sculpture after sculpture, invention after invention, and so on *ad infinitum*. Consider the following items.

Sigmund Freud's bibliography lists 330 articles and books. Thomas Edison obtained 1,093 patents, which remains the record at the U.S. Patent Office. Balzac, by working over 15 hours a day for 20 years, wrote 85 novels. Picasso created approximately 20,000 works over the course of his career. And J. S. Bach composed enough music to keep a copyist, working only 40 hours per week, busy for a career. Psychologist Frank Barron affirmed:

> The biography of the inventive genius commonly records a lifetime of original thinking, though only a few ideas survive and are remembered to fame. Voluminous productivity is the rule and not the exception among the individuals who have made some noteworthy contribution.

To convince the skeptical sloths, let's move to a higher plane of evidence. In lieu of specific cases, suppose we examine group statistics. Wayne Dennis studied contributors to disciplines as diverse as music, linguistics, infantile paralysis, gerontology/geriatrics, geology, and chemistry; he also examined books on all subjects in the Library of Congress. He found that the top 10% who were the most prolific in each field could be credited with about 50% of all the contributions to the field. In contrast, those among the 50% who were the least productive were responsible for only about 15% of all the work. There is even a law that expresses how much the elite monopolizes a creative endeavor. According to the Price law, if k is the number of persons active in a discipline, then the square root of this number ($\sqrt{k}$) approximates the size of that subset who produced half of the contributions. Thus, about 250 composers responsible for the music played in the classical repertoire. The square root of this number is 15.8. It turns out that a mere 16 composers put their names on half of all the pieces performed and recorded. The Price law holds for every major domain in the arts and sciences.

Furthermore, the most common occurrence is for individuals to make a *single* contribution to their fields. This means that the most productive individual is several times more prolific than those who are least productive. In the discipline of psychology, for example, the most prolific scientist boasts more titles than about 80 competitors in the bottom half of the population of psychologists. And, obviously, these figures understate the genuine status of the productive elite—for only those who contributed at least something to posterity are even counted in these tabulations. Yet sometimes the majority of potential contributors, as identified by their winning Ph.D.'s from major universities, publish nothing beyond their doctoral dissertations. In his classic book *The Man of Genius*, Cesare Lombroso claimed that "the appearance of a single great genius is more than equivalent to the birth of a hundred mediocrities." This assertion is not outlandish at all.

Given these facts, the luminaries of cultural history *must* be telling the truth. How else can they exhibit such astronomical output without budgeting their time in equal measure? Hence, we are brought back to the initial point: It takes work to become a renowned genius. These individuals are driven by huge motivational forces that far eclipse the impetus behind less accomplished colleagues. "Genius does what it must, and Talent does what it can," apologized Owen Meredith in his *Last Words of a Sensitive Second-Rate Poet*. So essential is this inexorable pressure that Francis Galton maintained that we cannot define genius without incorporating a motivational component:

> I mean those qualities of intellect and disposition, which urge and qualify a man to perform acts that lead to reputation. I do not mean capacity without zeal, nor zeal without capacity, nor even a combination of both of them, without an adequate power of doing a great deal of very laborious work. But I mean a nature which, when left to itself, will, urged by an inherent stimulus, climb the path that leads to eminence, and has strength to reach the summit—one which, if hindered or thwarted, will fret and strive until the hindrance is overcome, and it is again free to follow its labour-loving instinct.

Where does this drive come from? The answer to this question is one of the great mysteries of psychology. It could be that one or more of the motives already discussed is involved. The genius may be in the highest percentiles on the achievement motive, or the power motive, or maybe both together. Even the affiliation motive may participate if the creator fantasizes about acclaim as much as excellence, fortune, and prestige. Moreover, we certainly must be willing to credit the genius with some intrinsic motives as well. Geniuses cannot spend so many hours without an inherent passion for what they do. Therefore, we might do better to say that all the motives that can stimulate the energies of the human being all converge on a single activity, a monomaniacal preoccupation. Perhaps even some quirky needs—such as those dwelt upon by the psychoanalysts—may be included in this unified obsession. Only by the convergence of multiple forces can sufficient energy be rallied behind the prodigious labors of those figures who dominate the history of their disciplines.

Yet, in putting forward this explanation, we implicitly confess our ignorance. We are identifying not one motive, but a cornucopia of needs. In all likelihood, there can be no ultimate motive behind success.

CHAPTER 6

INFANTS, CHILDREN, AND TEENAGERS:
THE FAMOUS IN THEIR YOUTH

"The Child is father of the Man," said Wordsworth. This concisely expresses a basic tenet of developmental psychology: A person's childhood and adolescence provide vital clues about an individual's prospects in adulthood and old age. If we only knew the significant signs, we could raise our own children to join the greats of history. So how can we detect the antecedents of achieved eminence? We have two disparate methods at our disposal.

First, we can conduct a "longitudinal study." That is, we begin by examining a bunch of children or adolescents; we then repeat these assessments at regular intervals as the subjects pass through life's stages. Perhaps the most impressive longitudinal study ever conducted was that by Lewis Terman at Stanford University. In the early 1920s, Terman collected a sample of over 1,000 children from elementary schools in metropolitan California. These children scored at genius levels on a standard IQ test. They were then subjected to scrutiny from elementary school on.

Terman published the results in a series of volumes under the main title *Genetic Studies of Genius*. The initial measurements appeared in Volume 1, under the subtitle *Mental and Physical Traits of a Thousand Gifted Children*, published in 1925. Later studies of the same children came out between 1930 and 1959. Volumes 3, 4, and 5 were subtitled *The Promise of Youth: Follow-Up Studies of a Thousand Gifted Children*; *The Gifted Child Grows Up: Twenty-Five Years' Follow-Up of a Superior Group*; and *The Gifted Group at Mid-Life: Thirty-Five Years' Follow-Up of the Superior Child*. Even though the last report appeared after Terman's death in 1956, the study continued long after the instigator passed away. Indeed, one of the members of the sample, Robert Sears, grew up to become a distinguished developmental psychologist at Stanford, and thereby became linked to further follow-ups. Although Sears himself died in 1989, enough of his cohort still survives to serve as subjects for additional inquiries. The investigation may not end until the expiration of the last of these so-called "Termites."

Longitudinal investigations like Terman's are rare in the behavioral sciences. To launch one of these projects is time-consuming and expensive. To follow a group of children all the way to adulthood is no easy task. Subjects move to less accessible locations; attrition of the subject pool occurs when some get disgusted with serving as guinea pigs; and, naturally, some have the habit of inconveniently dying before the study ends. Besides all this, how many researchers want to start an investigation that they will not live to complete? Only younger psychologists can hope to see interesting results from the follow-ups, yet only older psychologists enjoy the job security that enables them to embark on high-risk lines of research.

Hence comes the second choice: the "retrospective study." Here the inquiry starts at the other end, with people who are already famous. Through questioning, these celebrities divulge the circumstances of their childhood. Francis Galton introduced this approach in 1874 with his book *English Men of Science*, in which he summarized the responses of Fellows of the Royal Society to the questionnaires he had sent them. Others may interview celebrities more directly, as Anne Roe did in her 1952 book *The Making of a Scientist*.

An alternative mode of retrospective analysis is also available: The psychologist can dig into the biographies of prominent personalities to determine the childhood and adolescent antecedents of their achievements. The first monumental application of this approach was *The Early Mental Traits of Three Hundred Geniuses* by Catherine Cox, who scrutinized the lives of renowned creators and leaders of Western civilization for developmental clues. Other investigators have followed in Cox's footsteps, surveying an array of developmental experiences that has grown ever more broad over the years. Cox's classic study obviously impressed her mentor, Lewis Terman; he had it inserted as Volume 2 in *Genetic Studies of Genius*, which appeared in 1926. Thus, the landmark retrospective inquiry is in the same set of volumes as the most ambitious longitudinal inquiry ever undertaken in this area.

Of course, retrospective studies have their own advantages and disadvantages. Although psychologists need not worry about attrition, they often must fret about the quality of the biographical data. Cox was dismayed to learn that someone as well known as Shakespeare had virtually nothing of value recorded about his childhood and adolescence. Indeed, there were years when Shakespeare apparently vanished off the face of the earth! Early biography was also skimpy for Luis de Camoëns, Jean Baptiste Colbert, Étienne de Condillac, John Knox, Ignatius Loyola, Niccolò Machiavelli, Francisco Pizarro, François Rabelais, and Titian! These luminaries made the first cut (enough fame), but not the second (essential data). Moreover, sometimes even when we possess rich information about a historical figure's childhood, we cannot always trust it. I have already discussed the memory distortions of hindsight bias in Chapter 3. After someone becomes world-renowned, there is often no shortage of parents, siblings, teachers, friends, and neighbors who saw the critical event that propelled the soul toward glory!

Because neither longitudinal nor retrospective methods are perfect, we should draw on both as much as possible. Happily, the findings of each method corroborate rather than contradict each other, with only minor exceptions. In this chapter I concentrate on developmental antecedents that fall naturally under three headings—family background, education, and marginality. With those facts under out belts, we can delve into one of the biggest puzzles in the psychology of greatness: Is genius born or made?

Hercules's Cradle: The Impact of Family Background

Like charity, the making of a notable creator, leader, or celebrity begins at home. The family environment serves as the "cradle of eminence." The home provides the child with the first experiences that shape development in one direction rather than another. Of course, family background can entail a host of possible factors. Even so, usually a handful of variables stand out as the most critical and universal. This is clear in Anne Roe's thumbnail sketch of the typical luminary in science:

> He was the first-born child of a middle-class family, the son of a professional man. He is likely to have been a sick child or to have lost a parent at an early age. He has a very high IQ and in boyhood began to do a great deal of reading. He tended to feel lonely and "different" and to be shy and aloof from his classmates.

A few of these developmental events and conditions may have been unique to the 64 scientists of repute whom Roe interviewed. Others may apply to famous scientists in general, but not to creators of other types, such as artists. Still other factors probably affect the development of famous personalities of whatever kind. Into this last class of influences fall three circumstances: (1) a person's ordinal position in his or her family; (2) the experience of traumatic events; and (3) the family provision for, and encouragement of, mental stimulation.

Oldest, Youngest, and In-Between

As we have seen in Chapter 2, Francis Galton's *Hereditary Genius* strove to show how achieved eminence runs in family lines. Yet scrutiny of family pedigrees reveals a peculiar fact: Many individuals have attained the utmost distinction, while their siblings have remained in the most dire obscurity. Look at the childhoods of Charles Darwin, Descartes, Cervantes, Rembrandt, Beethoven, Gandhi, or Sun Ixian. All had siblings, not one of whom was famous.

To be sure, famous siblings do exist. In mathematics we have the names of Jacques and Jean Bernoulli, in astronomy William and Caroline Herschel, in ballooning Joseph and Jacques Montgolfier, in cinematography August and Louis Lumière, and in aviation Orville and Wilbur Wright. In Chapter 2,

Table 2.2 has given contemporary examples. If we are willing to count those siblings who attained success in different fields, other cases are available. We can cite William James the psychologist and Henry James the novelist, or Ernst Heinrich Weber the physiologist and Wilhelm Edward Weber the physicist. All of these cases notwithstanding, it still must amaze us how few cases we can actually mention. Until recent times, when planned parenthood became a reliable option, only children were not very common. Yet in one study of more than 2,000 scientists and inventors, only 2% had equally famous siblings. Even if we allow for the lack of opportunities afforded the sisters of eminent men, that percentage still seems a bit low.

After all, if we believe that certain family environments favor the growth of genius, then shouldn't the benefits rain down on all children in the same household? If genetic endowment plays its part in the creation of future celebrities, shouldn't all offspring of the same parents enjoy equal odds of achieving recognition? Of course, we could explain the genetic inequalities by means of the doctrine of emergenesis discussed in Chapter 2. Yet, at the very least, we would expect identical twins to climb in tandem toward the pinnacles of fame. That event is exceedingly infrequent. One of the few instances involves Ann Landers and Abigail Van Buren, two prominent authors of advice columns in daily newspapers. So the enigma of the sibling dropouts remains.

Galton himself provided a potential resolution. Not long after *Hereditary Genius* appeared in 1869, Galton's genetic thesis came under attack. Among these critics was Alphonse de Candolle, a prominent French naturalist. Ironically, Candolle's own family might be taken to illustrate Galtonian pedigrees. His father was the famed Swiss botanist Augustin Pyrame de Candolle, and fame as a botanist was attained by his own son as well, Anne Casimir Pyrame de Candolle. Nevertheless, this middle Candolle documented some of the environmental factors that determine the appearance of eminent scientists. Innate capacity cannot be the whole story if the emergence of genius is governed by economics, climate, political milieu, and other global conditions.

Galton responded with the 1874 survey. By distributing questionnaires to nearly 200 English scientists of note, Galton hoped to discover the setting for greatness. Among the developmental factors he unearthed was ordinal position in the family. Notable scientists were disproportionately first-born children. To be sure, there were later-borns who managed to make it into the upper ranks. Galton himself was the last-born child in a large family. Still, the odds favored those born earliest. Primogeniture pointed to just one sibling to stand before the limelights of history.

This birth-order effect has been replicated many times in the century since Galton's survey. Of the 64 notable scientists interviewed by Roe, fully 39 were first-born, and 13 were at least second-born. Furthermore, of the 25 who missed out on primacy of birth, 5 were oldest sons, and 2 had an older sibling who had died in infancy or early childhood. Many of the rest were 5 or more years younger than their immediately older sibling. In general, first-borns usually represent 50% or more of the community of active scientists. The first-borns even exceed their later-born colleagues on various criteria of success. They are referred to more frequently in the scientific literature of their field. They receive higher creativity ratings at the hands of experts in their discipline. The first-borns even have a better chance of earning the Nobel Prize.

Nor is primogeniture restricted to science. In *A Study of British Genius* by Havelock Ellis, the same advantage was found for those who won an entry in *The Dictionary of National Biography*. Other studies have demonstrated that the advantage holds for achievement domains ranging from classical composers to American presidents, senators, and members of Congress. One recent inquiry found that nearly half of all notable creators, leaders, and celebrities of the 20th century were shown to be first-born children. Table 6.1 offers some representative examples in the various categories. But why the advantage? There are two main explanations.

TABLE 6.1. Ordinal Positions for Selected 20th-Century Celebrities

Only child: Lauren Bacall, Ingrid Bergman, Willy Brandt, André Breton, Martin Buber, John Cleese, Walter Cronkite, W. E. B. Du Bois, François Duvalier, Erik Erikson, Stan Freberg, Indira Gandhi, Lou Gehrig, Uri Geller, Arsenio Hall, Helen Hayes, Lillian Hellman, Howard Hughes, King Hussein (Jordan), Henry Miller, Flannery O'Connor, Cole Porter, Ezra Pound, Anthony Quinn, Vita Sackville-West, Jean-Paul Sartre, Charles Schulz, Haile Selassie, Frank Sinatra, Upton Sinclair, Alexander Solzhenitsyn, Gloria Swanson, François Truffaut, Peter Ustinov, Maurice Utrillo, Alan Watts, T. H. White.

First of: 2, James Agee, Muhammad Ali, Isaac Babel, Simone de Beauvoir, e e cummings, Bob Dylan, Edward Heath, Christopher Isherwood, Charles Ives, Carl Jung, Henry Kissinger, Sandy Koufax, Sylvia Plath, Wilhelm Reich, Theodore Roethke, Georges Simenon, Edward Steichen, Erich von Stroheim; 3, Nnambi Azikiwe, Leonard Bernstein, Julian Bond, Leonid Brezhnev, Benjamin Britten, Moshe Dayan, Henry Fonda, Martha Graham, Mata Hari, Jomo Kenyatta, Alfred Kinsey, Oskar Kokoschka, Alexander Korda, Shirley Maclaine, André Malraux, Carson McCullers, Margaret Mead, Mishima Yukio, Jan Myrdal, Anaïs Nin, John Sloan, Paul Tillich, Pierre Trudeau; 4, Cecil Beaton, Jimmy Carter, Gerald Ford, Che Guevara, Nikos Kazantzakis, Henry Luce, Jacqueline Kennedy Onassis, Drew Pearson, Edson Pelé, Vidkun Quisling, George Wallace, Jessamyn West; 5, Shirley Chisholm, Angela Davis, John Foster Dulles, Adolf Eichmann, Katherine Hepburn, Julian Huxley, Lyndon Johnson, Mickey Mantle, Piet Mondrian, Vladimir Nabokov, Oginga Odinga, David Sarnoff, Edgard Varèse, Yevgeny Yevtushenko; 6, Coco Chanel, Rose Kennedy, Norman Thomas; 7, Joyce Cary, Teilhard de Chardin, Nancy Mitford; 8, John O'Hara, Helena Rubinstein, Babe Ruth; 9, James Baldwin; 10, Grandma Moses; 11, Willie Mays; 14, Benny Bufano.

Middle child: Ingmar Bergman 2/3, Niels Bohr 2/3, Buckminster Fuller 2/3, Henry Cabot Lodge 2/3, Golda Meir 2/3, Jean Renoir 2/3, Tennessee Williams 2/3, George Zhukov 2/3; Christiaan Barnard 2/4, Francis Chichester 2/4, Isak Dinesen 2/4, Abba

(continued)

TABLE 6.1. (*Continued*)

Eban 2/4, Jimmy Hoffa 2/4, Hubert Humphrey 2/4, George McGovern 2/4, Joan Miró 2/4, Manfred von Richtofen 2/4, Grant Wood 2/4; Pierre Auguste Renoir 2/5; Cesar Chavez 2/6, Edmund Muskie 2/6; Georgia O'Keeffe 2/7; Augustus John 3/4, Louis Leakey 3/4, Eugene McCarthy 3/4, James Naismith 3/4, John Steinbeck 3/4, P. G. Wodehouse 3/4; Herbert Henry Asquith 3/5, Rosalind Franklin 3/5, Antoine de Saint-Exupéry 3/5; Bernadette Devlin 3/6; Alexander Neill 3/8; Leonard Woolf 3/9; Graham Greene 4/6, Louis Renault 4/6; Paramahansa Yogananda 4/8; Lillie Langtry 5/6, Edward G. Robinson 5/6; Mary Cassatt 5/7, Fidel Castro 5/7; Henry Moore 6/7; Lawrence Welk 6/8; Malcolm X 7/9; Nancy Astor 7/11; Frank Capra 8/9; Jiddu Krishnamurti 8/11; Lytton Strachey 11/13; Juan Gris 13/14.

Last of: 2, Fred Astaire, Bertolt Brecht, Alexander Calder, Marlene Dietrich, Alexander Dubček, Margot Fonteyn, Allen Ginsberg, Doris Lessing, Ronald Reagan, Sukarno, Elizabeth Taylor, James Thurber, Earl Warren, Evelyn Waugh; 3, Spiro Agnew, W. H. Auden, Marlon Brando, Rachel Carson, Jean Cocteau, Jacob Epstein, Greta Garbo, Judy Garland, Antonio Gramsci, Ho Chi Minh, Lady Bird Johnson, Janis Joplin, Vladimir Mayakovsky, Marilyn Monroe, Paul Muni, Sean O'Faolain, Laurence Olivier; 4, Roger Casement, Colette, Hélène Deutsch, Karl von Frisch, Otto Hahn, J. Edgar Hoover, Al Jolson, Ralph Nader, Joe Namath, Rudolph Nureyev, Pope Paul VI, Ravi Shankar, Isaac Bashevis Singer; 5, Elizabeth Arden, Jeane Dixon, C. S. Forester, Dag Hammarskjöld, Thor Heyerdahl, Käthe Kollwitz, Jackson Pollock, Paul Robeson, Andrew Wyeth; 6, Lou Andreas-Salomé, T. S. Eliot, Zelda Fitzgerald, Frédéric Joliot-Curie; 7, Evangeline Booth, Arthur Rubinstein; 9, Edward Kennedy.

Intellect?

Success of the highest order requires inordinate intelligence, an attribute that may correspond to ordinal position in the family. One gigantic inquiry looked at the intellectual ability of the *total* population of 19-year-old males born in the Netherlands. That provided about 400,000 subjects from which to generalize. Intelligence declined steadily from the first-borns to the last-borns; this decline was independent of family size and socioeconomic class. A second investigation was an even more colossal study of the nearly 800,000 students in the United States who took the National Merit Scholarship Qualifying Test. Again, first-borns surpassed middle children, who in their turn surpassed the last-borns. Beyond these examples, first-borns are overrepresented among child prodigies, and were overrepresented among the gifted children studied in Terman's longitudinal study. Primogeniture implies intellectual superiority.

This birth-order effect could explain why first-borns are so conspicuous among the notables: They have brains on their side. Hence, first-borns are more likely to go to college, to advance to graduate or professional school, and to enter the professions. First-borns are more likely to become Rhodes Scholars, and to enter the privileged career of the university professor. First-borns have higher odds of seeking science as a career. Whatever the details, first-borns are ideally positioned to dominate the entries of those listed in *American Men and Women of Science* and *Who's Who in America*. Their younger siblings, lacking the same level of intellectual ability, drop out early in the race to fame and fortune. They're just not up to snuff.

Unfortunately, we have not so much answered the initial question as rephrased it. For the moment, let us accept the possibility that younger siblings are intellectually inferior to older siblings. Whence arises this progressive decline as each successive child emerges from a mother's womb? Robert Zajonc has proposed the "confluence model" as a response. According to this model, the ordinal position of a child in the family decides the level of intellectual stimulation available in the early years. The first-born is stimulated by the social interactions of mature adults; the later-borns grow up in a home increasingly inundated by the immature activities of older siblings. Besides explaining the general ordinal drop in intelligence, the confluence model handles some of the finer features of the phenomenon. For instance, the model explains why successful later-borns often fall into one of two conditions: (1) They lost an older sibling early in development, or (2) a big age gap separates them from their older siblings. This pattern was observed among Roe's 64 scientists. In addition, the model accounts for the tendency for final prominence to be linked with early exposure to many adults in childhood.

These accomplishments notwithstanding, the confluence model has provoked a fair share of controversy. Sometimes the research vindicates the theory; at other times results run counter to the theory. Because this debate centers on everyday subjects, we need not enter this dispute here. Instead, we should consider whether the model is germane to a psychology of greatness.

And on this point we clearly cannot explicate the primogeniture advantage merely by citing contrasts in sibling intellectual development. In the first place, the first-born edge is not uniform. In the Ellis study of British genius, the birth-order effect was curvilinear. Although first-borns were overrepresented, so were the last-borns, even if not by so large a magnitude. Thus, the ordinal effect is out of order—first first-borns, then last-borns, then the middle children. This does not fit the confluence model. Second, in some domains firstborns have an edge even when intellectual ability is not required. For example, one study divulged that 9 out of 10 stripteasers were first-born daughters. Surely such behavior does not demand a premiere intellect! Moreover, in other areas it is the later-borns who predominate. For instance, later-borns are more likely to enter dangerous sports, such as professional football. Famed New York Jets quarterback Joe Namath was the last-born of four. Athletes engaging in less physically injurious sports do not exhibit this disproportion. All in all, any interpretation that hinges on intellectual development alone is not going to get us very far.

Personality?

Sigmund Freud was his mother's first-born son. Because his father's sons from a previous marriage were about Freud's mother's age, Freud was for all practical purposes the first-born of a second family. He certainly was his mother's favorite. Freud later remarked that "if a man has been his mother's undisputed darling he retains throughout life the triumphant feeling, the confidence in success, which not seldom brings actual success along with it." When Freud grew up and became famous, he gathered around himself a collection of disciples willing to accept the dogmas of their authoritative master. But many of the most outstanding of these followers eventually found themselves dissenting from the founder of psychoanalysis. Because Freud brooked no opposition, he often expelled these apostates after some heated exchange. Thus exiled and excommunicated, these ex-disciples would found their own brands of psychoanalysis. Among these rebels was Alfred Adler.

Unlike Freud, Adler was a later-born son. In fact, Adler's older brother was in many respects similar to Freud. Both were "Mama's boys" who could do no wrong; both did everything possible to live up to parental expectations. Hence, it is not surprising that Adler was the first important psychoanalyst to rebel against Freud's intellectual tyranny. Adler went on to advance an alternative scheme called "individual psychology." In Adlerian theory, sexual conflicts play a comparatively minor role in the genesis of the human personality. Instead, social interactions in early childhood figure much more prominently. Among these influences, sibling relationships have a major say in personality development. Adler claimed that the first-born never completely overcomes the birth of additional brothers and sisters. Since the later-borns attract so much parental attention, the first-born becomes a dethroned king. This implants in the first-born an incessant need to regain the center stage of parental affections—and so the first-born begins a crusade toward fame and fortune. Adler's theory can thus account for the supremacy of first-borns among the greats of history.

Owing to Adler's emphasis on sibling rivalries in personality development, the *Journal of Individual Psychology* has become an important repository of research on birth-order effects. For example, after showing the preponderance of first-borns in the U.S. Senate and House of Representatives, one Adlerian psychologist dutifully attributed this result to the intense approval-seeking behavior of the dethroned king. One intriguing feature of Adlerian theory is its implication that first-borns are not the same as only children. Only children do not suffer the usurpation of parental affections by younger siblings; in fact, they are first-borns and last-borns all rolled up in one. Adlerian inquiries have indeed discovered discrepancies between these two distinct types of first-borns. For example, despite the hegemony of first-borns among presidents of the United States, only children are extremely rare. Perhaps just Franklin D.

Roosevelt can legitimately count as a member of the species, and even he had an older half-brother. The closest only children usually get to the White House is the vice-presidency, where they are conspicuously represented. Presumably, only children, unlike the first-borns, lack ample experience in lording it over younger siblings—a skill of some value in winning the top spot on the ticket.

If one's goal is posterity's acclaim, it is clearly better to become president than vice-president. Nonetheless, Adlerian theory has the advantage that it allows later-borns to achieve greatness, albeit after their own fashion. If the first child is envious of the later children, the later-borns are jealous of the special status of the first-born. So the later-borns should display a certain rebelliousness against everything that their oldest sibling represents. The later in the sequence of births, the stronger this dissenting tendency.

There is an interesting case of this in psychology's history—the Allport brothers. The older, Floyd, was a pioneer in experimental social psychology; he sought rigorous scientific theories. Gordon, who was seven years younger, also made notable contributions to social psychology. But Gordon's approach was far more philosophical. Indeed, he was a leader in the movement that founded humanistic psychology, and at times he displayed rebellious, anti-science attitudes. That a sibling rivalry existed there can be no doubt. Once Gordon's wife tried to mediate by listing his brother's virtues. "And is he still stubborn, lazy, and procrastinating?" was Gordon's prompt reply.

This ordinal trend in defiance alone could account for the birth-order contrasts in intellectual development discussed earlier. Maybe it is not inferior ability that inclines later-borns to perform poorly on standardized tests, to achieve less in school, and to disfavor prestigious occupations. Rather, later-borns may find these first-born preoccupations to represent distasteful quests for authority and conformity.

In addition, those endeavors that welcome the more Bohemian personality should find many later-borns, and especially last-borns, knocking at the door. This helps explain the conspicuous presence of later-borns among artistic creators, such as creative writers. Albert Camus, Miguel de Cervantes, Fyodor Dostoevsky, T. S. Eliot, Ralph Waldo Emerson, Thomas Mann, Herman Melville, Michel de Montaigne, Gertrude Stein, Leo Tolstoy, Mark Twain, Voltaire, Walt Whitman, Oscar Wilde, and William Wordsworth provide some examples. Later-borns are more likely to become political revolutionaries as well. Fidel Castro was the fifth of his father's seven children; he and his younger brother Raúl led the Cuban revolution that overthrew the dictator Batista. Other later-borns who have in some way engaged in destroying (first-born) authority include Corazon Aquino, David Ben-Gurion, Simón Bolívar, Napoleon Bonaparte, Oliver Cromwell, Clarence Darrow, King David of Israel, Jefferson Davis, Charles De Gaulle, Alexander Dubček, Benjamin Franklin, Mahatma Gandhi, Adolf Hitler, Ho Chi Minh, Stonewall Jackson, Joan of Arc, Ayatollah Khomeini, Judas Maccabeus, Robert E. Lee, Vladimir Lenin, Jan Smuts, Leon Trotsky, and Lech Walesa. To this grouping we might also append the historic personalities who led religious movements: Moses, St. Francis Xavier, John Calvin, John Wesley, and Brigham Young.

We must not forget one thing: When we say that one birth order towers over others in an achievement domain, we are speaking only in a statistical sense. There are first-borns among revolutionaries, such as Mirabeau and Robespierre. And there are first-borns among creative writers, such as Goethe, Kafka, and Shakespeare. Similarly, there are later-born scientists, like Descartes and Darwin, and later-born statesmen, such as Bismarck, Cesar Borgia, Andrew Jackson, and Richelieu. These exceptions do not overturn the primary tenet, as long as the distributions of ordinal positions across careers departs from chance expectation. Moreover, often the aberrant cases furnish "exceptions that prove the rule."

In 1964, Irving Harris published a volume titled *The Promised Seed: A Comparative Study of Eminent First and Later Sons*. He gathered data on about 1,000 historical figures in several domains of distinction, such as politics, war, business, technology, science, religion, philosophy, and literature. Harris had no interest in counting the presence of first versus later sons. Instead, his argument was more subtle: When individuals of distinct birth orders enter the same field, the unique character of their respective contributions depends on their birth-order status. Hence, much of the book consists of contrasts between first and later sons who made their marks in the same annals. Thus, it contrasts Marx and Engels with Lenin and Trotsky; Grant and Hooker with Lee and Jackson; Freud and Jung with Adler and Rank; and Locke and Berkeley with Bacon, Hobbes, and Hume. In each pairing, Harris teased out the impression left by the stamp of early childhood experiences. Furthermore, though his investigation simplified discussion by concentrating on sons, every so often he mentioned how his principles would apply to daughters as well. Later-born daughters, such as Gertrude Stein or Mary Baker Eddy, also fit the theory.

Harris conducted no quantitative analyses of his subjects. He only tried to tie his conclusions in with psychological research on birth-order trends. The latter studies do reveal that birth order affects personality development in pertinent ways. Even better, if we examine famous people more closely, we can find data supporting the notion that ordinal position may influence the style of achievement for people working in the same field. For example, birth order predicts the personality traits of contemporary world leaders: Last-borns score extremely high on "nationalism, need for power, need for affiliation, distrust of others, and affectual orientation." The personality traits of American presidents also vary according to ordinal position: The later-borns have been more charismatic, for example. Birth order even affects the orientation of chief justices of the U.S. Supreme Court: First-borns have generally been the activists, middle-borns the consolidators.

Frank Sulloway has conducted the most material research in this vein. He focused on why some scientists accept novel theories while others, equally notable, reject any innovations. His subjects were nearly 3,000 participants in more than two dozen controversies that deeply divided the scientific community. Among the divisive issues were the Copernican system, preformation theory, spontaneous generation, circulation of the blood, the Newtonian revolution, mesmerism, uniformitarianism, phrenology, glaciation theory, germ theory, antisepsis, psychoanalysis, relativity theory, quantum hypothesis, continental drift, and acausality in physics. Sulloway then determined whether a scientist's birth order predicted the stand taken in a debate. In general, later-born scientists were much more quick to join the scientific avant-garde. First-borns, in contrast, tended to fight rear-guard actions against the encroachment of new ideas. These birth-order results were found even after such contaminants as a scientist's age, nationality, socioeconomic class, and political or religious beliefs were considered.

Sulloway's final model successfully predicts the position taken by 79% of the scientists studied. For instance, according to his prediction equation, Louis Agassiz only had about a 2% chance of supporting Darwin's theory of evolution by natural selection. Indeed, Agassiz was a fierce opponent of evolutionary theory. By comparison, Thomas Henry Huxley had a 98% chance of endorsing Darwin's ideas. When Huxley first read *The Origin of Species*, he remarked, "How extremely stupid not to have thought of that." Soon afterward Huxley became "Darwin's bulldog," effectively defending evolutionary theory against conservative attacks led by Sir Richard Owen and Bishop Wilberforce. If we look at the broad statistics, 83% of the proponents of the new theory were later-borns and only 17% were first-borns. Charles Darwin and Alfred Russell Wallace, the two founders of the theory, were both later-borns. Sulloway's equation actually predicts that Darwin enjoyed a 95% chance of accepting evolutionary theory, had Wallace beat him to the punch!

A crucial property of Sulloway's model is its explicit allowance for other influential factors. For example, one such factor concerns the social implications of the theory: Is it pro- or antiestablishment? Later-borns favor those ideas with liberal, reformist, or radical repercussions. Darwin's theory was of this nature. By flatly contradicting any literal interpretation of the Genesis story of creation, it threatened the powers that be. In contrast, when a new scientific concept leans toward more conservative or traditional views in politics or religion, the first-borns become its champions. The quinarian system of classification illustrates one such innovation in the history of science. This taxonomic scheme assigned all species to a hierarchical arrangement of circles within circles. The system was highly idealistic in a fashion compatible with the Biblical notion of an all-wise Creator. It was also static in its suggestion that species were unchanging. To a later-born naturalist, it probably sounded like yet another first-born plot to fortify the status quo.

This introduction of additional factors is critical. It is unlikely that birth order affects personality development without regard to other developmental variables. Investigators have found examples in domains besides science—such as the American presidency. Some chief executives have been closely affiliated with their predecessors in the Oval Office. Affiliation occurs when both the president and his predecessor belong to the same party. Such presidents are more likely to have been first-born sons who were paternal namesakes. As children, these future presidents may be more likely to identify with authority figures than later-born sons given different names from their fathers may be. As mature politicians, they will cozy up to their predecessors. Often this subservience adopts the guise of accepting an invitation to fill the vice-presidency. This was the case for John Adams, Calvin Coolidge, and Gerald Ford.

Building Character: Early Adversity

Beethoven's Fifth Symphony offers a metaphor for life. Composed in the ominous key of C minor, the work begins at once with the expression of conflict and struggle with the Fates. Despite changes of mood in succeeding movements, the Fate motive, "di-di-di-dah," always lurks in the background. Then, suddenly, the finale is announced with a triumphant fanfare in C major. Seemingly on the verge of defeat, Beethoven whips out the overwhelming sensation of victory. This symphony may serve as a metaphor for the emergence of genius as well. To attain success of the highest order, a person may have to suffer first. Samuel Butler sketched the developmental process in his novel *The Way of All Flesh*:

> In quiet, uneventful lives the changes internal and external are so small that there is little or no strain in the process of fusion and accommodation; in other lives there is great strain, but there is also great fusing and accommodating power; in others great strain with little accommodating power. A life will be successful or not according as the power of accommodation is equal to or unequal to the strain of the fusing and adjusting internal and external changes.

Retrospective studies of the biographies of historic figures often reveal frequent hardships in childhood and adolescence. Among these upsetting circumstances is parental loss. Examples can be seen in Table 6.2.

The most impressive proof of this developmental event is an ambitious study of 699 eminent figures of world history: 61% lost a parent before age 31, 52% before age 26, and 45% before age 21. Other studies, though less ambitious, have obtained similar results. One study scrutinized the creators and leaders who qualified for Cox's 1926 study, and found that orphanhood (the loss of one or both parents) plagued over one-fifth of these celebrities. Another investigation, also based on famous persons from all areas of accomplishment, discovered that nearly one-third lost their fathers early on. The orphanhood effect has been documented in more narrowly defined samples, too. Thus, studies of large samples of scientists suggest that the incidence of orphanhood is indeed high. In Roe's collection of great scientists, 15% had lost a parent before age 10. Among mathematicians, the percentages may be higher still: One-

TABLE 6.2. Instances of Parental Loss in the Lives of Historic Figures

Lost one or both parents in first decade:

Scientists: I. Barrow, Berzelius, Boyle, W. Bragg, Buffon, G. W. Carver, Cavendish, Copernicus, C.Darwin, d'Alembert, Eddington, Flamsteed, A. Fleming, Fourier, Fulton, Haller, Helmont, Humboldt, J. Hutton, Huygens, Jenner, Lord Kelvin, Kolmogorov, Laënnec, Lavoisier, Lobachevski, Maxwell, Newton, Paracelsus, Pascal, Priestley, Quetelet, J. Rennie, Count Rumford, Steinmetz, Steno, Telford, Volta, C. T. R. Wilson.

Thinkers: W. Blackstone, Confucius, Descartes, Hobbes, Hume, Leibniz, G.Marcel, Mencius, Montesquieu, Nietzsche, Rousseau, B. Russell, Śaṅkara, Sartre, Shinran, Spinoza, Swedenborg, Voltaire.

Writers: Baudelaire, Brontë sisters, Byron, Camus, Coleridge, Conrad, W. Cowper, Dante, Donne, Dumas *père*, Emerson, E. M. Forster, Gibbon, M. Gorky, Brothers Grimm, Hawthorne, Hölderlin, Hu Shih, Ben Jonson, Keats, Lermontov, Mallarmé, Maugham, G. Meredith, Molière, Montaigne, Neruda, Poe, Propertius, Racine, Solzhenitsyn, Steele, Stendhal, Sterne, Swift, Thackeray, Tolstoy, Wordsworth, Zola.

Artists: Canova, Delacroix, Diaghilev, D. W. Griffith, Fra Lippi, Masaccio, Michelangelo, Munch, Murillo, Raphael, Rubens.

Composers: J. S. Bach, Corelli, Puccini, Scriabin, Sibelius, Wagner.

Performers: C. Arrau, A. Blakey, Chaplin, B. Diddley, C. Eschenbach, C. Gayle, H. Irving, E. Kean, Paderewski, Pavlova.

Leaders: Alcibiades, St. Ambrose, Asquith, Atatürk, Baden-Powell, Bolívar, Catherine de Médicis, Danton, De Valera, Elizabeth I, Froebel, Genghis Khan, H. Hoover, Ivan the Terrible, A. Jackson, Juárez, Julian the Apostate, Kaunda, Kenyatta, R. E. Lee, Lincoln, Lloyd George, Louis XIV, Mary Queen of Scots, Muḥammad, Nelson, Nero, Pestalozzi, Peter the Great, Richelieu, Robespierre, E. Roosevelt, Shāpūr II, W. T. Sherman, Tecumseh, Victoria.

Lost one or both parents in second decade:

Scientists: Ampère, J. Bruner, M. Curie, H. Davy, Durkheim, Galois, J. Gibbs, W. R. Hamilton, J. Henry, Hooke, Humboldt, Joule, A. Keith, Lamarck, Leeuwenhoek, Malinowski, Mendeléev, Newcomb, J. J. Thomson, Tsiolkovsky, An Wang, J. Watt, Weierstrass, E. Whitney, W. Wundt.

Thinkers: St. Thomas Aquinas, Aristotle, St. Augustine, F. Bacon, Comenius, Erasmus, Frege, Hegel, Ibn Khaldūn, Kant, Melanchthon, R. Niebuhr, Santayana, Schopenhauer, Zhu Xi.

Writers: H. C. Andersen, Ariosto, Bellow, Bunyan, Calderón, Chateaubriand, J. F. Cooper, Dostoevsky, Dreiser, G. Eliot, H. Fielding, Frost, Gide, Goldsmith, Hugo, Jalāl ad-Dīn ar-Rūmī, Malamud, Mann, Melville, Petrarch, Plutarch, D. Richardson, R. Sheridan, T. Tasso, Turgenev, Mark Twain, H. Walpole.

Artists: Caravaggio, Claude Lorraine, J. L. David, Degas, Hiroshige, Magritte, Whistler.

Composers, Beethoven, Bruckner, F. Couperin, Handel, Liszt, Mussorgsky, Schoenberg, Schubert, Schumann, Tchaikovsky, von Weber.

Performers: P. T. Barnum, E. T. Booth, Duse, Garrick.

(continued)

TABLE 6.2. (*Continued*)

Leaders: Akbar the Great, Alexander the Great, St. Bernard, Julius Caesar, J. C. Calhoun, Charles XII, Chulalongkorn, Cleopatra, C. Coolidge, O. Cromwell, Eleanor of Aquitaine, Gustavus II Adolphus, A. Hamilton, Hannibal, Henry VIII, Hitler, Emperor Hong-wu, Sam Houston, Jefferson, Khrushchev, Lenin, Leo X, Emperor Leopold I, Lorenzo the Magnificent, St. Louis IX, Madame de Maintenon, Menelik II, Mohammed II the Conqueror, Monroe, Napoleon, Olivares, C. S. Parnell, Peel, Pericles, Philip II Augustus, W. Pitt the Elder and Younger, Pompey the Great, San Martin, Ranjit Singh, F. D. Roosevelt, T. Roosevelt, L. Sforza, Shi Huang-di, Wallenstein, Washington, Wellington, Zapata.

---

quarter lost a parent before age 10 and nearly one-third before age 14. The results for creative writers are even more dramatic: An inspection of the lives of such notables as Keats, Swift, Gibbon, and Thackeray showed that 55% lost a parent before age 15. In fact, another study found that the incidence of orphanhood for recipients of the Nobel Prize for literature was over eight times higher than that for winners of the Nobel Prize for physics. Orphanhood, especially the tragic early loss of the mother, is conducive to the development of reformers, philosophers, and religious figures in modern times.

Before we can say anything about these statistics, we first must know whether these rates exceed expectation. Despite some debate on this point, most comparisons indicate that the answer is yes. For instance, only about 6% of college students lost a parent by age 10—less than half the rate seen among Roe's famous scientists. Similarly, the incidence of early parental loss among British prime ministers up to 1940 was over twice as high as that for Peers living at the same time. Among those losing a parent before age 10 were Asquith, Balfour, Canning, Lloyd George, Perceval, Russell, the Duke of Wellington, and the Earls of Aberdeen, Liverpool, and Rosebery. All told, nearly 63% of those holding this highest office between Wellington and Chamberlain were orphans.

When we examine the general population, just two groups show orphanhood rates similar to those of the eminent—namely, juvenile delinquents, and depressive or suicidal psychiatric patients. These two exceptions suggest that Samuel Butler might have captured a profound truth. Some souls manage to accommodate the traumatic experiences of youth, while others lack the ego strength necessary to cope with the onslaught of personal events.

> The bereavement reaction can be an impetus for creative effort, a force for good, or it can have the effect of stunting personality growth and producing the concomitant antisocial acts, destruction of social relationships, and even the taking of one's own life.

One nice feature of this interpretation is that it explains why orphanhood is not a prerequisite for achieving greatness. Other traumatic events can provide alternative ways of producing the robust personality. Maybe a parent was alcoholic, or a favorite sibling was killed, or the household suffered many economic ups and downs. For instance, among those honored with the Nobel Prize for literature, over 30% "either lost at least one parent through death or desertion or experienced the father's bankruptcy or impoverishment." Illegitimacy may also be a factor. Famous "natural" children include Leon Battista Alberti, Frederick Douglass, Desiderius Erasmus, Jean Genet, Alexander Hamilton, James Kádár, T. E. Lawrence (Lawrence of Arabia), James MacDonald, Barnardo O'Higgins, Eva Perón, Shaka, Maurice Utrillo, Booker T. Washington, and William the Conqueror.

Trials and tribulations may also be of a more direct variety. Eminent people often must survive a physical or mental handicap. Eye disorders affected Aldous Huxley, Rudyard Kipling, Sean O'Casey, and Sygman Rhee. Blindness afflicted Homer, Helen Keller, Ved Mehta, Joaquin Rodrigo, Art Tatum, Ray Charles, and Stevie Wonder. Partial or total deafness struck early Thomas Edison and Konstantin Tsiolkovsky. Physical disabilities burdened Jane Addams, James DePreist, Joseph Goebbels, Karl Jaspers, Frida Kahlo, Itzhak Perlman, Joseph Stalin, Charles Proteus Steinmetz, Prince Talleyrand, Henri Toulouse-Lautrec, Carl Maria von Weber, and Kaiser Wilhelm II. Although Franklin D. Roosevelt was not crippled by polio until he was 39 years of age, his battle with the disease speaks for the personal strength that one gains upon victory. When asked whether he ever worried about things, he would sometimes say, "If you had spent two years in bed trying to wiggle your big toe, after that anything else would seem easy!"

Indeed, individuals can do more than merely adjust to severe handicaps. Some convert disabilities into unsurpassed skills. Adler spoke of "organ inferiority" driving persons to overcompensate. Wilma Rudolph, a victim of childhood polio, overcame her frailties to become the top female sprinter in the world. She earned her first Olympic medal at age 16, and four years later won three gold medals in the 1960 Olympics. Walt Davis, at eight years of age, suffered a case of infantile paralysis so severe that both legs and one arm were rendered immobile. Yet he became a world-class high jumper, setting five world records, and winning a gold medal at the 1952 Olympics. Finally, we have the example of Johnny Weissmuller. Although he was extremely sickly and frail as a youth, he struggled to become a world-class swimmer. Undefeated in competition from 1921 to 1928, he led the U.S. Olympic team in 1924 and 1928; during his career, he established 67 records. Then, after retiring from sports, he became the first actor to play Tarzan, starring in 19 films from 1932 to 1948. The famous yodeling yell echoing through the jungle announced to all in the theater audience that Weissmuller was no longer a wimp.

The before-and-after shot of the 90-pound weakling who becomes Charles Atlas is proverbial. It is the rags-to-riches legend of Horatio Alger clothed in athletic uniform. Similar stories are told of individuals in more intellectual realms of success. Demosthenes and Cicero both became the best orators of their day after overcoming speech impediments. Thomas Edison was thought to have a learning disability. Einstein was slow to speak, retarded in his comprehension of his world. Instances such as these remind us of Ralph Waldo Emerson's 1841 essay on "Compensation," in which adversity always has its eventual dividends: "Our strength grows out of our weakness." The inferiority complex becomes the impetus behind superior accomplishment.

There is a certain cosmic beauty in these ideas. Such notions sustain our confidence that we live in a just world. As in Beethoven's Fifth Symphony, tragedies in C minor set the stage for life's triumphant finale.

Booster Shots: Early Stimulation

Anne Roe's eminent scientists were very unlikely to originate in the lower strata of America's socioeconomic hierarchy. Not one came from a family where the chief breadwinner was an unskilled laborer, and only 3% had fathers who were skilled workers. In contrast, 53% were the sons of professional men. This incidence was 18 times greater than the proportion of professional parents in the general population. Even when we confine our attention to just science doctorates, those who have managed to become Nobel laureates are nearly twice as likely to have fathers who were professionals, managers, or proprietors. On the leadership side, a similar pattern holds. In the United States, for example, the log cabin myth is just that—pure myth. Between 1789 and 1934, 58% of the presidents, vice-presidents, and cabinet secretaries had fathers who were professionals, officials, or proprietors; only 4% of the fathers were wage earners, and 38% were farmers. In fact, for both U.S. presidents and justices of the U.S. Supreme Court, posthumous reputation is greatest for those who grew up in the upper echelons of American society. And the chief justice of the nation's highest court is especially likely to be an American blueblood. Finally, the same socioeconomic edge may be witnessed in endeavors beyond creativity or leadership. For instance, the top chess players of the world are most likely to emerge from homes where one or both parents enjoyed a university education.

Those studies that have examined a fuller range of achievement endeavors have found similar disparities. Of more than 300 contemporary creators, leaders, and celebrities, 80% emanated from business or professional homes, while only 6% ascended from dire poverty. And, as we saw earlier in regard to first-borns, we find a comparable bias in gifted children and child prodigies.

Why this preponderance? Roe and others have attributed this phenomenon to the "love of learning" that tends to pervade such homes. Parents in the professions know at first hand the value of an education. Accordingly, they cram the household of their geniuses-to-be with materials that stimulate them intellectually, aesthetically, and culturally. The parents themselves are more likely to have cultural and intellectual interests. This inspires them to maintain sizable home libraries, ample subscriptions to highbrow magazines, and mechanical or aesthetic hobbies guaranteed to attract the curiosity of a bright child.

In line with these provisions, parents of future achievers are more prone to encourage their children to explore the enriched environment. Indeed, parents frequently adopt a rather active role in propelling their offspring to precocious accomplishments. The fathers of Wolfgang Amadeus Mozart and John Stuart Mill did not sit idly by, waiting patiently for their sons to catch on. Rather, both pushed their chosen successors hard toward an early and prodigal mastery. Hence, at about six years of age the tiny Mozart was composing keyboard pieces, and the little Mill was writing a history of Rome.

In short, a stimulating home environment probably gives the child an early start on the expertise acquisition so essential to later success (see Chapter 3). Unhappily, as is the case for birth order and childhood trauma, plausible interpretations of these effects are multiple. One problem is obvious: The offspring of the higher castes are more likely to do well in school and to attain higher levels of formal training. Thus, one very real possibility is that education, and not social or economic rank by itself, bestows promise on a child. Consequently, our survey of developmental antecedents of greatness must leave the home for the schoolroom.

Students and Schools: The Impact of Education

For mediocre students past and present, Albert Einstein can serve as a patron saint. Like many disgruntled pupils throughout the history of education, Einstein was not particularly fond of the instructional methods that were current when he had to run the gauntlet. He once claimed that

> it is, in fact, nothing short of a miracle that the modern methods of instruction have not yet entirely strangled the holy curiosity of inquiry; for this delicate little plant, aside from stimulation, stands mostly in the need of freedom; without this it goes to wreck and ruin without fail. It is a very grave mistake to think that the enjoyment of seeing and searching can be promoted by means of coercion and a sense of duty.

Einstein found test time especially obnoxious:

> One had to cram all this stuff into one's mind for the examinations, whether one liked it or not. This coercion had such a deterring effect on me that, after I passed the final examination, I found the consideration of any scientific problems distasteful to me for an entire year.

Yet we should not be too quick to condemn the educational system that elicited Einstein's complaints. It may be specifically unwise for a student to quote Einstein as justification for failing grades in formal course work. Before we pass judgment on education, we first must examine the empirical research. Here we have three issues to address: (1) the quality of scholastic performance, (2) the quantity of formal education attained, and (3) the impact of self-education and extracurricular experiences.

Quality of Scholastic Performance

After someone attains world renown, a former teacher will sometimes express amazement. How could a pupil who held so little promise turn out to be so exceedingly successful years later? The mathematician Hermann Minkowski had this experience upon learning of Einstein's epochal achievements in theoretical physics: "For me it came as a tremendous surprise . . . for in his student days Einstein had been a lazy dog. He never bothered about mathematics at all." Are major innovators usually "lazy dogs" in school?

Empirical inquiries suggest a complex answer. On the one hand, research reveals that outstanding figures need not be the stellar pupils on which so many teachers stake their own immortality. In the first place, several studies have shown that a large proportion of famous people absolutely despised their educational experiences. In one group of 20th-century celebrities, about 60% hated school, making Einstein's opinion the majority viewpoint. Such dislike was especially rampant among mystics and psychics. Of those who found school a positive experience, most later attained fame in either science or politics. This discontent contrasts markedly with the positive feelings exhibited by many intellectually gifted children, like the ones Terman studied.

Besides the dissatisfaction, several researchers have found that scholastic attainments may not correspond to career accomplishments. Scientific achievement provides a good test case, because formal training is probably more essential to scientific creativity than to most other domains. Yet high grades in high school and college by no means guarantee success as a mature scientist. For example, one investigator scrutinized the undergraduate records of those elected as Fellows of the Royal Society. Their academic performance was usually poor, and decidedly no better than that of a comparison group of scientists who could not put F.R.S. after their surnames. Inquiries that examine a broader range of achievement domains allow us to generalize this conclusion. Singular creativity may not correspond to earning high marks in school and college. A high grade point average (GPA) is not a guarantee of sociocultural sainthood.

On the other hand, we cannot condemn scholars to oblivion simply because they boast straight-A averages. Among esteemed creators, leaders, and celebrities of modern times, fully one-fifth were honor students—over twice the proportion of such figures who repeatedly failed classes. Diverse problems also plague the researcher who tries to discern the linkage between school grades and adult success. For instance, some students may procure a stratospheric GPA by taking easy courses, while others sacrifice their class ranking by enrolling in really challenging classes. In addition, the most brilliant students may attend the most demanding universities, while their less capable high school classmates go to local community colleges. After all, the average IQs of undergraduates range from 108 in the least selective colleges to 132 in the elite institutions of higher education. That matches the gap between the intellect of the typical high school graduate and a person bright enough to join Mensa, a society of self-proclaimed "geniuses."

When investigators adjust for these and other contaminating factors, scholastic competence can sometimes predict adulthood success. College grades and honors can even predict professional eminence, including earning entries in *Who's Who*. The compatibility of studiousness and success is dramatically illustrated in a study of students who graduated from Wesleyan College between 1831 and 1899. Of those who qualified for Phi Beta Kappa, nearly one-third went on to achieve distinction. And nearly half of the class valedictorians or salutatorians attained success later in life. In contrast, of those who could claim no scholarly distinction whatsoever, fewer than 1 in 10 made it big in their careers. Of course, the association is seldom this strong. Yet seldom is the relationship negative, and whenever a negative association is found it is invariably weak.

In science, for example, each creator with an academic track record far below par is nullified by an equally accomplished scientist with intimidating scholastic achievements. Hence, there is nothing paradoxical about some notables' doing quite well as students. Marie Sklodowska, later Marie Curie, was two years ahead of her elementary school classmates in all subjects. She received a special gold medal when she graduated from the Russian *lycée* in Warsaw at age 16. Sigmund Freud was likewise at the head of his secondary school class, and graduated *summa cum laude*. J. Robert Oppenheimer graduated *summa cum laude* from Harvard with the highest honors ever awarded. Hence, all three exhibited scholastic fireworks without apparently compromising their later acclaim. These instances counterbalance the cases of Charles Darwin and Albert Einstein, whose academic attainments were much less noteworthy.

The same seesaw of example and counterexample is evident among historic leaders. To simplify the comparisons, let us look at the American presidents who graduated from Harvard. John Quincy Adams earned Phi Beta Kappa honors, but performed so poorly in the White House that he was defeated for re-election. He was the first president to suffer such defeat since his father John Adams had been similarly humbled 28 years earlier; John Adams had also been one of the better students in his Harvard Class. In contrast, Theodore Roosevelt, a Phi Beta Kappa like John Quincy, went down in the annals as one of the greatest presidents in U.S. history. Even so, Franklin D. Roosevelt, Teddy's distant cousin, was a mediocre Harvard student who still did excellently in the Oval Office. And finally we have the case of John F. Kennedy, who graduated with honors but was not a Phi Beta Kappa. His presidential accomplishments fall somewhere between those of the first two Harvard graduates. There doesn't seem to be any regularity here.

So what are we to make of this contradictory information? I think that we cannot make heads or tails of the data without weighing three factors:

1. Whether or not a future genius does well in formal school work depends very much on the atmosphere of the instructional system. For instance, according to those scientists Roe interviewed,

> Much of our educational system seems designed to discourage any attempt at finding things out for oneself, but makes learning things others have found out, or think they have, the major goal. . . . Once a student has learned that he can find things out for himself, though, bad pedagogy is probably only an irritant.

Hence, colleges that stress conformity to specified norms and dogmas, as some sectarian schools do, produce fewer of tomorrow's innovators.

2. Even within the same institution, teachers vary considerably in style and technique. In Roe's interview data, the favorite teachers were those who allowed students to cultivate their personal enthusiasms. Highly directive, authoritarian teaching methods only stifle what Einstein earlier called the "holy curiosity of inquiry." Donald MacKinnon noted that the esteemed architects that he interviewed

> were unwilling to accept anything on the mere say-so of their instructors. Nothing was to be accepted on faith or because it had behind it the voice of authority. Such matters might be accepted, but only after the student on his own had demonstrated their validity to himself.

As a result, their scholastic performance was uneven. They would often do poorly in classes where their instructors adopted an authoritarian style.

3. Grades are not the only means by which we can judge scholastic attainments. Other criteria are of equal if not superior utility in this regard. For instance, successful personalities often completed their higher education at some of the most prestigious institutions in the world. Attendance at elite colleges and universities is especially noticeable among eminent scientists. Undoubtedly, one cannot earn admission to such select institutions without showing uncommon scholastic aptitude early on. More important, perhaps, is the speed with which future notables pass through the system. In the sciences, for example, those with the most impressive odds of success are those who won their doctorates at an unusually early age. Thus, Max Planck received his doctorate, *summa cum laude*, at age 21. In fact, precocious receipt of a Ph.D. is among the best predictors of later achievement. In psychology, for instance, eminent contributors earned their degrees when they were five years younger than the average doctorate winner in the field. Evidently, future geniuses are already focused on pursuing their unique vision. They thus spend little time trying to win the respect of their teachers by earning top grades in courses that they deem irrelevant. Benjamin Bloom examined the differential patterns of success of those who had received their doctorates at the University of Chicago. He concluded that

> an individual who comes to a university with problems that he is really interested in, with some notion of himself as a research worker or scholar, and who is able to resist the student role of doing things because they are required or because he is told to do them is likely to be a most productive individual in his postgraduate career.

Naturally, early acquisition of a Ph.D. cannot provide a universally applicable predictor of acclaim. Many luminaries get by without a single set of initials behind their surnames. This raises the next issue.

Quantity of Formal Education

After Einstein completed his undergraduate education, he had no other choice but to accept a job with the Swiss Patent Office. Tucked away in one of the desk drawers at his office were several papers he would work on when his supervisor wasn't watching. Meanwhile, he hoped to improve his position by convincing the University of Zurich to award him a doctorate for one of his research contributions. The first thesis he offered was turned down; supposedly it was too short to qualify for a dissertation. Einstein's failure caused him to write to a friend, "I shall not become a Ph.D. . . . The whole comedy has become a bore to me." Nevertheless, the rejection did not discourage him from pursuing his independent path. By 1905, he had in hand four papers that were going to alter his career radically. Two were on more or less established topics—Brownian motion and the photoelectric effect. In the second of these, Einstein applied Planck's new quantum theory in a revolutionary way; it was this paper that the Nobel Prize committee cited when he received that honor 16 years later. A third paper was on a subject with which Einstein's fame is most intimately associated, the special theory of relativity. And the fourth paper was the least important, except for one curiosity: It was the same paper rejected earlier by the University of Zurich, with a single sentence appended. That addition was enough to earn him a Ph.D. The other three papers were adequate to assure him immortality. Obviously, picking up his doctorate was only a tangential enterprise in Einstein's quest for greatness.

The comments of other notables suggest that Einstein's experience may not be atypical. In the domain of creative writing, Vera Brittain advised: "The idea that it is necessary to go to a university in order to become a successful writer, or even a man or woman of letters (which is by no means the same thing), is one of those phantasies that surround authorship." Once a student has mastered the basics, additional education may be superfluous, if not downright hazardous. The danger arises because professors may not know what they are talking about. George Bernard Shaw warned, "He who can, does. He who cannot, teaches." And Henry David Thoreau cautioned, "There are nowadays professors of philosophy, but not philosophers."

There is plenty of anecdotal evidence for these accusations. Neither George Washington nor Abraham Lincoln had much formal education. Michael Faraday had to leave school when he was 14 years old, and even Isaac Newton never advanced beyond the bachelor's degree. In the 20th century, Harvard saw three of its students leave its hallowed halls to triumph without a diploma. Edwin Land dropped out, and proceeded to invent Polaroid lenses and the Polaroid Land Camera. Buckminster Fuller left under less pleasant circumstances, but still managed to devise the geodesic dome and a host of other inventions. Bill Gates, the third and most recent Harvard dropout, founded Microsoft Corporation, the goliath among computer software companies.

To advance beyond mere storytelling, we can cite the educational statistics gathered on more than 300 distinguished creators, leaders, and celebrities born between 1841 and 1948: 15% had an eighth-grade education or less, 11% had some high school, 19% completed high school, 9% endured some college, 19% actually earned an undergraduate degree, 4% acquired some knowledge in graduate school, and only 19% earned graduate degrees. In brief, the Ph.D.'s were well outnumbered by those who never walked across the stage at a high school commencement ceremony! From these data alone, it is plain that higher education is not a *sine qua non* for success.

We can add a further refinement to our discussion. The problem with citing mere percentages is that they tell us nothing about the relative success of those who have made it big. Not every famous scientist is grand enough to earn a Nobel Prize; not every American president goes down in the annals as a praiseworthy leader. Hence, we must study how acclaim in a field varies according to level of formal education. The first inquiry to gauge this relationship looked at the 301 creators and leaders who made up the Cox sample. These historical figures had already been ranked in achieved eminence by James McKeen Cattell back in 1903. Cox's published data, moreover, made it a simple matter to register how much formal training each received. Eminence was then plotted versus education, and a curve was fitted. Because creativity and leadership may require distinct amounts of education, the two domains were treated separately. Figure 6.1 shows the outcome.

For this group, renown as a leader was a negative function of formal education. Few of the greatest leaders of the sample—such as Napoleon or Lincoln—had ascended very high on the instructional ladder. The situation of creators was more ambiguous. At the beginning, formal education enhanced a leader's prospects. Yet the increments decreased until an optimal level was reached. Thereafter, further training brought about decrements in posthumous praise. Indeed, the lowest point on the curve was reserved for those assiduous souls who got their doctoral theses completed and approved!

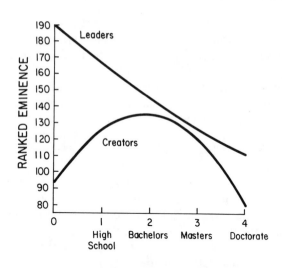

FORMAL EDUCATION

FIGURE 6.1. Ranked eminence versus formal education for 301 historic geniuses.

We can easily raise objections, however. Cox's sample comprised a rather motley collection of personalities spread over several nations and hundreds of years. Furthermore, all made their marks prior to the 20th century. Perhaps the complexities of modern life render higher education more pertinent to success. In addition, the breakdown into just two groups, creators and leaders, may have been excessively inclusive. For example, scientific and artistic creativity might visibly differ on the optimal level of training.

All these complaints are justified. Yet later investigations have made various adjustments without seriously qualifying the conclusions. Thus, 314 creators, leaders, and miscellaneous celebrities were scrutinized, most of whom won distinction in the latter half of the 20th century. For those who attained eminence in the arts and humanities, exactly the same curve emerged as seen for the creators in Figure 6.1. The peak was even at the same location. However, eminence in scientific occupations apparently required a bit more formal training before the optimum arrived; the maximum occurred about four years later, in fact. Finally, for modern leaders, it indeed appears true that higher education has more positive consequences for career development. Nowadays, the world is too complex to leave ignoramuses at the controls.

In Chapter 13 we shall inspect yet another study that endorses the inverted-U curves of the preceding two inquiries. So what does the turnaround signify? If you inspect Figure 6.1 closely, you will see that the optimum happens sometime between the junior and senior year of undergraduate education. In many university systems, the course work from the freshman to the senior year progresses from the broad and various to the specific and homogeneous. Getting the breadth is probably conducive to achievement, whereas the increased specialization may impair the creative mind. Later we can develop this interpretation further. For the moment, let us turn to the last issue.

Self-Education and Extracurricular Activities

Those who aspire toward greatness cannot ignore the need to procure expertise. When Einstein complained about oppressive school requirements, it was not because he wished to play his violin more often. Rather, ever since his earliest youth, Einstein was deeply engaged in his own self-education. By his 11th year, he was already perusing science, mathematics, and philosophy. Always fascinated with physics, he was incessantly pondering and absorbing. School too often deflected him from the dictates of his curiosity. So Einstein would often let his grades slide, in order to fulfill the more critical but informal obligations of his genius.

For achievers in general, self-education often assumes the form of omnivorous reading. In Terman's study, gifted children read much, read widely, and read hard. By elementary school, they would read a half dozen books per month. The volumes would span challenging topics, such as science, history, biography, poetry, drama, and travel. One study of contemporary luminaries found that at least half were voracious readers from childhood. In fact, early omnivorous reading is associated positively with later eminence. To have read widely is a hallmark of those who become widely read about.

To be sure, ample reading will not aid achievement in all domains. This is apparently true for the military, business, athletics, mysticism, and the arts. For these endeavors, the expertise integral to success cannot be obtained easily from books, but rather must be gotten from real-world sources. Future politicians, for example, will often indulge in such extracurricular activities as debating or editing the school paper. The school days of Lyndon Johnson and Richard Nixon exemplify this mode of extracurricular education.

Whatever the particular guise of an individual's self-education, the implication is clear: The aspiring person often must sacrifice formal course work whenever it interferes with this cardinal need. "I have never let my schooling interfere with my education," said Mark Twain. As a result, course grades will vary according to how well the assigned material fits the goals of self-instruction. In some domains, fortunately, special schooling is possible, so self-education can blend easily with institutional demands. There are schools of art and conservatories of music for the exceptionally talented. Accordingly, among famed creators, visual artists and composers are those most likely to have had special schooling. Picasso attended art academies at Barcelona and Madrid before launching his stellar career.

Poets and other literary creators, in comparison, are let loose on their own recognizance. They may attend writers' workshops from time to time, but otherwise they cannot cultivate their literary sensitivities in a suitable school or conservatory. Hence, poetry and fiction authors are especially likely to be prodigious consumers of the written word. They correspondingly tend to detest school, and to do poorly in it besides. Among American authors, Stephen Crane, Eugene O'Neill, William Faulkner, and F. Scott Fitzgerald all endured scholastic disasters in college. The negative attitude can be so potent that it is difficult to overcome even under the most auspicious circumstances. One might think that D. H. Lawrence would do well in a high school composition class. But no: He ranked 13th out of the 21 who took the course.

Given these facts, we should not expect greatness from the uneducated. The education will be there, but it will have been largely self-directed; it will have been specifically tailored for each aspirant's unique career path.

Outsiders: The Impact of Marginality

Like the Biblical voice crying out in the wilderness, major innovators often hail from the periphery of a discipline, culture, society, or political system. However, we cannot comprehend the impact of marginality without first recognizing that there is more than one way to be marginal. Marginality can be ethnic, sexual, geographic, and professional.

Minorities and Immigrants

Robert Park, a sociologist, pointed to the importance of population shifts in the making of history: "Every advance in culture, it has been said, commences with a new period of migration and movement of populations." An alternative to migration from outside is population mobility within, for

> the consequences . . . of migration and mobility seem, on the whole, the same. In both cases the 'cake of custom' is broken and the individual is freed for new enterprises and new associations. One of the consequences of migration is to create a situation in which the same individual . . . finds himself striving to live in two diverse cultural groups.

Park called the individual in this ethnic limbo the "marginal man" (or woman).

In Chapter 4, I have discussed Donald Campbell's "blind variation and selective retention" theory of creativity. In documenting his theory, Campbell referred to Park's conjecture, and gave it a more psychological cast. "Persons who have been uprooted from traditional culture, or who have been thoroughly exposed to two or more cultures, seem to have an advantage in the range of hypotheses they are apt to consider, and through this means, in the frequency of creative innovation." The marginal person should display more associative richness, divergent thinking, and other cognitive processes examined earlier. In a similar vein, the historian Arnold Toynbee spoke of the members of the "creative minority" who further human progress by their "withdrawal and return" relative to the majority culture. But is ethnic marginality really conducive to achievement?

In Western civilization, the most conspicuous evidence is the history of the Jews. Jews make up only between 1% and 3% of the population of Europe and the United States. Yet their presence in the lists of the eminent exceeds statistical expectations by a factor of 10 or more. This prominence holds especially for mathematicians, physicists, chemists, biomedical researchers, economists, lawyers, violin virtuosos, chess champions, and faculty members at prestigious universities. For instance, almost one out of five Nobel Prize recipients come from Jewish backgrounds. The proportion of Jews among the world's top chess players is more impressive still: seven out of ten. The Jewish edge probably has many sources, including the superior family environment often found in Jewish homes. Nevertheless, not the least of the material factors is the marginal position of Jews in Western culture. They are a Middle Eastern people transplanted into a European culture, enabling them to bring the novel insights of the ethnic outsider.

Jews are by no means unique. In Great Britain, for example, many famous scientists and inventors did not belong to the established Church of England; rather, they subscribed to one of the dissenting faiths. Joseph Priestley was a Nonconformist minister, John Dalton a Quaker, and Michael Faraday a Sandemanian. Likewise, in one study in the United States, the per capita representation of Unitarians among notable scientists was found to be well over 100 times greater than that of Methodists, Baptists, and Roman Catholics—the churches with the biggest memberships. Furthermore, if there are no creative minorities to rise from within, they can always be imported from alien lands. For example, research has found a significant proportion of notable mathematicians in the United States to be from immigrant backgrounds. More generally, among contemporary luminaries in a diversity of fields, about 19% were either first- or second-generation immigrants. In the United States alone, newcomers accounted for 44% of the eminent Americans. Indeed, their representation was seven times higher than those Americans descended from families that had been in the United States since shortly after the Revolution if not before. Thus, we may be able to look forward to a future Golden Age of U.S. culture, ignited by the recent influx of immigrants from Latin America and the Pacific Rim.

In crediting so much to ethnic outsiders, however, we must not raise our expectations too high. Oppression of the minority by the majority can certainly undo any potential advantage of ethnic marginality. Thus, Jews can easily rise above historical obscurity only in those nations where they enjoy at least the basic freedoms. For instance, there are fewer Jews in Switzerland than in Russia; yet the former are 83 times more likely to pick up a Nobel Prize in science than are the latter, on a per capita basis. That contrast illustrates the comparative status of Jews in the two societies.

Occasionally, the only way a minority can realize its creative potential is to break the chains of the majority. Suppressed nationalities seldom make monumental contributions to human civilization. This conclusion is expressed by the "Danilevsky law": "In order for civilization of a potentially creative group to be conceived and developed, the group and its subgroups must be politically independent." Hence, many nationalities achieve a climax of their creativity shortly after their liberation from foreign rule. The Golden Age of Greece followed upon the heels of the Persian Wars. The peoples of the Netherlands did not come fully into their own until they had separated from Spain. On the other side, the expansion of empires into "universal states" often proceeds at the expense of the cultural vitality of the enslaved peoples. Imperial Russia's effort to "Russify" its subject nationalities—and the Soviet empire's revised attempts to the same end—are prototypical.

So there should appear a positive relationship between political fragmentation and cultural creativity. Those times when a civilization area is broken into many sovereign nations should be those times when diverse achievements spring forth. Empirical evidence endorses this prediction, at least under a wide range of circumstances. Political fragmentation promotes more heterogeneity than is permissible in the typical imperial state. Think about the city-states of ancient Greece, or the tiny duchies and republics of Renaissance Italy.

When we examine political violence in Chapter 11, we shall learn of other means to mix up the cultural broth. Currently, however, it is more instructive to scrutinize another form of marginality.

Adherents to Unconventional Life Styles

Each society has its notions about what is acceptable sexual behavior. One often gets the impression, from reading the biographies of the rich and famous, that conformity to puritanical mores is seldom their cup of tea. One study of 20th-century celebrities found that fully 15% embraced unconventional life styles. Table 6.3 names some big names. Still, the real issue is not whether many notables followed alternative life styles; we cannot deny that fact. Instead, we should answer two questions.

First, does the incidence of an unconventional sexual orientation among the eminent exceed the rates found among the obscure? Unfortunately, it is extremely difficult to respond accurately to this query. Until recently, the repercussions of "coming out of the closet" were devastating. Wilde was imprisoned, and his reputation and livelihood were destroyed, when his liaison was revealed in a court of law. Tchaikovsky may have committed suicide to avoid a similar scandal on the threshold of revelation. There is a theory that Leonardo da Vinci was brought before the Inquisition because of rumors about his amo-

TABLE 6.3. Some Eminent Personalities Who Engaged in Unconventional Sexual Behaviors

Gay or bisexual men: Aeschylus, Edward Albee, Horatio Alger, Hans Christian Andersen, W. H. Auden, Francis Bacon, Brendan Behan, Benjamin Britten, Sir Richard Burton, Truman Capote, Giovanni Jacopo Casanova, Montgomery Clift, Jean Cocteau, Roy Cohn, Noël Coward, Hart Crane, James Dean, Michel Foucault, E. M. Forster, Emperor Hadrian, Jean Genet, André Gide, Allen Ginsberg, Dag Hammarskjöld, Keith Haring, Hugh Hefner, Rock Hudson, William Inge, Christopher Isherwood, Phillip Johnson, John Maynard Keynes, Charles Laughton, T. E. Lawrence, Leonardo da Vinci, Liberace, King Ludwig II of Bavaria, Norman Mailer, Robert Mapplethorpe, Christopher Marlowe, W. Somerset Maugham, Michelangelo, John Milton, Mishima Yukio, Vaslav Nijinsky, Alfred Nobel, Laurence Olivier, Pier Paolo Pascolini, Peter Pears, Philippe I (Duc d'Orléans), Cole Porter, Marcel Proust, Arthur Rimbaud, Ned Rorem, Peter Shaffer, Shaka, Algernon Swinburne, Peter Tchaikovsky, Bill Tilden, Michael Tippett, Paul Verlaine, Andy Warhol, Evelyn Waugh, Walt Whitman, Oscar Wilde, Tennessee Williams, and Ludwig Wittgenstein.

Lesbian or bisexual women: Natalie Barney, Elizabeth Bishop, Willa Cather, Colette, Marlene Dietrich, Eleonora Duse, Billie Holiday, Janis Joplin, Violetta Leduc, Carson McCullers, Edna St. Vincent Millay, Kate Millett, Victoria Sackville-West, Sappho, Bessie Smith, Gertrude Stein, Dorothy Thompson, Alice B. Toklas, and Virginia Woolf.

Participants in a ménage à trois: Lou Andreas-Salomé, Simone de Beauvoir and Jean-Paul Sartre, Augustus John, Vladimir Mayakovsky, Ezra Pound, Marguerite Radclyffe Hall, Lytton Strachey, and Paul Tillich.

"Latent" homosexuals: Emily Dickinson, George Eliot (Marian Evans), T. S. Eliot, F. Scott Fitzgerald, Sigmund Freud, J. Edgar Hoover, and Isaac Newton.

Note. Those listed as gay or lesbian are reputed to have engaged in at least one sexual encounter with someone of the same gender. Most so listed are or were confirmed homosexuals—usually by their own admission, especially in autobiographies or diaries.

rous occupations. On the other hand, the sexual norms in other times and places were such that someone could be homosexual simply because bisexuality was common recreation. Thus, it is hard to know how much weight we should assign to the sexual activities of many ancient Greeks. In such circumstances, perhaps we should be looking for those among the famous who were strictly heterosexual: *They* would be the marginals!

Second, what exactly is the causal connection between achievement and sexual preference? Perhaps neither causes the other. Instead, eminence and sexual marginality may be the result of a third factor underlying both attributes: To attain the highest success, a certain amount of personal independence is essential. To conform to all the dictates of one's culture is to condemn oneself to creative mediocrity. In fact, empirical studies show that creativity is linked with autonomy, or even a radical anticonformity. This is what makes ethnic marginality such a useful developmental force. A person standing at the intersection of two separate cultures can grab more freedom from the norms of either. Orphanhood and other kinds of childhood and adolescent trauma may fulfill a similar function, by disrupting the inculcation of traditional mores. The upshot of these and functionally equivalent experiences is to generate a personality who refuses to accept received opinions. This enables the person to embark on new, even grandiose schemes of achievement. The same process also creates an individual less willing to abide by societal prescriptions about acceptable sexual activities. An alternative life style can even advertise one's autonomous genius.

The advantage of this view is that it makes sexual preference part of a larger constellation of traits characterizing genius. For instance, outstanding creators are less likely to be married. Among great philosophers, for example, Hobbes, Descartes, Pascal, Spinoza, Locke, Leibniz, Voltaire, Kant, Schopenhauer, Kierkegaard, Santayana, and Wittgenstein were all bachelors. When the eminent are married, they are often unhappily so: Bertrand Russell walked down the aisle four times! The eminent are also more inclined to be androgynous. The males entertain more feminine traits, the females more masculine attributes. Socialization into stereotyped gender roles often betrays a broader acceptance of societal customs and prejudices.

This account also explains why sexual marginality may be less common in those avenues to success where adherence to conventional norms is more often mandatory. As the names listed in Table 6.3 show, alternative life styles are especially common among artists and authors. Such nonconformity is found frequently among actors and performers as well. Our politicians are another story altogether. A nation's leaders must obey societal expectations to have any hope of rising to the top; hence, among modern notables, political figures lead the most sexually conforming lives. In contemporary America, for example, each presidential candidate must go through the ritual of parading the loyal spouse and well-groomed kids before the TV cameras. It raises eyebrows in Peoria when the voters learn that someone is a confirmed bachelor (Jerry Brown) or a philanderer (Gary Hart). It will take a lot more "consciousness raising" before a self-proclaimed gay man or lesbian can run for the nation's highest office.

Thus, sexual marginality probably neither enhances or hinders creative success. Rather, it may be a symptom of underlying experiences that accelerate the development of genius. Even so, it is possible that under certain conditions marginality might take on a more active role. One study of 20th-century personalities examined the impact of a son's exposure to a dominating, possessive, or smothering mother. The developmental experience of being a "Mama's boy" could have two divergent outcomes. On the one hand, the son could grow up to become an illustrious poet. Since male poets quite often exhibit feminine traits, some cross-sex identification could be conducive to the sensitivity needed for poetic creativity. Oscar Wilde was a classic instance; his mother even clothed him in girl's outfits.

On the other hand, boys under these same circumstances can become dictators or military heroes. These men glorify their masculinity. As noted in Chapter 2, charisma in leaders is often associated with sexual prowess and military success. Are these machismo males overcompensating for a tendency toward "sissy" behaviors and interests? If so, this might explain the motives behind such "Mama's boys" as Gabriele D'Annunzio, Antonio Salazar, Gamal Abdul Nasser, Benito Mussollini, and Adolf Hitler, as well as Alexander the Great and Napoleon. Curiously, sometimes the disposition of the sensitive poet and the iron-fisted leader merge. Mussolini loved to read chivalric and martial poetry. Hitler wrote poetry and viewed himself as an artist.

The best case may be Gabriele D'Annunzio. He began his remarkable career as a notable Italian poet, novelist, and playwright. He even wrote plays for the famed actress Eleonora Duse, with whom he had a passionate love affair. After ending the relationship, D'Annunzio published an erotic novel disclosing their sexual escapades—a scandalous kiss-and-tell. But when World War I broke out, he became a soldier, sailor, and airman. In the third capacity he performed extravagant feats of heroism: He lost an eye in air combat and conducted a daring aerial reconnaissance over enemy territory, getting as far as Vienna! Contrary to the terms of the Versailles Treaty, he seized Fiume, serving as its dictator from 1919 to 1921. He ended his career as a staunch supporter of Mussolini's Fascist party, which heaped honors upon his head. D'Annunzio certainly made it clear that he was no "sissy."

Provincials

Besides ethnic and sexual marginality, a person can have peripheral status relative to the cultural, intellectual, or aesthetic centers of the day. In short, the individual may be a provincial rather than a cosmopolitan. The stereotype is that of a country bumpkin—a boor whose clothes are out of fashion, and who entertains others with his or her naiveté rather than refined repartee. We do not expect such imports from the provinces to accomplish marvels in a world that has already passed them by.

Although psychologists have conducted too little research on this question, what little we do have suggests that *this* stereotype, at least, strays not far from the truth. In artistic fields, creators born and raised in areas remote from the creative centers of their times usually fight a losing battle for recognition. In classical music, provincial composers are not only less prolific but also create less original compositions. In science, too, major metropolitan areas give birth to a larger proportion of luminaries than do rural regions.

Hence, if persons from the provinces wish to make their marks, they must transport themselves to the cultural capitol at the earliest possible speed. Those exceptional souls who have overcome this latent handicap have done just that.

Sir Ernest Rutherford was born in New Zealand, which was then something of a backwater in world science. Happily, he showed such brilliance that by age 24 he found himself studying under Nobel laureate J. J. Thomson at Cambridge University. Moving quickly to the leading edge of nuclear physics, he joined the ranks of the Nobel recipients, and ended his days as a Cambridge professor.

In the arts, innumerable provincial talents expanded themselves into fully cosmopolitan geniuses in the vital ambience of Paris. Irishman James Joyce and American Ernest Hemingway wrote some of their best fiction there. In Paris, Sergei Diaghilev, Pablo Picasso, Igor Stravinsky, Léonide Massine, George Balanchine, and Vaslav Nijinsky all worked together to produce revolutionary ballet—helping to propel each toward fame in the process. Parisian Nadia Boulanger, teaching just outside Paris at Fontainebleau, expanded the musical horizons of many American composers: Leslie Bassett, Arthur Berger, Easley Blackwood, Marc Blitzstein, Elliott Carter, Aaron Copland, David Diamond, Roy Harris, John Lessard, Douglas Moore, Walter Piston, Roger Sessions, Elie Siegmeister, and Virgil Thomson. These prominent artists all made their pilgrimages to that Mecca of modernity, Paris.

Trespassers and Interlopers

Perhaps the most crucial type of marginality is professional. Great innovations often come from those who were self-taught or else switched fields. The asset of professional marginality seems especially conspicuous in the sciences. Arthur Koestler, the author, claimed: "All decisive advances in the history of scientific thought can be described in terms of mental cross-fertilization between different disciplines." F. C. Bartlett, the psychologist, agreed: "It has often happened that critical stages for advance are reached when what has been called one body of knowledge can be brought into close and effective relationship with what has been treated as a different, and largely or wholly independent, scientific discipline." And Thomas Kuhn, a historian of science, elaborated:

> Almost always the men who achieve these fundamental inventions of a new paradigm have been either very young or very new to the field whose paradigm they change.... [F]or obviously these are the men who, being little committed by prior practice to the traditional rules of normal science, are particularly likely to see that these rules no longer define a playable game and to conceive another set that can replace them.

Corroborating these assertions are many telling anecdotes.

First, and as Bartlett suggested, scientists will often attain unexpected success because they introduce concepts, techniques, or thinking habits already assembled in another discipline. Helmholtz had to pursue a medical career even though his first love was physics, especially optics. Later he merged vocation and avocation when he invented the ophthalmoscope. Likewise, Landsteiner's prior experience in chemistry no doubt provided the base for his later isolation of blood groups. At times, the infusion of extradisciplinary ideas may reach outside the domain of science. Kekulé's original ambition was to become an architect. Although his career plans changed, his vivid visual imagery was probably a catalyst to his conceiving a structural basis for organic chemistry.

Second, and fitting Kuhn's statement, the key resource of marginality is often an ignorance that permits a fresh attack on a resistant problem. For example, in explaining his invention of a commercially successful process for steel production, Bessemer said this: "I had an immense advantage over many others dealing with the problem inasmuch as I had no fixed ideas derived from long established practice to control and bias my mind, and did not suffer from the general belief that whatever is, is right." The chance of this happening can be converted to a mode of argument. Once the French chemist Dumas urged his former pupil Pasteur to take on the problem of a disease that was decimating the French silk industry. Pasteur protested: "But I never worked with silkworms." Dumas reassured him: "So much the better." That marked the onset of Pasteur's exceptional odyssey from one domain of ignorance to another.

The abundance of quotes and anecdotes notwithstanding, empirical data are in short supply. However, two inquiries do suggest that professional marginality plays a role in scientific discovery that compares with ethnic marginality's place in general cultural creativity. One study showed that the innovators in X-ray astronomy were likely to have been marginal to the astronomical profession. The second study found a similar marginality effect concerning Alfred Wegener's theory of continental drift. In particular, the theory's opponents usually had many publications in mainstream geology, whereas the proponents often hailed from scientific disciplines outside the geosciences. A similar disparity concerns a daring hypothesis put forward in 1980: The episode that wiped out the dinosaurs at the end of the Cretaceous era was precipitated by a 10-kilometer asteroid striking the earth. This theory was advanced by Luis Alvarez, a nuclear physicist—a Nobel laureate, but a physicist nonetheless! The community of paleontologists was not amused.

Is Genius Born or Made?

In Shakespeare's *The Tempest*, the protagonist Prospero laments his failure to alter the base character of the savage monster Caliban:

> A devil, a born devil, on whose nature
> Nurture can never stick, on whom my pains,
> Humanely taken, all, all lost, quite lost . . .

This juxtaposition of the words "nature" and "nurture" is perhaps the first in the English language. The felicitous and attractive alliteration caught on in the discipline of psychology. The subtitle to Francis Galton's 1874 *English Men of Science* is *Their Nature and Nurture*. In explanation, Galton added,

> The phrase 'nature and nurture' is a convenient jingle of words, for it separates under two distinct heads the innumerable elements of which personality is composed. Nature is all that a man brings with himself into the world; nurture is every influence from without that affects him after his birth.

The comparative influence of environment and endowment is a central issue in developmental psychology. It is equally a critical question in understanding the origins of historic personalities. Below I re-examine the key findings of this chapter concerning this debate.

Nurtured Genius

Let us begin with the "nurture" position—that genius is made rather than born. We may start by distinguishing two types of geniuses. On the one hand, "analytical" geniuses are extremely articulate, logical, systematic, deliberate, self-disciplined, and well informed. They are supremely well adjusted to the demands of contemporary society and culture, and they thereby appear optimally successful from a contemporaneous perspective. On the other hand, "intuitive" geniuses are more rhapsodic, irrational, romantic, impulsive, and spontaneous. They are guided more by flashes of often unjustified and always unpredictable insights. They exhibit a profound distaste for any authority that exerts conformity pressures on their chaotic explorations and enthusiasms.

This contrast can be mapped onto others that we frequently hear about. Following Nietzsche's *The Birth of Tragedy*, we can say that analyticals are "Apollonian," the intuitives "Dionysian." Or, in line with Chapter 2's discussion, we might style these types "left-hemisphere" and "right-hemisphere," respectively. Closer still to mainstream psychology is the distinction between extraordinary intelligence and exceptional creativity—two attributes that need not go together.

Whatever the labels assigned to this contrast, we must recognize that analytical and intuitive geniuses represent two ends of a continuum. Geniuses may settle anywhere along this dimension, some mixing the two in equal measure. Where a given person stands on this continuum determines the domain in which he or she is most likely to achieve acclaim. To make the first cut, leaders must probably be more analytical, creators more intuitive in disposition. Within each of these groups, further partitions are possible. Status quo politicians and diplomats are likely to be more analytical, revolutionaries and political upstarts more intuitive. Similarly, among creators, scientific and artistic creativity in all likelihood differ. Yet some overlap is conceivable, too. Those scientists who stick to the received paradigm, and thus practice what Thomas Kuhn has called "normal science," will be more analytical than those scientists engaged in revolutionary science. Likewise, artists who conform to classic styles will be more analytical than those who seek romantic styles that put fewer constraints on self-expression. Thus, artists painting in an academic mode may actually be less intuitive than scientists who revolutionize their discipline.

With this scheme, we can interpret developmental antecedents according to where they would put a person on the analytical–intuitive dimension. That placement specifies where the individual can maximize acclaim. For example, first-borns lean more toward the analytical side, later-borns toward the intuitive side. Accordingly, first-borns are more likely to become status quo leaders and scientific creators, while later-borns are more likely to become revolutionaries and artistic creators. The disruptions caused by orphanhood and other traumatic experiences push the emerging genius toward the intuitive end. Thus, parental loss is more common among artists than scientists. Socioeconomic class enters the equation in the same fashion, with higher status corresponding to a more analytical mode of thinking. Again, this is reflected in the developmental outcomes seen in eminent personalities. We can also interpret the effects of education in this way. The reason why scientists require the most formal training is that the analytical skills inculcated in universities are more essential to success. Scholastic performance follows the same pattern. Finally, the various types of marginality operate in a parallel manner. Professional marginality, for example, favors revolutionary scientists more than it does practitioners of normal science.

Of course, in actual operation, these diverse factors would coalesce in the making of a remarkable personality. Birth order, early trauma, cultural enrichment, education, and marginality are all subject to tradeoffs as well. For example, individuals who already have everything else going for them do not need the final shock of orphanhood to set them on the right track. Hence, no one developmental event or condition is a sure bet in predicting later distinction. In fact, the child or adolescent may experience too much of a good thing, and end up one of the innumerable nonentities of history. For example, the resulting adult may be so intuitive as to lack all commitment and drive, fulfilling the life of a dilettante at best.

This theoretical scheme concentrates on the choice of domain, not on the size of success in the domain once it is chosen. Given a batch of geniuses in normal science, for instance, how do we predict who will attain the foremost heights? One possibility is that those enjoying the optimal mix of analytical and intuitive skills for the selected domain will emerge as the most successful. This means that the really accomplished figures will be those whose biographical backgrounds are most typical for the discipline. Hence, an artist who has suffered parental loss may have an edge over one who has not. Yet the evidence runs against this conjecture. The most acclaimed creators, leaders, or celebrities have biographies that are neither more nor less typical of those for their lesser-known colleagues.

A second possibility is that one or more developmental antecedents exist that affect attainments regardless of domain. All individuals, whether leaders or creators, scientists or artists, must have more of some attribute or skill to accomplish more. Yet it is not easy to identify the mysterious influence. Omnivorous reading does correlate with eminence in a wide array of fields—but not in all. The intense and unrelenting drive discussed in Chapter 5 may provide the missing factor. But this skirts the issue: Where does that phenomenal motivation come from in the first place? And, naturally, there may be some intellectual capacity behind the variation in attainments. This, too, begs the question. Whence arises these abilities?

Natural Genius

Francis Galton thought he had the answer to such unanswered questions: He ascribed exceptional accomplishment to natural ability. He stated this position most emphatically in his *Hereditary Genius*, but even in his *English Men of Science* the emphasis remains. Galton was willing to grant the environment merely a peripheral position in the creation of genius. So suppose we now speculate on how much genius is in one's genes.

We begin with an easy assumption: People vary in intellectual capacity. Some master, store, and retrieve information efficiently and accurately. Others execute the same tasks with more errors and less speed. If a person must master about 50,000 chunks of information to establish a base for achievement, then clearly a person who is much brighter can get that arduous business over with far sooner. Indeed, the greatest geniuses seem to require less time to pick up the disciplinary prerequisites. For example, we have already seen that illustrious scientists take less time earning their doctorates than do their less successful colleagues. In addition, the more impressive this intellectual wherewithal, the less time spent fulfilling the demands of formal education. This leaves additional time for self-education. The exceptionally brilliant can engage in extracurricular activities, including omnivorous reading, and win good grades and high honors at the same time. Given this added informal and self-directed study, the truly gifted are better prepared to follow their paths toward distinction.

Now let's add a second assumption: Much of a person's raw intellectual power is provided courtesy of the parents' DNA. (Heredity doesn't have to be everything; even a 50–50 split between nature and nurture will allow the following argument to proceed.) If this postulate is granted, the parents of those with amazing intellectual power should boast more natural ability themselves. They are the block from which the chip has been taken. If the likelihood is high that this capacity translates into life success, the parents of the great will occupy the most prestigious positions in society. Hence, luminaries may come from professional and middle-class homes simply because they share a common genetic proclivity for above-average intellectual ability.

This is effectively Galton's logic in *Hereditary Genius*, only with a broadened conception of success. Yet now let us push this argument one step further. We can argue that the family environment has no causal function as a developmental antecedent. If the homes of future notables are replete with culturally and aesthetically stimulating materials, these simply reflect the impressive intellectual caliber of their parents. Because they are brighter, they fill their homes with activities that satisfy their own curiosities. In other words, the cultural enrichment available in these homes is a symptom that a child has extremely intelligent parents. From this symptom we can infer that the child has probably inherited a similar level of intellectual aptitude. But if that child were kidnapped from the parents at birth and raised in a different family environment, the child's development would remain unaltered. Because he or she still enjoys superior genetic endowments, the stairway to acclaim will wait for the child's footsteps as before.

In more scientific terms, we can say that any association between enriched home environments in childhood and phenomenal accomplishments in adulthood is spurious. Both issue from an earlier and hidden factor—parental intelligence. Brighter parents construct more stimulating homes for themselves, and, less deliberately, pass their superior genes to their children. This concept applies to many other findings besides home enrichment. For instance, our original supposition was that omnivorous reading enables children and adolescents to get the proficiency necessary for adult achievements. Alternatively, we can surmise that avid consumption of books and magazines merely reflects the prior inheritance of an exceptional intellect. It is this intellect, and not the reading, that directly determines opportunities for later triumphs. The association between voracious reading and achieved eminence may be spurious.

What about the distinction between analytical and intuitive genius introduced earlier? In his essay on Abraham Cowley, Samuel Johnson claimed that "the true Genius is a mind of large general powers, accidentally determined to some particular direction." Johnson noted that it was Cowley's access to Edmund Spenser's *Faerie Queene*, placed on the window sill of his mother's room, that first directed him toward poetry. Also according to Johnson, it was a chance perusal of a treatise on painting by Jonathan Richardson that deflected the future Sir Joshua Reynolds toward a career in the visual arts. Many other examples of such "crystallizing experiences" can be found in the lives of illustrious individuals. For instance, Einstein felt that a magnet he received as a child helped propel him toward an interest in science.

Therefore, perhaps parents do affect the developmental course of their children. If a father and mother decorate the home with books about science and mathematics, give their children mechanical toys on their birthdays, and take them on trips to industrial museums, they may produce one or more scientific geniuses. But if the parents stock the house with easels and paints, play avant-garde music on the stereo, and pack the home library with thick books of art prints and literary anthologies, they may set their children along the contrary path to becoming artistic geniuses. The "large general powers" will have been deliberately rather than accidentally deflected toward either the analytical or the intuitive pole. Thus may nurture channel nature.

Yet the advocate of genetic endowment need not forfeit the fight. Children inherit more than just brains from their parents. Behavior geneticists have identified a whole inventory of personality traits that may pass down from generation to generation. Accordingly, it is feasible that genes decide not just the level of raw genius, but even where a person stands on the analytical–intuitive scale. Hence, the fact that eminent scientists come from different home environments than do eminent artists may again represent only a spurious relation. Parents with genes favoring scientific interests embellish their homes appropriately, and by sperm and egg pass that same proclivity to their offspring. Those progeny might still become distinguished scientists if they were separated from their parents and raised in a home characterized by frequent poetry readings and visits to art galleries.

The genetic provision for an analytical or intuitive inclination may even affect the course of formal education. Individuals who inherit an analytical style will love school, do well, and move far up the educational ladder. Individuals whose natural temperament is more intuitive will find formal training an incessant irritation, and will leave the system of analytical instruction at the earliest possible opportunity. So genes might give direct birth to the specific guise of genius. The events and conditions of childhood and adolescence could be mere symptoms, not causes.

Naturally, some of the developmental antecedents discussed in this chapter seem more recalcitrant from a genetic standpoint. What about orphanhood, marginality, or birth order? Very often, however, a careful analysis will disclose a secret opening for the intrusion of biological inheritance. Take orphanhood: Surely whether one or both parents died while their child is still a youngster is not something that can be inherited. But think again—a genetic link is actually conceivable. The parents of a famous personality are often older than average when their gifted child is born. Usually such parents are in their 30s when they settle down to raise a family. Since their life expectancy does not increase simply because they have delayed procreation by a decade or more, this implies a bigger risk that they will die before their brood leaves the nest.

This last point will provide us with a genetic interpretation if we assume that bright men and women plan their parenthoods wisely. Intelligence is probably associated with a willingness to put off a family until a person has (1) established a career, (2) found the best mate, and (3) built up adequate resources for bringing up children. In fact, both intelligence and eminence are associated with tardy fertility. Hence, we have another instance of potential spuriousness. Brilliant parents have children at older ages; because of their brilliance, their offspring will be brilliant too; and because of their delay in starting a family, their progeny may suffer parental loss. Orphanhood may be a sign, not an agent.

The same mode of reasoning can apply to other presumed antecedents of greatness, including the various kinds of marginality. In fact, the only developmental factor that stoutly resists a genetic interpretation is birth order. The Mendelian laws of inheritance are blind to whether an individual is first-born or later-born, middle child or only child. Galton acknowledged this difficulty in his *English Men of Science*. He saw ordinal position in the family as a matter of environment rather than endowment. Yet, with this rare exception, we cannot exclude genes as the agents of genius.

What is the truth? Are geniuses born or made? A definitive answer eludes us. Not until behavior genetics has finally exhausted itself in the pursuit of inherited traits can we gauge fully the extent to which endowment takes precedence over the environment. Moreover, it is not unlikely that nature and nurture interact in complex ways during human development. For example, people born with higher natural ability may possess a tenacious intellectual curiosity that drives them to read and explore, and thereby to expand their nurtured ability. Hence, the nature–nurture issue may be a controversy that can never be completely untangled. Even so, the absence of a secure theoretical reading should not blind us to the intrinsic value of the empirical results. At the minimum, the factors described here provide us with the means to identify those with the most promise of success. And at the maximum, we may have gotten some tips about how to coach our own offspring toward greatness. In either case, the child is prophet of the adult.

LIFE'S PRIME AND DEATH'S ADVANCE: A LIFE-SPAN PERSPECTIVE

Those who have not yet made their marks sometimes take comfort in the "myth of the belated magnum opus." In other words, they muse that it only takes a single great work—some trailblazing masterpiece or unprecedented accomplishment—to guarantee their place in the history books. So maybe they will finally get around to writing that novel that will knock all others off the shelves. Perhaps they will find the time to patent that gadget they have on the workbench in the garage. Or perchance they will finally run for a legislative office where they can ram through that revolutionary package of reforms they've been pondering all these years. Although the narrative details vary according to the aspiration, the plot outline is always the same: At last some wonderful achievement will propel these individuals from vexatious obscurity to instant applause.

Daydreamers still at the mercy of this delusion should ponder the words of Oliver Wendell Holmes Jr.: "If you haven't cut your name on the door of fame by the time you've reached 40, you might as well put up your jackknife." Although this warning is not entirely accurate, it is closer to the mark than the myth of the ninth-inning homer that will miraculously save life's big game. As noted in Chapter 5, attaining greatness is far from a one-shot affair. History does not operate on a one-per-customer basis. So, historic personalities have more than one notable event to their credit. The reputation of Wellington rests on far more than Waterloo, Lincoln's on more than the Gettysburg Address, and Edison's on more than the phonograph. Go ahead: Steal the *Republic* from Plato, the Fifth Symphony from Beethoven, the Sistine Chapel frescoes from Michelangelo, or *Hamlet* from Shakespeare. Their reputations would still tower above those of their contemporaries. Nobel laureate Max Born claimed that Einstein "would be one of the greatest theoretical physicists of all times even if he had not written a single line on relativity." In fact, when Einstein received his own Nobel Prize, his theory of relativity was not given specific credit! Yet, by then, Einstein's special theory of relativity was 16 years old and his general theory 6 years old. But he had accomplished so much else that the prize committee did not need to cite this work to justify casting a gold medal with his name.

Thus, making it big is a career. People who wish to do so must organize their whole lives around a single enterprise. They must be monomaniacs, even megalomaniacs, about their pursuits. They must start early, labor continuously, and never give up the cause. Success is not for the lazy, procrastinating, or mercurial. Hence, to comprehend fully what it takes to become a star, we must study achievers over the entire span of their productive lives.

I carry out such a life-span developmental scrutiny in this chapter. I start by reviewing what we know about the connection between age and achievement. Next I examine changes in the nature of one's career over the life course. Then I look at the closing years, including the aftermath of death.

Age and Achievement

Life has a beginning, a middle, and an end; careers do too. And the details of this simplistic delineation are complicated. For nearly all careers, we should speak at least of a continuous trajectory. This general trajectory consists of an onset, a curve of ascent, a peak, a curve of descent, and an endpoint. Although the career's start always happens years after life's debut, the career's end is often simultaneous with life's end. Within this overall path of achievement, we can isolate several career landmarks. For example, we can record when luminaries made their first and last contributions to history. We can also register when during the career their single most important contributions were made.

The word "contributions" is deliberately abstract. Their specific nature depends on the particular activity under view. The contributions may entail decisions, treaties, elections, revolutions, battles, conquests, reforms, laws, theories, discoveries, inventions, systems, monographs, novels, poems, plays, paintings, designs, compositions, products, songs, movies, shows, competitions, championships, trophies—or anything else that is largely discrete. Once we realize the diversity of forms these contributions may take, we should probably divide our discussion according to the principal domains of human achievement. Below I inspect creators, leaders, and celebrities separately.

Creators

Suppose we want to test the Holmes hypothesis about the 40th year marking the making or breaking point. We could rummage around the biographies of illustrious creators for confirmatory evidence. We might learn that Beethoven composed his Fifth Symphony, Michelangelo painted the Sistine Chapel, and Shakespeare wrote *Hamlet* all at about age 37. Even massive pieces like Tolstoy's *War and Peace* started to come out before the Holmes deadline. Yet evidence contradicting the 40th-year rule is easily summoned as well. Newton published his *Principia Mathematica* at age 45, Kant his *Critique of Pure Reason* at 57, and Copernicus his *Revolution of the Heavenly Spheres* at 70. Thus, we will get nowhere by compiling anecdote and antidote.

Another alternative is available to the psychologist. The approach has four steps: (1) Gather a collection of notable figures in a given creative domain; (2) compile a list of their accomplishments; (3) tabulate into consecutive intervals the number of achievements made in each age period; and (4) determine the career trajectory from the resulting curve. This line of attack was first tried in 1835 by Adolf Quetelet, and a second application dates back to 1874. So this more rigorous approach is now well over a century old. Nevertheless, the classic treatise using this method is the 1953 book *Age and Achievement* by Harvey C. Lehman. In this volume, Lehman tabulated the ups and downs in an awesome variety of activities, including the various scientific disciplines, many philosophical specialties, and the diverse genres of literature, art, and music. For each domain he calculated the overall age curve. The outcome is one of the most impressive research programs in the scientific study of achievement.

Lehman's published trajectories provoked a lot of controversy. Many did not like the implication that achievement declines in the closing years of a career. Furthermore, as in any pioneer effort, Lehman's inquiries were not without flaws. Nevertheless, work conducted in the decades since 1953 has remedied these technical difficulties. Lehman's main conclusions have been qualified and extended, but not flatly contradicted. I summarize these updated results under four headings: the productivity curve, quantity versus quality, interdisciplinary contrasts, and individual differences.

The Productivity Curve

Figure 7.1 shows the typical trajectory for productivity across the career. The vertical axis gives the output rate per year, while the horizontal axis specifies personal age. The curve summarizes the average career trajectory for thousands of creators, representing dozens of distinct endeavors in the arts and sciences. In fact, the data underlying the curve omit no important domain of creativity by which individuals may impress themselves upon posterity.

Plainly, productivity rises rapidly to a single peak, after which a gradual decline sets in. In more detail, the curve has three main features:

1. Output begins somewhere in the 20s. For instance, one study looked at the careers of notable 19th-century scientists and literary figures. The scientific greats included Darwin, Gauss, Helmholtz, Humboldt, Laplace, Liebig, Pasteur, Poisson, and Riemann; the literary greats included Balzac, Byron, Coleridge, Dickens, Goethe, Heine, Hugo, Ibsen, Poe, Schiller, Tolstoy, and Whitman. In both groups, the first offering was produced at about the mid-20s.

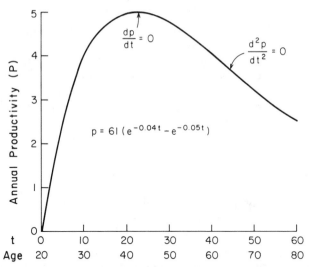

FIGURE 7.1. Curve that predicts annual productivity as function of career age (see original article for details about the mathematical model on which the figure is based).

    2. From that starting point, the curve ascends quickly to an optimum at some point near the 40th year, give or take half a decade. For example, among American scientists who won the Nobel Prize for their contributions, their most productive career decade was their 40s.

    3. After the career optimum is reached, the curve turns around and gradually approaches the point of zero output rate. In other words, after the initially rapid dropoff, the descent soon levels off. Because the decline is not nearly so precipitous as the ascent, creative individuals can be more productive in their 70s than they were in their 20s. Even so, the output rate is about half that seen at the career peak.

    The productivity curve in Figure 7.1 represents an average only. Hence, if it is used to predict the performance of a specific creator, we can merely speak of statistical odds. The curve does not dictate some iron-clad law that everyone must follow. In fact, research has documented some of the factors that affect the trajectory in specific instances. For example, in those disciplines where competition has become ever more fierce, output in the later years will sometimes fall below expectation. Older creators will sometimes find themselves trying to hold off an accelerating onslaught of whippersnappers, and eventually lose the battle. In addition, physical illnesses can also undermine productivity, making the later years less industrious than they might otherwise be. Death itself is the last word in output-inhibiting illness. Increased administrative duties can also vitiate creative performance, as can responsibilities of a more personal variety. Thus, productive output takes a nosedive when one's offspring tyrannize the household. Fertility and productivity are often incompatible.

These odds and ends notwithstanding, the curve in Figure 7.1 provides a rough picture of the careers of individual creators. For instance, this trajectory accurately fits the career course of Thomas Edison, as gauged by his output of patents. So, despite its crudeness, this curve still offers a good guideline of what to expect under ideal conditions.

Quantity versus Quality

Actually, before we can plot the data behind the typical trajectory in Figure 7.1, we must first consider a crucial question: Do we count all creative products, regardless of merit? Or do we restrict the tabulation to those pieces that left an enduring mark on the creative domain? In short, do we wish to examine indiscriminate quantity or to be more choosy about quality? In the first instance we would be studying mere productivity, whereas in the latter case our focus would be on true creativity. For any psychology of history, this is not an easy question to answer. On the one hand, the psychologist feels more comfortable counting all products, regardless of merit. Each product is then an objective behavior—an operant not all that different from a rat's pressing down a lever in a Skinner box. On the other hand, many of these products will exert no influence whatsoever on history. Therefore, to count worthless items along with the exceptional may result in a career trajectory that has nothing to do with the making of greatness. Thus, the theoretical contrast between quantity and quality is profound.

Fortunately, the empirical difference between personal productivity and social creativity is trivial if not nil. The age curve for acclaimed contributions has the same shape, on the average, as that for attempted contributions. Indeed, let us suppose that for each age interval we calculate the quotient of important works to the number of works produced, yielding a "quality ratio." This ratio of hits to total shots does not change in a regular pattern with age. The ratio neither increases nor decreases, nor exhibits any other form. This remarkable result suggests that quality is a function of quantity. The more pieces generated in a given age period, the higher the likelihood that one of those pieces will attain success. Not even outstanding creators can improve the odds with increased maturity. The ability to conceive *Hamlet* did not pre-empt Shakespeare from writing *Troilus and Cressida* immediately after. In the 1810s Beethoven could compose his last three symphonies and the *Missa Solemnis* alongside such forgettable pieces as *Leonore Prohaska, Der glorreiche Augenblick*, and *Wellington's Victory*. Throughout the career, success is a hit-or-miss affair. This linkage between quantity (productivity) and quality (creativity) we can call the "equal-odds rule."

Interdisciplinary Contrasts

The equal-odds rule has huge repercussions for understanding the placement of career landmarks in a creator's biography. To develop these implications, we must first examine a sin perpetrated by the curve shown in Figure 7.1: As a generic statement, it ignores the vast variation across disciplines in the expected career trajectories. In some fields creative productivity comes and goes like a meteor shower; the peak arrives early, and the decline is unkind. In other creative domains the ascent is more gradual, the optimum point is later, and the descent is more leisurely and merciful. For example, Figure 7.2 offers curves for science, art, and scholarship. Although all three trajectories follow the same pattern as that seen in Figure 7.1, the details vary substantially. For artists, the drop from crest to trough is depressing. The outlook for scholars, in contrast, is more optimistic; they don't even reach their career peaks until they enter their 60s. The trajectory for scientists falls in between.

Actually, the curves in this graph understate the true extent of the contrasts. The curves for each of the three domains were summed across separate curves for subdisciplines with each domain. Scholarship included historians, philosophers, and miscellaneous scholars; science included biologists, botanists, chemists, geologists, inventors, and mathematicians; and the arts included architects, chamber musicians, dramatists, librettists, novelists, opera composers, and poets. Each of these more specialized domains probably has its own characteristic trajectory. In the arts, for example, the curve for writing novels peaks much later than that for poetry writing. *The Brothers Karamazov* was written by a Dostoevsky who was 59 years old; *Les Misérables* came from the hand of a Hugo in his 60th year; and the second part of *Don Quixote* was pub-

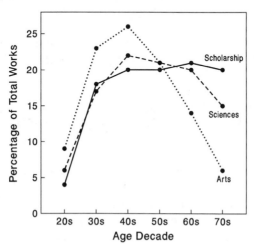

FIGURE 7.2. Empirical curves showing output in three domains as function of chronological age.

lished by a Cervantes who was 68 years of age. In contrast, William Blake lived to be 70, but probably wrote the best poems of his *Songs of Innocence* in his teens and 20s. And Coleridge, who lived to age 62, composed his contributions to *Lyrical Ballads* (including "The Rime of the Ancient Mariner") in his 20s. Critic H. L. Mencken alluded to examples like these in his utterance: "When one hears of a poet past thirty-five he seems somehow unnatural and obscene."

Even more dramatic, perhaps, are the contrasts seen in the sciences. For mathematical disciplines, such as pure mathematics and theoretical physics, the career course approximates that of the poets. Precocious peaks and spectacular descents are commonplace. This circumstance may have inspired Einstein's remark: "A person who has not made his great contribution to science before the age of thirty will never do so." Surely, this sets a more drastic deadline than that of Holmes! Paul Dirac said even more ominously:

> Age is, of course, a fever chill
> that every physicist must fear.
> He's better dead than living still
> when once he's past his thirtieth year.

Dirac himself received the Nobel Prize for physics when he was only 31, for work he had published when he was 25 years old. Einstein's own Nobel Prize recognized the contributions he had made when he was 26. And Newton's *annus mirabilis*, when he came up with many of the ideas that were to make him famous, was his 24th year. In contrast, creativity in the biological and earth sciences often peaks much later, with more gentle downward slopes. This is evident in the authors' ages for many classics in these fields: Darwin's *The Origin of Species* at age 50, Buffon's *Natural History* between ages 42 and 81, Lamarck's *Natural History of the Invertebrates* between ages 71 and 78, and Humboldt's *Cosmos* between ages 76 and 89.

If the age curves differ across scientific disciplines, then we would expect that the location of career landmarks would vary accordingly. By "career landmarks" I mean the first important contribution, the best contribution, and the last important contribution. Although this concept disregards quantity, where these landmarks are placed in a career depends on the curve for total productivity. To see how this is so, we need only apply the rule of equal odds. We can then make three observations:

1. *Age at first major contribution:* For those disciplines in which productivity increases faster than average, the number of attempts accumulates quite rapidly. This raises the chance of getting a hit in the early years. In contrast, in those disciplines where quantity increases more slowly, an individual will usually wait longer before the first quality idea appears.

2. *Age at best contribution:* On average, the location of the single best work corresponds to that period in a career in which an individual is most prolific overall. In those disciplines that exhibit earlier peaks in output, the most important contribution of a career should come earlier as well. By comparison, scientists working in fields with later productive optima should come out with their single most influential ideas at a later age.

3. *Age at last major contribution:* In fields with the most gradual declines, productivity will be sustained much later in life. This heightens the odds of producing a hit later as well. So those laboring in fields that demand more maturity can expect to contribute their last significant ideas when they are much older than average. On the other hand, in domains where the downward slope is steep, the odds of a senior colleague's leaving a mark on the discipline becomes vanishingly small. This was apparently the case in quantum theory, an enterprise so notorious for its early career peaks that it was styled *Knabenphysiks* ("boys' physics"). Many of its contributors were "over the hill" at ages when geologists and biomedical researchers would just be getting into stride!

Given this argument, the location of the three landmarks within a career should depend on a scientist's discipline. This is confirmed in Figure 7.3, which presents schematic career trajectories for 2,026 famous scientists spread across nine fields. The sample includes such names as Copernicus, Darwin, Descartes, Edison, Einstein, Freud, Galileo, Newton, and Pasteur, as well as many lesser lights. For each discipline four key events are depicted—the three career landmarks and death. The ages of first, best, and last contribution vary substantially across the several fields. The contrasts can be as large as 31% of the average length of a career. These differences are precisely what we would expect if (1) the age curves differ across disciplines and (2) the equal-odds rule applies to all disciplines in the same fashion.

Notice that mathematicians make their first impressions on history at the earliest age. This helps explain G. H. Hardy's observation that mathematicians become Fellows of the Royal Society at younger ages than do contributors to any other discipline. However, the data provide no support for Hardy's claim that he did "not know an instance of a major mathematical advance initiated by a man past fifty." The average age for the last important work in mathematics is 53. Moreover, the age for the final contribution may range anywhere between 21 and 81. So the very elderly are not excluded from the mathematical enterprise.

Individual Differences

The age range from 21 to 81 just mentioned spans 60 years. This is a huge spread of time within the context of a normal human life span. This range suggests that a critical qualification lurks behind all the preceding conclusions: The career trajectories may not be the same even for individuals struggling in the same endeavor. I am not talking about the influx of extraneous events, like those mentioned earlier. Rather, even under ideal conditions, two creators in the same domain can expect divergent career paths. This divergence has two sources.

First, if you re-examine Figure 7.1, you will note that the horizontal axis is actually defined in two separate ways. So far I have been speaking as if the curve

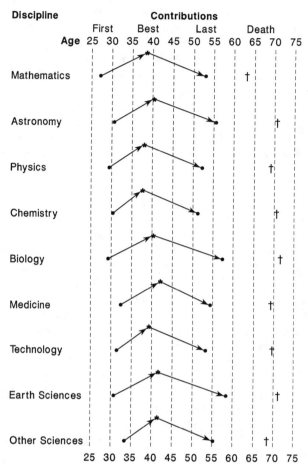

FIGURE 7.3. Career trajectories and landmarks for nine scientific disciplines.

is defined by chronological age. Yet this reading is misleading; both data and theory suggest that the trajectory is best described according to career age. The path of a productive life depends on when the career begins. Hence, the curve graphed in the figure starts not at birth but at the onset of the creative process. To be sure, chronological and career age will correlate very highly. Even so, individual differences in the *age at career onset* can have real repercussions. Those persons who, for whatever reason, get off to a late start can expect that the prime of their career will be delayed in equal measure. Late bloomers will prosper later.

To illustrate, Anton Bruckner was slow to find his true musical voice. It took an encounter with the operas of Richard Wagner to make him realize that the symphony was the form he should be pursuing. So in his 39th and 40th years he completed his first two symphonies—known as No. 0 and No. 00, since they were pure "juvenilia." His first symphonic masterworks did not appear until he was between 50 and 70 years of age. His whole career had shifted over at least 20 years from what represents "normal progress" in symphonic composition.

Second, we must recognize that some creators are far more prolific than colleagues within the same domain. One individual will generate idea after idea at a formidable sprint, while another will conceive new thoughts at a less hurried pace. When all other factors are held constant, the more prolific will end with a larger overall output. With a more impressive body of lifetime work, these fertile intellects will tend to enjoy weightier fame as well. For example, one study found that Nobel laureates among American scientists published at over twice the annual rate of a matched group of controls. Therefore, let us assume that the variation in output rate corresponds to individual differences in underlying creative *potential*. Our next question should be this: What is the impact, if any, of creative potential on the expected career trajectory?

The answer turns out to be simple. Given two individuals who launch their careers at the same chronological age and who work in the same discipline, the sole difference is the height of the curve. As is clear from Figure 7.1, the height of the curve indicates the annual output rate for a given career age. So the general shape of the curve can remain unchanged, while still allowing for more prolific production. In particular, if both age at career onset and discipline are the same, the career peak appears at the same location for both feverish and sluggish producers. A corollary of this fact concerns the middle career landmark: The age at which individuals produce their most acclaimed masterpiece does not depend on their creative potential. The best work appears at the same age, regardless of lifetime output or even ultimate eminence. For this career landmark, only the age at career onset and the domain of creativity are relevant factors.

Differences in creative potential *do* affect the placement of the other two landmarks, however. By the equal-odds rule, the greater the number of shots, the greater the number of hits on the average. Hence, the more productive a creator is at the beginning of the career, the sooner a true masterwork will appear. The same prediction holds for the concluding portion of the career: The more fecund the mind toward the end, the higher the odds that a lasting accomplishment will grace the final years. Thus, those persons who are highest in creative potential should produce their first important work sooner and their last important work later than is normal for their discipline. Data confirm this prediction, at least if we gauge creative potential by either lifetime output or posthumous distinction. The most prolific and successful creators get their first hit earlier and their last hit later.

Goethe offers a fine illustration. Phenomenally productive throughout his life, he first attained broad renown in 1774 with the publication of his *Sorrows of Young Werther*. He was then 25, yet had already been writing notable plays and poems for seven years. Then, 58 years later, in the final year of his life, he was putting the last touches on the second part of *Faust*!

Two individual-difference variables are thus of primary value in comprehending the career course—the age at career onset and the level of creative potential. These two factors operate independently of each other in delineating the career trajectory. Because these two factors are uncorrelated, we can devise a typology of career paths for creators working in the same discipline. We can then look at ideal types who are high or low on each variable in four possible combinations. Figure 7.4 gives the results.

Creators low in creative potential are depicted on the left-hand side of the figure, while those high in creative potential are shown on the right-hand side. By comparison, the trajectories in the top two graphs are for individuals who embarked on their careers when they were 20 years old, while those in the bottom two graphs waited until they were 30 years old. Moreover, vertical lines beneath each of the four curves demarcate the most likely location of the three career landmarks. Thus, we can picture more easily some of the predictions advanced earlier. For example, when career onset is held constant, greater creative potential is associated with an earlier first work and a later last work,

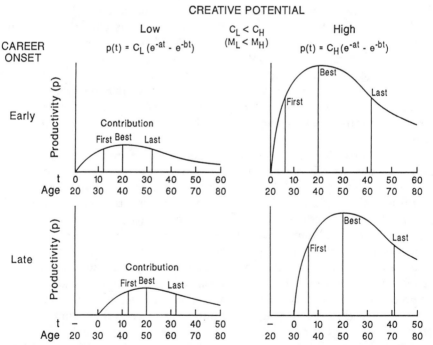

FIGURE 7.4. Career trajectories and landmarks for creators working in same field, but differing according to creative potential and age at career onset (see original article for details about the mathematical model on which the figure is based).

but there is no change at all in the placement of the single best work. On the other hand, if creative potential is held constant, an earlier career onset corresponds to an earlier best work. In addition, an earlier career onset means that the first and last work will appear sooner, too; all three landmarks shift by a decade. It is possible to derive some more complex predictions from this typology, but this would take us too far afield.

By allowing variation on just two straightforward factors, we can accommodate a variety of creative careers. When differences on these two variables are combined with the interdisciplinary contrasts in productivity curves, we can fix the gist of the career trajectory for any creative genius.

Leaders

Discovering how creativity varies over the life span is simple in comparison to tracing the changes in leadership. For creators, we can usually count products per unit of time. For leaders, on the other hand, it is not always obvious what exactly we should tabulate as annual output. Indeed, without enough care, the same analytical technique can lead us astray. For example, Lehman devoted his attention to leadership as well as creativity, but his results are not always meaningful. Most frequently, he would merely determine the ages at which leaders occupied various positions of power. Thus, he showed that many leaders were prone to be in their late 50s. This modal age held for British prime ministers and members of British cabinets, American chief executives and ambassadors, presidents of diverse republics scattered throughout the world, and famous naval commanders. But this fact alone tells us nothing about the performance of the individuals in these positions of leadership. For example, U.S. presidents have typically been in their late 50s on inauguration day, but there is no relation between an incumbent's age and his rating on a wide range of performance criteria, including posthumous reputation.

Sometimes Lehman tried to assess actual ability more directly, but ended up committing a logical fallacy. In one instance he determined the ages at which 198 military commanders fought 520 land battles. The subjects included such immortals as Alexander the Great, Julius Caesar, Frederick the Great, and Napoleon. The leaders were most likely to be in their early 40s. Therefore, we might conclude that the optimal age for demonstrating tactical genius is about the same as the best age for producing a creative masterpiece. Yet this inference is hazardous. Lehman did not compare the curve for winning commanders against the curve for their defeated opponents. The vanquished could have been born precisely the same year as the victorious. The "Iron Duke" of Wellington worsted Napoleon on the fields of Waterloo, but we cannot ascribe this victory to some special placement on some age curve. Both winner and loser were born in 1769, and less than five months apart at that!

We need a more direct comparison of victors and losers. For instance,

Lehman improved his analysis a bit when he turned to presidential candidates in the history of the United States. Rather than tabulate the ages of only those who garnered the most electoral votes, he added a parallel tabulation for those less fortunate. Curiously, the favorite age for running for the nation's highest office was the same for both groups—the late 50s. How winners and losers differed was more subtle. Those victorious in the November general election were more likely to be very close to this optimal age. Those defeated, in contrast, were either much younger or considerably older. George B. McClellan was 38 when he ran against Lincoln, and William Jennings Bryan was only 36 when he first campaigned for the presidency. These ages are close to the minimum age of 35 set by the U.S. Constitution. Both lost. At the other extreme, Peter Cooper was 85 when he ran unsuccessfully for the office. Hence, even if age bears no relation to presidential performance, it does seem pertinent to whether a candidate gets to take the oath on inauguration day.

Fortunately, other investigations have introduced further improvements in the analysis of leaders' careers. These inquiries suggest that the curve shown in Figure 7.1 can sometimes describe the careers of historic leaders as well as creators. For example, one study examined the political, military, and diplomatic triumphs of 25 hereditary monarchs of European history. The sample included such big names as Elizabeth I of England, Louis XIV of France, Margaret of Denmark, Frederick the Great of Prussia, Maria Theresa of the Habsburg Empire, Ivan the Terrible of Russia, and Süleyman the Magnificent of the Ottoman Empire. Their nations were best off when the reigning monarch was about 42 years old. A different study scrutinized 326 decisive land battles fought between 321 B.C. and A.D. 1905. On the average, the commander who was closest to his 45th birthday had the highest odds of success. Hence, for both political and military leadership, there appears an optimum age for making a (positive) mark. The early to middle 40s contains this peak.

A critical fact complicates this conclusion, however. In creative activities, the career peak depends on the discipline. The same holds for leadership, whether we look at political or religious leaders.

Making It in Politics

In society at large, felonies are largely the province of youth. With age, criminals mellow out, settle down, and—like famed outlaw Jesse James—may even toy with the prospect of becoming respectable members of their communities. The same hegemony may hold in politics as well. In the classic treatise *The Prince*, Machiavelli alleged that fortune is "a lover of young men, because they are less cautious, more violent, and with more audacity command her." Great leaders, as Tolstoy argued in *War and Peace*, may be little more than violent criminals glorified by some quirk in human events. And when it comes to becoming grandiose felons, youth has the edge. Benjamin Disraeli, the eminent British prime minister, once documented the case for Machiavelli's claim:

Almost everything that's great has been done by youth. . . . Why, the greatest captains of ancient and modern times both conquered Italy at five-and-twenty! Youth, extreme youth, overthrew the Persian Empire. Don Juan of Austria won Lepanto at twenty-five, the greatest battle of modern time . . . Gaston de Foix was only twenty-two when he stood a victor on the plain of Ravenna. Every one remembers Condé and Rocroy at the same age. Gustavus Adolphus died at thirty-eight. . . . Cortes was little more than thirty when he gazed upon the golden cupolas of Mexico. When Maurice of Saxony died at thirty-two, all Europe acknowledged the loss of the greatest captain and the profoundest statesman of the age. Then there is Nelson, Clive . . .

Yet these are examples of fierce souls who shook up the world in their mailed fists. Surely some politicians make their imprints by more gentle means? Yes, but when they do so, those leaders are older and wiser. Disraeli himself did not become prime minister of Great Britain until he was 64, nearly a quarter of a century after he penned the remarks above. Disraeli was a status quo politician, and a leader of the Conservative Party as well. The "angry young men" of politics, in contrast, take up more radical causes and pursue their ends by more tumultuous means.

The fury of youth is most unequivocal in the revolutionaries who overthrew tired or hated regimes. Robespierre was 33 when he was appointed public accuser in the early years of the French Revolution. Jefferson was the same age when his quill scratched out the Declaration of Independence. Castro was a year younger when his guerrilla forces marched victoriously into Havana. Both Lenin and Mao were in their 20s when they inaugurated their struggles for Communism. Illustrations can run on and on. One investigator found that among eminent revolutionaries, half were younger than 35 at the onset of their involvement, and almost 80% were younger than 45 years old. Compare these statistics with the measly percentage of status quo politicians who were so green: Fewer than 13% attained power before the age of 40.

Another way of revealing this disparity is to examine the trends in a single national entity. Lehman looked at the ages of American politicians both in the early years of its founding and in more contemporary times. These leaders were legislators in the Senate and House of Representatives (including House speakers), cabinet officers, Supreme Court justices, ambassadors, and army commanders. As the United States aged, so did its leaders. Nor are we talking about trivial differences. For example, the 544 members of Congress in 1925 were 10 years older than the 147 members who served back in 1799. In certain positions, the gap is more dramatic. Speakers of the House between 1789 and 1874 were usually in their 40s, whereas between 1900 and 1940 they were more likely to be in their 70s! We cannot attribute these shifts to altered life expectancies, either. In fact, under special circumstances, the trends may reverse: Governors of the American colonies tended to be about 20 years older than governors of the American states after the revolution. Yet colonial governors, as subordinates of the British crown, represented status quo positions. State governors, in contrast, are beholden to nobody!

The same pattern probably infected the Russian Revolution. Founded by comparatively young men—Lenin was 47 in 1917, Trotsky and Stalin 38—the Soviet Union became increasingly geriatric. By the Brezhnev era, bureaucrats well past retirement age crammed the Politburo. In time, an innovator in his early 50s rose to dismantle the decrepit system—Mikhail Gorbachev. And among his reforms was to put some relatively young blood back into the Politburo, such as Boris Yeltsin.

Making It in Religion

Disraeli did not say that youth is all blood and guts. The passage quoted above continued with another class of examples:

> Innocent III., the greatest of the Popes, was the despot of Christendom at thirty-seven. John de Medici was a Cardinal at fifteen, and according to Guicciardini, baffled with his statecraft Ferdinand of Arragon [sic] himself. He was Pope as Leo X. at thirty-seven. Luther robbed even him of his richest province at thirty-five. Take Ignatius Loyola and John Wesley, they worked with young brains. Ignatius was only thirty when he made his pilgrimage and wrote the "Spiritual Exercises."

Disraeli thus guessed that age shapes the achievements of religious leaders.
    There is plenty of anecdotal evidence for this influence. Luther was 34 when he nailed the 95 theses on the church door at Wittenberg, and John Wesley was 35 when he founded Methodism. We can go beyond Disraeli's examples, too. John Calvin was 27 when he wrote *Institutes of the Christian Religion*; George Fox was 23 when he founded the Quaker faith; and Joseph Smith was 25 when he found (by his account) *The Book of Mormon*. These figures were all Christians, and Jesus himself was about 30 at the height of his mission. Yet the primacy of youth is not confined to Christian leaders. Buddha was probably in his mid-30s when he founded one of the world's oldest religions. Of the world's great religious founders, Muḥammad may have been the oldest. And even then, Allah chose a man only 40 years old to serve as the prophet of Islam.
    Lehman studied this matter by looking at the careers of 54 leaders who founded religions, sects, or religious societies. The peak interval fell between the ages of 35 and 38, and none were 60 or older. On the other hand, Lehman told a rather different story about leaders of established faiths. Popes of the Roman Catholic Church were usually at least twice as old as Jesus when he died on the cross: Almost all were older than 50 years old, and nearly two-thirds were well in excess of 65 years. The favorite age range was 82 to 92! A similar pattern holds for leaders of other established churches. Brigham Young was twice as old as Smith when he took over Mormonism, and successive patriarchs in Salt Lake City have continued this monopoly of advanced maturity. As G. Stanley Hall concluded in his classic study of senescence, "men in their prime conceived the great religions, the old made them prevail."

What about Innocent III, Leo X, or Ignatius Loyola? These three led a religious flock over a thousand years old—certainly an established faith. Yet these men were behind major transformations in the institutional foundations of Catholicism. The pontificate of Innocent III established the Catholic Church as the supreme temporal and spiritual power in medieval Europe. Kings and emperors—Otto IV of Germany, Philip Augustus of France, and John of England—had to yield to his wishes. He also set in motion changes within the church that were to give rise to the Franciscan and Dominican orders. The papacy of Leo X was less spiritual, but profound nonetheless. Besides expanding the political power of the Vatican, Leo founded a Greek college and press in Rome; moreover, he began the construction of the new St. Peter's, becoming thereby a patron of the arts. Finally, St. Ignatius Loyola founded a new order, the Jesuits. In doing so, he made Roman Catholicism once more a dynamic, proselytizing faith that would send missionaries throughout the world.

So the broad scenario remains unchanged. In both politics and religion, the young are the heralds of change, the old the protectors of stability.

Celebrities

Creativity and leadership are the two chief routes to immortality. Yet other paths will often lead to fame and fortune far faster—the freeways to celebrity status. Celebrities may have an ephemeral acclaim, but at least they can reap the material benefits in their own lifetimes. After all, genuine fame, as Austin Dobson said, "is a food that dead men eat." Moreover, those who achieve the most phenomenal distinction in their own lifetimes may produce names for posterity, despite the transitory nature of their contributions. Examples include actors David Garrick and Sarah Bernhardt, dancers Vlaslav Nijinsky and Isadora Duncan, singers Enrico Caruso and Jenny Lind—even dandy George "Beau" Brummell.

Once more, Lehman did much of the pioneer research on this topic. I have already mentioned his work on movie stars in Chapter 2. Besides that, Lehman investigated the age curves for orators, movie directors, college and university presidents, and public hygienists. Here, however, I focus on just three domains —sports, chess, and business.

The Best in Sports

Lehman studied the age for peak proficiency at a diversity of physical skills— tennis, boxing, auto racing, rifle and pistol shooting, bowling, billiards, golf, football, and of course baseball. He even looked at state corn-husking championships! The broad picture for all these sports was the same: Athletic performance attained the highest point sometime in the late 20s or early 30s. Not only was the peak earlier than that usually found for creativity and leadership, but the decline was far more precipitous. As with creators and leaders, however, Lehman found that the most appropriate age curve was contingent on the domain. Outdoor tennis champions were the youngest; they were most often between the ages of 22 and 26, with their optimum in the latter part of the range. World champions at billiards, in contrast, were in their early 30s, with a peak at about age 35. In the latter sport, a player could even stay competitive until the 50th year or so.

Two investigators built upon Lehman's findings 25 years later, in 1988. They examined superathletes in track and field, swimming, baseball, tennis, and golf. The data spanned a range from 1894 to 1983, and included Olympic medalists as well as record holders and champions in professional sports. Again the age of peak performance was in the late 20s overall, and once more the range was large. In the 1988 study, the youngest champions were women swimmers, who peaked at 17. Janet Evans even became the world's top freestyle swimmer at age 15! The oldest champions were golfers of any gender, with a peak at about age 31. In running, moreover, the longer the distance, the older the champions. The optimum for baseball players was about the same as for long-distance runners, with a peak at about 28 years. Remarkably, the age curves were stable over nearly a century of data. In the 1896 Olympics, Ed Flack won the 1500-meter run at age 22; in the 1980 Olympics, the gold medal for the same event was given to the 24-year-old Sebastian Coe. This difference falls well within the Olympic-to-Olympic fluctuations in the age of champions for specific events.

Because peak ages are so consistent across time, biological factors must play a big part. Someone past 30 lacks the strength and stamina to survive in world-class competition. On the other hand, the variation in peak ages across different sports or events suggests that some require cognitive skills in addition to pure physical capacity. Competitive golf and billiards certainly leave more room for skillful players to compensate for any physical deficiencies. After all, these sports ask the body to do less anyway. Moreover, a really dedicated athlete can develop compensatory abilities fast enough to counterbalance any losses, at least for awhile.

The example of Nolan Ryan is already legendary. Until injury forced him to retire near the end of the 1993 season, he was one of the best pitchers in American baseball. In 1973 he set the record for the number of strikeouts. The next year, at age 27, his fastball was clocked at 100.8 miles per hour, the fastest on record. According to the statistics, Ryan should have entered the downhill slide of his career just a couple of years later. Yet he continued to perform at levels exceeding that of players much younger: As an athlete in his 40s, he was still breaking records. To pull this off, Ryan followed a severe regimen that few have the self-discipline to emulate. That was the only way he could stay competitive.

The Supreme at Chess

Lehman looked at the international chess tournaments held between 1851 and 1922. He identified 57 master players who finished first, second, or third in the competitions. Despite the common belief that chess favors the mature player, chess champions were most likely to be in their 30s. This basic conclusion has been extended in the elaborate investigations conducted by Arpad Elo. Elo first devised a sophisticated scheme for rating master players according to the quality and nature of the competition. He then applied this system to the careers of 30 masters born between 1830 and 1924. On this list were the names of such world chess champions as Wilhelm Steinitz, Emanuel Lasker, José Raoul Capablanca, Alexander Alekhine, Max Euwe, and Vassily Smyslov. When the performance ratings were plotted as a function of age, each chess master exhibited a curve not too different from that seen in Figure 7.1, but with a peak at about age 36.

Even so, the decline was often gradual. Competitive performance at age 63 was approximately equal to that at age 21. This helps explain the phenomenon of Emanuel Lasker, whom many consider the greatest all-time chess player. He became world champion in 1894 by defeating Steinitz, a title he held until he was defeated by Capablanca in 1921. Hence, not only was he champion for over a quarter of a century, but he was 53 years old when he lost this status. Even in his 60s, Lasker could win some classic games of chess.

Elo conducted a follow-up study that sampled more recent grand masters. The results generally fell in line with those just reported. However, one new finding concerned the remarkable career of Bobby Fischer, the world chess champion from 1972 to 1975, when he was between the ages of 29 and 32. According to Elo's rating system, Fischer was the strongest player in the history of chess. Moreover, his performance curve was still rising when he mysteriously forfeited his championship by default: His phobias and paranoia had herded him into seclusion in Los Angeles. So far his seclusion has only been interrupted by an unofficial "world championship" game held in war-torn Yugoslavia in 1992. Yet his career trajectory was aiming him toward the status of the greatest chess champion in the history of the game.

The Triumphant at Business

In comparison to either sports or chess, success as an entrepreneur seems a more accessible and convivial form of achievement. Many who would not dream of taking on the champions of chess or tennis still hope to get a big break in business some day. Moreover, many people, if given the choice between being rich or famous, would probably run with the money anyway. In addition, according to the trickle-down theory of economics, the wealthy make society and not just themselves more prosperous. Their enterprises create jobs for those who will always be employees rather than employers.

Given this reasoning, it is surprising that so little research has been done on the connection between age and business success. The only study I have come across is Lehman's own pioneer effort. In one analysis, Lehman examined the ages at which people attained enviable incomes. By consulting the records of the U.S. Treasury Department and *Who's Who in Commerce and Industry*, Lehman showed that the peaks came at about the same age as that for U.S. presidents, the late 50s. In another analysis Lehman studied those listed in *Who's Whos* and similar sources as the economic magnates of America; this time he found a somewhat later peak, somewhere in the 60s. This difference is not so much a discrepancy as a clue. People must first amass impressive wealth before they can receive recognition as giants of capitalism.

Indeed, the two peaks of income and influence do not tell the whole story. It takes years for investments to pay dividends. This is especially true for the biggest tycoons, who often invest in risky enterprises. As in politics and religion, taking exceptional risks is an obsession of youth. Thus, the roots of success are planted early. Andrew Carnegie's wealth was the result of financial decisions made in his 30s; a similar story can be told of John D. Rockefeller, Henry Ford, and many others. Hence, short of a winning lottery ticket, the average person should not expect a drastic improvement in his or her financial condition after the age of 40. Most of us possess our maximum disposable income by the time we reach middle age. That's when the investments we failed to make come back to haunt us with persistent if-I-only's!

Transformations and Transitions

Thus far, we have been counting achievements across the career as if all accomplishments were interchangeable. Yet, if we know anything at all about human development, it is that people change. Development does not suddenly cease in childhood or adolescence. Therefore, someone in the early years of a career is not the same person who draws that career to a close a few decades later. I am not speaking of minor transitions, either; the historic figure may have been radically transformed. Below I review two illustrations. The first involves shifts in life's themes. The second concerns luminaries' altered receptiveness to the illuminations of younger colleagues.

Life Themes

A young adult does not live the same life as someone who is middle-aged, and the latter's life contrasts sharply with that experienced in old age. These changes are manifest in the biographies of historic personalities. For example, one study looked at the lives of 10 great classical composers—Bach, Handel, Haydn, Mozart, Beethoven, Schubert, Chopin, Wagner, Brahms, and Debussy. Simultaneous with the course of their adulthoods were fluctuations in three other significant circumstances. First, composers got older; the stresses and strains of everyday living increased rapidly, attaining a peak in the 30s, and then declined. These woes entailed both family problems and professional difficulties. Second, the frequency and seriousness of various illnesses progressively increased, as their health deteriorated with age. Hence, the great composers did their work under ever-growing physical constraints. Third, the winning of honors, awards, and recognition displayed a peculiar pattern across the adult life span. Because most great composers were so precocious, they received much concrete praise in the early years of their careers. But the applause quickly died down as the composers entered a dry period. Happily, if the geniuses lived long enough, medals, prizes, and similar honors would once more come their way. Indeed, in the latter part of life this recognition exceeded anything they had experienced before. The public then honored them for what they had actually accomplished than for what their future might have promised. This underlines the tragedy of Mozart. After he had received so much praise as a child prodigy, his career entered the doldrums in terms of outside recognition. Dying in his mid-30s, he stood in the trough of fame. He had little contemporary appreciation to savor on his deathbed.

It's nice to know that even extraordinary individuals have their ups and downs. Yet these age trends are of restricted interest in comparison to the changes that take place in a creator's life work. What is important to a 30-year-old may seem trivial to the same person with twice that many birthdays, and vice versa. For example, the psychoanalyst Erik Erikson has argued that life consists of a series of crises. We resolve one dilemma only to find ourselves faced with another, more mature enigma. Thus, whereas an adolescent may be obsessed with establishing a self-identity, the young adult's preoccupation may be intimacy with others. With further maturity, the individual will dwell on what he or she will leave for the next generation, whether that progeny be biological or cultural. Finally, in old age, the person confronts death head on, and wavers between a sense of integrity and a profound despair. In the last years, he or she cannot help asking, "Did my life have any meaning?"

Erikson argues that these psychosocial crises represent universal patterns of the human life cycle. For instance, in one book he identified these issues in the life of Martin Luther. If so, then the themes addressed in the works of historic creators may reflect the progression in life's concerns. We do possess some tentative evidence that this is so. One study analyzed the topics treated by 81 classic plays—all the extant dramas of Aeschylus, Sophocles, Euripides, Aristophanes, and Shakespeare. Although the plays were thus separated by two millennia, a pattern still emerged. The younger dramatist discussed such practical matters as making prudent decisions in the world of human affairs, especially politics. The older dramatist tired of this world and thought more of the next. Doubts arose about the value of wealth, and the playwright contemplated the divine plan and the chance of mystical communion with that divine order.

A second study also examined plays, but this one concentrated solely on the 37 comedies, tragedies, and histories attributed to Shakespeare. Because the inquiry was so narrowly focused, it was possible to trace the thematic transformations in greater detail. These changes occurred between the *Henry VI* trilogy and *Henry VIII*—a period when Shakespeare was between 27 and 50 years of age. Over this interval, three types of trends emerged, regardless of the specific nature of the play he was writing:

1. Shakespeare simply lost interest in some topics as he matured. This was the case for the subject of competition in commerce and rivalry in politics. As he aged, his fascination with such practical affairs waned. This parallels what was found earlier for the four Greek playwrights as well.

2. Other themes began by attracting increased enthusiasm from Shakespeare's pen, only to fall by the wayside as he matured further. This curvilinear trend held for the Bard's treatment of romantic, chivalric, or courtly love. The same life transition was found for his discussion of the human being as an object of laughter or ridicule. The plays that he wrote in his early 30s—such as *The Taming of the Shrew, Romeo and Juliet*, and *A Midsummer Night's Dream*—illustrate these interests.

3. Shakespeare dared to approach still other themes only when he was yet older—in his late 30s and early 40s. This is the period of his great tragedies, such as *Hamlet, Othello, King Lear*, and *Macbeth*. He now fathomed the depths of conflict and struggle in human life. After this *Sturm und Drang* phase, Shakespeare moved away from such rugged material. *The Tempest* represents a dramatist with a more detached view of life and its crises.

These two studies of famous dramatists suggest that even great geniuses live lives. The works they leave behind reflect the stages through which they must pass. The themes they address undergo qualitative changes because their lives are changing in quality.

New Tricks

No one can stamp his or her mark on an unwilling audience. Therefore, one of the greatest obstacles that many innovators must face is the conservative nature of the human race. John Locke lamented that

> the imputation of Novelty is a terrible charge amongst those who judge of men's heads, as they do of their perukes, by the fashion, and can allow none to be right but the received doctrines. Truth scarce ever yet carried it by vote anywhere at its first appearance: new opinions are always suspected, and usually opposed, without any other reason but because they are not already common.

The history of science is especially notorious for the hardships tossed in the paths of those who venture to replace the old with the new. For example, Ignaz Semmelweis dared to suggest that deaths due to puerperal fever could be easily and dramatically reduced. All physicians had to do was wash their hands before dealing with patients. This was especially recommended after a doctor had just performed an autopsy on a victim of the disease. Despite ample clinical data to back up his claims, these suggestions were not welcomed by the medical establishment.

Jonathan Swift said, "When a true genius appears in the world you may know him by this sign, that the dunces are all in confederacy against him." If only it were so simple! For resistance to new ideas is by no means confined to the ignorant. Ironically, innovators themselves often become the central opponents of innovations. The difference is often one of age: The revolutionary of youth may mature into the stalwart defender of the establishment. As a consequence, advocates of novelty must expect a generation gap in the reception of their ideas. Charles Darwin recognized this fact when he anticipated the possible response to his theory of evolution by natural selection. In *The Origin of Species*, Darwin said that he did not "expect to convince experienced naturalists whose minds are stocked with a multitude of facts all viewed, during a long course of years, from a point of view directly opposite to mine." Instead, Darwin looked "with confidence to the future,—to the young and rising naturalists, who will be able to view both sides of the question with impartiality."

Almost a century later, Max Planck made a similar observation in his *Scientific Autobiography*. He had ample experience with trying to convince his conservative colleagues of the value of his quantum hypothesis. It took Planck two decades to persuade the scientific community that this was the right way to go. From this experience Planck concluded: "A new scientific truth does not triumph by convincing its opponents and making them see the light, but rather because its opponents eventually die, and a new generation grows up that is familiar with it." This proposition is styled "Planck's principle," and abundant anecdotes document its validity. Time after time, a younger scientist finds his or her great ideas attacked by an older scientist of considerable renown. Pasteur's biological theory of fermentation was strongly criticized by Liebig, 20 years his elder. Lord Rayleigh was 16 years older than Planck, and found the latter's quantum theory unacceptable.

This anecdotal evidence is backed up by some rigorous inquiries. One investigation studied who accepted and who rejected Darwin's theory of evolution. As Darwin suspected, the ages of naturalists did indeed affect their willingness to join the ranks of the evolutionists. Those fighting rear-guard actions against scientific progress were often those who had been in the avant-garde as youths. As an example, Adam Sedgwick's pioneer work in paleontology inspired Darwin to pursue his own interests in natural history. Yet when Darwin offered his evolutionary theory to the world, Sedgwick, Darwin's senior by 24 years, emerged as one of the theory's staunchest opponents. Hence, Planck's principle captures an important trend. But why?

As Darwin's quote hinted, it may be that age, strictly speaking, is not the key factor. Instead, other variables are the direct culprits, but these variables tend to go along with getting older. According to one sociologist,

> As a scientist gets older he is more likely to be restricted to innovation by his substantive and methodological preconceptions and by his other cultural accumulations; he is more likely to have high professional standing, to have specialized interests, to be a member or official of an established organization, and to be associated with a "school."

For example, one researcher looked at the response of geoscientists to the theory of continental drift. The scientist's age was not the direct determinant; rather, the opponents were those who had the most to lose by the adoption of the new theory. The resisters were well published in mainstream journals, and thus had their reputations on the line. The influence of age was thus indirect: Older scientists had longer bibliographies committed to the established paradigm.

Furthermore, we must not overlook the intellectual changes that happen to persons who have devoted decades to pursuing a particular line of thought. Sigmund Freud was 73 years old when he published *Civilization and Its Discontents*. Thus entering the final phase of his life and career, he admitted, "The conceptions I have summarized here I first put forward only tentatively, but in the course of time they have won such a hold over me that I can no longer think in any other way." In a similar fashion, Einstein had spent so much of his life contemplating a deterministic universe that he found it impossible to accept the probabilistic world of quantum physics. "God does not play dice" was his self-defense. Even though Einstein's work on the photoelectric effect had helped accelerate this movement, he became more and more isolated from his fellow physicists. By the end of his career, Einstein proposed a unified theory that colleagues considered preposterous.

Although Planck's principle was originally limited to scientific change, its applicability is broader. For instance, one study showed that the rule applies to scholarly endeavors besides science. An economic historian's age affected the probability of accepting cliometrics, the newfangled idea that econometrics might be applied to history. In 1978, a 35-year-old economic historian was almost three times more likely to practice cliometrics than a colleague 30 years older. Older historians wanted to retain the humanistic flavor of their discipline, while younger historians sought to convert it into a social science. Furthermore, the principle probably extends to domains beyond the academy of scholars; Supreme Court justices may become ever more conservative with age, for example. This age effect was especially conspicuous on the international scene in the early 1990s, when the Communist movement crumbled all around the globe. The holdouts were those powers ruled by revolutionaries who had first brought or helped to bring that discredited ideology to their nations: Fidel Castro in Cuba, Kim Il Sung of Korea, and Deng Xiaoping of China. Like the characters in George Orwell's *Animal Farm*, these revolutionaries defended the status quo against the forces of political change.

Moreover, while Planck's principle concerns the acceptance of new ideas, it may also offer insights into the creation of novelties. As historic personalities age, the channels of their creativity narrow. With time, the point is reached where the diversity of intellectual options constricts to a single path. Robert Benchley put this career fixation humorously: "It took me fifteen years to discover I had no talent for writing, but I couldn't give it up because by that time I was too famous." The outcome is not always so funny. Many once-great intellects discover themselves imitating their past achievements. Once that happens, their talent is dead. "People seldom improve," Oliver Goldsmith said, "when they have no model but themselves to copy."

Pablo Picasso may illustrate this pathetic progression. Once he was a dynamic artist at the forefront of change. Yet in the latter part of his life, the leading edge of art passed him by, leaving him trapped in self-imitation. There is a story that a dealer once asked him to authenticate a painting before a cautious customer. Picasso said that the piece was a forgery. When the dealer complained that the master had claimed earlier that the work was his own, Picasso responded honestly: "I often paint fakes."

The Closing Chapter: Achievement Late in Life

Discussion of Picasso's creative stagnation gives rise to a bigger question: At what age does outstanding achievement end? To respond, let's first review what we know about late-life potential. From there we will turn to a most amazing event, the swan-song phenomenon.

Winter Roses: Late-Life Potential

The Raw Facts

To appraise the prospects for achievement in the latter part of life, we must first examine what psychologists have learned from over a century of research on the topic. Four points are especially crucial:

1. Because the age curves differ terribly according to the domain of achievement, global statements about when a person is "over the hill" are simply meaningless. Leaders attain career peaks at higher ages than do creators, and variations exist within leadership and creativity activities as well. Thus, revolutionaries are younger than diplomats, poets younger than novelists. In some domains, in fact, the postpeak descent of the age curve is so minuscule that we can hardly speak of a decline at all. Status quo politicians and leaders of established faiths may stay capable until their final days, just as historians and philosophers may save their best works for last. One case is Talleyrand, the master French diplomat and politician. He entered public service under Louis XVI, and kept his head (and usually his influence) during the French Revolution, the Napoleonic era, and the restoration of the Bourbons. He played an instrumental role in the July Revolution, and then retired from politics at age 80! Another case is the Welsh thinker Bertrand Russell, who lived to be 98. During most of those years he was producing abstract and practical philosophy, continuing his output well into his 80s and 90s. Only in those areas where career trajectories are more meteoric will individuals have to fear the coming of old age. Even this worry is ameliorated by the next three facts.

2. If all other factors are held constant, an individual's career trajectory depends on when that career commenced. Those who get a late start will see their landmarks delayed in equal measure. As seen in Figure 7.4, those who began at age 30 rather than 20—but who are otherwise equal in creative potential—will generate their first, best, and last contributions a full decade later. Only those who get an exceptionally early start should feel anxiety over an early forced retirement. Yet even here a person can circumvent fate: Taking up a different career can rejuvenate creativity. Because the age curve depends on career age rather than calendar age, this switch resets the clock. Productivity gets a new lease on life.

A master of career changes was Benjamin Franklin—printer, writer, inventor, scientist, revolutionary, and diplomat. He changed his occupation so many times that he never had the leisure to lament being past his prime. Indeed, by having his activities overlap, he developed several careers at once! In his late 70s he was still inventing, devising bifocals to accommodate the failing eyesight of his 78th year. Just two years before his death at 84, he even affected the course of the Constitutional Convention.

3. The equal-odds rule casts a more favorable light on the last years of genius. As long as the individual continues to produce, the odds of getting a hit remain unchanged, on the average. Because the quality ratio of hits to total attempts does not decline with age, it may not even be meaningful to speak of an age decrement. Even if the rate of producing outstanding works declines, the rate of turning out mediocre works declines, too. Octogenarians may be offering fewer masterworks, but they are also filling up the world with less rubbish. Another way of expressing this point is to inspect the career product by product rather than year by year. On this basis, the likelihood that an octogenarian's product will become successful is no less than the likelihood for something produced during the creative prime.

4. Finally, we must throw into the prediction hopper the ever-present impact of individual differences. This variation is most easily discerned in historic creativity. Previously, I have introduced the notion of creative potential. Inspecting Figure 7.4 once more, we can see that differences in this potential have large implications for the career course. Given creators whose careers started simultaneously, those highest in creative potential will produce their first hits the soonest, and reach higher rates of output for both quantity and quality. More significantly, those highest in creative potential will prove more prolific in the latter part of life—and accordingly will produce their last masterpiece at an older age.

Individual differences are actually so large that they swamp the impact of age. A first-rate genius at 80 is worth more than a second-rate talent at half that age. Italian opera provides illustrations. At the low end of creative potential is Pietro Mascagni. At age 27 he produced his first, best, and last contribution to the repertoire, the brilliant *Cavalleria Rusticana*. Although he wrote other operas, this composition is the only one to exist beyond the realm of recital and concert excerpts. As he put it, "It is a pity I wrote *Cavalleria* first, for I was crowned before I became king." Contrast this with Giuseppe Verdi. His career began at about the same age as Mascagni's. But unlike Mascagni, Verdi did not sit still; he constantly developed himself as a musician and as a dramatist. As a result, he produced a series of masterpieces—from his first landmark, *Nabucco*, to his last landmark, *Falstaff*. The latter came 51 years after the first, and was written by a composer 80 years old. In between, he wrote several works that vie for the status of his single best opera—*Rigoletto*, *Il Trovatore*, *La Traviata*, *Aïda*, and *Otello*. And all are mainstays of the opera theater. Clearly, Verdi's creative potential was far higher than Mascagni's. Accordingly, he was crowned many times after becoming king.

These are the key facts. How do we interpret these findings?

The Range of Theories

Researchers have been trying to explain the postpeak declines for over a century. These accounts usually focus on creativity rather than leadership, though occasionally a theory may apply to both. In any case, four explanations may be the most worth reporting:

1. Lehman himself listed over a dozen possible factors. Perhaps the most important is the deterioration of energy and health with age. No doubt this happens, especially for athletes. Yet this extrinsic influence falls far short of a complete explanation. If physical well-being is so critical, why isn't the peak for creative output at about 30 rather than 40? Also, how can we account for contrasts across domains of achievement? Writing an epic novel probably takes more physical endurance than composing a lyric poem, so why aren't novels written by 30-year-olds and poems by 40-year-olds?

More importantly, although increasing physical handicaps can certainly impair the rate of output, it cannot explain why some persist despite overwhelming odds. Bach, Handel, and Delius went blind, and Beethoven and Smetana even became deaf, but all five still composed. The painter Renoir, crippled by arthritis in his later years, dictated instructions to an assistant. Another painter, Matisse, was eventually confined to a wheelchair, and so drew with a crayon attached to a long bamboo pole. Even more dramatic is the case of Franz Rosenzweig, the Jewish theologian. Suffering from progressive paralysis, he continued to work by devising a code by which he could communicate with eye movements alone. Similarly, the English theoretical physicist Stephen Hawking has persisted despite a disabling neuromotor disease. Admittedly, Rosenzweig was not an old man when his career raced against oblivion, nor is Hawking elderly. Even so, they demonstrate to all what can be accomplished by elders under often less stringent constraints. We should all contemplate these exemplars of endurance before making excuses about the infirmities of age.

2. Perhaps the decline is more mental than physical. "When the age is in, the wit is out," said Shakespeare. This implies a loss of intellectual capacity. Although there is much research on how performance on intelligence tests changes with age, it has yet to show that this explains the age decrements. For one thing, for those adults who stay intellectually active, the decrements are often small in comparison to the declines in achievement. Except when organic disorders strike, such as Alzheimer's disease, we are not talking about a metamorphosis of a genius into a moron. The same argument holds for declines in performance on creativity tests. Besides, the connection between test scores and success is not strong anyway (as we will see in Chapter 8). So wit may be more dim in old age, but it is not out. An awed observer once said of one aged playwright: "At 83 Shaw's mind was perhaps not quite as good as it used to be. It was still better than anyone else's."

3. If we cannot blame the brain, then how about ascribing the decline to motivation? Lord Byron grumbled, "years steal/Fire from the mind as vigour from the limb;/ And Life's enchanted cup but sparkles near the brim." The older individual may have lost enthusiasm for undertaking big enterprises. Alone, this explanation cannot take us very far. Before we can explain why the drive dissipates, we must ask where the motivation comes from in the first place. The most frequent answer is that historic figures are driven by a lust for fame and fortune. Once that desire is satisfied, the genius can settle into a cozy complacency. In a toned-down version, this is often the position advocated by sociologists, economists, and political scientists. In Chapter 3, for example, I have mentioned economic theories that interpret creativity as human capital. A person works hard to produce a handsome income. Thus, productivity tapers off in the latter part of life because the rewards become increasingly outweighed by the costs. Because senior citizens are less and less sure that they will reap the grain from the seeds now sown, they gradually cease to cultivate their creative gardens. Toward the very end, they can rest entirely on their laurels cut from past plantings.

Plausible though this seems, difficulties appear as well. This model cannot explain the behavior of the proverbial "starving artist in the attic." Why would a Paul Cézanne persist despite the absence of monetary rewards and universal renown? Moreover, let us contemplate some additional anomalies. Why would

Emily Dickinson write poetry without any desire to publish a single line? Why would Goethe wrap up and seal the second part of *Faust* for posthumous publication? Why would Cavendish carry out experiments in his private lab without any wish to announce his original findings to the world? Why did the mathematician Galois, facing death in a duel the next morning, stay up all night writing out his startling discoveries in higher algebra? Certainly, he would have been better off getting a good night's sleep! And apropos of death, just think of all the martyrs and heroes who performed fabulous feats of self-sacrifice—names like Socrates, Jesus, and Joan of Arc. None of their activities make sense if people are calculating utility functions to optimize their material benefits while minimizing their expenditures.

4. My own favorite explanation is that the career unfolds by the internal dictates of the very process by which people achieve. Exceptional accomplishments are contingent upon an individual's engagement in self-actualization or self-organization. This theory fits creative genius best. Each individual begins with an initial creative potential. This potential is actualized through the two-fold process of "ideation" and "elaboration." Ideation produces new ideas for creative projects, while elaboration converts these works-in-progress into actual contributions. Because the rates of ideation and elaboration depend on the materials manipulated by the creator, this theory handles contrasts across disciplines in career trajectories. For example, the ideation and elaboration rates are very fast for poetry and mathematics, very slow for history and geology. At the same time, by allowing for individual variation in creative potential and age at career onset, the theory can accommodate differences among creators working within the same discipline. This accommodation is evident in Figure 7.4, which was generated by this theoretical model, as was Figure 7.1. The equations that produced these contain only four parameters: the ideation rate (a), the elaboration rate (b), the initial creative potential (m), and the age at career onset (i.e., age when career age $t = 0$).

This final theory has the advantage that it makes extremely precise predictions—predictions that have withstood empirical tests. More important, the theory outlines a distinctive set of conditions under which late-life creativity should be strong. First, the higher the initial level of creative potential, the more creativity can be expected in the closing years of a career. Second, if we hold creative potential constant, we can expect that those who get a late start will have a late end as well. These two conditions are graphically portrayed in Figure 7.4. Third, if we hold creative potential and age at career onset constant, late-life creativity will be higher in those disciplines with slower ideation and elaboration rates. Hence arises the late creativity of historians and philosophers. Fourth and last, nothing except time and commitment prevents creators from resuscitating their creative potential. This requires that individuals constantly expose themselves to new and diverse ideas in their field. For instance, scientists who stay widely read throughout their careers are more likely to be productive late in life.

For an illustration, we might contrast Igor Stravinsky against Pablo Picasso.

Unlike the artist, the composer remained open to new ideas. Shortly after completing his opera *The Rake's Progress* in his neoclassic style, Stravinsky even took up the 12-tone technique of Arnold Schoenberg. This stylistic change astonished his admirers, not the least because Stravinsky and Schoenberg never got along when they were near neighbors in Los Angeles. Besides, Stravinsky was then entering his 70s. Yet one year after Schoenberg's death, Stravinsky became receptive to the serial technique of his rival. By rejuvenating his creativity, he could compose *Threni* in his 73rd year. His last masterpiece in this new style, *Requiem Canticles*, appeared in his 84th year. Stravinsky's creative potential had gotten a booster shot.

We should not consider the four explanations just outlined as mutually exclusive. Because creativity in the closing years is probably a complex function of many factors, no one theory can monopolize the phenomenon. The need for theoretical pluralism becomes especially obvious when we see what happens when geniuses have premonitions that they are about to die.

Swan Songs

Once we make adjustments for discipline, creative potential, and age at career onset, Figure 7.1 gives the most probable career trajectory for the "typical creative genius." Even so, we have overlooked one critical factor in the curve's construction: We have not considered the creator's proximity to death. For all appearances, productivity continues blithely on, albeit at an ever-slackening pace. Surely, we might expect some abrupt change as a historic personality faces the prospect of life's termination. So what does happen when an important figure nears the end of a life and a career?

One reaction may be a headlong drop in integrative complexity. In Chapter 3 I have discussed how we can tease out how effectively an individual processes information by applying content analysis to letters and documents. "Integrative complexity" as defined earlier, is a measure of a person's capacity to differentiate the intricacies of reality while at the same time integrating these complexities into a unified perspective. Peter Suedfeld carried out or supervised three studies showing how this gauge of intellectual functioning may shift when the Grim Reaper peers over the horizon. The first inquiry analyzed the correspondence of five British novelists—namely, Charles Dickens, George Eliot, George Meredith, Arnold Bennett, and Virginia Woolf. The complexity contained in their letters declined significantly in the last five years of their lives. The second looked at 85 addresses delivered by presidents of the American Psychological Association. Those distinguished psychologists who had the fewest years left to live scored the lowest on integrative complexity.

The final study again looked at correspondence, but this time the historic figures were more heterogeneous. Both creators and leaders were examined, such as Louis Brandeis, Lewis Carroll, Ruth Draper, Gustave Flaubert,

Sigmund Freud, Franz Kafka, Franz Liszt, Napoleon I, Marcel Proust, Mary Wollstonecraft Shelley, and Queen Victoria. One refinement was whether the person died suddenly, as by an accidental death, or only after a protracted illness that warned of death's coming well in advance. This distinction was critical. Those who saw the end coming showed a gradual drop in integrative complexity. The others, for whom the end came in a single pounce, maintained high levels of integrative complexity almost to the very end. Only in the last year was the drop conspicuous.

Judging from these findings, can we really entertain high expectations about the final years? Should any aged creator flirting with death be written off as an active force in history? On the contrary! Consider three points:

1. A peculiar twist often appears in the career trajectory of the creative genius. Contrary to the downhill slide depicted in Figure 7.1, the output of products toward the end of life fails to creep inexorably toward nothingness. Within the last few years, a sudden burst of creative vitality can emerge. I am not speaking here of the middle-aged either, but of octogenarians! It is like an ember on the coals of a dying fire unexpectedly exploding into flame, for a final flash of brilliance. To be sure, this upturn gets nowhere close to the acme of the career, nor is the burst any more than transient. Yet that it occurs at all must astonish us.

2. Art critics frequently comment on the late-life style of artistic geniuses. Rudolf Arnheim gave the example of *Christ Crowned with Thorns*, which Titian painted when he was nearing 90. When this painting is compared with another canvas on the same subject conceived in Titian's younger days, profound changes can be seen. In many late-life styles we can sense the artist expressing deeper thoughts and feelings with more economy of means. The basic principle seems to be "less is more." A similar phenomenon is reported by music critics as well. In Alfred Einstein's *Essays on Music*, a whole chapter treats the "Opus Ultimum." These last works need not be inferior to what composers offer under more auspicious life circumstances. They are qualitatively different, however, and frequently in an inspiring manner.

3. Some empirical data back up the critics' impressions. One inquiry examined 1,919 works by 172 classical composers. Those works that appeared toward the end of life differed on two objective attributes: (a) Their playing times were shorter, and (b) the melodic originality of their themes was lower. The latter characteristic was gauged by a computer analysis of melodic structure (see Chapter 4). Now we might conclude that these two traits of last works divulge a composer's failing creative powers. Yet that conclusion will not hold up. The same compositions also enjoy higher popularity in the classical repertoire, and they are even rated by musicologists as more profound. Thus, composers toward the end of life create compositions that say more with less. What is striking about these pieces is that the composer's age is irrelevant. These last-works effects can be seen in a Schubert or Mozart composition, despite the fact that neither man lived past his early 30s. The critical determinant is how much longer the composer has left to live. Hence, we can say that these events reflect a true "swan-song phenomenon."

Why the startling production of concise but sublimely effective masterpieces? I believe that this phenomenon gives us insight into what really drives exceptional achievement. Creative individuals are people driven by a sense of destiny. Their lives are rich in goals, plans, and aspirations. Their careers are characterized by what Howard Gruber has called a "network of enterprises." They have many projects going at once, all dedicated to working out the intellectual or aesthetic implications of a unique vision. The process could go on forever, except for the inevitability of death. Some moment in their lives makes them aware that the end draws nigh. Perhaps it is an obvious loss in vigor, or a pessimistic prognosis from a physician. Whatever the source, creators, like everybody else, begin to engage in a "life review." They look over their past, contemplate where they wished to aim their lives, and examine how far away they are from achieving their goals. They realize that among the current works-in-progress is some piece that will have to do as a last artistic testament. This final creation must wrap up all the loose ends of an all-too-brief existence. The last work must encapsulate the intent of an entire career. Time is running out, so they sing their swan song.

Certain conditions are imposed on the occurrence of this phenomenon. Undoubtedly, we cannot expect this to happen unless death is foreseen. Hence, Ernest Chausson, who rammed his head into a wall after losing control of his bicycle, would not be expected to display such a stylistic switch. Also, sometimes "false alarms" can occur when creators incorrectly infer that the end is at hand. Haydn's "Funeral" Symphony (No. 44) may exemplify this occasion. It was written after he had contracted a dangerous fever. He had even requested that the symphony's slow movement be played at his own funeral. But he lived 39 years more! In contrast, Schubert, who was succumbing to the advanced stages of syphilis, could produce true swan songs, including the songs collected posthumously to form the cycle entitled *Schwanengesang*. Similarly, Tchaikovsky, pondering the need to take his own life, could compose a suicide note in sound, the Sixth (*Pathétique*) Symphony. Other swan songs include the *Four Serious Songs* of the 63-year-old Brahms or the *Four Last Songs* of the 85-year-old Richard Strauss. Perhaps the most notable swan song, however, came from a composer still tragically young. Many of you may have seen Peter Shaffer's play *Amadeus* or the movie based on the play. As Mozart lovers know, the death scene depicted there was unhistorical. Ironically, however, historical truth here probably surpasses cinematic fiction.

Mozart, in the last six months of his life, may have had premonitions. These forebodings may have been intensified by an odd event that occurred in the summer of 1791. A mysterious stranger knocked on his door and commissioned the *Requiem* for an anonymous patron. Mozart was working on many other compositions at the time, but as his health began to fail, this explicit mass for the dead began to consume bigger hunks of his time. He began to suspect that the *Requiem* was to be his own. As far as scholars can determine, he only finished the first 12 of the 15 sections before succumbing. One of those sections he did live to complete was the chorus "Lacrymosa." This is a setting of the Latin text describing the tears shed as one prepares to leave this life and face God's judgment. To set these poignant words, Mozart conjured up a "melody almost too limpid for choral singing." On the afternoon of December 4, 1791, the day before Mozart passed away, he gathered some friends to sing through the *Requiem*, he himself taking the alto part. When the chorus reached the opening lines of the "Lacrymosa," he could not help breaking down, and laid the score aside to weep. A few hours later paralysis set in, and less than an hour after the midnight of the next day, Mozart was dead. Like the fabled swan, he had actually sung his last song.

In discussing swan songs, I have presumed that individuals try to culminate their life's work in a concentrated last statement. Yet something contrary seems feasible, too. During the life review that preoccupies persons writing their final chapters, they may come to realize that they have overlooked some talent or potential in that onrush to maturity. This realization may motivate a "last-chance syndrome." For instance, people in their golden years will often take up new hobbies, and find themselves performing quite well at creative activities. An example comes from recent times. At age 68, Elizabeth Layton had to figure out some way of combating thoughts of suicide, so she took up artistic expression. In doing so, she discovered a previously undeveloped talent. This discovery propelled her on an enterprise of special creativity at an age when most persons would have retired.

More rarely, the disabilities endured as one ages may be exploited as actual resources. A striking example is provided by the life and career of Michel Chevreul. He spent most of his life as a distinguished French chemist, making important discoveries about fatty acids. Then he decided to take up a new subject at an age when most people would be long dead. In his 90s, Chevreul became a pioneer gerontologist, with a specific interest in the psychology of aging! What he found out did not suffice to discourage him from his creative activities. Chevreul continued his productivity for the next decade. His last scientific paper appeared one year before his death at age 103.

Lives like these suggest that we can take our leave of life with a bang, not a whimper.

Death: The Sequel

Herodotus recounts the story of Croesus, king of Lydia. A ruler of fabled power and wealth, Croesus asked Solon, the wise Athenian lawgiver, whether Croesus was the happiest member of the human race. Solon warned him that people cannot be counted happy until their lives have ended happily. At best, the rich and famous are merely fortunate, for fortune always teeter-totters at the brink of historical caprice. Sure enough, Solon's warning proved prophetic. Croesus took on the Median Empire and lost all his wealth and power. Yet, ironically, by falling like Icarus or Phaethon from the empyrean heights to the plutonic depths, Croesus may have inadvertently insured himself more lasting fame. He became an immortal lesson of history.

This story tells us that the last act of a historic career is an agent's death. How one chooses to die is the final landmark, capping career and life in one instant. Just as we can count no persons happy until their deaths, we can gauge their fame only after that concluding moment is sealed. Indeed, often historic personalities fail to become bigger than life until after their deaths. Alive, Jesus of Nazareth was a provincial religious reformer of minor interest to Jews or Gentiles. After his crucifixion, he could grow into the Christ, and thereby expand into divine proportions. "Life levels all men: death reveals the eminent," said Shaw. Accordingly, we should learn much about important people by inspecting the impact of this last act.

A good place to begin is life span. How long an individual lives does more than convey the opportunities for affecting history. Duration on this planet may disclose secrets about the nature of a person's gift. To see how, let's start with the baseline. In Solon's speech to Croesus, he claimed that the allotted life span of the human was 70 years. Solon was not too far off the mark: The average life expectancy for famous personalities is about 65, give or take about 5 years. This figure may surprise those who think that humans in earlier periods of history lived short lives. Yet the belief is incorrect. The exceptional increase in the life span concerns an individual at birth. Owing to the decline in infant and child mortality, this general life expectancy has indeed grown phenomenally. In contrast, given a sample of people who survived to adulthood, the expected life span in civilized societies has always been in the 60s, not the 30s or 40s. Because most historic figures had to reach maturity to make names for themselves, their life expectancies have changed little over several centuries.

Given this stability, we can then inquire about discrepancies. Let's take a look at Cox's 301 creators and leaders. Their mean life span was 66 years; yet, for specific domains of achievement, the expectancies could be higher or lower. Thus for famous politicians, the life span was near Solon's figure, 70 years. Fully 30% lived to become octogenarians, while only 5% lived less than half a century. For creators, philosophers were the longest-lived, with a mean of 68 years, 14% reaching their 80s. Those entering other endeavors were less fortunate. Among the classical composers in her sample, the mean was about 62; not one reached 80, and nearly one-third died before their 50th birthday. Among the leaders, soldiers and revolutionaries came out short. Revolutionaries, especially, averaged about 51 years of age on their day of death, a mean about 11 years younger than that for famous commanders. More than two-fifths of the revolutionaries died before age 50, and not one lived to 80.

Clearly, being a revolutionary is hazardous to one's health. It's not hard to see why. Think about some of the key players in the French Revolution: Marat was stabbed to death in his bath at age 50; Robespierre was guillotined at age 36, and Danton at age 35. Nor does it take knife or blade to truncate the revolutionary's span of years. Mirabeau died at age 42 from natural causes, but his illness was probably aggravated by the precarious position he occupied as president of the National Assembly. Not long after he passed away, heads really began to roll in the squares of Paris.

Actually, we do not have to explain contrasts in life expectancies in terms of untoward events, such as assassinations, executions, or inordinate stress. Differences across domains may reflect systematic variation in typical career trajectories. For instance, as seen earlier, revolutionaries rise to power at younger ages than do diplomats and elected politicians. This precocity enables them to die younger and still leave their marks. The same principle applies to literary figures. Across the history of world literature, poets tend to live less long than prose authors. In English literature, for example, Dylan Thomas died at 39, Lord Byron at 36, Shelley at 30, Keats at 26, and Chatterton at 18. It is difficult to conjure up an equally notable novelist who died so young. The Russian novelist Lermontov, who lived only 27 years, is one of the rare exceptions. Yet the career peaks for poets come at more youthful ages than those for novelists; hence, poets can die prematurely and still leave something to posterity. It is for this reason, too, that classical composers and mathematicians live shorter lives than their brethren in the arts and sciences. In general, the more precocious the genius, the more an early death is permitted. Still, we cannot logically conclude from this that precocity causes early death.

Life span may unveil more matters than just area of accomplishment. Let's return to Cox's 301 creators and leaders. If we plot their posthumous reputations as a function of their age at death, we get the two curves shown in Figure 7.5. For the creators who wish to attain the greatest fame, dying at a middling age like 60 is ill advised. Their best options are either to die at a tragically young age or else hang in there until they become living monuments to their own past. In the former case, posterity can lament all the promise that was pitifully unrealized. In the latter case, younger contemporaries can make pilgrimages to the great matriarch or patriarch of the national culture. In the first case, we have a Mozart; in the second, a Goethe.

For leaders, the pattern differs: Little advantage accrues to those living to ripe old ages. Such figures have probably outlived their usefulness in world diplomacy, war, or politics. On the other hand, the asset of an early death is far more pronounced. Such personalities are often martyrs to a great cause. This can be an easy path to immortality for those lacking any other talents. "Martyrdom is the only way in which a man can become famous without ability," said Shaw.

Two further comments about Figure 7.5 are in order:

1. Although this represents only one study of the link between fame and life span, other data support the central conclusions. In Chapter 3 I have noted how politicians who die violently receive more of posterity's praise—indeed,

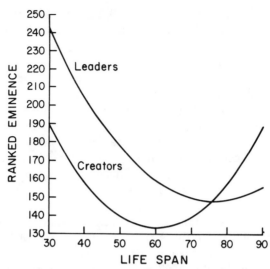

FIGURE 7.5. Ranked eminence as function of life span for 301 creators and leaders.

apotheosis. In addition, compatible results may be found in the daily newspaper. Empirical studies show that the amount of space granted a deceased celebrity in the obituary columns of *The New York Times* can be a curvilinear, U-shaped function of death age. The fewest lines of print are reserved for those who die at mediocre ages, as opposed to those who are tragically young or impressively old. Hence, we probably should take these curves seriously.

2. We probably should not take these curves *too* seriously. I would not recommend extrapolating the left-hand side of the two curves. These two functions are calculated for individuals who lived long enough to contribute a significant body of accomplishments. If we extrapolate back to even younger ages, it is extremely doubtful that a candidate will have a resumé long enough to be in the running. Chatterton committed suicide at 18, Galois died in a duel at 21, and Pergolesi succumbed to tuberculosis at 26. All three probably would have achieved greater fame had they lasted more years. Indeed, of these three, only Chatterton was sufficiently illustrious to join Cox's elite 301. But those who are still teenagers should not try what he did to take the shortcut to fame; they might not be so lucky. Even among recent ill-fated celebrities, James Dean and Freddie Prinze died at 24, Janis Joplin at 27, Jim Morrison and Jimi Hendrix at 28, and Rudolph Valentino at 31. Perhaps only one notable boasted a teenage death: Ritchie Valens died in a plane crash when he was 17.

Therefore, we must choose our life spans carefully. In fact, it may behoove us to do more than weigh out the correct amount of years. It may be advisable to plan the moment of death with an eye glancing toward posterity. How convenient for Mozart to be composing his *Requiem* on his deathbed! How dramatic for Beethoven to die as lightning and thunder rolled over Vienna, so he could raise his clenched fist one last time against the Fates! How smart for Copernicus to see the first copy of his heretical magnum opus on the day he died! I am not being facetious here, for sometimes historic personalities time their deaths with commendable precision.

Both John Adams and Thomas Jefferson had accomplishments to their credit before July 4, 1776. Still, their acceleration to national stature dates largely from that epochal moment. Even though Jefferson drafted the Declaration of Independence, Adams also served on the panel charged by the Continental Congress with drawing up that document. Both Adams and Jefferson signed the document on that first Independence Day—the only two presidents to have done so. Hence, as the 50th anniversary of the Declaration approached, both men received invitations to participate in the grand celebrations. Sadly, both were also too ill to accept. Jefferson, in fact, had already written the inscription for his tombstone, listing authorship of the Declaration of Independence as the foremost of his achievements. Lapsing into unconsciousness in early July, he awoke to ask his physician, "Is it the Fourth?" After being told, "It soon will be," Jefferson again lost consciousness; he died the next day, on July 4. Amazingly, John Adams died the very same day. Can there be any doubt that these two men chose their deaths to culminate their lives? For both Adams and Jefferson, their final breath was their swan song.

THE IMPORTANCE OF INTELLIGENCE

sychometrics is the science of psychological measurement. Psychometricians occupy themselves with devising accurate measures of individual
characteristics. The measures can assess judgments, values, attitudes,
motives, personality traits, and cognitive skills. The Thematic Apperception Test
so central to Chapter 5 counts as a psychometric instrument. In this chapter,
however, I discuss a rather different sort of test: the devices by which we assign
IQ scores to people. Indeed, in many respects, IQ tests are the most famous
and prototypical measures in the inventory of psychometrics. By the same token,
these instruments may be the most notorious of all psychometric techniques.

Here I focus on whether individual differences in intelligence predict the
attainment of greatness. I first look at the origins and nature of this concept in
the behavioral sciences, and then discuss whether psychometric IQ has any
utility for understanding achievement. From there I examine how we can rate
the intelligence of historic figures, and the relation between their rated intelligence and their performance. I then turn to some complications in using intelligence as an explanatory factor. The chapter ends with a discussion of those
individuals whose prodigious intellectual powers do not always translate into
historic acts—child prodigies, both famous and obscure.

Testing IQs in Contemporary Figures

In 1869, in *Hereditary Genius*, Francis Galton pioneered the psychological study
of historic creators, leaders, and celebrities. In 1874, in *English Men of Science*, Galton spearheaded the development of questionnaire methods—an
integral part of general survey techniques. And in 1883, in *Inquiries into Human
Faculty and Its Development*, Galton continued to position himself at the forefront of research. Among other novelties he introduced in this book was the
first systematic use of "anthropometric" instruments.

As pointed out in Chapters 2 and 5, Galton saw variation in natural ability
as the underlying cause of achieved eminence. So Galton tried to prove that
the famous came from family pedigrees marked by exceptional natural ability.

Yet, because natural ability was inferred rather than measured, Galton's demonstration was only indirect. By using anthropometric instruments, he hoped to gauge natural ability—even genius—more directly. After devising the first extensive test battery, he eventually administered the tests to more than 9,000 subjects. As a sign of Galton's own natural ability, he even managed to convince his testees to pay for the privilege of getting tested. He set up an exhibit at the International Health Exhibition, and charged three pence to the curious! Galton gauged the human faculties by such criteria as visual acuity, reaction time, and even strength of grip. Silly though these measures may now seem, they did have some theoretical justification. The British Empiricist school believed that the mind is a *tabula rasa* at birth. Therefore, the quality of an individual's intellect was thought to depend on the accuracy of the information it receives from the senses. Reaction time seems to fit common-sense notions about being "quick-witted," as well as more current ideas of information-processing speed. Even strength of grip may reflect a person's vigor and determination. Moreover, Galton's instruments were acceptably reliable for the time. For each person examined, he could provide precise scores that could be nearly duplicated on later testings. In modern psychometric terms, Galton's measures enjoyed reasonably good "reliability." The instruments were fairly free of gross errors.

Nevertheless, any psychometrician will explain that reliability is not enough; a psychological test must feature "validity" besides. A valid measure is one that actually measures what it purports to measure. On this criterion, Galton's anthropometric instruments failed miserably. This inadequacy was proven by one of his students, the American James McKeen Cattell. Cattell took Galton's tests to Columbia University, using them to assess the undergraduate population. If the tests really did size people up on natural ability, then we might expect them to predict scholastic performance. They didn't. In fact, scores on Galton's battery did not predict much beyond the immediate sphere of each test. Visual acuity predicted visual acuity, reaction time predicted reaction time, and so forth. One of the few contributions to survive from this era is the dog whistle, which Galton invented to assess a person's hearing. The only other contribution is the term "mental tests," which Cattell introduced in 1890 as a less tongue-twisting alternative to "anthropometric instruments." Aside from this, the Galton–Cattell tradition died.

The Origins of True Intelligence Tests

Meanwhile, a different series of events led to more valid indicators of Galton's elusive notion of natural ability. In 1904, the French government wished to improve the instruction of children whose educational development was retarded. In response, Alfred Binet worked with Théodore Simon to construct an intelligence test, which came out in 1905. The original purpose was to create a reliable and valid means to identify those children whose progress was slower than normal. Eventually, however, the goals expanded until the test became a more general gauge of childhood intelligence. The test could provide a single score that summarized a child's "mental age" (MA) in years and months. For children progressing normally through the school system, this score would match their chronological age (CA). On the other hand, the MA of retarded children would fall below their CA, while that of advanced children would reach higher. Because the Binet–Simon test assessed complex mental functions and cultural knowledge, unlike the Galton–Cattell measures, it enjoyed superior validity. Modern intelligence tests are descendants of this test.

One drawback of the Binet–Simon test was that it did not permit easy comparisons of children of different ages. The year after Binet died, a German psychologist, William Stern, offered a solution. First, he took a child's MA on the Binet–Simon test, and divided it by the same child's CA. To avoid ugly decimal fractions, he multiplied the resulting ratio by 100. The outcome was what Stern called the child's "mental quotient." For example, children whose MA and CA matched would receive a mental quotient of 100, the theoretical average for the entire population of human beings. In contrast, a 5-year-old with the mental capacity of a 10-year-old would earn a score of 200. Such a child would be twice as advanced as his or her peers.

In 1916, Lewis Terman took this development further. He began by adapting the Binet–Simon tests for American use. Because Terman was at Stanford University, the result was called the Stanford–Binet Intelligence Scale. Terman labeled the score produced by the Stanford–Binet a child's "intelligence quotient"; this is better known to the person on the street as the IQ. The score was still defined as IQ = (MA/CA) × 100. By testing children in the full range of ability, Terman worked to establish the IQ score as a meaningful way of characterizing differences in intelligence, from the retarded to the gifted. Influenced by Galton, Terman integrated the test results with Galton's theories of natural ability. In particular, Terman used his intelligence test to diagnose whether a child could be styled a genius—an IQ of 140 would put the child over the top. Thus, a five-year-old who thought like a seven-year-old would count as a genius-grade intellect. It was this criterion that Terman used to select the gifted children studied in his *Genetic Studies of Genius* series.

The history gets more involved, but to narrate the story further would take us too far afield. One additional development, however, must be mentioned. The original definition of IQ only makes sense when we are talking about children. Although intelligence tests were soon devised for adults—such as the Army Alpha and Beta tests taken by draftees during World War I—an IQ score cannot be calculated as a ratio of MA to CA. If you are five years old with the mind of a nine-year-old, you have reason to celebrate. But how would you feel if I told you that you were a 50-year-old with the mind of a 90-year-old? Yet the IQs would be 180 in both cases. Consequently, the IQ scores for adults are calculated according to how far above or below their peers they are. For example, if only 1 adult out of 100 does as well as you do on a general test, then you receive an IQ a bit over 140. Table 8.1 provides some additional examples for several representative IQ scores. This idea of replacing the MA/CA ratio with a "deviation quotient" was established by David Wechsler, who devised two of the most commonly used intelligence tests, the Wechsler Intelligence Scale for Children (WISC) and the Wechsler Adult Intelligence Scale (WAIS).

We need not go further into the subject than this. The procedures for "standardizing" test scores are complicated. It is enough to point out that the IQ score for an adult is not really a "quotient" any more. Instead, IQ has been reduced to an arbitrary number that indirectly reveals what percentage of the human race scores higher and lower than you do. Nevertheless, the IQ score, however it is calculated, is supposed to prophesy your prospects for success. Is this true?

TABLE 8.1. Implications of Approximate IQ Scores by Various Criteria

IQ	Meaning and consequence
228	Record IQ claimed by columnist Marilyn Jarvik (née Vos Savant).
176	Minimum score to be eligible for the Mega Society; only 1 person out of 1 million scores this high.
164	Minimum score for admission into the Four Sigma Society; only 1 person out of 30,000 attains this level.
158	Only 1 person out of 10,000 scores this high.
143	Broadly considered to represent a genius-level intellect; only the top 1% of the population scores this high; this is about the average IQ for those who earn Ph.D.'s in physics or who graduate with Phi Beta Kappa honors.
132	Minimum score to be eligible for the Mensa Society; this score or higher received by the top 2% of the population; it indicates borderline genius; this is about the average IQ for most Ph.D. recipients.
121	Minimum performance to be considered potentially gifted; this score places a person in the top 10% of the population; it is also about the average for college graduates in the United States.
116	Superior intelligence, in the top sixth of the population; this is the approximate average of individuals in professional occupations.
111	This score places an individual in the top third or quarter of the population; it is about the average for high school graduates, but such an individual would have only a 50–50 chance of graduating from college.
100	An average score. Theoretically, half the population should have scores higher than this, the other half lower.
95	Approximate average of semiskilled workers.
84	Bottom one-sixth of the general population scores at this level or below; high probability of becoming a high school dropout.
68	Bottom 2% of the general population: severe mental disabilities.

Note. These IQ scores use a standard deviation of 16. (A "standard deviation" is an indicator of average departure from the population mean. See later text for further explanation.)

How Much Success Can High Test Scores Buy?

Psychologists have reached a consensus on the Galton–Cattell measures: They don't work. Professional opinion about standard IQ tests is more divided. The reliability of these measures is not the problem; few psychometric instruments are as reliable as the best IQ tests. We can measure intelligence with less error than we can assess an individual's motives, values, or attitudes. What is less clear, however, is the validity of these instruments. What evidence have we that they indeed gauge some quality akin to Galton's natural ability? This question has plagued even the Binet-style tests from their very inception. Just look at what happened to Binet's compatriot Henri Poincaré. At a time

> when Poincaré was acknowledged as the foremost mathematician and leading popularizer of science of his time he submitted to the Binet tests and made such a disgraceful showing that, had he been judged as a child instead of as the famous mathematician he was, he would have been rated—by the tests—as an imbecile.

Something was and still is gravely amiss.

If we return to Table 8.1, we can glean three points:

1. IQ scores certainly determine whether you belong to a self-proclaimed intellectual elite. Some extremely exclusive societies have emerged that require stellar performance on IQ tests for admission. Mensa is the least restrictive; you only have to boast an IQ enjoyed by 1 out of 50 adults. Even so, some pretty illustrious people have belonged to this group: Sir Cyril Burt, Buckminster Fuller, Isaac Asimov, Sir Clive Sinclair, and James Fixx (author of *Games for the Superintelligent*). The Four Sigma Society, on the other hand, requires that you take a special test, since most IQ tests do not reach that high. The test is so difficult that you practically need a high IQ just to comprehend the instructions! And for the Mega Society—why bother to inquire if only a few dozen adults in the United States can qualify? Yet as anyone who has attended a meeting of one of these organizations can tell you, membership need not certify success. Indeed, some gatherings seem to amass the biggest collection of misfits and underachievers on this planet.

2. Table 8.1 evidently shows that IQ correlates with educational attainments as well. IQs of about 110, 120, and 130 line up as the means for high school diplomas, bachelor's degrees, and Ph.D.'s, respectively. In addition, IQ predicts scholastic performance, as seen in the high mean for those inducted into Phi Beta Kappa. Nonetheless, we have already learned that educational achievement has only a loose linkage with adulthood success.

3. It is equally clear that IQ squares up with occupational success. At least, those with higher IQs tend to work at more prestigious and often better-paying jobs. Professionals have IQs about 20 points higher than those of blue-collar workers. These inferences from Table 8.1 are strengthened when we present a more complete picture. The approximate median IQs for various occupations are as follows: accountant, teacher, and lawyer, 120; postal clerk, 115; store manager, tool maker, stock clerk, and machinist, 110; police officer, electrician, meat cutter, and sheet-metal worker, 105; machine operator, automobile mechanic, carpenter, baker, and truck driver, 100; cook, laborer, and barber, 95; miner, farm worker, and lumberjack, 90. Moreover, those whose scores are as far below average as the scores of people with Ph.D.'s are above average will often find it difficult to hold any job except the most unskilled.

Hence, we seem to be getting closer to a positive conclusion. If you are a lawyer, physician, engineer, scientist, or scholar, you are probably more likely to make your mark than if you are a trucker, janitor, or sanitation worker. There are exceptions, to be sure. Jimmy Hoffa was a grocery warehouse worker, Eric Hoffer a longshoreman, Cesar Chavez a migrant farm laborer. Yet these exceptions are probably rare in comparison to the proportion of professionals who make a mark on society or culture. Since a high IQ may be a prerequisite for entering the professions, excellent performance on one of these tests may predict adulthood accomplishment.

For example, 10% of lumberjacks have IQs of 70 or less, while another 10% have IQs above 110. In contrast, the bottom 10% of lawyers have IQs falling no lower than 110, while the top 10% in intellect reach above 130. These ranges just barely overlap. Only 1 out of 10 lumberjacks is as intelligent as the least bright lawyers. More critical, the range in IQs is much smaller in case pleading than in forest trimming. This narrower range holds despite the higher IQs available for lawyers. Moreover, the IQ ranges for lawyers, unlike that for lumberjacks, falls in the more restrictive portion of the intelligence distribution: Just the upper quarter of the human race is smart enough to pass the bar exam, whereas almost 98% of humanity can learn how to chainsaw a tree. Hence, you had better be brainy if your ambition is to become another Clarence Darrow, F. Lee Bailey, or Ralph Nader. Paul Bunyan alone became illustrious as a lumberjack, and he is a pure loggers' fantasy.

However, we must impose two qualifications on our chain of reasoning. First, many critics hold that IQ still fails to have any value for predicting the amplitude of success of individuals within the same occupation. It is one matter to say that you may need an IQ approaching 140 to become a physicist, and quite another to claim that those who make contributions to physics are intellectually superior to colleagues who do nothing to advance their field. Indeed, evidence suggests that within a given domain, IQ does not always correlate with the size of achievement. The second qualification spins off this complaint. Most studies of the relation between IQ and success concentrate on rather liberal signs of achievement. If you are doing well at your job, earn a decent income, and have received some nice citations or performance ratings here or there, you count as Mr. or Ms. Success. But what about really *big* success? How about winning a Nobel Prize? What about becoming a popular president or prime minister of a major world power? Here the predictive power of IQ can look rather deficient.

Take the subjects of the longitudinal study mentioned in Chapter 6—Terman's "Termites." This was a collection of children whose IQs averaged about 151. In the 35-year follow-up entitled *The Gifted Group at Mid-Life*, Terman could tell us whether his gifted children made good as adults. Because the Termites were now in their 40s, all had had enough time to strike gold with their careers. Moreover, for the most part, these were still people with genius-level IQs. So did any of these high-caliber brains make names for themselves?

Terman would like us to think so. Let's focus on the men in the sample, who had better career opportunities than the women. Of these gifted males, 70 earned listings in *American Men of Science*, and 3 were elected to the National Academy of Sciences; 10 had entries in the *Directory of American Scholars*, and 31 appeared in *Who's Who in America*. Of the latter 31, 13 were professors, 8 were business executives, and 3 were diplomats. The remainder included a landscape architect, an engineer, a writer and editor, a government official, a brigadier general in the U.S. Army, and a director of a large philanthropic foundation. Terman hoped to mount a final assault on our doubts by summarizing the accomplishments of these genius-level males:

> Nearly 2000 scientific and technical papers and articles and some 60 books and monographs in the sciences, literature, arts, and humanities have been published. Patents granted amount to at least 230. Other writings include 33 novels, about 375 short stories, novelettes, and plays; 60 or more essays, critiques, and sketches; and 265 miscellaneous articles on a variety of subjects. The figures on publications do not include the hundreds of publications by journalists that classify as news stories, editorials, or newspaper columns, nor do they include the hundreds, if not thousands, of radio, television, or motion picture scripts.

However, we must remember that Terman began with 857 males. Are these figures still striking when put on a per capita basis? Not nearly so. For instance, let us give Terman the benefit of the doubt and posit that all 2,000 scientific and technical publications were produced by the 70 who made it into *American Men of Science*. That implies that, on average, Terman's notable scientists produced about 29 publications by the time they had reached their mid-40s. In contrast, American Nobel laureates in the sciences averaged about 38 publications by the time they were 39 years old, and claimed about 59 publications by their mid-40s. That amounts to a twofold disparity in output. Hence, Terman's intellectual elite was not of the same caliber as the true scientific elite of the same nation and era.

One of the members of the true elite was William Shockley. Shockley was also among the elementary school children tested by Terman's researchers back in the early 1920s. However, his IQ score was not high enough to place him in the genius group, so he never had the distinction of being one of the 857 boys in the Terman collection of gifted children. Even so, he earned a Ph.D. from Harvard University. And after joining Bell Telephone Laboratories, he devised the point-contact transistor in 1947 and the junction transistor in 1948. For the former achievement, he shared the 1970 Nobel Prize for physics. Ironically, not one of the Termites received so high an honor.

Hence, a formidable IQ promises nothing, and a subgenius IQ is still an exploitable resource. As a final proof, let us look at the highest IQ score offered in Table 8.1. That belongs to Marilyn Jarvik (née Vos Savant). According to the *Guinness Book of World Records*, hers is the top score ever. When she was 10 years old, she received the highest possible score for 23-year-olds. And when later she took the test for admission to the Mega Society, she became its topmost scorer. Psychometrically, she is the brightest and the best of our species.

So what is she doing with her stratospheric cortex? She writes a Sunday magazine column called "Ask Marilyn," in which she gives answers to written inquiries that aim at stumping her genius. I am not trying to belittle her intelligence when I say that you may not need an IQ as high as hers to write her column. Hence, until she wins a Nobel or Pulitzer Prize for her efforts, we may have no option other than to conclude that she is an underachiever. She perhaps has the most "test smarts" of anyone in a nation approaching 300 million people. Among her compatriots, Marilyn's IQ is almost 60 points higher than that claimed by Nobel laureate Linus Pauling. But she has yet to match her intellectual inferior in the annals of history.

Gauging IQs in Historic Personalities

In assessing the impact of intellect on attainment, psychologists have not exhausted their options. Besides psychometrics, researchers can use "historiometric" techniques. Although we can consider Galton's *Hereditary Genius* as an illustration of this approach, the term was not actually defined until about 40 years later. In 1909, Frederick Woods offered "a new name for a new science." Historiometrics, he said, comprises those inquiries in which "the facts of history of a personal nature have been subjected to statistical analysis by some more or less objective method." Woods suggested that this method might contribute to the "psychology of genius"—an application that was demonstrated by no less a psychologist than Louis Terman himself.

In 1917 Terman published a paper entitled "The Intelligence Quotient of Francis Galton in Childhood." Now there can be no doubt that Galton's adulthood achievements confirmed his status as a genuine genius. Besides all the contributions mentioned earlier in this book, Galton developed a hand-held heliostat and devised a wave machine to capture the ocean's energy. Yet Terman was interested in whether Galton was a genius as a child. If Galton could have taken the Stanford–Binet, what would his IQ have been?

This may look like a quixotic quest until we remember how Terman defined IQ: as an authentic quotient—the ratio of MA to CA. Therefore, all

Terman had to do was scrutinize Galton's biography and compile a list of child-hood achievements. For each item, Terman could determine Galton's MA and CA, and from there obtain an IQ estimate. Galton's final IQ would be some kind of average of these separate estimates. For example, how would you grade the following letter?

MY DEAR ADÈLE,

I am . . . years old and I can read any English book. I can say all the Latin Substantives and Adjectives and active verbs besides 52 lines of Latin poetry. I can cast up any sum in addition and can multiply by 2, 3, 4, 5, 6, 7, 8, [9], 10, [11]. I can also say the pence table. I read French a little and I know the clock.

FRANCIS GALTON,
Febuary 15, 1827.

I have obviously omitted Galton's age. The numbers in brackets were those that Galton, in a display of second thoughts, erased from the letter; he used a knife to scratch out one number and, evidently finding this unsatisfactory, glued paper on top of the other number. Only one misspelling appears, the month that this letter was written.

Have you come up with an estimated mental age? Put it in months. Now Galton wrote the letter when he was four years old, but one day before his fifth birthday. So divide your estimate by 60, and then multiply that quotient by 100. Compare your figure with what Terman obtained by examining this and many other biographical tidbits. Terman surmised that Galton's childhood IQ was not too far from 200. During Galton's childhood, he was usually engaged in activities that are normally associated with children nearly twice his age.

Can Terman's procedure be generalized? Can we calculate IQ scores for, say, Leonardo da Vinci, Copernicus, Cervantes, Descartes, Newton, Napoleon, Beethoven, Lincoln, and other greats too dead to take the Stanford–Binet? If so, does a high IQ indeed confer an advantage in the competition for renown?

Cox's 301 Geniuses

As stated two chapters back, Volume 2 of Terman's *Genetic Studies of Genius* was written by Catherine Cox, one of his graduate students. In this volume, entitled *The Early Mental Traits of Three Hundred Geniuses*, Cox subjected 301 creators and leaders to historiometric rigors. The explicit model was Terman's calculation of Galton's IQ, but the sample was much larger and more diverse. She began with the 1,000 most eminent creators and leaders in the list compiled by James McKeen Cattell in 1903. Individuals were selected accord-ing to several objective factors. Those sampled had to be born since 1450, achieve eminence on their own rather than inherit a throne, receive the high-est eminence rankings, and the like. Those making the final cut included leaders such as Richelieu, Disraeli, Washington, Garibaldi, Cortés, and Luther, and creators such as Watt, Kepler, Spinoza, Montaigne, Calderón, Raphael, and Rossini. For each, Cox compiled a huge data base on early childhood and adolescent achievements. Although the raw data were deposited in the Terman archives at Stanford University, Cox abstracted the key facts in the published volume. No doubt, this is one reason the tome is 842 pages long!

From her abstract on John Stuart Mill, for example, we learn that he studied Greek at 3, read Plato at 7, began to master algebra and geometry at 8, and learned calculus at 11. At 5 he could debate the comparative prowess of Wellington and Marlborough, and at 6 he wrote a history of Rome. Cox then had three independent raters evaluate these data. The conclusion? Mill had an IQ of about 190. What he was doing at 5, the average person couldn't accomplish until 9 years and 6 months of age. After the same fashion, Cox's team provided IQ scores for the remaining 300 geniuses in her sample. As a further refinement, Cox corrected these estimates to accommodate errors and omissions in the biographies. In addition, she calculated two sets of IQs—one for ages 0–17 and the other for 17–26. This enabled Cox to gauge the stability of her IQ estimates.

If we overlook these niceties, the 301 unquestionably formed a bright club of important people. The average IQ was about 165, hinting that over half might qualify for the Four Sigma Society. Although none matched Marilyn Jarvik, more than a dozen reached high enough to meet the standards of the Mega Society. Goethe, for one, may have fallen only 20 IQ points short of Marilyn's score. On the other hand, the IQs for some other members of Cox's sample were not nearly so intimidating. Three Frenchmen, in particular, were no brighter than the typical college student—La Fontaine, Masséna, and Vauban. These cases and a few others notwithstanding, at least 96% could have joined the Mensa Society had they only lived long enough. By this loose definition of the term, the people who stamped their names on the monuments of history were certainly geniuses. More recent analyses have confirmed this judgment.

Yet this question is not the most interesting we might ask. In addition to just learning whether historic personalities were brilliant, we would also like to know whether the size of their IQ predicted the scope of their success. Obviously, they had to be smart to make a mark, but did the smartest people leave the biggest and most durable impressions? To illustrate, classical music buffs can contemplate the following IQ scores: Handel, Mozart, and Mendelssohn, 160; Beethoven and Wagner, 150; Weber, 145; Palestrina and J. S. Bach, 140; Gluck, Haydn, and Rossini, 135. Do these scores fit the relative merit of these 11 composers? Or let us ponder the IQs for eight early U.S. presidents: John Quincy Adams, 170; Jefferson, 160; John Adams and Madison, 150; Lincoln, 145; Washington, 130; Jackson, 120; and Grant, 115. Is this any better?

Plainly, our next task must be to take a more systematic approach to this matter.

What Do Precocious Intellects Achieve?

Cox wanted to determine whether differences in IQ could account for contrasts in fame. On first blush, her data do not lend themselves well to addressing this question. After all, her 301 formed an elite on both counts. It is very hard to get a respectable correlation between two measures when neither varies very much. This is one reason why IQ doesn't always predict occupational success. If a person needs an IQ above 130 to join a particular profession, IQs cannot differ much among professionals, at least not in comparison to the population at large. Instead of a potential spread of nearly 200 points, the actual range might be a mere 50.

Nevertheless, the variation in IQs, as we have seen, was fairly respectable for the 301 geniuses. In addition, the spread in fame was much greater than we might expect from the distinction of the sample. For instance, the most eminent leader was Napoleon, the least Philip Sheridan; the creators ranged from Voltaire to Harriet Martineau. Hence, there still may have been enough variation on both variables to produce an honorable correlation. In fact, Cox got a tolerably good result. The association between IQ and achieved eminence was about the same as that between, say, scores on the Scholastic Aptitude Test and college grade point average.

Other investigators have replicated this result with other samples. IQ is associated not only with increased fame, but also with such assets as superior versatility. The higher the IQ, the more domains in which an individual can succeed. This advantage of versatility is seen in the careers of Leonardo da Vinci, Michelangelo, Descartes, Pascal, Leibniz, Benjamin Franklin, Goethe, and Disraeli—all of whom could have been candidates for the Four Sigma Society. With more intellectual wherewithal, they could engage in more enterprises without risking the vitiating dissipation of the dilettante.

Besides operating as a generic resource for historic personalities, intelligence relates to success within more specific domains of achievement. For example, intelligence predicts distinction in several important types of political leadership. One study looked at 342 hereditary monarchs from European history between the Middle Ages and the Napoleonic era. Because a king, queen, or sultan may inherit a throne without demonstrating any special ability, the range of intellectual power among these individuals was far greater than that for most other forms of achievement. Some monarchs, like Charles II of Spain and Peter III of Russia, actually had subnormal brains. On the other hand, nothing prevents a monarch from being extremely brilliant as well. Hence, hereditary monarchs may offer a better test of the current hypothesis than the members of the Cox 301. In any case, for this sample, intelligence correlated positively with higher-rated leadership ability, a longer reign, and, most significantly, a more outstanding posthumous reputation.

Louis XIV of France, the Sun King, illustrated the cluster of traits that may adhere to the brilliant ruler. Considered the model of monarchy in his own and succeeding generations, both in France and in the rest of Europe, Louis was king for nearly three-quarters of a century. During that time he strengthened the central government, expanded French power and prestige, and made French culture the envy of the Continent. His was the age of Cassini, Corneille, Molière, Racine, Lully, Poussin, and Claude Lorraine.

The empirical findings on the American presidency are even richer. All presidents before George Bush have been rated on intellectual brilliance. High scores on this measure signify that a chief executive's mind was characterized by intelligence, sophistication, complexity, insight, curiosity, inventiveness, and both wide and artistic interests. These scores correlated well with the eight IQ scores that Cox published. The scores also enjoy a certain *prima facie* validity. For example, Warren Harding got the lowest rating on this measure. Harding was so dull that he often did not understand the speeches his ghost writers gave him to read. On the opposite end of the scale came Thomas Jefferson, philosopher, revolutionary, architect, scientist, accomplished violinist, agricultural expert, religious scholar, educator, and—oh, yes—president. Once John F. Kennedy gave a reception in honor of some Americans who had just won the Nobel Prize. He greeted them by noting that they represented, with only one exception, the most luminous collection of talents ever gathered under the White House roof. Kennedy excepted the occasions when Jefferson used to dine at the Executive Mansion alone. Interestingly, JFK scored the second highest in intellectual brilliance, albeit Jefferson stood head and shoulders above him. This evokes Sir Arthur Conan Doyle's dictum: "Mediocrity knows nothing higher than itself, but talent instantly recognizes genius." It is clear which of these leaders—Jefferson, Kennedy, and Harding—was the genius, which the talent, and which the mediocrity.

So if an incumbent had a genius-grade intellect, what did it get him? The most brilliant presidents tended to be more achievement-oriented, forceful, and idealistic. They were also more likely to display a creative and charismatic leadership style. Moreover, they had the highest odds of going down in history as great presidents. Out of hundreds of potential predictors of presidential greatness, intellectual brilliance emerged as one of the half-dozen most important. Jefferson, for example, is usually ranked in the top three or four all-time greats, whereas Harding nearly always falls at the bottom of the heap, even lower than Grant.

We can draw some conclusion after all: A high IQ is not irrelevant in understanding who becomes a big success. Although it is not the only factor, the higher a person's ability is, the bigger his or her impression on posterity.

Complications in Linking Intelligence to Achievement

The whole notion of IQ has sparked a hefty debate among psychologists. Many have doubted whether intelligence tests tell us anything valuable about human competence. Many more worry about cultural biases in these tests—biases that cast aspersions on members of certain ethnic groups. These complaints are not without justification. IQ is not everything. In preceding and succeeding chapters, I present a massive inventory of factors beyond the purview of the IQ score. In addition, few can question that it is impossible to devise a generic IQ test that scores all *Homo sapiens* with equal fairness. For maximum validity, we must tailor an IQ test to the specific environment to which an individual must adapt. Kids who must survive in the inner city should be quizzed on their "street smarts," not on who wrote *Faust*.

Nevertheless, we still have adequate reasons for concluding that intelligence goes along with outstanding achievement. The conclusion almost always holds when we confine ourselves to individuals within a single subculture and occupation. Furthermore, historiometric studies lead us to this same statement. In fact, I would like to argue that the inference is actually far stronger than it has been described thus far as being. Three complexities can cloud the correspondence between intellect and accomplishment: (1) the different distributions of IQ and achievement, (2) the formal relation between IQ and success, and (3) the multiple dimensions of intellect itself.

Extremes and Elites

In Chapter 5, I have discussed the highly elitist nature of historic achievement. A small percentage of the achievers accounts for a disproportionate amount of the contributions. This stands in stark contrast with intelligence, which has a more egalitarian distribution. The distribution of intelligence in the general population can be roughly described by the "normal curve" shown in Figure 8.1. There are other aspects of this figure that will prove valuable in the next section. But for now, let us concentrate on the overall shape of the curve defined by the combined shaded areas. In the depiction of this bell-shaped curve, the IQ scores are given on the horizontal axis; the probability of getting a particular score is given on the vertical axis.

Obviously, most people have IQ scores in the middling ranges, while only a small proportion have IQs far above or below this intellectual "middle class." We can specify the nature of the distribution more precisely. If IQ is distributed like the bell curve, then the most common score is 100. This is the "mode." Moreover, as many persons fall below this modal score as above it, making 100 the "median" as well. In addition, if we computed the average IQ across a large population of scores, the result would also be 100, which is the "mean." Equally important is the measure of the "dispersion" around the mean IQ; this is a gauge of how often and how far scores may depart from the average. The most frequently used indicator is the "standard deviation," which can be considered an average departure from the population mean. For many IQ tests, such as those underlying the IQ scores shown in Table 8.1, the standard deviation is taken at

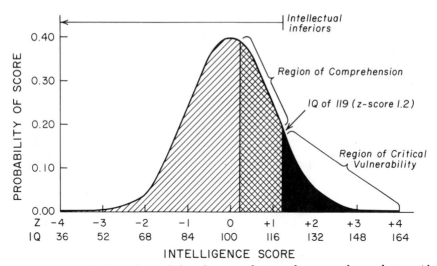

FIGURE 8.1. The hypothetical distribution of IQ in the general population. Also indicated are the consequences of having an IQ of 119 (see later text for further discussion).

about 16. However, this number is completely arbitrary; some IQ tests have standard deviations of 15, others of 20. For the curve shown in Figure 8.1, the standard deviation is also 16. As long as we know what we're talking about, it makes no real difference.

If IQ is normally distributed, the standard deviation tells us how many people we can expect within various intervals along the IQ scale. For example, about 68% of the population should fall within one standard deviation of the mean, or between 84 and 116. Fully 95% should have scores within two standard deviations of the mean, or between 68 and 132. And, lastly, almost 100% (actually 99.7%) should have scores within three standard deviations, or between 52 and 148. This is what makes admission into the Four Sigma Society so difficult. Sigma (σ) is the Greek letter chosen to represent the standard deviation. Thus, to join, a person must have an IQ *four* standard deviations above the mean—an extremely rare occurrence. If sigma equals 16, that requires an IQ of 164.

Because the standard deviation is so arbitrary, psychologists will sometimes express an individual's performance as a z score. This directly registers how many standard deviations above or below the mean a person scored. If the person's raw IQ score is above average, the z score is positive; if it is below average, the z score is negative. That way we can talk about a person's IQ (or other psychological attribute) without specifying the IQ test used. Raw IQ scores mean different things according to the test, but the z scores will have the same meaning.

Now let's get back to the main issue at hand. Given the normal curve in Figure 8.1, it is difficult to imagine how the output of notable contributions could be so elitist. The upper tail of the curve does not reach out far enough toward the right. To be sure, the actual distribution is not exactly normal. Its shape is that of a bell that has been squashed a little. But the distortion is still not enough to account for the discrepancy. In fact, the actual distribution of achievements across individuals is highly "skewed." That is, the right-hand tail reaches way out, as if "going for the gold." To appreciate the difference, we can examine Figure 8.2.

In order to produce this figure, a computer simulated two divergent distributions. Both distributions assumed that we were dealing with a population of 10,000 adult human beings. Both distributions were forced to have a mean of 100 and a standard deviation of 16. The computer first tried to reproduce the bell curve already seen. This was taken to represent the distribution of intelligence. This simulation yielded a more or less symmetrical distribution, as seen in the solid line in the figure. The lowest IQ score was 37 and the highest was 155, with a range of 118 points.

The computer next tried to reproduce what is called the "lognormal" distribution, which approximates the contrasts in observed productive output. As you can see from the dashed curve in the figure, the result was rather different. The distribution was no longer symmetrical, and the upper tail stretches

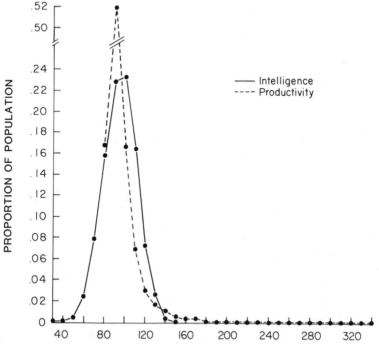

FIGURE 8.2. Theoretical distributions for intelligence and productivity, according to a computer simulation.

out almost indefinitely. Although the mean was still 100, the low score was now 87and the high score was 341, with a spread of 254 points. That high score is telling. Think of it as a PQ, or productivity quotient. Then out of 10,000 people, there can be 1 person with a PQ of 341, or a z score of 15! Contrast that with Marilyn Jarvik's puny IQ in Table 8.1. And in populations larger than 10,000, we should obtain PQs that are even more astronomical.

This exercise was abstract, but the point should be clear: The distribution of achievement is much more elitist than the distribution of intelligence. Because the two curves are so discrepant, we cannot expect IQ to explain all that we need to know about phenomenal success. Too many creators and leaders are more extraordinary than their intellects would suggest. Instead, other factors must be involved in the making of historic genius. By admitting this possibility, we can see how sometimes we may fail to appreciate the central role intelligence has to play.

In Chapter 2, I have discussed emergenesis, mentioning that this genetic process implies a multiplicative model of inheritance. Cyril Burt, William Shockley, and others have suggested that the same kind of mechanism might explain the crazy distribution of productivity. If output is a function of many factors operating *in conjunction*, then low scores on any one factor will bring down the final product. To illustrate, suppose that achievement is the upshot of a dozen factors, each rated on, say, a scale of 0–10. The highest level of accomplishment would be shown by someone high on all 12 requisites (10^{12}, or 10 multiplied by itself 12 times). Yet suppose that a person is extremely weak on just one of these factors, getting a zero score. Then the product of all 12 factors would be zero (for $0 \times 10^{11} = 0$). The chain may only be as strong as its weakest link.

By making achievement the product (rather than the sum) of independent factors, we have solved the distribution problem. Even when the factors entering such a product are normally distributed, the distribution of their joint product will not be. In fact, the product of the separate factors will be described by a lognormal distribution. By seeing intelligence as one of several multiplicative factors contributing to success, we get some bonuses with our purchase as well. For example, such a model enables us to understand how someone with a Mensa-level IQ may accomplish more than another with a Mega-level IQ. The IQ difference may be more than compensated for by the remaining factors going into the product. To go back to our hypothetical 12-factor model, 10 $\times 9^{11}$, where 10 represents the score on intelligence, yields a product 35% smaller than 9×10^{11}, where 9 now represents the intelligence score. Thus, the latter gets the edge in the bid for acclaim.

To offer a more concrete example of one potential tradeoff, we can return to Cox's 301 creators and leaders. She took a subset of 100 geniuses and scored them on 67 personality traits. She found that certain attributes allowed a person to achieve high distinction without the greatest IQ. In particular, "high but not the highest intelligence, combined with the greatest degree of persistence, will achieve greater eminence than the highest degree of intelligence with somewhat less persistence."

We must recall that Galton's notion of natural ability included determination and energy along with intellectual capacity. Although he did not say so, Galton's conception is compatible with the model just outlined. These three factors, and several other besides, may operate as a multiplicative product (rather than an additive sum). The outcome would be the extreme elitism apparent in lifetime achievements. This model enables a person to boast a PQ quite out of proportion to his or her IQ. The discrepancy may be surprisingly low or inordinately high. When PQ is a lot smaller than IQ, we have the classic underachiever. When the contrast is reversed, we obtain the so-called overachiever. We may have thus explained the comparative capacities and attainments of Marilyn Jarvik and William Shockley.

Triangles and Thresholds

The multiplicative model introduced above makes a prediction about how success may vary as a function of intelligence. When IQ is very low, the product of all the contributing factors will remain small, no matter what. Hence, an extremely low IQ exerts a kind of veto power over achievement. Notwithstanding the earlier anecdote about Poincaré, I know of no real case of an individual attaining distinction with a severely subnormal intellect. On the other hand, as IQ increases, the odds of greatness become ever more contingent on how a person scores on the other influences. If capacity on one or more of these other factors is dismal, then their combined product will be depressed, regardless of a high IQ. Suppose we were to take a sample of humans of widely divergent intellects, and plot their fame as a function of their IQs. We might get a "scatterplot" that looks like that in Figure 8.3.

This plot has two intriguing features. First, we can describe the distribution of points as a "triangular distribution." We cannot expect big events to come from those people with mediocre intellects. The highest eminence is reserved for those with the most impressive IQs. Nevertheless, the possession of an unusual intellectual power does not guarantee success; high intelligence is a necessary, but not a sufficient, condition for achievement. Hence, the data points form the triangle. Second, there is a point below which accomplishments become nil. In these depths, we are not speaking of also-rans any more, but of complete nonentities. This illustrates a "threshold function." Below a certain IQ, the contribution of intelligence to the product becomes zero. So the multiplicative product of all the separate factors becomes zero as well.

Triangular distributions and critical thresholds probably describe many key phenomena. For instance, research on the relation between creativity and intelligence suggests a similar distribution. Although it is extremely unlikely that

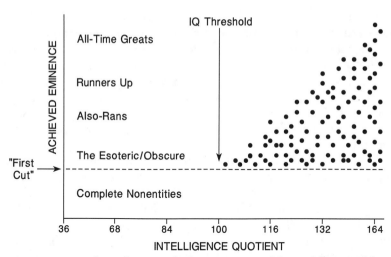

FIGURE 8.3. Hypothetical scatterplot between IQ and fame if described by a triangular distribution with a threshold function.

an unintelligent person can display exceptional creativity, a high IQ can correspond with any level of creativity, low to high. Furthermore, as long as the IQ is 120 or so, further increases in intelligence are less critical than other factors in creative personality. IQ functions like a threshold below which creativity becomes improbable.

Triangular and threshold functions produce relationships a bit more complicated than merely one factor's varying with another. Even so, matters can get more convoluted yet. After all, the results graphed in Figure 8.3 still imply that the brighter the better, in the main. Having a Mensa-level IQ or higher certainly can't do you any harm, and you enjoy a better chance of reaching the upper ranks. However, we can conceive of alternative functions in which increasing your IQ beyond a certain point will not help you any further along the path to good fortune. It could even happen that past an optimal level of intellect, additional cognitive power can only hurt your odds of greatness. Let me show how this might occur.

We want to know how intelligence might affect your odds of influencing a group of people. The more group members you influence, the more leadership you display. Now, we can consider three factors:

1. In all likelihood, group members are more easily persuaded by an intellectual superior than by an intellectual inferior. If you surpass everyone else in intelligence, you may be better at problem solving and more articulate in expressing your ideas. In contrast, it is easier to find factual and logical faults in the arguments of those far below on the intelligence scale. By this factor alone, the higher your IQ, the better.

2. However, those members of the group who are much beneath you in intelligence may not understand you. Your ideas may be too complicated and your language in expressing them too highbrow for the lower portions of the masses. Hence, among your intellectual inferiors, only those who are fairly close to you in intelligence will listen to you with an attentive ear. Those with appreciably lower intellects will simply stare at you in amazement, as you proceed to talk over their heads. As a rough rule of thumb, let's assume that it is easiest to convince others of your ideas when they are no more than one standard deviation below you in intelligence.

3. You must also look over your shoulder at *your* intellectual superiors. Not only are you more prone to defer to them in argument and confrontation, but they are also more likely to take you on in competition for the leadership role in the group. They will have the same assets that you enjoy, and more. Their problem-solving and critical skills will surpass yours, and their sophistication of expression will put you to shame. There is always the danger that they will beat you out in the scramble for the top slot.

If these three factors are combined, at what level of intelligence can you maximize the number of your appreciative adherents while you minimize the number of rivals and critics? For an answer, inspect Figure 8.1 once more. Here we see how the situation stands for a person with an IQ of 119. The cross-hatched area expresses the size of the group membership lying within the "region of comprehension" while remaining intellectual inferiors. The black-shaded area above IQ 119 indicates the size of the membership representing competitors for influence. This is the "region of critical vulnerability." The best IQ is one for which the comprehension region is as big as possible and the critical-vulnerability region is as small as possible. In more concrete terms, you want to increase the number of people who comprehend and appreciate you, while concomitantly decreasing the number of people who can tear you to shreds in open debate or in back-room negotiations. Suppose we skip the mathematics and go straight to the answer, which is shown in Figure 8.4.

The horizontal axis gives the IQ scores much as in Figure 8.1, but the vertical axis now gives the proportion of possible followers for a given IQ. Observe that you have no chance whatever of making a big impression if your IQ is close to the average of 100. Raise the IQ above this point, and the odds of attracting many adherents increases rapidly until the optimum arrives. After that point, more intellectual power detracts from influence. Beyond an IQ of 156, indeed, you would not do any better than if you had an IQ of about 103. Don't expect to become president of the United States if you're a Mensa, Four Sigma, or Mega member! The peak occurs at about an IQ of 119 (or about 1.2 standard deviations above the mean). Thus, the typical college graduate has about the right amount of mental prowess for attracting the largest flock.

The important point is that the predicted relation is described by a "curvilinear model." Moreover, many empirical studies confirm the central prediction that an IQ near 119 is the prescription for leader success. Or, more accu-

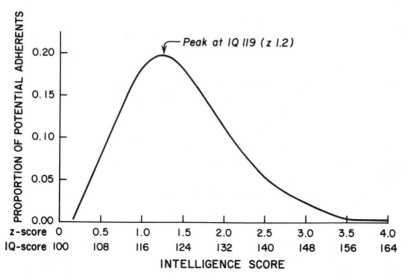

FIGURE 8.4. The expected proportion of potential followers as a function of intelligence, according to a theoretical model.

rately, the group leader usually has an IQ between 1.0 and 1.5 standard deviations above the group mean. This peak holds in social, military, industrial, and even political settings.

This inverted-U function can help us understand a quirk of American presidential leadership. Earlier, we have seen how U.S. chief executives who score high on intellectual brilliance are more prone to go down in history as truly great presidents. Yet these same giants of American politics tend to do *less* well in the Electoral College when they run for office. There is actually a negative relationship between intellectual brilliance and how many electoral votes are cast on a candidate's behalf. Jefferson just squeezed by in 1800, and was almost defeated by the man who then became his vice-president, Aaron Burr—an embarrassment that motivated the 12th Amendment to the Constitution. Woodrow Wilson, the only Ph.D. among the presidents, did even worse. Merely two out of five voters cast their ballots for him in 1912, and fewer than half favored his re-election in 1916. If it were not for political divisions among the opposing parties, there never would have been a President Wilson. John F. Kennedy, another intellectually brilliant candidate, beat Nixon by one of the smallest vote margins ever. Possibly, a person can be too bright to be president.

A refinement is overdue. When we place the peak IQ for influencing others at 119, we do so under the assumption that the IQs of the group membership are normally distributed, with a mean of 100. Sometimes this does not hold. For example, the average IQs of soldiers and sailors are somewhat lower than those of the rest of the population. Hence, less intelligence may be required of a military genius than in other guises of leadership. Accordingly, Cox found that the generals and admirals in her sample had the lowest mean IQs of all the leaders she studied—almost 20 points lower than those of revolutionaries, politicians, and religious figures. The IQs for Robert E. Lee and Napoleon were around 140, for Lord Nelson only 130, and for conquistador Hernando Cortés a mere 125. A commander cannot afford to be misunderstood.

It works the opposite way, too. Leta Hollingworth, a pioneer in the study of intellectually gifted children, gave a graphic example in a 1926 study. One of her subjects, a nine-year-old boy with an IQ of 190, was an outcast among his peers. Words like "capitulate," "reciprocal," and "naiveté" were part of his functional vocabulary. This same social isolate was later placed in a special-opportunity class whose membership boasted a mean IQ of 164. Suddenly, the nerd emerged as the class leader. His classmates actually understood what he was saying and could appreciate his brilliance. To borrow Doyle's terms, they were "talents" to his "genius."

The same heightening of the preferred IQ may show up in leadership domains. In U.S. presidential politics, a candidate must appeal to the general voter to win. This forces Americans to dip low into the pool of intellect. For instance, when voters were given a choice between an average guy like Dwight Eisenhower and an erudite and reflective Adlai Stevenson, "Ike" won hands down. Yet in parliamentary systems, such as Great Britain's, the prime minister is picked on a different basis. He or she must impress fellow members of Parliament rather than the populace at large. To be sure, the candidate must get elected to office, yet most party leaders stand for election at "safe" boroughs where rejection by the voters is unlikely. Hence, to become a leader among leaders, a prime minister must have an outstanding intellect relative to a raised baseline. Accordingly, the set of prime ministers should surpass the intelligence of the set of presidents.

Tentative evidence exists for this intriguing conjecture. The British prime ministers in the Cox sample were assigned IQs about a standard deviation higher than those of the American presidents in the same sample—a 15-point difference. And this gap may understate the contrast. The first five presidents in her sample were elected before the Electoral College became dominated by the ballot box. In the early years of American democracy, many of the electors were chosen by state legislatures rather than by the people directly. Not until the election of Andrew Jackson in 1828 did the selection of the chief executive more directly reflect the popular will. This shift may account for why the mean IQ of presidents Washington through John Quincy Adams was in almost the same league as the British prime ministers, whereas the mean IQ of presidents Jackson through Grant descended more than 20 points.

Using this new principle may also enable us to comprehend why creators can feature higher IQs than leaders. In the Cox sample, the difference was between 6 and 7 IQ points, or nearly half a standard deviation. The audience for creative ideas is far more restricted than that for the persuasive acts of leadership. Einstein did not have to convince everyone of the value of his theories, but only his fellow theoretical physicists. Even in those areas with broader appeal, such as literature, music, and the visual arts, creators must satisfy a more selective gathering of patrons, connoisseurs, aficionados, and critics. Moreover, creative geniuses have one option not available to leaders: They can pass over the heads of their contemporaries, appealing indirectly to posterity. Once a disgruntled musician trying to play some new quartets by Beethoven asked whether the master dared to call this stuff music. Beethoven's reply: "Oh, they are not for you, but for a later age!" If there are not enough people in the world today to appreciate a masterpiece, posterity can carry a bigger burden for the praise. Maybe, for example, only intellects well above Mensa level can appreciate Aristotle, Descartes, or Kant. But that should cause no worry, for the accumulation of appreciators over the generations will amount to millions of devotees.

Yet the curve for historic creativity may still follow the outlines of Figure 8.4, only with the curve shifted upward according to the discipline. The creative genius may still go beyond the pale of comprehension. Examples might include Joyce's *Finnegans Wake*, Schoenberg's 12-tone music, the tracts of Wittgenstein or Derrida, and some recent work on superstrings that causes even Nobel laureates in physics to scratch their heads.

Unity and Variety

It's now time to throw another monkey wrench into our cogitations. We have been viewing intelligence as a single homogeneous capacity, and assigning a single IQ score to each celebrity. This practice has a long history. Charles Spearman, back in 1927, introduced the notion of a "general intelligence" that underlies all demonstrations of intelligence. Today this single factor is still called "Spearman's *g*." Nevertheless, Spearman's scheme did not go unchallenged. L. L. Thurstone argued that the intellect could be broken down into several "primary abilities," such as memory, inductive reasoning, verbal comprehension, and perceptual speed. He claimed that these separate cognitive skills are basically independent of one another. Once more than one intelligence was permitted, the floodgates were swung open for the onrush of ever more. J. P. Guilford eventually proposed 120 distinct cognitive faculties. More recently, Robert Sternberg has tried to offer a more coherent but still comprehensive theory of intelligence. Yet his "triarchic model" assumes three complex components.

And it gets worse. IQ tests have generally focused on cognitive aptitudes. These abilities are readily assessed using psychometric measures. Even so, some critics claim that the full range of human intelligence is far more broad than the narrow realm of the standard IQ test. This position was taken by Howard Gardner in his 1983 book, *Frames of Mind: The Theory of Multiple Intelligences*. According to him, there are at least seven qualitatively distinct intelligences:

verbal, logical–mathematical, spatial–visual, bodily–kinesthetic, musical, intra-personal, and interpersonal. Only the first three of these are directly evaluated in the typical intelligence test. Yet all seven intelligences represent ways in which a person can display talent, even genius. In modern times, the seven roads to fame are exemplified by the careers of T. S. Eliot, Albert Einstein, Pablo Picasso, Martha Graham, Igor Stravinsky, Sigmund Freud, and Mahatma Gandhi.

Of course, a person may have strengths in more than one of the seven intelligences. Indeed, certain combinations may be essential for contributions in specific fields. Expert chess offers an example. One study of 55 grandmasters between André Dunican Philidor and Bobby Fischer found that a large per-centage had some link with mathematics or the exact sciences. Another study of 180 chess celebrities found that they exhibited a marked felicity with lan-guage; only 4% knew only one language, and 25% had mastered five or more. On the other hand, we should not expect these people to dance like Martha Graham, display the introspective probing of a Sigmund Freud, or demonstrate the social skills and wisdom of a Mahatma Gandhi. Many chess champions, in fact, are socially maladroit, neurotically defensive klutzes.

So let us grant that intelligence has multiple manifestations. Does that undo everything we have said? Fortunately, no. In the first place, many of the psy-chometric studies focus on achievements that use the very skills gauged by good IQ tests. In the sciences, for example, the verbal, logical–mathematical, and spatial–visual faculties are more critical than the other intelligences. Roe's 64 eminent scientists had median IQ scores of 166, 154, and 137 on tests of ver-bal, mathematical, and spatial thinking, respectively. And the middle score is an underestimate: Her famous physicists refused to take the math exam, be-cause it was insultingly easy! Performance on IQ tests seems to predict a wide range of activities in domains of creativity or leadership—as long as the domains require the skills that these tests measure.

Our discussions of distributions and functions also remain valid, with only slight qualifications. We can still speak of triangular scatterplots, threshold effects, and curvilinear, inverted-U relationships. The only difference is that we may confine the statements to a particular set of intelligences. Thus, when we are talking of musical creativity, we might compare the composer's musical IQ against the musical IQ of his or her audience. We might still get a curve like Figure 8.4. Furthermore, a theory of multiple intelligences can link up with the multiplicative model that generates the skewed distributions and triangu-lar scatterplots. We merely have to determine which of the seven intelligences enter the product. In those domains where more than one intelligence is man-datory, each intelligence enters the multiplication as a separate factor. For instance, if chess superiority requires logical–mathematical, spatial, and even linguistic prowess, all three intelligences would be factored into the equation along with the nonintellectual factors. There is nothing new here.

What about the historiometric studies? Is the work of Cox undermined by the idea that intelligence may be multidimensional? Not really. Think carefully about how Cox and her research assistants scored the 301 creators and leaders. They rummaged through the biographies, culling attainments that they could assign an MA as well as a CA. Cox imposed no preconceived idea of what specific accomplishments to examine. *De facto*, then, what her raters saw were achievements tailored for the specific intelligences of each youthful genius. J. S. Mill's biography was largely an inventory of his early mastery of linguistic, logical, and mathematical skills. Mozart's data listed mostly signs of musical precocity. Pascal's information concentrated on evidence of his advanced mathematical skills. And so forth. The intelligences in which these future geniuses were most adept as adults were almost invariably the same intelligences that distinguished their precocious years. Hence, Cox's IQs did not gauge the same intelligences. Mozart's IQ score was mostly musical, Pascal's largely mathematical.

Apparently, Cox's key conclusions survive unscathed. However, to comprehend more fully how multiple intelligences affect our conjectures, we must turn to the last topic of this chapter. If it is fair to say that the greatest geniuses are most likely to have been phenomenally precocious, is the reverse true? Is extraordinary precocity associated with exceptional adulthood achievement? In brief, do child prodigies become geniuses?

Prodigies versus Geniuses

By Mozart's 4th year, he could play the clavier, and by his 5th he began to compose little keyboard pieces. His first published composition came out when he was 7. By the time he had reached 15, his list of musical creations included sonatas, concerti, masses, symphonies, operettas, and an opera. So impressive was his progress that he was appointed a grand ducal concertmaster at age 13. Meanwhile, his career as a keyboard virtuoso continued in tours all over Europe. His performing career had started at age 6.

A comparable story can be told of Pascal. Like Mozart, he was tutored by his father. However, when Pascal's father obliged him to learn languages before mathematics, the son worked out the principles of elementary geometry on his own. Devising his own terminology, Pascal got as far as the 32nd proposition of Euclid before his father chanced upon his surreptitious activity. Amazed by what he saw, a tearful father decided to let his son pursue his natural inclinations. By the time he was 16, Pascal wrote an original work on conic sections. This was sent to Descartes for the latter's perusal. Although nearly 30 years Pascal's senior, and by this time a world-famous mathematician in his own right, Descartes showed symptoms of jealousy; he could not believe a 16-year-old capable of such an achievement. Three years later, at 19, Pascal invented a calculating machine. The rest of Pascal's biography becomes history.

There is no doubt that both Mozart and Pascal were child prodigies. They exemplify genuine success stories in which the child prodigy became a genius adult. Other examples—albeit often less dramatic—can be gleaned from Table 8.2. The athletes are included as illustrations of bodily–kinesthetic intelligence, for few are known for early intellectual brilliance. As Muhammad Ali once joked, "I only said I was the greatest, not the smartest."

Yet the story doesn't always have a happy ending. This becomes obvious when we inspect the phenomenon from the opposite end. What if we were to perform a longitudinal study of child prodigies to see what happens when they grow up? This is not as difficult as it first appears. Such studies are spontaneously undertaken by the print and electronic media. A true child prodigy is so newsworthy that he or she quickly attracts attention in the press and on the airwaves. The journalists will follow the poor prodigy around, waiting for a sign of weakness. The media take a special glee in showing how a childhood phenomenon becomes an adulthood mediocrity. Some prodigies stand still, while

TABLE 8.2. Child Prodigies and the Exceptionally Precocious among the Illustrious

Scientists: Svante Arrhenius, Arthur Cayley, Ferdinand Cohn, Enrico Fermi, Sigmund Freud, Francis Galton, Karl Gauss, Albrecht von Haller, William R. Hamilton, Theodore van Kármán, Lord Kelvin, John von Neumann, Simon Newcomb, Blaise Pascal, Jean Piaget, Julian Schwinger, Edward Teller, John D. Watson, Norbert Wiener.

Thinkers: Avicenna, Jeremy Bentham, Auguste Comte, Hugo Grotius, John Stuart Mill, Friedrich Schelling, Voltaire.

Writers: Brontë sisters, Rubén Darío, Samuel Johnson, Josephus, Giacomo Leopardi, Thomas Macaulay, Pablo Neruda, Alexander Pushkin, Arthur Rimbaud, John Ruskin, Edith Sitwell, Alfred Tennyson.

Artists: Jean-Michel Basquiat, Gian Lorenzo Bernini, Albrecht Dürer, Alberto Giacometti, Paul Klee, Andrea Mantegna, Mi Fei, Pablo Picasso.

Composers: Isaac Albéniz, Béla Bartók, Georges Bizet, Benjamin Britten, Ferruccio Busoni, Frederic Chopin, Henry Cowell, William Crotch, César Franck, Erich Korngold, Franz Liszt, Felix Mendelssohn, Claudio Monteverdi, Wolfgang Amadeus Mozart, Niccolo Paganini, Sergei Prokofiev, Mildós Rózsa, Camille Saint-Saëns, Roger Sessions, Richard Strauss, Georg Telemann, Henri Vieuxtemps, Carl Maria von Weber, Henri Wieniawski.

Performers: Enrique Bátiz, Sarah Chang, Charlie Chaplin, Harry Connick Jr., David Copperfield, Noël Coward, Bella Davidovich, Eleonora Duse, Vladimir Feltsman, W. C. Fields, Judy Garland, Jascha Heifetz, Michael Jackson, Edmund Kean, James Levine, Yehudi Menuhin, Midori, Shlomo Mintz, Tatum O'Neal, Mary Pickford, James Randi, Mickey Rooney, Elizabeth Taylor, Shirley Temple, Ellen Terry.

Chess masters: Bobby Fischer, Anatoly Karpov, Gary Kasparov, Judit Polgar, Samuel Rashevsky, Nigel Short, Boris Spassky.

Athletes: Boris Becker, Michael Chang, Nadia Comaneci, Babe Didrikson, Lottie Dod, Gertrude Ederle, Bob Matthias, Mike Tyson, Eldrich "Tiger" Woods.

others their age catch up. Will Rogers captured this idea when he confessed: "I was not a Child Prodigy, because a Child Prodigy is a child who knows as much when it is a Child as it does when it grows up."

Norbert Wiener provided an example in his own autobiography. He pointed out that in the year 1909, five infant prodigies were enrolled at Harvard. Besides Wiener himself (a 15-year-old graduate student), these included Adolf Augustus Berle, Cedric Wing Houghton, Roger Sessions, and the 11-year-old William James Sidis. Of these five, Wiener became a mathematical luminary, Berle a notable diplomat, and Sessions a famous composer. Sidis, in contrast, was an out-and-out failure. This outcome was surprising, for he seemed to have everything going for him. His father, Boris Sidis, was a psychologist and psychiatrist who, like the fathers of Mozart and Pascal, took a direct interest in his son's education. The senior Sidis tried to cultivate a child prodigy, and for a time it worked. In his first year as a Harvard undergraduate, the younger Sidis was invited to deliver a talk on four-dimensional regular figures before Harvard's Mathematics Club. It was an intellectual triumph. But when Sidis showed only limited success as a student, and finally became a university dropout, the newspapers had a field day. After a nervous breakdown, he refused to have anything to do with higher mathematics or anything else intellectual. He even declined to attend his father's funeral. In time, he became a human calculator at the Massachusetts Institute of Technology, getting paid to do routine arithmetic in the days before electronic computers performed such drudgery. Thus, he disappeared into obscurity, spurning publicity like the plague. Ironically, his greatest success may have been his precipitous failure. Otherwise, Wiener would have had no reason to mention him in his autobiography.

The story of Sidis can be told again and again, only with the name changed and the circumstances altered. Another dramatic example is Daisy Ashford. At a youthful 9 years, she wrote her popular masterpiece, *The Young Visiters*. By the time she was 14, her writing career was over! Why is it that some child prodigies grow up to become geniuses—like Mozart and Pascal, Sessions and Wiener—while others, like the young Sidis and Ashford, thoroughly fail to make a durable impression? There appear to be several factors.

In the case of Sidis, social and emotional problems may have interfered with his realizing his intellectual potential. This is especially an issue with prodigies in mathematics, music, and chess. Because a few children can attain adult-level mastery in these domains, they can enter a world that far outstrips their social development. To make matters worse, extreme child prodigies may actually be retarded in their acquisition of the basic social graces and acumen. Sidis, for one, acted younger than other 11-year-olds, and was far less mature than the average Harvard undergraduate. We don't know exactly why this retardation occurs, but the cause may lie in both the nature of the domain and the magnitude of a child's precocity. Mathematics, music, and chess are so abstract, so distant from worldly affairs, that prodigies may become lost in a private universe that prepares them little for practical living. Perhaps the very fact that a child is displaying so much precocity in some single domain also precludes him or her from having the time developing the necessary social skills. It doesn't help that pushy parents will often prevent their "budding genius" from playing with peers, who may impair their child's growth (or so Mom and Dad think). James Mills's deliberate social isolation of his son, J. S. Mill, is a classic instance of this parental sin.

This explanation fits with some of the points made earlier. Because intelligences are multiple, a child may not develop them all equally, or may even develop one or two at the expense of the others. This may make the prodigy not only average in some skills, but retarded as well. In an extreme case, the result may be a so-called "idiot savant." A savant is usually proficient at one task, while showing a subnormal intellect on everything else. Savants commonly specialize in the same intelligences seen in child prodigies—mathematics and music especially. This coincidence reinforces the proposition that the various intelligences are partitioned into separate brain modules. In any case, it could be that some child prodigies sacrifice too much in developing one particular mental faculty. There are probably thresholds for social intelligence below which it is impossible to attain success. According to the multiplicative model, this would wipe out any advantage to be gained from the extraordinary proficiency in some other capacity. The social and emotional maturity of Sidis may have been so low as to make the product of the factors nearly zero.

In addition, sometimes developmental changes intrude that place insurmountable obstacles in the path of the prodigy. Jean Piaget made a name for himself by describing the changes in a child's intellectual development. Thus, the stimulus-bound and highly concrete concepts of the child must be transformed into the more abstract, universal, and formal operations of the mature adult. Unfortunately, this means that child prodigies may master a domain in the wrong way or in an immature fashion. They must sooner or later translate their primitive expertise into a new format as they grow up. For instance, musically precocious children frequently undergo a "midlife crisis" in the transition from prodigies to proficient adults. They have started their musical careers at five or six, but their concrete competence must now metamorphose into a more formal expertise. Not every musical prodigy makes the change.

Up to now, we have been discussing circumstances and conditions that thwart a prodigy's development into a genius. Nonetheless, we must not overlook developmental events that thrust the prodigy forward. One example is the "crystallizing experience," briefly touched upon in Chapter 6. These experiences are special occasions that convert a desultory talent into a directed quest for excellence. In music, for example, a future composer may get the spark upon hearing a piece of music, or a future virtuoso may become entranced by the sound of a particular instrument. Thus, Wagner's hearing of Beethoven's *Fidelio* set him on the path to composition, just as Debussy's hearing of Wagner's *Tannhauser* overture inspired him the same way. The lifelong infatuations of Arthur Rubinstein and Yehudi Menuhin with their respective instruments—

piano and violin—were instances of love at first sight. Sadly, many potential geniuses twiddle their thumbs for a lifetime, waiting for something that really turns them on. Maybe the field in which they might attain greatness no longer exists, or will not exist for centuries.

Finally, the extra push may be more emotional or motivational. One drawback of extreme precocity is that success comes too easily. A child prodigy may thus attain a too-facile fame. This easy life does not provide adequate preparation for the struggles and frustrations of adulthood. Even the greatest geniuses must suffer many setbacks—incomplete projects, rejection slips, canceled commissions, inept rehearsals and poor performances, scathing critiques, and the like. Accordingly, it may not be a virtue that so many child prodigies lead overly protected lives. Sooner or later, they must gain the emotional stamina and motivational endurance to survive in the rough-and-tumble world. This reinforces what I have said earlier about the adverse family life that so often saddens the childhood of future geniuses (see Chapter 6). The early experience of orphanhood, for instance, may inoculate a gifted child against the hardships that must be endured in more mature years. Childhood traumas and disabilities may build a robust personality that can prevail over all of life's obstructions.

Dylan Thomas once complained, "There's only one thing that's worse than having an unhappy childhood, and that's having a too-happy childhood." Indulged and encouraged by his parents, Thomas was something of a poetic prodigy. The bulk of his lyric masterpieces were drafted by the time he attained majority. Yet, after moving from Swansea to London, he found himself utterly deficient in rudimentary survival skills. Can we wonder, then, that when the going got rough, Thomas got the bottle? His self-therapeutic alcoholism killed him in his 40th year.

We certainly can entertain more speculations about why not all prodigies become geniuses. Rather than do so, however, I would rather address an inverse issue. Let us look at the other end of the problem—at those individuals who have managed to achieve immortal status. Some of these undoubted geniuses were child prodigies, while others walked a more pedestrian developmental path. Who receives the higher acclaim? Should we expect less or more of geniuses who were prodigious youths? It just may be that any prodigy who gets through the obstacle course of childhood and adolescence will be optimally positioned for the most sensational triumphs. What is the truth?

A recent study of 120 classical composers provides the beginnings of an answer. Those studied were the most popular composers in the classical repertoire. The earliest was Palestrina, born in 1524; the most recent was Benjamin Britten, who died in 1976. Each composer was assessed on several career attributes. How famous did he become, and how many compositions of his entered the repertoire? What were the ages at which he began music lessons; commenced composition; composed his first, best, and last masterworks; and died? Figure 8.5 graphs some of the central findings.

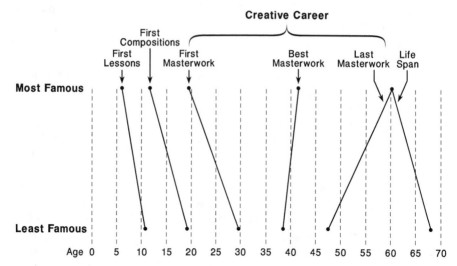

FIGURE 8.5. Typical career paths for the most and least famous of 120 classical composers.

This graph shows the divergent career trajectories for the most and least acclaimed composers. The upper portion indicates the typical career paths for the most famous composers, such as Bach, Beethoven, Brahms, Chopin, Debussy, Handel, Haydn, Mozart, Schubert, and Wagner. The lower portion reveals the typical trajectory for the also-rans, like Hugo Alfvén, Ferde Grofé, Anatol Liadov, Leo Sowerby, and Josef Suk. Although this figure is based on differences in eminence, the same conclusions hold when we plot the trajectories according to differences in the composers' lifetime output or annual productivity rates. Now let's interpret this graph, working backwards from the year of death.

First, we can see a strong tendency for the luminaries to die young—almost an eight-year contrast. However, we should not place too much emphasis on this point, for this effect can be largely attributed to the premature deaths of three top composers: Beethoven died at 57, Mozart at 35, and Schubert at 31. If these three were removed, the most and least famous would differ little in life span. Even so, this result does provide a dramatic backdrop to the next finding: The most popular composers produced their last career landmark at an older age. Hence, despite the abbreviated life spans, the great composers were older when their creativity gave up the ghost. Whereas their lesser competitors were quitting in their late 40s, the typical masters hung in there until their 60s. Indeed, the figure implies that the luminaries were usually still composing on their deathbeds. This was certainly true for Mozart, Bach, and many others.

Although we can see a modest tendency for the most notable composers to produce their best work at an older age, we can dismiss this as an important phenomenon. Individual differences in the age at which the middle career landmark appeared are too large to make this trend statistically reliable. On the other hand, the obvious proclivity of the great composers to score early hits is pronounced. On the average, an incontestable genius in music was 10 years ahead of his less conspicuous rivals. For the most famous, the first masterworks came in the late teens; for the least famous, these breakthroughs came in the late 20s. When we combine this information with what we know about the age of the last career landmark, we can see that the creative careers of the very famous were clearly longer. This contrast is apparent in the funnel shape of the two lines representing these two landmarks.

The really good stuff now arrives. The top-notch composers began composition at a younger age, and their formal training was also precocious. Whereas the least famous may have started to compose in their late teens, the most famous started as preteenagers. In fact, the least famous began their musical training at about the age that the most famous began composing. The most famous were already learning their trade at about six years of age. These results suggest that being a musical prodigy or near-prodigy is prophetic of later genius status. The earlier lessons and composition begin, the earlier the first masterwork, the later the last masterwork, the more total masterpieces produced, and the greater the posthumous reputation. Hence, if a musical prodigy gets somehow over the developmental hump, prospects are good for a most remarkable adulthood.

A couple of subtle findings hide in the graph as well. First, the number of years between the onset of composition and the first masterwork was smaller for the most famous. The gap was about three years. In the preceding chapter I have presented a theory that can account for this difference. Because the greater composers had higher creative potential, they produced ideas at a faster rate. Once they began to compose, they had to wait less before achieving a hit. Indeed, the study discussed here showed that the most famous composers produced at faster annual rates throughout their careers.

The second hidden result concerns the time lapse between the age at first lessons and the age at first composition. This was also smaller for the biggest stars in the classical repertoire; once more, the difference was about three years. This may not seem such a big deal, yet the contrast is ample when compared to the size of the hiatus. Lesser composers took more than 50% longer to gain the necessary musical skills for composition. In Chapter 3 we have seen that it takes time to master the 50,000 chunks of domain-germane information before a person can expect to make significant contributions. Yet this result suggests that the greatest composers, the prodigies and near-prodigies, can absorb new information at faster rates. It takes them less time than others to acquire the requisite expertise.

Should this suggestion surprise us? When Terman and others assessed psychometric IQ as a quotient of MA to CA, weren't they assuming that the intellectual prodigy masters information at faster rates? When Cox and other applied the same conceptual definition to estimate IQs of historic figures, didn't the same assumption justify the application? To gauge intellectual genius in childhood is tantamount to measuring how quickly a youth can assimilate a wealth of knowledge and skills. In fact, a current trend in research is to return to reaction times and related traits as clues to intellectual power. For example, researchers have shown that precocious children display faster speeds of information processing on objective laboratory tasks. Hence, the contrast in preparation time shown in Figure 8.5 may be part of a phenomenon that is much broader than musical creativity.

Great minds may be quick-witted after all. Francis Galton and James McKeen Cattell may have chosen their instruments unwisely, but at least they were not totally misguided. The dog whistle may be useless as a measure of IQ, yet some kind of reaction time assessment is certainly on the right track. The great figures of history do think fast, and early.

CHAPTER 9

THE IMPORTANCE OF PERSONALITY

s half the world knows, there are two kinds of people in this world: those who believe there are two kinds of people in this world, and those who don't. People in the first group love to split the human race down the middle. Some people are bright, others dull; some dominant, others submissive; some moral, others immoral; and so on to infinity. Psychologists are notably fond of dichotomous cuts. Many of these favorite "typologies" allow for only two basic types of personalities. Carl Jung, for example, introduced the classic separation of the introverts from the extroverts.

What about the people who don't believe there are two types of people? They, too, fall into two types. One type of nonbeliever maintains that all humans are effectively the same; whatever individual differences exist are trivial, transient, or superficial. This position is that favored by many cognitive psychologists who seek to understand the universal mind. As we have seen in Chapter 3, psychologists who study problem solving often stress that the world's greatest genius thinks no differently than the least remarkable of those reading these words. This idea has ancient roots. The founder of academic psychology, Wilhelm Wundt, was emphatic that the discipline should ignore individual variation. When James McKeen Cattell, Wundt's graduate student, wished to study individual differences in reaction time, Cattell was not allowed to carry out the experiments in his mentor's laboratory. Not surprisingly, as soon as Cattell got his Ph.D., he headed for England to do postdoctoral work under Francis Galton.

Galton represents the second type of person who believes that there are not two types of people—because there are more than two types. In his *Hereditary Genius*, Galton recognized at least seven grades of above-average natural ability, labeled A through G, and another seven grades of below-average ability, labeled a through g. Underlying this classification, however, was an underlying continuum from the most to the least intelligent. IQ scores provide an excellent example of such a continuous dimension. We can go ahead and devise a typology—such as "genius," "superior," "bright," "average," and "subnormal"— but this business is artificial. Intelligence is like the colors of the spectrum. We can speak of the primary colors red, yellow, and blue, but the rainbow is actually an undivided blend. The number of possible colors is infinite, because the wavelengths of light may vary indefinitely.

This chapter and the next are based on the assumption that individual differences in personality are real and consequential. Let us assume that people really do differ, and that this variation has something to do with a person's ultimate importance. Of course, I am not talking about contrasts in intelligence here; Chapter 8 has already taken care of that question. Nor can we any longer exhibit skepticism about such basic motives as power, achievement, and affiliation; Chapter 5 has dealt with those matters. But people can vary on more than intelligence and motivation. This chapter is therefore dedicated to that larger miscellany of personality.

The chapter advances from the narrow to the broad. It begins with an inventory of some specific traits. From that atomistic perspective it becomes ever more cosmic, eventually discussing the mentalities of whole cultures.

Tell-Tale Traits

Below I examine six sets of traits, ranging from the largely cognitive to the more social. All have historic repercussions.

Idealists and Dogmatists

In the late 1960s, a sociologist asked 571 professional historians to rate the American presidents. The experts assessed 33 chief executives between George Washington and Lyndon B. Johnson on seven traits. Among the seven dimensions was the trait of flexibility. Could the incumbent engage in the give-and-take often so desirable in world diplomacy and legislative negotiations? Or was the chief executive someone who always stubbornly resisted any temptations to bargain and compromise? According to the historians, the most flexible presidents were Kennedy, Lincoln, Jefferson, and Franklin D. Roosevelt. None of these executives were doctrinaire, and all were willing to change course if different paths might lead to better results. Jefferson, for instance, was rather willing to contradict his own political philosophy when he negotiated the Louisiana Purchase. On the other hand, among the most inflexible presidents were Hoover, Tyler, John Quincy Adams, and Jackson—four presidents who were seldom willing to give in to anybody. But even more obstinate than these four were Andrew Johnson and Woodrow Wilson. Johnson had to face impeachment because of his unyielding stance on Reconstruction. Wilson's comparable intransigence on the Versailles Treaty darkened the closing years of his own presidency.

Interestingly, the flexible presidents often came from distinct backgrounds. For example, they were more likely to come from large families, where the ability to get along with others was probably at a premium. This suggests that this trait may correspond to a larger cluster of personality traits; in fact, it does. The more flexible a president, the more he was likely to be moderate, restrained, friendly, attractive, and agreeable. However, the inflexible White House incumbents did have some character traits going for them as well; they displayed more forcefulness, achievement drive, initiative, dominance, and legislative activity. Nevertheless, the net effect of inflexibility was largely negative. The less flexible presidents used the veto power more often and saw more of their vetoes overturned by Congress. The inflexible incumbents also saw more of their appointments to the Cabinet and the Supreme Court rejected by the Senate. In short, they did not seem to have what it takes to work smoothly with legislators on Capitol Hill. Perhaps as an immediate consequence of this inaptitude, inflexible presidents had a higher likelihood of going down in history as controversial chief executives. Historians have reached a good consensus about the merits of Lincoln, FDR, and Washington, but they disagree adamantly about the presidencies of Hoover, Jackson, J. Q. Adams, Andrew Johnson, and Wilson.

Another of the seven traits was idealism. The historians rated each past president according to whether he was extremely idealistic or utterly practical. Wilson was hands down the most idealistic president, with J. Q. Adams coming in a poor second. In contrast, the most pragmatic presidents were Polk, Coolidge, and, to a lesser degree, Lyndon Johnson. As we might expect, the idealistic presidents were prone to exhibit a higher moral caliber than the pragmatic presidents. The former were less often sly, devious, manipulative, evasive, or unscrupulous.

An even more intriguing relationship connected these idealism ratings with the flexibility assessments: The most idealistic presidents were frequently the most inflexible besides. To be sure, there were exceptions: Kennedy was both flexible and idealistic. But overall, the pattern holds. Wilson typifies the linkage, as the most idealistic and most inflexible president ever. So we can combine these two traits into a single "dogmatism" dimension. Dogmatic chief executives were inflexibly idealistic, whereas nondogmatic incumbents were flexible and pragmatic types.

These presidents' dogmatism may have had roots in early childhood experiences. Whereas the flexibly practical tended to come from favorable socioeconomic backgrounds, the inflexibly idealistic often experienced severe physical and emotional deprivation. Wilson's childhood was horrid; FDR's was enviable. Dogmatism was also related to the amount of formal education a president received. If we plot the scores as a function of educational level, we get the curve shown in Figure 9.1. The most flexibly pragmatic presidents were those who got moderate amounts of academic training—some college but not too much. By comparison, the most inflexibly idealistic presidents were those who got either very little formal instruction or a great deal. The two most dogmatic presidents were Wilson and Andrew Johnson. The first got a Ph.D. from Princeton; the second was an illiterate until his wife taught him his letters in his late teens.

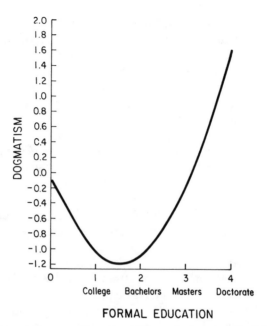

FORMAL EDUCATION

FIGURE 9.1. Dogmatism as a function of formal education for 33 U.S. presidents.

Unfortunately, we don't have many data points in the upper reaches of academic experience. Few of these presidents earned postgraduate degrees, and only one won a doctorate. Even so, this curve is almost the mirror image of that seen in Figure 6.1, where eminent creativity is plotted as a function of educational level. If dogmatism and creativity are inversely related—and empirical research suggests as much—then the inversion of their curves makes perfect sense. A modicum of a college education may facilitate a flexible, open, and innovative mind. In contrast, roots in academia may reinforce an ivory-tower rigidity to an even greater extent than the inflexibilities of outright ignorance. In line with this, those presidents who once served as college professors were also most prone to score high in dogmatism. Besides Wilson, who taught at Princeton, J. Q. Adams offers an example.

Is this sad news for any of my fellow professors who might want to run for the White House someday? Will the American people automatically dismiss anyone who comes on as a pig-headed utopian? Actually, the historical record suggests that Americans have a love–hate relationship with dogmatic incumbents. On the one side, the nondogmatic often come across as unscrupulous wheeler-dealer types whom few voters can thoroughly trust. On the other side, the dogmatic at least profess some principles on which they are willing to take a stalwart stand. This voter ambivalence takes two forms. First, when Americans have just endured a presidency directed by an apparently amoral politician, they seek a successor with irreproachable standards. And the pendulum can swing in the opposite direction, too. Thus, Harding replaced Wilson, who tired America with his moralizing proclamations. Second, Americans apparently want the victorious running mates for the nation's two highest offices to be complementary on dogmatism. If the presidential candidate is dogmatic, the vice-presidential candidate is nondogmatic, and vice versa. Hence, there was the odd pairing of the pragmatic Lincoln with the impractical Johnson. Therefore, the politically ambitious professor has two options: (1) wait for an election year in which Americans revolt against vile politicians in the Oval Office; or (2) become the running mate of someone whose political savvy balances out one's own academic abstraction.

Before we can cast our votes, we must answer one additional question. Who performs best in the White House—the inflexibly idealistic or the flexibly practical? Two suggestive findings are worthy of mention. In the first place, dogmatic presidents were more likely to rely on military force to accomplish their foreign policy goals. Because they lacked the capacity to dive into the diplomatic world of offers and counteroffers, they had to use brute strength to attain what negotiation did not achieve. The second finding is far less restrictive. A slight relationship exists between dogmatism and a president's standing with posterity. On the average, those rated as the greatest chief executives of American history are those at either extreme—the very dogmatic and the very nondogmatic. To state this relationship in a negative way, incumbents like Taft, Buchanan, and Madison—who were neither very idealistic nor very flexible—don't have much in their favor when historians mete out posthumous acclaim. Hence, it may not be politically dubious after all to vote for professors aspiring to be presidents!

Pessimists and Ruminators

Why do some people seem depressed most of the time? Well, among the many antecedents is a person's "explanatory style." Life is chock-full of untoward happenings, and few of us lead blissful lives. Yet we differ in how each of us chooses to explain life's adversities. Some people adopt a pessimistic explanatory style. These folks attribute unfavorable experiences to internal, stable, and global factors. They believe that adversity is caused by personal traits (internal), which are not susceptible to change (stable), and which are broad in their influence (global). Hence, a pessimistic explanatory style goes along with a feeling of hopelessness and despair. Such a style is, in fact, hazardous to people's well-being. It may cause them health problems, send them to a therapist, or drive them to suicide.

A pessimistic explanatory style also may manifest itself on the stage of history. Psychologists have devised a way of content-analyzing written materials for assessments of a person's explanatory style. The maiden application of this new technique focused on three historic occasions:

1. Transcripts of Lyndon B. Johnson's press conferences during the Vietnam War were analyzed. When Johnson adopted optimistic explanations for events, he was likely to take bold, even risky actions—acts that often escalated the conflict. His response to military setbacks was manic, not depressive. In contrast, when Johnson succumbed to a pessimistic explanatory style, his actions betrayed a person locked in the hold of helplessness and hopelessness. The notorious Tet offensive of early 1968 accelerated LBJ's decline toward depressive passivity. The culmination was his announcement that he would not run for re-election. He had become a victim rather than an agent of events.

2. Next, the investigators studied newspaper reportage of the 1984 Winter Olympics. The newspapers came from East and West Berlin. It was clear from watching the patrons in working-class bars that East Berliners showed more signs of depression than did West Berliners. Smiling, laughter, and free gestures were far more frequent in the West. The explanatory style in the sports pages of their respective newspapers mirrored this contrast. East Berlin was far more pessimistic and West Berlin optimistic in explaining the victories and defeats of their respective teams. What makes this disparity especially poignant is that the East Germans did so much better than the West Germans at the games—24 medals versus only 4! Moreover, the East Berlin papers were state-run rather than free enterprises. Hence, living in a Communist country even dampened the optimism of the powers that be, and virtually extinguished the optimism of the populace.

3. The last exploratory application returned to the United States. This time the investigators wondered whether explanatory style would predict success in presidential elections. They specifically analyzed the nomination acceptance speeches of the 20 Democratic and Republican candidates between 1948 and 1984. Besides measuring explanatory style, the researchers added a new factor, "rumination." A candidate scored high on "pessimistic rumination" when he not only made internal, stable, and global attributions, but mulled a lot over these attributions besides. This refinement is probably critical, for only when the candidate ruminated openly about his pessimism could his explanatory style affect voter response. In any case, out of the 10 elections examined, the candidate highest in pessimistic rumination lost in 9. The sole exception was the 1968 election, and even here Humphrey was only slightly higher than Nixon in optimism. Moreover, Humphrey started from behind in the polls, owing to the unpopularity of the Vietnam War, and still almost closed the gap between himself and Nixon by election day. Hence, the 1968 election does not undo the general finding that the bigger the difference in pessimistic rumination, the larger the contrast in the popular vote received in November.

The election of 1952 may epitomize the dramatic dissimilarity that can separate two candidates. In Eisenhower's acceptance speech we find upbeat, fighting expressions such as this: "Ladies and gentlemen, you have summoned me on behalf of millions of your fellow Americans to lead a great crusade—for freedom in America and freedom in the world." Adlai Stevenson, by comparison, reacted to his nomination almost as if he had caught the plague: "That my heart has been troubled, that I have not sought the nomination, that I could not seek it in good conscience, that I would not seek it in honest self-appraisal, is not to say I value it the less." The average voter must have wondered whether Stevenson would even cast a ballot in his own behalf!

This last application, like the first two, was described as only a pilot inquiry. Nonetheless, follow-up studies have confirmed and extended the basic thesis. Scores on pessimistic rumination successfully predicted the loser in presidential elections from 1900 to 1984. Out of the 22 elections, the pessimistic ruminator lost 18 times, and the size of the difference between the two candidates predicted the vote spread in the ballot box. Even after the researchers adjusted for many other factors that affected the election outcomes, the predictive power of pessimistic rumination remained. It seems that voters find depressive presidential candidates repulsive. They favor aspirants with more optimistic messages, leaders who believe they can take charge and solve all problems. As Napoleon advised, a politician must be "a dealer in hope."

More than cheerful confidence was operating here, however. There is also evidence that the pessimistic ruminators, in line with their attributions, adopted a more passive strategy. For example, the upbeat Truman in 1948 launched a "whistle-stop" campaign that led to an upset victory over his challenger, Dewey. A rather different incumbent ran for election in 1980: The downbeat Carter assumed an inert "Rose Garden strategy," and suffered a stunning defeat to the rhapsodic and vigorous Reagan. Hence, pessimistic rumination may well be symptomatic of a debilitating "give-up-itus" that vitiates a politician's competitive spirit.

Not surprisingly, a pessimistic explanatory style is associated with poor athletic performance as well. Athletes just can't compete when they feel they lack the necessary competence. The irony about this, of course, is that the glum prophecy becomes self-fulfilling and self-accelerating: They expect to lose, so they perform less well, so they lose. This then lowers their expectations on future occasions all the more. The negative feedback loop probably accounts for losing streaks in competitive sports and military conflicts. Indeed, one of the best predictors of success on the battlefield is whether a commander goes into the engagement with a winning or losing streak. One reason Napoleon won so many battles was that he almost always expected to win. Even after defeat, he would embrace an optimistic explanation. And because he and his soldiers behaved accordingly, he did not have to devote much time to explaining negative events!

Workaholics versus Beachcombers

We all know the stereotype: the hard-driven, aggressive, and competitive professional who has no time for anybody, not even his or her family. This workaholic behavior pattern has been the subject of considerable research.

In particular, psychologists have invented measures that distinguish two sorts of personalities, which are given the colorless titles "Type A" and "Type B." Type A persons feel there is never enough time to fulfill urgent responsibilities. They are extremely competitive and hostile toward others. In comparison, Type B persons are uncompetitive, amiable, and easy-going about their jobs. Whereas the prototypical Type A might be a chief executive officer for a Fortune 500 corporation, the prototypical Type B might be a California beachcomber.

Most of this research has been conducted in the subdiscipline of health psychology. Early studies suggested that the Type A behavior pattern was associated with a higher rate of coronary heart disease. This co-occurrence is, of course, consistent with commonplace notions about workaholics. Moreover, we can even think of historic examples. Lyndon Johnson was among the most Type A of all modern presidents; it's unsurprising that he died of a heart attack. Gustav Mahler offers a parallel example, in the realm of culture rather than politics. Unfortunately, more recent research shows that the connection between Type A and heart disease is more subtle. However, we need not resolve this debate here; our interest, rather, is in whether Type As are more likely to become VIPs than are Type Bs.

Empirical data suggest that the answer is yes. Nearly from the outset of life, the Type As appear destined for bigger accomplishments than their more mellow peers. The mothers of Type A personalities are much more emphatic about instilling in their children the desire to achieve. Not contradicting maternal expectations, Type As exhibit superior academic success in comparison to their Type B classmates. In addition, Type As tend to set challenging goals for themselves, which they work hard to accomplish. They strive to expand their mastery of difficult tasks. They also score higher on something called "self-efficacy"—the belief that they can achieve what they set their minds to do. As a result, Type As do indeed attain more career success. For instance, researchers with Type A personalities carry out more projects simultaneously, publish more articles, are cited more often by fellow professionals, and advance higher up the academic scale of rank and salary.

In one respect, the Type A edge should have been expected. I have already discussed in Chapter 5 the remarkable amount of time and effort geniuses devote to their careers. To spend as many hours as a genius does on a single-minded enterprise presupposes a mind driven by a sense of urgency. The eyes of the great are often on the hourglass; they are frantically trying to get out that final masterpiece, or even swan song, before the last grain of sand falls through. Besides the implicit time pressures, the most successful geniuses often succeed in the marketplace of ideas by a certain amount of ruthless aggressiveness. Geniuses are not meek, submissive souls. Just look at the lives of Beethoven and Stravinsky, Michelangelo and Picasso, Diaghilev and Martha Graham.

Curiously, a tradeoff should be apparent. The workaholics enjoy better odds of professional success. Yet they gain this advantage at some personal cost:

They could be shortening their lives. Obsessed with making their mark, the Type As may place their health on the block in an almost Faustian bargain. Their productive life thus can become a race against death. But the light is twice as bright when the candles burn at both ends!

Heroes and Adventurers

One of the oldest archetypes in human culture is that of the hero. The hero clashes with the Fates at tremendous personal risk. This archetype is richly portrayed in the mythology of ancient Greece: the legendary exploits of Perseus, the 12 labors of Hercules, Jason's quest for the Golden Fleece, the far-reaching wanderings and adventures of Odysseus. Other cultural traditions depict the same basic ideal, whether Gilgamesh of the Sumerians, Samson of the Hebrews, Siegfried of the Germanic peoples, or Ilya Muromets of the Russians. As popular immortals, these idols have become the centerpieces of heroic literature throughout the world. Of course, the archetype remains alive and well now—only these days the classic hero shows up on the silver screen and picture tube, in contemporary or futuristic attire. The archetype assumes the form of Indiana Jones in *Raiders of the Lost Ark* or Luke Skywalker in *Star Wars*. Many movie stars have carved out their careers as the living image of the primordial type: Charles Bronson, Clint Eastwood, Chuck Norris, Arnold Schwarzenegger, Sylvester Stallone, and John Wayne.

Yet I wish to focus on a more subtle form of heroism. The world of creative achievements is also a realm of heroic acts. These actions may spill no blood, but that does not make them less courageous. For great creators are great risk takers besides. This reality is often not fully appreciated, owing to a widely circulated myth about the creative genius: Too often we conceive of these luminaries as paragons of perfection. They supposedly conjure up magical creations with a "stroke of genius"—whether by a flash of insight or an exercise of intellectual brilliance. We too frequently see geniuses as infallible agents, as if they had some direct conduit to truth or beauty. This commonplace image is pure myth. Creative geniuses stumble; they trip; they make horrible mistakes. Their highest and most acclaimed successes are constructed on the low rubble of humiliating failures.

Actually, I have hinted at this reality back in Chapter 7 with the introduction of the equal-odds rule: Creativity (quality) is a mere function of productivity (quantity). On the average, those periods in a creator's career when the most products ensue are the same periods that see the most masterpieces. The quality ratio of hits to total attempts neither increases nor decreases with age. Not only does this principle apply to fluctuations in output with the career of a single genius; it also applies to contrasts across creative careers. Those individuals with the highest total output will, on the average, produce the most acclaimed contributions as well.

I know that this statement may elicit some skepticism. Aren't there "mass producers" who generate piece after piece of worthless trash? And aren't there also "perfectionists" who manage to offer the world nothing but polished gems? Yes, no doubt there are such people. Yet they only appear every once in a while. They are the exceptions rather than the rule. For example, one study found that American Nobel laureates published twice as many scientific papers as other scientists who were still worthy enough to make it into *American Men and Women of Science*. Other studies have determined that the number of citations a scientist receives in the work of fellow scientists is strongly associated with the total output of publications. In fact, the total number of publications predicts the amount of citations received by a scientist's three most acclaimed works. Moreover, this correspondence between quantity and quality holds over the long haul. For instance, the total length of the bibliography of a 19th-century scientist predicts how famous he or she is in the 20th century. Thus, a scientist who was then in the top 10% of the most productive elite had a 50% chance of earning an entry in a 1950s edition of the *Encyclopaedia Britannica*. In contrast, their less prolific colleagues only had a 3% chance of earning that distinction. Riemann could make a lasting impact on science with only 19 publications, and Mendel with only half a dozen, but instances like these are not frequent enough to overthrow the principle.

From this principle we can make this startling inference: The most successful creators are those with the most failures. Since the quality ratio is not proportionately higher for the more prolific, the supreme geniuses must have strewn their careers with mistakes and fiascoes. W. H. Auden put it well: "The chances are that, in the course of his lifetime, the major poet will write more bad poems than the minor." This holds for major creators in other domains. Take Albert Einstein as a case in point. In his crusade to overthrow quantum physics, he often made embarrassing gaffes. Once, after a long exchange with Niels Bohr, Einstein composed an elaborate argument that he thought would destroy the Copenhagen school. Bohr found a fatal flaw nonetheless: Einstein had neglected to consider the theory of relativity! Yet Einstein kept on going. He continued his search for a unified theory that ignored quantum physics. He could even defend his hopeless situation with the maxim "Science can progress on the basis of error as long as it is not trivial." Einstein was willing to sacrifice his reputation in the quest for his scientific Holy Grail.

The boldness of extraordinary genius often produces more than some miscarried experiments. This trait is responsible also for some rather sensational scenes in intellectual or aesthetic history. These episodes may not be as monumental as a military hero's risking all on the battlefield, but they are dramatic nonetheless. Think, for example, of the audience at the first performance of Igor Stravinsky's *Le Sacre du Printemps* in 1913. There was such an uproar of shouting, catcalls, and feet stamping, followed soon by fistfights and spitting, that the music was soon submerged in the pandemonium. Remember also that shortly after excerpts of James Joyce's *Ulysses* began to appear in an American literary journal in 1918, it was banned as pornography. Finally, recall the hostile response of those attending the notorious Armory Show of 1913. Marcel Duchamp's *Nude Descending a Staircase* was denounced as "an explosion in a shingle factory." Henri Matisse and Constantin Brancusi were hanged in effigy. Those exhibited excited the vociferous displeasure of no less a name than ex-President Theodore Roosevelt. Yet Stravinsky, Joyce, Duchamp, and the rest were undaunted by all the ruckus. They continued to take chances in pursuing their unique visions. Hence, the willingness to take creative risks often brings with it a special knack for alienating the public. The upshot is sometimes eventful scandal and protest.

The need to risk failure to gain success manifests itself beyond such impractical, cultural activities. Not all of Thomas Edison's 1,093 patents protected money-making contraptions. In fact, the amount of money he lost trying to devise a new method for extracting iron ore cost him all his profits from the electric light bulb. Henry Ford, Walt Disney, and Colonel Sanders each faced bankruptcy one or more times before becoming millionaires. Elvis Presley's first performance at the Grand Ole Opry got him fired. Golf celebrity Jack Nicklaus has won only a bit more than one-quarter of the tournaments he has entered. And what about the most praised American presidents? Jefferson's first attempt to win the presidency was a failure, as was Jackson's. Franklin Roosevelt was a losing vice-presidential candidate in 1920. And before Lincoln emerged victorious in the presidential election of 1860, he had lost more campaigns than he had won. Examples like these amply illustrate the cliché "Nothing ventured, nothing gained."

This willingness to take the hard knocks and punches on the road to success implies a good deal more about how to achieve greatness. If you wish to do so, you obviously must exhibit a rare self-confidence. To avoid discouragement, you need the ego strength of an Achilles or Siegfried. In addition, you must display an awesome persistence—a point touched upon in Chapters 5 and 6. When at first you don't succeed, you must try, try again. To use the motto of Hammer's music video, you've got to be "too legit to quit."

By thus looking at the qualities that belong to these notable risk takers, we can view these people as heroes who echo the legendary ancients.

Dominants and Extroverts

Our Paleolithic ancestors had it easy. Because they roamed around in hunter–gatherer groups, foreign affairs meant no more to them than conflicts and compacts with a few other groups in the vicinity. Nowadays we must live in a complex world of international politics. A nation's foreign policy must consider not just the interests of immediate neighbors, but the interests of nations thousands of miles away. How can the makers of foreign policy manage to comprehend this complexity?

One answer is to draw upon everyday experience. We all engage in interpersonal relationships. We have friends, as well as enemies or rivals. We form informal pacts and alliances. Indeed, these patterns of interpersonal activity began in elementary school, if not before. Moreover, by adulthood each of us has probably established a preferred style of interaction. Some of us may like to take charge, to dominate others. Others among us may be more willing to take on a subordinate role. Some of us may be highly extroverted, incessantly intruding our personalities upon the interactions that surround us. Others may adopt a more introverted stance toward our social world.

Our preferred orientation may then provide the model for our views of international affairs. If we like to push our peers around, we may want our nation to tell other nations who's boss. If we love to mix and gab at office parties, we may also like our nation to have a conspicuous presence in diplomatic exchanges on the world arena. Of course, if we just so happen to find ourselves in positions of power, we may find ourselves projecting our preferred interaction habits on the course of international affairs.

This, in outline, is the "interpersonal generalization theory" as it applies to foreign policy makers. This hypothesis has been subjected to an ingenious empirical test. Using biographical data, the investigator evaluated three dozen presidents and presidential advisors on two dimensions. First, the investigator determined whether a policy maker preferred a dominant mode of interaction with subordinates; in other words, did the individual like to lord it over underlings? Second, the policy makers were assessed according to whether they were primarily introverted or extroverted in human relations. The next step was to examine 62 cases of foreign policy debates in modern U.S. history. Some of these debates involved whether the United States should use its military might to impose its interests on other nations. One example was the debate between President Wilson and Secretary of State Bryan over the German U-boat actions during World War I. This altercation led to Bryan's resignation. Another set of policy debates specifically concerned the Soviet Union and nations of the Soviet bloc. For instance, President Eisenhower disagreed with Secretary of State Dulles over the former's desire to hold a summit conference with the Soviet leadership. In all of these debates, did a policy maker's interpersonal style shape the stance taken on the issue? Yes, indeed.

Those personalities who liked to reign over their inferiors were much more prone to recommend the use of military force to achieve American interests abroad. For example, in the period leading up to the Spanish-American War, Theodore Roosevelt (then assistant secretary of the Navy) advocated a more bellicose position than the more conciliatory policy chosen by President McKinley. Similarly, it made a difference whether a policy maker was extroverted or introverted. Hence, extroverts were more likely to recommend a more outgoing policy toward Soviet Union and the Soviet bloc. The introverts, in contrast, promoted a more isolationist point of view, one that questioned the value of negotiations and summit meetings. To be sure, there were exceptions.

The preferred pattern of interpersonal relationships did not provide an inviolable template for foreign policy recommendations. Even so, only one-fourth of the time did an official go against the grain of interpersonal preference. Clearly, social interaction strongly guided what policy makers saw as the most desirable framework for international relations.

The two dimensions were independent of each other. This fact provided the basis for a fourfold typology. That is, both the high- and low-dominance policy makers could be either extroverted or introverted, yielding four broad types of foreign policy orientations. Individuals illustrating the typology appear in Table 9.1. High-dominance introverts tried to confine potentially disruptive forces by establishing exclusive blocs, such as defensive alliances. In Wilson's conception, the League of Nations was an organization where the civilized countries could impose their will on the more barbarian members of the world community. Low-dominance introverts were more passively engaged in maintaining the status quo in international affairs. They produced such inept documents as the Kellogg–Briand Pact that "outlawed" war. Low-dominance extroverts, in contrast, operated as conciliators. Their involvement in foreign relations was both conspicuous and ineffectual. Their policies were not vigorously implemented—wishes without teeth. Lastly, high-dominance extroverts were international crusaders. They tried to reform international affairs by forcefully bringing all world powers into an inclusive system. The United Nations is a legacy of one such leader, Franklin D. Roosevelt.

It is not amazing that policy makers can behave this way. Interpersonal relationships provide a convenient metaphor for international affairs. Even so, what guarantee do we have that one policy maker's interpersonal style offers an adequate model for a particular policy issue at hand? Sometimes force is necessary, other times not. On some occasions an active role is the call of the hour, while other occasions dictate a passive wait-and-see attitude. Yet we have no assurance that the interpersonal orientation of a president or secretary of

TABLE 9.1. Personality Typology of Foreign Policy Orientations

	High dominance	Low dominance
Extroverts	World (integrating) leaders *Presidents*: L. Johnson, T. Roosevelt, F. D. Roosevelt, Kennedy *Secretary of state*: Byrnes *Policy advisor*: Hopkins	Conciliators *Presidents*: McKinley, Truman, Taft, Eisenhower, Harding *Secretaries of state*: Bryan, Hay *Policy advisor*: Stevenson
Introverts	Bloc (excluding) leaders *Presidents*: Wilson, Hoover *Secretaries of state*: Dulles, Hughes, Stimson, Acheson, Hull, Root *Policy advisor*: House	Maintainers *President*: Coolidge *Secretaries of state*: Herter, Marshall, Lansing, Sherman, Kellogg, Rusk *Policy advisor*: Kennan

state will just happen to coincide with the optimal strategy in a given situation. World-integrating and bloc-excluding leaders, even conciliators and maintainers, may all have their moments in history. But at a given moment a single politician may be out of synchrony with the times. Many have speculated whether Hitler's ambitious plans would have been nipped in the bud, had the other major European powers not been replete with conciliators at a critical juncture in history.

Saints versus Sinners

For ages, we have judged history in moral terms. The ancient Chinese historian Ban Biao saw in the coming and going of dynasties the hidden hand of the mandate of heaven. When rulers of one dynasty became corrupt and immoral, they lost their divine right to rule; soon a more virtuous leader would emerge, founding a new dynasty. The Hebrew prophets viewed the vicissitudes of Israel and Judah in similar terms. Amos, for example, condemned the otherwise successful reign of King Jeroboam II for the moral ills of contemporary society, and he prophesied doom accordingly. The Moslem historian Ibn Khaldūn continued this tradition in his 1377 philosophy of history. As he saw it, the rise and fall of Moslem dynasties was a cyclical process in which the heroic and ethical virtues of the nomad became perverted by the temptations of civilized life.

We moderns are no less inclined to judge events according to their ethical implications. The purpose of the trials at Nuremberg was to assign blame to those Nazi leaders who committed crimes against humanity. Hitler and his accomplices were branded as conspirators in an evil enterprise. More recently, Pol Pot of Cambodia, Saddam Hussein of Iraq, and Slobodan Milosevic of Serbia have earned widespread moral condemnation. Their genocidal brutalities have been compared to those of the Nazis. However, our applications of moral judgments to history may be misguided. As recorded in Chapter 3, it is too easy to succumb to self-centered moralizing. We all like to see ourselves as good, our enemies as bad. Therefore, we must ask whether psychological science can enable us to get more objective insights on this slippery question. Happily, behavioral scientists have probed this subject from more than one perspective.

First, several investigators have tried to extract moral lessons in the aftermath of the Holocaust. Some of this work has concentrated on the perpetrators of these grotesquely cruel events. Among the targets of ethical inquiry are (1) the Nazi physicians, like Josef Mengele, who participated in perhaps the most inhumane experiments ever conducted on human subjects; and (2) the Nazi officials, like Adolf Eichmann, who directed the institutions of genocide. One remarkable conclusion of these inquiries is the "banality of evil." That is, those responsible for immoral deeds are often quite ordinary people. They seldom fit the image of the psychopathic genius that permeates novels, movies, and television shows. Sometimes evil is not so much an active force as a passive agent permitted by the absence of good.

This surprising conclusion is underlined by studies of those altruists who risked their lives to help their Jewish neighbors and friends during the Holocaust. The rescuers tended to have had parents who instilled in them a strong sense of ethical obligation. "I learned to be good to one's neighbor," said one such hero, "to be responsible, concerned and considerate. To work—and work hard. But also to help—to the point of leaving one's work to help one's neighbor." Those who acquiesced in the horrors of the day lacked this behavioral commitment to rudimentary moral values. Their sin was usually one of omission, not commission.

Revealing though these inquiries are, we must become yet more rigorous. The work of Lawrence Kohlberg represents a major advance. Kohlberg has argued for the existence of six main moral stages, each stage representing a qualitatively distinct morality. As people develop from childhood through adulthood, they pass through these stages in an invariant sequence. Moreover, this sequence of stages reflects a progressive improvement in the adequacy of moral reasoning. Someone thinking at Stage 6 is displaying a higher level of morality than someone thinking at Stage 5 or lower. To see why, we need at least a thumbnail sketch of each stage.

1. *Obedience and punishment:* People (primarily children) obey those who have the power to punish them for transgressions against given rules. Because the rules are arbitrary rather than rational, they have no moral power divorced from the punitive authority that enforces them. Moreover, actions are judged by their physical repercussions rather than the intentions of their agents. Fortunately, not many adults are stuck at this primitive stage.

2. *Individualism, instrumental purpose, and exchange:* Ethical decisions are guided solely by what enables people to increase their pleasures and decrease their pains. Because they recognize that others are equally impelled by hedonistic goals, they are willing to enter reciprocal exchanges. Ethics is thus restricted to the narrow reciprocity principle: "I'll scratch your back if you scratch mine." This is effectively the code of Ayn Rand. Good and bad are defined in her "objectivist philosophy" according to a single, selfish soul— "*numero uno.*"

3. *Interpersonal accord, relationship preservation, and conformity:* People are seriously committed to maintaining close personal relationships. They also feel a moral responsibility to live up to expectations about what is good or nice behavior. They conform to general norms and expectations to earn social approval. This is the morality of the typical American junior high school student who looks to his or her peers for ethical guidance. It is also the first stage in which people adhere to moral conventions for their own sake. Stages 1 and 2, in contrast, are preconventional in Kohlberg's scheme.

4. *Social accord and system maintenance:* People feel it is their moral duty to obey the laws that must be observed by everyone in their society. These laws are necessary to preserve the social order. To disobey these legal prescriptions is to risk chaos. Thomas Hobbes, in his *Leviathan*, was a strong advocate of this ethical philosophy. Without obedience to the law, there would be "no arts; no letters; no society; and which is worst of all, continual fear, and danger of violent death; and the life of man, solitary, poor, nasty, brutish, and short." Interestingly, this is the highest stage that most American adults attain. It is the stage of "law and order."

5. *Social contract, utility, and individual rights:* This is the first of the postconventional stages, in which people move beyond the prescripts and statutes of society. Now they recognize and appreciate the diversity of opinions and values in a social system. Only by achieving some consensus, embedded in a social contract, can laws have some moral weight. Although people in this stage may see majority rule as a primary means of ensuring the "greatest good for the greatest number," they and everybody else have certain rights that cannot be arbitrarily terminated by a majority vote. As Thomas Jefferson expressed this restriction in the Declaration of Independence, we are all endowed with "certain unalienable Rights . . . among these are Life, Liberty and the pursuit of Happiness." In fact, the Declaration justified America's revolt from British rule by saying that Britain violated the implicit contract that bound Parliament not to infringe on such irrevocable rights. According to Kohlberg, the moral arguments that Socrates gave for why he had to drink the hemlock were Stage 5 in tone. By living in Athens as a citizen, he had implicitly consented to abide by its laws. Therefore, if convicted to die by a legitimate court of law, he must do so. Socrates could not morally accept the opportunity to escape that Crito afforded him.

6. *Universal ethical principles:* Very few people make it to this highest stage, in which moral standards are self-chosen principles that apply to all humanity. These principles are rooted in the fundamental belief in the essential and equal dignity of all human beings as rational actors. These abstract principles are then the final arbitrator of the justice of any law or contract. One way to describe Stage 6 is to think of a hypothetical party game of "ethical chairs." In a given moral dilemma, contemplate all the persons likely to be affected by a given ethical decision—including yourself. Imagine yourself in the position of each participant one by one. Each time ask yourself, "What is the best action to take?" If you give the same answer no matter whose chair you're sitting in, you are applying Stage 6 reasoning.

Thus, people at Stage 6 "put themselves in the other person's shoes." Perhaps they apply the Golden Rule of Jesus: "Do to others as you would have others do to you." Or they may cite the Silver Rule of Confucius: "Don't do to others what you don't want them to do to you." The outcome is much the same. When Lincoln spoke out against slavery, he argued that since he would not want to endure the life of a slave, he obviously could not stomach an existence as a slave master either. The Silver Rule orders us to drop the whip; the Golden Rule commands us to break the chains. Lincoln was at Stage 6.

One important history-making aspect of Stage 6 must be noted: A person's ethical conscience may dictate that he or she has a moral duty to disobey unjust laws. This was the position taken by Henry David Thoreau in his 1849 "Essay on Civil Disobedience." This was the principle applied by Mahatma Gandhi in his doctrine of *satyagraha*. This was also the implication articulated in Martin Luther King's 1963 "Letter from Birmingham Jail." In that last document, for instance, King followed St. Augustine by distinguishing between just and unjust laws. "A law is unjust . . . if the majority group compels a minority group to obey the statute but does not make it binding on itself. By the same token, a law in all probability is just if the majority is itself willing to obey it." Faced with the existence of an unjust law, King argued that one should not merely evade it; that is moral cowardice. Instead,

> One who breaks an unjust law must do so *openly, lovingly,* and with a willingness to accept the penalty. I submit that an individual who breaks a law that conscience tells him is unjust and who willingly accepts the penalty of imprisonment in order to arouse the conscience of the community over its injustice is in reality expressing the highest respect for law.

And so King's opposition to segregation laws got him incarcerated. For parallel reasons, Gandhi often found himself imprisoned during his crusades against South African racism and British imperialism. Similarly, Thoreau was locked up for refusing to pay a tax levied to support the U.S. invasion of Mexico, a war that Thoreau believed was morally reprehensible. For Thoreau, Gandhi, and King, universal ethical principles provided the means by which they left their distinctive moral stamp on the annals of civilization.

Naturally, the ethical imprint may not always be so elevated. When Lieutenant William Calley was tried for his role in the My Lai massacre, he gave Stage 4 excuses: He was only following orders; as a soldier, it was his legal (and moral) duty to obey. This was basically the same defense given by Colonel Oliver North when he was prosecuted in the wake of the Iran–Contra scandal of the Reagan administration. We can dip lower still. When Israel tried Adolf Eichmann for war crimes, Eichmann's reasons were Stage 2, even Stage 1: Obedience to Der Führer was either a virtue for its own sake, or at least something that was expedient if people wanted to save themselves. For example, Eichmann defended himself in the Israeli court with this Stage 1 sentiment:

> If I had sabotaged the order of the one-time Führer of the German Reich, Adolf Hitler, I would have been not only a scoundrel but a despicable pig like those who broke their military oath to join the ranks of the anti-Hitler criminals in the conspiracy of July 20, 1944.

Placing Eichmann's pusillanimous excuses alongside King's valorous actions renders more salient the frequent banality of evil.

The moral impression of Calley, North, and especially Eichmann is of a completely different order than that of Thoreau, Gandhi, and King. The long-term impact of Eichmann will probably exceed that of either Calley or North; the sheer magnitude of the immorality implied by organized genocide must cast a wide and dark shadow over human history. The more limited Stage 4 morality of Calley and North may not cast such a shadow. At the same time, we cannot doubt that the historic effects of the ethical lives of Thoreau, Gandhi, and King—especially the last two—probably exceed the effects of Calley's and North's actions. Does this imply that people are most likely to make their mark if they stand at the extremes of Kohlberg's ethical sequence? Is the relationship between historic influence and morality described by a curvilinear, U-shaped curve?

We have some evidence that this might be so. Psychologists have studied the moral development of those involved in the Free Speech Movement sit-in. This controversial event happened in 1965, at the University of California, Berkeley. Curiously, the campus radicals were not an ethically homogeneous group. On the one hand, the largest proportion of demonstrators were at Stage 6, with Stage 5 moralists almost as common. These students were obviously engaged in protesting an "unjust law," much as King advocated in his 1963 prison letter. On the other hand, the next most prominent group of activists were at Stage 2—sometimes even Stage 1! These participants were not guided by high ethical standards; they were just having immense fun behaving as amoral hooligans. Hence, the student radicals consisted of both moral giants and ethical idiots. The mediocre stayed in the dorms and studied.

This curvilinear relationship receives endorsement from an unanticipated quarter. Near the beginning of this century, Frederick Woods, the pioneer in historiometric methods, tried to assess members of royal families on "virtue." This is an old-fashioned, Victorian word for the possession of special qualities, of which moral caliber is certainly a central part. Later investigators over the decades since then have extended and refined this assessment. In particular, virtue scores have now been calculated for 342 kings, queens, emperors, kaisers, czars, and sultans. These absolute monarchs reigned over nations from Sweden and Denmark to Spain and Portugal, and from France and Scotland to Russia and Turkey. The virtuous rulers were more likely to be moral, prudent, well-meaning, and popular; the unprincipled rulers were more likely to be licentious, tyrannical, and treacherous. Moreover, a monarch's score on virtue tended to correlate, however modestly, with his or her score on intellect. This association parallels the modest tendency for a person's intelligence to correspond with a higher moral stage in Kohlberg's system.

Two other relationships are more fascinating. First, historic activity in a particular reign was a curvilinear, U-shaped function of a ruler's virtue. By "historic activity," I simply mean the sheer supply of notable events: conquests, battles, laws, reforms, executions, and similar occasions that make up the fabric of history. Second, the connection between eminence and virtue is summarized by the same U-shaped curve. By "eminence," I mean the leader's prominence in the nation's annals. Both of these curves were calculated after variable reign spans were considered.

Hence, there seem to have been two paths to monarchal greatness. The high road was to exhibit high moral caliber. Those who opted for this route went down in the history books as ethical paragons. The low road was to display not the slightest ethical scruple, and thus to be recorded as an moral ogre in royal robes. The two extremes are typified by St. Louis IX of France and Ivan the Terrible of Russia. Furthermore, no matter which choice the rulers made, their reigns were fraught with historic events. In the case of a saint, the era became a glorious one truly worthy of the Hebrew prophets and Chinese moralists—crusades for just causes both at home and abroad. In the case of a sinner, the era became equally glorious but most unworthy—tyranny, conquest, unprecedented dissipation. The choice thus seems to have been between fame or infamy. In contrast, the rulers who were neither good nor evil—who, like Hamlet, were "but indifferent honest"—fell by the wayside as the moral nonentities of the annals.

Earlier we have observed that the relation between presidential greatness and dogmatism is also described by a U-shaped curve: The most highly acclaimed chief executives of American history tended to be either inflexibly idealistic or flexibly practical. Even though this latter dimension is not the same as morality or virtue, it looks close enough to provide a striking parallel. The most successful presidents are either Stage 2 wheeler-dealer types who operated according to shrewd reciprocity, or Stage 6 preacher types who tried to raise the moral standard of American politics. The middling, conventional types were neither bad nor good, and attracted no admiration, negative or positive. It would appear that only devils and angels, not mere humans, can inspire awe.

Patterns of Character

There must be a better way of examining personality. We have been discussing trait after trait, but such a piecemeal discussion lacks coherence or insight. The whole seems less than the sum of its parts. We do not know how the various traits interrelate even when there appears to be some overlap in their content. For instance, what is the exact connection between being a Type A personality and having a preference for dominance in personal relationships? What is the precise association between dogmatism and morality?

An alternative does exist. Many psychologists have devised "personality inventories," which assess individuals on multiple traits simultaneously. The measured attributes are largely independent of one another. Someone taking the inventory may be high or low on one trait without necessarily being high or low on any of the others. Thus, interpretation need not worry about overlap among the separate dimensions on which personalities can vary. Moreover, measurements on each trait are "standardized"; that is, all scores are on the same scale. Hence, we can make such statements as "So-and-so is this many points above average on trait A but that many points below average on trait B." In fact, if the inventory contains enough distinct dimensions, we can draw a "personality profile." A profile is a graphic representation of the traits on which an individual scores high or low, as well as the size of the departure from the average. Figure 9.2 gives an example of a hypothetical profile.

Using this instrument, the investigators can assess a person on 14 different characteristics, labeled A through N. The score for each trait is assigned a point on the graph. Hence, this fictional individual has received a score of –1 on trait A, +1 on trait B, 0 on trait C, and so on. These scores have all been standardized such that 0 represents an average score in the general population. Numbers above or below 0 indicate how many standard deviations the person departs from the mean. A standard deviation is the gauge of variation introduced in Chapter 8.

To make a graph such as that in Figure 9.2 more visually effective, the separate points are often connected by straight lines to form a profile. The resulting profile gives a picture of a particular personality. People with similar personalities will look the same visually. Persons with diametrically opposed characters will yield profiles with lines all going in contrary directions. Furthermore, profiles may be constructed for groups rather than individuals. Instead of plotting single scores, we can plot group means. This enables us to compare the profiles of different types of people, such as leaders versus creators or scientists versus artists. Persons in one endeavor may score consistently higher on trait A in comparison to persons in another endeavor.

But where do we get the standardized scores to compute the individual or

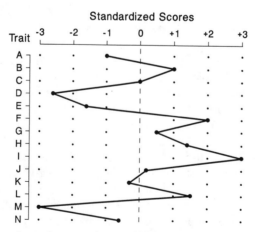

FIGURE 9.2. Hypothetical personality profile giving standardized scores on traits A through N.

group profiles? Again, Chapter 8 has specified the two major approaches to calculating IQ scores. Now we can examine the two principal methods for extracting profiles—the psychometric and the historiometric.

Contemporary Profiles

Psychometric inventories are commonplace. Dozens of them vie for use by both research and practicing psychologists. All are constructed by much the same methods. First, the psychometrician crafts a series of questionnaire items that gauge various aspects of personality: motives, values, interests, beliefs, activities, and so forth. Sometimes these questions are phrased so the person taking the test simply gives a true–false or yes–no response. For example, in the Minnesota Multiphasic Personality Inventory (MMPI), the subject has to agree or disagree with such statements as "I believe in God" and "I am a special agent of God."

Once a collection of items has been put together, the next step is to apply them to a representative batch of humanity. The test constructor usually discovers that responses on some items are related to responses to other items. Accordingly, the researcher applies a mathematical technique called "factor analysis," which objectively determines items that cluster into largely independent dimensions, or factors. Each item cluster then is said to measure a separate trait of the overall profile. Besides isolating which items make up which traits, factor analysis allows the psychometrician to assess the number of dimensions necessary to describe a human personality. The test maker now revises the instrument, and administers it to another sample of human beings. Norms can then be established for the personality inventory. With these norms in hand, the trait scores can be standardized. The test can thus be given to everyone under the sun, and the testees' personality profiles can be conveniently graphed. Of course, if we can persuade some illustrious personalities to take one of these standardized personality inventories, we can learn how their profiles differ from the rest of us.

To illustrate, R. B. Cattell devoted his career to developing the Sixteen Personality Factor Questionnaire (16 PF), which, as its name suggests, evaluates people on 16 different dimensions. These traits are expressed as "bipolar" factors; that is, high and low scores represent polar opposites. Thus, Simplicity contrasts with Shrewdness (Factor N), and Conservatism contrasts with Radicalism (Factor Q_1). The designations for some of the 16 factors are fairly straightforward, such as Low Intelligence versus High Intelligence (Factor B), Low Ego Strength versus High Ego Strength (Factor C), Low Dominance versus High Dominance (Factor E), and Low Guilt Proneness versus High Guilt Proneness (Factor O). In naming other factors, Cattell indulged a passion for what some laypersons might consider the quintessence of obscure jargon: Schizothymia versus Cyclothymia (Factor A), Threctia versus Parmia

(Factor H), and Praxernia versus Autia (Factor M). The intimidating terminology notwithstanding, these factors cover some important traits. For instance, Parmia means "boldness, spontaneity, and insusceptibility to inhibition," whereas Threctia signifies "shyness and high responsiveness to threat."

Besides having ordinary people take the 16 PF, Cattell and his colleagues have given this inventory to important people as well. For example, the 16 PF was given to 41 champions of the 1952 Olympic Games. By calculating an average score for this sample, the investigators obtained a profile typical of outstanding athletes. As a group, the champions were close to the general population on most dimensions. They stood out from the crowd on only four factors: They were low on Guilt Proneness (O), high on Parmia (H), higher still on Ego Strength (C), and extremely high on Dominance (E). This cluster appears to fit our common-sense ideas about what it might take to rise to the top in fierce Olympic competition. The picture is that of a "no-holds-barred, offer-no-quarter, me-first" victor.

This examination of Olympic champions was followed by another that focused on distinguished scientific researchers. The subjects were 46 physicists, 46 biologists, and 52 psychologists, all leaders in their fields. In comparison to normal adult males, these luminaries differed in several respects. Successful scientists were above average on Intelligence (B), Self-Sufficiency (Q$_2$), Dominance (E), Radicalism (Q$_1$), and Premsia (I). The last means the tendency to be tender-minded and sensitive. On the other hand, they were below normal on Guilt Proneness (O) and Group Superego (G). These scientists didn't spend much of their lives feeling guilty about not living up to society's moral standards. They also scored high on Desurgency (F), signifying that they were sober, serious, and prudent. Finally, they scored high on Schizothymia (A). That sounds like a grim diagnosis, given its superficial resemblance to the term "schizophrenic." Yet all it really means is that the scientists were cool, reserved, and detached introverts. They devoted more time to the silent recesses of the laboratory cubicle than to the noisy exchanges of the office party.

Although the scientists Cattell studied were certainly notable, he was not describing the sort of scientist who achieves greatness. Therefore, he wanted to know whether the personality profile evinced by contemporary scientists would fit the character pattern of the true greats of the past. So, as a hobby, Cattell began reading biographies of those whose names are permanently engraved in the annals of science. Among his subjects were Avogadro, Boyle, Cannon, Cavendish, Dalton, Darwin, Davy, Faraday, Humboldt, Lord Kelvin, Kepler, Lavoisier, Leibniz, Newton, Paracelsus, Pascal, Pasteur, Priestley, Scheele, and J. J. Thomson. On the basis of what he read, Cattell assigned ratings to the luminaries as if they had actually taken the 16 PF themselves. Their personality profiles were practically the same. Great scientists past and present could be described by the same broad character pattern.

In fact, other research using the 16 PF shows that key aspects of the profile apply to most types of extraordinary creativity. The same character pattern appeared in a sample of writers of imaginative literature and in another sample of artists worthy of entries in *Who's Who in American Art*. This congruence implies that certain character traits are probably essential rather than incidental to creative success. Take the proclivity toward extreme introversion, one of the most recurrent features of the generic profile.

Henry Cavendish, the notable physicist and chemist, illustrates how schizothymic a creative genius can be. Once, when he was coerced into attending a formal occasion, he found himself about to be introduced to some scientific celebrities from the Continent. Rather than endure the social chit-chat, Cavendish abandoned all amenities, turned away from his escorts, and sped down the hall, squealing like a bat. Cavendish ordinarily never said more than a handful of words to a man, and refused to utter anything to a woman. At home, he communicated to his female servants by written memos only, and fired instantly any servant who crossed his path. Cavendish even had a separate entrance added to his house so he could come and go without having to say "hello" or "goodbye" to another soul.

Admittedly, Cavendish went off the deep end on this trait. Even so, other notables, scientific and artistic, are more likely to avoid the entertainments of society than to seek them out. Such frivolous activities only interfere with the quiet contemplation necessary to consummate the most original ideas. When a friend badgered Charles Dickens with repeated invitations to attend social gatherings, Dickens protested:

> "It is only half-an-hour"—"It is only an afternoon"—"It is only an evening," people say to me over and over again; but they don't know that it is impossible to command one's self sometimes to any stipulated and set disposal of five minutes—or that the mere consciousness of an engagement will sometimes worry a whole day. These are the penalties paid for writing books. Who ever is devoted to an art must be content to deliver himself wholly up to it, and to find his recompense in it. I am grieved if you suspect me of not wanting to see you, but I can't help it; I must go in my way whether or no.

So preoccupied and dedicated must be the creative intellect that even the home hearth must not expect the attentiveness customarily due family life. Once when Karl Gauss was enthralled with a mathematical problem, a servant came in to advise him that his wife, who was quite ill, was about to breathe her last. He could only mutter, "Tell her to wait a moment till I'm through." Gauss was clearly deficient in Guilt Proneness and Group Superego as well!

Certainly there do exist creative geniuses who are cyclothymic rather than schizothymic—extroverts rather than introverts, to return to everyday terms. Alexandre Dumas *père* supposedly could write novels while enraptured in repartee. Yet creators like Dumas are much less frequent than creators like Cavendish, Dickens, and Gauss. The gregarious who fritter their time away at cocktail parties, social outings, and family get-togethers are less likely to leave enduring impressions on posterity. At death, their mouths are silenced forever, while the voices of deceased introverts speak on.

The other facets of the typical profile probably also facilitate the attainment of greatness, each trait after its own fashion. High Intelligence, Self-Sufficiency, Dominance, Radicalism, and Desurgency, in particular, join Schizothymia in composing the personality structure of the creative genius. Hence, those individuals whose personalities are most congruent with the generic profile have the best chances of climbing to the pinnacle of fame.

I don't want to exaggerate the resemblances. Although some features of 16 PF profiles stay fairly constant across domains of achievement, other traits may notably differ. For instance, eminent artists and writers, in comparison to distinguished scientists, are more emotionally unstable and sensitive, as well as more Bohemian in character. This contrast in profiles provides a personality basis for what C. P. Snow styled "the two cultures." The successful scientist becomes far too objective, unemotional, and analytical to have an outstanding appreciation for the arts. Charles Darwin admitted in his *Autobiography* that "now for many years I cannot endure to read a line of poetry; I have tried lately to read Shakespeare, and found it so intolerably dull that it nauseated me." Artists, on the other hand, cherish too much the personal, idiosyncratic, irrational, and emotional to entertain much regard for science. Coleridge once said, "The more I understand of Sir Isaac Newton's works, the more boldly I dare utter to my own mind . . . that I believe the Souls of 500 Sir Isaac Newtons would go to the making up of a Shak[e]speare or a Milton." So, despite the validity of the generic profile, scientific and artistic types belong to different clubs. Emotionality and sensitivity determine which membership card one holds.

Historical Profiles

By assessing deceased scientists on the 16 PF, R. B. Cattell was, in a sense, constructing a historiometric profile. The raw data came from biographies rather than the responses of live scientists to a personality questionnaire. The abstraction of personality traits from the life records of historic figures actually has a long history in psychology. Back in 1926, Catherine Cox assessed a subset of her 301 geniuses on 67 character traits. And in 1950, Edward L. Thorndike, the eminent psychologist, posthumously published ratings of 91 famous creators and leaders on 48 different personality attributes.

Unfortunately, in these inquiries no one tried to consolidate the profusion of traits into a more manageable set of broad dimensions. The profiles that Cox graphed in her study were monstrously complicated. Fortunately, the technique of factor analysis, which proves so useful in building psychometric profiles, can be applied to these biographical measures with equal success. For instance, factor analyses reveal that the 48 character traits in Thorndike's assessments can be collapsed into just four inclusive dimensions: Industriousness, Extroversion, Aggressiveness, and Intelligence. In other words, despite the diversity of traits, each can be assigned to one of four factors on which people may independently vary.

Psychometric and historiometric profiles have distinct advantages and disadvantages. Before we can appreciate the pros and cons, we need to examine in more detail a specific illustration of this alternative strategy. In this study, the goal was to assess 39 presidents of the United States on suitable personality dimensions. The inquiry began by abstracting from biographical materials descriptions of each president's personality. For example, the following passage is often quoted in presidential biographies:

> He was morally and physically courageous, even-tempered and conservative, secretive and sagacious, skeptical and cautious, truthful and honest, firm in his own convictions and tolerant of those of others, reflective and cool, ambitious and somewhat selfish, kind to all and good-natured, sympathetic in the presence of suffering or under an imaginative description of it, lived in his reason and reasoned in his life. Easy of approach and perfectly democratic in nature, [he] had a broad charity for his fellow-men and had an excuse for unreflective acts of his kind, and in short he loved justice and lived out in thought and act the eternal right. . . . I do not say that he never deviated from his own nature and his own rules. His nature, the tendency of it, is as I state. . . . [He] struggled to live the best life possible.

The author of this thumbnail sketch was William H. Herndon, who was describing his former law partner, Abraham Lincoln.

Personality descriptions such as this one were transcribed with all identifying material removed, so judges could not let their political prejudices contaminate their ratings. Next a team of independent judges converted the qualitative descriptions to quantitative assessments. Each judge was handed the Gough Adjective Check List (ACL), which consists of 300 adjectives arranged in alphabetical order from "absent-minded" to "zany." This list contains virtually any personality trait imaginable.

Usually psychologists use the ACL as a psychometric instrument. People take the test by checking off those descriptors that they believe apply to their own personalities; it is a self-rating system. In this inquiry, on the other hand, it was the judges who were evaluating all presidents from Washington through Reagan on the 300 adjectives. The judges used a 1-to-7 scale, where 7 signified that the adjective described the president perfectly, and 1 that the precise opposite was characteristic of the person. This practice echoes what Cattell did when he took the 16 PF for the long-deceased Newton, Galileo, and others.

Of course, not all adjectives were applicable. For example, how many chief executives can be described as "zany"? Most presidents (except Theodore Roosevelt) were given the lowest possible score on this trait (1). This is an illustration of a "floor effect" in measurement. In contrast, an adjective like "ambitious" exhibited a "ceiling effect." Not many American citizens rise to the nation's highest office without showing considerable amounts of ambition. Therefore, most presidents (except U.S. Grant) got the highest possible score on this trait (7). Because of floor and ceiling effects (and other problems), the judges could give meaningful scores on just 110 adjectives out of the original 300.

This is still a frightening number of traits—even worse that Cox's 67 or Thorndike's 48. It was certainly awkward to construct personality profiles for the 39 presidents using this many traits. Accordingly, factor analysis was used to consolidate the diverse traits into a more manageable number of character dimensions. This procedure was especially necessary because many of the traits just seemed to go together naturally. Some even measured more or less the same thing, albeit from opposite directions. Thus, presidents who scored high on "friendly" were extremely likely to score low on "unfriendly," and vice versa. The factor analysis did the trick: The 110 adjectives fell naturally into 14 different trait clusters. Many of these personality factors were bipolar as well. Table 9.2 shows the 14 dimensions with some of their most characteristic descriptors.

It may help to clarify the nature of these dimensions if I identify the presidents who stood out well above or below their colleagues. Theodore Roosevelt and Jackson were the lowest in Moderation; Polk was lowest on Friendliness; Jefferson scored the highest on Intellectual Brilliance, and Harding by far the lowest; Machiavellianism was most descriptive of Nixon, Lyndon Johnson, Van Buren, and Polk; Taylor displayed the least Poise and Polish; Grant had the lowest Achievement Drive; the highest Forcefulness was shown by Theodore Roosevelt and Lyndon Johnson; Kennedy, Reagan, and Lincoln were rather

TABLE 9.2. Dimensions of Presidential Personality According to ACL Descriptions

1. Moderation: "moderate," "modest," "gentle," "mild," "considerate," but not "temperamental," "outspoken," "argumentative," or "impatient"
2. Friendliness: "friendly," "outgoing," "sociable," "affectionate," but not "cold," "stern," "withdrawn," "shy," or "distrustful"
3. Intellectual Brilliance: "interests wide," "artistic," "inventive," "curious," "intelligent," "sophisticated," and "insightful"
4. Machiavellianism: "sly," "deceitful," "unscrupulous," "evasive," and "shrewd," but not "sincere" or "honest"
5. Poise and Polish: "poised," "polished," "formal," and "mannerly" but not "simple" or "unassuming"
6. Achievement Drive: "industrious" and "persistent" but not "quitting"
7. Forcefulness: "energetic," "active," and "determined"
8. Wit: "humorous," "witty," and "self-confident"
9. Physical Attractiveness: "handsome," "good-looking," and "attractive"
10. Pettiness: "greedy" and "self-pitying"
11. Tidiness: "methodical," "organized," and "thrifty"
12. Conservatism: "conservative" and "conventional"
13. Inflexibility: "stubborn," "persistent," "hard-headed," and "rigid"
14. Pacifism: "peaceable" but not "courageous"

conspicuous on Wit; Physical Attractiveness was a primary asset of Pierce, Fillmore, Kennedy, and Harding; Pettiness was Nixon's forte; anal-compulsive Tidiness described best Buchanan and Jefferson; Reagan was highest on Conservatism, Jefferson the lowest; Inflexibility plagued the personalities of Tyler, Wilson, and Andrew Johnson; and whereas Carter scored the highest on Pacifism, Theodore Roosevelt and Andrew Johnson scored the lowest.

To permit easy comparisons, the presidents' ratings on the 14 dimensions were standardized (as z scores). A zero means a president was average. A minus number tells us how much below average he was, a plus number how much above average. This is the same style as seen in Figure 9.2 above. In fact, once all the trait scores were made comparable, 14-factor personality profiles could be graphed for each of the 39 presidents. Such graphs allow us to spot the presidents who were most similar and most different in basic character. To illustrate, Figure 9.3 shows the resulting profiles for Franklin D. Roosevelt, Truman, and Eisenhower. Although these three presidents entered the White House in succession, their respective personality profiles were about as different as they could be.

I have said that FDR, Truman, and Eisenhower differed appreciably in their trait profiles. This is not a judgment call. Psychologists have designed techniques to gauge the similarities and differences among such profiles. The method known as "cluster analysis" will even group together those subjects with the most congruent highs and lows. Figure 9.4 shows the outcome of applying cluster analysis to the 14-factor profiles of the 39 presidents. Such a graph is called a "dendrogram," because of its tree-like design. Those presidents with the most similar profiles were grouped into clusters first, the most dissimilar presidents last. Profile similarities are depicted by the "cluster distance," which

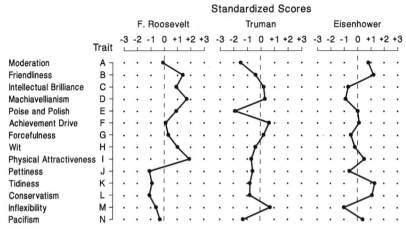

FIGURE 9.3. Personality profiles for three American presidents on 14 personality dimensions.

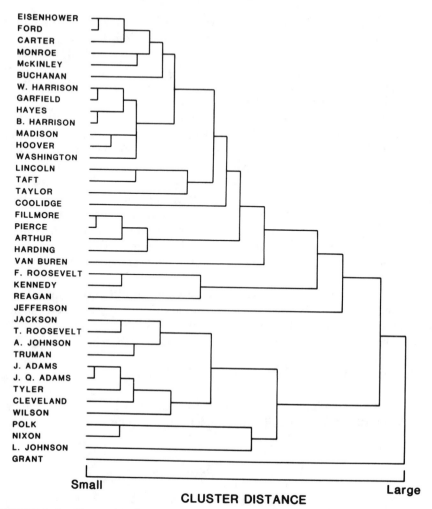

FIGURE 9.4. Clustering of 39 American presidents according to the similarity of their personality profiles.

records how long it took before two presidents (or clusters of presidents) were linked into a single cluster.

Notice that Eisenhower formed a cluster with Ford and later Carter—all "nice guys," to be sure, but a bit lackluster. Truman was grouped with a rather different cluster, one containing Andrew Johnson and, a little later, Theodore Roosevelt and Andrew Jackson. These were all somewhat immoderate, crude, inflexible, and belligerent types. Franklin D. Roosevelt was grouped with Kennedy and, again at some distance, Reagan. This cluster represented the more attractive, dynamic, optimistic, and outgoing style of presidency. Curiously,

Grant did not join his White House predecessors and successors until the very last moment. This hints that Grant's character pattern was quite unlike that of any other leader who placed his feet on a desk in the Oval Office. However, we cannot conclude from this disparity that Grant was automatically unfit to serve. Jefferson's profile was the second most discrepant from the rest; still, we cannot question his presidential competence.

These profiles do help us understand a president's performance, nonetheless. Several of these trait dimensions correlated with how a chief executive performed his duties. Therefore, certain profiles went along with specific achievements. For instance, successful legislators tended to score high in Machiavellianism, Forcefulness, Moderation, and Poise and Polish, but low on Inflexibility. That profile produced someone who could get the most bills through Congress while having the fewest vetoed bills overturned. At a less mundane level, a specific profile often yielded a charismatic presidency. Charisma was associated with high levels of Forcefulness, Machiavellianism, and Intellectual Brilliance, but low levels of Moderation and Conservatism.

Even a president's posthumous reputation is shaped by his distinctive profile. One example is whether a chief executive becomes highly controversial in the eyes of posterity. As mentioned earlier, a controversial president is a leader who provokes much disagreement among historians about whether his administration was good or bad for the country. Controversiality was associated with this profile: high on Achievement Drive, Forcefulness, Pettiness, and Inflexibility, but low on Moderation, Friendliness, and Wit. Controversial chief executives seemed to rock the boat too much, despite complaints that the waves were making others seasick. They lacked the grace and charm to phrase a disarming joke about their obnoxious preoccupations.

Psychometric profiles also permit us to anticipate an individual's activities. For instance, R. B. Cattell's 16 PF can be used to predict leadership ability. Hence, historiometric and psychometric profiles have much the same purpose and function in the psychology of history. Nevertheless, the two strategies also diverge significantly. Historiometric profiles are tailor-made for the celebrities. We don't know what the personality dimensions are until *after* we factor-analyze the many trait measurements. The psychometric profiles, in contrast, are based on everyday samples of humanity. Hence, the personality factors psychometricians come up with should apply (theoretically) to all the human race, famous, infamous, or nonfamous.

Which is better? On the one hand, the psychometric factors may have little utility when applied to specific types of achievement. Not all of the 14 personality dimensions found for the 39 presidents in this study have counterparts in the 16 PF, for example. Hence, if we did for the presidents what Cattell did for his eminent scientists, we might overlook some critical ways in which profiles predict success. On the other hand, because the psychometric profiles are standardized on the population of adults, we can make direct comparisons between celebrated and commonplace personalities. Thus, we know that creative geniuses are more introverted than the bulk of humanity. By comparison, when the historiometric approach is used, it is not always easy to make such statements. In Figure 9.3, the score of zero, which represents the baseline, does not describe the average Joe or Jane, but the average president instead. Yet it is improbable that those 39 presidents, as a group, were like all other Americans on these 14 dimensions. Even the most petty president, Nixon, just may have been less greedy and self-pitying than the norm for the American populace.

Because psychometric and historiometric profiles have distinct advantages and disadvantages, psychologists probably will always need both approaches in their endeavors to comprehend the makers of history.

Global Portraits

Whether we examine personality in terms of singular traits or a spectrum of profiles, the orientation of these inquiries is unequivocally atomistic. Each historical figure is sliced up into predetermined fragments; these tiny pieces are then reassembled to produce the final portrait for each individual. At best the result is a pointillist painting; at worst the outcome is a more puzzling application of analytical cubism. Nonetheless, another choice exists: We can apply a more holistic approach to understanding the character structure of important persons. Abraham Maslow's 1970 inquiry into "self-actualizing people" provides a perfect illustration.

As a primary agent in the emergence of humanistic psychology, Maslow was highly discontented with the image of humanity that was then prevalent in the discipline. Instead of examining the premiere exemplars of the species, psychologists dwelled too long on those representing the worst or least of what human beings can attain. Because "the study of crippled, stunted, immature, and unhealthy specimens can yield only a cripple psychology and a cripple philosophy," he argued, "the study of self-actualizing people must be the basis for a more universal science of psychology." To show how much closer to angels humans can appear if given a decent chance, Maslow gathered a collection of people he considered to be self-actualizers. Almost four dozen of the subjects were either historic personalities or public figures who had already staked their claim to fame by their achievements. Table 9.3 gives a partial list of Maslow's mixture of luminaries. By delving into their biographies, Maslow hoped to unearth the characteristics of people who function at their best.

Maslow's conclusions can be summarized as follows. Self-actualizers are far more efficient and comfortable than the rest of us in perceiving reality in all its manifestations—including politics and public affairs, science and philosophy, art and music. Generally, they are more accepting of themselves, of others, and of nature. They acknowledge flaws without sacrificing their ability to appreciate. As part of this, they have a sense of humor that is seldom hostile,

TABLE 9.3. Famous Self-Actualizers, According to Abraham Maslow

Political figures: George Washington, Thomas Jefferson, Abraham Lincoln, Eugene V. Debs, Eleanor Roosevelt

Reformers and humanitarians: Frederick Douglass, Harriet Tubman, John Muir, Jane Addams, Albert Schweitzer

Scientists and inventors: Benjamin Franklin, George Washington Carver, David Hilbert, Albert Einstein

Philosophers and thinkers: Thomas More, Baruch Spinoza, William James, Martin Buber

Poets and essayists: Johann Wolfgang von Goethe, John Keats, Ralph Waldo Emerson, Robert Browning, Walt Whitman, Aldous Huxley

Painters: Camille Pissaro, Pierre Renoir, Thomas Eakins

Composers and musicians: Franz Joseph Haydn, Fritz Kreisler, Pablo Casals

---

but often philosophical. They exhibit a simplicity, a naturalness, and a spontaneity in interactions with the world. They avoid the artificial or contrived manner. Nor are these persons who parade a fake sophistication by proclaiming their state of boredom. Rather, self-actualizers have a continued freshness of appreciation for the objects, events, and people bringing joy to their lives. They feel a vast sympathy or even affection for all humanity, and yet their friendships are most often few but deep. Their character structure is clearly democratic rather than authoritarian, and harbors a strong sense of right and wrong. At the same time, they display a desire for detachment, a certain need for privacy, which allows them to be solitary without adverse results. Accordingly, self-actualizers are autonomous, active agents of their own lives. They show a freedom that is independent of both culture and environment. They will usually transcend the limitations of any particular culture, actively resisting enculturation to preserve their independence. Their problem-solving activities concentrate on questions outside themselves, rather than being preoccupied with the defense and enhancement of a fragile ego. This helps them all to be intensely creative. Finally, most have encountered emotional events in their lives that might count as mystical, or at least qualify for the more neutral label of the "peak experience." This is a phenomenal feeling of unity and harmony that transcends the everyday consciousness of petty concerns and self. The peak experience becomes a central motivator of their lives. "The most beautiful thing we can experience is the mysterious," said Einstein, for "it is the source of all art and science."

An almost breathtaking sketch! Unhappily, Maslow found that self-actualizers were extremely rare in his contemporary populations. For example, fewer than 1 out of 3,000 students he studied qualified. Still, he did suggest ways in which we may become self-actualizers, providing hope for us mortals still engaged in self-improvement. Given the potential benefits of this vision, it may seem crass to draw attention to some of the problems plaguing Maslow's investigation. For instance, it is rather vague how Maslow got the specific sample of subjects, nor did Maslow rely on a rigorous analysis to get his global sketch of the typical self-actualizer. It looks as if Maslow simply assembled the biographies of personalities he happened to admire as a humanist, and then composed a generic tribute for them all.

Yet many people find the holistic methods of humanistic psychology more congenial than the atomistic techniques favored in the behavioral sciences. For these people, Maslow's work represents a fine instance of what psychologists can learn from the biographies of distinguished people.

Culture Mentalities

While we are being holistic, let's conclude this chapter by becoming more so. Up to now, our focus has been on the individual personality—on how people vary on particular traits, character profiles, or global dispositions. But can we also speak of the personality of an entire culture or civilization? For instance, when is it justified to claim (as two researchers have done) that some nation or period is extroverted, another introverted?

Let us return to the hypothetical trait profile shown in Figure 9.2. Recall that the points on the graph show the standardized scores for a single subject on each personality dimension in the inventory. Remember also that these points can represent group averages as well. It is this usage that has allowed us to talk about the typical Olympic champion or illustrious scientist. The profiles describe the mean scores received by all members of the group.

Why can't we calculate the average scores for all the members of a given culture or society? In principle, there is no reason we cannot do so. We might force every adult in the United States to take the 16 PF, and thereby get the personality profile of the generic American. We would find out whether this nation was higher than normal on Ego Strength and Self-Sufficiency, and lower than normal on Group Superego and Schizothymia. In practice, of course, such an enterprise is impossible. In the first place, it is difficult even to imagine the logistic problems that we would have to surmount to have millions of citizens take the 16 PF. The mass polio vaccinations of the 1950s would look Lilliputian by comparison. More importantly, because the norms for the 16 PF were based on a representative sample of American adults, the mean profile should be a straight line. The average person, on the average, must be average. Only by giving the 16 PF to a population on which the inventory was not standardized might we really learn something interesting. For example, it would be more instructive to distribute the test to all denizens of China, India, or Brazil—again, if we could pragmatically do so.

Fortunately, we have another line of attack at our disposal. We may rely on the predominant activities and artifacts of a time or place to characterize the preoccupations of its people. We have seen illustrations of this practice back in Chapter 5. Much of the work on the achievement motive entailed the use of cultural indicators. Fluctuations in the need for achievement within a nation were assessed through the content analysis of literature, graphic arts, folk tales, or children's readers. Changes in the entrepreneurial spirit were gauged by the distribution of exports, coal imports, patent applications, and growth in electrical consumption. Hence, if we choose carefully, we can indirectly assess large masses of individuals to determine their predominant group personality. And since we have repeatedly seen how personality traits affect individual achievement, shifts in the prevailing national character may leave an imprint on history. As an illustration, let us examine one of the most ambitious research projects ever conducted in the social sciences.

Pitirim Sorokin was not a psychologist, but a distinguished sociologist. Despite his professional affiliation, there is much psychology in his thinking and research. He was fascinated with the connection between the sociocultural system and the most prevalent personality of the age. This fascination is evident in his magnum opus, the four-volume *Social and Cultural Dynamics*, which came out between 1937 and 1941.

Sorokin believed that there are two main kinds of people in this world. Like Maslow's idea of self-actualizers, Sorokin's two species of personality encompass whole clusters of single traits. The two opposed types are as follows:

1. *The Sensate personality:* People with this disposition are highly extroverted. They direct their lives by their sense organs. Their epistemologies are empirical; that is, they believe that all knowledge comes through the five senses. Reality consists of material substance, which undergoes incessant flux. Only the individual human being has genuine existence; society is a mere conglomeration of these singular entities. Morality is thus individualistic, guided mostly by what increases pleasure and decreases pain. Despite these ethical guidelines, the subjective experience of volition is an illusion. Because everything is determined by impersonal physical laws, no person has true free will. We are all rats in a Skinner box.

2. *The Ideational personality:* Humans inclined this way are highly introverted. They govern their lives according to the dictates of their inner experience. Reason and especially mystical revelation take precedence over empirical data. The reality behind our illusory world consists of pure spirit or mind. This immaterial world is unchanging, eternal. Individualism must yield ground to the social system; the person is, like a single cell in a multicellular organism, dependent rather than autonomous. Morality stands on higher principles, especially the rule of love. Because each individual is granted the choice between good and evil, ethical responsibility is real rather than apparent. Each of us has the option to become a saint.

There are other personality types besides these two. Sorokin defined various transitional personalities, such as the Idealistic, the Cynical Sensate, and the Pseudo-Ideational. Still, Sensate and Ideational types express the most consistent clusters of personality traits. Naturally, most of us moderns may have more sympathy for the Sensate personality. According to Sorokin, this is the dominant type of current Western civilization. In contrast, ever since the Renaissance, the Ideational personality has been dismissed as an obsession of the Middle Ages. These "Dark Ages" were the time of cloistered mystics, monks, nuns, and clerics. Nevertheless, both types are obviously essential to an understanding of the course of human civilization across the globe.

In fact, Sorokin predicted that our present era of Sensate dominance is coming to a close. A new Ideational culture will replace it. The change is inevitable, for it has already happened more than once before. For example, the Ideational personality of medieval Christianity previously superseded the highly Sensate personality of the decadent Roman Empire. Sorokin specified a cause for these substitutions.

At the individual level, each type corresponds to the two main routes to personal happiness. On the one hand, you can try to satisfy all your desires. If you're thirsty, drink; if you're hungry, eat; if you're lustful, seduce; if you're covetous, acquire. This is the doctrine of hedonism—of the table, bed, and market. The basic commandment in this Epicurean code is "Eat, drink, and be merry" with "wine, women, and song," for "tomorrow you die." The drawback is that, in the words of the Rolling Stones, you may "get no satisfaction." That big deal may fall through; the sex object may reject your advances; that *nouvelle cuisine* may cause you indigestion. So, on the other hand, you can work at lowering your expectations. Reduce your wants to the barest minimum. Turn upon your own internal resources for strength and sustenance. What's within will always be there. No person, no circumstances can steal your peace with God, your union with the cosmic order, your blessed state of *nirvana* or *satori*. This is the doctrine of early Buddhism, and of ascetic philosophies everywhere. Because Diogenes of Sinope lived in a tub "like a dog" (*kunikos* in Greek), his own ascetic school became known as the Cynics. Diogenes was the fabled man who supposedly wandered the Athenian streets in broad daylight, holding a lamp while searching for an honest human. Having become famous for renouncing all worldly possessions, he was once approached by Alexander the Great, who asked whether this homeless person wanted anything. Diogenes just said to the conqueror, "Get out of my sun, you're casting a shadow on me."

For Sensate readers, the hardships of this second solution are conspicuous enough. What if you smell a delicious aroma wafting from a neighbor's kitchen? What about that sleek sports car you just saw advertised? What are you going to do about that luscious naked body leaning toward you at this very moment, deliberately tempting you away from more chaste thoughts? Not all of us can play St. Anthony and resist the myriad temptations of this material existence! And how quickly does a "Why not?" convert to an "I want more!"

Beware! The Stoic philosopher Epictetus warned: "Nothing is enough to the man for whom enough is too little."

In Sorokin's theory, the liabilities of either personality type lead to dissatisfaction. This eventually ushers in change on a grand scale. Enough Roman orgies, and the result is a large population with hangovers and sexually transmitted diseases who, worse yet, feel spiritually empty. Enough monotonous prayers in austere monastic cells, and the result is more and more souls turning away from salvation and toward the invitations of the body. Hence, when a whole civilization plunges toward one extreme type, it is just a matter of time before the pendulum will swing in the opposite direction. The oscillations will continue for as long as *Homo sapiens* occupies this planet.

These cyclical swings in the preponderant personality type have vast repercussions for intellectual, aesthetic, and social history. Sensate and Ideational people have different tastes and standards in almost everything. Sensate philosophers advocate empiricism, materialism, individualism, temporalism, determinism, and hedonistic or utilitarian ethics. Ideational thinkers promote rationalism and mysticism, idealism, collectivism, eternalism, free will, and the ethics of principles and love. So we have Epicurus, Lucretius, Locke, and Bertrand Russell on the one side, and Plato, Epictetus, Plotinus, St. Augustine, and St. Thomas Aquinas on the other. Sensate artists paint and sculpt highly realistic scenes of common people engaged in mundane activities. Erotic nudity is frequent to entice prurient interests, and artistic technique appeals to sensory pleasures. Ideational painters and sculptors try to capture the eternal world of pure spirit toward which all pure beings aspire. Everything becomes abstract, indefinite, ethereal. Hence, Sensate times can produce the erotic or naughty nakedness in the canvases and etchings of Fragonard, Goya, Delacroix, Courbet, Manet, Picasso, Dali, and Balthus. But Ideational times can produce the other-worldly mosaics, exquisite manuscript illustrations, inspiring stained-glass windows, and the lofty cathedrals of medieval Europe. It is actually telling that the latter works are anonymous, for the Ideational artist cares not for personal identity. A mere signature lacks cosmic significance.

We can compose similar statements for Sensate versus Ideational literature and music. In addition, whereas Sensate times favor scientific discoveries and technological inventions, Ideational times discourage such activities. After all, science and technology require an obsession with this world rather than a quest for the next. Sorokin even extended the pattern to encompass jurisprudence and politics. For instance, a Sensate *Zeitgeist* prefers the secular state, whereas an Ideational milieu supports a theocracy. The laws of the land reflect the spirit of the political system.

In general, all major cultural and social activities are at bottom the manifestation of a single underlying personality type. Because the pre-eminent personality type alters over history in a cyclical pattern, the sociocultural corollaries must follow suit. Sensate science, philosophy, literature, art, music, jurisprudence, and politics, as a coherent cluster of human achievements, alternate with their Ideational counterparts. These domains fluctuate together because they form a harmonious package. To piece together a workable culture from a Sensate component here and an Ideational component there would be the task of Sisyphus. Imagine the difficulty of placing Sensate pornography in an Ideational theocracy.

It is to Sorokin's credit that he had a Sensate side to his character. He did not offer his theory as a revelation from God or Allah; rather, he collected massive amounts of data on behalf of this thesis. Much of this documentation was quantitative. For instance, he had a team of professionals decide where 2,000 thinkers stood on the issues dividing Sensate and Ideational intellects. These thinkers ranged from classical Greece to the current century, and all the great minds of the Western intellectual tradition were represented. The resulting tabulations suggest that the rival philosophies have indeed played leapfrog with each other over the course of history. Empiricism has alternated with mysticism, materialism with idealism, individualism with collectivism, hedonistic with altruistic ethics, and so on.

This is not the place to undertake an exhaustive critique of Sorokin's theory and data. I wish to make just two points.

First, Sorokin's notion that civilization oscillates between the two personality types has come under serious challenge. One problem is that the cycles are too indistinct to command much credence. So indefinite are the fluctuations that they lack the inevitability required to certify prophecy. Don't hold your breath if you're waiting for the Ideational way of life to return to Western culture! A related problem is that the two personality types are not purely exclusive. Yes, it is rather tricky to live a Sensate life in an Ideational environment—being burned at the stake is a most unpleasant experience. Yet the antagonism fails to go in both directions. As the counterculture of the 1960s proved, it is possible for the mystically eager to live out their lives without becoming fuel for an *auto-da-fé*. Sensate societies are inherently more pluralistic than Ideational cultures.

The second point is more positive. Sorokin maintained that all domains of creative achievement express the same basic personality type. The various arts in a given era should therefore display a consistent style. No matter what the medium, all creations should stick to the same stylistic emphasis. In line with this idea, cultural historians and critics have often coined terms that apply to cross-media styles. The terms "baroque," "neoclassical," and "Romantic" are especially popular. We can accordingly speak about Romantic painting, poetry, architecture, and music as if these four forms of expression shared some common source of inspiration.

Carefully conducted experiments have shown that this usage has psychological justification. Using suitable excerpts and reproductions, the experimenters gave naive observers samples of poetry, painting, architecture, and music from the three artistic styles. The task was to sort the samples according to perceived similarity, ignoring the medium. Even though the raters found the stimuli quite exotic, they did quite well. They could see that a painting by Peter Paul Rubens, a poem by John Donne, an edifice by Gian Lorenzo Bernini, and a composition by George Frederick Handel belonged together (all baroque). Comparable groupings occurred for Jacques-Louis David, Alexander Pope, Jacques Germain Soufflot, and Franz Joseph Haydn (all neoclassical) and for Caspar David Friedrich, Victor Hugo, Sir Charles Barry, and Franz Liszt (all Romantic). The novices classified selections from the creative output of 60 painters, poets, architects, and composers. The three styles could nonetheless emerge from this diversity.

Is it then far-fetched to conclude that these cross-media styles mirror more fundamental shifts in the most popular personality of a time? Some eras desire elegance and restraint; others value fanciful elaboration and virtuosity; still others call for emotion, depth, and power. Talents with personalities typical for their periods then create artistic translations of the group mind. To be sure, the validity of cross-media styles provides only indirect support for Sorokin's hypothesis. His Sensate and Ideational styles are far more grand in scope. Even so, Sorokin's theory may partially explain the tsunamis on which these lesser styles ripple. No matter what the size of the wave, the attainments of human culture may betray the personality of a time and place.

THE SIGNIFICANCE
OF PSYCHOPATHOLOGY

Thus far, we have been rather kind to the illustrious personalities who have come under our scrutiny. For the most part, eminent creators and leaders have been portrayed as being pretty normal, or even supernormal. At this point, most of us would be neither ashamed nor inconvenienced to have a genuine genius as a close family member. However, in this chapter we cannot continue these pleasantries any further. We must instead inspect the more ugly underside of these phenomena. In particular, this chapter is devoted to the psychopathology of greatness. It begins by examining one of the oldest questions in the psychology of history: Is genius mad? This issue is related to another, which is discussed next: Are luminaries self-destructive? The final major topic concerns the impact of stressful events on the life and career of exceptional individuals. This subject leads to an inquiry that closes the chapter: To what extent is any mental illness that we spot in outstanding personalities merely the necessary cost of attaining greatness?

Madness and Genius

There is an age-old consensus that genius and madness are intimately aligned. Aristotle believed that "Those who have become eminent in philosophy, politics, poetry, and the arts have all had tendencies toward melancholia." Centuries later, Seneca stated that "no great genius has ever existed without some touch of madness." Nearly two millennia after Aristotle, the same conclusion was drawn by two leading English dramatists. Shakespeare wrote, "The lunatic, the lover, and the poet/Are of imagination all compact." And Dryden held, "Great Wits are sure to Madness near ally'd,/And thin Partitions do their Bounds divide."

With the coming of the Romantic age around 1800, the notion of the mad genius had become virtual dogma. By the century's end, this dogma was being endorsed by those who devoted their lives to studying pathological personalities. It was the prevailing opinion among the experts that genius is a mental disorder. This disorder was often ascribed to a congenital neuropathology. The most influential proponent of this view was the Italian criminologist Cesare Lombroso, whose classic *The Man of Genius* appeared in 1891. There he emphatically affirmed that genius could be linked with "degenerative psychosis," especially that of the "epileptic group."

Lombroso's judgments were repeated in the speculations of psychiatrists and psychologists throughout the world. Thus, an 1895 article published in the *Journal of Nervous and Mental Disease* listed the four possible results of an inferior genetic endowment:

> *First*, and most prominent in the order of frequency is an early death. *Second*, he may help swell the criminal ranks. *Third*, he may become mentally deranged and ultimately find his way into a hospital for the insane. *Fourth*, and least frequently, he startles the world by an invention or discovery in science or by an original composition of great merit in art, music or literature. He is then styled a genius.

And shortly after the turn of the century, William James could write that

> the nature of genius has been illuminated by the attempts . . . to class it with psychopathological phenomena. Borderland insanity, crankiness, insane temperament, loss of mental balance, psychopathic degeneration(to use a few of the many synonyms by which it has been called), has [*sic*] certain peculiarities and liabilities which, when combined with a superior quality of intellect in an individual, make it more probable that he will make his mark and affect his age, than if his temperament were less neurotic.

The advent of psychoanalysis did nothing to dispel this evolving consensus. Sigmund Freud departed little from the received tradition: As he saw it, creative genius is a sign of neurosis. Indeed, almost any variety of outstanding achievement is suspect, to a psychoanalyst's way of thinking. Hence, as we have seen in Chapter 5, when psychoanalysts conduct psychobiographical studies of historic personalities, they almost always end up providing clinical diagnoses of some tragic disorder. Leonardo da Vinci, Dostoevsky, Mary Baker Eddy, Woodrow Wilson, and the rest were all, in the last psychoanalysis, sick souls. The only real contrast between the psychoanalytic viewpoint and that of other psychiatrists concerns the origins of the sickness. The psychoanalysts believe that early childhood experiences, not genetic endowment, determine the development of mad genius.

Despite the popular view of genius as madness, a dissenting opinion emerged in the 1960s with the advent of humanistic psychology. Psychologists of this school saw creativity as a supreme form of mental health. Rather than being sicker than the rest of us, the creator is the one most sane. For instance, Abraham Maslow made it explicit that the attributes of the self-actualizer are practically the same as those of the creative personality. In fact, many of the self-actualizing individuals given in Table 9.3 made their names as creative geniuses. Maslow's image of genius looks diametrically opposed to the perspective passed down through the centuries.

An advantage of the humanistic image is that it avoids a paradox that plagues the mad-genius stereotype. By definition, creative geniuses are persons who manage to produce intellectual or aesthetic products that cinch their reputations with posterity. If subsequent generations can appreciate these ideas, does that mean that those appreciators are themselves crazy? After all, the patients of mental hospitals produce incoherent scribbles and paranoid theories that normal persons find impossible to accept. Indeed, this is usually how the unfortunates got themselves institutionalized in the first place. Maybe Macaulay captured a profound truth in his remark, "Perhaps no person can be a poet, or can even enjoy poetry, without a certain unsoundness of mind." Only this statement might apply to all creative domains, and include aficionados and connoisseurs in later generations. Then to create and to appreciate would both be acts of insanity. It would be like some grandiose *folie à deux*—a shared delusion that transcends the age!

Yet this last inference seems absurd. If the history of civilization is very much the record of creative achievements, then the annals must register a degenerative decline into mass psychosis. The larger the body of creative artifacts a culture has accumulated, the more insane must its people be. History would thus be regression rather than progression. So, by accepting the humanistic image of genius, we obliterate the paradox. If the geniuses are the healthiest among us, and their creations the products of self-actualizing beings, their marks on history will be more helpful than harmful. We may even use their lives to guide our own toward heightened well-being. Admiration for the great becomes a guise of self-improvement if not self-therapy.

Who's right? Should we reject historic geniuses as so many psychotics or neurotics? Or do they embody the best that *Homo sapiens* has to offer? Or is there some middle ground between these extremes? To answer, we must review three kinds of evidence: historiometric, psychiatric, and psychometric.

Historical Conjectures

On the surface, a resolution of the mad-genius debate is easy. We can just rummage around through the annals of history, and identify all the pathological notables we can find. Table 10.1 provides the outcome of one such survey. To simplify discussion, I have subdivided the persons according to the main fields in which they left their marks. In addition, I have sorted the many names into three principal diagnostic categories.

The first group contains those with conspicuous thought disorders. These individuals' concepts of reality were incongruent with the actual world. Symptoms might include hallucinations, delusions, and other psychotic symptoms.

TABLE 10.1. Eminent Personalities with Supposed Mental Illnesses

Schizophrenic disorders (and other cognitive psychoses):
Scientists: T. Brahe, Cantor, Copernicus, Descartes, Faraday, W. R. Hamilton, Kepler, Lagrange, Linnaeus, Newton, Pascal, Semmelweis, Weierstrass, H. Wells.

Thinkers: Kant, Nietzsche, Swedenborg.

Writers: Baudelaire, Lewis Carroll, Hawthorne, Hölderlin, S. Johnson, Pound, Rimbaud, Strindberg, Swift.

Artists: Bosch, Cellini, Dürer, Goya, El Greco, Kandinsky, Leonardo da Vinci, Rembrandt, Toulouse-Lautrec.

Composers: Donizetti, MacDowell, F. Mendelssohn, Rimsky-Korsakov, Saint-Saëns.

Others: M. Barrymore, de Sade, Goebbels, Herod the Great, Joan of Arc, Nero, Nijinsky, Shaka.

Affective disorders (depression, mania, or bipolar):
Scientists: Boltwood, Boltzmann, Carothers, C. Darwin, L. De Forest, J. F. W. Herschel, Julian Huxley, T. H. Huxley, Jung, Kammerer, J. R. von Mayer, V. Meyer, H. J. Muller, J. P. Müller, B. V. Schmidt, J. B. Watson.

Thinkers: W. James, J. S. Mill, Rousseau, Sabbatai Zevi, Schopenhauer.

Writers: Balzac, Barrie, Berryman, Blake, Boswell, V. W. Brooks, Byron, Chatterton, J. Clare, Coleridge, William Collins, Conrad, Cowper, H. Crane, Dickens, T. Dreiser, R.Fergusson, F. S. Fitzgerald, Frost, Goethe, G. Greene, Hemingway, Jarrell, Kafka, C. Lamb, J. London, R. Lowell, de Maupassant, E. O'Neill, Plath, Poe, Quiroga, Roethke, D. G. Rossetti, Saroyan, Schiller, Sexton, P. B. Shelley, C. Smart, T. Tasso, V. Woolf.

Artists: Michelangelo, Modigliani, Pollock, Raphael, Rothko, R. Soyer, Van Gogh.

Composers: Berlioz, Chopin, Elgar, Gershwin, Handel, Mahler, Rachmaninoff, Rossini, R. Schumann, Scriabin, Smetana, Tchaikovsky, Wolf.

Others: C. Borgia, Clive, O. Cromwell, A. Davis, J. Garland.

Personality disorders (including severe neuroses):
Scientists: Ampère, Cavendish, A. S. Couper, Diesel, Einstein, Frege, S. Freud, Galton, Heaviside, Huygens, Marconi, Mendel.

Thinkers: J. Austin, Beccaria, Comte, Descartes, Hegel, Hobbes, Hume, Kierkegaard, B. Russell, Spencer, Voltaire, Wittgenstein.

Writers: H. C. Andersen, E. B. Browning, R. Browning, Bunyan, Carlyle, Dickinson, Dostoevski, T. S. Eliot, Emerson, Flaubert, García Lorca, Gide, Allen Ginsberg, Gogol, Heine, G. M.Hopkins, A. Huxley, W. M. Inge, Melville, Pavese, Proust, S. Richardson, Rimbaud, Ruskin, Tennyson, de Tocqueville, Tolstoy, Verlaine, T. Williams, Zola.

Artists: Borromini, Bramante, Caravaggio, Cézanne, C. Chanel, Munch, Romney.

Composers: Beethoven, Bruckner, O. de Lasso, Schubert, Wagner.

Performers: S. Bernhardt, J. Dean, W. C. Fields, C. Gable, C. Grant, J. Joplin, M. Monroe, B. Powell.

Leaders: C. Barton, Bismarck, W. Churchill, M. B. Eddy, Göring, A. Gramsci, A. Hamilton, Hitler, H. Hughes, A. Krupp, H. Lee, R. E. Lee, Lincoln, Luther, Mussolini, Napoleon, Nightingale, Nixon, T. Roosevelt, W. Wilson, M. Wollstonecraft.

Note. Because almost all of these diagnoses are not based on objective clinical assessments, most are highly tentative.

287

Schizophrenics make up the largest proportion of this gathering, with a smattering of paranoids. The second group holds the most names. These people suffered from an emotional disequilibrium. Some experienced incapacitating states of depression; others had extremely unsettling episodes of mania; still others were victims of the bipolar (manic–depressive) syndrome. But the depressives dominate the collection. Depression is perhaps the disorder of choice among the great—Aristotle's "melancholia." The third and last group consists of those with severe personality problems, especially neuroses. However debilitating these disorders, the personalities in this group did not always require psychiatric attention or institutionalization. Even so, on more than one occasion their behaviors caused considerable chagrin to themselves, their loved ones, or their colleagues. For example, actress Sarah Bernhardt kept her own coffin at home to lie in; she was also reported to invite lovers to join her within its eerie confines.

Anyone familiar with some of the celebrities listed may complain about my including some favorite. Certainly the list is not infallible. One problem is that several of these individuals owed their mental ills to organic causes. Is it fair to brand a luminary as "nuts" when the brain has been taken over by some virus or bacterium? For example, sometimes Nietzsche's philosophy becomes the target of *ad hominem* arguments: We should not trust the ravings of a madman. Yet is this justified if his terminal insanity was the unlucky result of his early and infrequent indiscretions in houses of ill repute? The charge seems especially objectionable, given that his masterworks were all composed before the microbe did its nastiest business.

Another problem is that these personalities vary immensely in terms of the confidence we can place in their diagnoses. Some notables were insane enough to require treatment in an asylum; Hölderin, Pound, Donizetti, and von Mayer were such cases. Some even ended their lives both insane and institutionalized—such as Semmelweis, the Marquis de Sade, Fergusson, Schumann, Smetana, and Wolf. Others in the table definitely needed psychiatric help. Hemingway received electroshock therapy at the famed Mayo Clinic. Anne Sexton's psychiatrist aided her biographer, Diane Middlebrook, by giving the latter tape recordings of their therapy sessions. Gershwin got along so splendidly with his psychiatrist that they once went on a Mexico vacation together. And Rachmaninoff actually dedicated his Second Piano Concerto to his therapist, who directly inspired the composition's creation. In these instances, we cannot doubt that we are talking about troubled spirits.

In contrast, many others in the table are the recipients of posthumous diagnoses. These judgments may come from experienced psychiatrists, yet the evaluations are often based on skimpy information about symptoms. Can we legitimately infer that Hieronymous Bosch was psychotic by inspecting the bizarre imagery of his remarkable paintings? Controversy may brew over whether the symptoms were sufficiently real, intense, or frequent to warrant assigning them a pathological label. Hence, many of these diagnoses would not stand up in a court of law.

Even if we accept these diagnoses, they may not tell us much about the mad-genius question. We lack a baseline for comparison. A certain percentage of the general population will succumb to some type of mental or emotional difficulty at some time in their lives. So, despite the mass of names in the table, the percentage may be no higher than what we would see in any random gathering of personalities. After all, many thousands of people have had their names registered in the books of history. What we obviously need to do is to contrast the frequency of illness against the total supply of equally famous individuals. That would inform us whether the incidence of madness or eccentricity among such people is greater or less than would be expected merely by chance.

Some researchers have tried to make these comparisons. Among the first was the study that Havelock Ellis conducted of 1,030 British personalities. All subjects were of enough eminence to earn entries in the *Dictionary of National Biography*. According to his determinations, about 4% displayed some definite mental disorder, although this figure included senility along with insanity. About 8% suffered from extreme melancholia, *à la* Aristotle's claim. And about 5% exhibited some marked personality disorder. Finally, Ellis noted that 16% were imprisoned at some time in their lives. This statistic is only pertinent because Ellis conducted his study at the beginning of this century. As I have pointed out earlier, genius, insanity, and criminality were in those days seen as manifestations of the same underlying genetic syndrome.

These percentages may be high enough to cast doubts on the humanistic position. The heads and hearts of eminent people do not seem more robust than those of average human beings. They may even be more prone to infirmity, as Lombroso held. Moreover, some investigators suggest that the frequency of mental disorder may be unusually high in specific domains of achievement. For instance, the most cursory reading of Table 10.1 hints that creators and entertainers are more disposed toward instability than leaders are. Empirical studies confirm this inductive inference. It sounds logical that only under the rarest of conditions can a lunatic rise to supreme positions of power and then persevere there. In fact, most of the genuine instances of insanity in highest office involve hereditary monarchs, such as Charles VI (the Well-Beloved) of France and King George III of Great Britain. It is unlikely that these unhappy individuals would have survived as leaders in a democratic system. In 1972, presidential candidate George McGovern dropped Senator Thomas Eagleton of Missouri as his vice-presidential running mate when it was discovered that the latter had needed psychiatric help earlier in his career.

Even when we confine our attention to the creative geniuses listed, some activities may attract an inordinate share of off-center personalities. For instance, the number of writers with emotional problems looks conspicuous. But we must be cautious about making a generalization without some adequate baseline. In most samples of eminent personalities, poets, novelists, and essayists make up the largest group in any case, so this superfluity may merely reflect this abundance. Still, detailed studies have found that writers are indeed liable to such difficulties. Among eminent poets, almost half may show some pathological symptoms, and about 15% could be called psychotic without stretching the term's meaning. Shakespeare was evidently correct in saying that the poet and the lunatic are of a single mind. Similar proclivities may affect other types of artistic creativity as well. "What garlic is to salad, insanity is to art," said the sculptor Augustus Saint-Gaudens.

If we are willing to take these historical diagnoses on face value, we seem to have made some headway in resolving the debate. Nonetheless, no one should be convinced about the matter according to these data alone. Posthumous diagnoses offer the shakiest ground for scientific conclusions. What we need are statistics based on actual psychiatric assessments.

Clinical Diagnoses

Occasionally, a more systematic survey of luminaries who have received psychiatric diagnoses becomes possible. Such surveys unquestionably offer a more direct attack on the mad-genius issue. Furthermore, many of these inquiries confirm the conclusions drawn from the historiometric studies: Mental instability and creativity, at least, may be intimates. This affiliation is especially prominent among literary creators. For instance, one investigator looked at 15 writers who had attended the prestigious Writers Workshop at the University of Iowa. The writers were five times more likely to have been treated for affective disorders than were average persons, and virtually all 15 writers admitted extreme mood swings.

Another researcher concentrated on 47 eminent artists and writers of Great Britain. Over one-third had at some point needed psychiatric intervention for affective illness. These creators were often at the mercy of wild emotional vacillations, ranging from suicidal depression to hypomania. Poets were particularly vulnerable; half of them had required either drugs or hospitalization to handle a severe bout with depression. Of the various groups, the artists appeared the best off, and even they had had to seek psychotherapy at a higher-than-average incidence rate.

A third, more extensive inquiry was based on psychiatric diagnoses of about 19,000 persons from German-speaking nations. Of these, 294 were highly gifted artists and scientists, while another 151 were creators of lesser status. Not only was the incidence of schizophrenics, manic–depressives, and psychopaths higher among the creators than among the general population, but the gifted artists and scientists were more susceptible to abnormalities than their less distinguished colleagues. Greater eminence meant lesser sanity.

There is even some evidence hinting at the possible genetic basis for the disorders. One study was conducted in Iceland, a country with a population not much in excess of 200,000. This means that the mental hospital at Reykjavik can keep rather comprehensive records of psychotic citizens. At the same time, anybody who has become important boasts a listing in *Who Is Who in Iceland*.

The luminaries in the study had made their names as scholars, novelists, poets, painters, composers, and performers. It was accordingly possible to trace the genealogies of both achievement and insanity with a completeness impossible in gigantic nations like the United States. The family pedigrees were revealing: Relatives of schizophrenics were two to six times more likely to earn a place of creative distinction in Icelandic society. The incidence of deranged relatives definitely exceeded that occurring in families whose members had not left their marks. Parallel results emerged in the survey of German-speaking subjects mentioned above. Illustrious artists and scientists came from families where mental disorders were rampant—at least in comparison to pedigrees that produced less outstanding minds.

Although the psychiatric studies are more rigorous than the historiometric studies, they still have faults. Perhaps the most crucial objection concerns the reliability of clinical diagnoses. Psychiatrists do not always agree on the labels they assign the same patient. Indeed, psychiatrists may not always accurately distinguish healthy from unhealthy specimens of humanity. We need a more objective method.

Scientific Assessments

The third and last approach is perhaps the best. Rather than rely on the subjective judgments of psychiatrists, we can exploit the full power of psychometric methods. Many personality inventories are tailor-made for the diagnosis of clinical populations. In addition, these instruments often construct diagnoses with less error than the intuitive clinician may do. Happily, several psychologists have convinced eminent contemporaries to take these tests. The results corroborate the historiometric and psychiatric evidence.

The work at Berkeley's Institute for Personality Assessment and Research (IPAR) offers a fine starting point. Many big names have traveled to the IPAR to take the battery of tests waiting there. Among these measures is the Minnesota Multiphasic Personality Inventory (MMPI), which contains many scales that assess several aspects of pathology. The empirical results are striking: Distinguished creators show high scores on many of these scales. For instance, the creative architects who have visited the IPAR score higher than average on Psychopathic Deviation and Schizophrenia. This means that these people feature unusual thought processes, more open expression of their impulses, and a lack of social inhibition. The pathology of the creative writers is even more pronounced. In comparison to the general population, most are in the upper ranges on every pertinent scale of the MMPI. They score higher on Depression, Hypomania, Schizophrenia, Paranoia, Psychopathic Deviation, Hysteria, Hypochondriasis, and Psychasthenia. We need not dwell on each of these scales one by one; it suffices to say that the MMPI profile of these creators leans strongly toward psychopathology.

A similar pattern emerges when creators of note undergo different psychometric assessments. For example, creative personalities also score high on the Psychoticism scale of the Eysenck Personality Questionnaire (EPQ). This holds for both the arts and the sciences. In the first, successful artists score higher on Psychoticism than do nonartists. In the second, scientists scoring high on this dimension (1) publish more research and (2) receive more citations in the scientific literature. Even professional cartoonists score above normal! These findings signify that success is more often achieved by those disposed to be unconventional, nonconforming, antisocial, impersonal, unempathic, cold, egocentric, impulsive, aggressive, and tough-minded. This same cluster of traits points toward psychotic disorder.

Considered as a whole, this psychometric literature sheds light on why psychopathology may be so useful to the creative personality. An inclination toward illness may contribute to greatness in three ways:

1. Many of the traits associated with the Psychoticism scale should be conducive to the pursuit of a creative career. Major innovators must buck tradition to strike out on their own. They cannot be so wrapped up in pleasing people that they loose sight of their life's true mission. They must be persistent and self-centered to overcome the many obstacles placed in the path to greatness. In short, the personality profile characteristic of someone high in Psychoticism dovetails closely with the typical profile of the extraordinary creator, as traced in Chapter 9.

2. Those who score high on Psychoticism or the comparable MMPI scales think in unusual ways. Their associations are offbeat, almost bizarre. Their concepts are diffuse and inclusive, enabling them to connect ideas that others would see as quite irrelevant. Primary-process imagery abounds, even to a degree verging on the vulgarity of many schizophrenics. Anyone who has read Mozart's letters may recall examples. Often his correspondence overflowed with "clang associations," a frequent symptom of psychosis. Mozart loved to string words together according to their sound rather than their sense. This translation of a letter suggests Mozart's fondness for gibberish:

> Have you good *digestion*? Have you, perhaps, *congestion*? Can you tolerate me, do you *think*? Do you write with pencil or *ink*? Do you ever think of me, so far *away*? And are you not sometimes inclined to *felo de se*? You may have been *angry*, with me, poor *zany*, but if you will not *recognize me* I'll make a noise, will *scandalise ye*! There, you are laughing—*victoria*! Our *arsch* shall be emblems of peace between us. . . . *Adieu* little coz. I am, I was, I should be, I have been, I had been, I should have been, oh, if I only were, oh, that I were, would God I were; I could be, I shall be, if I were to be, oh, that I might be, I would have been, oh, had I been, oh, that I had been, would God I had been—what? A dried cod!

Francis Galton actually held that in his own creative meditations, words would appear "as the notes of a song might accompany thought." In general, these offbeat thinking patterns fit the processes described in Chapter 4.

3. Besides these cognitive riches, assessed psychopathology is often linked with manic states. These episodes give a creator the supreme energy, focused attention, and self-confidence often needed to complete the most ambitious projects. Beethoven would often compose his masterpieces in an elevated state of "rapture." For example, once his friend Schindler came to visit him while Beethoven was working on his grand *Missa Solemnis*:

> I arrived at the master's home in Mödling. It was 4 o'clock in the afternoon. As soon as we entered we learned that in the morning both servants had gone away, and that there had been a quarrel after midnight which had disturbed all the neighbors, because as a consequence of a long vigil both had gone to sleep and the food that had been prepared had become unpalatable. In the living-room, behind a locked door, we heard the master singing parts of the fugue in the *Credo*—singing, howling, stamping. After we had been listening a long time to this almost awful scene, and were about to go away, the door opened and Beethoven stood before us with distorted features, calculated to excite fear. He looked as if he had been in mortal combat with the whole host of contrapuntists, his everlasting enemies. His first utterances were confused, as if he had been disagreeably surprised at our having overheard him. Then he reached the day's happenings and with obvious restraint he remarked "Pretty doings, these, everybody has run away and I haven't had anything to eat since yesternoon!"

In fact, a detailed, empirical analysis of the career of another German composer, Robert Schumann, actually uncovered a conspicuous linkage between manic episodes and prolific output. Schumann's creative outpourings of 1840 and 1849, in particular, occurred during manic highs.

These psychometric findings, however, fall short of claiming that the creative genius is outright mad. For one thing, the IPAR researchers found that their subjects scored rather high on the MMPI scale of Ego Strength. This characteristic enables the personality to hold itself together, despite the onslaught of the pathological traits. Those low on Ego Strength let themselves disintegrate into incoherence. The creator has a conductor that keeps all the instruments of the rich orchestra playing together. The psychotic has no one standing on the podium. The normal person needs no director; there's only one player out there—nearly playing monotone!

It is imperative that a strong ego unify the personality into a tenacious whole. We have seen in Chapter 9 that geniuses are fantastic risk takers. Only a thick-skinned person can venture on new paths. It requires a big ego to stay the course while family, friends, colleagues, and critics advise the person to back off from his or her ambitions. It's not easy to accept many bombs en route to the few hits. The mad genius has the "right stuff" in these hard conditions, but the ego of the merely mad cannot pass muster. True psychotics do not take criticism well, and withdraw quickly from a hostile world.

Albert Rothenberg came across a poignant illustration in his psychiatric research. Having studied the creative process in both schizophrenic and authentic poets, he discovered a profound difference between the two: The former *"won't revise.* Not on your life, not in a million years." Their egos are so fragile, their poems so personally self-expressive, that they cannot change a single word without risking disintegration. They appear to say: "Take it or leave it! This poem is me! I won't change. It won't change." That attitude will not carry them far toward creative accomplishment. By contrast, the first draft of T. S. Eliot's *The Waste Land* was in deplorable shape. But, not being schizophrenic, Eliot was willing to follow the well-aimed advice of his wife and his friend Ezra Pound. Eliot thus could transform a rambling 800 lines into an epochal masterpiece just over half that length.

A second disparity between sane and insane may be the most provocative. Usually when creative geniuses take the MMPI, the EPQ, or some other diagnostic test, their scores on the pathology scales fall in a middle range. Creators exhibit more psychopathology than average persons, but less than true psychotics. They seem to possess just the right amount of weirdness. They are strange enough to come up with odd ideas, and to pursue those ideas no matter what the rest of the world says. Yet creators are not so outlandish that they lose all contact with reality. They are always hovering at the brink of madness. Dryden's phrase "thin Partitions" seems an apt metaphor.

This delicate connection between insanity and genius helps us understand the pedigrees isolated in the psychiatric studies. For those who come from a family background with unusual amounts of mental illness, their chances of becoming unstable themselves are noticeably increased. Yet that circumstance also enhances their odds of becoming a creative genius. Evidently, they must inherit just the right amount of the genetic proclivity. In the James family, the two brothers William and Henry picked up the optimal amount of mental instability (most likely from Henry James Sr.). Their younger siblings were less lucky. Alice, in particular, became "a cranky hysterical neurasthenic who essentially forced the people she cared about to take care of her by having spectacular nervous breakdowns and becoming a professional invalid."

Table 10.2 offers a more extensive list of families producing both madness and genius. Probably many more such pedigrees lurk behind the names that cram the history books. After all, most families would hush up any suggestions that such skeletons hide in *their* closets. If so, this phenomenon may go a long way toward explicating the problem of missing siblings—an issue introduced in Chapter 6. Many brothers and sisters of the rich and famous may be absent from the annals and almanacs because they abused drugs or alcohol, took their own lives at an early age, or found themselves constrained by straitjackets. Many of the remainder may not have inherited enough constructive insanity to make a name for themselves.

We can advance one step further in our speculations. Perhaps the genetic linkage between genius and madness accounts for the continued presence of otherwise deleterious genes in the human population. It is well known that certain harmful genes persist simply because they confer a survival advantage

TABLE 10.2. Examples of Family Lines Producing Both Eminent and Disturbed Personalities

Friedrich Adler: Mental illness affected both his mother and his sister.

Ethel, John, and Lionel Barrymore: Their father, Maurice, had a complete mental breakdown.

Ludwig van Beethoven: His father was an alcoholic, and his nephew attempted suicide.

Charlotte, Emily, and Anne Brontë: Besides their own affective disorders, their only brother, Patrick Branwell, was also depressive and died early from alcohol and opium abuse.

Lord Byron: Mood swings ruled his mother, while his father may have been a suicide; maternal grandfather was a melancholic who committed suicide, and another relative on his mother's side attempted suicide.

Charlie Chaplin: His mother, "Lily Hawley," lost all contact with reality.

Emperor Charles V: His mother was Joan the Mad.

Winston Churchill: His father, Lord Randolph, was manic–depressive.

Jean Cocteau: His father committed suicide.

Hart Crane: His mother had a total nervous collapse.

Honoré Daumier: His father died in an insane asylum.

Isak Dinesen: Her father committed suicide.

Albert Einstein: One son died in a Swiss mental clinic.

Peter and Jane Fonda: Their mother committed suicide; Peter attempted suicide, and Jane suffered from bulimia.

Allen Ginsberg: His mother was psychotic.

Graham Greene: He traced his own suicidal depressions to a manic–depressive grandfather.

King Hussein of Jordan: Psychosis present in his mother and father.

T. H. Huxley: Besides his own depressive states, his father died in an asylum; of his father's eight children, only T. H. and his sister could be considered normal; T. H.'s daughter, Marian, became extremely melancholic, lost her sanity, and died young; one grandson, Trevenen, was also melancholic and committed suicide; a second grandson, Julian, attempted suicide and suffered from depression; a third, Aldous, experimented with hallucinogenic drugs and the occult; several other temperamental disorders in the family.

William and Henry James: Besides William's considerable emotional difficulties, their sister Alice displayed hypochondriasis and pathological dependency; their father may have had a borderline personality disorder.

James Joyce: His daughter, Lucia, suffered from schizophrenia.

John, Robert, and Edward Kennedy: Their sister Rosemary had mental retardation and emotional disorders that eventually led to her getting a prefrontal lobotomy.

Charles Lamb: Besides his own problems, manic–depression afflicted his sister, Mary (who stabbed their mother to death).

René Magritte: His mother committed suicide.

Guy de Maupassant: His brother became a violent psychotic, and died in an asylum in 1889, but not before warning Guy that *he* was the crazy one in the family; Guy attempted suicide in 1892, was committed and placed in a straitjacket, and died in an asylum in 1893.

Margaret Mead: Her mother required professional treatment for depression.

(continued)

TABLE 10.2. (*Continued*)

Mishima Yukio: His maternal grandmother was a manic–depressive, his maternal grandfather an alcoholic.

Marilyn Monroe: Psychotic disturbances afflicted her mother, a grandmother, and an uncle.

Edvard Munch: One of his sisters was mentally ill.

Nero: Both his mother, Agrippina, and his maternal uncle, Caligula, were mentally deranged.

Friedrich Nietzsche: His father succumbed to a mental illness that he feared he would inherit.

Bronislava Nijinska: In addition to the schizophrenia that conquered her brother Vaslav Nijinsky, another brother suffered mental illness.

Eugene O'Neill: His mother was a drug addict, his son Eugene Jr. committed suicide, and another son, Shane, became emotionally unstable; he later disowned his daughter Oona for unacceptable behavior (at 18 she married Charlie Chaplin, who was her father's age).

Jean Piaget: His mother was extremely unstable.

Wilhelm Reich: Both of his parents committed suicide.

John Ruskin: Besides his own manic–depression, his grandfather's borderline madness ended in suicide.

Robert Schumann: Clinical depression affected both parents; there were two suicides among his first-degree relatives, and his own son spent most of his life in an asylum.

Mary Shelley: Her mother, the famed Mary Wollstonecraft (Mrs. Godwin), had a history of emotional disorders; her half-sister from the same mother, Fanny Imley, committed suicide.

Upton Sinclair: His father and two uncles were alcoholics; one of those uncles committed suicide.

Raphael and Moses Soyer: They had a psychotic mother.

Alfred Tennyson: His father was an alcoholic, and three brothers, Edward, Charles, and Septimus, all became mentally unstable.

J. M. W. Turner: His mother died insane.

Ethel Waters: Psychosis was present in her mother.

upon those who own only a partial set. For this reason, the gene that carries sickle-cell anemia is favored in African populations exposed to malaria. In contrast, the same gene is gradually disappearing among African-Americans, since malaria exerts less selective pressure for its retention.

Although there is more than one culprit behind psychosis, the same principle may apply. Those populations that have a higher incidence of mental instability may also harbor a bigger collection of creative geniuses. Presumably, the innovations of those geniuses have enough survival value to compensate for the societal costs of dementia. The insanity of a tragic minority is the price civilization pays to boast an exceptional rarity: a Michelangelo, Beethoven, Shakespeare, Tolstoy, Descartes, Copernicus, or Edison. And for those creators placed at the very edge of emotional coherence, derangement may be the final price they pay as well.

Self-Destructiveness and Greatness

Some years ago a *Robot Man* cartoon strip offered a curious "what if?" In the strip, Vincent Van Gogh hears a stranger knocking on his door. The stranger is a time traveler freshly returned from a later age where drugs have conquered mental illness. He hands Van Gogh a vial of futuristic antidepressant. Saying, "It's worth a try," the artist downs the medicine. Almost at once, Van Gogh thrusts his arms up with the words, "I feel better already! I feel like painting happy paintings! Like rolling surf and sunsets and clowns on black velvet and . . ."

However much we might lament the loss of this artistic genius, we could imagine this scenario unfolding differently. What if the visitor had practiced a wiser psychiatry, and put Vincent on a schedule of carefully increased dosages? Then there might exist a level of the drug that would alleviate the artist's debilitating depressions without destroying his creativity. We would still get vibrant scenes of open fields and whirling sky. He might even have taken new directions. Maybe he would have crossed the Atlantic to attend the 1913 Armory Show as a 60-year-old, world-renowned painter. All this could have happened simply because he would not have shot himself to death in 1890.

This hypothetical story pinpoints a critical omission in the foregoing discussion. We have said nothing about the most blatant act of insanity: suicide. As symptoms go, killing oneself may reveal more than all the scores on the MMPI. Furthermore, we have ignored a related symptom, the behavior somewhat euphemistically called "substance abuse." If a person lacks the courage to commit suicide outright, or feels that it would be immoral to do so, a whisky bottle can accomplish the same end more slowly. And if alcoholism is not the person's cup of tea, there's always drug addiction, whether to opium, heroin, cocaine, or whatever else. Finally, there is a more subtle means available: A person can just give up the desire to live.

Let's examine these three answers to Hamlet's famous question: "To be or not to be?"

Suicide

Table 10.3 lists some eminent people who committed suicide, as well as some celebrities who attempted suicide. This latter list, of course, probably understates the true proportion of failed suicides. Often such attempts are covered up by family and friends; only a completed suicide warrants an inquest by the coroner's office. Three other caveats are in order.

1. Whether a given death was self-inflicted may remain controversial. Some have suggested, for example, that Marilyn Monroe was murdered to keep her from revealing her alleged liaisons with John and Robert Kennedy. Others are still willing to argue that Tchaikovsky's imbibing of cholera-tainted water was inadvertent rather than deliberate—despite a documented instance of a

TABLE 10.3. Suicides and Suicidal Personalities among the Eminent

Actual suicides:

Scientists: E. Armstrong, H. Berger, B. B. Boltwood, Bridgman, Carothers, G. Eastman, E. Fischer, H. Fischer, Kammerer, L. Kohlberg, V. Meyer, J. P. Müller, S.-C. Deville, Pritikin, Turing, H. Wells.

Thinkers: Blount, Lucretius, Seneca.

Writers: Akutagawa, Berryman, Chatterton, H. Crane, Hemingway, Jarrell, H. Kleist, Koestler, M. J. de Larra, P. Levi, V. Lindsay, J. London, Lucan (Lucanus), Mayakovsky, Mishima, M. Lowry, Nerval, Pavese, Petronius, Plath, H. Quiroga, Sexton, V. Woolf, S. Zweig.

Artists: F. Borromini, R. W. Fassbinder, A. Gorky, Pollock, Rothko, Torrigiano, Van Gogh, Watanabe.

Composers: Tchaikovsky.

Performers: J. Barrymore, J. Garland, M. Monroe, F. Prinze, San no Rikyū, S. Vicious.

Leaders: Marcus Antonius, Boudicca, G. Boulanger, Brutus, Cassius, Castlereagh, Cato the Younger, Cleopatra, Demosthenes (the Orator), J. V. Forrestal, Goebbels, Göring, Hannibal, Hitler, A. Hoffman, Hung Xiuchüan, Isocrates, Rev. J. Jones, Kanoe, I. Kreuger, F. Krupp, R. La Follette Jr., Meng Tian, Nero, Oda Nobunaga, Rommel, Saigo, Vargas.

Attempted suicides:

B. Borg, Cardano, Clive of Plassey, W. Cowper, J. L. David, M. Foucault, P. Fonda, M. Gorky, G. Greene, J. Huxley, W. James, de Maupassant, J. R. von Mayer, I. Mechnikov, H. J. Muller, Napoleon III, Nasser, E. O'Neill, D. Parker, Robespierre, C. Saint-Simon, R. Schumann, Tōjō Hideki, E. Waugh, H. Wolf.

Note. For some of these figures, controversy still centers on whether the death was actually self-inflicted. Freddie Prinze's death was ruled a tragic accident.

suicide attempt earlier in his life. Yet others might debate whether Jackson Pollock's death in an automobile accident represented an act of self-destruction.

2. The suicides of many notables were carried out under extremely adverse circumstances. Therefore, we cannot count all such events as symptoms of underlying pathology. If someone faces certain death, can we deny the rationality of that person's choosing the time, place, and means? The Nazi suicides—Goebbels, Göring, and Hitler—illustrate this point well enough. Others in this situation include Marcus Antonius, Brutus, Cassius, Cato, Demosthenes, Hannibal, Nero, Oda Nobunaga, and Saigō Takamori. Indeed, some suicides were coerced by the explicit ultimatum of a ruler or victor. San no Rikyū, the Japanese tea master, and Seneca, the Roman writer, provide examples. In a different category are those personalities whose suicides precluded an excruciating death by some terminal illness. Physicist Percy Bridgman suffered from an incurable and painful disease. The suicide note left behind revealed that he chose that day to shoot himself because it was probably the last day he would

be physically capable of pulling the trigger. Arthur Koestler and Lawrence Kohlberg ended their lives for much the same reason.

3. The incidence of suicide is partly a function of cultural norms. Although the names in Table 10.3 do not comprise a representative sample of all suicides in history, both the absence and presence of certain cultures are suggestive. In Greco-Roman civilization, suicide was considered an honorable solution to an intractable predicament. Cleopatra, unlike her lover Marcus Antonius, might have been spared by the victorious Octavius, but the inevitable dishonor that would have been her lot was far more evil in her mind than a self-composed end. In Japanese civilization, suicide was even made into a fine art. *Seppuku* (or *hara-kari*) was a highly ritualized act by which the defeated could still triumph over the victor. Mishima Yukio's death illustrated the nobility (even if futility) of this course of action. On the other hand, other cultures look upon suicide with horror. Few Roman Catholics and Moslems, for example, have viewed it as a reasonable solution to the insurmountable. That disparity may largely explain the dearth of Irish, Italian, French, Spanish, Arabic, Persian, and Turkish surnames among lists of famous suicides. The paucity does not mean that these peoples enjoy a lower proportion of depressive personalities; it only means that any pathological inclination toward suicide must adopt a different form.

After we weigh these three points, the link between eminence and suicidal proclivities may appear weak. Only in a subset of instances can we clearly say that the suicide revealed a disordered personality. Carothers, Garland, Hemingway, Müller, Plath, Sexton, Van Gogh, and Woolf are perhaps the prime examples. Moreover, we still must confront the same problem that has permeated the entire chapter: Is the incidence of self-destruction higher among the eminent than in the population of nonentities?

To answer, we must first determine the suicide rate among the famous. One inquiry inspected more than 300 leaders, creators, and celebrities of the 20th century, and found that 2% had committed suicide and 3% had attempted suicide. Hence, about 1 out of 20 notables could be suicidal. The incidence may even be higher for artistic creators, such as writers. These statistics appear impressive. Also, this heightened risk fits the seeming preference for depressive disorders among the illustrious, as discussed earlier.

We'll return to this point shortly, when we examine substance abuse among luminaries. Right now, however, let us look at a tragic aftermath of celebrity suicide. In Goethe's best-selling novel *The Sorrows of Young Werther*, the protagonist shoots himself after falling hopelessly in love with a married woman. Notwithstanding the fictional nature of the example, this book immediately stimulated a rash of suicides among the youths of Europe. Imitators would even go so far as to dress in the same clothes as Werther did on the day of his suicide. This pathetic episode in literary history has provided a technical term in behavioral science—the "Werther effect." This occurs when a highly publicized suicide causes an increase in the occurrence of suicides in the general population. The Werther effect may operate by more subtle means, too, such as an increase of fatalities in automobile and airplane accidents. This might be called the Pollock path to biological oblivion.

In the Werther effect, not only may the exact cause of death vary, but so may the nature of the inciting event. Sometimes the precipitating incident is the actual self-destruction of a broadly admired celebrity. At other times the self-destructive act may involve an unknown, but the dramatic circumstances of the event make it widely publicized—and widely emulated. The front-page news creates more news of the same kind. At still other times the agent may be purely fictitious, as in the original Werther effect. For example, suicides portrayed in popular TV soap operas evidently increase auto accident fatalities in American adults. Whatever the specifics, suicidal "names in the news" can excite self-destructive propensities among the masses.

Happily, other big events can have an opposite effect. For instance, the suicide rate among Americans declines noticeably during presidential election years; the alienated are lifted temporarily out of their hopeless and isolated condition. This phenomenon, coupled with the Werther effect, proves how closely tied are the literal lives of the esteemed and the obscure.

Addiction

Substance abuse is one of the oldest sins of our species. The substance most frequently taken to excess in many cultures is alcohol. Precepts warning of the ills of alcoholism are as old as the Bible. The prophet Isaiah admonished the Hebrews (Isaiah 5:11):

> Woe to those who rise early in the morning,
>   that they may run after strong drink,
> who tarry late into the evening till wine inflames them!

Judging from the biographies of the great, Isaiah's advice has often been disregarded. Table 10.4 lists some reputed "problem drinkers," along with a collection of drug addicts; some pathetic souls are listed in both groups. Of course, the intensity of the disorder varied greatly among these personalities. Some had an obvious affinity toward excess, but managed to put the brakes on their indulgence whenever required. Others abandoned themselves to their habit. A few of these, like Jimi Hendrix, Janis Joplin, Elvis Presley, and John Belushi were killed by their addictions.

But, again, the critical question is whether the incidence of substance abuse is more conspicuous among the illustrious than in the population at large. Here the evidence is sketchy. Among creative writers, the rates of alcoholism clearly exceed those found in the general population. For example, about two-thirds of the Iowa Writers Workshop sample mentioned earlier in the chapter could

TABLE 10.4. Alleged Substance Abusers among Eminent Personalities

Alcohol:

Scientists: W. S. Hamilton, B. V. Schmidt.

Thinkers: Sartre, Seneca, Socrates.

Writers: J. Addison, Agee, W. H. Auden, Baudelaire, B. Behan, H. Belloc, Benchley, Bogan, Boswell, R. Burns, Capote, R. Chandler, Cheever, S. L. Clemens (Mark Twain), Coleridge, J. G. Cozzens, H. Crane, S. Crane, e e cummings, Dreiser, Faulkner, F. Scott Fitzgerald, D. Hammett, L. Hellman, Hemingway, Hugo, S. Johnson, Joyce, Kerouac, C. Lamb, R. Lardner, S. Lewis, J. London, R. Lowell, M. Lowry, Marquand, C. McCullers, St. Vincent Millay, J. Miller, C. Morley, Musset, J. O'Hara, E. O'Neill, D. Parker, Poe, W. S. Porter (O. Henry), E. A. Robinson, Roethke, D. Schwartz, Steinbeck, W. Stevens, A. C. Swinburne, Tennyson, D. Thomas, Thurber, Verlaine, T. Williams, E. Wilson, T. Wolfe.

Artists: de Kooning, A. Gorky, Kahlo, Modigliani, Pollock, F. Remington, Rothko, Toulouse-Lautrec, Utrillo.

Composers: Field, Glazunov, Gluck, Mussorgsky.

Performers: J. Barrymore, Beiderbecke, E. Clapton, N. Cole, J. Gleason, W. C. Fields, M. Griffith, D. Hopper, D. Johnson, E. Kean, C. Laughton, R. Mitchum, M. T. Moore, N. Nolte, C. "Bird" Parker, Piaf, B. Raitt, B. Smith, R. Starr, E. Taylor, R. Williams.

Leaders: Alexander the Great, U. S. Grant, Henry VIII, F. Pierce, W. Pitt the Younger, Emperor Severus.

Drugs:

W. H. Auden, D. Barrymore, J.-M. Basquiat, Baudelaire, J. Belushi, E. B. Browning, L. Bruce, J. Cash, Cocteau, N. Cole, M. Davis, DeQuincey, R. Dreyfuss, B. Dylan, Carrie Fisher, S. Freud, Jerry Garcia, J. Garland, Göring, M. Griffith, W. S. Halsted, Hendrix, B. Holiday, D. Hopper, H. Hughes, D. Johnson, J. Joplin, Kerouac, J. London, L. Minnelli, Modigliani, J. Morrison, Nightingale, C. "Bird" Parker, Piaf, E. Presley, K. Richards, Sartre, Utrillo, S. Vicious, R. Williams, T. Williams, B. and D. Wilson.

count as alcohol abusers. Indeed, many of the big names in Table 10.4 belong to novelists, poets, and essayists. According to this list, musicians, artists, and entertainers may also show some inclination to excessive drink. Scientists and politicians, on the other hand, seem less prone to this disorder, albeit exceptions do exist. Before his rise to fame in the Civil War, Grant was kicked out of the military for his lack of discipline in this regard.

If we accept the prevalence of substance abuse in some areas of achievement, the next question is this: Why? One possible answer is that alcohol and similar chemicals produce an altered state of consciousness that is conducive to the creative process. However, as pointed out in Chapter 2, no evidence exists that chemicals cause creativity. Even among literary giants, many did just fine without becoming enslaved by alcohol or any other drug; William Shakespeare, Marcel Proust, Thomas Mann, Isaac Singer, and Saul Bellow are examples. Even among those who did imbibe too much, few contended that alcohol facilitates creativity. Ring Lardner, F. Scott Fitzgerald, John Cheever, and many others usually saw alcohol as an ill, not an aid.

One psychiatrist probed the lives of 34 heavy drinkers of the 20th century—distinguished writers, artists, composers, and performers. Fewer than 1 out of 10 could claim a direct benefit from alcohol. Robert Lowell, for one, thought that drink stimulated his writing and that it helped moderate his manic-depressive symptoms. Still, drinking impaired creative productivity in over three-fourths of the sample. Jack London's literary prowess deteriorated as the alcohol concentration in his bloodstream accelerated. Fortunately, some came to recognize this liability and kicked the habit; John Cheever, for example, was able to do this before he died. So much for the myth of the inherently alcoholic artist!

So why the abuse? One response is opportunity: Writers lead solitary lives. Writing is best done alone, making it all too easy to place a bottle on the desktop. Artists and composers, too, may privately indulge without concern for their reputations. In contrast, scientists working at their labs and politicians at their offices are more subject to public scrutiny. It is intriguing that the two scientists in Table 10.4, Hamilton and Schmidt, came closer to fitting the pattern of the creative writer. The former was a mathematician, who could drink brandy in the privacy of his study. The latter was an astronomer, engaged in another solitary profession. How many of us would become alcoholics if we did not have to worry about colleagues smelling vodka on our breath?

Another reason involves the inevitable disappointments of celebrity life. I have repeatedly emphasized the heroic nature of exceptional achievement. To become a big-time success calls for a willingness to go for the long shot. The striving individual must face failure after failure on the way to fame and fortune. Alcohol and many other drugs can obviously soften the recurrent blows to self-esteem that these setbacks imply. Just got another rejection slip in the mail? Get out the shot glass, hypodermic, or pipe.

Even after society lionizes a luminary, he or she may not be safe. Achievers must often face the awesome pressure to equal or surpass what they have already accomplished. A Broadway playwright is only as good as the last play. A poet is judged most heavily by the most recent collection of poems. A novelist's latest piece of fiction had better be the best. Otherwise, critics and the public may descry the signs of creative decline. If a person has already produced something that's "a hard act to follow," how does he or she deal with this pressure? "Self-handicapping" may provide a way out.

Self-handicapping is a common phenomenon of everyday life. Maybe you are worried about how well you'll perform on an upcoming exam. So you deliberately sign up for overtime at work, the night before the exam. Crazy? No, because now when you blow the test you can always tell your friends, and fool yourself with, an excuse: "Naturally, I could have aced the exam if I'd only had more time to study." Research has amply documented this phenomenon. In competitive sports, for example, athletes will sometimes practice *less* before a big competition. It's better to lose because they didn't have time to do a proper workout than to suffer defeat when they are at the top of their form.

Self-handicapping has also been recorded in the behaviors of specific notables. One example comes from the domain of world chess—the "Deschapelles coup." When grandmaster Lebreton Deschapelles could no longer be confident that he could defeat all challengers, he refused to enter a match without first giving his opponent "pawn and move." Because the challenger would thus start the game with a one-piece advantage and the opening gambit, Deschapelles put himself in a no-lose situation. If he lost, it was because his adversary had the advantage; if he won, he was plainly the superior player.

Self-handicapping can sometimes lead to self-destructive behaviors. The fiasco that downed Gary Hart's bid for the 1988 Democratic presidential nomination may illustrate this extreme course of action. First, Hart virtually begged the press to spy on his private life, supposedly to dispel all rumors of his being a philanderer. He next had an attractive model, Donna Rice, spend a long night at his townhouse. Lo! She was seen and reported. Hart was obliged to withdraw his candidacy. This bizarre behavior makes sense if Hart feared election defeat more than sexual scandal. At least in the latter case, his picture was widely circulated in the mass media with an attractive female sitting on his lap. That may hurt the male ego less than rejection by the voters in the ballot box.

This brings us back to the use of addiction as a self-handicapping strategy. Alcohol abuse in the average person on the street can often be attributed to self-handicapping behavior. No one can really blame the person for failing to win that promotion if he or she is drunk all the time. Doesn't everyone know that alcoholism is a disease? The same unfortunate logic may afflict many celebrities as well. Many actors and actresses have showed up at the set thoroughly intoxicated—shortly after receiving an Academy Award. And reflect on the sad case of Truman Capote. His career culminated in his 44th year, when he published the best-seller *In Cold Blood*. After that grand success, Capote dissipated his life in alcohol and parties. He would speak of his next masterpiece, which all his fans awaited eagerly. Yet when he finally died nearly 20 years later, he left the mere scraps of a novel, *Answered Prayers*. Alcohol had enabled Capote to escape a somber responsibility. He could hide behind the bottle, and let the bottle take him from the world before the public could know the real reason for his handicap.

This motivation may be most likely to dominate those endeavors that meet three requirements. First, the domain should be extremely risky, with misses greatly outnumbering the hits. Second, the domain should emphasize a few big projects over many incremental contributions. Third, the domain should encourage extreme novelty, discouraging anyone from pursuing the same path. Hence, scientists may feel less need to handicap themselves than artists do. The rejection rates for submissions to scientific journals—especially in physics, chemistry, and biology—are much lower than in the arts and humanities. In addition, contributors in the sciences usually publish numerous small-scale journal articles rather than voluminous monographs. Lastly, scientists are not nearly under the same pressure to generate incessant novelties. In many fields, the advantage actually goes to those researchers who pursue all the ramifications of a single idea. Hence, these three factors may help make scientists less addiction-prone, as a group, than artists.

The Truman Capote example suggests a final cause of abuse: It is a guise of suicide, gradual but assured. In such cases, both substance abuse and suicide may be indications of an underlying depressive disorder. In many eminent lives, alcoholism or drug addiction was clearly a self-chosen means of self-annihilation. Artist Amedeo Modigliani made it explicit: "I am going to drink myself dead." A study of 70 famous American writers even showed that alcoholism works almost as well as a life shortener as suicide does. Whereas suicides had an average life expectancy 20 years shorter than that of nonsuicides, the average expected life span for alcoholics was 14 years shorter than that of nonalcoholics. We can conclude that the lethal efficiency of the bottle is 70% that of the gunshot, bridge jump, car wreck, or drug overdose.

Calendar Date and the Will to Live

Addiction entails much more than simply a desire for self-destruction. Many separate psychological processes are involved. Of these mechanisms, however, one deserves our special attention here. Besides accounting for why some unfortunates become addicted to alcohol and drugs, this process may also help determine the date on the calendar a celebrity selects to be his or her last.

Richard L. Solomon has proposed the "opponent-process theory" of acquired motivation. The theory focuses on a situation in which a person is repeatedly exposed to an affective stimulus. The stimulus may be pleasurable, like an alcohol buzz or a drug high. Or it may be noxious, like the intense heat of a sauna or the fear of a free fall in skydiving or bungee jumping. Whatever the details, the stimulus produces the expected affective sensation in the initial exposures. The drug creates the high; the free fall induces the terror. Furthermore, when the stimulus is withdrawn, an "affective contrast" appears. The drug experimenter gets a letdown from the heights; the skydiver delights in the sensation of feet planted on terra firma.

Yet repeated exposure to an affective stimulus causes a dynamic shift in the individual's reaction over time. First, the person undergoes progressive "hedonic habituation" to the stimulus; that is, with time, the experience loses its power to elicit the original affective response. In the case of substance abuse, we say that the individual builds up a "tolerance" to the drug. The person requires more and more to get the same charge. In skydiving, it is the fear response that gradually weakens. During the precipitous descent, the amply tested parachutist can savor the thrill rather than endure the panic.

Furthermore, a rather different change occurs once the stimulus is withdrawn. The affective contrast becomes ever more pronounced. For those addicted to drugs, the moderate displeasure of coming down is transformed into the agony of withdrawal pains. Increasingly, because the drug-induced ecstasy has been reduced to mere affective contentment, the addict eventually takes drugs mostly to avoid the distress of withdrawal. This aftermath is the "withdrawal syndrome." Nevertheless, a similar reversal takes place for negative stimuli after many outings. Thus, once the expert skydiver leaves the danger zone of free fall, the reaction is not just relief, but exhilaration.

These affective alterations happen because we are all designed to seek an emotional homeostasis. We therefore automatically counter a strong affective stimulus of one valence with an opposing force to balance it out. Hence, positive stimuli provoke negative reactions, negative stimuli positive reactions. With repetition, this opposing response largely cancels out the impact of the affective stimulus. The result is habituation. Emotional equilibrium is achieved. On the other hand, the opposing responses lag a bit behind the original stimulus. Affective reactions are sluggish. Accordingly, after the stimulus fades or disappears, the counterbalancing emotion remains in force, at least for a noticeable duration. Hence, as the impression of the stimulus is progressively attenuated, the affective contrast becomes increasingly exaggerated. The result is habituation coupled with the withdrawal syndrome.

Solomon has applied this opponent-process theory to an amazing diversity of phenomena. Besides drug addiction and parachuting, he has used his theory to interpret the temporal course of love, affection, sensation seeking, aesthetic appreciation, jogging, marathon running, and sauna bathing. However, I prefer to concentrate here on how this theory sheds light on the lives and deaths of the stars of human society. Imagine an event that occurs repeatedly, year after year, always on the same date—for example, your birthday. Probably when you were very young, this was a date you always looked forward to. In time, however, this event loses its luster, as in Thomas Moore's lament:

> "My birth-day" what a diff'rent sound
> That word had in my youthful ears!
> And how, each time the day comes round,
> Less and less white its mark appears!

By adulthood, in fact, your attitude toward birthdays may duplicate Alexander Pope's: "'Tis but the funeral of the former year." It comes to represent all the disappointments and failures of your accumulated past. So the very approach of your birthday may put you in a foul mood. Moreover, once your birthday has passed, you can breathe a sign of relief—an affective contrast. However, with repetition in your later years, the prebirthday anxiety may subside, while the postbirthday release may lessen.

Now, let us suppose that people are more likely to die when they are in negative or even depressed moods, and that death is less likely when they are in upbeat, positive moods. I am not speaking of suicide here, but merely a person's willingness to carry on with life. Then, given an ample collection of people, we should see a surge in deaths in the days just prior to their birthdays. Plus, we should discern a dip in deaths immediately after their birthdays. As people get older, the prebirthday surge should become less conspicuous, and the postbirthday dip should intensify.

There is evidence for this prediction. Two psychologists examined the deaths of people famous enough to have entries in *Who Was Who in America*. Those celebrities were selected who died within two weeks of their respective birthdays, yielding a sample of well over 4,000 lives. Overall, the incidence of death increased leading up to the birthdays, and dropped immediately afterward. Furthermore, the pattern differed when those who died relatively young were compared with those who died relatively old. The prebirthday surge was more dramatic for the younger than for the older personalities.

What about positive dates on the calendar? According to theory, the death dip should occur before the event, while the death surge should occur after. Moreover, the precise dip–surge pattern should change for the oldest members of our race. These predictions were confirmed in another study. This time the event was Christmas, presumably a festive holiday with positive emotional valence. The subjects were again more than 4,000 celebrities from *Who Was Who in America*, all of whom in this case all had died within four weeks of Christmas Day. For those who were under 72 years of age at their deaths, a pre-Christmas dip was followed by a post-Christmas surge. Those who died after passing their 72nd year exhibited a more exaggerated pattern. Other studies have often found dip–surge patterns in mortality rates for other holidays, both national and religious—such as Labor Day and Yom Kippur. Also, the dip–surge effect often holds for everyday populations as well as notables.

Before you start biting your fingernails whenever you glance over your appointment book, a caveat is in order. The effect is weak—so weak that it requires thousands of subjects to demonstrate its existence. It is also frail enough that the effect operates merely over a short interval. Only if you are dying within a couple of weeks of your birthday can this process do its work. Look at Beethoven, whose health began to deteriorate in the last year of his life. Although he had adequate vigor to live past his birthday on December 16, 1826, he certainly lacked the strength to hold out long enough to get within a few weeks of his next birthday. So he succumbed on March 26—long before he could enter any statistics on the dip–surge phenomenon. Solely those who are teeter-tottering on the threshold of oblivion are at the mercy of the mood swings predicted by opponent-process theory. Nonetheless, for those placed within the window of opportunity, this process of affective action–reaction may select the second date engraved on their tombstone.

Stress and Eminence

Admittedly, other events besides birthdays and holidays usually exert far bigger effects on the moment of death. These events are also much more distinctive and unpredictable. Specifically, people are often at risk when they are constantly bombarded by severe stress. Stress puts rare demands on the human body's capacity to cope. Hence, when the intensity or frequency of stress is great enough, people may become susceptible to physical pathologies that finish them off. A virus or bacterium that normally they would have defeated becomes their conqueror instead. A health liability that ordinarily would set up a marginal danger turns into a fatal terminator. At the funeral of President Kennedy, the ceremonial troops were commanded by an army captain who was only 27 years old. Yet 10 days after that traumatic episode—in his life and in the nation's history—he was himself dead from "cardiac irregularity and acute congestion." A historic tragedy had become a personal one.

If the captain had not been elevated to so prestigious a position, his own life story might have turned out less tragic. This lesson can be generalized: Those whose ambitions thrust them to the top must often forfeit the dream of longevity. Positions of power and prestige are amplified sources of chronic stress as well. Ruminate on the following three examples:

1. Among presidents of these United States, some enter office under more favorable conditions than others do. One index of auspicious circumstances is whether an incumbent was closely affiliated with his immediate predecessor. For example, Martin Van Buren was the handpicked successor to Andrew Jackson. On the other hand, James Polk was a dark-horse candidate for a Democratic Party that was trying to recapture the White House from the Whigs. If all other factors are held constant, a politician who becomes chief executive under the first condition has a less arduous task before him than one who faces the second condition. Many ex.·cutive appointments can be retained, and the same policies can be continued. Is it any surprise, then, that those in the first group tend to live longer than those in the second? For instance, both Van Buren and Polk served only one term in office. Yet Van Buren lived 21 years after his presidential retirement, and died well into his 79th year. Polk, in contrast, lived only 103 days after leaving office, dying from a bad case of diarrhea before he reached 54 years of age. In general, the 10 deceased presidents who entered office under less trying circumstances had a life expectancy of 78 years, with a retirement 22 years long. The dozen less fortunate chief executives could expect to live only to 68, with a retirement 12 years in length. All in all, stress costs a decade of life and leisure.

2. In an extensive study of hereditary monarchs, the age at ascending the throne was compared with the ruler's life span. On the average, the younger the king, queen, or sultan upon ascension, the shorter his or her life expectancy. Does this relationship betray the cruel strain of governing a nation? Does exposing themselves to such unrelenting distress earlier mark youthful monarchs for an early grave? Thus, Henry V had the misfortune of ascending the

English throne at age 26. Nine years later he was dead, worn out by the cares of government and conquest.

3. Now let us turn to that more sublimated form of politics and war: chess. Anyone who has watched a championship competition between two grandmasters knows that few duels can be more grueling. It is as much a physical contest as an intellectual one. And there is a cost: Those grandmasters who most often battled for supremacy shortened their lives by nearly a decade. Indeed, those competitors who made a profession out of the game died, on the average, about 10 years earlier than those grandmasters who pursued careers beyond the chess board. In the former group are unfortunates like Labourdonnais (45), Morphy (47), and Alekhine (54). In the latter wiser, and hence older, group are names like opera composer Philidor (69), literary critic Staunton (64), and mathematician Anderssen (61). As the life spans given in parentheses suggest, making a living at competitive chess can be hazardous to one's health.

Stress from Within

I think the argument is strong that frequent and intense stress can shorten lives. Yet the impact of stress does not have to be this dramatic. Ups and downs in stressors can affect physical well-being on a day-to-day basis. Most of us know the experience of coming down with a cold when we come under unusual stress. In fact, researchers in psychosomatic medicine have spent much effort trying to demonstrate the link between hassles and illness. One well-known example is the Social Readjustment Rating Questionnaire. This scale lists many events, both momentous and diminutive, that require people to make life adjustments. The person taking the test gets a certain number of points for each event. The points are assigned according to the amount of stress that must usually be endured. Here's a sample of items with their corresponding weights: minor violations of the law, 11; change in residence, 20; troubles with the boss, 23; beginning or ceasing formal schooling, 26; son or daughter leaving home, 29; gaining a new family member, 30; sexual difficulties, 39; marital reconciliation, 45; being fired from work, 47; marriage, 50; death of a close family member, 63; detention in jail, 63; marital separation, 65; divorce, 73; and death of spouse, 100.

The more intense a stressor is, the lower are its odds of occurrence. Even Elizabeth Taylor has changed residence more often than she's changed spouses. Hence, there is more than one way to collect life-change points. At one extreme, people can gather many minor hassles; at the other extreme, they may experience just one or two big events. In either case, should they accumulate many life-change units in a short span of time, their odds of coming down with a health problem increase. The specific outcome varies from person to person, according to idiosyncratic risks. Even so, the complaint is real. A person with a psychosomatic illness is not a hypochondriac.

This link between stress and physical health holds for all members of our species, notables included. This was shown in a study of 10 classical composers—Bach, Handel, Haydn, Mozart, Beethoven, Schubert, Chopin, Wagner, Brahms, and Debussy. Naturally, these personalities were no longer able to take the Social Readjustment Rating Questionnaire themselves; a psychologist thus took it for them, using detailed chronologies of their life histories. The biographies included information that was used to gauge fluctuations in their physical health over their adulthood life spans. As in the research on everyday subjects, the two measures were linked. The more life-change units accumulated in a given period of life, the higher the odds that the composer would succumb to a major physical illness.

What makes this relationship especially important is another reality pointed out in Chapter 7: Physical health is conducive to creative output. It is difficult for a person to keep up the heavy work schedule of the creative genius when an infirmity is keeping him or her in bed. Hence, stress does more than just shorten the number of years a person has to make a mark; it also can abbreviate the number of hours available each day for making the mark. Yet the frustrations and anxieties of living can accomplish even more than this: They can influence the very shape of the mark left behind.

Critics often argue that the arts represent a guise of emotional communication. Thus, Robert Frost warned the mere technician, "No tears in the writer, no tears in the reader." A poem, a painting, a composition—all art forms can convey to the appreciator an experience deeply felt by the work's originator. And of all vehicles of emotional expression, music may reign supreme. The very sound and shape of a melody can provide an intimate metaphor for the course of our deepest feelings. There is cross-cultural evidence that music offers an effective and universal form of affective expression. People can listen to music imported from the farthest reaches of this planet, and still identify the emotions that motivate the sounds. This is because "Music sounds the way emotions feel."

The emotional expressiveness of music was shown in another facet of the above-mentioned study of 10 composers. In Chapter 4 we have seen how a computer can measure the melodic originality of themes in the compositions that make up the classical repertoire. A melody scoring high in originality is rich in chromatic notes and unexpected intervals. Such melodies are more likely to be written in minor keys. These attributes are often associated with more tragic, melancholic, or tormented moods. In contrast, melodies scoring low in originality are more predictable, cheerful, easy-going, and upbeat.

The next question should be obvious. For these same 10 classical composers, we know when they suffered most and when life treated them well. We also know the melodic originality of the themes composed during their careers. So what is the connection between the two? It's positive. Melodic lines became the most tortuous when the composers' lives became the most tormented. It is as if the composers were engaged in self-therapy, and music was the medium of self-discovery. And if we are sensitive enough, we can share in the creators' self-disclosure. Tears in the creators, tears in the appreciators.

Stress from Without

Up to this point, I have emphasized the effects of largely personal stressors. The life changes are unique to the personality, rather than affecting thousands or millions across the board. This emphasis is consistent with the Social Readjustment Rating Questionnaire. All of its items concern private events rather than public affairs. Nevertheless, we must admit that some of the prime stressors in a person's life may originate outside the life of the individual. The sources of distress may be big events that cut across the lives of many unfortunates. For instance, researchers have documented the severe strains endured by those who lived near the Three Mile Island nuclear reactor—the power plant that had a partial meltdown on March 28, 1979. Certainly, the psychological ramifications of this nuclear accident can make the most stressful events in the Social Readjustment Rating Questionnaire appear trivial. How would it feel to believe that your child might some day die of cancer, owing to the accidental release of radioactive gases?

Calamities do not have to be human-made, of course. Natural disasters can also distribute intense stress across many people. Hence, several investigators have assessed the psychological damage inflicted by hurricanes, tornadoes, floods, fires, earthquakes, and other capricious devastations of nature. These catastrophic events definitely cause a severe "disaster stress reaction" in the populations affected. For instance, when Mount Saint Helens erupted on May 18, 1980, the town of Othello, Washington abruptly became the depository for tons of volcanic ash. Months later, the citizens showed the effects of this catastrophe. Mental illness had increased by 236%, the incidence of psychosomatic illnesses by 219%, and various stress-aggravated ailments by 198%. These changes were accompanied by big increases in alcohol abuse, domestic violence, and acts of criminal aggression, such as vandalism, disorderly conduct, and assaults. Natural disasters surely bode ill for a community's mental health.

Even these events are relatively local, compared to more global origins of strain. War is a prime example. Beethoven endured many problems in his life: failed negotiations with publishers, custody battles over his nephew Karl, concerts that went awry, devastating reviews, and the usual unrequited loves. Still, how do these compare to his having to listen to Napoleon's bombardment of Vienna, cowering in a basement, with pillows covering his fragile ears? Experiences of military conflict may not happen as often as the everyday hassles listed in the Social Readjustment Rating Questionnaire, but surely the points assigned to war's terrors must come at the top of any complete scale.

Because the next chapter discusses the psychological effects of historic aggression and violence, let us put this discussion on hold. But before advancing to Chapter 11, I'd like to pose a question.

Is Psychopathology the Cost of Greatness?

The earlier sections on mental illness have conveyed the strong impression that the etiologies are endogenous. That is, they have implied that certain people inherit a tendency toward madness, and that if this endowment is not potent enough to overpower an individual's ego, the insanity may be converted into genius. Nonetheless, this cannot be the whole truth. We have ample evidence that psychopathologies can have exogenous causes as well. Intense and frequent strain can do more than weaken one's immune system or raise one's blood pressure; these events can precipitate nervous breakdowns, too. Stressors can take personalities sitting at the edge of normality and push them off into madness.

Therefore, we must remain open to the prospect that many of the names listed in the tables of this chapter got there because they were simply overwhelmed by life's tests. That is, they may have been just like the rest of us regarding their interior resources, and life merely dished them out more than most people could handle. Recall what we have learned about the livelihood of greatness. The childhoods of the eminent are seldom benign; parental loss and other traumatic events may leave emotional scars that never heal. As adults, the famous must take stunning risks, chances that most people would not dare undertake. So they face recurrent failure, and even sometimes outright persecution. Even when success and acclaim rain upon their heads, the trials and tests do not cease. Their privacy may vanish, while their private lives become a mess. They may be lionized by the wrong people for the wrong reasons, making them feel unappreciated or even lonely. And the pressure of living up to ever-rising expectations and of always appeasing the fickle fans can make each day more arduous than the next. Even the very act of accomplishment can suck away precious reserves. The Social Readjustment Rating Questionnaire assigns 28 points for any "outstanding personal achievement." How many points should we give Beethoven's *Missa Solemnis*, Michelangelo's Sistine Chapel, Tolstoy's *War and Peace*, or Newton's *Principia Mathematica*?

I suspect that many of us could not have survived all the stresses that these luminaries went through without losing our own emotional equilibrium. I am not saying that the greats of history are never born with some tendencies toward madness; the pathological genealogies imply otherwise. I am only noting that all creatures, great and small, have their endurance limits—and that the really important personalities may have to endure a lot more than the rest of us. Perhaps genius is not always a fringe benefit of a tempered madness. Sometimes intemperate madness is an unsought penalty for genius.

CHAPTER 11

VIOLENCE AS A SHAPER
OF HISTORY

"**H**istory is little more than a picture of human crimes and misfortunes," said Voltaire. William Cullen Bryant called history "The horrid tale of perjury and strife,/Murder and spoil." The annals of human affairs are filled with conspiracies, assassinations, executions, massacres, riots, revolts, revolutions, invasions, and conquests. Thousands of "great" personalities have left their marks in human blood. Napoleon is prototypical. Tolstoy maintained in his *War and Peace* that Napoleon's acclaim rests mostly on his willingness to assume responsibility for collective murder. Napoleon gave the orders that allowed millions to become killers with impunity, and he bled France white in the process. Yet, owing to the scope and drama of this homicidal enterprise, Napoleon has gone down in the records as a "great man." By 1841, Thomas Carlyle could identify him as one of the few genuine heroes of history; by the beginning of this century, James McKeen Cattell could rank him as the most eminent personality in Western civilization. According to the amount of space received in biographical dictionaries, Napoleon has surpassed the less bellicose Shakespeare, Voltaire, Francis Bacon, Aristotle, Goethe, and Newton. In fact, in this century alone, "more than 200,000 volumes have been published on Napoleon and his times."

The example above concerns collective belligerence. Even so, violence can take place on a more individualistic level; this aggression, too, can serve as a vehicle for self-aggrandizement. John W. Hinckley Jr. hoped to impress actress Jodie Foster by killing President Reagan. Though he failed, he came close enough to get his name in the mass media and the history books. Because the world is chock-full of lost psyches desperate for a release from loneliness or obscurity, many will even confess to crimes that they could not have committed. Back in 1932, someone kidnapped and murdered the baby boy of famed aviator Charles Lindbergh. Unsolicited confessions were offered by more than 200 persons! Were there really that many nonentities who thought that notoriety was their only option in life?

In sum, individual and collective aggression plays a crucial role in the making of big people and events. Hence, we must devote a chapter to this nasty subject. Most of the following pages outline the causes of human violence. After that, I discuss the aftermath as well.

Causes of Violence

Violence comes from many sources. Yet from our standpoint, six factors stand out: population growth and the resulting rebelliousness toward authority figures; frustrated aspirations; intolerable weather; mob mentality; models of violence; and errors of judgment. These range from the emotional to the cognitive.

Crowded Streets and Young Rebels

Comparative psychologists have shown that extreme population density can lead to violent, self-destructive behaviors in animals. In one study, a mouse colony in a cage designed to hold 150 was allowed to grow until it became crammed with 15 times that amount; violent behaviors then appeared, including homicide, infanticide, and cannibalism. Societal critics frequently blame excessive population density for the violence suffered in human societies as well. Life in densely packed urban areas is often characterized by violent crimes and juvenile delinquency. The morning newspaper in any big city is replete with accounts of murders, muggings, rapes, and robberies. Of course, most of the aggressive acts committed in the metropolis merely contribute sterile tidbits to year-end crime statistics. Nevertheless, in another form, population pressure can motivate violence of long-term importance.

In Chapter 6, we have seen that revolutionaries are frequently later-born children. This implies that the leaders of revolts and rebellions come from large families. And this implication suggests a connection between population growth and large-scale domestic violence. Two historians have proposed a psychological model that delineates the way this causal linkage might work. The model argues that the key requisite for the outbreak of civil disturbances is an extraordinary surge in the population. The spurt must be well out of line with the increments that the nation's economy can easily accommodate. The especially critical part of this inordinate growth is the sharp increase in the number of young adult males. Criminologists have long known that members of this group make up by far the largest proportion of the population of violent criminals. This same group provides a functional reservoir of potential rioters, rebels, and revolutionaries. All that is necessary to convert this potential into actual collective violence is some means to alienate the youths from authority.

The needed alienation is a second by-product of extravagant growth in the population. High fertility rates mean overly large families; the result is intolerable familial tension. Sons display greater hostility toward their fathers. After all, these fathers must have difficulty bringing home the bacon while simultaneously attending to the emotional needs of their expanding brood. Since fathers represent their children's first authority figures, antagonisms toward fathers will generalize to animosity toward all powers that be. Rivalries among siblings also intensify, as each must compete more vigorously for restricted family resources. The only relationship to benefit from these pressures is that between mother and son. The emerging rebellious personality is thus often a "Mama's boy" who is alienated from other family members and vehemently opposed to the establishment. Once these familial and societal misfits grow up, the world is in for an awful surprise.

The creators of this intriguing model actually gathered data to check the central links in the developmental sequence. They looked at population statistics in France and England; and also examined the incidence of civil violence in the same two nations. They showed that a large jump in fertility rates was usually followed by violent turmoil after a lag of about 25 years. This was enough time for the sons so spawned to enter the stage of history. In France, for example, the revolutions of 1830, 1848, and 1871 all followed population spurts that took place 23, 26, and 29 years earlier, respectively. Moreover, the investigators went one step further: They attempted to gauge, however tenuously, the level of familial tension in the years intervening between population and aggression statistics. Using the biographies and autobiographies of literary figures, they showed that the ups and downs in family hostility and alienation pursued the expected course.

This model may explain the roots of the unruly baby-boom generation. Once demobilization began at the close of World War II, millions of soldiers came marching home to propagate the species. In many nations, the population spurt was unprecedented. We would therefore expect an increase in civil unrest as these offspring entered early adulthood. That was exactly what happened: In the United States, university students staged takeovers at Columbia, Harvard, and the University of California at Berkeley. Dramatic antiestablishment demonstrations occurred in Chicago during the 1968 Democratic convention. Kent State University became the site of a bloody confrontation after the Cambodian invasion of 1970.

To be sure, these events were mostly driven by the unpopular Vietnam War. But this was not the whole story. During this same period, poor blacks began rioting in America's urban ghettos, while the black intelligentsia tried to provide a radical foundation for the black protest. Angela Davis, for one, was 25 years old in 1969, when she first challenged the white establishment in California. Moreover, youth-led civil unrest was conspicuous in many other parts of the world during the late 1960s and early 1970s. Barricades again went up in the streets of Paris. The Red Guards launched the Cultural Revolution in China. The specific issues might shift from country to country—Communism, racism, imperialism, colonialism—but the key players belonged to the same cohort. The planet teemed with angry young lemmings storming over its surface, carrying placards and shouting slogans.

Thwarted Goals

What happened to all those zealots? Why aren't they still actively raising hell? One answer concerns a point made in Chapter 7: Revolution is mainly a young person's game. As people get older, they become more conservative. Just witness the case of Jerry Rubin, the one-time Yippie leader: By middle age, he had transformed himself into a businessman. Like him, former radicals become co-opted by the establishment.

Yet another explanation is possible: It could be that circumstances changed sufficiently that hostile feelings were no longer so blatantly provoked. This interpretation is most obviously valid with respect to the antiwar demonstrations. Once American participation in the Southeast Asian conflict diminished to the point at which young men ceased to be drafted into the military, the pool of potential protesters diminished dramatically. Young men could now pursue their life plans without worrying that their lives would be brought to a halt in the jungles of Vietnam. For African-Americans, too, conditions improved considerably. Although everything was (and remains) far from perfect, at least most minorities in America could look to their futures with augmented hope. Their life plans would be less often thwarted by unjust laws. Victims of racism even acquired legal recourse when employers or landlords engaged in more personal acts of discrimination. In brief, by the mid-1970s, life for the baby boomers had become less frustrating.

There is ample evidence, in fact, that frustration is a principal cause of aggression. When people set goals for themselves, and then encounter obstacles in their path, they are prone to lash out. Sometimes frustration-induced violence serves an adaptive or instrumental function: Swinging fists can clear the roadblocks in one's way. But the emotional function may be more important. Aggression provides catharsis. It's like losing your temper after a hard day at work. By ventilating the pent-up frustrations—by "letting off steam"—you feel better. We can comprehend many acts of historic violence in terms of this "frustration–aggression hypothesis." The first man to assassinate a U.S. President, John Wilkes Booth, was clearly frustrated over the defeat of the South in the Civil War. Similarly, the second man to become a presidential assassin—Charles Guiteau, who shot Garfield on July 2, 1881—was a frustrated office seeker. Moreover, when many people in the same geographical location are experiencing the same frustrations, the violence can become collective rather than just individual in nature.

We find a tragic illustration in the lynch mobs of the American South between 1882 and 1930. In the Southern economy, even after the Civil War, cotton was king. If the prices for cotton were good, farmers could make a decent living. They could buy that Ford that caught their fancy, or purchase that extra plot of land, or hire some additional help. When cotton prices dropped, in contrast, these aspirations were stymied. Aggression might be the immediate result. So was it any accident that fluctuations in the well-being of cotton farmers paralleled fluctuations in the lynching of blacks? Clearly, the descendants of former slaves provided convenient scapegoats for the descendants of former slave owners. Needless to say, using scapegoats as targets of accumulated frustration is not unique to the American scene. The Jews served much the same function in many European nations—before the Holocaust made this form of collective catharsis unfashionable.

Lynch mobs and pogroms are rather disorganized societal spasms. Nothing enduring comes from them, except perhaps for continued racial hatred. Yet the frustration–aggression linkage may trigger collective violence with more lasting results. In particular, many revolutions can be explicated in these terms. For example, a sociologist has put forward an intriguing "J-curve theory" of revolt. According to this model, people rarely rebel when conditions are horrid. When life is dependably hopeless, they cannot experience frustration, for they have no aspirations beyond survival. Instead, circumstances must first improve. If matters get progressively better, people begin to aspire to an even better life. Each year should be surpassed by the next. Children should be better off than the parents were. Once expectations are inclined to rise, the social order becomes more fragile. All it takes is some setback in the continuing progression to throw obstacles in everyone's path toward freedom, wealth, or status. This downturn then causes large masses of people to experience frustration, and then to express themselves through aggression. Hence, the result is collective violence when an ascending curve is unexpectedly converted to a curve in the shape of an inverted, backward J.

Many revolts and rebellions show this affective reaction. Dorr's Rebellion of 1842, the Russian Revolution of 1917, and the Egyptian Revolution of 1952 all happened when a period of steady gains was followed by a sudden reversal of fortunes. A more contemporary example occurred in the former Soviet Union. First came an era of ever-expanding hope in the late 1980s. This ascending portion of the curve was drawn by Gorbachev's liberal policies of *perestroika* (restructuring) and *glasnost* (openness). Then everything seemed momentarily lost with the attempted coup of August 1991. By kidnapping Gorbachev and taking over the Kremlin, the conspirators strove to alter the current course of Soviet history. That was a downward turn that most Soviet peoples were simply not prepared to accept. The hands on the clock could not be pushed back even by tanks in the streets. So the masses were prepared to fight for the new world they saw before them. The climax was the dissolution of the once-powerful Soviet Union.

Sultry Days

Let's imagine that the setting is ripe for violence. An extravagant burst in the population has produced a surfeit of alienated and hostile youths. A long-term rise in political freedom or economic welfare for a large mass of people has just been disrupted by a rapid reversal of status or subsistence. Society now becomes a powder keg, ready to explode on the slightest provocation. What lights the short fuse? The answer is literally heat. Shakespeare described the capacity of hot days to ignite aggression in *Romeo and Juliet*, where Benvolio warns Mercutio,

> I pray thee, good Mercutio, let's retire;
> The day is hot, the Capulets abroad,
> And, if we meet, we shall not scape a brawl.
> For now, these hot days, is the mad blood stirring.

Laboratory studies have shown that raising a room's thermostat does indeed increase the aggressiveness of its occupants. Moreover, correlational studies of real-world violence show conclusively that the higher the thermometer reading, the more likely aggression is. For example, violent crimes are more probable when the temperature is an enervating 90 degrees Fahrenheit than when it's in the cool 60s. By "violent crimes" I mean murder, rape, and aggravated assault; we can also include spouse abuse in this group. In contrast, nonviolent crimes, such as burglary, larceny, and motor vehicle theft, do not fluctuate with the digital readings outside the local bank. Moreover, the relationship between criminal aggression and temperature does not materialize in those neighborhoods where air conditioning is commonplace in homes, automobiles, workplaces, and recreational facilities.

Admittedly, these studies have focused on everyday crimes, not historic events. Even so, many infamous acts of criminal aggression do indeed take place during the steaming summer months. The July 2 on which Guiteau shot President Garfield was uncomfortably hot. And Robert F. Kennedy was shot by Sirhan Sirhan on June 5, 1968. Of course, not all assassinations take place in unpleasant weather. Nevertheless, it may be that summer killings are more likely to be crimes of passion, while historic homicides in other months are acts of calculation. Hence, the fact that John F. Kennedy was shot in November would fit the notion that Oswald's crime was coolly premeditated.

Besides, individual violence can take a more subtle but still highly public form. This can be seen on American baseball diamonds. Three social psychologists scrutinized 826 major league games played during the 1986, 1987, and 1988 seasons. The measure of aggression was the number of players at bat who were hit by a pitch. Angry pitchers often take out batters by a well-aimed fastball. Significantly, in this study, the odds that a player would be so victimized increased with the ambient temperature: Being hit by a pitch was almost twice as likely for games played in the 90s as for games when the temperature was below 70 degrees Fahrenheit. This link held up even after the investigators controlled for such contaminating factors as the number of wild pitches, passed balls, errors, walks, home runs, and attendance. In fact, temperature was the top overall predictor of this peculiar act of personal violence.

What makes the heat–aggression relationship especially consequential, however, is its association with collective violence. Americans often view the July 4 fireworks, which celebrate America's revolt from British rule, in shorts and T-shirts. Bastille Day, an analogous French holiday, occurs on July 14, another hot time of the year. A more current example can be found in the urban riots of African-Americans in the 1960s. The official *Report of the National Advisory Commission on Civil Disorders* made it clear: With only one exception, these disturbances began when the temperature was 80 degrees or more.

This last observation has led several social psychologists to document the "long, hot summer effect": the higher the ambient temperature, the higher the odds of civil disorders. This holds not just for American blacks, but for disgruntled peoples throughout the world. One study examined 836 uprisings that took place between 1791 and 1880. In Europe, July was the preferred month for unrest, whereas December and January were the quiet months. For South America this calendar pattern was reversed: The populace took to the streets in January, while everyone cuddled peacefully next to the home hearth on May and June. The heat must take the rap.

We don't know exactly why high temperatures so agitate the human spirit. One explanation is that excessive heat frustrates people. It's hard for them to do what they want, or to enjoy what they are doing, when the temperature and humidity are oppressive. Alternative explanations are legion. But one factor deserves our special attention: Summer months invite masses of human beings onto the streets, to escape the stifling closeness of sun-roasted homes and apartments. The availability of so many people may activate a whole different state of mind—one associated with mob psychology.

Anonymous Crowds

An astute reader may have noticed an oddity in the accounts above. All three factors reviewed so far are responsible for both individual and collective violence. Population pressure can produce intrafamily hostilities as well as revolutions. Frustration can yield both lone assassins and lynch mobs. A hot summer day can turn out murderers, rapists, and vicious baseball pitchers along with urban rioters. This picture hints that collective behavior is nothing more than the aggregate manifestation of individual behavior. If we know what makes single persons act out their anger, we will automatically know what underlies the violence of the masses. The whole is merely the sum of its parts.

Yet this simple-minded equivalence cannot be valid. We have ample reason to believe that people behave differently in a group than they would if they were alone—even when the circumstances are otherwise identical. Social psychologists who study altruistic behavior, for example, have done much research on the "bystander effect." A person who needs help is more likely to receive aid if there is only one bystander to the emergency than if there are several. There's something about the presence of other bystanders that inhibits any one bystander from taking the necessary action. For instance, "diffusion of responsibility" is more likely to increase with the number of spectators to the event. The more other bystanders there are, the more an individual bystander can say, "Let someone else get involved! I've got better things to do!" This excuse becomes much more difficult when there is only one witness to the victim's plight.

In fact, the original research on the bystander effect was inspired by a real event that took place in New York City back in 1964: the notorious Kitty Genovese rape–murder case. This young woman was nearly home when she was attacked by a knife-wielding assailant. The killer took 35 minutes to stab her to death. Despite her screams, no one came to her aid; no one even bothered to call the police until it was too late. Yet 38 witnesses were present at the event!

If groups can inhibit helping behavior in individuals, can they also go one step farther? Can submergence in a mob bring out the worst aggressive instincts in otherwise decent human beings? If so, we must acknowledge that the etiology of violence is not always the same for persons and masses. About a century ago, Gustave Le Bon, in his classic book *The Crowd*, tried to describe the singularities of the group mind. For example, the diffusion of responsibility that prevents people from intervening in emergencies can also free them from the usual restraints of civilization. Thus, "a crowd being anonymous, and in consequence irresponsible, the sentiments of responsibility which always controls individuals disappears entirely." Violent actions that people would not dream of undertaking alone suddenly become not only possible, but desirable. The anonymity of each individual coupled with the number of persons milling in the mob all imply that no one participant is accountable. Because the individuals cease to think as individuals, we say that they undergo "deindividuation." Once this mental conversion occurs, a person is free to become a barbarian.

Most readers can conjure up plenty of illustrations from newspapers and newscasts. In New York City, a group of teenagers went "wilding" through Central Park, attacked a female jogger, gang-raped her, and brutally beat her almost to death. In Ulster, a British soldier was yanked from his car by an angry mob and savagely beaten, and his bleeding, naked body was strung up, to the horror of other onlookers. Before a soccer match in Belgium, British fans stampeded their Italian opponents, crushing or suffocating 38 and seriously injuring hundreds more. Other prominent examples permeate the course of history: the Sicilian Vespers of 1282, in which mobs massacred 2,000 French, or the

St. Bartholomew's Day Massacre on 1572, in which 3,000 Huguenots were murdered in Paris alone. For me, the most monstrous instance is what happened to the famed Hypatia. Here was a woman whose beauty, eloquence, intellect, and (yet!) modesty were unrivaled by any female of the ancient world. She was a brilliant mathematician, astronomer, and philosopher. She headed the Neo-Platonist school at Alexandria, and was the last recorded member of the illustrious museum there. But as a renowned pagan, she became the focal point of tension between paganism and Christianity. In March of the year 415, a barbaric mob of Christian zealots dragged her down and hacked her into pieces.

Laboratory experiments have isolated some factors that can enhance the violent effects of deindividuation. Among the most significant is the role of clothing that conceals a person's identity. Members of the Ku Klux Klan are by no means foolish when they don their fearsome white hoods and robes. Such apparel assures anonymity, enabling them to leave conscience at home. Military uniforms can achieve much the same effect. According to a cross-cultural investigation, this perverse function can assume an exotic guise. The warriors of some cultures wear masks, paint their faces and bodies in rich colors and elaborate shapes, and put on special garments. Examples include the fierce-looking fighters of the New World, such as the Aztecs, Incas, and Comanches. Other cultures send the troops off to battle practically in their work clothes. If the extra military attire serves to deindividuate those in combat, we should expect such warriors to display extreme violence in warfare. That prediction holds up: On the average, deindividuated fighters are more prone to kill, torture, or mutilate their enemies. They don't often take prisoners, and when they do, their actions can be horrifying.

The anonymity of military uniforms is not the only parameter: The larger the collectivity, the higher the diffusion of responsibility. Lost in the crowd, any person can perform the most inhumane deeds with complete impunity. This second source of savagery is apparent in the behavior of white American lynch mobs toward black American victims. Some mobs are content merely to hang their unhappy prey from the limb of the nearest tree. Their anger then abates. Other mobs allow their violence to wax more ferocious. They may burn, lacerate, and even dismember the target of their fury. They may stretch out the execution, tormenting and torturing the victim, prolonging the agony. And what is a prime predictor of the action taken? The mob's size.

This last fact suggests an interesting notion. Perhaps the violence produced by deindividuation and the negligence produced by the bystander effect are two sides of the same coin. Get a few bystanders, and the chance for aid disappears; add some more bystanders, and the result is a deindividuated congregation ready to commit hideous acts. This continuum between constrained altruism and nurtured sadism is seen in an odd phenomenon of urban streets.

Sometimes deeply depressed persons will take an elevator to an upper floor of a tall building, climb out on a ledge, and try to summon up the courage to jump. When bystanders below realize what's happening, they look up in awe. Sometimes the story ends happily. On January 19, 1981, for example, boxing champion Muhammad Ali talked down a potential suicide from a ninth-floor window—to the cheers of the spectators. At other times the crowd below behaves more outrageously: The bystanders engage in "suicide baiting." They jeer and dare away at the wretch. Here's a story that ran in *The New York Times* on June 8, 1964:

> A Puerto Rican handyman perched on a 10th floor ledge for an hour yesterday morning as many persons in a crowd of 500 on upper Broadway shouted at him in Spanish and English to jump. Even as cries of "Jump!" and "Brinca!" rang out, policemen pulled the man to safety from the narrow ledge at 3495 Broadway, the north-west corner of 143rd Street.

Crowds do not bait potential victims often—maybe less than 10% of the time. But why do these deplorable episodes occur at all? According to the evidence, bystanders are most likely to turn bad under circumstances that are now familiar to us:

1. These events take place most often in the summer months. The bystanders may thus be in a foul mood already, owing to the heat.

2. This ill behavior arises most often when the victim has played Hamlet too long on the ledge. Many bystanders are missing appointments or forfeiting pleasures while waiting for the big event to happen. After a while, impatience grows, and with that increase comes frustration. So everybody eggs on a threatened suicide.

3. These episodes happen most frequently when those in the throng can become deindividuated. For example, a baiting crowd is most likely in the evening hours. At high noon, with the sun glaring at the warts, wrinkles, and freckles in everyone's face, it's hard for individuals to lose their identity. Anonymity needs darkness. Besides this, we must consider the crowd's size. The larger the number of bystanders present, the greater the resulting anonymity and diffusion of responsibility. Hence, crowds of 300 bystanders or more are most likely to urge the pathetic party to jump.

Research on baiting crowds introduces another concept, one sometimes confused with deindividuation—that of "dehumanization." Would-be suicides are most likely to be baited if they pick a ledge between the 6th and 12th floors. Above the 12th floor, persons on a ledge are too remote from the crowds below. Because they are out of earshot, they cannot be the object of insults and provocations. Below the 6th floor, the opposite happens: Bystanders can discern the faces of the would-be jumpers, spot their fear, and therefore sympathize with their predicament. Above all, the bystanders can appreciate that the potential suicides are flesh and blood, just as they themselves are, and not abstract stick figures in another universe. Between the 6th and 12th floors is the twilight zone of human cruelty. Persons standing on a ledge can now suffer dehumanization.

The members of the crowd can strip away the persons' humanity. The moral scruples that fellow humans deserve are operative no more.

Deindividuation is what happens to members of the crowd that makes them more violent. Dehumanization is what happens to the victims, to make them attractive targets of the violence. These two factors combined are the evil force behind the lynch mobs, gang rapes, and massacres that too often fill newspapers, newscasts, and history books. The victims become subhuman; the aggressors become inhuman.

Monkey See, Monkey Do: Models of Violence

Immersion in a crowd does more than cloak the individual in anonymity. Often, being with a large group of people means being exposed to *models* of aggressive behavior. Let us imagine that 10 or 15 youths (some of whom may not even know each other) are roaming the streets on a hot summer day. Nothing much is happening, except the vague ambience of frustration and hostility. Suddenly one of the teenagers picks up a rock and throws it through a store window. Another youth reaches into the display case thus exposed, and grabs a CD player. Pretty soon many others in the amorphous group follow suit, as everyone rushes down the main drag, smashing glass and stealing merchandise. The police now have an urban riot on their hands. The human proclivity for imitation causes a chain reaction. This process allows the fuller exploitation of the available anonymity.

This brings us to a central psychological explanation for aggressive behaviors—"social learning theory." First developed by Albert Bandura, this theory says that people are prone to imitate the actions of others, including violent acts. They are especially likely to mimic models when those models are seen as prestigious or powerful. Violent actions also elicit emulation when those behaviors bring benefits—when the model "gets away with it."

Models can enlarge people's aggressiveness in two ways. First, novel aggressive acts may be acquired through "observational learning." Thus, some youths in the group described above may never have realized that it only takes a brick and a free hand to confiscate a new TV at the local appliance store. Second, models can enable people to undergo "disinhibition." Everyone has a rich repertoire of aggressive skills—skills that are seldom if ever used. Through punishment, whether direct or vicarious, most people have learned to inhibit their hostile impulses. Seeing one human being acting out his or her anger frees others to do the same. They are unleashed to do what was always latent within.

No doubt both observational learning and disinhibition are critical factors in violent behavior. Sometimes these social learning processes are responsible for aggressive actions of major proportions. To see how these processes may operate, let us examine examples drawn from four kinds of events—movies, news, sports, and politics.

Some appalling crimes have been inspired by films shown on television or in the movie theaters. In 1974, the movie *Born Innocent* appeared on TV. A few days later, a little girl in California was violently assaulted; her attackers used a method similar to that depicted in the film. In 1977, a scene from the TV series *Kojak* inspired a Florida teenager to murder an 82-year-old woman after the same fashion. When the boy appeared in court, he pleaded innocent by reason of "television intoxication." In 1984, a husband set his wife ablaze after seeing such an act portrayed in the TV movie *The Burning Bed*. In a 1988 trial, another teenager admitted that he had gotten the idea to bludgeon a class-mate to death from watching the videotape docudrama *Faces of Death*. Perhaps the most historic example took place in 1981, when John W. Hinckley Jr. modeled himself after a cab driver in the movie *Taxi Driver*. This character, a Vietnam War veteran, "flips out" and decides to assassinate a political candidate. Following suit, Hinckley tried to kill President Reagan.

Of course, these are all anecdotes, not findings. Nevertheless, there is ample evidence that the violence acted out on the TV tube or movie screen can provoke violence in the world beyond the den or theater. Moreover, movies and TV shows are by no means the sole source of aggressive models; the evening news often puts some dramatic murders at center stage. In fact, widely publicized homicides tend to cause a rise in criminal violence. Even worse, a truly sensational serial killer can inspire a string of "copycat" murders. This effect was seen even before the days of TV and movies. Back in 1888, when Jack the Ripper became the first mad slasher to stain the history books, the public had to rely on the newspapers alone. Geraldo Rivera could not visit the gruesome scenes with video cameras. Even so, the printed narrations were enough to incite others to pattern themselves after Jack's *modus operandi*.

Naturally, much of the time on TV news and the space in newspapers is allotted to covering events besides killings. Even so, many of these alternative subjects offer food for aggressive thoughts. This is particularly true for sports. A game, competition, or championship fight is, at bottom, little more than an elevated form of violence. In boxing there may be rules that must be followed, and gloves to cushion the blows, but a punch from a heavyweight is a mean experience nonetheless. Some have argued that big-time sports events have a redeeming social value. Spectators supposedly experience "catharsis" from watching professionals brutalize each other; that is, aggressive impulses are harmlessly released through the vicarious process of identifying with the vic-tor. Social learning theory argues the opposite: The athletes are still providing violent models that can stimulate disinhibition.

Judging from research, the social learning theorists have the more accurate view. For example, shortly after a heavily publicized boxing match, there is an increase in homicides in the general population. Prize fights involving Muhammad Ali were especially likely to excite homicidal acts days afterward. Albeit innocently, Ali was an inciter of murder.

Even when the side spectators support in a sporting event is the side that wins, there's no reason to believe that the spectators will curtail their aggressive instincts. This was shown in a study of football fans who viewed the 1969 Army–Navy game. This is one of the classic annual matchups in the sport; therefore, if a spectator strongly identifies with one side, and that side emerges victorious, we might expect some catharsis. Still, whether a fan rooted for the winner (Army) or the loser (Navy), the same general level of disinhibition resulted. Fans on both sides of the field became more aggressive, not less. Hockey and wrestling are other sports besides boxing and football that increase rather than decrease aggression in the public. Anyone who wishes to promote a sport with the least in lethal aftershocks should schedule swimming or gymnastics.

Sports violence can generalize to actions far removed from the playing field or stadium. Other peoples and other nations may become the targets of violent intent as well. One cross-cultural inquiry looked closely at the bellicosity found in societies captivated by combative sports. These are games that plunge athletes into aggressive, warlike contact. Competitors may try to inflict physical harm on their opponents, or in some other way simulate the actions of warriors on the battlefield. Whatever the specifics, societies that engage in such recreational activities are more likely to go to war with their neighbors. The association between the Roman legions and the gladiators of Rome is perhaps prototypical. The fearsome Aztecs, too, were notorious for both imperial conquests and gladiatorial contests.

In modern times, combative sports assume less terrifying forms, such as soccer, ice hockey, and American football. Still, we should not underestimate the connection between sport and battle in these less cruel sports. In the summer of 1969, a war broke out between Honduras and El Salvador. The conflict escalated from the violence surrounding an important soccer match. The result was what historians style the Soccer War.

This brings us to politics as a final source of aggressive models. Frequently, the big events in public affairs are violent acts; thus, political violence breeds more violence. After President Kennedy's assassination in November 1963, there was a significant rise in the crime rate. This may seem a trivial example, as it may merely have involved lowly types getting courage from another lowly type, Lee Harvey Oswald. Still, leaders in positions of supreme power can ape the aggression of other leaders in power. A politician or general who seizes power in a *coup d'état* inadvertently provides a role model for others farther down in the hierarchy. Accordingly, usurpers may themselves suffer usurpation. A study of 342 monarchs found that those who left a trail of blood on their rise to the top often left a second trail on the way down—their own. For instance, Richard III murdered his way to the English throne, only to fall himself at Bosworth Field. "All who take the sword will perish by the sword," Jesus warned (Matthew 26:52).

If Jesus's admonition were true, why would anyone pick up their weapons? A cardinal principle of social learning is that people only copy models who avoid punishment for their crimes. Unfortunately, Jesus exaggerated: Not *all* violent agents in history bring doom upon themselves, but only *some*. Many usurpers, even the most brutal, manage to live to ripe old ages. For every Hitler and Mussolini, there is a Franco, Stalin, Mao, or Tito. Unless punishment is meted out by an insomniac Zeus well stocked with lightning bolts, it may not deter those willing to venture beyond the pale of morality. Ironically, it is easier to stimulate violence via models than to prevent violence through direct retaliation.

This odd asymmetrical impotence undermines capital punishment. The logic behind this legal practice is obvious: If villains knew that they would face the death penalty, were they to murder someone, they would think twice about taking that course of action. Logical as this deterrence-based argument sounds, the research suggests that such executions have little effect on homicides. Although we may spot a momentary dip in capital offenses after an execution, the decline is too transient to have lasting value. Moreover, this respite from killing requires that the execution be well publicized in the mass media. A potential murderer must see the criminal's body on the front page of the newspaper—strapped to an electric chair or hanging from a scaffold—to fear society's decrees, however briefly.

Why the ineffectiveness? Thucydides hinted at an answer in his *The History of the Peloponnesian War*. He recorded a debate on how to punish the Mitylenians, who had just rebelled against Athenian hegemony. One recommendation was to massacre all the town's adult males, and to put all women and children on the slave market. This would offer a grim lesson to any other denizens of the empire who might also contemplate rebellion. A level-headed opponent of this bloody deterrence reasoned as follows:

> Now of course communities have enacted the penalty of death for many offenses far lighter than this: still hope leads men to venture, and no one ever yet put himself in peril without the inward conviction that he would succeed in his design. Again, was there ever city rebelling that did not believe that it possessed either in itself or in its alliances resources adequate to the enterprise? All, states and individuals, are alike prone to err, and there is no law that will prevent them; or why should men have exhausted the list of punishments in search of enactments to protect them from evildoers? . . . Either then some means of terror more terrible than this must be discovered, or it must be owned that this restraint is useless.

Human beings will calculate the rewards and costs of different actions, each weighted by the probabilities of various outcomes. Few insurrections occur when the odds of success look nil. Few homicides happen when execution for the crime appears certain. Still, peoples and persons can misjudge the likelihood of the worst-case scenario. It only takes one successful revolt to undo the argument for the more cautious course, one unsolved case of homicide to give hope to a rogue planning murder. Much to humanity's dismay, disinhibition is often more potent than deterrence.

Losing Perspective

I have just spoken as if potentially violent persons or nations engage in a rational cost–benefit analysis. Only if the expected rewards outweigh the probable costs will the decision maker resort to aggression. Yet, as Thucydides suggested, nothing assures that these logical analyses will be faultless. Humans can always overestimate the advantages of homicide or conflict while underestimating the advantages of peaceful solutions. People can error in otherwise cool judgments. Hence, to comprehend aggressive behaviors more fully, we must delve into possible lapses in the human information-processing system.

We have already explored one applicable concept: "integrative complexity." I have defined this notion in the earlier discussion of cognition (Chapter 3). High complexity indicates that a decision maker carefully weighs all the relevant perspectives on an issue and then integrates them into a single, coherent position. Low complexity, in contrast, means that a person considers only one viewpoint, which is maintained with dogmatic tenacity. Chapter 3 has outlined how the letters and speeches of historic figures can be scored for integrative complexity, as well as how this cognitive variable can help us understand the long-term success of revolutionaries, victory in presidential elections, and triumph on the battlefield. This same factor can lead to the outbreak of war besides.

Military conflict often results when an international crisis gets out of hand. A string of unexpected events suddenly traps world leaders in a difficult decision-making quandary. The decision makers must face a complex situation in which multiple issues are at stake: national honor and security; personal prestige and ambition; and the economic, diplomatic, and military repercussions of various courses of action. Each leader must fathom his or her own options while concomitantly pondering the intentions and capacities of all other participants in the crisis. It is like a gigantic chess match, with multiple players, and with not all pieces visible on the board. Hence, to resolve the dispute without activating military resources demands unusual intellectual flexibility and agility. Each leader must imagine the point of view of all other parties, simultaneously scrutinizing a host of contingencies and scenarios. Participants in the conflict must leave others honorable means to retreat from open confrontation.

None of these conditions are likely to be met if each antagonist adopts a rigidly egocentric and self-righteous stance. Thus, nonviolent solutions to international crises may require that the decision makers on all sides exhibit the highest levels of integrative complexity. This prediction was confirmed in two separate inquiries.

The first study scrutinized two types of international crises. On the one hand, some crises led to an outbreak of war. One such crisis occurred in 1914, after the Archduke Ferdinand of Austria–Hungary was assassinated by a Serbian nationalist; this resulted in World War I. Another crisis that went bad was that leading to the 1950 Korean conflict. On the other hand, other crises were resolved without bloodshed. Included in this group were the 1911 Moroccan crisis, the 1948 Berlin blockade, and the 1962 Cuban missile crisis. The diplomatic exchanges surrounding these critical moments in history were scored for integrative complexity. The results were clear. When the diplomats exhibited very low levels of complexity, one or more parties were more likely to resort to force to settle the dispute. Moreover, when the preliminary phase of a crisis was contrasted with the climax phase, a significant pattern emerged: A cool-headed resolution of a crisis usually corresponded with an increase in the intricacy of intercourse. It was as if each participant was trying hard to comprehend the positions of all adversaries. For example, during the Cuban missile crisis, the American side was represented by President Kennedy and Secretary of State Rusk. The Soviet side consisted of Premier Khrushchev; Gromyko, the minister for foreign affairs; and Zorin, the Soviet ambassador to the United Nations. These decision makers all raised the complexity of their communications, and in doing so they averted World War III. The world leaders who bumbled their way into the catastrophe of World War I were much less wise; they actually showed a decrease in complexity.

The second investigation focused on the Middle East. The area around Palestine has seen four big wars since the state of Israel declared its existence in 1948. For each occasion, speeches delivered in the United Nations General Assembly were scored for integrative complexity. The speeches represented the positions of most nations directly or indirectly involved, such as Israel, Egypt, Syria, the United States, and the Soviet Union. Except for the Soviet Union, the leadership of all countries evinced a dramatic drop in complexity before the initiation of armed hostilities. In fact, the largest prewar reductions in information-processing sophistication were shown by the United States and Israel. However, these two nations also displayed the highest baseline levels of complexity under peacetime conditions.

These two inquiries and subsequent studies imply that the construct of integrative complexity has more than explanatory utility; it also has predictive power. If we spot complexity decreasing in leaders' speeches as an international crisis unfolds in the newspapers, we had better get provisions for the bomb shelter. Not only do such declines prophesy an escalation of the diplomatic altercations into all-out war, but they can also herald a surprise attack. This usage was suggested by a study of 18 such events in the 20th century. The surprise attacks included Germany's invasion of the Soviet Union in 1941 (Case Barbarossa); the Japanese assault on Pearl Harbor in 1941; the Soviet Union's crushing of the Hungarian revolution and the "Prague Spring"; the 1961 Bay of Pigs incursion led by U.S.-supported Cuban exiles; Egypt's launching of the 1973 Yom Kippur War; and Argentina's occupation of the Falkland (Malvinas) Islands in 1982. Speeches by the leaders of the nations involved were gathered from the period prior to the day of each surprise attack. The leaders of the aggressor nations exhibited a clear decline in complexity in the months and weeks leading up to the assault. Curiously, the leaders of the attacked nations showed evidence that they suspected danger. In the week just before each enemy's surprise, each victim often increased the complexity of diplomatic communications. Victims evidently get a whiff of the hostile atmosphere, and try to ameliorate tensions by adopting more even-handed positions. Unfortunately, this integrative-complexity aerosol seldom suffices.

I must confess an inherent ambiguity in this interpretation. It has been assumed that reduced integrative complexity in decision makers is a cause of military violence. Losing breadth of perspective, leaders unthinkingly plunge their nations into organized carnage; their rationality fails them at a crucial juncture in international affairs. Nevertheless, we could just as well argue for a contrary causal account. Perhaps the real agent is an underlying emotional state. Because intense stress and emotional turmoil can lower the efficiency of information processing, integrative complexity may be an effect rather than a cause. When an international conflict raises a people's rage to a fever pitch, the ability to handle intricate data may fall by the wayside. This stored-up anger also soon manifests itself in a declaration of war or a surprise attack.

In support of this alternative hypothesis, we can cite one fact: Even individuals not directly involved in foreign affairs may show changes in integrative complexity in response to current events. For instance, one study measured the complexity in editorials that appeared in the *Bulletin of the Atomic Scientists* between 1947 and 1974. This assessment varied according to the hands on the clock uniquely featured in this magazine. This clock's hands registered how close the world was to the midnight of nuclear war. Nevertheless, those writing these editorials were not the incumbent policy makers in the U.S. Departments of State or Defense. A second study examined the private correspondence of British novelists. This indicated that the complexity seen in these letters was partially contingent on Great Britain's war status. Much bloodshed meant lower complexity. Yet Charles Dickens, George Eliot, George Meredith, Arnold Bennett, and Virginia Woolf lacked portfolios in the governments responsible for the martial events.

Rather than choose one account over the other, we may find that the best solution is to say that it works both ways. Poor judgment makes the world more dangerous. This raises the emotional ambience, which in its turn inhibits good decision making. Reason goes into a tailspin while emotion escalates upwards. The upshot is war.

Effects of Violence

Violent acts often have important repercussions. Some of these are temporary in nature; the effects turn up during or shortly after the aggressive events, only to dissipate within a year or so. In contrast, really momentous acts of violence may have ramifications that extend for generations.

The Transient Impact

Any mention of brief effects must acknowledge the obvious: Violent acts have victims, and families of victims. Yet other effects are less obvious. Let's scrutinize the more subtle reactions to three kinds of violence—namely, political instability, civil disturbances, and international war.

The Shadows of Political Chaos

When Oswald killed John F. Kennedy in 1963, it was not just Jacqueline Kennedy who suffered, but the entire nation as well. This universal pain was witnessed in a commonplace reaction throughout the country: Many Americans had a compelling need to affiliate with others. Through mutual commiserations, Americans hoped to alleviate the anguish. Many of the flashbulb memories mentioned in Chapter 3 entail recollections of such shared, and hence softened, grief.

Another repercussion lasted longer and yet was less patent. The citizens of Dallas felt guilty that their city was the site of a national tragedy. This guilt caused extensive stress, which manifested itself in both health problems and pathological behaviors. In the years immediately after the assassination, deaths caused by heart disease in Dallas increased dramatically, in spite of the fact that the cardiac mortality rates in other parts of the country were actually declining. Moreover, in 1964 the Dallas suicide rate jumped 20%! This change could not be explained by the usual factors that often explain fluctuations in suicide rates; furthermore, the increase in the rest of the nation was only 1%. Nor are such reactions unique to Dallas. The people of Memphis also showed a large increase in coronary deaths immediately after the assassination of Martin Luther King.

The citizens of both cities may have suffered these ill effects because they did not deal properly with the historic episodes. Both cities failed to grapple with their respective assassinations until many years later. At the time, no monuments were erected; no memorials were dedicated; not even any streets were renamed. Everyone in those tragic locales behaved as if denial was the preferred coping mechanism. As many clinical psychologists will tell you, this is not an effective way of dealing with pain. The people should have worked through their emotional turmoil rather than repressed it. Supposedly, the reason we have funeral ceremonies is to give the bereaved an opportunity to undergo the necessary catharsis. Dallas and Memphis did not carry out the public observances that, through the proper choice of symbolic expressions, would have performed the needed group therapy for their citizens.

Assassinations of heads of state are not the sole form of political instability. A *coup d'état*, a revolt by a nation's military, or some other interjection of extralegal chaos into a system of government are also examples. Disorder and disruption among a nation's power elite, in fact, can have some powerful long-term consequences, as we will see shortly. Right now, let us examine a more delicate effect of such unseemly events.

Many creative individuals cannot maintain a splendid isolation when a political system succumbs to anarchy. After all, creators often gravitate to a nation's capital, putting them right in the midst of the unauthorized activities. Accordingly, the breathtaking happenings in the political arena will frequently have echoes in the products that emerge from a creator's brush, chisel, or pen. Shakespeare's career illustrates what I mean. In London, the Bard's company performed in Southwark, a short ride from the hub of the British monarchy at Westminster. Moreover, many of the plays that Shakespeare wrote for the Globe and other theaters dealt with kings and queens, both domestic and foreign, ancient and more recent. On occasion, his dramas would even entertain the royal person, whether Queen Elizabeth I or King James I. Therefore, the thematic material of Shakespeare's plays would often reflect the more disturbing events in British politics. He could not ignore the dangerous rebellion of the Earl of Essex, the Queen's one-time favorite. Nor could Shakespeare stay inert upon learning of the Guy Fawkes "Gunpowder Plot" to blow up Parliament as the King stood within. Hence, plays composed during these troubled times were more likely to address such profound questions as "the duties of command and obedience in family life," "patterns of love and friendship in the family," the "myth of the royal personage . . . and the burdens of monarchy," and, lastly, "the natural and the unnatural or monstrous."

For those of us who grew up under a democracy rather than a monarchy, this collection of themes may not make a lot of sense. So let's put ourselves in Shakespeare's shoes. He lived in an age of hereditary monarchs. This political institution is founded on familial relationships among individuals with a particular aristocratic pedigree. In addition, royal rule is presumed to embody the natural order of human affairs. James I himself was a proponent of the "divine right of kings." In this milieu, conspiracies against the sovereign were necessarily evil. The great playwright thus underlined the abnormality of any ambition to override this divine, family-based order. By tailoring his themes to the events, Shakespeare probably won appreciative applause from most of his audiences. Unintentionally, he also may have served as the therapist for his fellow Londoners. His dramatic allusions to current events might have provided the type of therapy that the residents of Dallas and Memphis sadly lacked.

The Aftermath of Civil Unrest

In terms of impact, political instability is sometimes a weak agent. Although many people are affected, few people are involved. This contrasts strikingly with riots, revolts, and revolutions, in which large masses of people take to the streets and highways. Sometimes the explicit goal is to overthrow a regime, other times to create a new nation. But the core aspect of these big occasions is the same: The populace—not a lone politician, general, or assassin—will decide the course of history.

Given the scope of these events, it is not surprising that they overflow into the world outside politics. Creativity will pursue different paths when there are barricades blocking the boulevards, mobs flinging open prison gates, and new-fangled flags waving over the nation's capital. Civil disturbances will leave an imprint on a nation's literature, arts, and music—even the high fashions that adorn its women. Many times these influences require no sophistication to detect. The impact of the 1830 July Revolution upon Delacroix is clear to anyone looking at his famous painting *Liberty Leading the People, 1830*. Even his political sympathies can be identified.

Other effects are more subtle. For instance, civil disturbances can affect the creative outpourings of classical composers, even when the music is abstract rather than descriptive. One investigator examined 1,935 works in the standard repertoire, and determined whether a piece was composed under conditions of political unrest. Revolts and rebellions favored more accessible melodic material. This dip toward "easy listening" made the pieces more popular with hoi polloi; the compositions later became some of the war horses of the concert hall. Yet for much the same cause, these works have frequently earned low marks from musicologists, who see these compositions as more superficial than profound. An example is the accessible *Symphonie Fantastique*. Berlioz composed this favorite of music appreciation courses in the same year that Delacroix painted his *Liberty*.

The Scars of International War

Frequently, when nations choose to battle it out for military supremacy, the products of the creative mind will also adjust to reflect the times. For example, one study scrutinized how World War II affected the music of modern classical composers. Some of these composers found themselves trying to create music in a war zone, with artillery rounds buzzing and aerial bombs pounding. Béla Bartók, Arthur Honegger, Olivier Messiaen, Darius Milhaud, Francis Poulenc, Dmitri Shostakovich, Richard Strauss, and Ralph Vaughan Williams fall into this group. Others composed under less stressful conditions. Samuel Barber, Lukas Foss, Paul Hindemith, Arnold Schoenberg, and William Schuman are examples. The compositions analyzed included Bartók's Sixth String Quartet, Messiaen's *Quartet for the End of Time*, Strauss's *Metamorphosen*, Barber's Second Essay for Orchestra, Schoenberg's *Survivor from Warsaw*, and Schuman's *Prayer in Time of War*. Those pieces emerging from the war zone could be easily distinguished from the others: The melody lines and rhythmic patterns were more irregular, and dynamic contrasts were more pronounced. The turmoil of the occasion was engraved in sound.

Naturally, other forms of creative expression alter under the strain of war. The thematic content of plays and poems changes. And fashion designers change what high-society women consider the chic look. Yet another effect is more critical: Warfare affects not just the qualitative aspects of creative output, but also the quantity. In both art and science, war inhibits individual creativity. Even in the more applied sciences, such as medicine, the net effect of military activity is negative. World Wars I and II were especially devastating in their suppression of the creative spirit; most kinds of productivity suffered all over the globe. The good news is that these negative effects are fairly short-lived. If a war is not too long or brutal, creative output will soon return to its prewar levels.

Perhaps it is almost silly to speak of these results. Who cares about war's impact on the quality and quantity of creativity? Certainly no head of state is going to shelve military plans just because artistic styles will change! Even any loss in creative output can be tolerated as an allowable short-term cost of mounting an attack. Nevertheless, warfare's impressions are more material and pernicious than this. Most unquestionable are the severe economic costs. Yet the psychological costs may be greater still. Thousands, even millions of soldiers experience the degradation of war; they have seen at first hand human nature in its most inhuman form. The combination of deindividuation with dehumanization has prodded them to commit acts that they never thought any human being could conceive. They have seen close buddies fall victim to the horrors of war. The results are individuals who have undergone a transformation from civilization to barbarism. They are not reconverted before demobilization lets them loose on civilian populations.

Most of us have read stories of Vietnam War veterans afflicted with "post-traumatic stress syndrome." Unable to return to a normal existence, many veterans suffer from depression, anxiety, and alcoholism. Occasionally, one last straw will crack a veteran's fragile self-restraint, and he will go berserk with a semiautomatic rifle. A small-scale war hero regresses into a mass murderer and suicide. However dramatic, these episodes of pointless slaughter constitute the tip of an iceberg of war-induced peacetime violence.

One thorough cross-national study sifted through crime data from all over the world. The findings were clear: An increase in postwar homicide was a consistent by-product of organized violence. Moreover, the specific evidence was most compatible with a "legitimization-of-violence model." That is, "the presence of authorized or sanctioned killing during war has a residual effect on the level of homicide in peacetime society." There certainly is no reason to believe that demobilized soldiers experience some catharsis that enables them to transform into pacifists. The Rambo character played by Sylvester Stallone in several films is more typical.

Some patriots are inclined to believe that this sad situation is confined to the Vietnam War—that it was the price Americans paid for not supporting their fighters 100%. But this result is universal. Throughout history, roving bands of mercenaries have often dedicated themselves to rape and pillage as a privilege of peacetime maladjustment. In the United States alone, the American Revolution, the Civil War, World Wars I and II, and other conflicts have all trained soldiers for future civilian violence. "In 1949 a combat veteran named Howard Unruh, who had won marksman and sharpshooter ratings during World War II, went on a rampage in Camden, New Jersey, killing twelve people with a souvenir pistol." During the Civil War, William Quantrill led a band of Confederate irregulars in a series of daring and vicious raids. After the war, several of the veterans made a career of violence; among these guerrilla graduates were Frank and Jesse James. Legalized violence later invites illegitimate violence.

The Enduring Legacy

When we scan the big picture, the most salient long-term effects of violence are apparently political. The boundaries of nations shift on the map. Governments convert from one dynasty or system to another. Soldiers on the move have effaced whole peoples from the face of the earth. Without denying the significance of these prodigious effects, we must again recognize less eye-catching results of historic violence. For a psychology of history, two realms of effects hold special fascination: creativity and ideology.

Creativity Waxes and Wanes

We have already seen that political violence can cause momentary declines in the production of masterworks in the arts and sciences. Such events offer an environment unsuitable for creative thought. Nevertheless, we must also recognize that political violence provides the context for the development of future creators. Accordingly, sometimes the full impact of these events will not be seen until the youths of today become the adults of tomorrow. Not the current generation but the next may bear the full brunt of the turmoil. Because about two decades separate a creator's developmental period from his or her productive period, we will have to wait 20 years for these effects to follow. Despite the delay, the results will last longer. A whole generation of creators will enter maturity with their personalities indelibly shaped by the big happenings of their youth. Not until that cohort fulfills its historic destiny, and passes away into the obituary columns, will room be granted to the next cohort—one bearing the impression of a more tranquil past.

Take political instability: the occurrence of military revolts, *coups d'état*, political assassinations, arbitrary executions, and other signs of anarchy among the power elite. The impact of these conspicuously violent activities on adult creators is transient and weak. A genius can always find some sheltered cove somewhere on the planet from which to conceive masterpieces in exile. Children and adolescents still developing their special talents are less fortunate; unable to escape, they can evolve a world view that is antithetical to certain kinds of creative expression. Hence, two decades after a major eruption of political anarchy, we often see an abrupt drop in the number of creative geniuses. This decline is most conspicuous in those disciplines that stress logical, systematic, and long-range goals, such as science or philosophy. For instance, after an infusion of political instability, the number of illustrious philosophers often shrinks in the next generation. Furthermore, those few thinkers who do appear are usually not of the highest caliber. In the visual arts, on the other hand, political anarchy is less detrimental to creative development. Artistic luminaries can grow up in times of political chaos with minimal cost. Whereas Kant spent his entire life within 50 miles of quiet Königsberg, Michelangelo grew up in the chaos of Florence and its environs—the time of the Pazzi Plot and Savonarola.

The aftermath of collective violence is not always negative, however. Civil disturbances embrace the masses in a fashion that can have different implications for personal development. Because anyone can stand behind the barricades, people can gain an enhanced sense of personal control over events. Revolutionaries can set up a regime that is more responsive to the wishes of the populace. Furthermore, general unrest opens opportunities for diverse nationalities to express themselves, or even to seek national autonomy. Revolts and rebellions against the culturally oppressive imperial state can stir up the intellectual and aesthetic broth, exposing developing talents to new alternatives, perspectives, and traditions. Therefore, 20 years after civil disturbances, the world frequently sees a new Golden Age of creative activity. This influx in the next generation occurs across all major creative domains. The rejuvenation of creativity is particularly prominent when the populace directs its violence against imperial regimes.

Interestingly, if this pattern continues to hold through the second decade of the 21st century, Eastern Europe should eventually show this long-term effect. From the Adriatic to the Baltic to the Pacific, the nations that emerged from the Soviet bloc should become hotbeds of creative innovation.

Ideologies Come and Go

Among the transient effects of violence were changes in the themes and images that conveyed in poetry, drama, and other literary forms. Can big-time violence similarly affect the prevalent beliefs of an era? According to Pitirim Sorokin's "law of polarization,"

> The overwhelming majority of the population in normal times is neither distinctly bad nor conspicuously virtuous, neither very socially-minded nor extremely anti-

social, neither markedly religious nor highly irreligious. In times of revolution this indifferent majority tends to split, the segments shifting to opposite poles and yielding a greater number of sinners and saints, social altruists and antisocial egoists, devout religious believers and militant atheists. The "balanced majority" tends to decrease in favor of extreme polar factions in the ethical, religious, intellectual, and other fields. This polarization is generated by revolutions in all fields of social and cultural life.

To test Sorokin's idea, one psychologist examined more than 2,000 thinkers from the Western intellectual tradition. These thinkers participated in the principal philosophical debates from ancient Greece to the 20th century. Although their advocated positions were indeed responsive to civil unrest, the reaction was not instantaneous. Instead, history had to wait until the youths exposed to the turmoil matured into adult thinkers. Not the current generation, but rather the later generation, reflected the political disorder in its intellectual thinking. In particular, 20 years after a rash of civil disturbances, Western civilization saw an increase in thinkers who advocated extreme and contradictory positions: rationalism versus empiricism, idealism versus materialism, eternalism versus temporalism, realism versus nominalism, collectivism versus individualism, free will versus determinism, and principled versus hedonistic ethics. The civil conflict of one generation was sublimated into the intellectual combat of the next generation.

International war also deflected philosophical debate along different paths. The study found that about two decades after a bloody conflict, philosophers were *less* inclined to propose that knowledge comes from sensory data, that reality is ever-changing, that abstract concepts are mere linguistic conventions, that the individual has supremacy over society, and that the pleasure principle should be the basis for ethical decisions. This configuration of suppressed beliefs may have been the developmental result of wartime propaganda. When nations found their existence threatened by a foreign power, they may have tried to reinforce blind faith in a lasting political system that was real rather than symbolic. Furthermore, collective survival demanded patriotic self-sacrifice and the subordination of personal desires to the general good.

The cross-generational linkages found in this study between war and ideas were not all one-directional, however. A certain philosophical milieu often supported the military enterprise. Materialistic and skeptical thinkers, in particular, might provide the ideological justification for warfare. Such ideas evidently infused a generation with the cynicism needed to put a low price on human life. If material values reigned supreme, and all truths were relativistic, what difference would casualty figures make? This phenomenon will receive further documentation in the next chapter, when we review research on the authoritarian personality.

This one exception notwithstanding, the main influences were found to run from collective aggression to philosophical thought. Wars and civil disturbances left a durable imprint on the youths who would emerge as the key intellects of the next generation. Ideology mirrored prior violence.

Caveats: Psychology's Limits

Before we leave this subject, we must glance over our shoulders at psychology's neighbors in the social sciences. Many political scientists, sociologists, anthropologists, economists, and historians would take issue with the conclusions of this chapter; they would claim that it stresses puny psychological factors at the expense of gigantic political, sociological, cultural, economic, and historical forces.

These bigger agents are especially crucial for a broad understanding of collective forms of aggression, such as civil and foreign wars. If psychological processes participate in these gross causal sequences, the mind may serve more as an intermediary than as a director of events. For example, the connection between integrative complexity and the peaceful resolution of crises may capture a mere fragment of a more encompassing diplomatic and military process. In this process, the decision makers become mere pawns rather than agents. Even more individualistic forms of aggression can also include systemic factors among the determinants. For instance, the frustration–aggression hypothesis cannot tell the whole story about why blacks were the targets of lynch mobs in the American South. We need a larger body of theory to explain why the mobs singled out African-Americans. These added considerations may take us well beyond the confines of psychological science.

Thus, whenever we try to explicate historic acts of aggression, we must be ever wary of committing the "fundamental attribution error" (see Chapter 3). That is, we must not become so preoccupied with the wishes and traits of historic actors that we overlook severe situational constraints on their behaviors. Frequently, there are so many external forces impinging on people that their internal inclinations don't count for much. Many international wars, for example, result from long-term economic, diplomatic, military, and even cultural rivalries. Often the decision makers in an international crisis find themselves tangled up in an intricate web of material necessities, alliance commitments, and historic precedents. Then leaders do not lead, but follow the course of events. About a year before the Civil War ended, the nation's commander-in-chief, Abraham Lincoln, wrote, "I claim not to have controlled events, but confess plainly that events have controlled me."

Compare World Wars I and II. The second of these conflicts can boast visible agents: Hitler, Mussolini, and Tōjō were very much in charge. The first conflict seems different, however. Most participants did not actively seek a military solution to the looming crisis. Certainly Kaiser Wilhelm II, who bore the brunt of the blame after the war ended, lacked the causal status of Chancellor Hitler. World War I, unlike World War II, lacked any "evil genius." There was plenty of incompetence and arrogance spread around the various European capitals in 1914. But basically, there was little agreement between what the leaders sought and what they got. They were pawns to the Fates—Fates named Political Science, Sociology, Anthropology, Economics, and History.

Their sister Psychology was taking a break, resting for the more sinister events that transpired in 1939.

Because psychological processes so often take a back seat while systemic forces do the driving, psychologists must be wary about becoming social reformers or political pundits. Occasionally, psychologists may move too rashly from the laboratory to the real world. Before they do so, they should work out the details about how the individual mind articulates with the mechanisms identified by other disciplines. For example, in 1962, the year of the Cuban missile crisis, psychologist Charles E. Osgood published *An Alternative to War or Surrender*. In this volume he presented his solution to the Cold War. The strategy goes by the acronym "GRIT," which stands for "graduated and reciprocated initiatives in tension" reduction. According to this approach, one side in a political conflict can ease tensions by taking a carefully calculated unilateral move toward conciliation. The hope is that this gesture will inspire an equal concession on the other side. All parties thus make piecemeal adjustments in their military and diplomatic postures. Little by little, the dangerous strains dividing two powers shrink to manageable proportions. Osgood wrote his book in the hope that it would do its part toward calming the East–West conflict.

Now there is good laboratory evidence that GRIT can work. At least the strategy can increase cooperation in dyads playing games, such as the ubiquitous Prisoners' Dilemma game. Moreover, analyses of world diplomacy in the Cold War era show that GRIT was sometimes practiced by actual politicians. When it was applied, the strategy appeared to do the job rather nicely. Yet the underlying systemic issue remains: The apparent success of GRIT does not mean that Osgood can claim a practical triumph of applied psychology. There are two main problems.

First, larger systemic factors may govern whether world leaders are open to suggestions from behavioral science research. Some circumstances may favor leadership that is responsive to such advice, even to the point of recruiting "think tanks" for that very purpose. Other conditions may produce politicians who turn a deaf ear to political psychologists, just as many Hebrew kings refused to listen to their prophets. Because psychologists cannot control these contextual influences, they must resign themselves to the fact that they will frequently be ignored by those in power.

Second, the bigger political, societal, cultural, economic, and historic forces may actually underlie an automatic implementation of the very procedure that a psychologist advocates. For example, when the stresses of the broad situation dissipate enough, the decision makers can adopt higher levels of integrative complexity. This expanded sophistication in information processing then enables the politicians to take the point of view of their opponents. This enriched outlook, finally, allows the decision makers to see the wisdom in (1) advancing conciliatory initiatives and (2) reciprocating the concessions offered by other nations. In this causal scenario, GRIT is a repercussion of the mammoth but largely subterranean forces operating beyond the realm of individual psychology. This makes the political psychologist more of a commentator on change, and less of an agent.

Of course, there may be places where psychologists can play a constructive role in restricting violence. I am only urging caution. We cannot always ask the paltry psyche to take on the Goliaths of aggression; too often it's our tiny slingshot versus their monstrous spears and shields! Only on the rarest of occasions is a psychological process likely to be a future King David.

THE INFLUENCE OF ATTITUDES AND BELIEFS

Hamlet reminds Polonius that "there is nothing either good or bad, but thinking makes it so." Hamlet is suggesting how our attitudes shape our evaluations of the world around us. The objective world just is, whereas the subjective world varies from person to person, according to each individual's attitudes. Moreover, these attitudes provide the impetus behind human actions. Indeed, a single-minded adherence to an all-encompassing belief can drive people to phenomenal heights of achievement. Think of the mountains moved in the name of some religion or ideology. Buddhism, Christianity, Islam, Marxism, and other attitudinal systems have nudged countless individuals onto history's stage. Some historic actors even get the lead roles in the scripts by which new cultures and societies play out before the world. By mouthing the ideals of the French Revolution early in his career, Napoleon enthralled millions among the oppressed peoples of Europe.

Hence, any psychology of history must consider the place of attitudes and beliefs in the making of history. This chapter touches upon three essential facets of this topic: public opinion, ideology, and authoritarianism. It closes with a discussion of a most troublesome question in the field: Given the compelling impact of attitudes, can we change them?

Public Opinion

Even the most ruthless dictator must remain sensitive to public opinion. Napoleon himself called public opinion "the thermometer a monarch should constantly consult." Heads of state who lose contact with the people's voice may die or be dethroned. Leaders in modern democracies are therefore fortunate: They have access to two credible clues to public opinion. First, citizens can respond to the queries of the pollster, stating how they stand on certain key issues of the day. Second, voters can express their beliefs by casting ballots for their favorite candidates on election day.

Popularity in the Polls

Nowadays we have come to think that pollsters provide accurate portraits of voter opinions. Political candidates will even consult the polls to see which way the wind blows. Yet this faith was not always justified. It took a while for survey methodology to reach the point where it accurately portrayed the mind of the people. Early pollsters, in fact, could make some horrible mistakes. An infamous example is the *Literary Digest* survey that predicted a landslide victory of Alfred Landon over Franklin D. Roosevelt in the 1936 presidential election. Among the few pollsters who did successfully predict the outcome, however, was George Gallup. In the process of developing modern survey methods, Gallup built up the nation's largest political polling organization. The phrase "Gallup poll" became almost as generic as the term "Kleenex."

Moreover, the Gallup poll takes on other challenges besides predicting presidential elections. Since 1941, in particular, the Gallup organization has given the American public the same question to ponder: "Do you approve or disapprove of the way the incumbent is handling his job as president?" From the Truman administration on, the Gallup poll has posed this question about once a month. We thus have a trustworthy and detailed record of how the American people have perceived the leadership of the person in the Oval Office.

Watching the monthly ups and downs in presidential popularity is more than a recreational activity. The incumbent's approval rating has genuine political reverberations. Most obviously, popular presidents are more likely to get elected to a second term in office. Even when the incumbent is not running for another term, the president's party has better odds of returning a replacement to the White House. Furthermore, chief executives who enjoy high approval ratings can often use their popularity as a lever to push bills through Congress. Members of the House and Senate do not take lightly the wishes of a president with a clear mandate to legislate. The reverse can occur, too: Unpopular presidents had better keep their mouths shut about their legislative preferences. This perverse switch occurred in the case of President Nixon. Owing to the Watergate scandal, his approval rating fell to one-third in late 1973. This meant that each time he advocated certain energy proposals, public support for those policies actually declined!

What determines the incumbent's approval rating? There are five key factors: voter alienation over time, economic factors, international affairs, armed conflicts, and negative events in general.

Alienated Adherents?

Back in 1796, Thomas Jefferson offered this prophecy: "No man will ever bring out of the Presidency the reputation which carries him into it." This certainly held for George Washington, and for most of the presidents since him. This inexorable decline in reputation appears in the approval ratings of modern presidents. At the beginning of the first term, an incumbent's performance may easily earn the approval of more than two-thirds of survey respondents. This honeymoon with the public soon wears thin. On the average, each successive year means a drop of about six percentage points. However, much of the decline occurs in the first couple of years, and then levels off. Only if the people elect the incumbent to a second term will the president recoup most of that loss.

Two explanations have been offered for this phenomenon. One is more sociological in nature. To get elected to the White House, a candidate must put together a coalition of diverse interest groups. These groups support the candidate in the hope that they will see a change in national policies affecting their constituencies. Unhappily, the separate goals of the various members of the coalition may be incompatible. A president can't please everybody; satisfying one demand may compel him to betray another. So, when the incumbent tries to translate campaign promises to administration achievements, he is doomed to alienate adherents one by one, losing popularity in the process.

The second explanation is more psychological. Inauguration day is a moment of hope for millions of Americans. They greet the new administration with high expectations. These expectations are inflated by a naive credence in the idealism and optimism of the presidential campaign. In time, disillusionment replaces these far-fetched hopes. The incumbent fails to live up to the unrealistic wishes of the American populace. Anticipation is converted into cynicism. The approval ratings reflect the violated hopes.

These two interpretations are not mutually exclusive. The president's standing with the public may drop owing to both the practicalities of group coalitions and the irrationalities of individual voters. Moreover, both explanations fit the explanation given in Chapter 3 about rhetoric in presidential campaigns. We have seen there that the integrative complexity of campaign speeches is noticeably lower than that of the same politician's policy speeches once he gets into the Oval Office. The candidate oversimplifies political realities; this raises the hopes of both coalitions and voters. The incumbent engages in more complex excuse making. This hedging estranges certain constituencies, and disillusions voters whose expectations were exorbitantly high.

Economic Slumps?

On November 6, 1928, Herbert Hoover won 444 electoral votes to Alfred E. Smith's 87. He thus entered the White House with a landslide victory. On November 8, 1932, Hoover won only 59 votes to Franklin Roosevelt's 472. Hoover thus was booted out of the White House by a more sweeping landslide. What caused an almost exact reversal of fortune in just four years? When Hoover ran in 1928, he promised "A chicken in every pot, a car in every garage." The opposite happened: Few in 1932 could afford poultry, and even fewer automobiles. Prices on the New York Stock Exchange crashed on October 29, 1929;

soon millions of Americans were thrown out of work, as unemployment reached 13 million by the end of 1932. American industry limped along at half capacity. All around the country, the jobless set up ramshackle settlements called "Hoovervilles." "Hunger marchers" and a "Bonus Army" descended on the nation's capital in the hope of relief. While the Great Depression worsened, the incumbent merely repeated like a broken record that prosperity was just around the corner.

George Gallup was not conducting polls that early, so we lack approval ratings for Hoover's administration. Yet, if we judge by the 1928 and 1932 election results, his popularity must have plummeted. Moreover, we can extrapolate from research showing that the incumbent's approval rating is very much at the mercy of the economist's statistics. Changes in disposable income, unemployment, inflation, and other indices of material well-being can seriously undermine the president's standing with the American people. For example, an increase of 1% in the annual inflation rate can translate into a decrease of almost four percentage points in the polls.

The impact of the economy on the president's approval ratings has two curious quirks. First, the impact is often asymmetrical: An incumbent usually loses more by a worsening economy than he gains by an improving economy. When material well-being is already at an acceptable level, Americans evidently focus on other political issues besides the state of the economy. Only when citizens begin to worry about their next paycheck do the unemployment and inflation statistics prove germane to their evaluations of administration performance. Second, America's two main political parties are differently vulnerable to the latest statistics in the business section of the daily newspaper. For instance, bad unemployment statistics harm Republicans more than Democrats in the Oval Office. This difference results from the common belief that the Republican Party represents those Americans who never fear for their jobs. This belief may date from the Hoover administration.

But why does the economy affect presidential popularity at all? Again, two main explanations are possible. The "pocketbook citizen" hypothesis holds that economic hard times bring direct hardships for individual Americans, so they hold the incumbent responsible for all their financial difficulties. In contrast, the "sociotropic citizen" hypothesis views Americans more favorably. Citizens presumably use the state of the national economy as a criterion for judging the incumbent's leadership. They see the president's ability to solve economic problems as a fair test of his political competence. Under the first hypothesis, citizens act out of pure self-interest; the recurrent question is "What have you done for *me* recently?" Under the second, citizens are less self-centered; the issue is "what have you done for the *nation* recently?"

Happily, detailed analyses of survey data suggest that the president's approval ratings vary more for sociotropic than for pocketbook reasons. The typical respondent to a Gallup poll adopts a patriotic rather than an egoistic attitude in judging the incumbent's effectiveness. Perhaps we can extrapolate this comforting finding back to 1932. Even American voters who still had jobs probably lost confidence in Hoover as the president who could lead America out of the doldrums. If only the unemployed had voted for Roosevelt, Hoover would have been re-elected easily. However, the question was not the amount of cash in the wallet, but the amount of leadership in the White House.

International Crises?

A bizarre phenomenon occurred in the aftermath of the Bay of Pigs fiasco of 1961. President Kennedy was forced to accept the blame for an unmitigated military and diplomatic disaster. He gracefully assumed responsibility by quoting from the film *The Desert Fox*: "Victory has a hundred fathers and defeat is an orphan." Did his willingness to admit "paternity" in this case inflict severe damage on Kennedy's fledgling approval rating? Quite the contrary! His popularity in the polls actually shot up.

This positive effect is by no means unique. The Bay of Pigs invasion provoked an international crisis, and any president's standing in the polls usually rises with the onset of such crises. The gain is normally about five to seven percentage points. This "rally-around-the-flag" effect holds for five types of crises: (1) specific military interventions, like Lyndon B. Johnson's decision to send troops to the Dominican Republic; (2) major developments in military conflicts already in progress, like the Inchon landing in the Korean War; (3) significant diplomatic developments, such as the announcement of the Truman Doctrine; (4) important technological breakthroughs with international repercussions, like the Soviet launching of Sputnik I; and (5) summits between the American chief executive and the leader of the Soviet Union, such as the Camp David meeting between Eisenhower and Khrushchev. It makes little difference whether the events are good or bad. They just have to be earthshaking. Hence, the Bay of Pigs episode, debacle though it was, could still elicit the rally-around-the-flag effect among patriotic Americans.

Of course, by subsuming the Bay of Pigs under this more general phenomenon, we have not actually explained the event's impact on JFK's popularity. We still need an explanation for the rally-around-the-flag effect. One interpretation is that an event that threatens all Americans tells us that we all share a common fate with the president. Sharing the same fate is an important influence on a person's attractiveness. In addition, many crises give America's commander-in-chief the opportunity to display the essential qualities of charismatic leadership. Charisma is best revealed when a leader faces an emergency with strength and resolve.

Both explanations are compatible with a key feature of the rally-around-the-flag effect: It's transient. A president cannot build up a powerful and enduring mandate by provoking a conflict with other nations. Any upsurge in popularity soon dissipates by about six percentage points per year. Further, if a crisis drags on, it ceases to be a credit to the incumbent, and may even become an albatross around his neck. The hostage crisis in Teheran first boosted President Carter's standing with Americans. In time, however, this very predicament helped make him a one-term chief executive.

The temporary nature of the rally-around-the-flag effect is not the only reason incumbents may not wish to foment conflicts to jack up a sagging image in the polls. Such provocative actions are dangerous besides. A crisis may easily get out of hand. Fortunately for the president, if not for the American people, the incumbent can sometimes benefit from more modest manipulations of American jingoism. Approval ratings can increase by one percentage point for every billion dollars the president adds to the defense budget. This effect is more generous than we can explain according to any economic advantages of military spending. Therefore, we may best describe this result as a miniversion of the rally-around-the-flag effect. By advocating the purchase of more bombers, tanks, and other military hardware, the incumbent can represent himself as a figure of power and determination. President Carter tried to scale down U.S. strategic forces under the SALT II agreement, and looked like a wimp. President Reagan supported a massive peacetime buildup, including the new MX intercontinental ballistic missile system and the futuristic Strategic Defense Initiative ("Star Wars"), and came across as a presidential Rambo.

Of course, this device is not without risk either. It may escalate an arms race with rival nations. And that race may end in war. But that event, too, may affect people's attitudes toward the president.

Military Conflicts?

Heads of state seeking more support at home have often sought war with states abroad. All loyal citizens then rally around their flag and their leader. William H. Seward, Abraham Lincoln's secretary of state, actually suggested that the new Republican administration provoke a war with Great Britain—so that the Southern states would remain in the Union.

Seward must have been weak in history. War doesn't always make the nation's leader a rallying point for good will. Many denizens of New England were staunchly opposed to the War of 1812; they derisively called it "Mr. Madison's War." Similarly, many Northerners could not support the Mexican-American War. Even Lincoln's war to preserve the Union was attacked by Northern "Copperhead" Democrats: Antidraft sentiment exploded in mob violence. Not until the Spanish-American War did the United States endorse a military enterprise with intense nationalistic feeling. So wars are not always reliable foci for rally-around-the-flag effects.

Because Gallup's regular assessment of presidential popularity only dates from the Truman administration, we can investigate the impact of merely two big-time wars—the Korean and Vietnam conflicts. Of these two, the Vietnam War may have been especially potent as a shaper of public opinion. Television made this the first living-room war. Each night we could see on our TV screens the bloody reality of guerrilla warfare and counterinsurgency campaigns. Each night we would register the body counts and kill ratios.

In any case, both U.S. conflicts with Asian opponents undermined the approval ratings of the incumbents responsible. The Korean War cost Truman about 18 percentage points in the polls. This drop was certainly enough to dissuade Truman from seeking a second full term, had he had any inclination to do so. The Vietnam War deducted about 12 percentage points from Lyndon Johnson's approval rating. Johnson himself thought that this unpopular "police action" cost him about 20 percentage points. The American people were especially sensitive to news about casualty figures. Hearing that "our boys" were dying on the other side of the Pacific "to fight someone else's war" was not likely to induce the public to support the struggle. In addition, Americans soon became touchy about the incessant bomber missions over North Vietnam, first introduced by LBJ after the Gulf of Tonkin Resolution and fully maintained by Nixon. In Johnson's case, at least, the incumbent's popularity paid dearly for these sorties over Haiphong Harbor, Hanoi, and other military targets.

We should be cautious about generalizing from these two wars to others that came earlier in the annals of America. The United States became mired in what were really internecine conflicts among single peoples, the Koreans and the Vietnamese. The lines drawn were ideological rather than cultural, linguistic, geographical, or historical. Moreover, the United States was never directly threatened by either North Korea or North Vietnam. Both conflicts lacked a dramatic provocation equivalent to the Japanese attack on Pearl Harbor (World War II) or the German torpedoing of U.S. shipping on the Atlantic (World War I). Instead, American soldiers were fighting thousands of miles away from home for a rather abstract principle—the "domino theory" of international Communism. According to this theory, the Communists' onward movement could only be stopped by a vigorous policy of containment. Yet, owing to diplomatic niceties, the United States had to apply considerable restraint in releasing its military might. These were not all-out wars in which the full resources were brought to bear on the enemy. We were not fighting Japan or Germany, but two underdeveloped nations with superpower allies. General MacArthur's inability to see the larger conformation of the Korean conflict forced President Truman to dismiss him as military commander. By underlining the ambiguity of "limited war," this dismissal did nothing to make the war more popular.

Given the nature of these two conflicts, we might better view them as instances of the final determinant of attitudes toward the incumbent.

Adverse Headlines?

The president's approval rating is vulnerable to more than just alienated adherents, economic slumps, international crises, and military conflicts. For example, strikes of organized labor against major U.S. industries can subtract about three percentage points from the incumbent's popularity. In addition, events unique to a single presidency can exert obvious influences on contemporary American opinion. The scandal that followed the Watergate break-in and later cover-up cost Nixon at least 10 percentage points in the Gallup poll. If we combine these phenomena with some of these described above, a theme emerges: The public may not appreciate chief executives who preside when the newspaper carries lots of bad news. Because the president is the most conspicuous personality in the nation, the negative affect associated with such noxious events rubs off on him. If the country is suffering, the incumbent's reputation must suffer.

The process operating here is probably emotional conditioning, which has been described in Chapter 3. There exists ample evidence that if stimuli are associated with circumstances that produce a state of positive or negative emotion, those stimuli may gain the capacity to elicit the same reaction. For example, we are actually less favorably disposed toward a stranger whom we meet while bad news is emanating from the radio. This affective conditioning is too primal to be rational. Negative circumstances influence our responses, regardless of whether the target of our emotional associations is actually responsible for the pleasure or pain.

This irrational aspect of conditioning brings us back to the White House resident. Whether we are avid readers of newspapers or we rely on the evening news for our information, we all are bombarded with accounts of events that may affect our emotional equilibrium. Sometimes the news is largely bad; other days it is mostly good. Most days, as well, the president stays before us. He is delivering a policy speech here, attending a ceremony there, or fishing or golfing at some other place. Therefore, according to affective conditioning, the incumbent's popularity should climb when the news is largely favorable and should slide when the news is mostly unfavorable. Research confirms this expected linkage between attitudes and events.

To be sure, maybe these associations are justified. After all, isn't the president a maker of history? Still, if the emotional associations are primarily irrational in origin, it should not matter much whether the president is personally responsible for the good or bad events. This is in fact the case: News that results directly from executive action carries about the same weight as news arising from sources beyond the incumbent's control. People are not especially discriminating about assigning responsibility for their moods. One of Iago's more cynical observations in Shakespeare's *Othello* applies here: "Reputation is an idle and most false imposition; oft got without merit, and lost without deserving." Then again, no one promised the president that public life would be fair. Herbert Hoover and his ilk, from Martin Van Buren to Jimmy Carter, learned this the hard way.

Success in the Voting Booth

Defenders of democracy often argue that it is the most rational system of government. Each citizen is the best judge of his or her own self-interest. Each voter can best discern the candidate who will realize that self-interest. When ballots are cast on election day, the opinions of millions are translated into winners and losers. The victors can then claim to speak for the "will of the people." As an index of public opinion, the ballot box is unsurpassed; otherwise, government would be better run according to the opinion polls. A "pollsterocracy" would eclipse democracy.

Unfortunately, this argument does not stand up well to scrutiny. In the first place, the ballot box only registers the voice of the people when voting is mandatory—that is, when all eligible voters must go to the polls. Many nations, including the United States, impose fewer demands on their citizens. Casting a ballot or staying home is a personal option. Yet when only a minority opt to express their opinions, the election may no more represent the public's attitudes than would the latest *Literary Digest* survey. Hence, we cannot understand the relation between the vote and public opinion without first asking why citizens choose to vote at all.

One answer is the "rational voter" model: People cast ballots because their votes may make a difference. This sounds logical—too logical. Seldom is the decision to participate in representative democracy based on clear logic. Four examples from American presidential politics fix this point:

1. If pollsters announce that an election is too close to call, the voters should flock to the polls. Who would want to stay home only to learn that their political idol lost by a single vote? In contrast, if the contest is so lopsided that the outcome is never in doubt, why should voters waste their time? The inevitable is going to happen no matter what they do. Yet the closeness of elections does not appreciably affect the size of the voter turnout. This null effect holds for both the primaries and the general election.

2. In a similar vein, we might think that voters would turn out in droves for those elections that offer a choice between two polarized views about the nation's future. If the two leading candidates advocate diametrically opposed or even antagonistic policies, the ballot box should determine the fate of America. On the other hand, when the contestants represent pretty much the same middle-of-the-road positions, rational voters can more readily excuse themselves with a peremptory "Why bother?" The nation's direction will not change course no matter who shows up on inauguration day. Yet ideological disparities among candidates affect voter turnout not one iota.

3. In the 1980 contest, the TV networks announced early projections of a Reagan victory while the polls were still open in the Mountain and Pacific time zones. Carter soon broadcast his concession speech before the polls had closed. Yet this double whammy left voter turnout unaffected. Westerners continued to wait their turn at the voting places.

4. When voters calculate the odds that a particular candidate might win the presidency, personal preferences should not matter. Aspirants do not win simply because voters expect them to. Even so, most voters ignore this logical irrelevance. Instead, once they decide who's got their vote, they perceive their candidate of choice as having the best shot at the White House. In fact, people are four times more likely to believe that their preferred contestant will win rather than lose. Furthermore, the preference is what mostly determines the probability, not the other way around. Wishful thinking is the culprit here, not some bandwagon effect. And yet, if voters really expect their choice to emerge the victor, why would they even bother to manipulate a voting machine? Is it rational to assume this responsibility of citizenry when a candidate is going to sit in the Oval Office even if his supporters stay home?

Psychologists have offered a partial interpretation for such behaviors. But, if anything, the explanation fits better an "irrational voter" model, in which the guilty party may be a voter's illusion. People may view their votes as diagnostic of what the rest of the voters will do. They may believe that their preferred candidate will enter the White House as long as all like-minded voters cast their ballots. Therefore, voters go ahead and vote to prove to themselves that others of the same opinion will behave likewise, and victory belongs to all. It is a simple if specious match: similar opinions, similar actions. This diagnostic purpose implies that voters do not always turn out to push their rational self-interests. They often show up at the polls to reinforce a genial world view.

This discussion of *why* citizens vote must make us wonder about *whom* they vote for. If voters are not entirely rational when deciding whether or not to vote, should we expect those who actually cast their ballots to behave more wisely? To answer, let us inspect three related aspects of U.S. presidential politics: nomination, election, and re-election.

Getting Nominated

In America today, it is not easy to win the nomination to run for president on behalf of a major political party. It usually requires that the presidential candidate win primaries and caucuses in many contests throughout the country. Moreover, except when an incumbent president seeks re-election, the nomination process normally begins with many aspirants within both major parties. In addition, many if not most candidates are comparative unknowns at the national level. So, to capture enough delegates to clinch the nomination demands that a candidate emerge early from the pack, and then gather enough momentum that no rival can catch up. How does a particular candidate garner this essential advantage?

One interesting study traced out some of the factors distinguishing the victor from the also-rans. The investigator studied the 1976 presidential season over a 15-week period. The focus was on the Democratic primaries, owing to the swarm of aspirants. There were 18 candidates all told, including the six "front-runners"—Carter, Harris, Jackson, McCormack, Udall, and Wallace. Three variables provided useful predictors of vote outcome:

1. Regional exposure was important. This means that the candidate held an elective office—such as governor or senator—that made his name familiar to those living in the region where the primary was held. For example, Jimmy Carter had such exposure in Florida, North Carolina, Georgia, and Tennessee, while Jerry Brown had that advantage in Nevada and California.

2. Campaign expenditures were critical. This factor had twice as much predictive power as did regional exposure. The more a contender could spend on TV spots, posters, travel, and appearances, the bigger his vote share.

3. Success in earlier primaries predicted success in later primaries. American voters were inclined to choose a winner, as identified by the voters on prior primary Tuesdays. Plainly, at the beginning of the primary season, this factor had little weight. There was no track record yet. But after the New Hampshire primary, this variable assumed ever-increasing influence. In fact, toward the end of the primary season, actual electoral performance became the single most crucial determinant. The bandwagon began rolling. As a result, as the candidate neared the end of the trial, campaign expenditures could be reduced. Donations could be piggy-banked for the general election in November.

Do these three predictors have anything in common? A strong argument can be made that these antecedents of success reflect a more fundamental phenomenon in psychology—the "repeated-exposure effect." As noted in Chapter 4, much evidence suggests that when a person is exposed repeatedly to a hitherto neutral stimulus, the individual becomes more favorably attracted to that stimulus. Familiarity breeds liking, not contempt. Furthermore, this process affects both interpersonal attraction and attitude change. Since a candidate is trying both to look attractive ("I'm a great person!") and to change your opinion ("Vote for me, my policies are best!"), repeated exposure thus expedites success in two different ways.

The three predictors of primary victories all can be seen as vehicles to repeated exposure. Regional exposure obviously makes a candidate's name a more likely household word. Campaign expenditures make his or her face and ideas better known among the public. Success in earlier primaries elevates his or her presence in the newspapers and newscasts. Furthermore, we might subsume under this same process other factors that we know can contribute to nomination victory. For instance, national war heroes have good odds of winning the top spot on a party's ticket; Eisenhower was a case in point. War heroes enjoy the distinctive virtue of national exposure, not merely regional exposure.

Admittedly, repeated exposure is not the only possible explanation for these findings. Maybe the better candidates attract more campaign contributions before the primary season begins, and then translate this material resource into delegate counts. Nevertheless, repeated exposure probably explains at least a part of what's going on during the nomination procedure. We then have here another illustration of the irrational voter. Whenever momentum builds mostly by this psychological process, the political bandwagon may turn onto some arbitrary paths. Thus, when the first primaries are held in states where only one candidate has regional exposure, that contestant's campaign gets a jump start that can convert into a permanent head start. Worse, by the end of the primary season, disparities among the candidates in delegates won can be utterly out of sync with genuine contrasts in political merit. The intrinsic leadership of the ultimate victor may be only slightly greater than that of an opponent at the bottom of the heap. Yet the delegate count may differ by an order of magnitude or more.

Winning Election

Once ambitious politicians have won nomination, they must campaign all over the nation, recruiting voters to cast ballots in the November election. Who is likely to garner the most support?

One criterion must be attitude similarity. We find persons more attractive whose attitudes are similar to ours. We are also more easily persuaded by people whom we see as similar. Moreover, it is a cardinal principle of representative democracy that leaders speak for all whenever they speak for themselves. Theodore Roosevelt advised, "The most successful politician is he who says what everybody is thinking most often and in the loudest voice." In fact, the data partially endorse this hypothesis. Candidates whose positions on the issues are closest to the dominant opinion of registered voters will ordinarily do better on election day. Even though the candidates from the two leading parties seldom differ much on the issues—the "Tweedledum versus Tweedledee" phenomenon—this effect can decide election results. In 1960, for example, Kennedy beat Nixon by the narrowest popular vote margin in U.S. history. Kennedy's victory was possible because racial issues had not yet assumed a prominent place in American politics. If these issues were as conspicuous in the 1960 campaign as they were to become in the 1968 election, Kennedy would have lost the South and the presidency.

Yet what happens when a third-party candidate seeks the nation's highest office? In the 1968 presidential election, for instance, George Wallace challenged both Republican Richard Nixon and Democrat Hubert Humphrey. Wallace expressed the opinions of many racist and disgruntled Americans. Potential Wallace voters faced a dilemma not encountered by Nixon and Humphrey supporters: They had to choose between sincere and strategic voting. In "sincere voting," citizens vote for the candidate who most nearly advocates their own beliefs without regard to practicalities. In "strategic voting," by comparison, citizens consider the practical reality that a third-party candidate has never yet moved into the White House. Hence, strategic voters cast their ballots for that presidential aspirant who (1) has a genuine chance of winning and (2) most closely approximates their views on the issues of the day. Strategic voters thus appear more rational than the sincere voters, who throw away their ballots in a "protest vote."

Even so, sincere rather than strategic voting is the prevalent behavior at the ballot box. People vote their opinions rather than their common sense. We may partly explicate this behavior in terms of the preference–expectation link mentioned earlier. Voters prefer the candidate who embodies their views, and then these same voters exaggerate their preferred candidate's prospects for victory. So, for most citizens, the distinction between sincere and strategic voting breaks down. Many Wallace supporters really convinced themselves that he would be the next president of the United States.

Another complication is more profound. Attitude similarity is not the sole basis for candidate–voter similarity. Candidates whose personality characteristics are most like our own also earn our endorsements; "birds of a feather flock together." Take the 1980 contest between Reagan and Carter. Many voters saw Carter as the more compassionate of the two candidates. Moreover, some of these voters perceived themselves as compassionate people. The compassionate voted for the compassionate.

Complicating discussion still further is another fact: Voters often look for personal qualities that they believe to be pertinent to effective performance in the Oval Office. No matter what the voter's own disposition, a candidate must convey the image of strength, activity, competence, and trustworthiness. In 1980 and 1984, many people voted for Reagan *not* because his beliefs were most compatible with their own, but because he looked more "presidential" than either Carter or Mondale.

Therefore, voters use criteria other than attitude similarity when casting their ballots. Indeed, a candidate's personal characteristics are often more crucial in winning votes than the candidate's positions on the issues. Even completely arbitrary traits—such as looks, age, race, gender, and surname—may motivate a decision to prefer one politician over all others. Does this mean that attitude similarity plays a small part in voting behavior? No, because there's a catch: People do not accurately perceive the opinions of their preferred candidates. Once a voter takes a liking to a politician for reasons having nothing to do with the issues, that voter then distorts his or her perception of the politician's stance. The stronger the preference, the greater the distortion. Thus, in 1980 Carter's supporters overlooked discrepancies between their opinions and his. Reagan's supporters did the same. By exaggerating how much their favorite candidate agrees with their own beliefs, voters convince themselves that they are voting rationally.

This act of voter self-deception may provide an interpretation for something discussed earlier in this chapter: the relentless decline in the incumbent's approval rating. If citizens vote for candidates for reasons besides attitude similarity, then the mandate received in the ballot box may inflate the incumbent's true support. An unfortunate president may be put into the White House by many voters who do not strongly support the candidate's policy positions.

Accordingly, when the candidate becomes president, many Americans are in for a big surprise. Ironically, the incumbent may then alienate many adherents simply by living up to his campaign promises!

Earning Re-Election

Re-election is a different story from nomination and election. When voters cast ballots for new aspirants to an office, they must predict how each candidate will perform. On the other hand, once a politician has served a term in office, the voters can engage in "retrospective voting." They can look back at the leader's actual performance, and judge whether they want more of the same. If the answer is negative, voters can then "throw the rascals out" by supporting challengers in the next election. Moreover, the politician who already occupies a given office automatically enjoys a special edge denied the first-time candidate—the "incumbency advantage." Unless voters have good cause for throwing an incumbent out of office, the incumbent usually expects electoral support upon seeking re-election. After all, the incumbent has had plenty of opportunity to screw things up if he or she were really incompetent. So why shouldn't the rational voter adopt the rule "If it ain't broke, don't fix it"?

This incumbency advantage is immediately apparent in the U.S. presidency. American chief executives can cash in their incumbency for a 6–10% edge in the voting booth. Even an incumbent vice-president gains a vote lead of about 4% should he seek the presidency. Accordingly, only 10 presidents in American history have actually lost when they ran for a second term: John Adams, John Quincy Adams, Van Buren, Cleveland, Benjamin Harrison, Taft, Hoover, Ford, Carter, and Bush.

Hence, any analysis of re-election must begin with the incumbency advantage as a baseline. We then must ask what factors deflect the incumbent's chances away from this baseline. In addition, we must separate these factors into two groups. First, some variables affect the chances that an incumbent will earn his party's renomination to run for another term. If things look grim, the party in power will dump an incumbent so it can put up a candidate with superior prospects. In U.S. history, for instance, Tyler, Fillmore, Pierce, and Arthur were all denied the opportunity to serve a second term by unappreciative colleagues in their respective political parties. Second, other variables influence the odds that an incumbent, once renominated, will stay in office with the best wishes of the general electorate.

For a sitting president of the United States, renomination becomes more likely if the incumbent has managed to sign lots of legislation during his first term. Hence, we do expect incumbents to get something accomplished during their first administration if they want to continue. Furthermore, an incumbent's party should also dominate the Congress. Because unpopular presidents cost their party congressional seats in the midterm elections, the party leaders are certainly not going to risk further losses. In addition, the incumbent's support in Congress is an excellent guide to his chances of winning a second term in the general election.

To get renominated, an incumbent also should have been considered "presidential material" before entering the White House. By this I mean that the politician made an active quest for the nation's highest office by running in primaries and influencing caucuses. In contrast, some presidents were "dark horse" candidates who were drafted by a deadlocked convention. Polk was the first, but Pierce offers an even better case in the present context. Moreover, some incumbents were "accidental presidents"—vice-presidents who succeeded to office on the death or resignation of their predecessors. Many of these were not serious presidential contenders before their selection as vice-president. Fillmore, Andrew Johnson, Arthur, and Ford are examples. In any case, incumbents who were not viewed as presidential material before becoming president probably lack a strong and widely dispersed following among the American electorate. They had meager exposure, and their performance in the White House has done nothing to improve matters, often because they have served abbreviated terms.

To turn to re-election prospects, incumbent presidents are more likely to return to the Oval Office when they happen to be serving as the country's wartime commander-in-chief. Voters in the 1864 election accepted Lincoln's advice not to "swap horses while crossing the stream." The precedent actually has earlier origins. Jefferson won a second term in the midst of the war with Tripoli; Madison was similarly rewarded shortly after the outbreak of the War of 1812. In this century, Franklin Roosevelt was elected to an unprecedented fourth term during World War II. And even the controversial Vietnam War may have proved an asset when Nixon sought a second term in 1972. Wartime incumbents are handed a rare chance to exhibit power, toughness, determination, and other features of charismatic leadership (see Chapters 2, 5, and 9). Incumbents themselves seem aware of this advantage. Presidents who are up for a second term under wartime conditions will often employ military force in a more visible fashion during an election year. A show of military force becomes a show of political competence.

But we are dilly-dallying around the crucial factor that underlies both renomination and re-election. Victor Hugo may have derisively exclaimed, "Popularity? It's glory's small change"—but the incumbent's approval rating is the single most important predictor of his success on election day. Thus, all the factors that sway an incumbent's standing in the Gallup polls will contribute directly to his re-election prospects. The president is especially vulnerable to events that affect his performance ratings in the months leading up to the general election. The people have short memories.

The most important influence on approval rating is probably the state of the economy. No incumbent, presidential or otherwise, wants to face the American voters in November when the latest economic statistics are atrocious. Such is the presumed basis for the "political business cycle," in which prosperity has a suspicious tendency to be synchronized with election years. There is evidence, for instance, that Truman's upset victory over Dewey was partly purchased. The real disposable income per capita fell between 1946 and 1949, except in 1948, the year Truman sought re-election. Through shrewd use of economic policy, the incumbent pumped up the economy just enough to give American voters more cash in their pockets when they cast their ballots at the polls. In the 1992 election year, incumbent Bush tried the same tactic by changing the withholding formula for the federal income tax—but the boost to the American economy was too little, too late.

Unfortunately, when the economy is badly sputtering, the incumbent's hands are often tied. Hoover really had little power to turn the Great Depression around before the election of 1932. Even if his political philosophy had allowed drastic federal interventions, American industry would have continued its descent. After all, the depression continued even after FDR launched his New Deal programs. What made Hoover's re-election defeat somewhat unjust was that the responsibility for the stock market crash was not really his. He had to pay the price for economic policies pursued by his predecessor, Calvin Coolidge. Hoover's story is similar to that of another one-term president, Van Buren. The "Little Magician" bore the brunt of the disaster precipitated by Andrew Jackson's dearth of economic acumen.

The impact of economic news is often overlooked by the political pundits and amateurs who like to read election results as if they were tea leaves. The election of 1980 provides a wonderful illustration. Reagan's impressive landslide victory over the incumbent, Carter, inspired many observers to announce that Americans had shifted dramatically toward the right wing of the political spectrum. Yet detailed analysis suggests otherwise. We can safely attribute Carter's downfall to the poor economic performance of his administration. The real per capita disposable income dropped by 3% in that election year; this was the first time this had happened since Roosevelt vanquished Hoover in 1932. Therefore, the people were rejecting Carter's economic policies rather than endorsing Reagan's conservative ideology.

There is a vital lesson here: We must be wary about inferring public opinion from election results. When voters cast their ballots at the polls, they base their decisions on a host of attitudes and beliefs. Single-issue elections are a rarity, especially at the national level. Accordingly, victory and defeat provide only ambiguous cues about the views of the average citizen. So when an incumbent loses his bid for another term to some challenger, not everything he stands for is repudiated, nor is everything the winner advocates vindicated. When a candidate takes on and defeats an incumbent, the challenger can never know for sure what in his platform has received the mandate of the American people. This lesson probably applies to democratic systems all over the globe. It is definitely unsafe to draw big inferences about a people's attitudes from big election results.

What is more tricky to decide is whether the retrospective voter is a rational voter. Of course, it appears wise to retain an incumbent who hasn't committed any irretrievable blunders. Even so, is the citizen's self-interest served by placing so much emphasis on the incumbent's most recent successes and failures? Doesn't this invite dangerous manipulation of foreign and domestic policies to achieve short-term rather than long-term advantages? And is it smart to respond to events over which the incumbent has no control?

Ideology

From examining voter attitudes about presidents or candidates, we now move to examine those persons whose attitudes create historic events more directly. These are the representatives whom we elect to legislative offices at the national level. The main objects of our attention here are the distinguished politicians who serve in the U.S. Senate. I make two points: First, and more obviously, ideology often determines a senator's policy; second, and less clearly, intellectual sophistication influences a senator's ideology. To make the second point, I invite back an old friend introduced in earlier chapters—integrative complexity.

The discussion begins with a narrow but critical issue in foreign policy. The discourse is then enlarged to encompass the political spectrum under which we can subsume all issues, whether foreign or domestic. Moreover, these conclusions extend well beyond the U.S. Senate. The same principles apply to figures as diverse as representatives to the British Parliament, justices of the U.S. Supreme Court, and members of the former Soviet Politburo.

Isolationists versus Internationalists

According to the U.S. Constitution, the Senate claims a central place in the making of foreign policy. The Senate offers its "advice and consent" to the President. Besides confirming appointments to diplomatic positions, the Senate must give its approval to treaties negotiated between the president and the heads of foreign states. Therefore, the Senate floor often becomes the battleground for contending views on America's proper place in international politics. One of the more persistent of these battles involves the debate between isolationists and internationalists. Should the United States ignore events in realms beyond its shores? Or should it assume a more active role in international affairs? If senators believe the former, they should reject treaties that form "entangling alliances" with other world powers. If they believe the latter, senators should not only approve those alliances, but also back the commitment of economic and military aid to foreign nations.

In debating these issues, why do some senators take the isolationist stance while others adopt the internationalist position? The concept of integrative complexity provides a potential answer. As you will recall, someone low on complexity can only see the world from a single point of view. In contrast, someone high on complexity can simultaneously consider a multitude of perspectives, and then unify these into a harmonious framework.

Hence, if senators are low on integrative complexity, they will see international affairs in a simplistic fashion: First there's the United States; then there's everybody else. On the other hand, if senators are high on this variable, they will view global politics in a more complex manner. The United States is but one of the world's powers. Each power has a distinct national interest that cuts across alliances, ideologies, traditions, and geographies. It is too simple-minded to claim that other nations are either for us or against us. Stalwart friends shade imperceptibly into intractable enemies, and this shading varies unpredictably according to the prevalent diplomatic question of the hour. A nation as supreme as the United States must take an active role in international affairs to help maintain the delicate balance of forces that serves the cause of world peace. Ultimately, no nation wins, and all nations lose, when that intricate equilibrium is destroyed. So we should predict that isolationists score low on integrative complexity, while internationalists score high.

Philip Tetlock tested this prediction using the speeches delivered in the U.S. Senate during the 82nd Congress (1951–52). This Senate had to grapple with the proper place of the United States in the postwar world. America seemed at the crossroads between enlarging its internationalist future or shrinking to its isolationist past. Many issues pertaining to diplomatic and military commitments remained unresolved. Senator Robert A. Taft, son of former President Taft, opened the first session of the 82nd Congress by attacking Truman's foreign policy. Supporters of the incumbent's internationalist convictions rose to the defense. There followed three months of argument on both sides of the question. All told, 35 senators were articulate on U.S. foreign policy. Using key votes as a guide, Tetlock classified these policy leaders as outright isolationists, ambivalent isolationists, and nonisolationists. Senators Dirkson and McCarthy were typical of the first group; Taft and Brewster of the second; and Humphrey, Fulbright, Connally, Kefauver, and Sparkman of the third. The speeches of all 35 politicians were then analyzed for integrative complexity.

The results were clear. The outright isolationists scored lowest on complexity; their policy statements were the simplest of all. On the other side, the nonisolationists scored the highest. Their remarks on the Senate floor accommodated many perspectives at once in a comprehensive outlook on international affairs. The integrative-complexity scores of the ambivalent isolationists came between these two extreme groups.

Tetlock went one step further. He also measured the attitudes of the speakers toward the two big powers around which the world was then polarizing—the United States and the Soviet Union. The isolationists had extremely contrasting feelings: The United States was the epitome of good, the Soviet Union the embodiment of evil. The nonisolationists, by comparison, had more balanced attitudes toward ingroup and outgroup. The leader of the free world was not always in the right; the leader of the Communist bloc was not invariably wrong. Again, the ambivalent isolationists had attitudes more in the middle.

Foreign policy ideology does thus appear to emerge from a leader's basic capacity to handle the complexities and ambiguities of world affairs. Simplistic thoughts forge primitive policies. Nonetheless, Tetlock was aware that an alternative explanation could obscure these results. Most of the isolationists were Republicans, including "Mr. Republican" himself, Senator Taft. Yet the 82nd Congress was controlled by a Democratic majority, and the incumbent was a Democrat as well. This forced the Republicans to express opposition viewpoints. Conceivably, an out-of-power minority uses straightforward arguments as a rhetorical strategy. In this case, Republicans may have been more interested in appealing to the American people than in persuading their Senate colleagues. They acted as if they were looking at the next election for a mandate, which would require lower integrative complexity, as we have seen in Chapter 3. This interpretation makes spurious any link between isolationism and low complexity. If the Republicans were in power, perhaps their attacks on the internationalists would have been conceptually rich.

To tease out the most likely explanation requires that we expand our analysis in two ways. First, we need to examine how integrative complexity relates to a politician's placement on the political spectrum. Second, we must scrutinize how occupying the minority position affects the complexity of speeches delivered before legislative bodies.

Right Wing versus Left Wing

We can place the Senate debates between the internationalists and isolationists in a more inclusive context. Many of the isolationists belonged to the conservative side of the political spectrum. They wished to preserve what they held to be the sacrosanct principles of the American republic, such as George Washington's admonition in his Farewell Address to eschew commitments with other nations. Rather than get entangled in other people's business, the United States should concentrate its energies on Christianity, capitalism, and the Constitution. These are the "three C's" of classic American conservatism.

In contrast, many of the internationalists were of a more liberal persuasion. They could appreciate better the relativism inherent in any evaluation of other peoples and governments. The religious beliefs, economic systems, and political frameworks of other world states deserve respect and understanding even when they conflict openly with our own. Liberals appreciate the essential pluralism of international affairs because they are committed to pluralism at home. They wish to open America to those left out of the mainstream—women, minorities, the disadvantaged, the oppressed. If this means that one or more of the three C's must be soft-pedaled or stretched, then so be it! For liberals, the American way is symbolized by the Statue of Liberty, not a cross, smoke-stack, or piece of parchment.

When isolationism and internationalism are linked with the bigger dimen-sion on which political attitudes vary, this debate becomes part of a larger set of issues. The political spectrum governs the position one takes on such ques-tions as states' rights, civil rights, free speech, gun control, affirmative action, abortion, school busing, bilingual education, prayer in schools, deregulation of industry, capital gains taxes, free trade, social security benefits, and immigra-tion policy. Thus, we need to understand the psychological foundations of this ideological variation. Why are some leaders located on the right-wing, conser-vative side, while others align themselves with the left-wing, liberal side? Why do yet others land someplace in the middle, becoming the moderates or middle-of-the-roaders?

In part, the solution to this riddle may again lie in the notion of integra-tive complexity. Philip Tetlock and his colleagues pursued this lead in a series of provocative inquiries. These investigations began with a study of the U.S. Senate of the mid-1970s. Using actual voting records, Tetlock classified the senators as liberal, moderate, or conservative. He then assessed the senators' policy statements delivered before their colleagues for integrative complexity as well. To insure that differences among the senators could not be attributed to other causes, Tetlock adjusted for such contaminants as age, education, party affiliation, and years of Senate service. Even with these corrections, the con-servative senators expressed their attitudes in more simplistic terms than did their moderate and liberal rivals. This result fits perfectly with the earlier find-ing that isolationism was advocated by senators who displayed below-average complexity.

This result may look too pat to those who sit with the right wing on most issues—and who feel their side is usually correct. Besides, any unbiased viewer of politics must admit that the extreme left wing can also hold a respectable num-ber of conceptual simpletons. American Communists used to do a fantastic job of sticking to the monotone party line promulgated by the former Soviet Union. So maybe this research reflects political bias rather than scientific objectivity.

Tetlock was well aware of these difficulties. But he also recognized a prob-lem with concentrating on the U.S. Senate: This body does not include all ideo-logical extremes. The center of gravity of American politics is clearly right of center. Unlike the parliaments of most other democracies, the U.S. Senate has never included a Communist—or, for that matter, any true socialist. On the other hand, the Senate has put out the welcome mat for some rather extreme right-wingers. Even today, the most liberal senator is probably closer to the political center than is the most conservative senator. An Edward Kennedy, for instance, is more middle-of-the-road than a Jesse Helms. Therefore, Tetlock wanted to examine a legislative body featuring a wider array of opinions.

The British House of Commons is far more inclusive than the U.S. Sen-ate. A sizable number of socialists vie for political power with moderates and conservatives. Tetlock scored 89 members of Parliament (MPs) for integrative complexity. Instead of using public speeches, this time Tetlock took advantage of some confidential interviews that had been previously conducted by another researcher. Classification of the MPs went beyond just identification with either the Labour or the Conservative Party. They were further divided into extreme socialists, moderate socialists, moderate conservatives, and extreme conservatives. This was based on how they stood on two divisive issues: (1) How much should the government regulate the economy? (2) How much should the government provide for social welfare?

The empirical results confirmed expectations. The extreme conservatives were very similar to the extreme socialists in their low integrative complexity. MPs from both of these groups expressed simpler opinions than those advocated by either the moderate socialists or the moderate conservatives. So, if we look far enough on either side of the ideological continuum, the extremists displayed a consistent proclivity toward simplicity. Only those in more centrist positions supported attitudes that were differentiated, multidimensional, and integrated. These findings replicate and extend Tetlock's results from the mid-1970s senators. The results also support the "ideologue hypothesis." This maintains that the extremists of any stripe, whether right-wing or left-wing, will exhibit the same cognitive style; at both ends of the spectrum, we may expect to discover individuals who are rigid and dogmatic. Ideologues are too intolerant of ambiguity to show any appreciation for the inescapable complexities of their social and political worlds. By comparison, those who defend conciliatory positions do so because they see reality in far less dichotomous, black–white terms.

Before we accept the ideologue hypothesis, we must weigh a fact that we have so far ignored. At the close of the preceding section, I have mentioned something that might confound the linkage of low complexity with isolationist foreign policy: Most of the isolationists came from a political party that was out of power. Low integrative complexity may represent an effective rhetorical strategy for the minority opposition. Clearly, the same snag may occur here. To clarify matters, we must allow the contending parties to switch roles. If the outsiders take over the government, their rhetoric should become more complex; by contrast, those in the ousted party should invoke more simplistic arguments, now that they are no longer accountable for their actions. The opponents should become mirror images of each other. In fact, maybe extremists score low on complexity solely because they seldom muster a large enough following to allow them to set up their own government. In Chapter 3, we have seen that successful revolutionaries can suddenly change their cognitive tune once their new regimes consolidate power.

To explore this further, Tetlock and his associates returned to the U.S. Senate. Altogether, they scrutinized five congresses. In three of these, the moderates and liberals dominated the legislative branch (the 82nd, 94th, and 96th); in the other two, the conservatives took control (the 83rd and 97th). Therefore, we can ask whether there was a flip-flop from the 82nd to the 83rd Congress, and from the 94th and 96th to the 97th. Complexity scores came from speeches delivered on the Senate floor. The senators themselves were classified as liberal, moderate, or conservative. This was done according to how their voting records were rated by the Americans for Democratic Action (a liberal political organization whose ratings are diametrically opposed to those of the Americans for Constitutional Action, a conservative group). What happened to senators in these three groups when they switched positions with their political opponents?

In general, both the moderates and the liberals were found to be mouthing more simplistic rhetoric when they were thrown out of power. Moreover, the conservatives did get more complex when handed the reins of government. Yet the scores were not completely reversed. In the 97th Congress, conservative senators were at about the same level as the liberals, and they were still below the moderates. In the 83rd Congress, furthermore, both the liberals and the moderates stayed well above the conservatives in the complexity of their policy statements. Hence, whether politicians are in or out certainly affects their rhetoric, but stylistic shifts are not the whole story either. Under the most auspicious conditions, the conservatives preserve something of their hallmark preference for the straight and narrow.

Let's not be too harsh on the staunch conservatives in the U.S. Senate. If Americans elected Communists to serve on Capitol Hill, and if Communists ever assumed power, we would expect the same behavior. An extreme left-wing Senate would look like an extreme right-wing Senate. Those in power would find it difficult to see reality from multiple perspectives, even when they have to engage in excuse making. Admittedly, I have just stated that successful revolutionaries undergo such a conversion; even so, I suspect that the conversion is never total. Genuine ideologues simply lack the cognitive apparatus to ape those who feel comfortable dwelling in the eternal ambiguities of centrist positions. Indeed, many revolutionaries, once the old regime succumbs to their onslaughts, cannot find a place for themselves in the new revolutionary government. They are more idealistic than pragmatic.

The key conclusions in these studies have been developed in additional inquiries. For example, one study scrutinized the Canadian House of Commons from 1948 and 1988. Integrative-complexity scores were calculated for members of both the government and opposition parties. Because another study had already shown that Liberals scored higher than Conservatives on complexity, the investigators focused on how switching back and forth between government and opposition status changed the rhetoric of policy statements. As expected, the Conservatives and Liberals did indeed swap rhetoric when they exchanged places in ruling Canada. Moreover, the gap in complexity between government and opposition grew as more and more time elapsed since the last election. Those in power became increasingly complex; those out of power became increasingly simple. On the other hand, when neither party won a majority in the House of Commons and some power sharing was required, both parties became more complex. When politicians have to share the limelight with their political enemies, it behooves them to learn the enemies' lines as well as their own.

Researchers have moved beyond the confines of legislative bodies in representative democracies. For instance, Tetlock and his colleagues looked at the U.S. Supreme Court to see whether the same principles would apply to the judicial mind. They specifically examined the integrative complexity of the judicial opinions written by the 25 justices who sat on the bench between 1946 and 1978. Every effort was made to control for such extraneous factors as a judge's age, religion, quality of law school attended, and the circumstances under which the opinions were written. Taking everything into consideration, the Supreme Court justices behaved very much like the members of the U.S. Senate and the MPs of the British or Canadian House of Commons. First, justices with liberal or moderate voting records showed more complex styles of thought than did justices with more conservative voting records. Second, dissenting opinions were usually more simplistic than the opinions written by the court majority. Thus, there are two independent stimulants to simplicity: ideological extremity and opposition status.

One final investigation deserves attention, owing to the complete change of venue. Tetlock and a collaborator decided it was time to move away from democratic systems. If integrative complexity is to have any value as a correlate of ideological stance, it must be shown to operate in governments that are very different from the representative democracies of the United States, Great Britain, and Canada. So they studied the politicians who guided the Soviet Union in the mid-1980s, most of whom were Politburo members. Because they were now dealing with a Communist regime, the analysis tipped toward the other end of the spectrum. As members of the Communist Party, all Soviet politicians were technically extreme left-wingers. Even so, these leaders could be divided into two groups, the traditionalists and the reformers.

Traditionalists defended the Soviet system inherited from the Brezhnev era. This was a system with a ponderous bureaucracy, an ailing economy, and an outmoded ideology. Among the traditionalists were such figures as Nikolai Tikhonov, Dinmuhammad Kunayev, Vladimir Shcherbitsky, and Grigory Romanov. In contrast, the reformers wanted to revamp the system from the ground up. The most conspicuous member of this group was Mikhail Gorbachev, who eventually implemented the revolutionary ideas of *glasnost* and *perestroika*. Other reformers included Nikolai Ryzhkov, Eduard Shevardnaze, and Boris Yeltsin. Although it may look strange to employ the designation, the traditionalists were comparable to our conservatives. Like members of the American right wing, they were dedicated to preserving their heritage intact. Instead of the three C's, however, the traditionalists had only the one C, Communism. The reformers, on the other hand, were more like our liberals or even moderates. They were willing to compromise ideological purity for the sake of practical results. This willingness to sacrifice the Marxist–Leninist ideology went so far as to introduce the principles of democratic politics and the free-market economy.

If these parallels have been drawn correctly, we should expect the reformers to exhibit more integrative complexity than the traditionalists. The investigators found that this was precisely the case. In addition, if what we have learned from democratic governments can be applied to this one-party regime, we should expect some shifts when the reformers gained supremacy over the traditionalists. This also took place. During the Chernenko period, when the traditionalists reigned supreme, the reformers occupied the opposition role. In the Gorbachev period, the reformers switched places with the traditionalists. The rhetoric of the reformers was responsive to the shift, for the increase in complexity was dramatic. The traditionalists changed very little across the two periods. This may seem surprising, yet we must realize that the traditionalists were already so simplistic that they really had little room to maneuver. Besides, as we have seen for members of the U.S. Senate, conservatives exhibit more "trait-like" stability in their style of thought. With old-line Soviet traditionalists and American conservatives, "what you see is what you get." Both bend little with shifts in the political wind.

Chapter 3 has illustrated how complexity relates to revolutionary success, military victory, and presidential rhetoric. Chapter 11 has shown how complexity can help us understand the resolution of international crises and the launching of surprise attacks. Now, this chapter has shown how complexity relates to the ideologies in the U.S. Senate and Supreme Court, the British and Canadian Parliaments, and the former Soviet Politburo. Few psychological variables have so many manifestations in history. But the next has even more.

Authoritarianism

According to the ideologue hypothesis, extremists at either end of the political spectrum will display the most simplistic attitudes. Those closer to the political center, in contrast, will exhibit a highly differentiated and integrative style of thought. This trend is only distorted, not obliterated, when extremists usurp power from the moderates. What's happening here? Philip Tetlock developed an interesting interpretation—the "value pluralism" model. This model can be summarized as follows: The stand we take on various political issues depends very much on our value systems. Some of us simplify our decisions by making one specific value our topmost concern. Others of us may try to juggle a multitude of values, with no clear priority among them. If we stick to a single value, we have no need to think in a complex manner. Yet if we try to maximize more than one value simultaneously, we will often have no other choice but to show integrative complexity. This is because for many issues two or more values may come in conflict; the only way we can resolve this conflict is to consider all the tradeoffs, and then arrive at a tenuous compromise among the competing criteria. The ideologue is someone who highlights one value at the expense of all others. The moderate is someone who is willing to engage in the more demanding value-juggling act.

Tetlock argued that two values cause the most contention: freedom and equality. People who value freedom believe that everybody should be allowed to do what they please, with the fewest restrictions possible. People who value equality believe that extreme disparities in power and opportunity are unacceptable in any democratic society. On many issues, these two values recommend rather contrary decisions. Should big capitalists be allowed free rein, even if this means that the rich will get richer and the poor get poorer? Do landlords have the right to rent to whomever they want, even if it means that they can deny an apartment to a Hispanic family or a homosexual couple?

For people whose beliefs lie in the middle of the political spectrum, the resolution of issues like these is not easy. They must weigh competing considerations. Within limits, for example, employers should be free to hire whomever they want. Yet some line must be drawn between reasonable hiring practices and those that discriminate against certain members of our society. Where is that boundary? Can employers be obliged to engage in reverse discrimination if minority-group members are underrepresented in their company? Should there be quotas? For ideologues, in contrast, such issues are nonissues. Because ideologues on the right stress the primacy of freedom, government has no business telling people how to run their businesses. And because ideologues on the left stress the primacy of equality, government must intervene to preserve the equality of all citizens.

The value pluralism model clearly explains the connection between complexity and ideological position. Nonetheless, it cannot be the whole story. One problem is that it is a purely cognitive theory, yet attitudes and beliefs often have a potent emotional component. It is one matter to say that someone is prejudiced, for instance, and quite another to claim that this person is bigoted. The latter implies a fanatical opinion that goes beyond more intellectual stereotypes. In addition, viewers of the political scene often conclude that right-wing extremists are qualitatively different from left-wing extremists. The former appear both rigid and rabid. Whereas leftists may have a coherent ideology that calls for change, the rightists appear obsessed by the desire to turn back the clock. Whereas the leftists' plans are in the future tense and volatile, the rightists' plans are in the past tense and fixed.

Therefore, we need to spend more time inspecting the basis of right-wing beliefs. This takes us to the extraordinary studies that have been done on the authoritarian personality. This part of the chapter begins by discussing this phenomenon as a stable *trait* of character. It ends by showing that authoritarianism also functions as an ever-changing *state* that responds to political and economic conditions. Both discussions return us to the attitudes of the average person on the street.

Narrow Minds: Authoritarianism as a Trait

However inadvertently, Adolf Hitler's rise in Germany was a enormous boon to American science. As the Nazi forces spread over the European continent, many first-rate intellects emigrated to safer lands, especially the United States. Some emigrés were Jews who found themselves the targets of virulent anti-Semitism. Others were advocates of political viewpoints that made them *persona non grata* with the anti-Communist, antiliberal Nazi Party. Practically overnight, the country filled up with first-rate scientists. American psychology, too, gained some major figures. Not only did practically the entire Gestalt school come over en masse, but the United States gained several distinguished psychoanalytic thinkers besides.

Some of these immigrating psychologists, like T. W. Adorno and Else Frenkel-Brunswik, settled on the West Coast, joining the staff at the University of California at Berkeley. They thus became part of an ambitious research project that probed the personality basis of beliefs. In 1950, this work culminated in one of the classics in the study of attitudes, *The Authoritarian Personality*. This inquiry began with a series of interviews of average Joes and Janes. In line with the preoccupations of the time, these interviews aimed at discerning the beliefs most supportive of fascist policies and practices. The interviews led to the development of several attitudinal measures that gauged various aspects of this right-wing allegiance. Hence, the Anti-Semitism Scale gauged whether an individual held extremely biased stereotypes about Jews. Because anti-Semitic people often expressed negative opinions about other ethnic groups, the investigators proceeded to develop the Ethnocentrism Scale as well. This assessed whether an individual was strongly prejudiced toward conventional, majority-culture values. In addition, a Politico-Economic Conservativism Scale measured more directly a person's standing on the political spectrum. A conservative inclination was shown to go along with both ethnocentric and anti-Semitic beliefs.

These scales reflected a sensitivity to what had just happened in Europe. The investigators were acutely aware of the evils of anti-Semitism, ethnocentrism, and right-wing extremism. Moreover, the Berkeley researchers went a step further, this time revealing the influence of psychoanalytic theory. They devised the F Scale, which measured a person's "potentiality for fascism." This scale gauged more than just attitudes. The basic premise behind the F Scale was the existence of an "authoritarian personality syndrome." The attitudes measured by the other scales were thought to be merely symptoms of this more comprehensive character trait. This trait was seen as by no means superficial; on the contrary, the syndrome was viewed as deeply rooted in the individual's personality.

In particular, authoritarianism receives nourishment from unconscious impulses that the person is constantly trying to repress. Many aspects of the authoritarian personality, in fact, are straightforward manifestations of standard psychoanalytic defense mechanisms. For example, authoritarians have difficulty accepting their sexual desires. Because repressed sexual thoughts are always bubbling to the surface, threatening their fragile egos, authoritarians often resort to "projection": They believe that *other* people are preoccupied with sex. Hence, those who score high on the F Scale are most likely to endorse the item "No matter how they act on the surface, men are interested in women for only one reason." By projecting their unfulfilled wishes upon others, authoritarians preserve their ego stability.

A defensive obsession with sex is not the only symptom that makes up the authoritarian personality. High scorers on the F Scale are conspicuous in their "conventionalism," for they believe that people must conform rigidly to the middle-class norms of the majority culture. They also score high on "authoritarian submission," or the need to submit themselves to the will of a leader, especially a leader characterized by "power and toughness." In line with this and with their adherence to conventions, they support "authoritarian aggression" against those who refuse to obey authority or to follow the dictates of the majority culture. They display considerable "stereotypy," which means that they classify people into rigid and often dichotomous groups—good versus evil, Christian versus Communist, white versus black, Gentile versus Jew, and so forth. They also exhibit "superstitious" beliefs (such as a belief in astrology), which place the locus of control outside the individual. At the same time, authoritarians rate high on "cynicism" and "destructiveness." That is, they have rather negative attitudes about human nature, and the base nature of humanity justifies the use of violence. For instance, those scoring high on the potentiality for fascism are more likely to express the opinion that "Human nature being what it is, there will always be war and conflict."

Finally, authoritarians score high in "anti-intraception." Because they have so much going on in the subterranean realms of their brains that they are trying perpetually to keep the lid on, they don't like to look closely into their own inner workings or those of others. "When a person has a problem or worry, it is best for him not to think about it, but to keep busy with more cheerful things" is one of the statements that elicit the agreement of high F Scale scorers. Needless to say, they don't appreciate psychologists, and especially psychoanalysts, who delve into portions of the psyche where no one belongs. The Socratic "Know thyself" is not one of their maxims.

In essence, fascists are people who are out of tune with themselves. They have big chips on their shoulders; accordingly, they need to dump on outgroup members to maintain their self-esteem. Hence, the persons who lined up to support Hitler and the Nazi Party were sick people. The Holocaust was the symptom of a whole nation's becoming mentally ill. The potentiality for fascism was realized as overt authoritarianism on a continental scale.

Naturally, the Berkeley researchers were not primarily interested in explaining what happened in Europe during World War II. The authoritarian syndrome is not a mere historical curiosity. Contemporary people, including

Americans, can score quite high on the F Scale, too. So psychologists can use this instrument to understand current political and social beliefs and behaviors. The F Scale has become one of the most popular measures in the social sciences, and those who have applied this scale have found that it predicts a diversity of attitudes and actions. Consider three sets of findings:

   1. Scores on the F Scale indicate how someone is going to vote on election day. In the 1984 presidential campaign, authoritarians preferred Ronald Reagan, nonauthoritarians Walter Mondale. Likewise, authoritarians preferred Reagan over Carter and Anderson in 1980, Nixon or Wallace over Humphrey or McCarthy in 1968, and Nixon over Kennedy in 1960. They were more likely to want General Douglas MacArthur to run for president of the United States in 1952. In general, those who score high on the F Scale vote for conservative or even reactionary candidates in democracies all over the globe.

   2. Authoritarians also take different stands on various foreign policy issues. They are especially disposed to advocate the use of military force to solve international conflicts. For instance, a day after a plane was hijacked to Cuba in July 1961, authoritarians had greater odds of endorsing Senator Smathers's direct threat to Fidel Castro: "if the plane is not released in 24 hours we're coming after it." Those scoring higher on the F Scale were also more likely to lend their unequivocal support to American involvement in the Vietnam War. Thus, on October 15, 1969, when activists proclaimed a Moratorium Day in protest of the Vietnam War, college students with low F Scale scores were less likely to show up for class.

   3. F Scale scores predict a person's likely position on domestic questions as well. In the 1950s, for example, high scorers were more opposed to the introduction of socialized medicine. They were are also more favorably disposed toward the controversial requirement that faculty members at the University of California submit to a compulsory "loyalty oath." In the 1990s, moreover, authoritarians in the United States advocate highly conservative positions on such issues as drugs, abortion, child abuse, AIDS, homelessness, higher education, the environment, the trade deficit, and the space program. Finally, authoritarians are more prone to defend sexist, racist, or heterosexist policies, such as discrimination against women, blacks, or homosexuals. In regard to the last attitude, one item on the F Scale notes the belief that "Homosexuality is a particularly rotten form of delinquency and ought to be severely punished." Those who know their history will recall that the pink triangle that now proudly proclaims the gay and lesbian movement began in Nazi Europe. It had the same status as the yellow star of David forced upon European Jews: Both badges were free tickets to the gas chambers.

   Besides all this, high scores on the F Scale correlate with such dispositions as dogmatism, conservatism, militarism, nationalism, and religiosity. Therefore, authoritarians are inclined toward the same opinions as individuals rating high on these traits, which together form an inclusive personality complex. For example, the trait may affect how much credence people place in the evening news or in official police explanations of riots. The higher their authoritarianism, the more gullible they are about the statements of authority figures. More intriguingly, the disposition may partially determine who among the great a person most admires. Right-wingers are prone to admire religious figures, military leaders, athletes, and popular entertainers, whereas left-wingers are prone to admire scientists, inventors, poets, and dispensers of high art. Back in the 1930s, conservatives looked up to U. S. Grant, Babe Ruth, and Bing Crosby, while radicals revered Marie Curie, Charles Steinmetz, Lord Byron, Isadora Duncan, and Enrico Caruso. Conservatism even predicts the sort of poetry people most prefer: Whereas liberals like complex compositions that are rich in meaning, conservatives like far more simplistic and accessible constructions. Hence, insofar as authoritarianism predicts placement on the conservative–radical spectrum, it can predict the choice of favorite persons and poems besides.

This chapter lacks the space to review all the provocative findings and irksome controversies in this research. Like any innovative researchers, the Berkeley investigators made their fair share of methodological mistakes. Furthermore, those unsympathetic with psychoanalytic theory may prefer a different theoretical explanation for the phenomenon. And many conservatives may object to the focus on right-wing authoritarianism when the extreme left-wing may provide striking parallels.

Still, when we carefully weigh all the data and debates, we cannot doubt that the studies of the authoritarian personality capture a vital truth. Political and social attitudes are not entirely cerebral. Beliefs are often grounded in emotional processes, and sometimes these processes are pathological. Because these beliefs are embedded so deeply in a person's constitution, they operate as stable personality traits. More importantly, people act on these beliefs, so extremist attitudes translate into extremist behaviors. Fill up a nation with enough authoritarians, and the rise of right-wing extremism becomes almost guaranteed. Add a few more, and neofascist groups may go from radical fringe to majority party. The upshot can be another Adolf Hitler, Holocaust, or even world war. And another tragic nation may see its outstanding citizens escape abroad rather than suffer oppression at home.

Scary Times: Authoritarianism as a State

So where do authoritarians come from? Research on this issue often adopts a developmental framework. Presumably, distinct child-rearing practices create future adults who manifest the key symptoms of the syndrome. For example, those who grow up to score high on the F Scale often have parents who are strict and rigid disciplinarians. Authoritarians come from the kind of home where the saying "Spare the rod and spoil the child" is both practiced and preached. Nevertheless, we must recall the nature–nurture issue discussed in

Chapter 6. A genetic component may partially support the emergence of these personalities. Hence, both nature and nurture may do their distinctive part in filling society with individuals with a high potentiality for fascism.

Yet this cannot tell the whole story. Judging from history, the magnitude of authoritarianism exhibited by a nation or people can vary dramatically from generation to generation. The free-wheeling experimentation of Germany under the Weimar Republic was followed shortly by the goose-step regimentation of the Nazi regime. These quick movements suggest that authoritarianism operates as a transient state as well as an enduring trait. At any given time, a population will have a certain range of authoritarian personalities, but certain external conditions will shift the mean level either up or down. In particular, when individuals face extremely stressful events, any latent authoritarian tendencies are amplified. Thoughts become more rigid, emotional reactions intensify, and dormant prejudices fly out of the darkness. Authoritarianism may be a coping behavior that people use when they confront events that threaten their livelihoods, even their very lives.

Actually, we have already encountered a similar phenomenon in the research on integrative complexity. Threatening circumstances usually undermine a person's power to process information in sophisticated ways. Similarly, ample research proves that menacing events can raise the level of authoritarian symptoms in the populace. A pioneer investigator in this area was Stephen Sales, who conducted two fascinating inquiries.

In the first study, Sales recorded how ups and downs in the economy affected the rates at which people converted to different Christian denominations in the United States. He divided the sects into two groups, the authoritarian and the nonauthoritarian. Authoritarian churches enforce absolute obedience to theological doctrine and moral prescription. Those church members who stray from the flock find themselves excommunicated, shunned, or in some other overt manner branded as heretics. In contrast, nonauthoritarian churches allow their members much latitude of personal conscience. A wide range of beliefs and behaviors is accepted without condemnation. As hypothesized, Sales found that economic hardship inspired membership growth in authoritarian churches, while economic prosperity encouraged expansion in the less authoritarian forms of Christianity. These relationships held up for the entire United States, such as the shift toward authoritarian churches that occurred during the Great Depression; these effects also appeared in the history of a single city—Seattle, Washington. In the latter case, Seattle was chosen owing to the volatile nature of its economy. Unemployment figures in this city can swing wildly according to how well a single corporation is doing—namely, Boeing Aircraft.

In the second study, Sales isolated cultural indices of the several symptoms of the authoritarian syndrome. Among other things, he gauged the power and toughness of favorite comic strip characters, the cynicism displayed in articles in popular magazines, the severity of punishment meted out for sex crimes, the sales figures for books on superstitious topics, and the intensity of anti-intraception as reflected in aversion toward the disciplines of psychology and psychoanalysis. During the Great Depression, these signs of heightened authoritarianism became more prominent in American culture. The modal personality had shifted toward a fascist disposition.

Later researchers have only reinforced the argument. In one study, a troubled economy was linked with the popularity of 1,761 prime-time television shows from 1950 to 1974. When Americans felt insecure about their material well-being, they preferred programs featuring tough and powerful authority figures. Many of these TV characters enforced conformity to "truth, justice, and the American way." Furthermore, such effects can go beyond the confines of popular culture. Another study found that threatening circumstances influenced the appearance of parapsychological research in professional journals; here parapsychology was taken as an index of superstitious beliefs. Further research has shown that threat even affects politics. When conditions get bad, Americans favor presidential candidates who score high in the need for power. When the country seems to be going down hill, voters want a strong, tough leader in the White House. Hence, it was no accident that the United States became a breeding ground of authoritarian demagogues during the Great Depression. A figure like Louisiana's Huey Long would have been a fish out of water during more auspicious times.

We must bear in mind that the external threat need not be economic; the danger may be political or military as well. In addition, the specific symptoms of authoritarianism may alter with shifts in cultural meanings. For example, in today's America, some superstitious beliefs have become associated with the New Age subculture—a nonauthoritarian conglomeration of free thinkers, occultists, and mystics. As a consequence, the popularity of a belief system like astrology is no longer closely tied with threatening circumstances. A similar shift has occurred regarding harsh punishment for sex offenders. This has become a feminist issue rather than a matter of sex-tinged authoritarian aggression.

But the most significant point is that the phenomenon of threat-enhanced authoritarianism is by no means restricted to the United States of America. This association between condition and state may be universal. For instance, one study examined the canons issued by a dozen ecumenical councils of the Roman Catholic Church. The more threatening the circumstances that motivated a council, the more dogmatic the canon that it issued. A second illustration may be more provocative.

Two psychologists looked at the relationship between economic threat and superstition in Germany between 1918 and 1940. They measured threat using indicators of real wages, unemployment, and industrial production. They assessed superstition by counting the number of magazine articles on astrology and mysticism. In line with everything else we've seen so far, a deteriorating economy occasioned an increase in superstitious interests. Things got particularly bad, of course, when the Great Depression hit Germany. By 1932, unemployment had reached an outrageous 45%. Under such deplorable circumstances, shouldn't we expect that other symptoms of extreme authoritarianism would crop up as well? Specifically, wouldn't the German people appeal to a leader who exhibited the utmost in power and toughness? Well, in January of the very next year, the Germans made Adolf Hitler their chancellor. Soon hundreds of antiauthoritarian scientists and psychologists would seek refuge in the United States. Our examination of research on the authoritarian personality has come full circle!

Can We Change the World?

Clearly, people vary among themselves and across situations in their attitudes. This variation is also responsible for behaviors with historic repercussions. Given this centrality, we can appreciate why so many psychologists have studied possible ways to change a person's beliefs. Attitudes have behavioral effects, and some of those effects may be antithetical to a harmonious society. Racist and sexist beliefs, in particular, are not mere matters of personal preference, like one's favorite ice cream; rather, these beliefs can sanction discriminatory behaviors with gigantic moral and legal repercussions. Therefore, by building an inventory of attitude change techniques, psychologists can aspire to make history. They can use the methods to make this world a better place to live.

This benevolent aspiration must admit an obstacle, however. Attitude change techniques are less effective than most people realize. Even the most dramatic interventions often prove ineffective. The much-feared brainwashing methods that the Communist Chinese used during the Korean War are guilty of false advertising. It would be hard to imagine methods more intense than these; the targets were bombarded with an unrelenting attack on the whole basis of their existence. Even so, the effects of these methods were seldom permanent under normal circumstances. In fact, the recent failure of Communist regimes all over Eastern Europe betrays how ineffective attitude change techniques can really be. The full armament of propaganda technology was applied to entire generations of citizens. Everyone thought that George Orwell's novel *1984* presaged the future condition of the human race. And yet this unprecedented onslaught on people's beliefs failed to make an enduring impression on the minds of these peoples. If monolithic, persistent, and committed regimes could not convince the masses that they were living in a utopia, how effective can we expect persuasion attempts to be in more open, pluralistic societies?

Indeed, research carried on in democratic countries unveils the impotence of even the mass media in changing people's preconceived ideas. For example, today most of us living in industrialized nations get our information from TV. We may watch the morning or evening news, and even catch a few special reports. Even so, the impact of TV news on people's opinions is limited. Only a small proportion of TV watchers count as genuine news aficionados who must get a daily dose of Dan Rather or Tom Brokaw. In addition, even those who have caught a particular news broadcast can seldom recall the key news stories of the day! Evidently, a person can sit in front of a TV set for a half hour without really processing the sights and sounds thrown toward the living room couch!

Of course, we could argue that the daily fare of the newscast is bland stuff. Viewers become quickly habituated to car bombings, plane crashes, and mass murders. Perhaps only the most dramatic stories can shake watchers out of their intellectual lethargy. Moreover, perhaps only these big events will get enough viewers glued to the tube to make a bona fide difference in opinion nationwide. Empirical research paints a more ambivalent picture.

For instance, researchers on the mass media have repeatedly examined the effect of presidential debates on voter preferences. Pundits often cite the first televised debate between Nixon and Kennedy as a critical event in the 1960 campaign. It made the youthful JFK look as if he would not be out of place in the White House. Big results are also ascribed to the 1976 debate between Ford and Carter, and the 1980 debate between Carter and Reagan. Nonetheless, the analyses reveal something very different. For the most part, viewers see what they expect to see; the person they already favor tends, in their opinion, to win the debate. Only those viewers who are undecided may make up their minds according to the outcome of the spectacle. This means that presidential debates are more effective in initial attitude formation than in authentic attitude change. The undecided may make up their minds, but the rest have their minds already made up. For the latter, the presidential debates serve largely to reinforce their opinions.

This ineffectiveness holds for other kinds of news programming besides news specials. For example, many Americans in the 1970s watched a TV rendition of Alex Haley's *Roots* and the sequel, *Roots: The Next Generation*. These miniseries traced the history of black slavery and white racism in the United States. The audiences for these special programs broke all viewing records, and the drama was unforgettable. Still, a viewer's reactions largely reflected preexisting attitudes. Americans of African heritage might have felt vindicated, but doors opening onto Main Street America were not swung wide open simply because whites saw blacks whipped and chained.

A later made-for-TV movie on a different subject is often touted as having a big impact on public opinion. This was *The Day After*, which portrayed in gruesome detail the likely aftermath of a nuclear exchange between the world superpowers. This special was watched by millions, and it apparently packed quite a wallop in developing antinuclear attitudes. People became aware of the unequivocal danger that they had hitherto largely ignored. Yet we don't know for sure whether this TV movie represents an incontestable instance of attitude change. Many of the viewers who were most impressed by the film may have been least informed on the issue. And, in any case, evidence for long-term effects is lacking.

These may not be the best examples, admittedly. After all, neither the two *Roots* miniseries nor *The Day After* represented real current events. What about those times when real history-making events cause millions to become riveted to their TV sets? Well, we often see notable effects. For instance, when the Watergate tapes divulged President Nixon's complicity in the cover-up, the percentage of Americans who wanted him removed from office increased by 15% in three days. Similarly, the Chernobyl nuclear accident of April 1986 altered significantly the antinuclear attitudes of those exposed to the drifting radioactive clouds. Such victims were less likely to believe industry proclamations that nuclear energy was safe energy.

Even so, these very examples pinpoint some of the restrictions on such effects. In the Nixon case, a very specific event was tied to an extremely narrow issue. Many Americans felt that if the incumbent committed a felony, he should be removed from office. The tapes provided the evidence necessary to invoke that principle. Hence, the more basic belief—in the constitutional powers of the presidency—had not really altered. The Chernobyl incident also tied a specific datum to a particular conclusion, but added another factor: Those who had changed their minds were people directly affected by the event narrated on the TV screen. The reality was concrete, not abstract. Furthermore, the event's impact on antinuclear beliefs tended to dissipate over time. Once the radioactive risk had been removed, people could return to their everyday lives, and their commitments could stray into oblivion.

There are many other factors that prevent momentous occasions from having the attitudinal influence we might otherwise expect. One problem is that people often have short memories. Earlier in this chapter, I have listed a sizable number of important circumstances that can raise or lower an incumbent president's approval rating. Yet these influences often operate only briefly. In time, their impact will decrease until public opinion returns to some baseline level. Hence, one year after American troops came home from victory in the Persian Gulf War, President Bush's approval rating hit a depressing low. Memories of that triumph had faded in the face of all the other (preponderantly bad) news that had occupied the headlines since. The influences that have durable effects on public opinion are precisely those that persist over time and that affect people directly. A chronically weak economy provides an obvious illustration. Long waits in unemployment lines or expensive visits to grocery stores can refresh the memory on a regular basis.

Another problem is more elementary: People do not always think the way we suppose. In particular, many theories of attitude change assume that people are driven by a need for consistency—that they like to have their beliefs, feelings, and behaviors congruent with one another. When a person finds an inconsistency, he or she should experience dissonance, and therefore should strive to change some opinions so the cognitions can be more consonant.

People don't always behave like this, however. They seem to tolerate an abundance of self-contradictions. For instance, on July 19, 1969, Senator Edward Kennedy drove off a bridge in the wee hours of the morning. A female passenger in the car, Mary Jo Kopechne, drowned, largely because of the senator's negligence in getting immediate help. Notwithstanding all the immoral and even criminal implications of the incident, many Kennedy supporters managed to swallow the sudden lump in their throats. Without altering their support,

> 65% admitted the possibility, if not the probability, that the girl's life could have been saved had he not delayed; 20% admitted the possibility that he was aware of this when he did delay; and 64% thought that his delay was probably or definitely based, at least in part, on his concern for his reputation.

Over twenty years since that fatal accident at Chappaquidick, Kennedy remains a senator from Massachusetts.

To be fair, the willingness to forgo cognitive consonance is not restricted to liberals. Conservatives, too, exhibit the same inclination. Hence, one study conducted during the 1968 presidential campaign found that supporters of George Wallace were actually *less* likely to obey a new law than were supporters of either Nixon or Humphrey. What made this finding remarkable was that Wallace was the "law and order" candidate!

If human beings are not obsessed with consistency, they are also immune from those attitude change strategies that rely on this motivation. Information campaigns can present raw facts that contradict cherished beliefs, yet the public may proceed along its merry way as if nothing had happened. How can people be so oblivious to the most minimal dictates of rationality?

One explanation is seen in the thought structure of the authoritarian personality. These individuals hold inconsistent beliefs by keeping them apart in "logic-tight compartments." For instance, those who maintain anti-Semitic attitudes tend to believe that (1) Jews are always trying to intrude on Gentiles and (2) Jews are always trying to separate themselves from Gentiles! Both beliefs can't be true. Any consistency is emotional only.

Yet the authoritarians have no monopoly on attitudinal inconsistencies. Let's go back to the phenomenon of integrative complexity. Persons high on this attribute can accommodate a wide range of seemingly contradictory opinions. Although the most complex thinkers integrate this diversity into a coherent package of attitudes, this integration may not be immediately obvious to those with simpler minds or contrary persuasions. Even worse, the very tolerance of ambiguity may lead complex thinkers to accept and to announce contradictory opinions. They will take these inconsistencies on faith, feeling at an intuitive level that a unity underlies any apparent incongruities. In defense, some may evoke Emerson's warning in "Self-Reliance":

> A foolish consistency is the hobgoblin of little minds, adored by little statesmen and philosophers and divines. With consistency a great soul has simply nothing to do. . . . Speak what you think now in hard words and tomorrow speak what tomorrow thinks in hard words again, though it contradict everything you said today.—'Ah, so you shall be sure to be misunderstood.'—Is it so bad then to be

misunderstood? Pythagoras was misunderstood, and Socrates, and Jesus, and Luther, and Copernicus, and Galileo, and Newton, and every pure and wise spirit that ever took flesh. To be great is to be misunderstood.

And Walt Whitman proclaimed in his "Song of Myself":

> Do I contradict myself?
> Very well then I contradict myself,
> (I am large, I contain multitudes.)

The lofty mind thus strives to encompass all opinions, not to foreclose truth in a stupid quest for a superficial certainty. For people like Emerson and Whitman, attitude change methods based on consistency theories look absurd.

If attitudes are so hard to alter, why have attitudes changed? Surely they have. Religions, ideologies, and philosophies of life have come and gone over the centuries. No one alive today continues to think Paleolithic thoughts. The answer may be simple, or, rather, complex. Few attitudes stand alone. Each belief we have is embedded in an intricate matrix of beliefs. Moreover, we ourselves, as embodiments of one configuration of beliefs, are enmeshed in an elaborate network of interpersonal relationships, social roles, and cultural traditions. Accordingly, any puny attempt to change one attitude is almost doomed to fail. The belief may shift a little one way or another, but in doing so it is thrown out of disequilibrium with the larger complex of attitudes, interactions, and customs. So the change becomes transient; the lone aberrancy is killed by the manifold interdependencies.

In sum, we cannot change attitudes without first changing the belief complexes, relationships, and groups that grant those attitudes their *raison d'être*. This may require political, economic, and cultural events far bigger than a propaganda poster, campaign spot, news broadcast, or TV special.

IMITATION, AFFILIATION, GROUP DYNAMICS, AND LEADERSHIP

Aggression and attitudes are only two of many topics studied by social psychologists. Actually, social psychologists bridge two disciplines, psychology and sociology. While many researchers will identify themselves as psychologists, a respectable number consider themselves sociologists instead. Yet the two social psychologies are by no means the same. The psychologist concentrates on individual thoughts, feelings, and behaviors, whereas the sociologist concentrates on group decisions, norms, and actions. In fact, many sociologists believe that their psychological colleagues put too much emphasis on the individual. Psychologists supposedly commit the sin of "psychological reductionism"; that is, Group phenomena are reduced to the psychology of single brains. In contrast, the sociologists argue, for many human activities "the whole is greater than the sum of its parts." Certain properties emerge from groups that are not mere aggregations of psychological processes in each group member. These group-emergent behaviors are beyond psychology.

Thus, it must be clear that a social psychology of history stands at the outer boundaries of any psychological science. One step further, and we will be entering the foreign land of the sociology of history. Nonetheless, residing within our frontiers are four prominent topics that still reserve a place for the historic actor. In particular, this chapter examines (1) imitation and emulation; (2) affiliation, attraction, interaction, and intimacy; (3) group dynamics; and (4) leadership. It ends with a discussion of whether creativity embodies a special form of leadership.

Admiration, Imitation, and Emulation

Several times in this book, I have discussed Francis Galton's 1869 *Hereditary Genius*. This book troubled those who felt that a genetic explanation placed too much emphasis on the individual as an agent of grand events. Because biological endowment belongs to a single person, claims that some special people are born great may erroneously downplay the impact of bigger, sociocultural forces. One of Galton's most illustrious critics, Alfred Kroeber, hailed from the discipline of cultural anthropology. Kroeber contended that the culture takes primacy over the individual in any account of human beliefs, emotions, and actions, and that historic geniuses are no exception to this rule. As noted back in Chapter 4, Kroeber first attacked the genius theory by citing the phenomenon of duplicate discoveries and inventions. Yet Kroeber's main attack came in 1944, when he published *Configurations of Culture Growth*. Like *Hereditary Genius*, this has become a classic in the study of eminent achievers.

The two volumes have much in common. Both contain chapters that deal with the main areas of accomplishment, such as art, science, and politics. Both have chapters replete with long lists of notable figures from several nationalities and historic eras. Yet once the reader goes beyond a quick thumbing through of the pages, stark contrasts between the two books appear. Galton simply listed famous people in alphabetical order, an array that nicely depicts family pedigrees (see Table 2.1). By comparison, Kroeber first separated his notables by nationality, and then listed them in strict chronological order. Table 13.1 presents a characteristic example. Kroeber's layout emphasizes each individual's ties to a specific culture and a period. Moreover, whereas Galton's chapter titles suggest a focus on individuals, Kroeber's chapter titles underline the prevalence of cultural systems. For instance, Galton's book has a chapter entitled "Painters"; the Kroeber book has one called "Painting." Although Kroeber plainly used Galton's book as a model for his own treatise, Kroeber made both dramatic and subtle changes to reflect an opposed outlook.

In fact, Kroeber's explicit goal was to prove that the genetic theory of genius was plain wrong. Genius does not appear in isolation; rather, one genius clusters with others of greater and lesser fame in adjacent generations. These clusters Kroeber called "configurations." When a configuration reaches a crest, a Golden Age of creative activity is the result; when the configuration descends to a trough, a Dark Age occurs. Now, if genius were the upshot of inherited ability, it should be spread more evenly from generation to generation. After all, the traits available in the population gene pool cannot fluctuate wildly in any short period.

If genetics cannot explain the leapfrogging of Golden and Dark Ages, what can? Kroeber offered one explanation that should make social psychologists smile. He argued that geniuses cluster in history because the key figures of one generation emulate those in the immediately preceding generations. Kroeber quoted an ancient though obscure Roman historian, Velleius Paterculus, who said:

> Genius is fostered by emulation, and it is now envy, now admiration, which enkindles imitation, and, in the nature of things, that which is cultivated with the highest zeal advances to the highest perfection; but it is difficult to continue at the point of perfection, and naturally that which cannot advance must recede.

TABLE 13.1. Configuration for American Literature, According to Kroeber

Rise from 1800–1840 (births 1771–1795):

Charles Brockden Brown	(1771–1810)
Daniel Webster	(1782–1852)
Washington IRVING	(1783–1859)
James Fenimore COOPER	(1789–1851)
Fitz-Greene Halleck	(1790–1867)
William Cullen BRYANT	(1794–1878)
Joseph Rodman Drake	(1795–1820)

Culmination from 1840–1860 (births 1796–1823):

William Hickling Prescott	(1796–1859)
Ralph Waldo EMERSON	(1803–1882)
William Gilmore Simms	(1806–1870)
Henry Wadsworth LONGFELLOW	(1807–1882)
John Greenleaf WHITTIER	(1807–1892)
Oliver Wendell HOLMES	(1809–1894)
Edgar Allan POE	(1809–1849)
Margaret Fuller	(1810–1850)
Harriet Beecher Stowe	(1811–1896)
John Lothrop Motley	(1814–1877)
Richard Henry Dana	(1815–1882)
Henry David Thoreau	(1817–1862)
James Russell Lowell	(1819–1891)
Herman Melville	(1819–1891)
Walt WHITMAN	(1819–1892)
Donald Grant Mitchell (Ik Marvel)	(1822–1908)
Francis Parkman	(1823–1893)

Decline from 1860 on (births from 1825 on):

Bayard Taylor	(1825–1878)
Emily Dickinson	(1830–1886)
Samuel Clemens (Mark Twain)	(1835–1910)
Thomas Bailey Aldrich	(1836–1907)
William Dean Howells	(1837–1920)
Bret Harte	(1839–1902)
Edward Rowland Sill	(1841–1887)
Henry James	(1843–1916)
Sidney Lanier	(1842–1881)

Note. Literary figures Kroeber thought particularly important have their surnames printed in capital letters. Because Kroeber collected his primary data in the 1930s, he probably lost perspective on the late 19th and early 20th centuries. Besides underestimating authors like Dickinson, Clemens, and James, he missed out on the literary giants of the glorious 1920s (and depressive 1930s). Certainly Theodore Dreiser, F. Scott Fitzgerald, William Faulkner, Sinclair Lewis, Eugene O'Neill, Edna St. Vincent Millay, Ernest Hemingway, Langston Hughes, John Steinbeck, and others formed a second crest of literary creativity rivaling that of nearly a century before.

And as in the beginning we are fired with the ambition to overtake those whom we regard as leaders, so when we have despaired of being able either to surpass or even to equal them, our zeal wanes with our hope; it ceases to follow what it cannot overtake, and abandoning the old field as though pre-empted, it seeks a new one.

Thus, as each generation builds upon the one before it, it attains a high point of perfection that stymies further growth. The tradition degenerates into empty imitation, as the most creative minds move on to greener pastures.

This basic process has been cited often since Roman times. The idea is implicit in Newton's remark, "If I have seen further than other men, it is because I stood on the shoulders of giants." The notion is also compatible with contemporary ideas about imitation and social learning. Furthermore, if it were valid, this concept would save the phenomenon of genius for psychology. Emulation would be a social-psychological process, entailing one person's becoming enthralled by the accomplishments of another person. But how true is this explanation? To weigh the evidence, we must acknowledge that imitation follows two routes. First, those who aspire to greatness can admire and ape the achievements of predecessors at a distance, without personal contact. Indeed, these idols may no longer walk among the living. Second, aspirants can interact in the more intimate capacity of disciples, apprentices, or pupils. Predecessors who influence development indirectly we may loosely style "models"; those who act directly we can call "mentors."

Models of Greatness

Person to Person

Judging from anecdotal evidence, those whose attainments oblige our admiration often emulated models whom they themselves admired as sources of inspiration. The young John Coltrane, before becoming a famous jazz saxophonist, would repeatedly listen to recordings of Charlie Parker's improvisations. With a picture of "Bird" hanging in his room, Coltrane would try to play each note on his own instrument. Albert Einstein also had *his* idols looking over him while he worked in his study; the portraits were of Newton, Faraday, and Maxwell. People who leave their marks seem prone to admire remarkable predecessors.

We also have scientific evidence for the impact of models, coming from two distinct sources. We can start by scrutinizing the historical clusterings of genius. Like Kroeber, we can examine the ups and downs in the appearance of big-time achievers in a particular society and domain. We then discover that the number of notables in one generation is a positive function of the number of models available in the preceding generation. The helpful impact of model availability holds in both Western and Eastern civilizations. The effect works for both creativity and leadership. The more potential models who are around when the gifted are first developing their talents, the better the chance that the latter will themselves become idols for others to emulate. Great politicians admire the great politicians of their youth. Great philosophers admire the great thinkers from whom they received the truth seeker's torch. It is most difficult to develop talent into genius in a vacuum. So, as Kroeber thought, it is this modeling process that partly accounts for why luminaries cluster into configurations.

These conclusions, however, come from aggregated data. The researchers counted the number of achievers appearing in consecutive generations; they then calculated how much the count in one generation correlated with that in the preceding generation. Nevertheless, if we systematically study information drawn from many biographical entries, complementary findings appear. Eminent personalities were usually exposed, very early in life, to illustrious predecessors. Even better, the availability of many appropriate models in childhood and adolescence often accelerates the emergence of precocious creativity. Mozart is a good example: His father made sure that young Wolfgang met the main composers of the day, such as K. P. E. Bach and Joseph Haydn. These were the giants on whose shoulders Mozart could stand. And few composers were more precocious than he!

Even so, we must recognize that models can also have a stifling effect on achievement. As art critic Clive Bell warned, "genius-worship is the infallible sign of an uncreative age." Outstanding predecessors may appear such paragons of perfection that their followers are intimidated rather than inspired. Although Johannes Brahms began writing his first symphony before his 30th year, it took him years to complete it. Even after finishing the first movement, he lamented, "I will never write a symphony." The completed product did not emerge until he was 43 years old, an age at which Beethoven had already penned his first eight symphonies. The deceased Beethoven was indeed the culprit. Brahms once complained: "You will never know how the likes of us feel when we hear the tramp of a giant like Beethoven behind us." Not surprisingly, when Brahms finally offered his first symphony to the world, the music critic Hans von Bülow hailed it as Beethoven's *Tenth* Symphony. The imitations were sometimes obvious. The main theme in the last movement of the Brahms First Symphony echoes the "Ode to Joy" theme in the last movement of Beethoven's Ninth Symphony! Fortunately for Brahms, he eventually got out from underneath the master's heavy hand. Otherwise he would not have become, as von Bülow put it, one of the "three B's" of classical music, with Bach and Beethoven.

Somehow, developing talents must assimilate models without becoming enslaved or silenced by them. Those snared by their models simply regurgitate what they have feasted on. Those who are truly nourished by these banquets actually digest the nutrients, converting them into muscle and nerve. With that added strength, the emulator moves forward. "Immature poets imitate; mature poets steal; bad poets deface what they take, and good poets make it into something better, or at least something different," said T.S. Eliot.

Why does one talent take the path to enervating imitation, while another pursues the high road to invigorating emulation? Investigations have teased out two conditions that can make famous models gifts rather than curses.

First, models are more conducive to personal development if an aspirant admires more than one. Those who focus all their adulation on a single paragon often end up as blind imitators. Few individuals make an impression on posterity simply by aping one illustrious predecessor. But when developing youths multiply the sources of inspiration, they enhance the diversity of influences; this raises the odds that they can avoid debilitating imitation. They can then advance beyond their models. For example, the dominating presence of Sir Isaac Newton most likely squelched creative mathematics in Great Britain for over a century. Mathematicians on the European continent, in contrast, had many more first-rate intellects to respect beyond Newton, such as Leibniz and the Bernoulli family. This enabled French, German, and Italian creators to carry higher mathematics much further. Only when British mathematicians began looking on the other side of the English Channel for models were they able to catch up with the advances that had left them behind.

Second, the ambitious youth can emulate predecessors who are more remote in cultural or historical circumstances. It is easier to mimic forerunners who made their mark under a comparable milieu. In comparison, exemplars who worked in a *Zeitgeist* more remote cannot be simply copied, because the template must be adjusted to new conditions. For instance, a primary agent of the artistic Renaissance was the revived appreciation of Greco-Roman art. This enabled artists to break away from the stranglehold of the Byzantine and Gothic traditions. Because Renaissance artists were Christians, not pagans, they could not adopt ancient techniques and standards wholesale. Initially, the subject matter had to be drawn from the Old and New Testaments, not Hesiod or Ovid. This provided the stimulating challenge that culminated in a Michelangelo. The results were a Moses enthroned like Zeus, a David as erect as Apollo—all without the slightest glimmer of mere replication.

These two considerations can enter a tradeoff relationship. Those with talent who must admire near contemporaries should emulate many rather than few. However, if they select models further removed from them in space and time, then fewer paragons can be tolerated without loss. There is thus some truth to Voltaire's words, "Originality is nothing but judicious imitation." People who entertain ambitions in the realm of historic greatness must painstakingly pick their paragons.

Idea to Idea

We must note a final feature of generation-to-generation modeling. The spotlight thus far has been pointed at how models affect the amount and weight of creativity in the next generation. Yet the key figures in one generation can strongly shape the specific *content* of the following generation's activity. This is apparent in intellectual history. Most obvious is the manner in which the philosophical commitments of one generation continue in the next generation of thinkers. For example, the number of epistemologists who argue for empiricism relates positively to the number who take the same stance two decades later. The same clustering occurs for virtually all intellectual positions, such as rationalism, mysticism, idealism, materialism, determinism, individualism, and utilitarian ethics.

This apparent inertia in the flow of ideas is not so potent, however, as to stifle change in philosophical traditions. In fact, the beliefs of one generation can influence the next generation's beliefs in a more negative way. For instance, a generation of thinkers who favor extreme empiricism often antedates a generation in which thinkers espouse skepticism. Once intellectuals start believing that all human knowledge comes from the sense organs, the next step in the history of ideas is to voice doubts about whether human beings can really know anything at all about the reality beyond the senses. Hence, rather than endorse the opinions of immediate predecessors, the new generation can decide to introduce contrary viewpoints. This process is akin to the Hegelian notion of thesis and antithesis.

If the new generation can offer antitheses to the preoccupations of their models, then the alternatives can really open up. There are more ways to reject an idea than to endorse it. Sometimes in the history of ideas, the statement of antitheses to earlier theses causes the intellectual community to undergo philosophical polarization. For example, let us suppose a given generation of philosophers emphatically argues for a Sensate system of beliefs (see Chapter 9). Specifically, let's say that these thinkers propose the following: Human beings can know only what their senses tell them. The primary basis of existence is matter rather than spirit. Because the world is in constant flux, nothing is stable or trustworthy. Even abstract ideas are merely arbitrary names for things, without roots in reality itself. Only individuals have any existential reality, since a higher sense of community is absent. All individuals lack freedom of choice. Instead, they are driven by fate or the inexorable laws of nature. Absolute moral principles have no force. Ethical decisions are merely driven by the pursuit of pleasure and the avoidance of pain.

What personal philosophy would *you* develop if you were exposed to this cluster of ideas as a youth? If your reaction recapitulates what has repeatedly happened in the history of Western philosophy, you can go in two opposing directions. On the one hand, you can advocate a total skepticism toward everything. Your reply to a pessimistic world view is a *Weltanschauung* even more depressing. You doubt the truth of all before you. On the other hand, you can counter pessimism with optimism: You can take up "fideism." As a fideist, you express an emphatic belief in God or other spiritual reality. You accept free will and higher moral values. Yet these beliefs do not reflect a firm conviction that derives from reason and evidence; instead, your creed stems from a desperate need to believe. Fideists must act *as if* God exists, *as if* they control their lives—all in a gigantic "leap of faith."

We don't know why some people opt for skepticism while others choose fideism. But it remains a curiosity of history that models can cause such a bifurcation in beliefs. This probably happens when the opinions of the models create a profound malaise in the intellects of the emergent generation.

Mentors to Greatness

A more personal touch may enhance the benefits of modeling. Rather than admire at a distance, a youth may become a student, pupil, apprentice, or disciple under one or more distinguished predecessors. Such a predecessor then becomes a teacher, master, or mentor. We have ample evidence that this special social interaction can have a most desirable impact on creative development. A study of Nobel laureates found that more than 50% had served an apprenticeship under at least one other recipient of that honor. Because the new laureates would function in turn as mentors for the next generation of scientific talent, the ultimate outcome is often an extensive "family pedigree" of mentor–apprentice relationships. Figure 13.1 depicts one such lineage, which began with Lord Rayleigh. It is clear in this graph that J. J. Thomson, Rutherford, Born, and Bohr were especially prolific in the production of outstanding scientists.

We can find comparable mentoring effects beyond the physical sciences, including psychology. Mentoring is a major contributor to success in the arts as well. In general, if a person has studied under a distinguished mentor, this raises the odds that the pupil also will attain distinction. Those who work directly under illustrious predecessors often launch their careers earlier and exhibit a more prolific level of output for the rest of their lives. Moreover, the teacher–pupil relationship is a two-way street. Having many intellectual offspring who are extraordinary is a good way of securing a place in the history books. At times, being a mentor is the mentor's main claim to fame. Nadia Boulanger was once a competent composer, but her posthumous reputation was assured by the esteemed students she produced. Her former pupils became some of the key composers of the 20th century. Besides the dozen-plus Americans listed in Chapter 6, she cultivated the creativity of Lennox Berkeley, Jean Français, Igor Markevitch, and Darius Milhaud.

In scrutinizing the effects of models, we have seen that the influence is not always salutary. Adulation of paragons can elicit an imitativeness destructive of later achievement. The same ambivalence holds for mentoring: A disciple must master all that's good in the mentor's craft without becoming subservient to the mentor's achievements. Again, as in the case of modeling, certain conditions help determine whether the net impact of mentoring will be positive or negative. Three circumstances deserve special mention:

1. Prospective pupils should draw upon many mentors rather than just one. The same advice has been given in the choice of models, and for the same

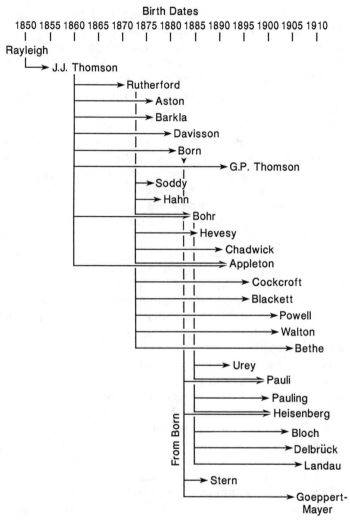

FIGURE 13.1. Mentor–student relationships among some Nobel laureates in physics.

reason. With many mentors on which to base their personal growth, talented youths are less likely to follow the suicidal path toward mere replication. Instead, they will be obliged to synthesize the diversity represented by their training. A synthesis of techniques or styles or ideas may be a pupil's key to fame.

  2. Disciples should work under those who are at the peak of their career. The plurality of Nobel laureates, for example, studied under mentors who were in their late 30s or early 40s. Mentors at their career peaks are more prolific, and thus their profuse activity introduces an atmosphere of ideational richness. New ideas are buzzing about with stimulating excitement. In contrast, mentors in the last stage of their careers may be working on far fewer projects, with less exhilarating effects on youthful apprentices. In addition, mentors in their prime are less likely to have succumbed to Planck's principle (see Chapter 7). They will be more accepting of the rash ideas of enthusiastic youths. So ideational richness will accompany ideational openness.

3. Aspirants should have a strong talent. A pupil who has unperturbable self-assurance and a strong sense of direction, coupled with an immense capacity for pursuing his or her own idiosyncratic ideas, is less likely to buckle under a mentor's grip. Those with lesser skills have more to fear. George Gershwin once made an observation about musical schooling that is applicable here: "Many people say that too much study kills spontaneity in music, but although study may kill a small talent, it must develop a big one. In other words, if study kills a musical endowment, that endowment deserves to be killed."

If pupils possess a prodigious gift, this sometimes means that they must rebel against the impositions of the more formidable class of mentors. When the American James McKeen Cattell went to Germany to study under Wilhelm Wundt, the very "father of psychology," Cattell found that the Herr Professor would not permit experiments on individual differences in his laboratory. Wundt was also accustomed to assign the dissertation topics for his graduate students. Rather than turn away from the inquiries that would later make Cattell famous, Cattell simply conducted the necessary experiments in his own apartment. He would not let Wundt kill his talent.

We should not overlook another aspect of mentoring: A mentor can be a parent besides. This possibility is implicit in Figure 13.1; G. P. Thomson was the son of J. J. Thomson. Nor is the effect confined to father–son pairs. The chip-off-the-old-block effect also holds for Nobel laureate Irène Joliot-Curie, the daughter of two laureates, Marie and Pierre Curie. But because of Pierre's tragic death in a street accident, it was Marie who played the principal mentoring role.

The very existence of parent–child mentoring raises a new issue in the debate between Kroeber's culture configurations and Galton's hereditary genius. Galton's family pedigrees could merely represent a special case of Kroeber's clusters of genius. If emulation of luminaries fuels the path to eminence, this will generate many mentor–apprentice pairs. A subset of these will just happen to have the same surnames. After all, as mentors go, parents are exceedingly convenient. Therefore, social learning theory rather than behavior genetics may provide the more thorough account of the pedigrees. The old nature–nurture issue raises its troublesome head once more.

Affiliation, Attraction, and Interaction

In some ways, the influence of models and mentors on greatness cannot count as a full-fledged social-psychological process. The impact is perhaps more developmental than social. Although an ambitious youth may become attached to paragons and masters, he or she eventually assimilates the expertise, and then moves to the realm of adulthood self-actualization. Modeling and mentoring then cease to exist as social factors in grown-up geniuses. The latter are free to become loners and isolates. Wordsworth said that Newton was "a mind forever/ Voyaging through strange seas of thought alone." If so, social psychology may provide no useful explanatory principles, once we look at actual accomplishments.

For the sociologically disposed, this conclusion is simply unacceptable. For example, the sociology of science places much emphasis on the role played by the scientific community in the making of knowledge. Scientists are not just a bunch of nerds sequestered in isolated cubicles. They become colleagues and associates; they form collaborations; they enter competitive rivalries and disputes. Even what counts as a "discovery" is subject to negotiation and arbitration by the "invisible college" of fellow scientists. For the sociologist, the lone genius is a myth nurtured by the reductionist propaganda of the psychologist.

Newton himself illustrates this point. Paranoid recluse though he was, he could not divorce himself from the scientists of his time. Besides "standing on the shoulders" of dozens of distinguished predecessors, he rubbed shoulders with dozens of eminent contemporaries. These included rivals and competitors, correspondents and colleagues, and even a handful of intimates. Among these professional associates were celebrities such as Jean Bernoulli, Bradley, DeMoivre, Flamsteed, Halley, Hooke, Leibniz, Locke, MacLaurin, Römer, Wallis, and Wren. Nor were these social interactions merely peripheral irritations in Newton's solitary career. Edmund Halley, for example, largely deserves the credit for getting Newton's monumental *Principia* into print.

Moreover, we can advance beyond anecdote. There is evidence that the society a genius keeps can shape adulthood triumphs.

Colleagues, Collaborators, and Rivals

When we probe the lives of notables in almost any area of historic achievement, it soon becomes apparent that most are surrounded by many other contemporaries, great and not so great. Thus, one study examined 10,160 eminent creators, leaders, and celebrities in the history of Chinese civilization. Those periods that produced the most first-class exemplars of creativity or leadership were those that produced the most also-rans in the same domain. This congruence held for mathematicians, scientists, religious leaders, philosophers, essayists, novelists, dramatists, poets, sculptors, architects, and artisans, as well as for famous officials, soldiers, rebels, assassins, royalty, eunuchs, scholars, and occultists. A master poet like Li Bo, for example, was enveloped by dozens of minor literary talents of the Tang dynasty.

This contemporaneous clustering of supernova, stars, planets, comets, and asteroids is characteristic of Western civilization as well. In fact, I have already suggested as much in introducing the Price law in Chapter 5. Price's original way of phrasing this principle was that "the total number of scientists goes up as the square, more or less, of the number of good ones." By a "good scientist" he meant someone who makes enormous contributions to scientific knowledge. Hence, as a scientific enterprise grows, the number of also-rans actually increases at a faster rate than the number of all-time greats. This informs us that during Golden Ages, the top-notch intellects not only are encircled by other top-notch intellects, but also find themselves batting at swarms of cultural gnats.

We already know that the Price law applies to domains besides science, including artistic endeavors. The same principle is germane to leadership as well. Shakespeare gave an example in *Julius Caesar*, a play that describes an era full of master politicians. Rome was the home of Pompey the Great, Cicero, Marcus Antonius (Mark Antony), Octavius, and many others, in addition to the title character. All scrambled for slices of the ever-expanding imperial pie. Among the gnats were the conspirators who would soon butcher Caesar in the Senate. In the play, one of the aspiring tyrannicides, Cassius, addresses Brutus in lines of memorable envy:

> Why, man, he doth bestride the narrow world
> Like a Colossus, and we petty men
> Walk under his huge legs and peep about
> To find ourselves dishonourable graves.

So Cassius, Casca, Cinna, Trebonius, Ligarius, and Marcus and Decius Brutus took their places in history by cutting down the Colossus whose standing in those same annals was already assured.

This example raises a critical issue. It's one matter to say that the big, the little, and the middling huddle together in historical time. It's another matter to comprehend the status of the relationships. Undoubtedly, at times the interactions can be hostile. Yet the social experiences also may be more collaborative. Julius Caesar was not without allies, and eventually these friends were to cause the deaths of the conspirators. Hence, to understand better what happens, we must again move from the aggregate level to the more one-on-one level. What kind of dyadic relationships foster success? Two studies offer responses.

The first looked at the lives of 772 great and not-so-great artists in Western civilization. These painters and sculptors included names as gigantic as Michelangelo, and as paltry as Hendrick Bloemaert. The relationships each artist entered into with fellow artists were determined. Some of these interactions involved predecessors and successors, but others entailed contemporaries— rivals, collaborators, associates, and copupils. The frequency of such professional connections correlated positively with an artist's posthumous acclaim. Antagonistic relationships were almost as conducive to long-term success as were cooperative relationships. Even a mind like Michelangelo's could apparently benefit by sometimes hostile rivalries with Leonardo, Raphael, and even lesser artists.

The second study scrutinized the lives of 2,026 scientists and inventors. Again the range in eminence was wide, from towering monuments like Isaac Newton down to thin bricks like William Higgins. Once more a host of relationships were assessed, and comparable results emerged: The more salient the individual in the history of science and technology, the larger the number of social relationships he or she could claim. The most illustrious contributors had more associates, collaborators, and other positive professional contacts. They also had more rivals and competitors. And it was not just posthumous reputation that correlated with having a rich collection of relationships. Even when two scientists equal in ultimate fame were compared, the one with more relationships (both positive and negative) also exhibited more lifetime productivity. Thus, we are not speaking of some bias in the perceptions of posterity; those whose names were most often connected with other names were behaviorally different besides. Those with more connections, even antagonistic ones, were more prolific in the offering of original ideas.

To sum up, more than some diffuse social ambience is responsible for putting the leviathans and the minnows in the same tank. Actual social interactions must be taking place as well. Moreover, for both artists and scientists, the quantity of interactions rather than their quality seems crucial. For those who wish to achieve greatness, the number of professional contacts appears more critical than the relative fame of those contacts. For example, as long as a genius takes a rival seriously, that competitor can push the genius to greater heights—even though later generations may wonder about why the behemoth fussed so much about the small fry. The once hidden brilliance of Descartes was released by a fortuitous public debate with the now obscure Chandoux. Furthermore, we have reason to believe that this social influence operates on the great individuals' behavior. Those affected actually do more to earn their posthumous reputations. Three processes might induce these results: social facilitation, social comparison, and social stimulation.

Excitement?: Social Facilitation

Sometimes people will perform better when there are other people around. The others may be either members of an audience or a set of fellow actors. For example, according to a classic 1898 study of the bicycle records kept by the Racing Board of the League of American Wheelmen, cyclists raced faster when competing than when racing alone. Can this "social facilitation effect" account for the positive impact of contemporaries on creative performance? Probably not. The presence of others is a benefit only when people are performing a well-learned and often-practiced behavior. Riding a bicycle, lifting weights, and other activities in sports are examples. Anyone who has played in competitive sports knows how often an athlete must practice, and practice, and practice. Hence, athletic achievements are boosted by spectators and competitors. In contrast, being surrounded by an audience or by fellow actors will produce a "social interference effect" if the performance is not adequately rehearsed. The presence of others appears to strengthen the enactment of high-probability behaviors while weakening the realization of low-probability behaviors.

Yet, as noted in Chapter 4, the creative process itself requires an extensive infusion of low-probability mental operations. Remote associations, intuitive ideas, unusual visual imagery, and other features of creative thought are not operations that can be made habitual. Hence, we would expect the most original ideas to emerge from moments of solitude. Only at a later stage, when the new conception undergoes more routine verification and elaboration, may we expect social facilitation effects to take place. Albert Einstein was not expressing a freakish opinion when he professed that his own work style did not lend itself to social interaction. "I am a horse for a single harness, not cut out for tandem or teamwork," he said, "for well I know that in order to attain any definite goal, it is imperative that *one* person should do the thinking and commanding."

Endorsement?: Social Comparison

If creators do not socialize to take advantage of social facilitation effects, then we must look elsewhere for an explanation. In the sciences, many important ideas emerge from collaborative projects. This is notably the case in "big science"—domains such as high-energy physics and biomedical research. For some disciplines, in fact, studies conducted by multiple investigators are actually more influential than those introduced by single investigators. So some benefits must accrue from collaboration.

One interpretation is that individuals must engage in the process of "social comparison." This process occurs whenever someone feels uncertain about some personal opinion or ability. He or she then looks to similar others to obtain usable feedback. This process may be unusually important in the sciences, where the costs of error are most severe. No respectable scientist wishes to risk his or her reputation by offering mistaken ideas to the scientific community. Accordingly, the more collaborators who are working on a project, the more cross-checks against potentially embarrassing mistakes. To be sure, these safeguards may weed out revolutionary innovations as well. If Einstein had had to become a "team player" from the onset of his career, he might not have come up with his iconoclastic theories. Even so, science is a game whose players are risk-adverse. Scientists worry more about sins of commission than about sins of omission.

A more profound form of social comparison operates in the arts. An artistic creation is itself a form of self-expression. As such, we may view an art work as a direct act of social comparison. The artist may be filled with emotional turmoil, plagued with existential angst, or obsessed by some highly personal feeling or image. Whatever the specific source of the uncertainty, the artist may need to share that experience with others to validate its reality. If so, without other artists working in the same expressive medium, the social comparison function may vanish altogether. Poet W. H. Auden hinted at this dependence:

> The ideal audience the poet imagines consists of the beautiful who go to bed with him, the powerful who invite him to dinner and tell him secrets of state, and his fellow-poets. The actual audience he gets consists of myopic schoolteachers, pimply young men who eat in cafeterias, and his fellow-poets. This means that, in fact, he writes for his fellow-poets.

I believe this helps us understand better the role of social context in creative genius. Great creators need an audience of appreciators. If it were otherwise, they could retreat to caves and there enter an autistic world of futile artistic muttering. But social feedback goes with the business. By successfully "wowing" others with their aesthetic impressions, artists receive social confirmation. Still, artists realize that their aesthetic experiences are too intimate and too profound to impress widely. Only a select group can fully fathom that inner world. That elite consists of fellow artists who are best positioned to nod their heads in assent or shed some tears in sympathy. Mass judgment and popular acclaim may not be spurned, naturally; someone has to help pay the bills. Yet even the most deafening applause of the public may carry less force than a single sigh from a kindred spirit.

This would explicate the gross features in the clustering of genius. Creators of all grades are prone to be contemporaries because all creators, great and small, need an appreciative elite who are targets of self-expressive social comparisons. All participants inspire each other to attain ever more venturesome heights of self-expression. Each probes the limits of self-knowledge and technique. The also-rans and nonentities, therefore, are by no means irrelevant to the collective enterprise. All are comrades in arms.

In addition, this process may explain some of the finer aspects of the phenomenon as well. Take Japanese literature as an example. Some of the greatest creators in this tradition were women: Lady Murasaki, Sei Shōnagon, Lady Komachi, and dozens more. Like geniuses of other types, however, these female luminaries formed configurations, such as the grouping during the Heian period. What is interesting is how the women clustered. Literary females did not necessarily appear when Japanese society opened up to female achievement in general. It was not a matter of generic opportunities. Instead, literary females emerged when literary activity among the males underwent a conspicuous rebirth. The female participants formed part of a more inclusive Golden Age in literary achievements. Thus, the women depended on an audience distinguished by endeavor rather than by gender. The great female writers composed for their fellow writers more than for nonwriters of their own sex.

Incitement?: Social Stimulation

We may not have yet placed our finger on the most critical process. The most crucial advantage of an abundance of similar minds may be the intellectual stimulation it affords. Without the influx of creative ideas from others in the field, the intellect will eventually run dry. As Sir Joshua Reynolds counseled in his *Discourses on Art,*

> The greatest natural genius cannot subsist on its own stock: he who resolves never to ransack any mind but his own, will be soon reduced, from mere barrenness, to the poorest of all imitations; he will be obliged to imitate himself, and to repeat what he has before often repeated. When we know the subject designed by such men, it will never be difficult to guess what kind of work is to be produced.

The implication is that a Golden Age represents a free exchange of advanced ideas among a sizable collectivity of creators. The intercourse allows all participants to rejuvenate their creative potential constantly—much as sexual intercourse revitalizes the gene pool with new genetic combinations.

This third interpretation can account for some key features of the phenomenon. Consider the following four implications of social stimulation:

1. It explains why a Golden Age can consist of contemporaries of widely varying degrees of merit. Not only do the lesser figures gain inspiration from the great names of their day, but the impetus can work in the opposite direction as well. Anyone who has read the biographies of illustrious creators will often come across the names of less renowned contemporaries to whom subjects are indebted. Debussy felt the impact of Satie; Picasso's career cannot be severed from that of Braque. The disparities can even be far greater than this. For a time, Sigmund Freud was intellectually dependent on a crank like Wilhelm Fliess.

2. It explains the co-occurrence of men and women when creativity revives in a particular field. Intellectual and aesthetic stimulation need not be gender-bound. A man may not confess a feminine inspiration, yet the influence will be there nonetheless.

3. It explains why profitable rehabilitation may come from both rivals and allies. Whatever the reluctance to admit openly the impact of competitors, the incitement will still be there. How many times has it happened that one luminary vigorously attacked the ideas of some opponent, only to sneak those very ideas into his or her own work when no one was looking?

4. It explains why lifetime productivity is associated with the number of disciplinary contacts. Besides producing more, those embedded in a rich mesh of creators also have longer careers as well. Geniuses who live in a world boiling over with creativity may resuscitate their creative potential faster than they can use it up. So they may never descend to that poignant self-imitation that Reynolds warned against.

Social stimulation has one final advantage over many alternative interpretations: It remains consistent with the notion that creative geniuses are reclusive people. Luminaries don't have to be extroverts to soak up the best of their milieu. They can dip in and out at will, as when Van Gogh briefly shared a room with Gauguin. By a cycle of withdrawal and return, they extract new inspiration from the next round of quasi-gregarious activity, and then ensconce themselves in some cell safe from the distractions of society, high or low. This recurrent pattern resolves the paradox inherent in saying that introverts require social connections to maximize their creativity.

Intimates

The social relationships examined above are all professional. Yet we must also note that associations of a more intimate nature have a special place in the pursuit of a successful career. In the visual arts, for example, there exists a correlation between how famous an artist becomes and how many fellow artists he or she can claim as friends. A parallel pattern holds in the sciences. Even Sir Isaac Newton, despite his misanthropy, entered into close relationships (albeit often transient) with James Bradley, Abraham DeMoivre, David Gregory, Edmund Halley, John Locke, Brook Taylor, and Christopher Wren. He was not an island unto himself.

These conclusions were drawn from studies of 772 painters and sculptors and 2,026 scientists and inventors. Lamentably, much less research has been conducted on how personal relationships spur on exceptional leadership in politics, war, business, or religion. This near-absence is deplorable, because what little evidence we do have suggests that interpersonal relations among leaders can have historic reverberations. For instance, one study revealed that a falling out between Fidel Castro and Che Guevara may have preceded the latter's decision to leave Cuba in the summer of 1965. Despite official statements to the contrary, content analysis deciphered a decline in Castro's warm feelings toward his one-time intimate long before Guevara's fateful move to lead a new revolution in Bolivia.

The connection between intimacy and leadership is not the only gaping hole in our knowledge. We also know too little about the impact of the most intimate relationships of all. Sexual relations are the impulse behind much history. Just look at Marcus Antonius and Cleopatra, Abelard and Héloïse, Eleanor and Franklin Roosevelt, Marie and Pierre Curie, Simone de Beauvoir and Jean-Paul Sartre, Georgia O'Keeffe and Alfred Stieglitz, and (perhaps) Anaïs Nin and Henry Miller. In these examples we are speaking of near-equals. In other instances, one member of the pair lurks in the background but exerts an impressive influence nonetheless. Thus, we can cite the "woman-behind-the-man" phenomenon. Take Mary Todd and Abraham Lincoln, Marie-Anne and Antoine Lavoisier, and, most recently, Nancy and Ronald Reagan. Some women even inspired more than one man. Cosima Liszt (Hans von Bülow and Richard Wagner), Alma Schindler Mahler (Gustav Mahler, Franz Werfel, and Walter Gropius), and Lou Andreas-Salomé (Friedrich Nietzsche and Rainer Maria Rilke) may offer good examples. Cases like these often authenticate James M. Barrie's remark, "Every man who is high up loves to think that he has done it all himself; and the wife smiles, and lets it go at that."

Nevertheless, we must not overlook the reverse inspiration, a "man-behind-the-woman" phenomenon. Because of the severe handicaps that talented females must face in a male-dominated society, the encouragement and support of a close male companion can sometimes ease a woman's path to eminence. Now we can conjure up cases in which we might consider the female the more capable of the pair: Virginia and Leonard Woolf, Dorothy Richardson and Alan Odle, Enid Bagnold and Sir Roderick Jones, Käthe and Karl Kollwitz, Hélène and Felix Deutsch, Helen Hayes and Charles MacArthur. Furthermore, now that homosexual relationships are out in the open, we must also acknowledge the "man-behind-the-man" and the "woman-behind-the-woman" phenomena. Gertrude Stein and Alice B. Toklas may offer the best example among lesbians. Among gay men, W. H. Auden, Christopher Isherwood, and Francis Bacon (the artist) received support from live-in others of the same sex.

Few empirical inquiries directly address this fascinating issue. One investigation traced the lives of the women in Terman's sample of childhood geniuses, and found many who assumed the role of the woman behind the man. Another analysis looked at first ladies in the White House; it found that presidents' wives who became their spouses' political partners were most likely to ensure a prominent place in history for themselves and their husbands. But, certainly, more research must be done. We must learn in what ways *the* significant other can leave a mark on *that* Significant Other who leaves a mark on history.

Group Dynamics

In discussing the "person-behind-the-VIP" phenomenon, we must not ignore a undeniable difficulty. Many individuals associated with the rich and famous may enjoy an acclaim that is more parasitic than symbiotic. These persons gain celebrity status by linking themselves with bona fide luminaries, but they may make little direct contribution to the success of those persons on which their own reputations depend. Examples include all those people who have written best-selling revelations about some parent or lover, deceased or living. Who would even have read a book by Patti Davis, were her parents not named Nancy and Ronald Reagan? In a similar vein, where would Michael Chaplin be without his father, Charlie; Mary de Rachewiltz without her father, Ezra Pound; Svetlana Alliluyeva without her father, Stalin; or Nadezhda Krupskaya without her husband, Lenin? Who would have heard of Jessica Hahn without her tryst with evangelist Jim Bakker, or Donna Rice without her rendezvous with Gary

Hart? One study of the White House occupants found that the reputations of first ladies gained more from association with distinguished men in the Oval Office than presidents' reputations gained by association with distinguished first ladies.

Social psychologists have a cute term for this business: "BIRGing," for "Basking in Reflected Glory." It's a commonplace way of making a favorable impression on others as well as boosting our own egos. Many of us will engage in "name dropping" or relate stories about "a friend who has a cousin who once met" some VIP. Yet BIRGing assumes another form, which takes us to the subject of this part of the chapter. Often we BIRG by identifying with some successful group—even though we have made no direct contribution to the group's success. For example, in one study researchers watched BIRGing in action in large-enrollment courses in introductory psychology. The study took place on seven university campuses—Arizona State, Louisiana State, Notre Dame, Michigan, Pittsburgh, Ohio State, and Southern California. On the Monday after the Saturday football game, the investigators simply monitored the clothing worn by the students. If the class came after a big win, students were more likely to don some article that proclaimed their identification with the school, such as a sweatshirt emblazoned with "University of . . ." Indeed, the bigger the margin of victory, the more such emblems and identifications filled the lecture hall. As far as personal self-esteem is concerned, *"our* team's victory Saturday night" marks a big event that elicits an obvious response in what apparel students yank out of the closet. When the sales of American flags went up after the U.S. victory in the Persian Gulf War, BIRGing adopted the guise of patriotism rather than school spirit.

BIRGing implies that personal identity can become submerged under group identity. Individuals may lose themselves in other ways as well. Let's look at four examples: social loafing, the home-court advantage, decision-making pathology, and contagion and rumor.

Loafing on the Job

Imagine that 12 members of a college fraternity are practicing for a tug-of-war contest. To practice, they tie a thick rope to a dynometer that measures the amount of force applied by the pulling agents. The dozen brothers on the team have all been pretested and shown to be equally strong. Now, as part of the drill, they begin to pull one by one on the rope, watching the dynometer as they increase the number of pullers. One brother on the rope, and the meter reads 100 pounds. Yet two brothers will pull a bit less than 200 pounds, three much less than 300 pounds, four far less than 400 pounds, and so on. The whole is less than the sum of its parts. This is called the "Ringlemann effect."

This effect happens for two main reasons. The first is "coordination loss." Because it's hard to coordinate all the separate pullers, one brother may be adjusting his grip on the rope and another consolidating his footing in the grass at the very instant that the remaining 10 are yanking at the max. So they exert only 1,000 pounds' effort. The need for coordination is one reason why crew teams drag along otherwise free-riding coxswains.

The second factor is more interesting: "social loafing." This is similar to the diffusion-of-responsibility concept discussed in Chapter 11. Because the tug-of-war entails a collective effort, no one person is accountable for victory or defeat. The responsibility for gaining or losing ground in the competition is distributed equally among all dozen teammates. This means that at any one moment a particular player can feel free to relax without the embarrassment of disclosure. The upshot is also the Ringelmann effect.

Now tug-of-war may be a common Greek contest, but it's not an Olympic event. Can we find an example in the domain of historic behavior? Yes, though the illustration comes from an unlikely quarter: the songs produced by the most celebrated rock group in the history of popular culture. In 1966 John Lennon raised an uproar when he boasted, "We're more popular than Jesus Christ now. I don't know which will go first. Rock and roll or Christianity." We can't say either, but the astronomical success of the Beatles is unquestionable. A whole generation of teenagers throughout the world grew up with their lyrics, antics, and albums. Even today—after the group split up, Lennon was killed, Paul McCartney composed a classical *Liverpool Oratorio,* and Ringo Starr ended up as a miniature conductor on a children's TV show—their popularity remains. Diluted arrangements of their melodies have even attained the status of elevator music in office buildings.

This body of creative products offers a unique opportunity to check for social loafing. First, 162 of the Beatles' songs were written by John Lennon and Paul McCartney, either individually or as a song-writing team. Of these, Lennon wrote 70 and McCartney 45; the remaining 47 were collaborative efforts. This separation by itself would not help us, were it not for a second key fact: Lennon and McCartney began working together when each was 16 years old. They then made a compact that their songs would come out as group products, no matter who actually created a piece. Only after 1967, when the Beatles began to show signs of disintegration, was the authorship of new songs labeled or implied. When the group finally broke up, Lennon revealed who wrote which of the earlier songs as well. Finally, not all the songs were hits. As pointed out many times, creativity is a hit-or-miss affair. Even the most magnificent genius makes mistakes or produces forgettable ideas. Lennon and McCartney were no exceptions. Only about a third of their total output attained the distinction of selection for placement on single records. In addition, even among those songs that made it as singles, only a subset soared to the top of the charts (according to *Billboard Magazine*). "Hey Jude" was a far bigger hit than "I'll Get You," for example.

Given these data, everything is set for us to discover the occurrence of social loafing. In the post-1967 years—when songs were overtly identified as either

Lennon, McCartney, or Lennon–McCartney creations—the cowritten songs were much less popular than the pieces that were individually written. The two song masters loafed. This difference did not appear in the earlier songs, and we wouldn't expect it to. Because all earlier songs came out under the collective Lennon–McCartney signature, there was no more reason to loaf on the jointly written efforts than on the individually conceived songs. Moreover, we cannot ascribe these quality differences to coordination loss. For the pre-1967 songs, the co-composed songs were actually *better* than those coming from a single hand. Therefore, social loafing may provide a reasonable explanation for the relative popularity of the songs in the Lennon–McCartney corpus.

Earlier, we have seen that coauthored scientific papers are often more influential than single-author papers. Why don't we see social loafing in science too? A basic contrast works here. In the creation of rock songs, Lennon and McCartney were near-equivalents. Each could produce the lyrics and melodies necessary for a hit song. Hence, collaboration was not essential to the product; each could loaf without fear of identification. In the creation of scientific journal articles, the conditions are often very different. Each author is usually a specialist in one specific domain or technique; each donates one piece to the overall product. No one investigator can carry out the whole project alone. Frequently, too, the individual contributions can be recognized by fellow professionals. Other experts know that scientist A provided sample X, that scientist B ran analysis Y, and that scientist C wrote grant proposal Z. These circumstances make it less likely that social loafing will undermine the quality of the collective product.

Still, social loafing can occur in the sciences. When it does, it assumes a pernicious form. For "big science" to succeed, each collaborator must trust his or her colleagues to exhibit the utmost in scientific conscientiousness. If one contributor does sloppy work, or even resorts to forging data, the whole group suffers. Many cases of fraud in science involve such multiple-investigator projects. Recently a Nobel laureate, David Baltimore, suffered the humiliation of having to retract published work, owing to the shenanigans of a junior collaborator. This event is much worse than creating a rock-and-roll song that never gets anywhere on the charts!

Home Games

In addition to their absence from the Olympic Games, tug-of-war contests are decidedly intramural. The winning fraternity during Greek Week seldom travels to another campus to compete for some conference championship. In serious sports, by comparison, such tours are an integral part of the season. Whether we are speaking of baseball, basketball, or any other sport, the season oscillates between two kinds of competitive matches: home games and road games. This raises the question about what kind of performance we can expect under the divergent circumstances. Is there a "home-field advantage," or does the edge go to the visiting team? The answers are complex.

On the one hand, the home-court advantage permeates sports. Even teams that do poorly all season will often have better than a 50–50 chance of winning on the home turf. In fact, as a predictor of victory on the playing field, the home-game advantage has about the same influence as the actual athletic prowess of the teams' players. This resource has many sources, but one involves the fans in the stands. The boos and jeers of the home-team spectators can undermine the performance of the visiting team. This is especially true for indoor games, like basketball.

On the other hand, there can be a home-field *dis*advantage, too. This may occur when the match is important, especially when the outcome will decide the championship. The expectations of the home fans can then become so high that the home team may "choke under pressure" and lose. For example, in the National Basketball Association playoffs between 1967 and 1982, the home team emerged victorious 7 times out of 10 in the first four games. But when it was necessary time to play a decisive seventh game, the team playing on its own court won only two times out of five. A similar pattern appears in American baseball. In the first two games of the World Series, the home team wins 60% of the time. Yet in the final game that decides the series, the visiting team comes out on top at about that same rate.

No matter which way the advantage goes, the very existence of home-team effects suggests that winning a championship is not decided by strictly athletic merits. Sometimes one team will climb to the top of the heap because of how the season's travel schedules happen to work out. These effects also show the wisdom of having championship games played on neutral turf, as is done in the Super Bowl of American professional football.

I have suggested in Chapter 11 that competitive team sports are behavioral metaphors for military combat between national armies. Should we then find home-turf effects in the world of warfare? The one study conducted on this question found a clear answer: On the battlefield, the invaders have the most going for them. Armies defending their homelands bask in fewer victories and suffer more crushing defeats.

We could interpret this disadvantage as a special kind of "choking under pressure," but I think another process may be working. Aggressive forces are normally led by commanders who assume the initiative on the battlefield. In contrast, those defending a nation are more often commanded by generals who adopt a more conservative, even complacent military strategy. The defenders may, ironically, believe too strongly in the myth of the home-court advantage! France's experience with the supposedly impregnable Maginot Line at the outset of World War II is a classic case. That's why the best defense really is a good offense. Israel's success in holding off her Arab neighbors is perhaps the best modern model. In the 1973 Yom Kippur War, the Israeli response to a surprise attack was to invade Egypt and Syria. Israel's southern forces crossed the Suez

Canal, while its northern forces got within 20 miles of Damascus. The two Arab powers then acceded to a cease-fire.

So home ground can often be a liability, whether the combat is real or metaphorical. And this peril is often strongest when the stakes are highest.

Stupid Decisions

If home defense is often disadvantageous in combat, then shouldn't aggressors usually win? If so, then something must be amiss. Anyone familiar with 20th-century military history would wonder why the parties that have started major wars have usually gone down in defeat. Germany went belly up in World Wars I and II. Japan lost all its conquests in the Pacific and its Chinese and Korean acquisitions besides. North Korea's incursion into South Korea was thrown back. Argentina's takeover of the Falkland (Malvinas) Islands became an unmitigated disaster for its naval forces. The Iraqi conquest and subsequent loss of Kuwait constitute only the most recent example.

However, on closer examination, these facts do not contradict the earlier conclusions. We must impose an elementary distinction between winning battles and winning wars. The first exploits immediate tactical advantages; the second builds upon enduring strategic assets. The aggressive powers mentioned above were quite successful in the early phases of their campaigns of conquest. It was only later that the tides turned against them. The reversals began because the strategic cards were stacked against the aggressors from the outset.

Admiral Yamamoto, a key architect of the Japanese attack on Pearl Harbor, understood this difference very well. He knew that Japan could succeed in crippling the naval forces anchored in Hawaii. But he also realized that Japan probably could not win a protracted war against the full economic and military might of the United States. If the Japanese decision makers had weighed all the evidence as carefully as Yamamoto had, the surprise attack might never have happened. Their failure to consider the repercussions completely and objectively meant that within only a few years, Japan found itself occupied by a foreign power for the first time in its history.

Why did those who made these big decisions commit such disastrous mistakes? If leaders were so smart, they would never launch wars they couldn't win. What makes these outcomes especially enigmatic is that the decisions were seldom made by a single mind. Instead, the calamitous decisions came from discussions that involved a nation's key decision makers. Although we might expect that even a bright person might have an occasional lapse in common sense, shouldn't others in the group have served as a check on cognitive neglect? If the separate perceptions and reservations of many decision makers were pooled, any rash idea should have suffered quick extinction in the deliberation room.

However, we have seen in connection with social loafing that the whole can sometimes be less than the sum of its parts. A cowritten Lennon–McCartney song may be inferior to one composed by either Lennon or McCartney separately. Could the same happen in group decision making? If we put a bunch of clever politicians in a chamber and gave them a problem to solve, could they come up with a solution worse than that produced by anyone of them working alone? If the answer is yes, then some group dynamic is the culprit.

Political psychologist Irving Janis proposed just such an explanatory process. He discovered the group dynamic by studying what went on in actual historic decisions. Some of these involved momentous miscalculations, such as President Kennedy's authorization of the Bay of Pigs invasion. To help tease out the pathology, Janis also investigated group decisions that came out right, such as President Kennedy's handling of the Cuban missile crisis about a year later. Table 13.2 lists some additional historic events that have been scrutinized by various researchers perplexed by decision-making pathologies.

On the basis of these detailed analyses, Janis proposed a process called "groupthink." Groupthink occurs when decision makers exhibit certain symptoms. For example, the group members will often display an "illusion of invulnerability," seeing themselves as incapable of error. They express belief in the moral superiority of their ingroup, and exhibit crudely drawn stereotypes about the enemy. Individual doubts about the wisdom of group proposals are subjected to self-censorship in the interest of maintaining the *esprit de corps*. Any dissenters from the majority position quickly face direct pressures to conform. This business of suppression is often taken up by self-appointed "mindguards." The group thereby attains a unanimity that is more apparent than real. On the surface everyone agrees with the group decision, while privately many decision makers entertain severe doubts.

These doubts are justified. When decision makers show the signs of groupthink, their judgments prove faulty on several counts. They do not com-

TABLE 13.2. Historic Events Scrutinized for Group Decision-Making Pathology

Date	Event	Groupthink
1914	French nonpreparation for German Schlieffen Plan	Yes
1938	Chamberlain's Munich Agreement with Hitler	Yes
1941	American nonpreparation for Pearl Harbor attack	Yes
1947	Marshall Plan for reconstruction of Western Europe	No
1950	UN invasion of North Korea	Yes
1961	Bay of Pigs invasion	Yes
1962	Cuban missile crisis	No
1964	Decision to escalate Vietnam War	Yes
1973	White House cover-up of Watergate break-in	Yes
1980	Failed attempt to rescue U.S. hostages in Iran	Yes
1986	Decision to launch the *Challenger* space shuttle	Yes
1986	Exchange of arms for hostages (Iran–Contra scandal)	Yes

pletely examine alternative courses of action, and they seldom reappraise rejected alternatives later in the deliberations. The members also do not fully explore the risks associated with the favored course; nor does the group develop effective contingency plans, should the recommended course of action fail to meet its objectives. The members do not scrutinize all the necessary data, and what information they do examine is processed in a biased fashion. The upshot is a group decision with low odds of success.

Janis also listed the settings that lead to groupthink. It is most likely to occur when the group is highly cohesive—so tight that it insulates itself from outside input. Groupthink is also inflated when the leader is highly directive, taking a strong stance at the outset of the group debates. Usually, too, the group does not arrange for the unbiased appraisal of all pros and cons for various potential actions. Finally, the group is often under external threat to decide quickly. As we have seen in Chapter 12, a threatening climate can make people more compliant to authority figures, such as the group leader. These conditions all help insure that group members become obsessed with attaining a consensus that fits the leader's views rather than reality.

Given these causes and effects, Janis offered several suggestions on how to combat groupthink. For instance, the leader should maintain complete impartiality as the discussion begins. The leader should invite the expression of objections and reservations. The group should, from time to time, invite outside experts to participate in the discussions; this will provide some "reality testing" for the favorite group proposals. The group should even identify at least one member to play the role of "devil's advocate" by challenging the wisdom of the group's ideas.

The groupthink hypothesis has inspired much discussion and research. Two follow-up studies are especially valuable because they introduced quantitative techniques in investigating the phenomenon. The first study applied content analysis to materials describing decisions that either were or were not contaminated by groupthink. When groupthink confounded the decision makers, the information processing displayed lower integrative complexity. The members were too simple-minded to arrive at good solutions to the crisis before them. The second study investigated the presidential decision-making process during 19 post-World War II international crises. Pertinent documents were scored for symptoms of decision-making pathology. The resulting decisions were also scored for the effectiveness of the outcomes. As predicted, the larger the number of symptoms of poor information processing, the higher the chance that the results would be adverse.

All this is not to say that the original conception of groupthink has survived unscathed. Recent studies have necessitated significant qualifications. For example, some circumstances are more conducive to groupthink than others are. Decision makers are most likely to succumb to this group pathology when (1) the leader actively promotes a particular proposal, (2) the group insulates itself from outside input, (3) there is strong pressure within the group to conform to the group's norms, and (4) the group membership is highly homogeneous in composition. Other conditions, such as external threat and time pressure, are less essential for the phenomenon to appear.

Nevertheless, even with these qualifications, Janis obviously pinpointed an important group dynamic. When groupthink occurs, decision makers will arrive at conclusions far beneath the intelligence of even the least capable member of the group. The result is very often a historic blooper.

Rumor Mills

Those old enough to recall any of the big events listed in Table 13.2 may remember a curious phenomenon. When something big happens—whether a disaster, riot, assassination, or invasion—rumors often run rampant. All sorts of false stories circulate. These stories become amplified well out of proportion to the truth. It's not just ideas that become distorted; people become emotional, and others catch the fear, terror, or anger as if it were some viral contagion. The mob mind and heart end up blowing the whole business out of proportion.

The group can even create bogus big events. In 1969, the word spread that Paul McCartney had died in an automobile accident, and that his place in the Beatles had been taken by an exact double. Despite McCartney's protest that reports of his death were very much exaggerated, it became a surprisingly difficult rumor to shake. As Hesiod said, "Gossip is mischievous, light, and easy to raise, but grievous to bear and hard to get rid of." So the oddest coincidences were twisted to conform to the gossip. Rumor mongers scanned album covers of *Sergeant Pepper* and *Abbey Road* for secret proofs of Paul's demise.

A more recent case had more serious repercussions. In 1980, some devout Christians concluded that the moon and stars logo for Procter and Gamble products was actually a secret emblem for devil worshipers. The man in the moon's bearded head supposedly held the numerals 666, which identify Satan in the Bible's book of Revelation. Even as late as 1991, the story went around that the president of Procter and Gamble had appeared on *The Phil Donahue Show*. Right there, before a national audience, the president had confessed that his corporation subsidized the Church of Satan. None of this was true!

These two rumors were relatively harmless. Unhappily, this is not always the case. Shakespeare warned how

> Rumour is a pipe
> Blown by surmises, jealousies, conjectures,
> And of so easy and so plain a stop
> That the blunt monster with uncounted heads,
> The still-discordant wavering multitude,
> Can play upon it.

A slight misunderstanding between client and broker can thereby explode into a frenzy of selling, which culminates in a stock-market crash. Even worse, an already exaggerated report can expand with retelling until it becomes the impulse behind an uncontrollable mob, bent on unrestrained violence. The civil disorders of the 1960s offer many examples. According to the official government analysis of these disorders,

> Rumors significantly aggravated tension and disorder in more than 65 percent of the disorders studied by the Commission. Sometimes, as in Tampa and New Haven, rumor served as the spark which turned an incident into a civil disorder. Elsewhere, notably Detroit and Newark, even where they were not precipitating or motivating factors, inflaming rumors made the job of police and community leaders far more difficult.

Given the deaths, injuries, and property damage that were the products of these disturbances, we are no longer dealing with quaint manifestations of ignorance. Rumors can make history, tragic history.

Social psychologists recognized the potential seriousness of this phenomenon early on. One of the earliest investigations is also one of the classics in the field: a book titled *The Invasion from Mars*. This volume came out in 1940, not long after Germany marched into Poland and not long before Japan attacked Pearl Harbor. But the study dealt with another military incursion altogether, and from another planet no less! This invasion happened on radio.

In 1938, Orson Welles produced a popular radio show called *The Mercury Theatre*. One day, for Halloween entertainment, Welles aired a dramatic adaptation of the science fiction novel *The War of the Worlds*, by H. G. Wells. For those who knew what was happening, this radio drama would threaten nothing greater than their imaginations. Yet for those who tuned in by chance, what they heard often made them fear for their lives. They listened to news bulletins that repeatedly interrupted, and eventually pre-empted, the "regularly scheduled programming." These bulletins informed the listener that the Martians had sent an invasion force against our planet. Using their death rays, these strange creatures were taking over the northeastern United States.

The most fascinating aspect of this broadcast is how its impact was amplified by rumor and contagion. People who were not listening to the radio were caught up by the onslaught of events. Here are four victims' reports:

1. "I was resting when an excited person phoned and told me to listen to the radio, that a big meteor had fallen. I was really worried."

2. "I don't think we would have gotten so excited if those couples hadn't come rushin' in the way they did. We are both very calm people, especially my husband, and if we had tuned in by ourselves I am sure we would have checked up on the program but they led me to believe it was any station."

3. "When I came out of the telephone booth, the store was filled with people in a rather high state of hysteria. I was already scared but this hysterical group convinced me further that something was wrong."

4. "My wife kept outwardly calm too. But there were so many people around that neither of us had a chance to collect our wits and see what was really the matter."

People dropped what they were doing, rushing home to have a few last moments with their loved ones before the Martians arrived. The world was coming to an end. The aliens would reign supreme on the earth. All this panic resulted from an utterly fictitious event! *The War of the Worlds* thereby became the most notorious broadcast in the history of radio.

Research has shown how rumor can disseminate with much less impetus than this. Word may spread about mass poisonings or bloody massacres, for example, without the slightest evidence. Even when this process follows upon the heels of a true calamity, the effects can be no less sensational. After an earthquake, rumors may spread that floods are on the way, or that a cyclone is coming, or that another earthquake has been forecast—or that all these things are soon to happen. A release of radioactive steam at a nuclear plant soon becomes a core meltdown. A minor disaster becomes an imminent catastrophe.

Fortunately, psychologists have made some headway in understanding the processes involved. This phenomenon requires a distinctive convergence of several different factors. The general population must be replete with anxious individuals. These anxious people should be plagued by uncertainty about the course of recent events, whether social or environmental. These uncertain, anxious individuals should also have some personal involvement in the rumor's message. Finally, these anxious, uncertain, involved persons should be credulous enough to swallow stories that are often clearly absurd. So there must be a confluence of anxiety, uncertainty, involvement, and credulity.

This distinct configuration explains why rumors are more commonplace during times of war, natural disaster, or economic instability. It accounts for why rumors usually concern what may be happening to *us* rather than to *them*. It also accommodates the fact that some people are especially susceptible to this monster. Sadly, this explanation also advises us that rumors will always be with us. As long as the world is a threatening place filled with gullible people, there will be plenty of psychological material for making mountains out of molehills. Hence, events often make impressions on the masses that are larger than reality warrants.

Leadership

In an individualistic concept of leadership, certain key people dramatically shape the world. Among the advocates of this view was the historian and essayist Thomas Carlyle. In his 1841 book *On Heroes, Hero-Worship, and the Heroic in History*, he proclaimed "The history of the World is but the Biography of great men." If we were to get a list of notable leaders and study their lives in detail, we would have thus mastered the history of the human race. Presumably, scrutiny of these great lives would also reveal what it takes to become a maker of political, military, economic, or religious events.

Indeed, much of this book has been devoted to this very task of decipherment. In chapter after chapter, we have examined the attributes of those individuals who attain greatness as leaders. These factors include genetic endowment; integrative complexity; power, achievement, and affiliation motives; developmental experiences such as birth order, orphanhood, education, and marginality; a leader's age and intelligence; and such assorted traits as dogmatism, explanatory style, dominance, extroversion, morality, and psychopathology. Obviously, because we are trying to develop a psychology of history, we cannot take the position that individuals are superfluous to the creation of big events. That would contradict the book's contents.

Nevertheless, we must admit that a psychology of history cannot exclude social factors altogether. Certainly few social psychologists believe that the individual's activities are miraculously isolated from the impact of situational forces. So let us look at how these contextual factors affect the expression of leadership. But we must also look at how the leader's personal characteristics can interact with external opportunities. Sometimes a big act of leadership is the joint product of individual and situation.

The Right Place, the Right Time

If Thomas Carlyle is the classic advocate of the "great-person" theory of leadership, Leo Tolstoy is an exemplary promoter of the opposing viewpoint. In his monumental novel *War and Peace*, Tolstoy flatly contradicted Carlyle's claim that Napoleon was one of those people whose biography is history. According to Tolstoy, Carlyle got it backwards: Napoleon's biography was a mere manifestation of history's impersonal and deterministic unfolding. To make this case, Tolstoy devoted many pages to proving that Napoleon had very little if any control over the course of events, military or otherwise. For example, Tolstoy analyzed at length the epic battle of Borodino, proving to his satisfaction that the action was decided by the soldiers doing the fighting, not by Napoleon doing the commanding. Group dynamics, not leadership, ordered where the colors would advance, and ordained where they would fall.

Because Napoleon is such a prototypical example of exceptional leadership, Tolstoy felt free to generalize:

> A king is history's slave . . . In historic events, the so-called great men are labels giving names to events, and like labels they have but the smallest connection with the event itself. Every act of theirs, which appears to them an act of their own

will, is in a historical sense involuntary and is related to the whole course of history and predestined from eternity.

Because eminent leaders have no causal role in history, they serve only as convenient tags for big events. Leaders don't become eminent by making history; rather, historians make some leaders eminent when they write history. Instead of the leader's mind manifesting itself in history, the leader's name wins a place in the historian's mind. Leaders are mere eponyms—handy names for epochs in history.

This idea fits with something learned back in Chapter 3: Wartime leaders attain more conspicuous places in the annals of history than do peacetime leaders. This holds for monarchs, presidents, and prime ministers. Furthermore, this eponymic theory fits other facts not yet mentioned. For instance, on the average, the most famous rulers of history have longer tenures in office than their less illustrious predecessors and successors do. Among great monarchs, the archetypical case is Louis XIV (the Great), who reigned for almost three-quarters of a century. Clearly, the more time a leader spends as the nation's head of state, the more events will collect under his or her name. This accumulation then enhances the leader's historic utility as an eponym. Yet the leader's personal responsibility for those events may be minimal. In hereditary monarchies, specifically, the all-time big names merely reap the benefits of youthful ascension to the throne coupled with unusually robust health. If these two advantages are in force, and the era is one of intense military and political agitation, we have the recipe for an undeserved greatness.

Although this eponymic theory may enjoy empirical support, Carlyle could raise an objection. These data only deal with a leader's posthumous reputation. Of course, arbitrary factors may decide a leader's usefulness as a label for historic events. Yet successful leadership consists of more than some greatness ratings decades or centuries down the road; it also entails actual behavioral performance. If we narrow our attention to a leader's objective impact on contemporaries rather than posterity's subjective evaluations, psychological variables may have a larger part to play—even the lead role. This argument fits what we have seen earlier in this book. Most of the personality traits associated with leadership are linked with specific criteria rather than global assessments.

We apparently have a way out of the quagmire. If we get trapped in a debate about why some politicians go down in the annals as great leaders, we can argue that they were lucky to be at the right place at the right time. "There are no great men," said Admiral Halsey, "only great challenges that ordinary men are forced by circumstances to meet." But should the conversation get more specific, we can begin talking about the right person. Personal traits do have a say in why some leaders adopted aggressive foreign policies or why other leaders proved so effective as legislators.

We cannot salvage the psychology of greatness so easily, however. Tolstoy certainly thought that the context accounts for more than just historical acclaim.

The situation may determine more narrowly defined indicators of leadership as well. Even the outcome of a battle is dictated independently of the will of any so-called military genius. In addition, there is no shortage of data proving how vulnerable a leader's performance is to external circumstances beyond anyone's control. One illustration should suffice to make the point. The example comes from studies of presidential leadership that discerned the "vice-presidential succession effect."

One of the peculiarities of the American presidency is that there are two different routes to residence at 1600 Pennsylvania Avenue. Most commonly, presidents enter office after winning election in the November election. These are the duly elected chief executives. Less common are the "accidental presidents" who have entered the Oval Office through the back door. Each of these was serving as the nation's vice-president when the duly elected president left office before completing his term. Of the 39 presidents from Washington to Reagan, almost one-quarter were accidental: Tyler, Fillmore, Andrew Johnson, Arthur, Theodore Roosevelt, Coolidge, Truman, Lyndon Johnson, and Ford. Except in the last instance, the predecessor died in office, whether by assassination or natural death. Only Ford assumed the presidency upon the incumbent's resignation.

Curiously, the accidental presidents to date did not perform very well as American chief executives; at least, they failed by four objective behavioral criteria. First, when they were compelled to veto a bill passed by Congress, these incumbents were more likely to see their veto overturned. This is a slap in the face that legislators on Capitol Hill apply only sparingly. Second, when these incumbents appointed someone to fill a vacant Cabinet post, they had higher odds of having that nominee rejected by the Senate. This is another rare technique for humiliating a sitting president, for normally executives are allowed to pick their own helpers. Third, the Senate likewise tended to reject the incumbents' appointments to the U.S. Supreme Court. Indeed, in Andrew Johnson's case, Congress finally shrank the size of the nation's highest judicial body so that the incumbent would have no vacancies to fill! Fourth and last, an accidental president was rarely nominated to run for another term in office. Of the duly elected presidents, only 27% were denied a shot at a second term. But of the nine accidental presidents, 44% suffered this disgrace. Why this stark contrast?

An advocate of the great-person theory would have a ready answer. The vice-presidency is a relatively powerless position that cannot attract the nation's best leaders. The first vice-president, John Adams, was the first to complain; he bitterly remarked, "My country has in its wisdom contrived for me the most insignificant office that ever the invention of man contrived or his imagination conceived." Too often, moreover, conventions select the vice-presidential running mate to balance out the ticket ideologically or geographically. So accidental presidents may come from inferior stock than the duly elected presidents.

There is absolutely no empirical support for this conjecture. Studies have directly compared the two kinds of presidents on a diversity of relevant factors; they differ on none. There are no important differences in biographical background, prior political experience and competence, motivational disposition, broad personality profile, specific leadership style, or a host of other variables. Another datum is equally damaging: For those accidental presidents who managed somehow to get themselves elected to their own terms, the performance deficits vanished. Once the unfortunate became a duly elected president, the rates of overturned vetoes and rejected appointments descended to baseline levels.

Hence, this phenomenon most likely shows what happens when a person is at the wrong place at the wrong time. The problem with being an accidental president is that it is an extremely weak political position to be in. He hasn't been elected by anybody. Most voters had their eye on the candidate who occupied the top spot on the ticket in the general election. This means that an accidental president lacks the mandate enjoyed by even the most junior member of Congress. Aggravating matters further is the Constitution's failure to spell out exactly the vice-president's status upon moving up a notch. When the first accidental president, John Tyler, assumed the duties of the presidency, his fellow politicians wanted to call him the *acting* president. Poor Tyler was even ridiculed as "His Accidency."

Thus, vice-presidential succession brings into the White House a leader who lacks legitimacy in the eyes of his governmental colleagues. This purely situational factor explains why the hapless incumbent faces so many difficulties with other members of the federal government. It also accounts for why the disadvantage disappears once he receives his own mandate. Finally, it explains the lack of applicable contrasts in biography, experience, capacity, personality, or style. The vice-presidential succession effect tells us how the context can determine performance even on specific, objective, and contemporaneous benchmarks.

The Right Person, Place, and Time

Not all writers state the issue in exclusive terms. Rather than chattering about individual versus situation or genius versus *Zeitgeist*, some thinkers substitute the conjunction "and" for the preposition "versus." Psychology and sociology can combine in the creation of notable people and events. This convergence is suggested in Hegel's comment:

> The great man of the age is the one who can put into words the will of his age, tell his age what its will is, and accomplish it. What he does is the heart and essence of his age, he actualizes his age.

The merger is also implicit in Machiavelli's advice to the shrewd politician that "he will be successful who directs his actions according to the spirit of the times." The genius may be the person who exploits the *Zeitgeist* for personal advantage.

Actual research admonishes us to weigh carefully both individual and situation. Victory on the field of battle provides an example. Which general emerges victorious is partly based on personal attributes, such as age, experience, and aggressiveness. To this list we can add integrative complexity, as detailed in Chapter 3. Still, the victor is also affected by such obvious situational factors as army size. "God is always for the big battalions," said Voltaire. An earlier section of this chapter has described the home-field disadvantage, another situational input.

Even a military mind as exalted as Napoleon's could not escape strategic and tactical constraints. Although his success rate in battle exceeded that of all other French generals, the fluctuations in his success rate paralleled those of his military colleagues. When other French armies were victorious, the army under Napoleon's personal command had better odds of success. But when Napoleon's colleagues were not doing so well *vis-à-vis* France's enemies, Napoleon's chances for victory dimmed in rough proportion. Sometimes these concurrent events were even connected directly. Marshal Grouchy's failure to prevent General Blücher from joining forces with the Duke of Wellington sealed Napoleon's devastating defeat at Waterloo.

In these military examples, success or failure resulted from the summation of individual and situational variables. The right person happened to be in the right place at the right time. The effects of individual and situation can get more complex than simple addition, however. The effects may multiply, as in the multiplicative functions introduced in Chapter 8. The same individual may be the right person at one place and time, but the wrong person under contrasting circumstances. Individual and situation may have to dovetail in a more specific fashion for a person to gain fame and fortune.

Two examples follow; both regard aspects of presidential leadership. The first concerns election success, and the second legislative achievement.

The Ballot Box

In an ideal democratic system, the best leader would receive the most votes in the ballot box. However, what voters consider the "best person for the job" varies according to the circumstances. Most obviously, the candidate must advocate policies that most citizens find palatable—a criterion that may shift from one election to the next. Aspirants must match the populace on more subtle criteria as well. For instance, most of Chapter 5 has been devoted to reviewing the research on the motive triad—the power, achievement, and affiliation motives.

A politician's score on these three needs can influence performance both as a candidate and as an incumbent. David Winter has shown that these motives also affect a candidate's chances in November. In particular, the congruence between the president's motive profile and that of the American people predicts (1) the percentage of the popular vote received, (2) the margin of victory over the runner-up candidate, and (3) the odds of winning re-election to a second term in office. Voters want a national leader whose instincts are the same as their own. Ironically, this is not a desirable outcome, however democratic the result. For the congruence between a president's motive profile and that of the populace predicts *inferior* leadership in the White House. The right person for the ballot box is the wrong person for the Oval Office!

In this illustration, the characteristics of the leader depend on the modal personality of the people. If most Americans are high in affiliation, medium in power, and low in achievement, the candidate should display the same configuration. However, also governing election success is the match between the politician and the political conditions beyond the world of voter disposition. Let us return to the subject of birth order, introduced in Chapter 6. The relationship between birth order and success cannot be stated in simple terms, because the association depends on the type of success required. Being a first-born will be an advantage under one set of conditions, but a drawback under a contrary set.

This same contingency occurs in presidential elections. Sometimes the election takes place during times of international crises or war. In this case, Americans seek a strong leader, so a first-born has the advantage. At other times the political *Zeitgeist* favors peaceful reconciliation of conflicting interests in both foreign and domestic arenas. Now the need is for a leader who is open to flexible bargaining and negotiation; *ergo*, the middle-born child becomes the person of the hour. At still other times the nation may be facing social disruption and potential chaos, such as happened during the Great Depression. That brings the only child into the fray.

These remarks are not mere speculations by some Adlerian psychoanalyst. Data on U.S. presidents support this pairing of birth order with political *Zeitgeist*. For example, the top contenders for the presidency usually have the same ordinal positions in their families (especially when we focus on sons only). Thus, in the 1860 election, the three primary candidates—Lincoln, Douglas, and Breckinridge—were only sons. More recently, in the 1988 election, both Bush and Dukakis were second-born sons. Furthermore, the matching holds for British prime ministers as well. Winston Churchill is a prime case. A first-born with a domineering personality, he only found a secure place in the British government when his country was at war. He became minister of munitions during World War I and served as the prime minister in World War II—in the latter instance with immense distinction.

All of this evidence together should help us understand a curious fact of political history in democratic societies. Occasionally, a politician of the highest caliber somehow never makes it into the nation's highest office. The history of the United States alone is riddled with the names of political leaders who never quite made it over the last hurdle: Henry Clay, James G. Blaine, William Jennings Bryan, Charles Evans Hughes, Adlai Stevenson, Barry Goldwater, and Hubert Humphrey. These were not candidates of fringe parties, but the nominees of vigorous political organizations. Nor were these individuals "fly-by-nights" in national politics. Yet they all shared the misfortune of having been out of step with their times. They may also have shared the ability to have been great presidents under different circumstances.

And what about the flip side of the coin? What of those elected president not because they were especially suited for the position, but because they happened to comply with the superficial demands of the political *Zeitgeist?* What about the likes of Pierce, Harding, and other small leaders thrust into a job too big for them? Perhaps these historic embarrassments are the political equivalents of once best-selling authors whose books now cannot even be found in Salvation Army stores.

The Roll Call Vote

Chapter 9 has shown that a chief executive requires a special cluster of personality traits to earn recognition as a great president. The chief executive must be moderate and flexible, and yet forceful and Machiavellian. At the same time, much of the president's success in shaping the nation's laws is contingent on contextual factors beyond his control. The two most unmistakable constraints are (1) the size of the president's electoral mandate in the general election and (2) the extent to which the incumbent's party controls the two houses of Congress. Neither of these factors have to reflect with any accuracy the personal qualities of leadership the incumbent can potentially display.

It would be most convenient if these individual and situational variables worked in an additive fashion. We could then just sum up the separate resources in any prediction of legislative performance. But it's not so simple. The impact of individual factors depends on the situational factors, and vice versa. One salient case concerns the executive's eagerness in using his veto power, and the legislature's willingness to overturn his vetoes.

In general, inflexible incumbents must often resort to this last-ditch tactic in exerting their will over legislation. Such rigid incumbents also see a significant number of their vetoes overridden by Congress. Even so, the two situational variables just mentioned interact (in a multiplicative manner) with presidential flexibility in determining the frequency of uncooperative exchanges between White House and Capitol Hill.

The first contextual factor is the size of the incumbent's electoral mandate. For highly flexible presidents, the scope of victory in the November election affects how often they rely on the veto power. The bigger the margin in the Electoral College, the more bills the incumbent sends back to Congress for reconsideration. In contrast, unswayable presidents fail to weigh the size of their electoral mandate when deliberating whether to reject a piece of legislation that has just landed on their desk. This obliviousness is most unwise, of course. For the incumbent's mandate gauges the magnitude of his national constituency, and the latter serves as a counterweight to the more provincial constituencies of a single member of the House or Senate. In any case, this interaction shows how a personality trait, obstinacy, can moderate the association between situation and performance. An unusual rigidity on the president's part can swamp the otherwise robust connection between an incumbent's electoral backing and veto use.

The second interaction effect involves the size of the representation of the president's party on Capitol Hill. The amount of party control moderates the association between any pigheadedness and the rate at which executive vetoes are overturned. For those chief executives who boast exceptional flexibility, the relation between the degree of congressional support and the number of overridden vetoes is negligible. The adaptable incumbents can deftly bargain and negotiate, notwithstanding the dearth of allies they can count upon. This supple adaptation to political reality is foreclosed for the more bullheaded executives. Accordingly, the association between party control and veto overrides now becomes rather tangible. An obstinate president is very much at the mercy of those who rule the roost in Congress. If the context is genial, no one ever needs to suspect that the president hides a tragic flaw. Only when the legislative context turns more hostile will this personality quirk erupt. Once the blemish appears, the incumbent assumes the uncomfortable status of an obstructionist president. He gives bills the thumbs down, knowing full well that Congress will not sustain the vetoes.

This last interaction can be called the "Johnson-Wilson effect." The name recognizes America's two most uncompromising presidents, Andrew Johnson and Woodrow Wilson. Sadly, both politicians could claim a respectable number of personal virtues. Both could evince effective leadership under the proper conditions. Yet both fell completely apart when faced with potent opposition. In particular, when their supporters formed only a minority in Congress, these two men reverted to stubborn and self-defeating behaviors. Among these leader pathologies was their excessive and fruitless reliance on the veto power. At a more singular level, senseless intransigence also forced Johnson to endure impeachment proceedings. And Wilson suffered the defeat of his diplomatic masterpiece, the Treaty of Versailles. Their presidencies self-destructed.

Creators as Leaders

There is something missing from our analysis of leadership. Although the chapter begins by discussing achievement in a diversity of domains, its focus has become narrower and narrower. By the time the topic of leadership comes up, an entire mode of accomplishment has dropped out completely. That neglected realm is outstanding creativity. There is an excuse for this negligence: When social psychologists discuss leadership, they usually restrict this phenomenon to its political, economic, social, and religious manifestations. So I am only following accepted practice.

This practice is unacceptable, however. According to the current definition of leadership, we may have no other choice but to view creativity as a specific type of leadership. A leader is that group member whose influence on group attitudes, performance, or decision making greatly exceeds that of the average member of the group. Under this conception, a president, prime minister, dictator, or monarch is clearly a leader. So is the chief executive officer of a Fortune 500 corporation, the coach of a professional hockey team, the director of a major charitable foundation, or the founder of a new religious sect. Moreover, the wider and more enduring the leader's impact, the more leadership we can say the leader displayed. Adolf Hitler's leadership would rate higher than Ernst Röhm's by this criterion.

Well, can't we apply the same concept to creators? A scientist, thinker, writer, artist, or composer must make a broad and lasting impression to etch a name in the tablets of human culture. This necessity is implicit in Alfred North Whitehead's apotheosis of one ancient Greek philosopher: "The safest general characterization of the European philosophical tradition is that it consists of a series of footnotes to Plato." This claim may seem extreme, but it contains a grain of truth. Moreover, comparable statements may be composed for creators of other types. Cases include Newton's impact on the mathematical sciences, Michelangelo's effect on the visual arts, and Beethoven's influence on musical expression. In addition, we can gauge the caliber of genius by the scope of that consequence—just as we do for leaders. Hence, Albert Einstein would score higher on the creativity scale than would the much less persuasive Friedrich Hasenöhrl.

This linkage between creativity and leadership is by no means a novel idea. Nearly a century has passed since scholars first tried to rank the most eminent figures of history—a task that still attracts participants today. Chapter 1 has given the example of the 1987 book *The 100: A Ranking of the Most Influential Persons in History*. Because both creators and leaders are included on these lists, the tacit assumption must be that a common basis exists on which we can meaningfully compare these celebrities. The common denominator is influence, and to assess influence is to evaluate leadership. That's what puts Muḥammad, Lenin, Genghis Khan, and Bolívar on the same scale as Aristotle, Darwin, Kalidasa, Bach, and Hokusai. These people may not all weigh the same, but they all have weight—as leaders.

This argument is no analytical legerdemain. I have not speciously identified some ethereal category that only loosely subsumes the two key means by which personalities leave big marks on history. Throughout this book, we have examined many examples of variables and processes that participate in the making of geniuses of all species. Genetic endowment, reinforcement schedules, motivation, birth order, childhood trauma, marginality, age, intelligence, risk taking, self-actualization, depression, social learning, authoritarianism, and emulation—I could cite many more instances. Although these factors sometimes have different results for creators than for leaders, the results are often much the same, even indistinguishable.

Furthermore, the evidence presented in this volume actually understates the overlapping etiologies. Because of the topic limitations imposed in Chapter 1, I have not digressed too far from the luminaries who define the *raison d'être* of this book. Nevertheless, studies of more mundane human beings have found some other common features. For example, experimental investigations have found that creativity may be aided by cognitive and motivational factors that we know succor leadership as well. Shared facilitators include the need for power and conceptual complexity.

Social psychologists have long considered leadership a legitimate and important disciplinary topic. Creativity has not been. Creativity has been studied by many cognitive, personality, developmental, and educational psychologists, but only a few social psychologists have gotten involved. This oversight is a misfortune. If we are correct in holding that creators are leaders of a specific kind, then the social psychology of creativity must become a respected subfield. Should that happen, the psychologists' understanding of both creativity and leadership should expand.

CHAPTER 14

EPILOGUE: HAS THE
PSYCHOLOGIST SUCCEEDED?

The psychology of history has already expanded our understanding of greatness. We now know a lot about those individuals whose actions, thoughts, and feelings design the present and document the past. We have also amassed a wealth of information about how these persons affect those of us obliged to experience history in the making. Moreover, the full panoply of psychological science has proved applicable, whether to the agents or to the recipients of big events. Parallel to each class of significant happenings or personalities is an impressive set of psychological processes. Some factors are more psychobiological, others more cognitive, and still others more social, but we cannot deny their participation. If we want to comprehend the movers and the shakers, or at least understand our reactions to all the movement and shaking going on, we cannot disregard the lessons of psychology.

Still, this whole enterprise is not immune from criticism. Five questions, in particular, most threaten the present enthusiasm.

Do Behavioral Laws Even Exist?

If there were no laws of behavior, there would exist no behavioral science. The psychology of history would then lack foundation. Yet psychology has gathered enough findings in the past century or so to qualify as a genuine psychological *science*. To be sure, these results have a somewhat different status than do the laws that populate the physical sciences. Behavioral laws are statistical rather than deterministic in nature; they only tell us what happens "on the average" or "over the long run." Still, this is telling us a lot. According to Sherlock Holmes, "You can never foretell what any man will do, but you can say with precision what an average number will be up to. Individuals may vary, but percentages remain constant."

Therefore, we need not get defensive about psychology's limitations. This is especially true insofar as psychology is not the sole science that can offer only regularities and patterns instead of inviolate principles. No one doubts that medicine counts as a science. Its status is secure even when your personal physician can merely tell you what the *probable* results are for any dietary practice, exercise program, daily habit, drug prescription, or surgical intervention. Even in the physical sciences, determinism will often yield ground to probabilities. This has been true in the realm of quantum physics ever since the Heisenberg uncertainty principle was formulated.

Naturally, the critic can argue on. All this research is fine and dandy, but psychology concentrates on subjects who are contemporaries, and rather normal ones at that. Once psychologists move their analytical equipment onto the stage of history, their supposed statistical patterns may disappear. Collingwood cautioned in *The Idea of History*:

> To regard such a positive mental science as rising above the sphere of history, and establishing the permanent and unchanging laws of human nature, is therefore possible only to a person who mistakes the transient conditions of a certain historical age for the permanent conditions of human life.

All "findings" may be context-bound.

In defense, almost all the research reviewed in this book was based on the actual events and people of history. It did not merely involve some shaky extrapolations from the transient episodes of modern life to historic occasions and personalities. Furthermore, the book's statistical laws have emerged from the examination of cases drawn from many nationalities and historical periods. This cross-cultural and transhistorical breadth has helped to insure that the patterns transcend any one place or time.

Critics may now attack from a different angle. Instead of challenging science, they can question the value of historical data. Perhaps history and biography are too riddled with error and prejudice to provide secure ground for a behavioral science. A comprehensive answer to this objection is impossible in this small space. I have, in fact, devoted an earlier book to this very matter: *Psychology, Science, and History*. Rather than summarize the main arguments, let me just touch upon one illustrative issue.

Many skeptics believe that history is capricious. They maintain that who makes it into the annals and who doesn't is a matter of chance; moreover, the allotments of greatness and obscurity are unstable, changing unpredictably over time. As a result, different levels of achievement are not informative about any behaviors that might impart success. For instance, some scholars have advanced the "Ecclesiastes hypothesis." This is based on the Biblical passage (Ecclesiastes 9:11) that cynically holds, "The race is not to the swift, nor the battle to the strong, neither bread to the wise, nor yet riches to men of understanding, nor yet favor to men of skill; but time and chance happeneth to them all." If the Ecclesiastes hypothesis were true, psychologists could not expect to build a science on the behavior of so-called historic personalities.

My response to this complaint is twofold. First, this entire book can be considered a contradiction of the thesis that personal qualities supply nothing in the quest for fame. Each chapter has added to the inventory of traits and processes that enhance an individual's prospects for acclaim. Metaphorically at least, the swift win the race, the strong win the battle, and so on down the other corridors to applause.

Second, so conspicuous is the intrusion of these stable attributes that they constrain the supposed caprice of history. Notwithstanding the occasional cases of "neglected genius"—Gregor Mendel and J. S. Bach are perhaps the favorite examples—posthumous reputation does not alter randomly across time. On the contrary, the stability of fame endures across decades, even centuries. Furthermore, this stability partly springs from the life work that achievers have offered the world. Happenstance does participate in the making of reputations, to be sure, but these extrinsic contaminants are not the whole story. Hence, in contradiction to the Ecclesiastes hypothesis, time and chance does not determine all.

To sum up, behavioral laws really do exist, and they do make history.

Doesn't Sociocultural Context Determine All?

Philosophers of history might raise a different set of issues. Thinkers like Ban Biao, Ibn Khaldūn, Giambattista Vico, Herbert Spencer, Auguste Comte, Oswald Spengler, and Arnold Toynbee all held that principles akin to behavioral laws actually exist. But these laws concern the behavior of whole civilizations. The individual, as a fragment of the larger sociocultural system, merely goes along for the ride, like flotsam in an ocean current. The context, or the *Zeitgeist*, becomes the true agent of history.

Of all such philosophical positions, the most provocative is probably the doctrine of cycles. According to the Emperor Marcus Aurelius, "all things from eternity are of like forms and come around in a circle." For some philosophers, history is no exception; it is forever repeating itself in cycles of birth, growth, maturity, decay, and death. The finest thumbnail sketch of this position was penned by Lord Byron:

> There is the moral of all human tales;
> 'Tis but the same rehearsal of the past,
> First Freedom, and then Glory—when that fails,
> Wealth—Vice—Corruption,—Barbarism at last:—
> And History, with all her volumes vast,
> Hath but *one* page.

For the sake of argument, let's assume that large cyclical forces decide the forms of creativity and leadership that individuals can pursue at a certain instant and locus in history. One circumstance, and military conquest is the order of the day. Another, and it's time for epic poetry. Does this automatically render psychology irrelevant? No! Let us consider two items:

1. The cyclic movements account for *what* rather than *who*. It's one matter to say that a specific moment favors scientific creativity, and quite another to identify which of millions of individuals in the population will rise to the top as the celebrated scientists of the time. For example, we might accept Sorokin's claim that the scientific revolution was but one ripple on the larger wave of Sensate culture. Yet that admission does not tell us why Newton rose higher than Hooke in the achievements that mark that crucial epoch. That leaves an opening for the psychologist.

2. In some domains of achievement, extreme success may actually depend on bucking the sociocultural trends. For instance, Chapter 4 has shown how a computer can calculate the originality of the thousands of melodies that make up the classical repertoire. If we fit a trend line to these originality scores for all 15,618 themes in the sample, we obtain the curve seen in Figure 14.1. The computer thus can spy an ascending cyclical pattern in the prominence of unpredictable melodic constructions in classical music. Yet which compositions leave the biggest mark on the repertoire? Should the work contain melodies that fall as close as possible to this oscillating baseline? Or should the melodies depart from the cycle?

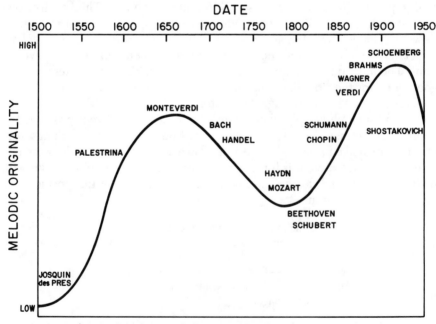

FIGURE 14.1. Upward cycle in melodic originality for 15,618 themes in the classical repertoire.

The second alternative is correct. The most popular pieces in the classical repertoire consist of thematic material that went against the stylistic norms at the time of composition. Nor is this result unique to music. The most famous philosophers in the Western intellectual tradition are those who refused to conform to the mainstream positions of their day. In the arts and humanities at least, the big cycles only dictate what to expect from the also-rans and nonentities of civilization.

These points are not dependent on the truth or falsity of cyclical theories. Despite the occurrence of noncyclic environmental influences, we cannot infer that context determines everything, while the individual counts as an explanatory nothing. For example, social scientists often argue that human cultural achievements depend on the acquisition of material wealth. The Golden Age of Greece was largely financed by the Athenian empire. The Italian Renaissance was partly bought by the bankers of Florence. And we can marshal evidence for this hypothesis. Even so, this interpretation cannot exclude the individual from the cultural equation. As before, strict economics may not explain why some creative spirits climbed higher than the rest. In addition, the material base may only set the minimum conditions for achievement. Once that threshold level of posterity is met, the cultural creators take off on their own. The process of imitation and emulation is but one of many forces that provide the additional thrust. Psychologists remain employed.

We must mull over one last consideration. When the impersonal milieu is evoked as an explanatory agent, the application may be too broad to fit single cases. What may very well hold for the nation or civilization as a whole may not accurately describe the context for an individual within the cultural area. This critical point has been verified in studies of philosophical creativity in Chinese history. What was happening in China in general was less important in the emergence of genius than what was happening in the specific locality where a thinker developed and prospered. Even in times of political chaos and oppression, there might survive isolated pockets of tranquility that allowed intellects full freedom of expression.

The heterogeneity raises an intriguing issue: To what extent do great minds pick their environments to uphold their genius? Thinkers like Confucius wandered around the courts of China, looking for a prince who would favor their ideas. Similar peregrinations are commonplace in the history of civilization. Ionian Greek philosophers, artists of the Italian Renaissance, American writers of the "lost generation," and intellectuals of Nazi Europe—all sought more propitious settings. The same thing is now happening to distinguished scientists of the former Soviet Union; many are seeking new homes for their first-class science. In these instances, the person chooses the context instead of letting the context warp the person. It may even be a sign of genius that such people design their world to satisfy their needs.

Are the Predictions and Explanations Good Enough?

Critics of the behavioral sciences love to dwell on one handicap: Because behavioral laws are statistical rather than deterministic, a "plus or minus" rides on every forecast. In contrast, the exact sciences (such as physics or chemistry) will often make precise predictions, and then confirm the predictions to an accuracy of several decimal places. If behavioral scientists cannot make good predictions, others may infer that they should have little confidence in the explanatory power of their theories. Much must be left out if events cannot be predicted exactly.

Yes, we must admit that there is going to be some amount of error in a psychologist's forecasts. Human beings are extremely complex entities. They think, feel, and behave in phenomenally intricate settings. To juxtapose this situation against that of the physicist or chemist is not playing fair. Physical scientists isolate their systems from disturbing influences, and that simplifies their analyses. As soon as they leave the cubicles and the test tubes, matters become too intricate even for them. Thus, a thorough physics of a ski jump or a pitched baseball is beyond anyone's predictive powers. At least, we cannot expect any better precision than that which we find in the behavioral sciences. Sometimes psychology actually exhibits a precision that surpasses that in physics! This is especially true when we compare established fields within psychology to frontier endeavors such as high-energy physics.

More importantly, psychology's predictive and explanatory power is not all that bad. In Chapter 4, we have seen that we can use theory to predict the observed frequencies of various grades of multiples (the duplicate discoveries discussed there). The discrepancies between observations and predictions are actually rather small. This heightens our confidence that the theory underlying the predictions has captured some modicum of truth. Other examples could be given. For instance, our ability to predict which presidents will go down in history as stellar leaders is actually rather outstanding: We can account for about 82% of the contrasts in posthumous reputation. Also, what errors we make are too small to have practical consequence. The equations call no bad president good, and label no good president bad.

I confess that we cannot always do this well. Sometimes we can only account for about 25% of what's going on. Often our predictive and explanatory power dips to 5% or less. Even so, these figures are rather respectable, whatever a critic might think. Psychology's ability to treat history actually exceeds medicine's ability to treat many diseases. Furthermore, even smaller effects than this can have important repercussions. A fascinating case is that of batting averages in American baseball. Although players and fans may brag about this statistic, its predictive value for a single time at bat is minuscule—about one-third of one percent! Does this mean that big hitters like José Canseco are vastly overpaid? Not at all, for seasons are seldom dictated by a single hit, walk, or strikeout. Therefore, game after game, the advantage of an exceptional batting average stockpiles. Not just hits, but home runs and runs batted in accrue. At the end, this accumulation may ultimately decide which team wins the pennant. So even small events can have big effects if those events build up in this way.

I am not claiming that psychology can now predict and explain everything we want to know about history. Nor do I assert that psychology ever will. I maintain only that psychology's predictive and explanatory power already suffices to make it a respectable approach to understanding greatness.

Is the Enterprise Elitist?

Rather than fault this book's contents on scientific grounds, some critics may take aim at its subject matter. Doesn't it put too much emphasis on the preeminent names while ignoring the masses? Hasn't it slighted the many anonymous individuals who also make history? For example, some have argued that modern science does not depend on genius any more. Instead, the edifice of scientific truth is built by many minor workers, each of whom adds one brick. This pleasantly egalitarian view is named the "Ortega hypothesis," after the Spanish thinker José Ortega y Gasset. He once said that

> it is necessary to insist upon this extraordinary but undeniable fact: experimental sciences has progressed thanks in great part to the work of men astoundingly mediocre, and even less than mediocre. That is to say, modern science, the root and symbol of our actual civilization, finds a place for the intellectually commonplace man and allows him to work therein with success.

Even working scientists sometimes express the same opinion. One example is the statement by Nobel laureate Howard Florey that

> science is rarely advanced by what is known in current jargon as a "break-through," rather does our increasing knowledge depend on the activity of thousands of our colleagues throughout the world who add small points to what will eventually become a splendid picture much in the same way that the Pointillistes built up their extremely beautiful canvasses.

Unhappily for the levelers among us who insist on democratic equality, the facts contradict the Ortega hypothesis. Remember the Price law (mentioned back in Chapter 5 and elaborated in Chapter 13), according to which a small percentage of scientists accounts for most of the contributions. And this is true of every creative discipline besides science. Indeed, in only slightly altered form, the Price law probably applies to leadership as well. No matter where we look, the same story can be told, with only minor adjustments. Identify the 10% who have contributed the most to some endeavor, whether it be songs, poems, paintings, patents, articles, items of legislation, battles, films, designs, or anything else. Count up all the accomplishments that they have to their credit. Now tally the contributions of the remaining 90% who struggled in the same area of achievement. The first tally will equal or surpass the second. Period. The important people deserve their acclaim.

Even though I defend our interest in the principal figures of past and present, this does not mean that the psychology of history allows that interest alone. The annals of human culture consist of events as well as people. Although some big events are the products of historic personalities, not all are. Hence, many pages of this book have been devoted to important happenings that are the products of the masses. For example, we have examined the motivational makeup of the masses and the authoritarian activities of the populace. We have also looked at riots and lynch mobs, rumor and contagion. These and other phenomena scattered throughout this volume turn our attention to how certain psychological processes enable small people to produce big events.

Psychology of history escapes the charge of excessive elitism in one more manner. We have often concentrated on how historic events and personalities affect the conglomerate of unnamed individuals. Among these phenomena of wide impact are beauty and power, flashbulb memories, suicide and disease, population pressure, economic frustration, stifling heat, public opinion, voter behavior, and basking in reflected glory. In addition, many of the processes discussed in this book are of equal relevance for both notables and nonentities. These include behavior genetics, handedness, drugs, race and gender, birth order, education, age, intelligence, explanatory style, Type A personality, morality, deindividuation, diffusion of responsibility, social learning, social loafing, and the home-court advantage. All in all, much in the preceding chapters is far from elitist.

A complete psychology of history, indeed, must encompass all *Homo sapiens*. Whatever our specific role, we all participate in its making.

Hasn't a Lot Been Left Out?

Despite the diversity and richness of results presented in these pages, much remains untold. We all can name types of historic events that and people who have been granted too little attention in this volume. We know hardly anything about the origins of major religious figures, whether founders, apostles, popes, patriarchs, saints, or heretics. We also have only scanty information on what makes for extraordinary success as an entrepreneur. Other domains of achievement have been ignored altogether. What about the patrons and connoisseurs who have played such an essential role in the creation of magnificent art, music, and literature? What causes the crucial emergence of a Pericles or Maecenas, the many Medicis or Pope Julius II, Louis XIV of France or Christina of Sweden, Nadezhda von Meck or Peggy Guggenheim? No one knows. Nor can we say much about why certain scientific theories are so influential, why only a handful of operas are played yearly across the globe, or why specific artistic master-works become icons of our civilized existence.

Our ignorance of celebrities and achievements in popular culture is no less astonishing. We know too little, if anything, about movie stars, cinematographers, directors, and producers; rock stars, jazz musicians, and classical virtuosos; folk artists, hairdressers, clothes designers, interior decorators, and artisans; wine makers, chefs, and restaurateurs; raconteurs, comics, clowns, mimes, and acrobats; team owners, coaches, and professional athletes; plus famous detectives, lawyers, eccentrics, dandies, models, playboys, sex symbols, martial artists, and those distinctive spirits who try to win entries in the *Guinness Book of World Records*. And can I mention notorious mass murderers, assassins, con artists, and Mafia bosses?

Yet why complain? Why should we not regard these overlooked forms of fame or infamy as critical research sites available for any psychologist willing to take on the challenge? Perhaps this book's most glaring omissions will inspire some readers to make their own marks on the psychology of history!

Notes

The notes and references provided in the following pages focus on those sources that document specific findings in the psychology of history. Except for direct quotations, documentation is not given for material that can be readily found in general reference works in either psychology or history.

Chapter 1

What Is Psychology? "the science of mental life": James 1890/1952, 1.

What Is History? "History is . . . bunk": *Who Said What When* 1991, 259. "The newspaper": Auden & Kronenberger 1966, 236. *The 100*: Hart 1987. *Brush Up Your Shakespeare!*: Macrone 1990. "Ode to Shakespeare": Giles 1923/1965, 418. Table 1.1: Most data fromHendrickson 1988.

What Is a Psychology of History? Psychohistory: Runyan 1982, 1988b. Leonardo: Freud 1910/1964. Interview: Roe 1952; cf. Eiduson 1962; Zuckerman 1977. Institute for Personality Assessment and Research: Barron 1969; MacKinnon 1962. Presidential popularity: Kernell 1978; Mueller 1973. Literary change: Martindale 1973. Discovery programs: Langley et al. 1987; cf. Boden 1991. Archives: Simonton 1990e. Early archival studies: Galton 1869; Quetelet 1835/1968. Obedience: Milgram 1963. Nazi war criminals: Arendt 1963; Gilbert 1950; Lifton 1986. Calley case: Kelman & Hamilton 1989.

Chapter 2

Genes and Genius. "Time, place, and action": Dryden 1693/1885, 60.

Galton's Eugenics. "the opinion of contemporaries": Galton 1892/1972, 77. Table 2.1: Adapted from Galton 1869. "could add the names" Galton 1892/1972, 261. Figure 2.1: Data from several sources, including Galton 1869. "There are far more": Galton 1892/1972, 294.

A Sequel? "relatives of distinction": Bramwell 1948, 150, the research discussed. Royalty: Woods 1906. Woods revisited: Simonton 1983d.

A Critique? Against Galton: Gould 1981. "He stands for fame": Young 1725–28/1854, 351. Reputation and natural ability: Simonton 1991b.

Identical versus Fraternal Twins. Key findings: Bouchard et al. 1990; Waller et al. 1990.

Emergenesis and Genius. "the self-perceived ability": Lykken 1982, 370. Emergenesis: Lykken 1982; Lykken et al. 1992. "probably depends on": Lykken 1982, 370. Creativity test: Waller et al. 1993.

Right and Left. "When a cast of the right side": Fancher 1979, 52–53. "Gall's own skull": Fancher 1979, 53. Einstein's brain: Storfer 1990, 390. "The apparent absence": Springer & Deutsch 1989, 28.

One Brain or Two? Dissent: Hines 1991, Ehrenwald 1984. Third Rasumovsky: Masserman 1984. Complex fantasy: Hoppe 1989; Hoppe & Kyle 1990. Magic synthesis: Arieti 1976. "I think the most significant . . . activities": Sagan 1977, 185.

One Hand or Two? Beni Hasan: Dennis 1958. Art: Coren & Porac 1977. Madonna and Child: Uhrbrock 1973. Table 2.3: Data from Barsley 1970; Fincher 1977. Art students: Beaton 1985. Sports: Porac & Coren 1981. Mathematical precocity: O'Boyle & Benbow 1990.

Drugged Success? "Combining a little orange juice": Davis & Maurice 1931, 361. Alcohol and creativity: Rothenberg 1990. "when the wine is in": Becon circa 1550/1844, 375. "Kubla Khan": Schneider 1953. Experiments on psychedelics: Berlin et al. 1955; Harman et al. 1966. "Nitrous oxide and ether": James 1902, 387.

Sleepless Ambitions? "great men and geniuses": Hartman 1973, 68. "Many times I have found": Nixon 1962, 105.

Organic Failures? "After my death": Magagnini 1991, B1. "Toscanini's fumble": Klawans 1988, ch. 5. *Woodrow Wilson and Colonel House*: George & George 1956. Opposition: Weinstein 1981; Weinstein et al. 1978. Reply: George & George 1981. Cognitive Impairment Scale: Gottschalk et al. 1988. "President Reagan had . . . higher levels": Gottschalk et al. 1988, 616.

Ethnicity and Gender. Possible biases: Gould 1981; Shields 1975.

Race and Racism. "the average intellectual standard": Galton 1892/1972, 394. "the average ability": Galton 1892/1972, 397. "The Jews have the best average brain": Harnsberger 1972, 295. "At all times": Wiener 1953, 11–12. Race rankings: Rushton 1988; cf. Anderson 1991; Weizmann et al. 1990; Zuckerman 1990. Afrocentrism: Asante 1988. Balanced view: Gates 1992. Racial differences in IQ: Storfer 1990, ch. 6. High-IQ black girl: Witty & Jenkins 1935. Nutrition: Eysenck 1991. "What history and ethnology seem to teach": Hertz 1928/1970, xi. Jewish and Japanese intellects: Storfer 1990, chs. 14–15. "even in recent years": Berenson 1954, 179.

Women and Sexism. Overview: Ochse 1991. Famous women in the West: Cattell 1903; Eisenstadt 1978. Female scientists: Simonton 1991a; cf. Cole 1987. Female composers: Simonton 1991b. Female writers: Cattell 1903; Cox 1926; Simonton 1992a.

Chromosomes and Hormones. Cognitive differences: Maccoby & Jacklin 1974. Closing of gender gap: Feingold 1988; cf. Halpern 1989. Variability hypothesis: Shields 1975. Evidence for Geschwind & Galaburda 1987 theory: Benbow & Stanley 1980, 1983; Felson & Trudeau 1991; but see Kimball 1989.

Cultures and Societies. Socialization practices: Barry et al. 1957. Mills College: Helson 1990. "who were successful in careers": Helson 1990, 49. Brothers: Helson 1980. "He that hath wife and children": Bacon 1597/1942, 29. Marriage and family: Hayes 1989, 312–13; cf. Goertzel et al. 1978; Kyvik 1990; Tomlinson-Keasey 1990. Prejudiced judgments: Fidell 1970; Glick et al. 1988. "I would venture to guess": Woolf 1929, 51. Females in Japan: Simonton 1992a. "Face-ism": Archer et al. 1983. Modern art: O'Kelley

1980. *Time* covers: Johnson & Christ 1988. Obituaries: Kastenbaum et al. 1976–77; Kearl 1986–87; Spilka et al. 1979–80. "One is not born": de Beauvoir 1949/1968, 267.
Power. Charisma: Cell 1974. Mayoral election: Berkowitz et al. 1971. Presidential elections: Simonton 1987e. Re-election: Simonton 1981. Greatness: Holmes & Elder 1989; McCann 1992; Simonton 1981, 1986g. War heroes: Simonton 1986g, 1986h, 1991f. Wartime presidents: Nice 1984; Simonton 1986g, 1986h, 1991f. Absolute monarchs: Simonton 1984g. Charisma: Cell 1974. Violent death: Simonton 1981, 1984g, 1991f. Heights: Ellis 1926. *Hereditary Genius*: Galton 1869. Male versus female leaders: Simonton 1984g.
Love. Evolutionary theory of sexual attraction: Buss 1988. "lonely hearts": Harrison & Saeed 1977. "had it been shorter": Pascal circa 1662/1952, 202. "Beauty like hers is genius": Rossetti 1881/1888, 185. Composite photographs: Galton 1883; Langlois & Roggman 1990; cf. Alley & Cunningham 1991. Ideal female face: Cunningham 1986. "Age cannot wither her": Shakespeare circa 1595–1611/1952, vol. 26, 321. Age, beauty, and fertility: Buss 1988. Actors vs. actresses: Lehman 1953, ch. 10. 1992 Oscars: Connolly 1992. *Charlie's Angels*: Kendrick & Gutierres 1980. Counterarguments: Howard et al. 1987; Travis & Yeager 1991. Stripteasers: Skipper & McCaghy 1970. Female figure trends: Garner et al. 1980; Silverstein et al. 1986.
The Conquistador and the Tyrant: Sociopolitical Systems. Gender and aggression: Hyde 1986. Cross-cultural survey: Whiting & Edwards 1973. Physical harm: Eagly & Steffen 1986. Weapons, hunting, and warfare: D'Andrade 1966. "man has within him": Einstein & Freud 1933, 6. Phallic symbol: Eibl-Eibesfeldt 1972. *The Fates of Nations*: Colinvaux 1980. "The fates of whole peoples": Colinvaux 1980, 13. "Social oppression": Colinvaux 1980, 85. "Aggressive war": Colinvaux 1980, 93. Sex-role diversity: Mead 1963. Male–female roles: Eagly 1987; Eagly & Steffen 1986. Men–women and need to dominate: Winter 1988a. "Nature, Mr. Allnutt": Agee et al., 1951, 69.
Psychobiological Psychobiography? "In Leonardo's case": Freud 1910/1964, 85. Erikson 1958 on Luther; cf. Erikson 1969. King George III: Runyan 1988a. "From his father": Jones 1953, 3–4. Season of birth and mental illness: Dalen 1975; Eysenck & Nias 1982. Season of birth and eminence: Huntington 1938; cf. Kaulins 1979. Cosmobiology: Eysenck & Nias 1982.

Chapter 3

"the influence of affective factors": Gardner 1987, 6.
The Black Hat: Learning Negative Affect. Connotations: Adams & Osgood 1973. Table 3.1, *The Three Faces of Eve*: Thigpen & Cleckley 1957. Black uniforms: Frank & Gilovich 1988. "It was aptly billed": Noland 1991, D1.
The Insidious Smile: Learning Positive Affect. "A person presumably is expected": Fang 1972, 27. Facial expressions in 1984: Mullen et al. 1986. Analyzing newscasters' nonverbal communications: Friedman, DiMatteo, & Mertz 1980; Friedman, Mertz, & DiMatteo 1980. Additional evidence: McHugo et al. 1985. Media as biased: Vallone et al. 1985. Actual objectivity: Clancy & Robinson 1985.
Skinnerian Conditioning. "100 most important people": Robinson 1970.
Campaign Rhetoric. Campaign speeches: West 1984; cf. Goggin 1984. Controversial positions: Campbell 1983. Visual image: Rosenberg et al. 1986.

Creative Output. "The true artist": Shaw 1903, 22. "The nobel is a ticket": Amabile 1983, 13. "I believe that you": Allen 1949, 231. "Genius is born": quoted in Esar 1949/ 1989, 217. Motivation definitions: Amabile 1983, 15. Creative writers: Amabile 1985. Sociological models: Allison et al. 1982; Allison & Stewart 1974. Economic models: Diamond 1984, 1986; Levin & Stephan 1991. Investment and psychoeconomic models: Rubenson 1990; Rubenson & Runco 1992; Sternberg & Lubart 1991; Walberg 1988. Cumulative advantage: Allison et al. 1982; Allison & Stewart 1974. "The Matthew effect": Merton 1968, 58. Mathematical models: Allison 1980; Simon 1955; Price 1976. Literary analyses: Skinner 1972. Insight: Epstein 1990. "No man but a blockhead": Boswell 1791/1952, 302. Direct application of learning theory to creative output: Ohlsson 1992.

Perceiving People. El Greco: Arnheim 1986, 160. Perception and politics: Jervis 1976. Historical analogies: Gilovich 1981; cf. Schuman & Rieger 1992; Spellman & Holyoak 1992.

Good versus Bad. Negativity bias: Lau 1982, 1985. 1984 election: Klein 1991. Explanation: Lau 1985. Empirical tests: Lau 1985. Implication: Klein 1991.

Them versus Us. Prestige suggestion: Lorge 1936. Responses to "I hold that a little rebellion": Asch 1952, 422. Hostile media: Vallone et al. 1985. Studies of newspaper reports: Winter 1987a. U.S.–Soviet perceptions: Bronfenbrenner 1961; cf. Suedfeld 1992. Mirror-image wars: White 1968, 1969, 1977. Wars 1913–1968: White 1969. For sports parallel, see: Hastorf & Cantril 1954.

Remembering Things and Happenings. Nonsense syllables: Ebbinghaus 1885/ 1913.

Memory as Expertise. Mnemonists: Luria 1968. Aitken: Hunter 1977. "It is all right": Marek 1975, 193.

Capacity Needed: 50,000 Chunks. Morphy's memory: Halacy 1970, 83. Chess studies: Chase & Simon 1973; de Groot 1978; Holding 1985. Chess players' memory: Chase & Simon 1973. Basketball: Allard et al. 1980. Devi: Jensen 1990. "No, Hardy!": Snow 1969, 37. 50,000 chunks: Simon & Chase 1973.

Time Needed: 10 Years. Time needed: Simon & Chase 1973. Unseasoned players: Holding 1985, 32–33. Mozart: Blom 1974. Musical preparation: Hayes 1989b, 293– 99; cf. Simonton 1991b. See also: Bloom 1985; Pressey & Combs 1943.

Flashbulbs. "I was seated": Brown & Kulik 1977, 74. "My father and I": Colegrove 1899, 247–48. Definition: Brown & Kulik 1977. Table 3.2: Events studied in Brown & Kulik 1977; Colegrove 1899; Neisser 1982, 1986; Neisser & Harsch 1992; Pillemer 1984; Rubin & Kozin 1984; Thompson & Cowan 1986; Winograd & Killinger 1983; Yarmey & Bull 1978. JFK, Evers, Malcolm X, King, and Wallace assassinations: Brown & Kulik 1977. Errors: Neisser 1982; cf. Neisser & Harsch 1992. Interpretations: McCloskey et al. 1988; Winograd & Killinger 1983. "Now print!": Brown & Kulik 1977. Emotion: Pillemer 1984. Benchmarks: Neisser 1982; cf. Pillemer 1984; Winograd & Killinger 1983. "we remember" and "the term 'flashbulb'" Neisser 1982, 48.

Autobiographies. "I can remember": F. Darwin 1892/1958, 43. "when you put down": Day 1949, 264. Memory of eminent psychologists: Mackavey et al. 1991. John Dean: Neisser 1981. Egocentrism: Greenwald 1980. Turning points: Ross & Sicoly 1979.

Hindsights. "I began by telling the President": Neisser 1981, 154, who discusses Dean. Hindsight bias: Fischhoff 1975. Nixon's trips: Fischhoff & Beyth 1975. Gubernatorial elections: Synodinos 1986. Presidential elections: Leary 1982. "known to have predicted" and "missed by just 6 hours": Kerr 1991, 253.

Attribution: Judging People and Events. Warren Commission report: Warren Commission 1964. "people have an irrational need": McCauley & Jacques 1979, 637, who conducted the experiment.

It's Not Their Fault!: Attributions about Others. JFK: Sokolsky 1964. Presidential greatness: Kenney & Rice 1988; Simonton 1987e, 1991f. Equivalences use: Simonton 1986h. Generality of effect: Simonton 1986c. Monarchs' eminence: Simonton 1984g. Assassinated presidents' traits: Simonton 1986g, 1986h, 1988d. Assassination attempts: Simonton 1986g, 1991f; cf. Holmes & Elder 1989; Simonton 1981. King assassination: Rokeach 1970.

It's Not My Fault!: Self-Serving Attributions. Sports: Lau & Russell 1980; cf. Mann 1974; Winkler & Taylor 1979. Wisconsin: Kingdon 1967. Watts riots: Sears & McConahay 1973.

Two Sides of Every Question: Simple versus Complex Thinking. PCT stems: Schroder et al. 1967, 25. "Stiff trade tariffs" and "Saudi Arabia seeks": both in Tetlock et al. 1984, 983. Revolutionaries: Suedfeld and Rank 1976. Robert E. Lee: Suedfeld et al. 1986. Presidential elections: Tetlock 1981b; cf. Wallace & Suedfeld 1988. Simple vs. complex campaign messages: West 1984. Hitler's DQ: Ertel 1985.

Mental Twists and Turns in History? Memory for presidents: Brown & Siegler 1991; Roediger & Crowder 1976. Impressions of presidents: Anderson 1973. Presidential rating survey: Murray & Blessing 1983; see also Murray & Blessing 1988. Scandal: Simonton 1986g, 1986h, 1991f; cf. Kenney & Rice 1988. Wartime leaders: Nice 1984; Simonton 1984g, 1987e. "My argument is that": Hardy 1903–08/1978, 88. "marked by the rare advantage": Gibbon 1776–88/1952, vol. 1, 32. For more illustrations, see: Ballard & Suedfeld 1988; Cell 1974; Simonton 1986c, 1987e, 1990e. "And glory long": Byron 1818–23/1949, 156.

Chapter 4

Problem Solving. "Most writers—poets in especial": Poe 1846/1884, 159. "It is my design": Poe 1846/1884, 160. Commonality of genius: Boden 1991; Hayes 1989; Perkins 1981; Weisberg 1992.

Laboratory Models of Creativity. Gestalt theory: Wertheimer 1945/1982. "required to handle": Simon 1973, 479. "On eight occasions": Simon 1986, 7. Balmer's formula: Qin & Simon 1990, 305. "interested in how" and "In order to follow": Qin & Simon 1990, 283.

Computer Imitations of Genius. Background of AI: Boden 1991; Crevier 1993.

Chess Players? Computer chess: Levy & Newborn 1982. Computer vs. Kasparov: Waldrop 1989. Computer vs. Polgar: "Computer beats chess whiz" 1993. Human strategy: Holding 1985.

Expert Systems. Expert systems: Duda & Shortliffe 1983. COOKER: Turpin 1988. MYCIN: Buchanan & Shortliffe 1984. Creative expert systems: MacCrimmon & Wagner 1987.

Discovery Programs. "Heuristically programmed": Clarke 1968, 95. Discovery's logic: Simon 1973. Discovery programs: Langley et al. 1987. Program names: Shrager & Langley 1990. BACON: Bradshaw et al. 1983. KEKADA: Kulkarni & Simon 1988. Faraday: Tweney 1990. Milieu: Simonton 1988e. Problem finding: Csikszentmihalyi 1988. "Galileo formulated the problem": Einstein & Infeld 1938, 95.

Originality. Campbell's model: Campbell 1960. "when it was only": Dryden 1664/ 1926, 1. "It takes two": Hadamard 1945, 30. Extensions: Eysenck 1993; Kantorovich 1993; Kantorovich & Ne'eman 1989; Martindale 1986a, 1990; Shrader 1980; Simonton 1988e, 1993a, 1993b; Stein & Lipton 1989.

What Creators Tell Us. Examples: Perkins 1981; Root-Bernstein 1989. Anthology: Ghiselin 1952. Questionnaires/interviews: Hadamard 1945; Platt & Baker 1931; Roe 1952.

Imagination and Associative Richness. "must have a vivid intuitive imagination": Planck 1949, 109. "a scientist of high achievement": Price 1963, 107. "Instead of thoughts": James 1880, 456. "a powerfully developed" and "more is required": Mach 1896, 167. Evidence: Gough 1976.

Intuition and Unconscious Processes. Quotes from "necessary to construct" to "unknown to us": Hadamard 1945, 28–29. "Then I turned my attention": Poincaré 1921, 388. "a manifest sign": Poincaré 1921, 389. Incubation: Wallas 1926. Introspections: Helmholtz 1898. "Ideas rose in crowds": Poincaré 1921, 387. Quotes from "the hooked atoms" to "new combinations": Poincaré 1921, 393. "The role of the preliminary . . . work": Poincaré 1921, 393–94.

Sensory Imagery and Dreams. Psychoanalytic theory: Freud 1908/1959. "regression in the service of the ego": Kris 1952. Primary-process thinking: Suler 1980. Quotes from "combinatory play" to "reproduced at will": Hadamard 1945, 142–43. "It is a serious drawback": Hadamard 1945, 69. "I turned my chair": Findlay 1948, 37. "One phenomenon is certain": Hadamard 1945, 8.

Janusian and Homospatial Thinking. Mirror images: Rothenberg 1979. "actively conceiving two or more opposite . . . ideas": Rothenberg 1979, 55. Einstein and Bohr: Rothenberg 1987. "One of the favorite maxims": Bohr 1967, 328. "actively conceiving two or more discrete entities": Rothenberg 1979, 69. Simulation: Rothenberg 1986.

Serendipity and Exploration. Table 4.1: Data from Austin 1978; Cannon 1940; Koestler 1964; Mach 1896; Shapiro 1986. "Serendipity": Cannon 1940. "Chance favors only": Beveridge 1957, 46. "were *seen* numbers of times": Mach 1896, 169. "a first principle": Skinner 1959, 363. "instinct for arresting exceptions": F. Darwin 1892/1958, 101. "I was struck by the obsession": Chipp 1968, 429. "Sometimes for several years": Chipp 1968, 595. Art students: Getzels & Csikszentmihalyi 1976. "We are all agreed": Cropper 1970, 57.

The Unending Search for the New. Other inventories: Beveridge 1957; Boden 1991; Koestler 1964; Perkins 1981; Root-Bernstein 1989. Martindale's theory: Martindale 1975, 1984b, 1986a, 1990. "Beneath your fair head": Martindale 1975, 71, italics removed. "I love you opposite the seas": Martindale 1975, 88. Simulation: Martindale 1973. "A pencil is like _____" responses: Martindale 1990, 348. Italian painting: Martindale 1986b. Classical music: Martindale & Uemura 1983. Literature: Martindale 1975, 1984a, 1990.

Aesthetic Merit. "as civilisation advances": Macaulay 1825/1900, 7. "Literature is news": Pound 1934, 15.

Great Art from the Outside. Canon problem: Gates 1992.

Name Dropping? Literature: Sherif 1935; cf. Asch 1948; Babad 1977; Bernberg 1953; Etaugh & Sanders 1974. Quality variations: Das et al. 1955. Self-confidence: Michael et al. 1949. Hungarian stories: Simonton 1988a. Basis of tastes: Martindale et al. 1988. Reputations over generations: Simonton 1991d.

Acquired Tastes? "Jukebox": Brickman & D'Amato 1978. Infant rats: Cross et al. 1967. Performance frequences: Moles 1958/1968, 29.

Great Art from the Inside. Oedipal conflict: Jones 1949. Gestalt studies: Arnheim 1962, 1971, 1986. Mondrian: Noll 1966.

Are There Musical Masterworks? "Music is the arithmetic of sounds": *Who Said What When* 1991, 252. Musical style: Paisley 1964; cf. Knopoff & Hutchinson 1983; Longuet-Higgins 1987, chs. 7–13; Youngblood 1958. "melody is the main thing": Landowska 1964, 336; cf. Karno & Konečni 1992. Computer ratings of masterworks: Simonton 1980c, 1980d, 1984h, 1986a. Table 4.2: Adapted from Simonton 1984h, Table 3, 13. Repertoire popularity: Simonton 1980d, 1983b, 1989c. Figure 4.1: Adapted from Simonton 1983b, Figure 1, 43. For a literary parallel, see: Kammann 1966.

Do Literary Masterpieces Exist? Shakespeare's plays: Derks 1989; Simonton 1983a, 1986f. "Poetry is as exact a science": *Who Said What When* 1991, 170. "bear the unmistakable stamp" and "are no better than": Evans 1974, 1747. "Let me not": Craig & Bevington 1973, 482. First sonnet study: Simonton 1989b. "I wish our clever young poets": Coleridge 1835, 84, italics removed. Second sonnet study: Simonton 1990c. "The most striking characteristic": Macaulay 1825/1900, 14. Short stories: Martindale 1988.

Duplicate Discoveries. Table 4.3: Data from Kroeber 1917; Ogburn & Thomas 1922; others. Priority disputes: Merton 1968. "discoveries and inventions become . . . inevitable": Merton 1961a, 306. "it was discovered in 1900": Kroeber 1917, 199. "Is great intelligence required" and "A consideration": White 1949, 212. "the basic difference": Price 1963, 69. Accounts: Boring 1963; Kroeber 1917; Lamb & Easton 1984; Merton 1961a, 1961b; Ogburn & Thomas 1922.

Four Questions about Multiples. "a failure to distinguish": Schmookler 1966, 191. See also: Constant 1978; Kuhn 1977, ch. 4. "have come to look": Zuckerman 1977, 203. Central message: Patinkin 1983. Artistic multiples: Stent 1972. Scientific idiosyncrasies: Holton 1971–72. "a mathematician will recognize": Koestler 1964, 265. "the claw of the lion": Asimov 1982, 153. "the last infirmity of nobel minds": McKenna 1983, 66. Study of 264 multiples: Merton 1961b. "social evolution is a resultant": James 1880, 448. "implications cannot be connected": Stent 1972, 84. "all the ideas are simple": Daintith et al. 1981, 531. "If Watson and Crick had not existed": Stent 1972, 90.

Three Characteristics of Multiples. Multiple grades: Simonton 1978a. Monotonic decline in grades: Kroeber 1917; Merton 1961b; Ogburn & Thomas 1922; Simonton 1979a. Skewed distribution of grades: Price 1963; Simonton 1978a, 1986e. Probabilistic models: Brannigan & Wanner 1983a; Price 1963; Schmookler 1966; Simonton 1978a, 1979a, 1986i. Communication models: Brannigan & Wanner 1983b; Simonton 1986d, 1986i, 1987c. Multiples participation: Simonton 1979a. Quotes from "great scientific genius" to "degrees of talent": Merton 1961b, 484. Qualification to Merton: Simonton 1979a. More discussion: Simonton 1987c; Simonton 1988e, ch. 6.

Chapter 5

"science of historical motivation": deMause 1981, 179. Clinical interpretation: Kohut 1986. Criticisms: Simonton 1983e; Stannard 1980.

Economic Prosperity and the Need for Achievement. "money is the sinews": Cohen & Cohen, 1960, 294. "art and literature flourish": Davis 1941, 572. *The Achieving Society*: McClelland 1961. "something for its own sake": McClelland 1984, 228.

Rich Peoples. Stories of 45 cultures: Child et al. 1958. Entrepreneurs: McClelland 1961. Study of 39 nations: McClelland 1961. "One day the tortoise": McClelland 1984, 432. Criticisms: Finison 1976; Frey 1984; Mazur & Rosa 1977.

Wealthy Times. U.S. achievement: deCharms & Moeller 1962. World literature: Bradburn & Berlew 1961; Cortés 1960; McClelland 1961. Doodles: Aronson 1958. Paintings: Davies 1969; McClelland 1961. National wealth: Bradburn & Berlew 1961; Cortés 1960; McClelland 1961.

Profitable Corporations. Car companies: McClelland 1984, 452–56. "nothing is as practical": Lewin 1947, 8. Training: McClelland & Winter 1969; McClelland 1984, 553–66.

Political Leadership and the Need for Power. Power and politicians: Lasswell 1948. "concern with impact": Winter 1980, 77.

The White House. First study: Donley & Winter 1970. Motivational studies: Wendt & Light 1976; Winter 1973, 1987b; Winter & Stewart 1977. Specific presidents: Winter 1987b. Unless otherwise indicated, findings come from the preceding sources. Charisma: House et al. 1991; Simonton 1988d. Assassination: Simonton 1986h; Wendt & Light 1976; Winter 1973. Powerful, charismatic presidents: Simonton 1986h. Great decisions: Winter 1987b. Greatness: Winter 1987b; Winter & Stewart 1977; cf. Holmes & Elder 1989; House et al. 1991; Simonton 1987e. Achievement-motivated presidents: Wendt & Light 1976 and Winter & Stewart 1977, unless otherwise noted. Machiavellianism: Simonton 1986h. Political creativity and neuroticism: Simonton 1988d. Affiliation-oriented presidents: Winter 1987b; Winter & Stewart 1977; cf. Hermann 1980a. Optimal motive profile: Spangler & House 1991; Winter 1980; Winter & Stewart 1977. Barber's typology: Barber 1977; cf. Simonton 1986h, 1988d; Winter 1987b.

The Campaign Trail. 1976 candidates: Winter 1982. 1988 candidates: Winter 1988b. "From one generation to the next": Winter 1988b, 22. "We must defeat the merger maniacs": Winter 1988b, 22.

The International Scene. Southern Africa: Winter 1980. Quotes from "initiation, continuation" to "than to wait": Winter 1980, 81. County officials: Browning & Jacob 1964. Activists: Rothman & Lichter 1980. Politburo: Hermann 1980a. Heads of state: Hermann 1980b. "The greater the leaders' need": Hermann 1980b, 31.

Group Fantasy Analysis. "Freud postulated": Cocks & Crosby 1987, 310. *The History of Childhood*: deMause 1974. Group motives: McClelland 1961, 1975. Don Juan: Winter 1973.

Psychobiography. Wilson: Freud & Bullitt 1967. "Hitlerature": Binion 1976; Langer 1972. Nixon: Brodie 1983; Chesen 1973; Mazlish 1972. Mazlish's 1972 claims: Elms 1976, 109. Potential problems: Elms 1988. Winter and Carlson's study of Nixon: Winter & Carlson 1988. "In May 1970": Winter & Carlson 1988, 77. Bush and Gorbachev: Winter et al. 1991a, 1991b.

The Ultimate Motive for Greatness? "You must have no dependence": Reynolds 1769–90/1966, 37. "As is the case in all branches": Pavlova 1956, 118. Long hours: Boyce et al. 1985; Chambers 1964; Hargens 1978; Manis 1951. Specific hours: Simon 1974. Quotes from "driving absorption" to "anything else": Roe 1952, 25. Simon's 100 hours: Hayes 1989a, 137. "genius is one per cent.": *Oxford University Press Dictionary of Quotations* 1953/1985, 195. "The only place": *Who Said What When* 1991, 341. "Work,

Finish, Publish": Beveridge 1957, 161. "The biography of the inventive genius": Barron 1963, 139. Dennis study: Dennis 1955. Price law: Price 1963, ch. 3; cf. Lotka 1926; Simonton 1984d. Composers: Moles 1958/1968. Elitist productivity: Davis 1987; Dennis 1955; Shockley 1957. Psychologists: Dennis 1954c; cf. Wispé 1965. Post-Ph.D. publications: Bloom 1963. "the appearance of a single great genius": Lombroso 1891, 120. "Genius does what it must": *Oxford University Press Dictionary of Quotations* 1953/ 1985, 337. "I mean those qualities": Galton 1892/1972, 77.

Chapter 6

"The Child is father of the Man": Wordsworth 1807/1928, 79. Terman volumes (except vol. 2): Terman 1925; Burks et al. 1930; Terman & Oden 1947, 1959. Recent studies: Holahan 1984–85; Oden 1968; Tomlinson-Keasey & Little 1990; Tomlinson-Keasey et al. 1986; Vaillant & Vaillant 1980. Retrospective studies: Galton 1874; Roe 1952; cf. Bloom 1985; Zuckerman 1977. Successors to Cox 1926: Goertzel & Goertzel 1962; McCurdy 1960; Raskin 1936; Walberg et al. 1980.

Hercules's Cradle: The Impact of Family Background. "cradle of eminence": Goertzel & Goertzel 1962. Various family factors: see Goertzel & Goertzel 1962; Goertzel et al. 1978. "He was the first-born child": Roe 1952, 22. General review: Simonton 1987b.

Oldest, Youngest, and In-Between. Siblings in Science: Simonton 1992c. Identical twins: Gedda 1951/1961. Candolle's attack: Candolle 1873. Galton's survey: Galton 1874. Birth order: Adams 1972; Altus 1966; Schachter 1963. 64 scientists: Roe 1952. Half or more of great scientists: Chambers 1964; Eiduson 1962; Helmreich et al. 1980; Rubin 1970; Terry 1989. Citation rates: Helmreich et al. 1980. Creativity ratings: Helson & Crutchfield 1970. Nobel Prize: Clark & Rice 1982. *A Study of British Genius* (rev. ed.): Ellis 1926. Composers: Schubert et al. 1977. National politics: Wagner & Schubert 1977; Zweigenhaft 1975. Celebrities of 20th century: Goertzel et al. 1978. Table 6.1: Data largely from Goertzel et al. 1978; Lucaire 1991.

Intellect? Netherlands: Belmont & Marolla 1973. National Merit Scholarship Qualifying Test: Breland 1974. Prodigies: Feldman with Goldsmith 1986. Gifted: Terman 1925. Education: Altus 1966; Schachter 1963. Scientific careers: West 1960. Eminence: Schachter 1963. Confluence model: Zajonc 1986; cf. Retherford & Sewell 1991. Exposure to adults: Walberg et al. 1980. Curvilinear effect: Ellis 1926. Stripteasers: Skipper & McCaghy 1970. Dangerous sports: Nisbett 1968. Personality development: Albert 1980; Stewart 1977.

Personality? "if a man has been": Clark 1980, 19. Dethronement: Adler 1938. Individual psychology: Bliss 1970; Eisenman 1964; Wagner & Schubert 1977; Zweigenhaft 1975. Senate and House: Zweigenhaft 1975. U.S. presidents: Wagner & Schubert 1977. Vice-presidency: Wendt & Muncy 1979. "And is he still": Stagner 1988, 374. Writers: Bliss 1970. Revolutionaries: Stewart 1977, 1991; Walberg et al. 1980; cf. Hudson 1990. Harris's argument: Harris 1964. Personality differences: Eisenman 1987; Ernst & Angst 1983. "nationalism, need for power": Hudson 1990, 597. American presidents: Simonton 1986h, 1988d. Chief justices: Weber 1984. Sulloway's study: Sulloway 1990. Paternal namesakes: Barry 1979.

Building Character: Early Adversity. "In quiet, uneventful lives": Butler 1903/ n.d., 288. Hardships: Goertzel & Goertzel 1962. Table 6.2: Data from several sources, such as Eisenstadt et al. 1989; Goertzel et al. 1978; Illingworth & Illingworth 1969, 34–35; Silverman 1974; Woodward 1974. Study of 699 figures: Eisenstadt 1978. Cox 1926: Albert 1971. Follow-up study: Walberg et al. 1980; cf. Goertzel et al. 1978. Scientists: Berry 1981; Eiduson 1962; Roe 1952; Silverman 1974; cf. Woodward 1974. Mathematicians: Roe 1952. Writers: Brown 1968; cf. Martindale 1972. Literary Nobel laureates: Berry 1981. Mother loss: Simonton 1986b. Critical view: Woodward 1974. College students: Roe 1952. Prime ministers: Berrington 1974; Rentchnik 1989. Juvenile delinquents and psychiatric patients: Eisenstadt 1978; cf. Brown 1968; Tomlinson-Keasey et al. 1986. "The bereavement reaction": Eisenstadt 1978, 220. Broader view: Goertzel & Goertzel 1962. "either lost at least one parent": Berry 1981, 387. Handicaps: Goertzel & Goertzel 1962. "If you had spent two years": Boller 1981, 266. "Our strength grows": Emerson 1841a/1941, 163.

Booster Shots: Early Stimulation. Statistics: Roe 1952. Professional homes: Berry 1981; Chambers 1964; Eiduson 1962; Elliott 1975; Helson & Crutchfield 1970; Moulin 1955; Taylor 1963; West 1961; Wispé 1965. Nobel laureates: Zuckerman 1977. American politicians: Matthews 1954. Presidents and justices: Baltzell & Schneiderman 1988, 1991; cf. Holmes & Elder 1989. Chief justices: Baltzell & Schneiderman 1991. For world leaders generally: Blondel 1980. Chess players: Elo 1978. Broader samples: Cox 1926; Raskin 1936; Simonton 1976a. Sample of 300 moderns: Goertzel, Goertzel & Goertzel 1978. The gifted: Terman 1925; Tomlinson-Keasey & Little 1990. Prodigies: Feldman with Goldsmith 1986. Stimulation: Goertzel & Goertzel 1962; Howe 1982; Roe 1952; Walberg et al. 1980; cf. Schaefer & Anastasi 1968. Encouragement to explore: Walberg et al. 1980. Parental training: McCurdy 1960; cf. Bloom 1985. Class and education: Simonton 1976a; Terman 1925; Terman & Oden 1947.

Students and Schools: The Impact of Education. "it is, in fact": Schlipp 1951, 17. "One had to cram": Hoffman 1972, 31.

Quality of Scholastic Performance. "For me it came": Seelig 1958, 28. School hated: Goertzel et al. 1978. Mystics and psychics: Simonton 1986b. Positive responses: Goertzel et al. 1978. Science: Chambers 1964; cf. Schaefer & Anastasi 1968. Grades and scientific success: Gaston 1973, 51; Hoyt 1965; MacKinnon 1960; Razik 1967; Taylor 1963; Taylor et al. 1963. F.R.S.: Hudson 1958. GPA in general areas: Baird 1968; Bednar & Parker 1965; Guilford 1959; McClelland 1973. Honor students: Goertzel et al. 1978. Methodological issues: Barrett & Depinet 1991. Mean IQs in colleges and universities: Cronbach 1960. Mensa: Serebriakoff 1985. High grades or honors and success: Barrett & Depinet 1991; Cohen 1984. Wesleyan College: Nicholson 1915. Reviews: Bretz 1989; Cohen 1984; Dye & Reck 1989; Samson et al. 1984. Poor and excellent students in science: Baird 1968; Chambers 1964; Owens 1969; Taylor & Ellison 1967; Taylor et al. 1963. Educational atmosphere: Torrance 1962. "Much of our educational system": Roe 1952, 82. Sectarian schools: Thistlethwaite 1963. Best teachers: Roe 1952; cf. Schaefer & Anastasi 1968; Thistlethwaite 1963. "were unwilling to accept anything": MacKinnon 1962, 494. Prestigious institutions: Blackburn et al. 1978. Especially among notable scientists: Helmreich et al. 1980; Wispé 1965; Zuckerman 1977. Youthful winners of doctorates: Albert 1975; Blackburn et al. 1978; Eagly 1974; Harmon 1963; Lyons 1968; Visher 1947. Eminent psychologists and age at Ph.D.: Lyons 1968; Simonton 1992b; Wispé 1965. "an individual who comes": Bloom 1963, 258.

Quantity of Formal Education. "I shall not become a Ph.D.": Hoffman 1972, 55. "The idea that it is necessary": Brittain 1948, 7. "He who can, does": Shaw 1903, 230. "There are nowadays": Thoreau 1854/1942, 39. More than 300, 1841–1948: Goertzel et al. 1978. Figure 6.1: Data from Simonton 1976a; figure itself reprinted from Simonton 1983c. Additional analyses: Simonton 1983c; Simonton 1984d, ch. 4; Simonton 1987b. 314 celebrities: Simonton 1984d, ch. 4. Scientific vs. artistic creativity: Simonton 1988e.

Self-Education and Extracurricular Activities. Gifted reading habits: Terman 1925; cf. Schaefer & Anastasi 1968. Celebrities' voracious reading: Goertzel et al. 1978. Reading and eminence: Simonton 1984d, 74. Reading unnecessary: Goertzel et al. 1978; Simonton 1986b. Politicians' extracurricular activities: Goertzel et al. 1978. "I have never let": Harnsberger 1972, 553. Uneven course grades: MacKinnon 1960. Schooling in art and music: Simonton 1986b. Authors' voracious reading: Simonton 1986b. Authors' detesting school: Goertzel et al. 1978. Collegiate failures: Goertzel & Goertzel 1962.

Minorities and Immigrants. Quotes from "Every advance in" to "cultural groups": Park 1928, 881. "Persons who have been uprooted": Campbell 1960, 391. "Creative minority": Toynbee 1946. Jewish eminence: Arieti 1976, 325–36; Hayes 1989, Table 4; Veblen 1919. Jewish laureates: Berry 1981. Jewish chess players: de Groot 1978. U.S. science and religious affiliation: Lehman & Witty 1931. Immigrants among mathematicians: Helson & Crutchfield 1970. Immigrants among famous moderns: Goertzel et al. 1978. Swiss vs. Russian Jews: Berry 1981. Suppressed nationalities: Kroeber 1944. "In order for civilization": Sorokin 1947/1969, 543. "Universal states": Toynbee 1946. Political fragmentation: Naroll et al. 1971; Simonton 1975b, 1976f. Heterogeneity: Simonton 1976d.

Adherents to Unconventional Life Styles. Unconventional life styles: Goertzel et al. 1978. Table 6.3: Data from Goertzel et al. 1978; Lucaire 1991; others. Creativity in homosexuals: Domino 1977; cf. Rothenberg 1990, ch. 9. Creativity linked with autonomy, anticonformity: Crutchfield 1962; Helson & Crutchfield 1970; MacKinnon 1978; Roe 1952. Marriage: Ellis 1926; Goertzel et al. 1978; McCurdy 1960. Androgyny: Barron 1963; Helson 1980; MacKinnon 1978; cf. Harrington & Anderson 1981. Mothers: Goertzel & Goertzel 1962. Feminine poets: Martindale 1972.

Provincials. Artistic fields: Simonton 1984a. Classical music: Simonton 1977b, 1986a. Science: Berry 1981.

Trespassers and Interlopers. Outsider innovations: Hughes 1958. Marginality in science: Hudson & Jacot 1986. "All decisive advances": Koestler 1964, 230. "It has often happened": Bartlett 1958, 58. "Almost always the men": Kuhn 1970, 90. "I had an immense advantage": Beveridge 1957, 5. "But I never" /"So much the better": Asimov 1982, 423. X-ray astronomy: Simonton 1984e; cf. Gieryn & Hirsh 1983. Continental drift: Stewart 1986.

Is Genius Born or Made? "A devil": Shakespeare circa 1595–1611/1952, vol. 27, 543. "The phrase 'nature and nurture'": Galton 1874, 12.

Nurtured Genius. Intuitive vs. analytical genius: Simonton 1988e, ch.3. Intelligence vs. creativity: Getzels & Jackson 1963; Wallach & Kogan 1965. Normal vs. revolutionary science: Kuhn 1970. Domain selection vs. achievement: Simonton 1986b. Biographical typicality: Simonton 1986b.

Natural Genius. Variation in expertise acquisition: Simonton 1991b. Environmental variables reflect genetic dispositions: Plomin & Bergeman 1991; Scarr & McCartney 1983; Simonton 1991c. "The true Genius": Johnson 1781, 5. Crystallizing experiences: Walters & Gardner 1986. Home environments of gifted adolescents: Schaefer & Anastasi 1968. Age of parents at birth of their celebrated child: Ellis 1926; Raskin 1936; Simonton 1992c; Visher 1947. Fertility of exceptional people: Ellis 1926; Simonton 1992c.

Chapter 7

"If you haven't cut your name": Lehman 1953, 185–86. "would be one of the greatest": Hoffman 1972, 7. Career aspect of achievement: Wallace & Gruber 1989.
   Creators. Successor to Quetelet 1835/1968: Beard 1874. *Age and Achievement*: Lehman 1953. Critics of Lehman: Bullough et al. 1978; Cole 1979; Dennis 1954d, 1956a, 1966. Lehman's defense: Lehman, 1956, 1958, 1962, 1963, 1966a, 1966b. Technical problems: Simonton 1988b, 1989a, 1990e.
   The Productivity Curve. Curve's fit and Figure 7.1: Simonton 1984b; cf. Bayer & Dutton 1977. Age at career onset: Raskin 1936; cf. Albert 1975; Simonton 1991a, 1991b, 1992b. Nobel laureates: Zuckerman 1977; cf. Cole 1979; Lehman 1953; Simonton 1992b. Possible high productivity at end: Dennis 1966; Lehman 1953; Simonton 1988b. Competition: Dennis 1954d; Simonton 1977a, 1980d. Illness: Lehman 1953; Simonton 1977a. Administrative duties: Garvey & Tomita 1972; Roe 1965, 1972; Stern 1978. Fertility: Hargens et al. 1978; McDowell 1982.
   Quantity versus Quality. Debate: Dennis 1954d; Lehman 1956. Empirical equivalence: Simonton 1977a, 1985b, 1988b. Equal-odds rule (originally styled the constant-probability-of-success principle): Simonton 1977a, 1985b, 1988b. Further evidence: Davis 1987; Over 1989, 1990.
   Interdisciplinary Contrasts. Figure 7.2 Data from Dennis 1966; figure itself reprinted from Simonton 1990e, Figure 5.3, 120. Poetry vs. novel writing: Dennis 1966; Simonton 1975a, 1989a. "When one hears of a poet": *Who Said What When* 1991, 253. Contrasts across disciplines: Abt 1983; Adams 1946; Cole 1979; Dennis 1956b; Hermann 1988; Lehman 1963, 1966a, 1966b; Levin & Stephan 1989; Manniche & Falke 1957; Moulin 1955; cf. Christensen & Jacomb 1992; Shin & Putnam 1982. "A person who has not made": Brodetsky 1942, 699. "Age is, of course": Jungk 1958, 27. Other career landmark studies: Lindauer 1993b; Pressey & Combs 1943; Raskin 1936; Zhao 1984; Zhao & Jiang 1986; Zusne 1976. Formal derivation of landmarks: Simonton 1991a, 1991b. Figure 7.3: Data from Simonton 1991a, Table 2, 126. F.R.S.: Hardy 1940/1969. "not know an instance": Hardy 1940/1969, 72. Last work in mathematics: Simonton 1991a.
   Individual Differences. Chronological vs. career age: Bayer & Dutton 1977; Lyons 1968; Simonton 1984a, 1988b, 1989a. Correlation of chronological and career age: Bayer & Dutton 1977. American Nobel laureates: Zuckerman 1977. Formal definitions of creative potential: Simonton 1984a, 1988b, 1989a. Creative potential and career trajectories: Simonton 1991a, 1991b, 1992b. Age at best work independent of output and fame: Raskin 1936; Simonton 1991a, 1991b, 1992b; Zusne 1976; cf. Horner et al. 1986. Correlation between creativity and the first and last landmarks: Simonton 1984a, 1989a, 1991a, 1991b, 1992b; cf. Christensen & Jacomb 1992; Dennis 1954b; Over 1982a, 1982b, 1988. Figure 7.4: Reprinted from Simonton 1991a. More detailed, and mathematical, deductions: Simonton 1991a, 1991b. Empirical demonstrations: Simonton 1984a, 1989a, 1991a, 1991b, 1992b.
   Leaders. Lehman's leadership studies: Lehman 1953, ch.11; cf. Oleszek 1969. Presidents: Simonton 1981, 1986g, 1987e; cf. Murphy 1984. Monarchs: Simonton 1984f. Military victory: Simonton 1980a.
   Making It in Politics. "a lover of young man": Machiavelli 1513/1952, 36. "Almost everything that's great": Disraeli 1849, 118–19. Revolutionaries: Rejai 1979. Status quo leaders: Blondel 1980. American leaders: Lehman 1953.
   Making It in Religion. "Innocent III., the greatest": Disraeli 1849, 119. Statistics: Lehman 1953, 173–74. "men in their prime": Hall 1922, 420.

Celebrities. "is a food that dead men eat": Dobson 1913, 569.

The Best in Sports. Lehman on sports: Lehman 1953, ch. 16. Follow-up: Schulz & Curnow 1988.

The Supreme at Chess. Lehman on chess: Lehman 1953, 18; cf. Buttenwieser 1935; de Groot 1978, 354; Draper 1963; Rubin 1960. Elo's study: Elo 1965. His follow-up: Elo 1978.

The Triumphant at Business. Lehman on business: Lehman 1953, ch. 10. Income peak at 40: Stolzenberg 1975.

Life Themes. Study of 10 composers: Simonton 1977a. Luther: Erikson 1958. Topics of 81 plays: Simonton 1983a. Shakespeare: Simonton 1986f.

New Tricks. "The imputation of Novelty": Locke 1690/1952, 85. "when a true genius appears": Esar 1949/1989, 196. Quotes from "expect to convince" to "question with impartiality": Darwin 1860/1952, 240. "A new scientific truth": Planck 1949, 33–34. Reception of Darwin's theory: Hull et al. 1978. Complications: Messerli 1988; Stewart 1986. "As a scientist gets older": Barber 1961, 601. "the conceptions I have summarized": Freud 1929/1952, 790. "God does not play": Hoffmann 1972, 193. Cliometrics: Diamond 1980. Acceptance rates: Whaples 1991. Another study: Oromaner 1977. Judicial conservatism: Schubert 1983; cf. Tetlock et al. 1985. "It took me fifteen years": Esar 1949/1989, 28. "People seldom improve": Esar 1949/1989, 83.

The Raw Facts. Further discussion: Simonton 1988b, 1990a, 1990b. "It is a pity": Ewen 1965, 863.

The Range of Theories. Lehman's interpretations: Lehman 1953, ch. 20. "When the age is in": Shakespeare circa 1595–1611/1952, vol. 26, 520. Cognitive changes: Simonton 1988b, 1990a. "At 83 Shaw's mind": *Who Said What When* 1991, 256. "years steal/Fire": Byron 1812–16/1905, 186. Fourth model: Simonton 1984b, 1988b, 1988e, 1991a, 1991b. Continued reading: Dennis & Girden 1954.

Swan Songs. Novelists: Porter & Suedfeld 1981. APA presidents: Suedfeld 1985. Sudden vs. slow death: Suedfeld & Piedrahita 1984. Burst of creative vitality: Haefele 1962; cf. Davis 1953. Late-life style: Arnheim 1986; Lindauer 1992, 1993a. "Opus Ultimum": Einstein 1956, ch. 5. Swan-song phenomenon: Simonton 1989c. "Network of enterprises": Gruber 1989. "melody almost too limpid": Blom 1974, 181. Layton: Ryan 1989.

Death: The Sequel. "Life levels all men": Shaw 1903, 240. Life expectancies: Cox 1926; Raskin 1936; Simonton 1975a, 1977b, 1991a, 1991b, 1992a; Sorokin 1925, 1926. Changes in life expectancy: Barinaga 1991. The 301 geniuses: Cox 1926. Poets vs. prose authors: Simonton 1975a. Composers and mathematicians: Simonton 1977b, 1991a. Precocity: Simonton 1977b, 1991a; Zhao & Jiang 1986. Figure 7.5 Data from Simonton 1976a; figure itself reprinted from Simonton 1984d, Figure 3, 89. "Martyrdom is the only way": Esar 1949/1989, 181. Obituary columns: Mills 1942; Lehman 1943. Adams and Jefferson quotes: deGregorio 1989, 51.

Chapter 8

Testing IQs in Contemporary Figures. Galton's tests: Galton 1883. Cattell's work: Cattell 1890.

The Origins of True Intelligence Tests. Table 8.1: Data from several sources, especially Storfer 1990 and Cronbach 1960. Illustrious members of Mensa: Serebriakoff 1985.

How Much Success Can High Test Scores Buy? "when Poincaré was acknowledged": Bell 1937, 532. IQ and occupational achievement: Tomlinson-Keasey & Little

1990. IQs for occupations: Stewart 1947 (these are Army General Classification Test scores rescaled to a standard deviation of about 16). Skepticism about IQ: McClelland 1973; cf. Barrett & Depinet 1991; Dreher & Bretz 1991. Null or weak results regarding correlation between IQ and creative success within careers: Bayer & Folger 1966; Bloom 1963; Cole & Cole 1973, 69–70; Helson & Crutchfield 1970; Jones 1964. Termites' IQs: Terman 1925. "Nearly 2000 scientific and technical papers": Terman & Oden 1959, 147. Figures for American Nobel laureates calculated from Zuckerman 1977, 302. Marilyn Jarvik: McFarlan 1989, 26.

    Gauging IQs in Historic Personalities. "a new name": the title of Woods 1909. "the facts of history": Woods 1909, 703. "psychology of genius": Woods 1911. "MY DEAR ADÈLE": Cox 1926, 42.

    Cox's 301 Geniuses. Cox's study: Cox 1926. Cattell's list: Cattell 1903. Similar studies and follow-ups: Raskin 1936; Simonton 1976a; Sorokin 1925, 1926; Walberg et al. 1980; Woods 1906. Composers' and presidents' IQs (uncorrected estimates for ages 0–17): Cox 1926.

    What Do Precocious Intellects Achieve? Intelligence–eminence correlation: Simonton 1976a, 1991e; Walberg et al. 1980. Versatility: Simonton 1976a; cf. Raskin 1936; White 1931. Monarchs: Simonton 1983d, 1984g; cf. Woods 1906, 1913. Presidents: Simonton 1986h. "Mediocrity knows nothing higher": *Who Said What When* 1991, 578. Presidential brilliance: Simonton 1986h, 1988d, 1991f; cf. McCann 1992.

    Complications in Linking Intelligence to Achievement. Criticisms: Gould 1981; McClelland 1973; cf. Barrett & Depinet 1991; Simonton 1990e.

    Extremes and Elites. Figure 8.1: Reprinted from Simonton 1985a, Figure 1, 534. Actual distribution: Burt 1963. Figure 8.2: Reprinted from Simonton 1988e, Figure 4.1, 66 (distributions obtained via Monte Carlo methods). Multiplicative model: Burt 1943; Shockley 1957; Simonton 1988e. "high but not the highest": Cox 1926, 187.

    Triangles and Thresholds. Triangular function: Guilford 1967. Threshold IQ of 120: Barron & Harrington 1981; MacKinnon 1962. Curvilinear model: Simonton 1985a. Figure 8.4: Reprinted from Simonton 1985a, Figure 3, 540. Winning votes: Simonton 1986h. Low IQs of generals and admirals: Cox 1926. Boy with 190 IQ: Hollingworth 1926. Presidents vs. prime ministers calculated from: Cox 1926. Creators vs. leaders: Simonton 1976a. "Oh, they are not for you": Knight 1973, 67.

    Unity and Variety. 120 factors: Guilford 1967. Triarchic theory: Sternberg 1985. Seven intelligences: Gardner 1983. Seven exemplars: Gardner 1993. Grandmasters: de Groot 1978. Chess celebrities: Elo 1978. Scientists' IQ scores: Roe 1952.

    Prodigies versus Geniuses. Precocious youths: Bloom 1985; Feldman with Goldsmith 1986; Radford 1990. Table 8.2: Data from several sources, including Cox 1926, Radford 1990. "I only said I was the greatest": Van Lange 1991, 693. "I was not a Child Prodigy": Day 1949, 4. Sidis: Montour 1977; Wiener 1953, 131–35. Savants: Howe 1989. "Midlife crisis": Bamberger 1986. Crystallizing experiences: Walters & Gardner 1986. Finding one's life work: Ebersole & DeVogler-Ebersole 1985. "There's only one thing worse": Ferris 1977, 49. Study of 120 composers: Simonton 1991b. More evidence on the speed of expertise acquisition for the talented: Bloom 1985. Processing speed: Jensen et al. 1989.

Chapter 9

    Idealists and Dogmatists. Ratings of 33 presidents: Maranell 1970. Inflexibility correlates: Simonton 1986h, 1988d. Idealism and morality: Simonton 1986h. Dogmatism: Simonton 1981, 1986g; Wendt & Light 1976. Background: Wendt & Light 1976. Education: Simonton 1983c. Figure 9.1: Reprinted from Simonton 1983c, Figure 2, 155. Creativity: Simonton 1983c. Professors: Simonton 1981. Attitudes toward dogmatism: Simonton 1987e. Military intervention: Wendt & Light 1976. Presidental greatness: Simonton 1987e.

Pessimists and Ruminators. Exploratory studies: Zullow et al. 1988. Quotes from Eisenhower and Stevenson: Zullow et al. 1988, 677. 1900–84 elections: Zullow & Seligman 1990. "a dealer in hope": McKenna 1983, 107. Athletic performance: Seligman et al. 1990. Winning streaks: Simonton 1980a.

Workaholics versus Beachcombers. Mothers: Matthews et al. 1977. Scholastic success: Ovcharchyn et al. 1981. Challenging goals: Ward & Eisler 1987. Mastery orientation: Matthews et al. 1980. Self-efficacy: Taylor et al. 1984. Researcher achievements: Matthews et al. 1980; Taylor et al. 1984. Aggressiveness and success: Simonton 1991e.

Heroes and Adventurers. Equal-odds rule: Dennis 1954a; Simonton 1984d, 1985b. Perfectionists vs. mass producers: Cole & Cole 1973. American Nobel Laureates: Zuckerman 1977; cf. Helson & Crutchfield 1970. Publication and citation: Davis 1987; Cole & Cole 1973; Helmreich et al. 1980; Simonton 1984i, 1992b. Three most cited works: Cole & Cole 1973. Bibliographies of 19th-century scientists: Dennis 1954a; cf. Dennis 1954c. "The chances are": Bennet 1980, 15.

Dominants and Extroverts. Interpersonal generalization theory: Etheredge 1978. Table 9.1: Data from Etheredge 1978, Table 1, 439.

Saints versus Sinners. Nazi physicians: Lifton 1986. Eichmann: Arendt 1963; Von Lang & Sibyll 1983. "Banality of evil": Arendt 1963. Rescuers: Oliner & Oliner 1988. "I learned to be good": Oliner & Oliner 1988, 164. Six stages: Kohlberg 1984. "no arts; no letters": Hobbes 1651/1952, 85. "A law is unjust": King 1963/1968, 145. "One who breaks": King 1963/1968, p. 146. "If I had sabotaged": Kohlberg 1984, 54. Free Speech protesters: Haan et al. 1968; cf. Nassi 1981; cf. O'Conner 1974. Virtue measures: Simonton 1983d, 1984g; Thorndike 1936; Woods 1906. Monarchs: Simonton 1983d. Intelligence: Simonton 1983d; Thorndike 1936; Woods 1906. Activity and eminence: Simonton 1984g.

Contemporary Profiles. "boldness, spontaneity": Cattell 1965, 372. "shyness and high responsiveness": Cattell 1965, 375. Olympic athletes: Cattell 1965, 242–43; see also Butt & Cox 1992; Kroll & Peterson 1965; Mahoney & Avener 1977; Morgan 1980. Distinguished scientists: Cattell 1963, 1965. General pattern: Cattell 1963. "It is only half-an-hour'": Allen 1948, 230. "Tell her to wait": Asimov 1982, 415. Artistic vs. scientific profiles: Cattell & Butcher 1968. Two cultures: Snow 1960. "now for many years": F. Darwin 1892/1958, 53–54. "The more I understand": Coleridge 1801/1956, 709.

Historical Profiles. Cox traits: Cox 1926. Thorndike factors: Thorndike 1950; see also Knapp 1962; Simonton 1991e. Presidents' profiles: Simonton 1986h. "He was morally and physically courageous": Armbruster 1982, 172–73. ACL: Gough & Heilbrun 1965. Table 9.2: Reprinted from Simonton 1986h, Appendix, 159–60. Figure 9.3: Data from Simonton 1986h. Cluster analysis in Figure 9.4: Reprinted from Simonton 1986h, Figure 1, 155. Legislative success: Simonton 1986h. Charisma: Simonton 1988d. Controversality: Simonton 1986h. 16 PF and leadership: Cattell & Stice 1954.

Global Portraits. "the study of crippled . . . specimens": Maslow 1970, 180. Table 9.3: Information from Maslow 1970. "The most beautiful thing": Maslow 1970, 154.

Culture Mentalities. Societal extroversion–introversion: Lynn & Hampson 1975. Sorokin's work: Sorokin 1937–41. Reanalyses of Sorokin's data: Klingemann et al. 1982; Simonton 1976c, 1976g, 1978b. Ideationals in Sensate times: Simonton 1976c. Cross-media styles: Hasenfus et al. 1983.

Chapter 10

Discussion: Becker 1978; Prentky 1989; Richards 1981; Rothenberg 1990.

Madness and Genius. "Those who have become eminent": Andreasen & Canter 1974, 123. "no great genius": Seneca n.d./1932, 285. "The lunatic, the lover, and the poet": Shakespeare circa 1595–1611/1952, vol. 26, 370. "Great Wits are sure": Dryden 1681, 6. *The Man of Genius*: Lombroso 1891. "*First*, and most prominent": Babcock 1895, 752. "the nature of genius": James 1902, 22–23. Self-actualizers: Maslow 1959, 1972. "Perhaps no person can be a poet": Macaulay 1825/1900, 9.

Historical Conjectures. Table 10.1: Data from many sources, especially Arieti 1976; Babcock 1895; Goodwin & Jamison 1990, ch.14; Prentky 1980; Rothenberg 1990; and others. Ellis's 1904 study: Ellis 1926. Leaders vs. creators: Goertzel et al. 1978; cf. Ludwig 1992. Contrasts among creative fields: Ludwig 1992. Mad poets: Martindale 1972. "What garlic is to salad": Esar 1949/1989, 174.

Clinical Diagnoses. Writers Workshop: Andreasen & Canter 1974; Andreasen 1987. British creators: Jamison 1989. Germans: Juda 1949. Iceland: Karlson 1970. Pedigrees: McNeil 1971; Myerson & Boyle 1941; Richards et al. 1988.

Scientific Assessments. Psychometric advantage: Faust 1984; Meehl 1954. Architects and writers: Barron 1969; MacKinnon 1962. Artists: Götz & Götz 1979a, 1979b. Researchers: Rushton 1990. Cartoonists: Pearson 1983. Thinking patterns: Woody & Claridge 1977. "Have you good *digestion?*": Mersmann 1928/1972, 88–90. "as the notes of a song": Hadamard 1945, 69. Manic advantage: Jamison 1989; Richards 1981. "I arrived at the master's home": Forbes 1967, 735. Schumann: Slater & Meyer 1959. Ego Strength: Barron 1969. "*won't revise.* Not on your life": Rothenberg 1990, 63. "a cranky hysterical neurasthenic": Strouse 1988, 90. Genius–madness gene: Hammer & Zubin 1968.

Self-Destructiveness and Greatness. "It's worth a try" and "I feel better already" Richards 1990, 300.

Suicide. The 300: Goertzel et al. 1978. Writers: Andreasen 1987. Werther effect: Phillips 1974; cf. Wasserman 1984. Automobile and airplane accidents: Phillips 1979, 1980a, 1982. Celebrity suicides: Stack 1987a. Front-page suicides: Ishii 1991. Soap opera suicides: Phillips 1982. Presidential elections: Boor 1981; Boor & Fleming 1984; Lester 1990; cf. Masterton & Platt 1989; Wasserman 1983.

Addiction. Table 10.4: Data from Ludwig 1990, Rothenberg 1990, and many others. Iowa Writers Workshop: Andreasen 1987. Heavy drinkers: Ludwig 1990. Opportunity: Rothenberg 1990. Self-handicapping in sports: Rhodewalt et al. 1984. Deschapelles: Berglas 1985, 235. Hart: Berglas 1988. Single-mindedness: Crane 1965; Simonton 1992b. "I am going to drink myself dead": Murray & Murray 1959, 214. Alcoholic writers: Lester 1991; cf. Davis 1986.

Calendar Date and the Will to Live. "My birth-day": Moore circa 1820/1929, 530. "'Tis but the funeral": McKenna 1983, 24. *Who Was Who in America*, birthdays: Harrison & Kroll 1989–90. *Who Was Who in America*, Christmas: Harrison & Kroll

1985–86. Original work on dip–surge phenomenon: Phillips & Feldman 1973. Subsequent specific work on eminent: Harrison & Moore 1982–83; Zusne 1986–87. Everyday subjects: Baltes 1977–78; Marriott & Harshberger 1973. Famous vs. nonfamous: Labovitz 1974. Critique: Schulz & Bazerman 1980; but see Harrison & Kroll 1989–90.

Stress and Eminence. "cardiac irregularity": Engel 1991, 771. Presidency: Barry 1983–84. Monarchy: Sorokin 1925, 1926. Chess: Barry 1969.

Stress from Within. Life change items and weights: Holmes & Holmes 1970, Table 1, 123. Life-change scale for composers: Simonton 1990e, Table 3.11, 78. Illness: Simonton 1977a, 1989b. Productivity: Simonton 1977a. "No tears in the writer": Frost 1949, vi. Cross-cultural studies: Child 1972. "Music sounds the way emotions feel": Child 1968, 861. Recent evidence: Thompson & Robitaille 1992. Melodic originality: Simonton 1977a, 1987a.

Stress from Without. Three Mile Island: Baum et al. 1983; Hartsough & Savitsky 1984; Houts et al. 1988. Mount Saint Helens: Adams & Adams 1984.

Chapter 11

"History is little more": Sproul 1953, 412. "The horrid tale": Sproul 1953, 45. Carlyle rating: Carlyle 1841. Cattell ranking: Cattell 1903. "more than 200,000 volumes": Godechot 1974, 838.

Crowded Streets and Young Rebels. Rodent colonies: Marsden 1972. Fertility and violence: Matossian & Schafer 1977.

Thwarted Goals. Lynchings: Hepworth & West 1988; Hovland & Sears 1940; Mintz 1946. J-curve theory: Davies 1962. Relative deprivation: Crosby 1976; Thompson 1989.

Sultry Days. "I pray thee": Shakespeare circa 1595–1611/1952, vol. 26, 301. Research review: Anderson 1989. Criminal violence: Anderson 1987; Anderson & Anderson 1984; Bell & Fusco 1986; Cotton 1986; DeFonzo 1984; Harries & Stadler 1983, 1988; Perry & Simpson 1987; Rotton & Frey 1985. Spouse abuse: Michael & Zumpe 1986. Pitchers: Reifman et al. 1991. Official report: Kerner 1968. Heat and riots: Baron & Ransberger 1978; Carlsmith & Anderson 1979. Seasons for riots: Lombroso 1899/1911.

Anonymous Crowds. "a crowd being anonymous": Le Bon 1896, 30. Warriors' garb: Watson 1973. Lynch mobs: Mullen 1986. "A Puerto Rican handyman": Mann 1981, 704. Suicide baiting: Mann 1981.

Monkey See, Monkey Do: Models of Violence. Media violence: Huesmann & Malamuth 1986. Newsworthy homicides: Phillips 1980a, 1983, 1986; Phillips & Hensley 1984. Boxing: Miller et al. 1991; Phillips 1983. Debate: Baron & Reiss 1985a, 1985b; Phillips & Bollen 1985. Army–Navy game: Goldstein & Arms 1971. Safe sports: Goldstein & Arms 1971; Arms et al. 1979. Combative sports: Sipes 1973. Monarchs: Simonton 1984g. Death penalty: Archer & Gartner 1984, ch.6; Bailey 1980, 1990; Bailey & Peterson 1989, 1990; King 1978; McFarland 1983; Phillips 1980b; Stack 1987b. Same may apply to war: Levy & Morgan 1986; cf. Simonton 1976e. "Now of course": Thucydides circa 400 b.c./1952, 427–28.

Losing Perspective. Crisis decision making: Midlarsky 1984. First study: Suedfeld & Tetlock 1977. Second study: Suedfeld et al. 1977. Further studies: Ballard 1983; Raphael 1982; Wallace & Suedfeld 1988. For complex, long-term interplay between two nuclear powers: Tetlock 1985. Surprise attacks: Suedfeld & Bluck 1988. *Bulletin of the Atomic Scientists*: Suedfeld 1980. Novelists: Porter & Suedfeld 1981; cf. Milburn & McGrail 1992.

The Shadows of Political Chaos. Affiliation: Cole 1965. Dallas and Memphis: Pennebaker 1990, ch. 11. Shakespeare: Simonton 1986f; cf. Simonton 1983a. Quotes from "the duties of command" to "unnatural or monstrous": Simonton 1986f, 500–1.

The Aftermath of Civil Unrest. Arts and fashions: Martindale 1975; Richardson & Kroeber 1940; Simonton 1977c, 1986f, 1990d. Musical compositions: Simonton 1986a.

The Scars of International War. War zone music: Cerulo 1984. Arts and fashions: Simonton 1977c, 1986f, 1990d. Creative output: Price 1978; Simonton 1976b, 1976e, 1980b, 1986f. Economic costs: Beck 1991. Post-traumatic stress: Centers for Disease Control 1988; Davidson & Baum 1985. Postwar homicides: Archer & Gartner 1984, ch. 4. "the presence of authorized . . . killing": Archer & Gartner 1984, 96. "In 1949 a combat veteran": Archer & Gartner 1984, 75.

The Enduring Legacy. Technique behind next two sections: Simonton 1984c.

Creativity Waxes and Wanes. Future creators: Simonton 1975b. Top thinkers: Simonton 1976f. Effects of rebellion against imperial regimes: Simonton 1975b; cf. Kavolis 1966.

Ideologies Come and Go. "The overwhelming majority": Sorokin 1947/1969, 487. Philosophical beliefs: Simonton 1976g.

Caveats: Psychology's Limits. Systemic factors: Archer & Gartner 1984; Russett 1972; Singer 1981. "I claim not to have controlled": Lincoln 1864/1940, 809. Wilhelm and Hitler: Waite 1990. Osgood's book: Osgood 1962. Real-world evidence: Etzioni 1967; Gamson & Modigliani 1971.

Chapter 12

"there is nothing": Shakespeare circa 1595–1611/1952, vol. 27, 43.

Public Opinion. "the thermometer": McKenna 1983, 155.

Popularity in the Polls. Election: Brody & Sigelman 1983; Rosenstone 1983; Sigelman 1979. Legislation: Bond & Fleisher 1984; Rivers & Rose 1985; Zeidenstein 1985. Nixon: Page & Shapiro 1984. Pioneer studies: Kernell 1978; Mueller 1970, 1973; cf. Brody 1991.

Alienated Adherents? "No man will ever bring": Frost 1988, 175. Popularity declines: Kernell 1978; Mueller 1970, 1973; Stimson 1976; cf. Brody 1991. Coalitions: Mueller 1970, 1973. Expectations and disillusion: Sigelman & Knight 1983, 1985a; Stimson 1976.

Economic Slumps? Economic conditions: Kenski 1977; Kernell 1978; MacKuen 1983; Monroe 1978; Mueller 1970, 1973; Norpoth 1984. Some complexities: Hibbs 1982a, 1982b; Hibbs et al. 1982; Lanoue 1987; Monroe 1984; Nice 1992; Sigelman & Knight 1985b. Asymmetry: Mueller 1970; cf. Bloom & Price 1975. Republicans vs. Democrats: Hibbs 1979; Kenski 1977; Kernell & Hibbs 1981. Pocketbook vs. sociotropic citizens: Kinder 1981; Kinder & Kiewiet 1979; Lewis-Beck 1985; Markus 1988; cf. Feldman 1982; Kramer 1971. For replication outside U.S.: Hibbs 1982b.

International Crises? "Victory has a hundred fathers": Taylor 1972, 526. Crisis: Hibbs 1982a; Kernell 1978; Mueller 1970, 1973. Defense spending: Monroe 1978.

Military Conflicts? War and support: Kick 1983; Morgan & Bickers 1992. War and popularity: Hibbs 1982a; Kernell 1978; Mueller 1970, 1973; cf. Nice 1992.

Adverse Headlines? Labor strikes: Mueller 1970. Watergate: Hibbs 1982a; Kernell 1978; Norpoth 1984. Radio news: Veitch & Griffitt 1976; cf. Veitch et al. 1977. Good vs. bad news and incumbent popularity: Brody & Page 1975. Some limits: Simon & Ostrom 1989. "Reputation is an idle . . . imposition": Shakespeare circa 1595–1611/ 1952, vol. 27, 219.

Success in the Voting Booth. Attitudes and voting behavior: Kelley & Mirer 1974. Closeness and turnout: Foster 1984; cf. Glazer & Grofman 1992. Closeness and turnout in primaries: Norrander & Smith 1985. Closeness of candidate positions: Poole & Rosenthal 1984. The 1980 election: Carpini 1984; Carter 1984. Preferences and expectations: Abramowitz & Stone 1984; Bartels 1985; Granberg & Brent 1983. Voter's illusion: Quattrone & Tversky 1984.

Getting Nominated. Study of 1976 presidential season: Grush 1980. Regional and home-state advantages: see also Holbrook 1991; Lewis-Beck & Rice 1983. Campaign expenditures and bandwagon effect: see also Aldrich 1980; Bartels 1985; Norrander & Smith 1985. Repeated exposure and election success: Grush et al. 1978. War heroes: Simonton 1985c.

Winning Election. "The most successful politician": Frost 1988, 163. Attitude similarity: Byrne et al. 1969; Krosnick 1988; Poole & Rosenthal 1984. Kennedy–Nixon election: Rosenstone 1983. Sincere vs. strategic voting: Poole & Rosenthal 1984. Political activists may be more sensible, however, than voters: Abramowitz & Stone 1984; Stone & Abramowitz 1980. Personality similarity: Leitner 1983; cf. Winter 1987b. Effective-leader image: Kinder et al. 1980. Personal attributes: Glass 1985; Miller et al. 1986. Arbitrary criteria: Abelson et al. 1982; Efran & Patterson 1974; O'Sullivan et al. 1988; Piliavin 1987; Sigelman & Sigelman 1982. Assimilation of positions: Brent & Granberg 1982.

Earning Re-Election. Incumbency advantage: Rosenstone 1983. Predictors of re-nomination and re-election: Simonton 1986g. Show of force: Stoll 1984. "Popularity?": *Who Said What When* 1991, 180. Economics: Abramowitz 1985; Bloom & Price 1975; Campbell 1985; Cuzán & Bundrick 1992; Erikson 1989; Holbrook 1991; Kiewiet 1983; Kinder & Kiewiet 1979; Lewis-Beck 1985; Lewis-Beck & Rice 1984; Monroe 1979. Political business cycle: Tufte 1978; cf. Brown & Stein 1982; Browning 1985; Chappell & Keech 1985; Davidson et al. 1992. Truman's strategy: Rosenstone 1983. 1980 election: Hibbs 1982c; cf. Miller & Wattenberg 1985.

Isolationists versus Internationalists. The 82nd Congress: Tetlock 1981a.

Right Wing versus Left Wing. Mid-1970s Senate: Tetlock 1983. British MPs: Tetlock 1984. Parallel evidence: Ertel 1985. Five congresses: Tetlock et al. 1984. Revolutionaries: Suedfeld & Rank 1976. Liberals vs. Conservatives in Canadian House of Commons: Suedfeld et al. 1990. Switching roles in Canadian House of Commons: Pancer et al. 1992. U.S. Supreme Court: Tetlock et al. 1985. Soviet politicians: Tetlock & Boettger 1989.

Authoritarianism. Value pluralism: Tetlock 1983, 1984. Equality vs. freedom: Rokeach 1973; see also Mahoney et al. 1984.

Narrow Minds: Authoritarianism as a Trait. *The Authoritarian Personality:* Adorno et al. 1950. Follow-ups: Altemeyer 1981, 1985; Eckhardt 1991; Kreml 1977. Voter preferences: Byrne & Przybyla 1980; Leventhal et al. 1964; McCann 1990a; McCann & Stewin 1986; Milton 1952; Schweidiman et al. 1970. Senator Smathers: Williams

1963. Vietnam War: Izzett 1971; cf. Karabenick & Wilson 1969. Socialized medicine: Mahler 1953. Loyalty oath: Handlon & Squier 1955. 1990s: Peterson et al. 1993. Prejudicial attitudes: Rigby 1988. Authoritarianism, dogmatism, conservatism, and religiosity: Eckhardt 1991; cf. Altemeyer 1981, 1985. Gullibility before authority: Levy 1979; McCarthy & Johnson 1962. Admired people: Lentz 1939. Poetry preferences: Gillies & Campbell 1985. Critiques: Christie & Jahoda 1954; Kirscht & Dillehay 1967; Kreml 1977; McKinney 1973. More on right-wing authoritarianism: Altemeyer 1981, 1985.

Scary Times: Authoritarianism as a State. Child rearing: Adorno et al. 1950; Altemeyer 1981, 1985. Genetic basis: Kreml 1977; cf. Eysenck 1954. Authoritarian churches: Sales 1972. Authoritarian culture: Sales 1973. Prime-time TV: Jorgenson 1975. Parapsychology: McCann & Stewin 1984. Power-hungry leaders: McCann 1991; McCann & Stewin 1987; cf. McCann 1990b, 1991. Broader conception of threat: McCann 1991; McCann & Stewin 1990. Cultural meaning shifts: Doty et al. 1991. Ecumenical councils: Rokeach 1960. Supersition in Germany: Padgett & Jorgenson 1982.

Can We Change the World? Brainwashing: Hunter 1953; Lifton 1961; Schein et al. 1961. TV news watchers: Robinson 1971. News recall: Neuman 1976. Presidential debates: Kraus 1962, 1979. *Roots* and *Roots: The Next Generation* viewers: Ball-Rokeach et al. 1981; Hur & Robinson 1978. *The Day After* viewers: Schofield & Pavelchak 1989. Watergate tapes: Laing & Stevenson 1976; cf. Sweeney & Gruber 1984. Chernobyl accident: Verplanken 1989. "65% admitted the possibility": Silverman 1971, 176; cf. Riley & Pettigrew 1976. Wallace supporters: Wrightsman 1969. Failed information campaigns: Hyman & Sheatsley 1947. Other assessments of media impact on attitudes: Atkin 1969; Erikson 1976; Hurd & Singletary 1984; Iyengar et al. 1984. Anti-Semitic stereotypes: Adorno et al. 1950. "A foolish consistency": Emerson 1841b/1941, 127. "Do I contradict myself?" Whitman 1855/1942, 100.

Chapter 13

Admiration, Imitation, and Emulation. Table 13.1: Data from Kroeber 1944, 609. "Genius is fostered by emulation": Kroeber 1944, 18. "If I have seen": Asimov 1982, 282.

Person to Person. Modeling across generations: Simonton 1975b, 1976d, 1976g, 1988c. Exposure to models: Walberg et al. 1980. Individual-level modeling: Simonton 1977b, 1984a, 1992c; Wispé 1965. Negative effects: Sheldon 1979, 1980; Simonton 1976f, 1977b. "genius-worship is the . . . sign": Bell 1913/1958, 112. Brahms quotes: Ewen 1965, 693. "Immature poets imitate": Eliot 1920/1975, 153. Two conditions: Simonton 1984a, 1992c. "Originality is nothing": Esar 1949/1989, 209.

Idea to Idea. Intellectual history: Simonton 1976g, 1978b.

Mentors to Greatness. Nobel laureates: Zuckerman 1977, ch. 4. Figure 13.1: Data from Zuckerman 1977, Figure 4.3, 103. Sciences generally: Simonton 1992c. Psychology: Simonton 1992b; Wispé 1965. Visual arts: Simonton 1984a. Negative effects: Sheldon 1979, 1980. Enhancements: Simonton 1984a, 1992c. "Many people say": *Musical Heritage Review* 1991, 48. Galton and Kroeber: Simonton 1988c.

Affiliation, Attraction, and Interaction. "a mind forever": Asimov 1982, 231. Newton: Simonton 1992c.

Colleagues, Collaborators, and Rivals. China: Simonton 1988c. "the total number of scientists": Price 1963, 53. "Why, man": Shakespeare circa 1595–1611/1952, vol. 26, 570. Artists: Simonton 1984a. Scientists: Simonton 1992c; cf. Simonton 1992b.

Excitement?: Social Facilitation. Cyclists: Triplet 1898. "I am a horse": Sorokin 1963, 274.

Endorsement?: Social Comparison. Collaboration: Beaver 1986; Diamond 1985; Lawani 1986; Smart & Bayer 1986; Zuckerman 1977. Social comparison: Suls & Fletcher 1983. "The ideal audience": Auden 1948, 176. Literary women in Japan: Simonton 1992a.

Incitement?: Social Stimulation. "The greatest natural genius": Reynolds 1769–90/ 1966, 90. Career length: Simonton 1992c; cf. Simonton 1992b.

Intimates. Artists: Simonton 1984a. Scientists: Simonton 1992c. Castro and Guevara: Ramirez & Suedfeld 1988. "Every man who is high up": Esar 1949/1989, 25. Terman's women: Tomlinson-Keasey 1990. First Ladies: Simonton 1993c.

Group Dynamics. White House occupants: Simonton 1993c. BIRGing: Cialdini et al. 1976. Historical example: Harrison et al. 1988.

Loafing on the Job. "We're more popular than Jesus Christ": *Who Said What When* 1991, 310. Beatles: Jackson & Padgett 1982.

Home Games. Home-court advantage: Greer 1983; Schwartz & Barsky 1977. Recent review: Courneya & Carron 1992. Choking: Baumeister & Showers 1986; Baumeister & Steinhilber 1984. Battlefield: Simonton 1980a.

Stupid Decisions. Groupthink: Janis 1982. Recent review: t'Hart 1991. Table 13.2: Events in Janis 1982; t'Hart 1991. Lower integrative complexity: Tetlock 1979. Poor information processing: Herek et al. 1987, 1989. Qualifications: McCauley 1989. Recent refinements: Tetlock et al. 1992.

Rumor Mills. McCartney, Procter and Gamble rumors: Rosnow 1991. "Gossip is mischievous": Rosnow & Fine 1974, 64. "Rumour is a pipe": Shakespeare circa 1595–1611/1952, vol. 26, 467. "Rumors significantly aggravated tension": Kerner 1968, 326. *The Invasion from Mars*: Cantril 1940. Quotes from "I was resting" to "really the matter": Cantril 1940, 140–42, italics removed. Reviews: Rosnow 1980, 1991.

Leadership. "The history of the World": Carlyle 1841, 1.

The Right Place, the Right Time. "A king is history's slave": Tolstoy 1865–69/1952, 343–44. Eponyms: Simonton 1984g. Years in office: Simonton 1984g, 1987e, 1991f; see also Sorokin 1925, 1926. Vice-presidential succession effect: Simonton 1985c. "My country has . . . contrived": Frost 1988, 248. No differences: Simonton 1985c, 1986g, 1986h, 1987e, 1988d.

The Right Person, Place, and Time. "The great man of the age": Hegel 1821/1952, 149. "he will be successful": Machiavelli 1513/1952, 35. "God is always": *Oxford University Press Dictionary of Quotations* 1953/1985, 557. Battlefield: Simonton 1980a. Napoleon: Simonton 1979b.

The Ballot Box. Motives: Winter 1987b. Birth order: Stewart 1977.

The Roll Call Vote. Assessment: Edwards 1985. Situational factors: Simonton 1987e. Inflexibility: Simonton 1987d.

Creators as Leaders. Definition of a leader: Simonton 1985a. "The safest general characterization": Whitehead 1929/1978, 39. *The 100*: Hart 1987. Similar effects for creators and leaders: Simonton 1991e; cf. Simonton 1976a. Power motive: Fodor 1990. Cognitive complexity: Charlton & Bakan 1988–89. A social psychology of creativity: Amabile 1983.

Chapter 14

Do Behavioral Laws Even Exist? "You can never foretell": Myers 1990, 5. "To regard such a . . . science": Collingwood 1946, 224. *Psychology, Science, and History*: Simonton 1990e. Ecclesiastes hypothesis: Turner & Chubin 1976, 1979. Stability of fame: Farnsworth 1969; Helmreich et al. 1981; Over 1982c; Rosengren 1985; Simonton 1990e, 1991d.

Doesn't Sociocultural Context Determine All? "all things from eternity": Aurelius circa 175/1952, 258. "There is the moral": Byron 1812–16/1905, 228. Cycles: Gray 1958, 1961, 1966; Lowe & Lowe 1982; Marchetti 1980; Peterson & Berger 1975; Rainoff 1929; Sorokin & Merton 1935. Figure 14.1 and research: Adapted from Simonton 1980d, Figure 1, 976. Cultural achievements and economics: Dressler & Robbins 1975; Inhaber 1977; Kavolis 1964; Rainoff 1929; Simon & Sullivan 1989. China: Kuo 1986, 1988.

Are the Predictions and Explanations Good Enough? Psychology vs. physics: Hedges 1987. Presidential greatness: Simonton 1986h, 1987e, 1991f. Psychology vs. medicine: Rosenthal 1990. Batting averages: Abelson 1985.

Is the Enterprise Elitist? Ortega hypothesis: Cole & Cole 1972. "it is necessary to insist": Ortega y Gasset 1932/1957, 110–11. "science is rarely advanced": Crowther 1968, 363. Ortega hypothesis studies: Cole & Cole 1972; Green 1981; Oromaner 1985.

Table 4.2 is adapted from Simonton 1984h; copyright 1984 by Dean Keith Simonton. Figure 4.1 is adapted from Simonton 1983b; copyright 1983 by the Music Educators National Conference. Figure 6.1 is reprinted from Simonton 1983c; copyright 1983 by Dean Keith Simonton. Figure 7.1 is reprinted from Simonton 1984b; copyright 1984 by Academic Press, Inc. Figure 7.2 is reprinted from Simonton 1990e; copyright 1990 by Yale University Press. Figure 7.4 is reprinted from Simonton 1991a; copyright 1991 by the American Psychological Association. Figure 7.5 is reprinted from Simonton 1984d; copyright 1984 by Harvard University Press. Figure 8.1 is reprinted from Simonton 1985a; copyright 1985 by the American Psychological Association. Figure 8.2 is reprinted from Simonton 1988e; copyright 1988 by Cambridge University Press. Figure 8.4 is reprinted from Simonton 1985a; copyright 1985 by the American Psychological Association. Figure 9.1 is reprinted from Simonton 1983c; copyright 1983 by Dean Keith Simonton. Table 9.2 is reprinted from Simonton 1986h; copyright 1986 by the American Psychological Association. Figure 9.4 is reprinted from Simonton 1986h; copyright 1986 by the American Psychological Association. Figure 14.1 is adapted from Simonton 1980d; copyright 1980 by the American Psychological Association.

REFERENCES

Abelson, R. P. 1985. A variance explanation paradox: When a little is a lot. *Psychol. Bull.*, 97, 129–33.

Abelson, R. P., Kinder, D. R., Peters, M. D., & Fiske, S. T. 1982. Affective and semantic components in political person perception. *J. Pers. Soc. Psychol.*, 42, 619–30.

Abramowitz, A. I. 1985. Economic conditions, presidential popularity, and voting behavior in midterm congressional elections. *J. Polit.*, 47, 31–43.

Abramowitz, A. I., & Stone, W. J. 1984. *Nomination politics*. New York: Praeger.

Abt, H. A. 1983. At what ages do outstanding American astronomers publish their most cited papers? *Publ. Astronom. Soc. Pacific*, 95, 113–16.

Adams, B. N. 1972. Birth order: A critical review. *Sociometry*, 35, 411–39.

Adams, C. W. 1946. The age at which scientists do their best work. *Isis*, 36, 166–69.

Adams, F. M., & Osgood, C. E. 1973. A cross-cultural study of the affective meanings of color. *J. Cross-Cult. Psychol.*, 4, 135–56.

Adams, P. R., & Adams, G. R. 1984. Mount Saint Helens's ashfall: Evidence for a disaster stress reaction. *Amer. Psychol.*, 39, 252–60.

Adler, A. 1938. *Social interest*, J. Linton & R. Vaughan, trans. London: Faber & Faber.

Adorno, T. W., Frenkel-Brunswik, E., Levinson, D. J., & Sanford, R. N., eds. 1950. *The authoritarian personality*. New York: Harper.

Agee, J., Collier, J., & Huston, J. 1951. *The African Queen* [Screenplay]. Hollywood, CA: Script City.

Albert, R. S. 1971. Cognitive development and parental loss among the gifted, the exceptionally gifted and the creative. *Psychol. Rep.*, 29, 19–26.

Albert, R. S. 1975. Toward a behavioral definition of genius. *Amer. Psychol.*, 30, 140–51.

Albert, R. S. 1980. Family positions and the attainment of eminence: A study of special family positions and special family experiences. *Gifted Child Q.*, 24, 87–95.

Aldrich, J. H. 1980. *Before the convention*. Chicago: University of Chicago Press.

Allard, F., Graham, S., & Paarsalu, M. E. 1980. Perception in sport: Basketball. *J. Sport Psychol.*, 2, 14–21.

Allen, W., ed. 1949. *Writers on writing*. New York: Dutton.

Alley, T. R., & Cunningham, M. R. 1991. Averaged faces are attractive, but very attractive faces are not average. *Psychol. Sci.*, 2, 123–26.

Allison, P. D. 1980. Estimation and testing for a Markov model of reinforcement. *Sociol. Meth. Res.*, 8, 434–53.

Allison, P. D., Long, J. S., & Krauze, T. K. 1982. Cumulative advantage and inequality in science. *Amer. Sociol. Rev.*, 47, 615–25.

Allison, P. D., & Stewart, J. A. 1974. Productivity differences among scientists: Evidence for accumulative advantage. *Amer. Sociol. Rev.*, *39*, 596–606.

Altemeyer, B. 1981. *Right-wing authoritarianism*. Winnipeg: University of Manitoba Press.

Altemeyer, B. 1985. *Enemies of freedom*. San Francisco: Jossey-Bass.

Altus, W. D. 1966. Birth order and its sequelae. *Science*, *151*, 44–48.

Amabile, T. M. 1983. *The social psychology of creativity*. New York: Springer-Verlag.

Amabile, T. M. 1985. Motivation and creativity: Effects of motivation orientation on creative writers. *J. Pers. Soc. Psychol.*, *48*, 393–99.

Anderson, C. A. 1987. Temperature and aggression: Effects on quarterly, yearly, and city rates of violent and nonviolent crime. *J. Pers. Soc. Psychol.*, *52*, 1161–73.

Anderson, C. A. 1989. Temperature and aggression: Ubiquitous effects of heat on occurrence of human violence. *Psychol. Bull.*, *106*, 74–96.

Anderson, C. A., & Anderson, D. C. 1984. Ambient temperature and violent crime: Tests of the linear and curvilinear hypotheses. *J. Pers. Soc. Psychol.*, *46*, 91–97.

Anderson, J. L. 1991. Rushton's racial comparisons: An ecological critique of theory and method. *Canad. Psychol.*, *32*, 51–60.

Anderson, N. H. 1973. Information integration theory applied to attitudes about U.S. presidents. *J. Educ. Psychol.*, *64*, 1–8.

Andreasen, N. C. 1987. Creativity and mental illness: Prevalence rates in writers and their first-degree relatives. *Amer. J. Psychiat.*, *144*, 1288–92.

Andreasen, N. C., & Canter, A. 1974. The creative writer: Psychiatric symptoms and family history. *Compreh. Psychiat.*, *15*, 123–31.

Archer, D., & Gartner, R. 1984. *Violence and crime in cross-national perspective*. New Haven, CT: Yale University Press.

Archer, D., Iritani, B., Kames, D. D., & Barrios, M. 1983. Face-ism: Five studies of sex differences in facial prominence. *J. Pers. Soc. Psychol.*, *45*, 725–35.

Arendt, H. 1963. *Eichmann in Jerusalem*. New York: Viking.

Arieti, S. 1976. *Creativity*. New York: Basic Books.

Armbruster, M. E. 1982. *The presidents of the United States and their administrations from Washington to Reagan*, 7th ed. New York: Horizon Press.

Arms, R. L., Russell, G. W., & Sandilands, M. L. 1979. Effects on the hostility of spectators of viewing aggressive sports. *Soc. Psychol. Q.*, *42*, 275–79.

Arnheim, R. 1962. *Picasso's Guernica*. Berkeley: University of California Press.

Arnheim, R. 1971. *Art and visual perception*. Berkeley: University of California Press.

Arnheim, R. 1986. *New essays on the psychology of art*. Berkeley: University of California Press.

Aronson, E. 1958. The need for achievement as measured by graphic expression. In J. W. Atkinson, ed., *Motives in fantasy, action, and society*, 249–65. Princeton, NJ: Van Nostrand.

Asante, M. K. 1988. *Afrocentricity*, new rev. ed. Trenton, NJ: Africa World Press.

Asch, S. E. 1948. The doctrine of suggestion, prestige and imitation in social psychology. *Psychol. Rev.*, *55*, 250–76.

Asch, S. E. 1952. *Social psychology*. New York: Prentice-Hall.

Asimov, I. 1982. *Biographical encyclopedia of science and technology*, 2nd rev. ed. New York: Doubleday.

Atkin, C. K. 1969. The impact of political poll reports on candidate and issue preference. *Journ. Q.*, *46*, 515–21.

Auden, W. H. 1948. Squares and oblongs. In R. Arnheim, W. H. Auden, K. Shapiro, & D. A. Stauffer, eds., *Poets at work*, 163–81. New York: Harcourt, Brace.

Auden, W. H., & Kronenberger, L. 1966. *The Viking book of aphorisms*. New York: Dorset Press.

Aurelius, M. circa 175. Meditations. In R. M. Hutchins, ed., *Great books of the Western world*, vol. 12, 251–310. Chicago: Encyclopaedia Britannica, 1952.

Austin, J. H. 1978. *Chase, chance, and creativity*. New York: Columbia University Press.

Babad, E. Y. 1977. Effect of source of information as a function of age, professional relevance, and experience. *Psychol. Rep.*, *41*, 231–36.

Babcock, W. L. 1895. On the morbid heredity and predisposition to insanity of the man of genius. *J. Nerv. Ment. Dis.*, 20, 749–69.

Bacon, F. 1597, 1620. *Essays and the new Atlantis*. Roslyn, NY: Black, 1942.

Bailey, W. C. 1980. A multivariate cross-sectional analysis of the deterrent effect of the death penalty. *Sociol. Soc. Res.*, *64*, 183–207.

Bailey, W. C. 1990. Murder, capital punishment, and television: Execution publicity and homicide rates. *Amer. Sociol. Rev.*, *55*, 628–33.

Bailey, W. C., & Peterson, R. D. 1989. Murder and capital punishment: A monthly time-series analysis of execution publicity. *Amer. Sociol. Rev.*, *54*, 722–43.

Bailey, W. C., & Peterson, R. D. 1990. Murder, capital punishment, and television: Execution publicity and homicide rates. *Amer. Sociol. Rev.*, *55*, 628–33.

Baird, L. L. 1968. The achievement of bright and average students. *Educ. Psychol. Meas.*, *28*, 891–99.

Ball-Rokeach, S. J., Grube, J. W., & Rokeach, M. 1981. "Roots: The next generation"— who watched and with what effect? *Publ. Opin. Q.*, *45*, 58–68.

Ballard, E. J. 1983. Canadian prime ministers: Complexity in political crises. *Canad. Psychol.*, *24*, 125–29.

Ballard, E. J., & Suedfeld, P. 1988. Performance ratings of Canadian prime ministers: Individual and situational factors. *Polit. Psychol.*, *9*, 291–302.

Baltes, M. M. 1977–78. On the relationship between significant yearly events and time of death: Random or systematic distribution? *Omega*, *8*, 165–72.

Baltzell, E. D., & Schneiderman, H. G. 1988. Social class in the Oval Office. *Society*, *25*, 42–49.

Baltzell, E. D., & Schneiderman, H. G. 1991. From rags to robes. *Society*, *28*, 45–54.

Bamberger, J. 1986. Cognitive issues in the development of musically gifted children. In R. J. Sternberg & J. E. Davidson, eds., *Conceptions of giftedness*, 388–413. Cambridge, England: Cambridge University Press.

Barber, B. 1961. Resistance by scientists to scientific discovery. *Science*, *134*, 596–602.

Barber, J. D. 1977. *The presidential character*, 2nd ed. Englewood Cliffs, NJ: Prentice-Hall.

Barinaga, M. 1991. How long is the human life-span? *Science*, *254*, 336–38.

Baron, J. N., & Reiss, P. C. 1985a. Reply to Phillips and Bollen. *Amer. Sociol. Rev.*, *50*, 372–76.

Baron, J. N., & Reiss, P. C. 1985b. Same time, next year: Aggregate analyses of the mass media and violent behavior. *Amer. Sociol. Rev.*, *50*, 347–63.

Baron, R. A., & Ransberger, V. M. 1978. Ambient temperature and the occurrence of collective violence: The "long, hot summer" revisited. *J. Pers. Soc. Psychol.*, *36*, 351–60.

Barrett, G. V., & Depinet, R. L. 1991. A reconsideration of testing for competence rather than for intelligence. *Amer. Psychol.*, *46*, 1012–24.

Barron, F. X. 1963. The needs for order and for disorder as motives in creative activity. In C. W. Taylor & F. X. Barron, eds., *Scientific creativity*, 153–60. New York: Wiley.

Barron, F. X. 1969. *Creative person and creative process*. New York: Holt, Rinehart & Winston.

Barron, F. X., & Harrington, D. M. 1981. Creativity, intelligence, and personality. *Ann. Rev. Psychol.*, 32, 439–76.

Barry, H. 1969. Longevity of outstanding chess players. *J. Genet. Psychol.*, 115, 143–48.

Barry, H. 1979. Birth order and paternal namesake as predictors of affiliation with predecessor by presidents of the United States. *Polit. Psychol.*, 1, 61–66.

Barry, H. 1983–84. Predictors of longevity of United States presidents. *Omega*, 14, 315–21.

Barry, H., Bacon, M. K., & Child, I. L. 1957. A cross-cultural survey of some sex differences in socialization. *J. Abnorm. Soc. Psychol.*, 55, 327–32.

Barsley, M. 1970. *Left-handed man in a right-handed world*. London: Pitman.

Bartels, L. M. 1985. Expectations and preferences in presidential nominating campaigns. *Amer. Polit. Sci. Rev.*, 79, 804–15.

Bartlett, F. 1958. *Thinking*. New York: Basic Books.

Baum, A., Gatchel, R. J., & Schaefer, M. A. 1983. Emotional, behavioral, and physiological effects of chronic stress at Three Mile Island. *J. Consult. Clin. Psychol.*, 51, 565–72.

Baumeister, R. E., & Showers, C. J. 1986. A review of paradoxical performance effects: Choking under pressure in sports and mental tests. *Eur. J. Soc. Psychol.*, 16, 361–83.

Baumeister, R. E., & Steinhilber, A. 1984. Paradoxical effects of supportive audiences on performance under pressure: The home field disadvantage in sports championships. *J. Pers. Soc. Psychol.*, 47, 85–93.

Bayer, A. E., & Dutton, J. E. 1977. Career age and research—Professional activities of academic scientists: Tests of alternative non-linear models and some implications for higher education faculty policies. *J. Higher Educ.*, 48, 259–82.

Bayer, A. E., & Folger, J. 1966. Some correlates of a citation measure of productivity in science. *Sociol. Educ.*, 39, 381–90.

Beard, G. M. 1874. *Legal responsibility in old age*. New York: Russell.

Beaton, A. 1985. *Left side, right side*. London: Batsford.

Beaver, D. de B. 1986. Collaboration and teamwork in physics. *Czech. J. Physics, B 36*, 14–18.

Beck, N. 1991. The illusion of cycles in international relations. *Internat. Stud. Q.*, 35, 455–76.

Becker, G. 1978. *The mad genius controversy*. Beverly Hills, CA: Sage.

Becon, T. circa 1550. *Catechism, with other pieces written by him in the reign of King Edward the Sixth*, J. Ayre, ed. Cambridge: Cambridge University Press, 1844.

Bednar, R. L., & Parker, C. A. 1965. The creative development and growth of exceptional college students. *J. Educ. Res.*, 59, 133–36.

Bell, C. 1913. *Art*. New York: Capricorn Books, 1958.

Bell, E. T. 1937. *Men of mathematics*. New York: Simon & Schuster.

Bell, P. A., & Fusco, M. E. 1986. Linear and curvilinear relationships between temperature, affect, and violence: Reply to Cotton. *J. Appl. Soc. Psychol.*, 16, 802–7.

Belmont, L., & Marolla, F. A. 1973. Birth order, family size, and intelligence. *Science, 182*, 1096–1101.

Benbow, C. P., & Stanley, J. C. 1980. Sex differences in mathematical ability: Fact or artifact? *Science, 210,* 1262–64.

Benbow, C. P., & Stanley, J. C. 1983. Sex differences in mathematical reasoning ability: More facts. *Science, 222,* 1029–31.

Bennet W. 1980, January–February. Providing for posterity. Harvard Magazine, 13–16.

Berenson, B. 1954. *Aesthetics and history.* Garden City, NJ: Doubleday.

Berglas, S. 1985. Self-handicapping and self-handicappers: A cognitive/attributional model of interpersonal self-protective behavior. In R. Hogan & W. H. Jones, eds., *Perspectives in personality,* vol. 1, 235–70. Greenwich, CT: Jai Press.

Berglas, S. 1988. Self-handicapping behavior and the self-defeating personality disorder: Toward a refined clinical perspective. In R. C. Curtis, ed., *Self-defeating behaviors,* 261–88. New York: Plenum Press.

Berkowitz, W. R., Nebel, J. C., & Reitman, J. W. 1971. Height and interpersonal attraction: The 1969 mayoral election in New York City. *Proc. 79th Ann. Convent. Amer. Psychol. Assoc., 6,* 281–82.

Berlin, L., Guthrie, T., Weider, A., Goodell, H., Wolff, H. G. 1955. The effects of mescaline and lysergic acid on cerebral processes pertinent to creative activity. *J. Nerv. Ment. Dis., 122,* 487–91.

Bernberg, R. 1953. Prestige suggestion in art as communication. *J. Soc. Psychol., 38,* 23–30.

Berrington, H. 1974. Review article: *The Fiery Chariot*: Prime ministers and the search for love. *Brit. J. Polit. Sci., 4,* 345–69.

Berry, C. 1981. The Nobel scientists and the origins of scientific achievement. *Brit. J. Sociol., 32,* 381–91.

Beveridge, W. I. B. 1957. *The art of scientific investigation,* 3rd ed. New York: Vintage.

Binion, R. 1976. *Hitler among the Germans.* New York: Elsevier.

Blackburn, R. T., Behymer, C. E., & Hall, D. E. 1978. Correlates of faculty publications. *Sociol. Educ., 51,* 132–41.

Bliss, W. D. 1970. Birth order of creative writers. *J. Indiv. Psychol., 26,* 200–2.

Blom, E. 1974. *Mozart.* London: Dent.

Blondel, J. 1980. *World leaders.* Beverly Hills, CA: Sage.

Bloom, B. S. 1963. Report on creativity research by the examiner's office of the University of Chicago. In C. W. Taylor & F. X. Barron, eds., *Scientific creativity,* 251–64. New York: Wiley.

Bloom, B. S., ed. 1985. *Developing talent in young people.* New York: Ballantine Books.

Bloom, H. S., & Price, H. D. 1975. Voter response to short-run economic conditions: The asymmetric effect of prosperity and recession. *Amer. Polit. Sci. Rev., 69,* 1240–54.

Boden, M. A. 1991. *The creative mind.* New York: Basic Books.

Bohr, H. 1967. My father. In S. Rozental, ed., *Niels Bohr,* 325–35. Amsterdam: North-Holland.

Boller, P. F., Jr. 1981. *Presidential anecdotes.* New York: Oxford University Press.

Bond, J. R., & Fleisher, R. 1984. Presidential popularity and congressional voting: A reexamination of public opinion as a source of influence in Congress. *West. Polit. Q., 37,* 291–306.

Boor, M. 1981. Effects of United States presidential elections on suicide and other causes of death. *Amer. Sociol. Rev., 46,* 616–18.

Boor, M., & Fleming, J. A. 1984. Presidential election effects on suicide and mortality levels are independent of unemployment rates. *Amer. Sociol. Rev., 49,* 706–7.

Boring, E. G. 1963. *History, psychology, and science*, R. I. Watson & D. T. Campbell, eds. New York: Wiley.

Boswell, J. 1791. *The life of Samuel Johnson, LL.D.* In R. M. Hutchins, ed., *Great books of the Western world*, vol. 44. Chicago: Encyclopaedia Britannica, 1952.

Bouchard, T. J., Lykken, D. T., McGue, M., Segal, N. L., & Tellegen, A. 1990. Sources of human psychological differences: The Minnesota study of twins reared apart. *Science, 250,* 223–28.

Boyce, R., Shaughnessy, P., & Pecker, G. 1985. Women and publishing in psychology. *Amer. Psychol., 40,* 577–78.

Bradburn, N. M., & Berlew, D. E. 1961. Need for achievement and English economic growth. *Econ. Dev. Cult. Change, 10,* 8–20.

Bradshaw, G. F., Langley, P. W., & Simon, H. A. 1983. Studying scientific discovery by computer simulation. *Science, 222,* 971–75.

Bramwell, B. S. 1948. Galton's *Hereditary genius* and the three following generations since 1869. *Eugenics Rev., 39,* 146–53.

Brannigan, A., & Wanner, R. A. 1983a. Historical distributions of multiple discoveries and theories of scientific change. *Soc. Stud. Sci., 13,* 417–35.

Brannigan, A., & Wanner, R. A. 1983b. Multiple discoveries in science: A test of the communication theory. *Canad. J. Sociol., 8,* 135–51.

Breland, H. M. 1974. Birth order, family-configuration, and verbal achievement. *Child Dev., 45,* 1011–19.

Brent, E., & Granberg, D. 1982. Subjective agreement with the presidential candidates of 1976 and 1980. *J. Pers. Soc. Psychol., 42,* 393–403.

Bretz, R. D., Jr. 1989. College grade point average as a predictor of adult success: A meta-analysis and some additional evidence. *Publ. Personnel Manage., 18,* 11–22.

Brickman, P., & D'Amato, B. 1975. Exposure effects in a free-choice situation. *J. Pers. Soc. Psychol., 32,* 415–20.

Brittain, V. 1948. *On being an author.* New York: Macmillan.

Brodestsky, S. 1942. Newton: Scientist and man. *Nature, 150,* 698–99.

Brodie, F. M. 1983. *Richard Nixon.* Cambridge, MA: Harvard University Press.

Brody, R. A. 1991. *Assessing the president.* Stanford, CA: Stanford University Press.

Brody, R. A., & Page, B. I. 1975. The impact of events on presidential popularity: The Johnson and Nixon administrations. In A. Wildavsky, ed., *Perspectives on the presidency,* 136–48. Boston: Little, Brown.

Brody, R. A., & Sigelman, L. 1983. Presidential popularity and presidential elections: An update and extension. *Publ. Opin. Q., 47,* 325–8.

Bronfenbrenner, U. 1961. The mirror image in Soviet–American relations: A social psychologist's report. *J. Soc. Issues, 17*(3), 45–56.

Brown, F. 1968. Bereavement and lack of a parent in childhood. In E. Miller, ed., *Foundations of child psychiatry,* 435–55. Oxford: Pergamon Press.

Brown, N. R., & Siegler, R. S. 1991. Subjective organization of U.S. presidents. *Amer. J. Psychol., 104,* 1–33.

Brown, R., & Kulik, J. 1977. Flashbulb memories. *Cognition, 5,* 73–99.

Brown, T. A., & Stein, A. A. 1982. Review article: The political economy of national elections. *Comp. Politics, 14,* 479–97.

Browning, R. P., & Jacob, H. 1964. Power motivation and the political personality. *Publ. Opin. Q., 28,* 75–90.

Browning, R. X. 1985. Presidents, congress, and policy outcomes: U.S. social welfare expenditures, 1949–77. *Amer. J. Polit. Sci.*, *29*, 197–216.

Buchanan, B. G., & Shortliffe, E. H., eds. 1984. *Rule-based expert systems*. Reading, MA: Addison-Wesley.

Bullough, V., Bullough, B., & Mauro, M. 1978. Age and achievement: A dissenting view. *Gerontologist*, *18*, 584–87.

Burks, B. S., Jensen, D. W., & Terman, L. M. 1930. *Genetic studies of genius: Vol. 3. The promise of youth: Follow-up studies of a thousand gifted children*. Stanford, CA: Stanford University Press.

Burt, C. 1943. Ability and income. *Brit. J. Educ. Psychol.*, *12*, 83–98.

Burt, C. 1963. Is intelligence distributed normally? *Brit. J. Stat. Psychol.*, *16*, 175–90.

Buss, D. M. 1988. Love acts: The evolutionary biology of love. In R. J. Sternberg & M. L. Barnes, eds., *The psychology of love*, 100–8. New Haven: Yale University Press.

Butler, S. 1903. *The way of all flesh*. Roslyn, NY: Black, n.d.

Butt, D. S., & Cox, D. N. 1992. Motivational patterns in Davis Cup, university and recreational tennis players. *Internat. J. Sport Psychol.*, *23*, 1–13.

Buttenwieser, P. 1935. The relation of age to skill of expert chess players. *Psychol. Bull.*, *32*, 529. (Abstract.)

Byrne, D., Bond, M. H., & Diamond, M. J. 1969. Response to political conditions as a function of attitude similarity–dissimilarity. *Human Relat.*, *22*, 251–62.

Byrne, D., & Przybyla, D. P. J. 1980. Authoritarianism and political preferences in 1980. *Bull. Psychon. Soc.*, *16*, 471–2.

Byron, G. G., Lord. 1812–16. Childe Harold. In E. H. Coleridge, ed., *The poetical works of Lord Byron*, 141–241. London: Murray, 1905.

Byron, G. G., Lord. 1818–21. *Don Juan*. London: Lehmann, 1949.

Campbell, D. T. 1960. Blind variation and selective retention in creative thought as in other knowledge processes. *Psychol. Rev.*, *67*, 380–400.

Campbell, J. E. 1983. Ambiguity in the issue positions of presidential candidates: A causal analysis. *Amer. J. Polit. Sci.*, *27*, 284–93.

Campbell, J. E. 1985. Explaining presidential losses in midterm congressional elections. *J. Politics.*, *47*, 1140–57.

Candolle, A. de. 1873. *Histoire des sciences et des savants depuis deux siècles*. Geneva: Georg.

Cannon, W. B. 1940. The role of chance in discovery. *Scient. Monthly*, *50*, 204–9.

Cantril, H. 1940. *The invasion from Mars*. Princeton, NJ: Princeton University Press.

Carlsmith, J. M., & Anderson, C. A. 1979. Ambient temperature and the occurrence of collective violence: A new analysis. *J. Pers. Soc. Psychol.*, *37*, 337–44.

Carlyle, T. 1841. *On heroes, hero-worship, and the heroic in history*. London: Fraser.

Carpini, M. X. 1984. Scooping the voters? The consequences of the networks' early call of the 1980 presidential race. *J. Politics.*, *46*, 866–85.

Carter, J. 1984. Early projections and voter turnout in the 1980 presidential election. *Publ. Choice*, *43*, 195–202.

Cattell, J. M. 1890. Mental tests and measurements. *Mind*, *15*, 132–41.

Cattell, J. M. 1903. A statistical study of eminent men. *Pop. Sci. Monthly*, *62*, 359–77.

Cattell, R. B. 1963. The personality and motivation of the researcher from measurements of contemporaries and from biography. In C. W. Taylor & F. Barron eds., *Scientific creativity*, 119–31. New York: Wiley.

Cattell, R. B. 1965. *The scientific analysis of personality*. Baltimore: Penguin.

Cattell, R. B., & Butcher, H. J. 1968. *The prediction of achievement and creativity*. Indianapolis: Bobbs-Merrill.

Cattell, R. B., & Stice, G. F. 1954. Four formulae for selecting leaders on the basis of personality. *Human Relat.*, 7, 493–507.

Cell, C. P. 1974. Charismatic heads of state: The social context. *Behav. Sci. Res.*, 9, 255–305.

Centers for Disease Control, Vietnam Experience Study. 1988. Health studies of Vietnam veterans: I. Psychosocial characteristics. *J. Amer. Med. Assoc.*, 259, 2701–7.

Cerulo, K. A. 1984. Social disruption and its effects on music: An empirical analysis. *Soc. Forces*, 62, 885–904.

Chambers, J. A. 1964. Relating personality and biographical factors to scientific creativity. *Psychol. Monogr.: Gen. Appl.*, 78(Whole No. 584), 1–20.

Chappell, H. W., Jr., & Keech, W. R. 1985. A new view of political accountability for economic performance. *Amer. Polit. Sci. Rev.*, 79, 10–27.

Charlton, S., & Bakan, P. 1988–89. Cognitive complexity and creativity. *Imag. Cog. Pers.*, 8, 315–22.

Chase, W. G., & Simon, H. A. 1973. Perception in chess. *Cog. Psychol.*, 4, 55–81.

Chesen, E. S. 1973. *President Nixon's psychiatric profile*. New York: Weyden.

Child, I. L. 1968. Esthetics. In G. Lindzey & E. Aronson, eds., *The handbook of social psychology*, 2nd ed., vol. 3, 853–916. Reading, MA: Addison-Wesley.

Child, I. L. 1972. Esthetics. *Ann. Rev. Psychol.*, 23, 669–94.

Child, I. L., Storm, T., & Veroff, J. 1958. Achievement themes in folk tales related to socialization practice. In J. W. Atkinson, ed., *Motives in fantasy, action, and society*, 479–92. Princeton, NJ: Van Nostrand.

Chipp, H. B., ed. 1968. *Theories of modern art*. Berkeley: University of California Press.

Christensen, H., & Jacomb, P. A. 1992. The lifetime productivity of eminent Australian academics. *Internat. J. Geriat. Psychiat.*, 7, 681–6.

Christie, R., & Jahoda, M., eds. 1954. *Studies in the scope and method of "The authoritarian personality."* Glencoe, IL: Free Press.

Cialdini, R. B., Borden, R. J., Thorne, A., Walker, M. R., Freeman, S., & Sloan, L. R. 1976. Basking in reflected glory: Three (football) field studies. *J. Pers. Soc. Psychol.*, 34, 366–75.

Clancy, M., & Robinson, M. J. 1985. General election coverage: Part I. *Publ. Opin.*, 7(6), 4–54, 59.

Clark, R. D., & Rice, G. A. 1982. Family constellations and eminence: The birth orders of Nobel Prize winners. *J. Psychol.*, 110, 281–87.

Clark, R. W. 1980. *Freud*. New York: Random House.

Clarke, A. C. 1968. *2001: A space odyssey*. New York: New American Library.

Cocks, G., & Crosby, T. L., eds. 1987. *Psycho/history*. New Haven, CT: Yale University Press.

Cohen, J. M., & Cohen, M. J. 1960. *The Penguin dictionary of quotations*. New York: Penguin.

Cohen, P. A. 1984. College grades and adult achievement: A research synthesis. *Res. Higher Educ.*, 20, 281–93.

Cole, D. 1965. Affiliative behavior at the time of the president's assassination. *Psychol. Rep.*, 16, 326.

Cole, J. R. 1987. Women in science. In D. N. Jackson & J. P. Rushton, eds., *Scientific excellence*, 359–75. Beverly Hills, CA: Sage.

Cole, J. R., & Cole, S. 1972. The Ortega hypothesis. *Science*, 178, 368–75.

Cole, S. 1979. Age and scientific performance. *Amer. J. Sociol.*, *84*, 958–77.

Cole, S., & Cole, J. R. 1973. *Social stratification in science*. Chicago: University of Chicago Press.

Colegrove, F. W. 1899. Individual memories. *Amer. J. Psychol.*, *10*, 228–55.

Coleridge, S. T. 1801. Letter to T. Poole. In E. L. Griggs, ed., *Collected letters*, vol. 2. Oxford: Clarendon Press, 1956.

Coleridge, S. T. 1835. *Specimens of the table talk*, vol. 1. London: Murray.

Colinvaux, P. 1980. *The fates of nations: A biological theory of history*. New York: Simon & Schuster.

Collingwood, R. G. 1946. *The idea of history*. Oxford: Clarendon Press.

"Computer beats chess whiz." 1993, August 22. *Sacramento Bee*, A2.

Connolly, C. 1992, March 26. Older actresses seem to have disappeared from the movie screen. *Sacramento Bee*, E7.

Constant, E. W., II. 1978. On the diversity of co-evolution of technological multiples: Steam turbines and Pelton water wheels. *Soc. Stud. Sci.*, *8*, 183–210.

Coren, S., & Porac, C. 1977. Fifty centuries of right handedness: The historical record. *Science*, *198*, 631–32.

Cortés, J. B. 1960. The achievement motive in the Spanish economy between the 13th and 18th centuries. *Econ. Dev. Cult. Change*, *9*, 144–63.

Cotton, J. L. 1986. Ambient temperature and violent crime. *J. Appl. Soc. Psychol.*, *16*, 786–801.

Courneya, K. S., & Carron, A. V. 1992. The home advantage in sport competitions: A literature review. *J. Sport Exercise Psychol.*, *14*, 13–27.

Cox, C. 1926. *Genetic studies of genius: Vol. 2. The early mental traits of three hundred geniuses*. Stanford, CA: Stanford University Press.

Craig, H., & Bevington, D., eds. 1973. *The complete works of Shakespeare*, rev. ed. Glenview, IL: Scott, Foresman.

Crane, D. 1965. Scientists at major and minor universities: A study of productivity and recognition. *Amer. Sociol. Rev.*, *30*, 699–714.

Crevier, D. 1993. *AI: The tumultuous history of the search for artificial intelligence*. New York: Basic Books.

Cronbach, L. J. 1960. *Essentials of psychological testing*, 2nd ed. New York: Harper & Row.

Cropper, W. H. 1970. *The quantum physicists*. New York: Oxford University Press.

Crosby, F. 1976. A model of egotistical relative deprivation. *Psychol. Rev.*, *83*, 85–113.

Cross, H. A., Halcomb, C. G., & Matter, W. W. 1967. Imprinting or exposure learning in rats given early auditory stimulation. *Psychonom. Sci.*, *7*, 233–4.

Crowther, J. G. 1968. *Science in modern society*. New York: Schocken Books.

Crutchfield, R. 1962. Conformity and creative thinking. In H. E. Gruber, G. Terrell, & M. Wertheimer, eds., *Contemporary approaches to creative thinking*, 120–40. New York: Atherton Press.

Csikszentmihalyi, M. 1988. Motivation and creativity: Toward a synthesis of structural and energistic approaches to cognition. *New Ideas Psychol.*, *6*, 159–76.

Cunningham, M. R. 1986. Measuring the physical in physical attractiveness: Quasi-experiments on the sociobiology of female facial beauty. *J. Pers. Soc. Psychol.*, *50*, 925–35.

Cuzán, A. G., & Bundrick, C. M. 1992. Selected fiscal and economic effects on presidential elections. *Presid. Stud. Q.*, *22*, 127–34.

Daintith, J., Mitchell, S., & Tootill, E. 1981. *A biographical encyclopedia of scientists*, vol. 1. New York: Facts on File.

Dalen, P. 1975. *Season of birth*. New York: Elsevier.

D'Andrade, R. G. 1986. Sex differences and cultural institutions. In E. E. Maccoby, ed., *The development of sex differences*, 174–204. Stanford, CA: Stanford University Press.

Darwin, C. 1860. *The origin of species by means of natural selection*, 2nd ed. In R. M. Hutchins, ed., *Great books of the Western world*, vol. 49, 1–251. Chicago: Encyclopaedia Britannica, 1952.

Darwin, F., ed. 1892. *The autobiography of Charles Darwin and selected letters*. New York: Dover, 1958.

Das, J. P., Rath, R., & Das, R. S. 1955. Understanding versus suggestion in the judgment of literary passages. *J. Abnorm. Soc. Psychol.*, *51*, 624–28.

Davidson, L. M., & Baum, A. 1985. Implications of post-traumatic stress for social psychology. *Appl. Soc. Psychol. Ann.*, *6*, 207–32.

Davidson, L. M., Fratianni, M., & Von Hagen, J. 1992. Testing the satisficing version of the political business cycle 1905–1984. *Publ. Choice*, *73*, 21–35.

Davies, E. 1969, November. This is the way Crete went—Not with a bang but a simper. *Psychol. Today*, 43–47.

Davies, J. C. 1962. Toward a theory of revolution. *Amer. Sociol. Rev.*, *27*, 5–19.

Davis, H. T. 1941. *The analysis of economic time series*. Bloomington, IN: Principia Press.

Davis, R. A. 1953. Note on age and productive scholarship of a university faculty. *J. Appl. Psychol.*, *38*, 318–19.

Davis, R. A. 1987. Creativity in neurological publications. *Neurosurgery*, *20*, 652–63.

Davis, R. H., & Maurice, A. B. 1931. *The caliph of Bagdad*. New York: Appleton.

Davis, W. M. 1986. Premature mortality among prominent American authors noted for alcohol abuse. *Drug Alc. Dep.*, *18*, 133–38.

Day, D., ed. 1949. *The autobiography of Will Rogers*. Boston: Houghton Mifflin.

de Beauvoir, S. 1949. *The second sex*, H. M. Parshley, trans. & ed. New York: Knopf, 1968.

deCharms, R., & Moeller, G. H. 1962. Values expressed in American children's readers: 1800–1950. *J. Abnorm. Soc. Psychol.*, *64*, 136–42.

DeFonzo, J. 1984. Climate and crime: Tests of an FBI assumption. *Environ. Behav.*, *16*, 185–210.

deGregorio, W. A. 1989. *The complete book of U.S. presidents*, 2nd ed. New York: Dembner Books.

de Groot, A. D. 1978. *Thought and choice in chess*, 2nd ed. The Hague: Mouton.

deMause, L. 1974. *The history of childhood*. New York: Bedrick Books.

deMause, L. 1981. What is psychohistory? *J. Psychohist.*, *9*, 179–84.

Dennis, W. 1954a. Bibliographies of eminent scientists. *Scient. Monthly*, *79*, 180–83.

Dennis, W. 1954b. Predicting scientific productivity in later maturity from records of earlier decades. *J. Gerontol.*, *9*, 465–67.

Dennis, W. 1954c. Productivity among American psychologists. *Amer. Psychol.*, *9*, 191–94.

Dennis, W. 1954d. Review of *Age and achievement*. *Psychol. Bull.*, *51*, 306–8.

Dennis, W. 1955. Variations in productivity among creative workers. *Scient. Monthly*, *80*, 277–78.

Dennis, W. 1956a. *Age and achievement*: A critique. *J. Gerontol.*, *9*, 465–67.

Dennis, W. 1956b. Age and productivity among scientists. *Science*, *123*, 724–25.

Dennis, W. 1958. Early graphic evidence of dextrality in man. *Percept. Mot. Skills*, *8*, 147–49.

Dennis, W. 1966. Creative productivity between the ages of 20 and 80 years. *J. Gerontol.*, *21*, 1–8.

Dennis, W., & Girden, E. 1954. Current scientific activities of psychologists as a function of age. *J. Gerontol.*, *9*, 175–78.

Derks, P. L. 1989. Pun frequency and popularity of Shakespeare's plays. *Emp. Stud. Arts*, *7*, 23–31.

Diamond, A. M., Jr. 1980. Age and the acceptance of cliometrics. *J. Econ. Hist.*, *40*, 838–41.

Diamond, A. M., Jr. 1984. An economic model of the life-cycle research productivity of scientists. *Scientometrics*, *6*, 189–96.

Diamond, A. M., Jr. 1985. The money value of citations to single-authored and multiple-authored articles. *Scientometrics*, *6*, 315–20.

Diamond, A. M., Jr. 1986. The life-cycle research productivity of mathematicians and scientists. *J. Gerontol.*, *41*, 520–25.

Disraeli, B. 1849. *Coningsby, or the new generation.* London: Longmans, Green.

Dobson, A. 1913. *Collected poems.* London: Paul, Trench, Trübner.

Domino, G. 1977. Homosexuality and creativity. *J. Homosex.*, *2*, 261–67.

Donley, R. E., & Winter, D. G. 1970. Measuring the motives of public officials at a distance: An exploratory study of American presidents. *Behav. Sci.*, *15*, 227–36.

Doty, R. M., Peterson, B. E., & Winter, D. G. 1991. Threat and authoritarianism in the United States, 1978–1987. *J. Pers. Soc. Psychol.*, *61*, 629–40.

Draper, N. R. 1963. Does age affect master chess? *J. Roy. Stat. Soc,,* *126*, 120–27.

Dreher, G. F., & Bretz, R. D., Jr. 1991. Cognitive ability and career attainment: Moderating effects of early career success. *J. Appl. Psychol.*, *76*, 392–97.

Dressler, W. W., & Robbins, M. C. 1975. Art styles, social stratification, and cognition: An analysis of Greek vase painting. *Amer. Ethnol.*, *2*, 427–34.

Dryden, J. 1664. Epistle dedicatory of *The rival ladies.* In W. P. Ker, ed., *Essays of John Dryden*, vol. 1, 1–9. Oxford: Clarendon Press, 1926.

Dryden, J. 1681. *Absalom and Achitophel.* London: Davis.

Dryden, J. 1693. Epistle to Congreve. In W. Scott & G. Saintsbury, eds., *The works of John Dryden*, vol. 11, 57–60. Edinburgh: Paterson, 1885.

Duda, R. O., & Shortliffe, E. H. 1983. Expert systems research. *Science*, *220*, 261–68.

Dye, D. A., & Reck, M. 1989. College grade point average as a predictor of adult success: A reply. *Publ. Personnel Manage.*, *18*, 235–41.

Eagly, A. H. 1987. *Sex differences in social behavior.* Hillsdale, NJ: Erlbaum.

Eagly, A. H., & Steffen, V. J. 1986. Gender and aggressive behavior: A meta-analytic review of the social psychological literature. *Psychol. Bull.*, *100*, 309–30.

Eagly, R. V. 1974. Contemporary profile of conventional economists. *Hist. Polit. Econ.*, *6*, 76–91.

Ebbinghaus, H. 1885. *Memory: A contribution to experimental psychology*, H. A. Roger & C. E. Bussenius, trans. New York: Teachers College of Columbia University, 1913.

Ebersole, P., & DeVogler-Ebersole, K. 1985. Meaning in life of the eminent and the average. *J. Soc. Behav. Pers.*, *1*, 83–94.

Eckhardt, W. 1991. Authoritarianism. *Polit. Psychol.*, *12*, 97–124.

Edwards, G. C., III. 1985. Measuring presidential success in Congress: Alternative approaches. *J. Politics*, *47*, 667–85.

Efran, M. G., & Patterson, E. W. J. 1974. Voters vote beautiful: The effects of physical appearance on a national election. *Canad. J. Behav. Sci.*, *6*, 352–56.

Ehrenwald, J. 1984. *The anatomy of genius: Split brains and global minds*. New York: Human Sciences Press.

Eibl-Eibesfeldt, I. 1972. Similarities and differences between cultures in expressive movements. In R. A. Hinde, ed., *Nonverbal communication*, 297–312. Cambridge, England: Cambridge University Press.

Eiduson, B. T. 1962. *Scientists*. New York: Basic Books.

Einstein, A. 1956. *Essays on music*. New York: Norton.

Einstein, A., & Freud, S. 1933. *Why war?* London: Peace Pledge Union.

Einstein, A., & Infeld, L. 1938. *The evolution of physics*. New York: Simon & Schuster.

Eisenman, R. 1964. Birth order and artistic creativity. *J. Indiv. Psychol.*, *20*, 183–85.

Eisenman, R. 1987. Creativity, birth order, and risk taking. *Bull. Psychonom. Soc.*, *25*, 87–88.

Eisenstadt, J. M. 1978. Parental loss and genius. *Amer. Psychol.*, *33*, 211–23.

Eisenstadt, J. M., Haynal, A., Rentchnick, P., & De Senarclens, P. 1989. *Parental loss and achievement*. Madison, CT: International Universities Press.

Eliot, T. S. 1920. Philip Massinger. In F. Kermode, ed., *Selected prose of T. S. Eliot*, 153–60. London: Faber & Faber, 1975.

Elliott, C. A. 1975. The American scientist in antebellum society: A quantitative view. *Soc. Stud. Sci.*, *5*, 93–108.

Ellis, H. 1926. *A study of British genius*, rev. ed. Boston: Houghton Mifflin.

Elms, A. C. 1976. *Personality in politics*. New York: Harcourt Brace Jovanovich.

Elms, A. C. 1988. Freud as Leonardo: Why the first psychobiography went wrong. *J. Pers.*, *56*, 19–40.

Elo, A. E. 1965. Age changes in master chess performance. *20*, 289–99.

Elo, A. E. 1978. *The rating of chessplayers, past and present*. New York: Arco.

Emerson, R. W. 1841a. Compensation. In *The best of Ralph Waldo Emerson*, 147–69. New York: Black, 1941.

Emerson, R. W. 1841b. Self-reliance. In *The best of Ralph Waldo Emerson*, 119–46. New York: Black, 1941.

Engel, G. L. 1991. Sudden and rapid death during psychological stress: Folklore or folk wisdom? *Ann. Internal Med.*, *74*, 771–82.

Epstein, R. 1990. Generativity theory and creativity. In M. Runco & R. Albert, eds., *Theories of creativity*, 116–40. Newbury Park, CA: Sage.

Erikson, E. H. 1958. *Young man Luther: A study in psychoanalysis and history*. New York: Norton.

Erikson, E. H. 1969. *Gandhi's truth: On the origins of militant nonviolence*. New York: Norton.

Erikson, R. S. 1976. The influence of newspaper endorsements on presidential elections. *Amer. J. Polit. Sci.*, *20*, 207–33.

Erikson, R. S. 1989. Economic conditions and the presidential vote. *Amer. Polit. Sci. Rev.*, *83*, 567–73.

Ernst, C., & Angst, J. 1983. *Birth order*. New York: Springer-Verlag.

Ertel, S. 1985. Content analysis: An alternative approach to open and closed minds. *High School J.*, *68*, 229–40.

Esar, E., ed. 1949. *The dictionary of humorous quotations*. New York: Dorset Press, 1989.

Etaugh, C., & Sanders, S. 1974. Evaluation of performance as a function of status and sex variables. *J. Soc. Psychol.*, *94*, 237–41.

Etheredge, L. S. 1978. Personality effects on American foreign policy, 1898–1968: A test of interpersonal generalization theory. *Amer. Polit. Sci. Rev.*, *78*, 434–51.

Etzioni, A. 1967. The Kennedy experiment. *West. Polit. Q.*, *20*, 361–80.

Evans, G. B., ed. 1974. *The Riverside Shakespeare*. Boston: Houghton Mifflin.

Ewen, D. 1965. *The complete book of classical music*. Englewood Cliffs, NJ: Prentice-Hall.

Eysenck, H. J. 1954. *The psychology of politics*. London: Routledge & Kegan Paul.

Eysenck, H. J. 1991. Raising IQ through vitamin and mineral supplementation: An introduction. *Pers. Indiv. Diff.*, *12*, 329–33.

Eysenck, H. J. 1993. Creativity and personality: Suggestions for a theory. *Psychol. Inquiry*, *4*, 147–48.

Eysenck, H. J., & Nias, D. K. B. 1982. *Astrology*. London: Smith.

Fancher, R. E. 1979. *Pioneers of psychology*. New York: Norton.

Fang, I. E. 1972. *Television news*, rev. & enlarged ed. New York: Hastings House.

Farnsworth, P. R. 1969. *The social psychology of music*, 2nd ed. Ames: Iowa State University Press.

Faust, D. 1984. *Limits of scientific reasoning*. Minneapolis: University of Minnesota Press.

Feingold, A. 1988. Cognitive gender differences are disappearing. *Amer. Psychol.*, *43*, 95–103.

Feldman, D. H., with Goldsmith, L. T. 1986. *Nature's gambit*. New York: Basic Books.

Feldman, S. 1982. Economic self-interest and political behavior. *Amer. J. Polit. Sci.*, *26*, 446–66.

Felson, R. B., & Trudeau, L. 1991. Gender differences in mathematics performance. *Soc. Psychol. Q.*, *54*, 113–26.

Ferris, P. 1977. *Dylan Thomas*. London: Hodder & Stoughton.

Fidell, L. S. 1970. Empirical verification of sex discrimination in hiring practices in psychology. *Amer. Psychol.*, *25*, 1094–98.

Fincher, J. 1977. *Sinister people*. New York: Putnam.

Findlay, A. 1948. *A hundred years of chemistry*, 2nd ed. London: Duckworth.

Finison, L. J. 1976. The application of McClelland's national development model to recent data. *J. Soc. Psychol.*, *98*, 55–59.

Fischhoff, B. 1975. Hindsight ≠ foresight: The effect of outcome knowledge on judgment under uncertainty. *J. Exp. Psychol.: Human Percept. Perform.*, *1*, 288–99.

Fischhoff, B., & Beyth, R. 1975. "I knew it would happen": Remembered probabilities of once-future things. *Organ. Behav. Human Perform.*, *13*, 1–16.

Fodor, E. M. 1990. The power motive and creativity of solutions to an engineering problem. *J. Res. Pers.*, *24*, 338–54.

Forbes, E., ed. 1967. *Thayer's life of Beethoven*, rev. ed. Princeton, NJ: Princeton University Press.

Foster, C. B. 1984. The performance of rational voter models in recent presidential elections. *Amer. Polit. Sci. Rev.*, *78*, 678–90.

Frank, M. G., & Gilovich, T. 1988. The dark side of self- and social perception: Black uniforms and aggression in professional sports. *J. Pers. Soc. Psychol.*, *54*, 74–85.

Freud, S. 1908. Creative writers and day-dreaming. In J. Strachey, ed. & trans., *Standard edition of the complete psychological works of Sigmund Freud*, vol. 9, 141–53. London: Hogarth Press, 1959.

Freud, S. 1910. *Leonardo da Vinci and a memory of his childhood*, A. Tyson, trans. New York: Norton, 1964.

Freud, S. 1929. Civilization and its discontents, J. Riviere, trans. In R. M. Hutchins, ed., *Great books of the Western world*, vol. 54, 767–802. Chicago: Encyclopaedia Britannica, 1952.

Freud, S., & Bullitt, W. C. 1967. *Thomas Woodrow Wilson*. Boston: Houghton Mifflin.

Frey, R. S. 1984. Does n-Achievement cause economic development? A cross-lagged panel analysis of the McClelland thesis. *J. Soc. Psychol.*, *122*, 67–70.

Friedman, H. S., DiMatteo, M. R., & Mertz, T. J. 1980. Nonverbal communication on television news: The facial expression of broadcasters during coverage of a presidential election campaign. *Pers. Soc. Psychol. Bull.*, *6*, 427–35.

Friedman, H. S., DiMatteo, M. R., & Mertz, T. J. 1980. Perceived bias in the facial expressions of television news broadcasters. *J. Communic.*, *30*(4), 103–11.

Frost, E., ed. 1988. *The bully pulpit*. New York: Facts on File.

Frost, R. 1949. *Collected poems*. New York: Holt.

Galton, F. 1869. *Hereditary genius*. London: Macmillan.

Galton, F. 1874. *English men of science: Their nature and nurture*. London: Macmillan.

Galton, F. 1883. *Inquiries into human faculty and its development*. London: Macmillan.

Galton, F. 1892. *Hereditary genius*, 2nd ed. Gloucester, MA: Smith, 1972.

Gamson, W. A., & Modigliani, A. 1971. *Untangling the Cold War*. Boston: Little, Brown.

Gardner, H. 1983. *Frames of mind: The theory of multiple intelligences*. New York: Basic Books.

Gardner, H. 1987. *The mind's new science*. New York: Basic Books.

Gardner, H. 1993. Seven creators of the modern era. In J. Brockman, ed., *Creativity*, 28–47. New York: Simon & Schuster.

Garner, D. M., Garfinkel, P. E., Schwartz, D., & Thompson, M. 1980. Cultural expectations of thinness in women. *Psychol. Rep.*, *47*, 483–91.

Garvey, W. D., & Tomita, K. 1972. Continuity of productivity by scientists in the years 1968–1971. *Sci. Stud.*, *2*, 379–83.

Gaston, J. 1973. *Originality and competition in science*. Chicago: University of Chicago Press.

Gates, H. L., Jr. 1992. *Loose canons*. New York: Oxford University Press.

Gedda, L. 1951. *Twins in history and science*, M. Milani-Comparetti, trans. Springfield, IL: Charles C Thomas, 1961.

George, A. L., & George, J. L. 1956. *Woodrow Wilson and Colonel House: A personality study*. New York: Day.

George, J. L., & George, A. L. 1981. *Woodrow Wilson and Colonel House*: A reply to Weinstein, Anderson, and Link. *Polit. Sci. Q.*, *96*, 641–65.

Geschwind, N., & Galaburda, A. 1987. *Cerebral lateralization*. Cambridge, MA: MIT Press.

Getzels, J., & Csikszentmihalyi, M. 1976. *The creative vision*. New York: Wiley.

Getzels, J., & Jackson, P. W. 1963. The highly intelligent and the highly creative adolescent: A summary of some research findings. In C. W. Taylor & F. X. Barron, eds., *Scientific creativity*, 161–72. New York: Wiley.

Ghiselin, B., ed. 1952. *The creative process*. Berkeley: University of California Press.

Gibbon, E. 1776–88. *Decline and fall of the Roman Empire*. In R. M. Hutchins, ed., *Great books of the Western world*, vols. 40–41. Chicago: Encyclopaedia Britannica, 1952.

Gieryn, T. F., & Hirsh, R. F. 1983. Marginality and innovation in science. *Soc. Stud. Sci.*, *13*, 87–106.

Gilbert, G. M. 1950. *The psychology of dictatorship*. New York: Ronald Press.

Giles, H. A., ed. 1923. *Gems of Chinese literature*. New York: Dover, 1965.

Gillies, J., & Campbell, S. 1985. Conservatism and poetry preferences. *Brit. J. Soc. Psychol.*, *24*, 223–27.

Gilovich, T. 1981. Seeing the past in the present: The effect of associations to familiar events on judgments and decisions. *J. Pers. Soc. Psychol.*, *40*, 797–808.

Glass, D. P. 1985. Evaluating presidential candidates: Who focuses on their personal attributes? *Publ. Opin. Q., 49*, 517–34.

Glazer, A., & Grofman, B. 1992. A positive correlation between turnout and plurality does not refute the rational voter model. *Qual. Quant., 26*, 85–93.

Glick, P., Zion, C., & Nelson, C. 1988. What mediates sex discrimination in hiring decisions? *J. Pers. Soc. Psychol., 50*, 178–86.

Godechot, J. 1974. Napoleon. In *Encyclopaedia Britannica: Macropedia*, 15th ed., vol. 12, 831–39. Chicago: Encyclopaedia Britannica.

Goertzel, M. G., Goertzel, V., & Goertzel, T. G. 1978. *300 eminent personalities*. San Francisco: Jossey-Bass.

Goertzel, V., & Goertzel, M. G. 1962. *Cradles of eminence*. Boston: Little, Brown.

Goggin, M. L. 1984. The ideological content of presidential communications: The message-tailoring hypothesis revisited. *Amer. Polit. Q., 12*, 361–84.

Goldstein, J. H., & Arms, R. L. 1971. Effects of observing athletic contests on hostility. *Sociometry, 34*, 83–90.

Goodwin, F. K., & Jamison, K. R. 1990. *Manic–depressive illness*. New York: Oxford University Press.

Gottschalk, L. A., Uliana, R., & Gilbert, R. 1988. Presidential candidates and cognitive impairment measured from behavior in campaign debates. *Publ. Admin. Rev., 48*, 613–19.

Götz, K. O., & Götz, K. 1979a. Personality characteristics of professional artists. *Percept. Mot. Skills, 49*, 327–34.

Götz, K. O., & Götz, K. 1979b. Personality characteristics of successful artists. *Percept. Mot. Skills, 49*, 919–24.

Gough, H. G. 1976. Studying creativity by means of word association tests. *J. Appl. Psychol., 61*, 348–53.

Gough, H. G., & Heilbrun, A. B., Jr. 1965. *The Adjective Check List manual*. Palo Alto, CA: Consulting Psychologists Press.

Gould, S. J. 1981. *The mismeasure of man*. New York: Norton.

Granberg, D., & Brent, E. 1983. When prophecy bends: The preference–expectation link in U.S. presidential elections, 1952–1980. *J. Pers. Soc. Psychol., 45*, 477–91.

Gray, C. E. 1958. An analysis of Graeco-Roman development: The epicyclical evolution of Graeco-Roman civilization. *Amer. Anthropol., 60*, 13–31.

Gray, C. E. 1961. An epicyclical model for Western civilization. *Amer. Anthropol., 63*, 1014–37.

Gray, C. E. 1966. A measurement of creativity in Western civilization. *Amer. Anthropol., 68*, 1384–1417

Green, G. S. 1981. A test of the Ortega hypothesis in criminology. *Criminology, 19*, 45–52.

Greenwald, A. G. 1980. The totalitarian ego: Fabrication and revision of personal history. *Amer. Psychol., 35*, 603–18.

Greer, D. L. 1983. Spectator booking and the home advantage: A study of social influence in the basketball arena. *Soc. Psychol. Q., 46*, 252–61.

Gruber, H. E. 1989. The evolving systems approach to creative work. In D. B. Wallace & H. E. Gruber, eds., *Creative people at work*, 3–24. New York: Oxford University Press.

Grush, J. E. 1980. Impact of candidate expenditures, regionality, and prior outcomes on the 1976 Democratic presidential primaries. *J. Pers. Soc. Psychol., 38*, 337–47.

Grush, J. E., McKeough, K. L., & Ahlering, R. F. 1978. Extrapolating laboratory exposure research to actual political elections. *J. Pers. Soc. Psychol., 36*, 257–70.

Guilford, J. P. 1959. Traits of creativity. In H. H. Anderson, ed., *Creativity and its cultivation*, 142–61. New York: Harper.

Guilford, J. P. 1967. *The nature of human intelligence.* New York: McGraw-Hill.

Haan, N., Smith, M. B., & Block, J. 1968. Moral reasoning of young adults: Political–social behavior, family background, and personality correlates. *J. Pers. Soc. Psychol., 10,* 183–201.

Hadamard, J. 1945. *The psychology of invention in the mathematical field.* Princeton, NJ: Princeton University Press.

Haefele, J. W. 1962. *Creativity and innovation.* New York: Reinhold.

Halacy, D. S. 1970. *Man and memory.* New York: Harper & Row.

Hall, G. S. 1922. *Senescence.* New York: Appleton.

Halpern, D. F. 1989. The disappearance of cognitive gender differences: What you see depends on where you look. *Amer. Psychol., 44,* 1156–58.

Hammer, M., & Zubin, J. 1968. Evolution, culture, and psychopathology. *J. Gen. Psychol., 78,* 151–64.

Handlon, B. J., & Squier, L. H. 1955. Attitudes towards special loyalty oaths at the University of California. *Amer. Psychol., 10,* 121–27.

Hardy, G. H. 1940. *A mathematician's apology.* Cambridge, England: Cambridge University Press, 1969.

Hardy, T. 1903–08. *The dynasts.* London: Macmillan, 1978.

Hargens, L. L. 1978. Relations between work habits, research technologies, and eminence in science. *Sociol. Work Occup.,* 5, 97–112.

Hargens, L. L., McCann, J. C., & Reskin, B. F. 1978. Productivity and reproductivity: Fertility and professional achievement among research scientists. *Soc. Forces,* 57, 154–63.

Harman, W. W., McKim, R. H., Mogar, R. E., Fadiman, J., & Stolaroff, M. J. 1966. Psychedelic agents in creative problem-solving: A pilot study. *Psychol. Rep.,* 19, 211–27.

Harmon, L. R. 1963. The development of a criterion of scientific competence. In C. W. Taylor & F. X. Barron, eds., *Scientific creativity,* 44–52. New York: Wiley.

Harnsberger, C. T., ed. 1972. *Everyone's Mark Twain.* New York: Barnes.

Harries, K. D., & Stadler, S. J. 1983. Determinism revisited: Assault and heat stress in Dallas, 1980. *Environ. Behav.,* 15, 235–56.

Harries, K. D., & Stadler, S. J. 1988. Heat and violence: New findings from Dallas field data, 1980–1980. *J. Appl. Soc. Psychol.,* 18, 129–37.

Harrington, D. M., & Anderson, S. M. 1981. Creativity, masculinity, femininity, and three models of psychological androgyny. *J. Pers. Soc. Psychol.,* 41, 744–57.

Harris, I. D. 1964. *The promised seed: A comparative study of eminent first and later sons.* New York: Free Press.

Harrison, A. A., & Kroll, N. E. A. 1985–86. Variations in death rates in the proximity of Christmas: An opponent process interpretation. *Omega,* 16, 181–92.

Harrison, A. A., & Kroll, N. E. A. 1989–90. Birth dates and death dates: An examination of two baseline procedures and age at time of death. *Omega,* 20, 127–37.

Harrison, A. A., & Moore, M. 1982–83. Birth dates and death dates: A closer look. *Omega,* 13, 117–25.

Harrison, A. A., & Saeed, L. 1977. Let's make a deal: An analysis of revelations and stipulations in lonely hearts advertisements. *J. Pers. Soc. Psychol.,* 35, 257–64.

Harrison, A. A., Struthers, N. J., & Moore, M. 1988. On the conjunction of national holidays and reported birthdates: One more path to reflected glory? *Soc. Psychol. Q.*, *51*, 365–70.

Hart, M. H. 1987. *The 100: A ranking of the most influential persons in history*. Secaucus, NJ: Citadel Press.

Hartman, E. L. 1973. *The functions of sleep*. New Haven, CT: Yale University Press.

Hartsough, D. M., & Savitsky, J. C. 1984. Three Mile Island: Psychology and environmental policy at a crossroads. *Amer. Psychol.*, *39*, 1113–22.

Hasenfus, N., Martindale, C., & Birnbaum, D. 1983. Psychological reality of cross-media artistic styles. *J. Exp. Psychol.: Human Percept. Perform.*, *9*, 841–63.

Hastorf, A. H., & Cantril, H. 1954. They saw a game: A case study. *J. Abnorm. Soc. Psychol.*, *49*, 129–34.

Hayes, J. R. 1989a. Cognitive processes in creativity. In J. A. Glover, R. R. Ronning, & C. R. Reynolds eds., *Handbook of creativity*, 135–45. New York: Plenum Press.

Hayes, J. R. 1989b. *The complete problem solver*, 2nd ed. Hillsdale, NJ: Erlbaum.

Hedges, L. V. 1987. How hard is hard science, how soft is soft science? *Amer. Psychol.*, *42*, 443–55.

Hegel, G. W. F. 1821. *The philosophy of right*, T. M. Knox, trans. In R. M. Hutchins, ed., *Great books of the Western world*, vol. 46, 1–150. Chicago: Encyclopaedia Britannica, 1952.

Helmholtz, H. von. 1898. An autobiographical sketch. In *Popular lectures on scientific subjects, second series*, E. Atkinson, trans., 266–91. New York: Longmans, Green.

Helmreich, R. L., Spence, J. T., Beane, W. E., Lucker, G. W., & Matthews, K. A. 1980. Making it in academic psychology: Demographic and personality correlates of attainment. *J. Pers. Soc. Psychol.*, *39*, 896–908.

Helmreich, R. L., Spence, J. T., & Thorbecke, W. L. 1981. On the stability of productivity and recognition. *Pers. Soc. Psychol. Bull.*, *7*, 516–22.

Helson, R. 1980. The creative woman mathematician. In L. H. Fox, L. Brody, & D. Tobin, eds., *Women and the mathematical mystique*, 23–54. Baltimore: Johns Hopkins University Press.

Helson, R. 1990. Creativity in women: Outer and inner views over time. In M. A. Runco & R. S. Albert, eds., *Theories of creativity*, 46–58. Newbury Park, CA: Sage.

Helson, R., & Crutchfield, R. S. 1970. Mathematicians: The creative researcher and the average Ph.D. *J. Consult. Clin. Psychol.*, *34*, 250–57.

Hendrickson, R. 1988. *The dictionary of eponyms*. New York: Dorset Press.

Hepworth, J. T., & West, S. G. 1988. Lynchings and the economy: A time-series reanalysis of Hovland and Sears 1940. *J. Pers. Soc. Psychol.*, *55*, 239–47.

Herek, G. M., Janis, I. L., & Huth, P. 1987. Decision making during international crises: Is quality of process related to outcome? *J. Confl. Resolut.*, *31*, 203–26.

Herek, G. M., Janis, I. L., & Huth, P. 1989. Quality of U.S. decision making during the Cuban missile crisis. *J. Confl. Resolut.*, *33*, 446–59.

Hermann, D. B. 1988. How old were the authors of significant research in twentieth century astronomy at the time of their greatest achievements? *Scientometrics*, *13*, 135–38.

Hermann, M. G. 1980a. Assessing the personalities of Soviet Politburo members. *Pers. Soc. Psychol. Bull.*, *6*, 332–52.

Hermann, M. G. 1980b. Explaining foreign policy using personal characteristics of political leaders. *Internat. Stud. Q.*, *24*, 7–46.

Hertz, F. 1928. *Race and civilization*, A. S. Levetus & W. Entz, trans. New York: Ktav, 1970.

Hibbs, D. A., Jr. 1979. The mass public and macroeconomic performance: The dynamics of public opinion toward unemployment and inflation. *Amer. J. Polit. Sci.*, *23*, 705–731.

Hibbs, D. A., Jr. 1982a. The dynamics of political support for American presidents among occupational and partisan groups. *Amer. J. Polit. Sci.*, *26*, 312–32.

Hibbs, D. A., Jr. 1982b. Economic outcomes and political support for British governments among occupational classes: A dynamic analysis. *Amer. Polit. Sci. Rev.*, *76*, 259–79.

Hibbs, D. A., Jr. 1982c. President Reagan's mandate from the 1980 elections: A shift to the right? *Amer. Polit. Q.*, *10*, 387–420.

Hibbs, D. A., Jr., Rivers, R. D., & Vasilatos, N. 1982. The dynamics of political support for American presidents among occupational and partisan groups. *Amer. J. Polit. Sci.*, *26*, 312–32.

Hines, T. 1991. The myth of right hemisphere creativity. *J. Creat. Behav.*, *25*, 223–27.

Hobbes, T. 1651. *Leviathan*. In R. M. Hutchins, ed., *Great books of the Western world*, vol. 23, 43–283. Chicago: Encyclopaedia Britannica, 1952.

Hoffman, B. 1972. *Albert Einstein*. New York: Plume.

Holahan, C. K. 1984–85. The relationship between life goals at thirty and perceptions of goal attainment and life satisfaction at seventy for gifted men and women. *Internat. J. Aging Human Dev.*, *20*, 21–36.

Holding, D. H. 1985. *The psychology of chess skill*. Hillsdale, NJ: Erlbaum.

Holbrook, T. M. 1991. Presidential elections in space and time. *Amer. J. Polit. Sci.*, *35*, 91–109.

Hollingworth, L. S. 1926. *Gifted children*. New York: Macmillan.

Holmes, J. E., & Elder, R. E. 1989. Our best and worst presidents: Some possible reasons for perceived performance. *Presid. Stud. Q.*, *19*, 529–57.

Holmes, T. S., & Holmes, T. H. 1970. Short-term intrusions into the life style routine. *J. Psychosom. Res.*, *14*, 121–32.

Holton, G. 1971–72. On trying to understand the scientific genius. *Amer. Scholar*, *41*, 95–110.

Hoppe, K. D. 1989. Psychoanalysis, hemispheric specialization, and creativity. *J. Amer. Acad. Psychoanal.*, *17*, 253–69.

Hoppe, K. D., & Kyle, N. L. 1990. Dual brain, creativity, and health. *Creat. Res. J.*, *3*, 150–7.

Horner, K. L., Rushton, J. P., & Vernon, P. A. 1986. Relation between aging and research productivity of academic psychologists. *Psychol. Aging*, *1*, 319–24.

House, R. J., Spangler, W. D., & Woycke, J. 1991. Personality and charisma in the U.S. presidency: A psychological theory of leader effectiveness. *Admin. Sci. Q.*, *36*, 364–96.

Houts, P. S., Cleary, P. D., & Hu, T. 1988. *The Three Mile Island crisis*. University Park: Pennsylvania State University Press.

Hovland, C. J., & Sears, R. R. 1940. Minor studies in aggression: 6. Correlation of lynchings with economic indices. *J. Psychol.*, *9*, 301–10.

Howard, J. A., Blumstein, P., & Schwartz, P. 1987. Social or evolutionary theories? Some observations on preferences in human mate selection. *J. Pers. Soc. Psychol.*, *53*, 194–200.

Howe, M. J. A. 1982. Biographical evidence and the development of outstanding individuals. *Amer. Psychol.*, *37*, 1071–81.

Howe, M. J. A. 1989. *Fragments of genius*. New York: Routledge.

Hoyt, D. P. 1965. *The relationship between college grades and adult achievement* (Amer. Coll. Test. Prog., Res. Rep. No. 7). Iowa City, IA: American College Testing Program.

Hudson, L. 1958. Undergraduate academic record of Fellows of the Royal Society. *Nature, 182*, 1326.

Hudson, L., & Jacot, B. 1986. The outsider in science. In C. Bagley & G. K. Verma, eds., *Personality, cognition and values*, 3–23. London: Macmillan.

Hudson, V. M. 1990. Birth order of world leaders: An exploratory analysis of effects on personality and behavior. *Polit. Psychol., 11*, 583–601.

Huesmann, L. R., & Malamuth, N. M., eds. 1986. Media violence and antisocial behavior [Special issue]. *J. Soc. Issues, 42*(3).

Hughes, E. C. 1958. *Men at their work*. Glencoe, IL: Free Press.

Hull, D. L., Tessner, P. D., & Diamond, A. M. 1978. Planck's principle: Do younger scientists accept new scientific ideas with greater alacrity than older scientists? *Science, 202*, 717–23.

Hunter, E. 1953. *Brain-washing in Red China*, new & enlarged ed. New York: Vanguard Press.

Hunter, I. M. L. 1977. An exceptional memory. *Brit. J. Psychol., 68*, 155–64.

Huntington, E. 1938. *Season of birth*. New York: Wiley.

Hur, K. K., & Robinson, J. P. 1978. The social impact of "Roots." *Journ. Q., 55*, 19–24, 83.

Hurd, R. E., & Singletary, M. W. 1984. Newspaper endorsement influence on the 1980 presidential election vote. *Journ. Q., 61*, 332–38.

Hyde, J. S. 1986. Gender differences in aggression. In J. S. Hyde & M. C. Linn, eds., *The psychology of gender*, 51–66. Baltimore: Johns Hopkins University Press.

Hyman, H. H., & Sheatsley, P. B. 1947. Some reasons why information campaigns fail. *Publ. Opin. Q., 11*, 413–23.

Illingworth, R. S., & Illingworth, C. M. 1969. *Lessons from childhood*. Edinburgh: Livingstone.

Inhaber, H. 1977. Scientists and economic growth. *Soc. Stud. Sci., 7*, 514–26.

Ishii, K. 1991. Measuring mutual causation: Effects of suicide news on suicides in Japan. *Soc. Sci. Res., 20*, 188–95.

Iyengar, S., Kinder, D. R., Peters, M., & Krosnick, J. A. 1984. The evening news and presidential evaluations. *J. Pers. Soc. Psychol., 46*, 778–87.

Izzett, R. R. 1971. Authoritarianism and attitudes toward the Vietnam War as reflected in behavioral and self-report measures. *J. Pers. Soc. Psychol., 17*, 145–48.

Jackson, J. M., & Padgett, V. R. 1982. With a little help from my friend: Social loafing and the Lennon–McCartney songs. *Pers. Soc. Psychol. Bull., 8*, 672–77.

James, W. 1880. Great men, great thoughts, and the environment. *Atlantic Monthly, 46*, 441–59.

James, W. 1890. *The principles of psychology*. In R. M. Hutchins, ed., *Great books of the Western world*, vol. 53. Chicago: Encyclopaedia Britannica, 1952.

James, W. 1902. *The varieties of religious experience*. London: Longmans, Green.

Jamison, K. R. 1989. Mood disorders and patterns of creativity in British writers and artists. *Psychiatry, 52*, 125–34.

Janis, I. L. 1982. *Groupthink*, 2nd ed. Boston: Houghton Mifflin.

Jensen, A. R. 1990. Speed of information processing in a calculating prodigy. *Intelligence, 14*, 259–74.

Jensen, A. R., Cohn, S. J., & Cohn, C. M. G. 1989. Speed of information processing in academically gifted youths and their siblings. *Pers. Indiv. Diff., 10*, 29–34.

Jervis, R. 1976. *Perception and misperception in international politics*. Princeton, NJ: Princeton University Press.

Johnson, S. 1781. *The lives of the most eminent English poets*, vol. 1. London: Bathurst et al.

Johnson, S., & Christ, W. G. 1988. Women through *Time*: Who gets covered? *Journ. Q.*, 65, 889–97.

Jones, E. 1949. *Hamlet and Oedipus*. New York: Gollancz.

Jones, E. 1953. *The life and work of Sigmund Freud: Vol. 1. The formative years and the great discoveries, 1856–1900*. New York: Basic Books.

Jones, F. E. 1964. Predictor variables for creativity in industrial science. *J. Appl. Psychol.*, 48, 134–36.

Jorgenson, D. O. 1975. Economic threat and authoritarianism in television programs: 1950–1974. *Psychol. Rep.*, 37, 1153–54.

Juda, A. 1949. The relationship between highest mental capacity and psychic abnormalities. *Amer. J. Psychiat.*, 106, 296–307.

Jungk, R. 1958. *Brighter than a thousand suns*, J. Cleugh, trans. New York: Harcourt Brace.

Kammann, R. 1966. Verbal complexity and preferences in poetry. *J. Verb. Learn. Verb. Behav.*, 5, 536–40.

Kantorovich, A., 1993. *Scientific discovery: Logic and tinkering*. Albany: State University of New York Press.

Kantorovich, A., & Ne'eman, Y. 1989. Serendipity as a source of evolutionary progress in science. *Stud. Hist. Philos. Sci.*, 20, 505–29.

Karabenick, S. A., & Wilson, W. 1969. Dogmatism among war hawks and peace doves. *Psychol. Rep.*, 25, 419–22.

Karlson, J. I. 1970. Genetic association of giftedness and creativity with schizophrenia. *Hereditas*, 66, 177–82.

Karno, M., & Konečni, V. J. 1992. The effects of structural interventions in the first movement of Mozart's Symphony in G Minor K. 550 on aesthetic preference. *Music Percept.*, 10, 63–72.

Kastenbaum, R., Peyton, S., & Kastenbaum, B. 1976–77. Sex discrimination after death. *Omega*, 7, 351–59.

Kaulins, A. 1979. Cycles in the birth of eminent humans. *Cycles*, 30, 9–15.

Kavolis, V. 1964. Economic correlates of artistic creativity. *Amer. J. Sociol.*, 70, 332–41.

Kavolis, V. 1966. Community dynamics and artistic creativity. *Amer. Sociol. Rev.*, 31, 208–17.

Kearl, M. C. 1986–87. Death as a measure of life: A research note on the Kastenbaum–Spilka strategy of obituary analysis. *Omega*, 17, 65–77.

Kelley, S., Jr., & Mirer, T. W. 1974. The simple act of voting. *Amer. Polit. Sci. Rev.*, 68, 572–91.

Kelman, H. C., & Hamilton, V. L. 1989. *Crimes of obedience*. New Haven, CT: Yale University Press.

Kendrick, D. T., & Gutierres, S. E. 1980. Contrast effects and judgments of physical attractiveness: When beauty becomes a social problem. *J. Pers. Soc. Psychol.*, 38, 131–40.

Kenney, P. J., & Rice, T. W. 1988. The contextual determinants of presidential greatness. *Presid. Stud. Q.*, 18, 161–69.

Kenski, H. C. 1977. The impact of economic conditions on presidential popularity. *J. Politics*, 39, 764–73.

Kernell, S. 1978. Explaining presidential popularity: How ad hoc theorizing, misplaced emphasis, and insufficient care in measuring one's variables refuted common sense and led conventional wisdom down the path of anomalies. *Amer. Polit. Sci. Rev.*, 72, 506–22.

Kernell, S., & Hibbs, D. A. 1981. A critical threshold model of presidential popularity. In A. Wildavsky, ed., *Perspectives on the presidency*, 49–71. Boston: Little, Brown.

Kerner, O., chair. 1968. *Report of the National Advisory Commission on Civil Disorders*. New York: Bantam.

Kerr, R. A. 1991. The lessons of Dr. Browning. *Science, 253,* 622–23.

Kick, E. L. 1983. World-system properties and military intervention–internal war linkages. *J. Polit. Milit. Sociol., 11,* 185–208.

Kiewiet, D. R. 1983. *Macroeconomics and micropolitics*. Chicago: University of Chicago Press.

Kimball, M. M. 1989. A new perspective on women's math achievement. *Psychol. Bull., 105,* 198–214.

Kinder, D. R. 1981. Presidents, prosperity, and public opinion. *Publ. Opin. Q., 45,* 1–21.

Kinder, D. R., & Kiewiet, D. R. 1979. Economic discontent and political behavior: The role of personal grievances and collective economic judgments in congressional voting. *Amer. J. Polit. Sci., 23,* 495–527.

Kinder, D. R., Peters, M. D., Abelson, R. R., & Fiske, S. T. 1980. Presidential prototypes. *Polit. Behav., 2,* 315–38.

King, D. R. 1978. The brutalizing effect: Execution publicity and the incidence of homicide in South Carolina. *Soc. Forces, 57,* 683–87.

King, M. L. 1963. Letter from Birmingham Jail. In *Annals of America*, vol. 18, 143–49. Chicago: Encyclopaedia Britannica, 1968.

Kingdon, J. W. 1967. Politicians' beliefs about voters. *Amer. Polit. Sci. Rev., 61,* 137–43.

Kirscht, J. P., & Dillehay, R. C. 1967. *Dimensions of authoritarianism*. Lexington: University of Kentucky Press.

Klawans, H. L. 1988. *Toscanini's fumble*. Chicago: Contemporary Books.

Klein, J. G. 1991. Negativity effects in impression formation: A test in the political arena. *Pers. Soc. Psychol. Bull., 17,* 412–18.

Klingemann, H.-D., Mohler, P. P., & Weber, R. P. 1982. Cultural indicators based on content analysis: A secondary analysis of Sorokin's data on fluctuations of systems of truth. *Qual. Quant., 16,* 1–18.

Knapp, R. H. 1962. A factor analysis of Thorndike's ratings of eminent men. *J. Soc. Psychol., 56,* 67–71.

Knight, F. 1973. *Beethoven and the age of revolution*. New York: International.

Knopoff, L., & Hutchinson, W. 1983. Entropy as a measure of style: The influence of sample length. *J. Music Theory, 27,* 75–97.

Koestler, A. 1964. *The act of creation*. New York: Macmillan.

Kohlberg, L. 1984. *The psychology of moral development*. San Francisco: Harper & Row.

Kohut, T. A. 1986. Psychohistory as history. *Amer. Hist. Rev., 91,* 336–54.

Kramer, G. H. 1971. Short-term fluctuations in U.S. voting behavior, 1896–1964. *Amer. Polit. Sci. Rev., 65,* 131–43.

Kraus, S., ed. 1962. *The great debates*. Bloomington: Indiana University Press.

Kraus, S., ed. 1979. *The great debates, 1976*. Bloomington: Indiana University Press.

Kreml, W. P. 1977. *The anti-authoritarian personality*. Oxford: Pergamon Press.

Kris, E. 1952. *Psychoanalytic explorations in art*. New York: International Universities Press.

Kroeber, A. L. 1917. The superorganic. *Amer. Anthropol.*, *19*, 163–214.

Kroeber, A. L. 1944. *Configurations of culture growth*. Berkeley: University of California Press.

Kroll, W., & Peterson, K. H. 1965. Personality factor profiles of collegiate football teams. *Res. Q.*, *36*, 433–40.

Krosnick, J. A. 1988. The role of attitude importance in social evaluation: A study of political preferences, presidential candidate evaluations, and voting behavior. *J. Pers. Soc. Psychol.*, *55*, 196–210.

Kuhn, T. S. 1970. *The structure of scientific revolutions*, 2nd ed. Chicago: University of Chicago Press.

Kuhn, T. S. 1977. *The essential tension*. Chicago: University of Chicago Press.

Kulkarni, D., & Simon, H. A. 1988. The process of scientific discovery: The strategy of experimentation. *Cog. Sci.*, *12*, 139–75.

Kuo, Y. 1986. The growth and decline of Chinese philosophical genius. *Chin. J. Psychol.*, *28*, 81–91.

Kuo, Y. 1988. The social psychology of Chinese philosophical creativity: A critical synthesis. *Soc. Epistemol.*, *2*, 283–95.

Kyvik, S. 1990. Motherhood and scientific productivity. *Soc. Stud. Sci.*, *20*, 149–60.

Labovitz, S. 1974. Control over death: The Canadian case. *Omega*, *5*, 217–21.

Laing, R. B., & Stevenson, R. L. 1976. Public opinion trends in the last days of the Nixon administration. *Journ. Q.*, *53*, 294–302.

Lamb, D., & Easton, S. M. 1984. *Multiple discovery*. England: Avebury.

Landowska, W. 1964. *Landowska on music*, D. Restout, ed. & trans. New York: Stein & Day.

Langer, W. C. 1972. *The mind of Adolf Hitler*. New York: Basic Books.

Langley, P., Simon, H. A., Bradshaw, G. L., & Zythow, J. M. 1987. *Scientific discovery*. Cambridge, MA: MIT Press.

Langlois, J. H., & Roggman, L. A. 1990. Attractive faces are only average. *Psychol. Sci.*, *1*, 115–21.

Lanoue, D. J. 1987. Economic prosperity and presidential popularity: Sorting out the effects. *West. Polit. Q.*, *40*, 237–45.

Lasswell, H. D. 1948. *Power and personality*. New York: Norton.

Lau, R. R. 1982. Negativity in political perception. *Polit. Behav.*, *4*, 353–78.

Lau, R. R. 1985. Two explanations for negativity effects in political behavior. *Amer. J. Polit. Sci.*, *29*, 119–38.

Lau, R. R., & Russell, D. 1980. Attributions in the sports pages. *J. Pers. Soc. Psychol.*, *39*, 29–38.

Lawani, S. M. 1986. Some bibliometric correlates of quality in scientific research. *Scientometrics*, *9*, 13–15.

Le Bon, G. 1896. *The crowd*. London: Benn.

Leary, M. R. 1982. Hindsight distortion and the 1980 presidential election. *Pers. Soc. Psychol. Bull.*, *8*, 257–63.

Lehman, H. C. 1943. The longevity of the eminent. *Science*, *98*, 270–73.

Lehman, H. C. 1953. *Age and achievement*. Princeton, NJ: Princeton University Press.

Lehman, H. C. 1956. Reply to Dennis' critique of *Age and achievement*. *J. Gerontol.*, *11*, 128–34.

Lehman, H. C. 1958. The chemist's most creative years. *Science*, *127*, 1213–22.

Lehman, H. C. 1962. More about age and achievement. *Gerontologist, 2*, 141–48.

Lehman, H. C. 1963. Chronological age versus present-day contributions to medical progress. *Gerontologist, 3*, 71–75.

Lehman, H. C. 1966a. The most creative years of engineers and other technologists. *J. Genet. Psychol., 108*, 263–70.

Lehman, H. C. 1966b. The psychologist's most creative years. *Amer. Psychol., 21*, 363–69.

Lehman, H. C., & Witty, P. A. 1931. Scientific eminence and church membership. *Scient. Monthly, 33*, 544–49.

Leitner, L. M. 1983. Construct similarity, self-meaningfulness, and presidential preference. *J. Pers. Soc. Psychol., 45*, 890–94.

Lentz, T. F. 1939. Personage admiration and other correlates of conservatism–radicalism. *J. Soc. Psychol., 10*, 81–93.

Lester, D. 1990. Suicide and presidential elections in the USA. *Psychol. Rep., 67*, 218.

Lester, D. 1991. Premature mortality associated with alcoholism and suicide in American writers. *Percept. Mot. Skills, 73*, 162.

Leventhal, H., Jacobs, R. J., & Kudirka, N. Z. 1964. Authoritarianism, ideology, and political candidate choice. *J. Abnorm. Soc. Psychol., 69*, 539–49.

Levin, S. G., & Stephan, P. E. 1989. Age and research productivity of academic scientists. *Res. Higher Educ., 30*, 531–49.

Levin, S. G., & Stephan, P. E. 1991. Research productivity over the life cycle: Evidence for academic scientists. *Amer. Econ. Rev., 81*, 114–32.

Levy, D., & Newborn, M. 1982. *All about chess and computers.* Rockville, MD: Computer Science Press.

Levy, J. S., & Morgan, T. C. 1986. The war-weariness hypothesis: An empirical test. *Amer. J. Polit. Sci., 30*, 26–49.

Levy, S. G. 1979. Authoritarianism and information processing. *Bull. Psychonom. Soc., 13*, 240–42.

Lewin, K. 1947. *The research center for group dynamics.* New York: Beacon House.

Lewis-Beck, M. S. 1985. Pocketbook voting in U.S. national election studies: Fact or artifact? *Amer. J. Polit. Sci., 29*, 348–56.

Lewis-Beck, M. S., & Rice, T. W. 1983. Localism in presidential elections: The home state advantage. *Amer. J. Polit. Sci., 27*, 548–56.

Lewis-Beck, M. S., & Rice, T. W. 1984. Forecasting presidential elections: A comparison of naive models. *Polit. Behav., 6*, 9–21.

Lifton, R. J. 1961. *Thought reform and the psychology of totalism.* New York: Norton.

Lifton, R. J. 1986. *The Nazi doctors.* New York: Basic Books.

Lincoln, A. 1864. Letter to A. G. Hodges. In *The life and writings of Abraham Lincoln,* P. V. D. Stern, ed., 807–9. New York: Modern Library, 1940.

Lindauer, M. S. 1992. Creativity in aging artists: Contributions from the humanities to the psychology of old age. *Creat. Res. J., 5*, 211–31.

Lindauer, M. S. 1993a. The old-age style and its artists. *Emp. Stud. Arts, 11*, 135–46.

Lindauer, M. S. 1993b. The span of creativity among long-lived historical artists. *Creat. Res. J., 6*, 231–39.

Locke, J. 1690. *An essay concerning human understanding.* In R. M. Hutchins, ed., *Great books of the Western world,* vol. 35, 83–509. Chicago: Encyclopaedia Britannica, 1952.

Lombroso, C. 1891. *The man of genius.* London: Scott.

Lombroso, C. 1899. *Crime.* Boston: Little, Brown, 1911.

Longuet-Higgins, H. C. 1987. *Mental processes*. Cambridge, MA: MIT Press.

Lorge, I. 1936. Prestige, suggestion and attitudes. *J. Soc. Psychol.*, *7*, 386–402.

Lotka, A. J. 1926. The frequency distribution of scientific productivity. *J. Wash. Acad. Sci.*, *16*, 317–23.

Lowe, J. W. G., & Lowe, E. D. 1982. Cultural pattern and process: A study of stylistic change in womens dress. *Amer. Anthropol.*, *84*, 521–44.

Lucaire, E. ed. 1991. *The celebrity almanac*. New York: Prentice-Hall.

Ludwig, A. M. 1990. Alcohol input and creative output. *Brit. J. Addict.*, *85*, 953–63.

Ludwig, A. M. 1992. Creative achievement and psychopathology: Comparison among professions. *Amer. J. Psychother.*, 46, 330–56.

Luria, A. R. 1968. *The mind of a mnemonist*, L. Solotaroff, trans. New York: Basic Books.

Lykken, D. T. 1982. Research with twins: The concept of emergenesis. *Psychophysiology*, *19*, 361–73.

Lykken, D. T., McGue, M., Tellegen, A., & Bouchard, T. J., Jr. 1992. Emergenesis: Genetic traits that may not run in families. *Amer. Psychol.*, *47*, 1565–77.

Lynn, R., & Hampson, S. L. 1975. National differences in extraversion and neuroticism. *Brit. J. Soc. Clin. Psychol.*, *14*, 223–40.

Lyons, J. 1968. Chronological age, professional age, and eminence in psychology. *Amer. Psychol.*, *23*, 371–74.

Macaulay, T. B. 1825. Milton. In I. Gollancz, ed., *Critical historical essays*, vol. 1, 3–66. London: Dent, 1900.

Maccoby, E. E., & Jacklin, C. N. 1974. *The psychology of sex differences*. Stanford, CA: Stanford University Press.

MacCrimmon, K. R., & Wagner, C. 1987. Expert systems and creativity. In J. L. Mumpower, O. Renn, L. D. Phillips, & V. R. R. Uppuluri, eds., *Expert judgment and expert systems*, 173–93. Berlin: Springer-Verlag.

Mach, E. 1896. On the part played by accident in invention and discovery. *Monist*, *6*, 161–75.

Machiavelli, N. 1513. *The prince*, W. K. Marriott, trans. In R. M. Hutchins, ed., *Great books of the Western world*, vol. 23, 1–37. Chicago: Encyclopaedia Britannica, 1952.

Mackavey, W. R., Malley, J. E., & Stewart, A. J. 1991. Remembering autobiographically consequential experiences: Content analysis of psychologists' accounts of their lives. *Psychol. Aging*, *6*, 50–9.

MacKinnon, D. W. 1960. The highly effective individual. *Teach. Coll. Rec.*, *61*, 367–78.

MacKinnon, D. W. 1962. The nature and nurture of creative talent. *Amer. Psychol.*, *17*, 484–95.

MacKinnon, D. W. 1978. *In search of human effectiveness*. Buffalo, NY: Creative Education Foundation.

MacKuen, M. B. 1983. Political drama, economic conditions, and the dynamics of presidential popularity. *Amer. J. Polit. Sci.*, *27*, 165–92.

Macrone, M. 1990. *Brush up your Shakespeare!*. New York: Harper & Row.

Magagnini, S. 1991, July 14. Brain may be key to curbing violent crime, experts say. *Sacramento Bee*, B1, B5.

Mahler, I. 1953. Attitudes toward socialized medicine. *J. Soc. Psychol.*, *38*, 273–82.

Mahoney, J., Coogle, C. L., & Banks, P. D. 1984. Values in presidential inaugural addresses: A test of Rokeach's two-factor theory of political ideology. *Psychol. Rep.*, *55*, 683–86.

Mahoney, M. J., & Avener, M. 1977. Psychology of the elite athlete: An exploratory study. *Cog. Ther. Res.*, *1*, 135–41.

Manis, J. G. 1951. Some academic influences upon publication productivity. *Soc. Forces*, 29, 267–72.

Mann, L. 1974. On being a sore loser: How fans react to their team's failure. *Austral. J. Psychol.*, 26, 37–47.

Mann, L. 1981. The baiting crowd in episodes of threatened suicide. *J. Pers. Soc. Psychol.*, 41, 703–9.

Manniche, E., & Falk, G. 1957. Age and the Nobel Prize. *Behav. Sci.*, 2, 301–7.

Maranell, G. M. 1970. The evaluation of presidents: An extension of the Schlesinger polls. *J. Amer. Hist.*, 57, 104–13.

Marchetti, C. 1980. Society as a learning system: Discovery, invention, and innovation cycles. *Technol. Forecast. Soc. Change*, 18, 267–82.

Marek, G. R. 1975. *Toscanini*. London: Atheneum.

Markus, G. B. 1988. The impact of personal and national economic conditions on the presidential vote: A pooled cross-sectional analysis. *Amer. J. Polit. Sci.*, 32, 137–54.

Marriott, C., & Harshberger, D. 1973. The hollow holiday: Christmas, a time of death in Appalachia. *Omega*, 4, 259–66.

Marsden, H. M. 1972. Crowding and animal behavior. In J. F. Wohlwill & D. H. Carson, eds., *Environment and the social sciences*, 5–14. Washington, DC: American Psychological Association.

Martindale, C. 1972. Father absence, psychopathology, and poetic eminence. *Psychol. Rep.*, 31, 843–47.

Martindale, C. 1973. An experimental simulation of literary change. *J. Pers. Soc. Psychol.*, 25, 319–26.

Martindale, C. 1975. *The romantic progression: The psychology of literary history*. Washington, DC: Hemisphere.

Martindale, C. 1984a. Evolutionary trends in poetic style: The case of English metaphysical poetry. *Comput. Humanit.*, 18, 3–21.

Martindale, C. 1984b. The evolution of aesthetic taste. In K. J. Gergen & M. M. Gergen, eds., *Historical social psychology*, 347–70. Hillsdale, NJ: Erlbaum.

Martindale, C. 1986a. Aesthetic evolution. *Poetics*, 15, 439–73.

Martindale, C. 1986b. The evolution of Italian painting: A quantitative investigation of trends in style and content from late Gothic to the Rococo period. *Leonardo*, 19, 217–22.

Martindale, C., ed. 1988. *Psychological approaches to the study of literary narratives*. Hamburg: Buske.

Martindale, C. 1990. *The clockwork muse: The predictability of artistic change*. New York: Basic Books.

Martindale, C., Brewer, W. F., Helson, R., Rosenberg, S., Simonton, D. K., Keeley, A., Leigh, J., & Ohtsuka, K. 1988. Structure, theme, style, and reader response in Hungarian and American short stories. In C. Martindale, ed., *Psychological approaches to the study of literary narratives*, 267–89. Hamburg: Buske.

Martindale, C., & Uemura, A. 1983. Stylistic evolution in European music. *Leonardo*, 16, 225–28.

Maslow, A. H. 1959. Creativity in self-actualizing people. In H. H. Anderson, ed., *Creativity and its cultivation*, 83–95. New York: Harper & Row.

Maslow, A. H. 1970. *Motivation and personality*, 2nd ed. New York: Harper & Row.

Maslow, A. H. 1972. A holistic approach to creativity. In C. W. Taylor, ed., *Climate for creativity*, 287–93. New York: Pergamon Press.

Masserman, J. H. 1984. Foreword. In J. Ehrenwald, *The anatomy of genius*, xi–xiii. New York: Human Sciences Press.

Masterton, G., & Platt, S. 1989. Parasuicide and general elections. *Brit. Med. J.*, *298*, 803.

Matossian, M. K., & Schafer, W. D. 1977. Family, fertility, and political violence, 1700–1900. *J. Soc. Hist.*, *11*, 137–78.

Matthews, D. R. 1954. *The social background of political decision-makers*. Garden City, NY: Doubleday.

Matthews, K. A., Glass, D. C., Rosenman, R. H., & Bortner, R. W. 1977. Competitive drive, pattern A, and coronary heart disease: A further analysis of some data from the Western Collaborative Group Study. *J. Chronic Dis.*, *30*, 489–98.

Matthews, K. A., Helmreich, R. L., Beane, W. E., & Lucker, G. W. 1980. Pattern A, achievement striving, and scientific merit: Does pattern A help or hinder? *J. Pers. Soc. Psychol.*, *39*, 962–67.

Mazlish, B. 1972. *In search of Nixon*. New York: Basic Books.

Mazur, A., & Rosa, E. 1977. An empirical test of McClelland's *Achieving society* theory. *Soc. Forces*, *55*, 769–74.

McCann, S. J. H. 1990a. Authoritarianism and preference for the presidential candidate perceived to be higher on the power motive. *Percept. Mot. Skills*, *70*, 577–78.

McCann, S. J. H. 1990b. Threat, power, and presidential greatness: Harding to Johnson. *Psychol. Rep.*, *66*, 129–30.

McCann, S. J. H. 1991. Threat, authoritarianism, and the power of United States presidents: New threat and power measures. *J. Psychol.*, *125*, 237–40.

McCann, S. J. H. 1992. Alternative formulas to predict the greatness of U.S. presidents: Personological, situational, and zeitgeist factors. *J. Pers. Soc. Psychol.*, *62*, 469–79.

McCann, S. J. H., & Stewin, L. L. 1984. Environmental threat and parapsychological contributions to the psychological literature. *J. Soc. Psychol.*, *122*, 227–35.

McCann, S. J. H., & Stewin, L. L. 1986. Authoritarianism and Canadian voting preferences for political party, prime minister, and president. *Psychol. Rep.*, *59*, 1268–70.

McCann, S. J. H., & Stewin, L. L. 1987. Threat, authoritarianism, and the power of U.S. presidents. *J. Psychol.*, *121*, 149–57.

McCann, S. J. H., & Stewin, L. L. 1990. Good and bad years: An index of American social, economic, and political threat 1920–1986. *J. Psychol.*, *124*, 601–17.

McCarthy, J., & Johnson, R. C. 1962. Interpretation of the "City Hall riots" as a function of general dogmatism. *Psychol. Rep.*, *11*, 243–45.

McCauley, C. 1989. The nature of social influence in groupthink: Compliance and internalization. *J. Pers. Soc. Psychol.*, *57*, 250–60.

McCauley, C., & Jacques, S. 1979. The popularity of conspiracy theories of presidential assassination: A Bayesian analysis. *J. Pers. Soc. Psychol.*, *37*, 637–44.

McClelland, D. C. 1961. *The achieving society*. New York: Van Nostrand.

McClelland, D. C. 1973. Testing for competence rather than for "intelligence." *Amer. Psychol.*, *28*, 1–14.

McClelland, D. C. 1975. *Power*. New York: Irvington.

McClelland, D. C. 1984. *Human motivation*. Glenview, IL: Scott, Foresman.

McClelland, D. C., & Winter, D. G. 1969. *Motivating economic achievement*. New York: Free Press.

McCloskey, M., Wible, C. G., & Cohen, N. J. 1988. Is there a special flashbulb-memory mechanism? *J. Exp. Psychol.: Gen.*, *117*, 171–81.

McCurdy, H. G. 1960. The childhood pattern of genius. *Horizon*, *2*, 33–38.

McDowell, J. M. 1982. Obsolescence of knowledge and career publication profiles: Some evidence of differences among fields in costs of interrupted careers. *Amer. Econ. Rev.*, *72*, 752–68.

McFarlan, D., ed. 1989. *Guinness book of world records*. New York: Bantam.

McFarland, S. 1983. Is capital punishment a short-term deterrent to homicide?: A study of the effects of four recent American executions. *J. Crim. Law Criminol.*, *74*, 1014–30.

McHugo, G. J., Lanzetta, J. T., Sullivan, D. G., Masters, R. D., & Englis, B. G. 1985. Emotional reactions to a political leader's expressive displays.*J. Pers. Soc. Psychol.*, *49*, 1513–29.

McKenna, M. 1983. *The Stein and Day dictionary of definitive quotations*. New York: Stein & Day.

McKinney, D. W., Jr. 1973. *The authoritarian personality studies*. The Hague: Mouton.

McNeil, T. F. 1971. Prebirth and postbirth influence on the relationship between creative ability and recorded mental illness. *J. Psychol.*, *39*, 391–406.

Mead, M. 1963. *Sex and temperament in three primitive societies*. New York: Morrow.

Meehl, P. 1954. *Clinical versus statistical prediction*. Minneapolis: University of Minnesota Press.

Mersmann, H., ed. 1928. *Letters of Wolfgang Amadeus Mozart*, M. M. Bozman, trans. New York: Dover, 1972.

Merton, R. K. 1961a. The role of genius in scientific advance. *New Scient.*, *12*, 306–8.

Merton, R. K. 1961b. Singletons and multiples in scientific discovery: A chapter in the sociology of science. *Proc. Amer. Philos. Society*, *105*, 470–86.

Merton, R. K. 1968. The Matthew effect in science. *Science*, *159*, 56–63.

Messerli, P. 1988. Age differences in the reception of new scientific theories: The case of plate tectonics theory. *Soc. Stud. Sci.*, *18*, 91–112.

Michael, R. P., & Zumpe, D. 1986. An annual rhythm in the battering of women. *Amer. J. Psychiat.*, *143*, 637–40.

Michael, W. B., Rosenthal, B. G., & De Camp, M. A. 1949. An experimental investigation of prestige-suggestion for two types of literary material. *J. Psychol.*, *28*, 303–23.

Midlarsky, M. I. 1984. Preventing systemic war: Crisis decision-making amidst a structure of conflict relationships. *J. Confl. Resolut.*, *28*, 563–84.

Milburn, M. A., & McGrail, A. B. 1992. The dramatic presentation of news and its effects on cognitive complexity. *Polit. Psychol.*, *13*, 613–32.

Milgram, S. 1963. Behavioral study of obedience. *J. Abnorm. Soc. Psychol.*, *67*, 371–78.

Miller, A. H., & Wattenberg, M. P. 1985. Throwing the rascals out: Policy and performance evaluations of presidential candidates, 1952–1980. *Amer. Polit. Sci. Rev.*, *79*, 359–72.

Miller, A. H., Wattenberg, M. P., & Malanchuk, O. 1986. Schematic assessments of presidential candidates. *Amer. Polit. Sci. Rev.*, *80*, 521–40.

Miller, T. Q., Heath, L., Moican, J. R., & Dugoni, B. L. 1991. Imitative violence in the real world: A reanalysis of homicide rates following championship prize fights. *Aggress. Behav.*, *17*, 121–34.

Mills, C. A. 1942. What price glory? *Science*, *96*, 380–87.

Milton, O. 1952. Presidential choice and performance on a scale of authoritarianism. *Amer. Psychol.*, *7*, 597–98.

Mintz, A. 1946. A re-examination of correlations between lynchings and economic indices. *J. Abnorm. Soc. Psychol.*, *41*, 154–60.

Moles, A. 1958. *Information theory and esthetic perception*, J. E. Cohen, trans. Urbana: University of Illinois Press, 1968.

Monroe, K. R. 1978. Economic influences on presidential popularity. *Publ. Opin. Q.*, *42*, 360–69.

Monroe, K. R. 1979. Econometric analyses of electoral behavior: A critical review. *Polit. Behav.*, *1*, 137–73.

Monroe, K. R. 1984. *Presidential popularity and the economy*. New York: Praeger.

Montour, K. 1977. William James Sidis, the broken twig. *Amer. Psychol.*, *32*, 265–79.

Moore, T. circa 1820. My birth-day. In A. D. Godley, ed., *The poetical works of Thomas Moore*, 530–31. London: Milford, 1929.

Morgan, T. C., & Bickers, K. N. 1992. Domestic discontent and the external use of force. *J. Confl. Resolut.*, *36*, 25–52.

Morgan, W. P. 1980, July. Test of champions: The iceberg profile. *Psychol. Today*, 92–99, 102, 108.

Moulin, L. 1955. The Nobel Prizes for the sciences from 1901–1950: An essay in sociological analysis. *Brit. J. Sociol.*, *6*, 246–63.

Mueller, J. E. 1970. Presidential popularity from Truman to Johnson. *Amer. Polit. Sci. Rev.*, *64*, 18–34.

Mueller, J. E. 1973. *War, presidents and public opinion*. New York: Wiley.

Mullen, B. 1986. Atrocity as a function of lynch mob composition. *Pers. Soc. Psychol. Bull.*, *12*, 187–98.

Mullen, B., Futrell, D., Stairs, D., Tice, D. M., Baumeister, R. F., Dawson, K. E., Riordan, C. A., Radloff, C. E., Goethals, G. R., Kennedy, J. G., & Rosenfeld, P. 1986. Newscasters' facial expressions and voting behavior of viewers: Can a smile elect a president? *J. Pers. Soc. Psychol.*, *51*, 291–5.

Murphy, A. B. 1984. Evaluating the presidents of the United States. *Presid. Stud. Q.*, *14*, 117–26.

Murray, P., & Murray, L. 1959. *A dictionary of art and artists*. Baltimore: Penguin.

Murray, R. K., & Blessing, T. H. 1983. The presidential performance study: A progress report. *J. Amer. Hist.*, *70*, 535–55.

Murray, R. K., & Blessing, T. H. 1988. *Greatness in the White House*. University Park: Pennsylvannia State University Press.

Mus. Herit. Rev., 1991, *15*(13), 48.

Myers, D. G. 1990. *Social psychology*, 3rd ed. New York: McGraw-Hill.

Myerson, A., & Boyle, R. D. 1941. The incidence of manic–depressive psychosis in certain socially important families: Preliminary report. *Amer. J. Psychiat.*, *98*, 11–21.

Naroll, R., Benjamin, E. C., Fohl, F. K., Fried, M. J., Hildreth, R. E., & Schaefer, J. M. 1971. Creativity: A cross-historical pilot survey. *J. Cross-Cult. Psychol.*, *2*, 181–88.

Nassi, A. J. 1981. Survivors of the sixties: Comparative psychosocial and political development of former Berkeley student activists. *Amer. Psychol.*, *36*, 753–61.

Neisser, U. 1981. John Dean's memory: A case study. *Cognition*, *9*, 1–22.

Neisser, U. 1982. Snapshots or benchmarks? In U. Neisser, ed., *Memory observed*, 43–48. San Francisco: W. H. Freeman.

Neisser, U. 1986. Remembering Pearl Harbor: Reply to Thompson and Cowan. *Cognition*, *23*, 285–86.

Neisser, U., & Harsch, N. 1992. Phantom flashbulbs: False recollections of hearing the news about *Challenger*. In E. Winograd & U. Neisser, eds., *Affect and accuracy in recall*, 9–31. New York: Cambridge University Press.

Neuman, W. R. 1976. Patterns of recall among television news viewers. *Publ. Opin. Q.*, *40*, 115–23.

Nice, D. C. 1984. The influence of war and party system aging on the ranking of presidents. *West. Polit. Q.*, *37*, 443–55.

Nice, D. C. 1992. Peak presidential approval from Franklin Roosevelt to Ronald Reagan. *Presid. Stud. Q.*, *22*, 119–26.

Nicholson, F. W. 1915. Success in college and in later life. *School & Society*, *2*, 229–32.

Nisbett, R. E. 1968. Birth order and participation in dangerous sports. *J. Pers. Soc. Psychol.*, *8*, 351–53.

Nixon, R. M. 1962. *Six crises*. Garden City, NY: Doubleday.

Noland, E. 1991, September 23. Raiders can't pass Falcons' test. *Sacramento Bee*, D1, D6.

Noll, A. M. 1966. Human or machine: A subjective comparison of Piet Mondrian's *Composition with Lines* (1917) and a computer-generated picture. *Psychol. Rec.*, *16*, 1–16.

Norpoth, H. 1984. Economics, politics, and the cycle of presidential popularity. *Polit. Behav.*, *6*, 253–73.

Norrander, B., & Smith, G. W. 1985. Type of contest, candidate strategy, and turnout in presidential primaries. *Amer. Polit. Q.*, *13*, 28–50.

O'Boyle, M. W., & Benbow, C. P. 1990. Handedness and its relationship to ability and talent. In S. Coren, ed., *Left-handedness*, 343–72. Amsterdam: Elsevier.

Ochse, R. 1991. Why there were relatively few eminent women creators. *J. Creat. Behav.*, *25*, 334–43.

O'Conner, R. E. 1974. Political activism and moral reasoning: Political and apolitical students in Great Britain and France. *Brit. J. Polit. Sci.*, *4*, 53–78.

Oden, M. H. 1968. The fulfillment of promise: 40-year follow-up of the Terman gifted group. *Genet. Psychol. Monogr.*, *77*, 3–93.

Ogburn, W. K., & Thomas, D. 1922. Are inventions inevitable? A note on social evolution. *Polit. Sci. Q.*, *37*, 83–93.

Ohlsson, S. 1992. The learning curve for writing books: Evidence from Professor Asimov. *Psychol. Sci.*, *3*, 380–82.

O'Kelley, C. 1980. Sex-role imagery in modern art: An empirical examination. *Sex Roles*, *6*, 99–112.

Oleszek, W. 1969. Age and political careers. *Publ. Opin. Q.*, *33*, 100–3.

Oliner, S. P., & Oliner, P. M. 1988. *The altruistic personality*. New York: Free Press.

Oromaner, M. 1977. Professional age and the reception of sociological publications: A test of the Zuckerman–Merton hypothesis. *Soc. Stud. Sci.*, *7*, 381–88.

Oromaner, M. 1985. The Ortega hypothesis and influential articles in American sociology. *Scientometrics*, *7*, 3–10.

Ortega y Gasset, J. 1932. *The revolt of the masses*, M. Adams, trans. New York: Norton, 1957.

Osgood, C. E. 1962. *An alternative to war or surrender*. Urbana: University of Illinois Press.

O'Sullivan, C. S., Chen, A., Mohapatra, S., Sigelman, L., & Lewis, E. 1988. Voting in ignorance: The politics of smooth-sounding names. *J. Appl. Soc. Psychol.*, *18*, 1094–1106.

Ovcharchyn, C. A., Johnson, H. H., & Petzel, T. P. 1981. Type A behavior, academic aspirations, and academic success. *J. Pers.*, *49*, 248–56.

Over, R. 1982a. Does research productivity decline with age? *Higher Educ.*, *11*, 511–20.

Over, R. 1982b. Is age a good predictor of research productivity? *Austral. Psychol.*, *17*, 129–39.

Over, R. 1982c. The durability of scientific reputation. *J. Hist. Behav. Sci.*, *18*, 53–61.

Over, R. 1988. Does scholarly impact decline with age? *Scientometrics*, *13*, 215–23.

Over, R. 1989. Age and scholarly impact. *Psychol. Aging*, *4*, 222–25.

Over, R. 1990. The scholarly impact of articles published by men and women in psychology journals. *Scientometrics*, *18*, 71–80.

Owens, W. A. 1969. Cognitive, noncognitive, and environmental correlates of mechanical ingenuity. *J. Appl. Psychol.*, *53*, 199–208.

The Oxford University Press dictionary of quotations, 2nd ed. 1953. New York: Crescent Books, 1985.

Padgett, V., & Jorgenson, D. O. 1982. Superstition and economic threat: Germany 1918–1940. *Pers. Soc. Psychol. Bull.*, *8*, 736–41.

Page, B. I., & Shapiro, R. 1984. Presidents as opinion leaders: Some new evidence. *Policy Stud. J.*, *12*, 649–61.

Paisley, W. J. 1964. Identifying the unknown communicator in painting, literature and music: The significance of minor encoding habits. *J. Communic.*, *14*, 219–37.

Pancer, S. M., Hunsberger, B., Pratt, M. W., Boisvert, S., & Roth, D. 1992. Political roles and the complexity of political rhetoric. *Polit. Psychol.*, *13*, 31–43.

Park, R. E. 1928. Human migration and the marginal man. *Amer. J. Sociol.*, *33*, 881–93.

Pascal, B. circa 1662. *Pensées*, W. F. Trotter, trans. In R. M. Hutchins, ed., *Great books of the Western world*, vol. 33, 171–352. Chicago: Encyclopaedia Britannica, 1952.

Patinkin, D. 1983. Multiple discoveries and the central message. *Amer. J. Sociol.*, *89*, 306–23.

Pavlova, A. 1956. Pages of my life. In A. H. Franks, ed., *Pavlova*, 111–27. New York: Burke.

Pearson, P. 1983. Personality characteristics of cartoonists. *Pers. Indiv. Diff.*, *4*, 277–78.

Pennebaker, J. W. 1990. *Opening up*. New York: Morrow.

Perkins, D. N. 1981. *The mind's best work*. Cambridge, MA: Harvard University Press.

Perry, J. D., & Simpson, M. E. 1987. Violent crimes in a city: Environmental determinants. *Environ. Behav.*, *19*, 77–90.

Peterson, B. E., Doty, R. M., & Winter, D. G. 1993. Authoritarianism and attitudes toward contemporary social issues. *Pers. Soc. Psychol. Bull.*, *19*, 174–84.

Peterson, R. A., & Berger, D. G. 1975. Cycles in symbol production: The case of popular music. *Amer. Sociol. Rev.*, *40*, 158–73.

Phillips, D. P. 1974. Influence of suggestion on suicide: Substantive and theoretical implications of the Werther effect. *Amer. Sociol. Rev.*, *39*, 340–54.

Phillips, D. P. 1979. Suicide, motor vehicle fatalities, and the mass media: Evidence toward a theory of suggestion. *Amer. J. Sociol.*, *84*, 1150–74.

Phillips, D. P. 1980a. Airplane accidents, murder, and the mass media: Towards a theory of imitation and suggestion. *Soc. Forces*, *58*, 1001–24.

Phillips, D. P. 1980b. The deterrent effect of capital punishment: New evidence on an old controversy. *Amer. J. Sociol.*, *86*, 139–48.

Phillips, D. P. 1982. The impact of fictional television stories on U.S. adult fatalities: New evidence on the effect of the mass media on violence. *Amer. J. Sociol.*, *87*, 1340–59.

Phillips, D. P. 1983. The impact of mass media violence on U.S. homicides. *Amer. Sociol. Rev.*, *48*, 560–68.

Phillips, D. P. 1986. Natural experiments on the effects of mass media violence on fatal aggression: Strength and weakness of a new approach. In L. Berkowitz, ed., *Advances in experimental social psychology*, vol. 19, 207–50. New York: Academic Press.

Phillips, D. P., & Bollen, K. A. 1985. Same time, last year: Selective data dredging for negative findings. *Amer. Sociol. Rev.*, *50*, 364–71.

Phillips, D. P., & Feldman, K. A. 1973. A dip in deaths before ceremonial occasions: Some new relationships between social integration and mortality. *Amer. Sociol. Rev.*, *38*, 678–96.

Phillips, D. P., & Hensley, J. E. 1984. When violence is rewarded or punished: The impact of mass media stories on homicide. *J. Communic.*, *34*(3), 101–16.

Piliavin, J. A. 1987. Age, race, and sex similarity to candidates and voting preference. *J. Appl. Soc. Psychol.*, *17*, 351–68.

Pillemer, D. B. 1984. Flashbulb memories of the assassination attempt on Ronald Reagan. *Cognition*, *16*, 63–80.

Planck, M. 1949. *Scientific autobiography and other papers*, F. Gaynor, trans. New York: Philosophical Library.

Platt, W., & Baker, R. A. 1931. The relation of the scientific "hunch" to research. *J. Chem. Educ.*, *8*, 1969–2002.

Plomin, R., & Bergeman, C. S. 1991. The nature of nurture: Genetic influence on environmental measures. *Behav. Brain Sci.*, *14*, 373–86.

Poe, E. A. 1846. The philosophy of composition. In *The works of Edgar Allan Poe*, vol. 5, 157–74. London: Routledge, 1884.

Poincaré, H. 1921. *The foundations of science*, G. B. Halstead, trans. New York: Science Press.

Poole, K. T., & Rosenthal, H. 1984. U.S. presidential elections 1960–80: A spatial analysis. *Amer. J. Polit. Sci.*, *28*, 282–312.

Porac, C., & Coren, S. 1981. *Lateral preferences and human behavior*. New York: Springer-Verlag.

Porter, C. A., & Suedfeld, P. 1981. Integrative complexity in the correspondence of literary figures: Effects of personal and societal stress. *J. Pers. Soc. Psychol.*, *40*, 321–30.

Pound, E. 1934. *ABC of reading*. New Haven, CT: Yale University Press.

Prentky, R. A. 1980. *Creativity and psychopathology*. New York: Praeger.

Prentky, R. A. 1989. Creativity and psychopathology: Gamboling at the seat of madness. In J. A. Glover, R. R. Ronning, & C. R. Reynolds, eds., *Handbook of creativity*, 243–69. New York: Plenum Press.

Pressey, S. L., & Combs, A. 1943. Acceleration and age of productivity. *Educ. Res. Bull.*, *22*, 191–96.

Price, D. 1963. *Little science, big science*. New York: Columbia University Press.

Price, D. 1976. A general theory of bibliometric and other cumulative advantage processes. *J. Amer. Soc. Inform. Sci.*, *27*, 292–306.

Price, D. 1978. Ups and downs in the pulse of science and technology. In J. Gaston, ed., *The sociology of science*, 162–71. San Francisco: Jossey-Bass.

Qin, Y., & Simon, H. A. 1990. Laboratory replication of scientific discovery processes. *Cog. Sci.*, *14*, 281–312.

Quattrone, G. A., & Tversky, A. 1984. Causal versus diagnostic contingencies: On self-deception and on the voter's illusion. *J. Pers. Soc. Psychol.*, *46*, 237–48.

Quetelet, A. 1835. *A treatise on man and the development of his faculties*. New York: Franklin, 1968.

Radford, J. 1990. *Child prodigies and exceptional early achievers*. New York: Basic Books.

Rainoff, T. J. 1929. Wave-like fluctuations of creative productivity in the development of West-European physics in the eighteenth and nineteenth centuries. *Isis*, *12*, 287–319.

Ramirez, C. E., & Suedfeld, P. 1988. Nonimmediacy scoring of archival materials: The relationship between Fidel Castro and "Che" Guevara. *Polit. Psychol.*, *9*, 155–64.

Raphael, T. D. 1982. Integrative complexity theory and forecasting international crises. *J. Confl. Resolut.*, *26*, 423–50.

Raskin, E. A. 1936. Comparison of scientific and literary ability: A biographical study of eminent scientists and men of letters of the nineteenth century. *J. Abnorm. Soc. Psychol.*, *31*, 20–35.

Razik, T. A. 1967. Psychometric measurement of creativity. In R. L. Mooney & T. A. Razik, eds., *Explorations in creativity*, 301–9. New York: Harper & Row.

Reifman, A. S., Larrick, R. P., & Fein, S. 1991. Temper and temperature on the diamond: The heat–aggression relationship in major league baseball. *Pers. Soc. Psychol. Bull.*, *17*, 580–85.

Rejai, M. 1979. *Leaders of revolution*. Beverly Hills, CA: Sage.

Rentchnick, P. 1989. Orphans and the will for power. In M. Eisenstadt, A. Haynal, P. Rentchnick, & P. De Senarclens, *Parental loss and achievement*, 35–69. Madison, CT: International Universities Press.

Retherford, R. D., & Sewell, W. H. 1991. Birth order and intelligence: Further tests of the confluence model. *Amer. Sociol. Rev.*, *56*, 141–58.

Reynolds, J. 1769–90. *Discourses on art*. New York: Collier, 1966.

Rhodewalt, F., Saltzman, A. T., & Wittmer, J. 1984. Self-handicapping among competitive athletes: The role of practice in self-esteem protection. *Basic Appl. Soc. Psychol.*, *5*, 197–210.

Richards, R. 1981. Relationships between creativity and psychopathology: An evaluation and interpretation of the evidence. *Genet. Psychol. Monogr.*, *103*, 261–324.

Richards, R. 1990. Everyday creativity, eminent creativity, and health: "Afterview" for CRJ issues on creativity and health. *Creat. Res. J.*, *3*, 300–26.

Richards, R., Kinney, D. K., Lunde, I., Benet, M., & Merzel, A. P. C. 1988. Creativity in manic-depressives, cyclothymes, their normal relatives, and control subjects. *J. Abnorm. Psychol.*, *97*, 281–88.

Richardson, J., & Kroeber, A. L. 1940. Three centuries of women's dress fashions: A quantitative analysis. *Anthropol. Rec.*, *5*, 111–50.

Rigby, K. 1988. Sexist attitudes and authoritarian personality characteristics among Australian adolescents. *J. Res. Pers.*, *22*, 465–73.

Riley, R. T., & Pettigrew, T. F. 1976. Dramatic events and attitude change. *J. Pers. Soc. Psychol.*, *34*, 1004–15.

Rivers, D., & Rose, N. L. 1985. Passing the president's program: Public opinion and presidential influence in Congress. *Amer. J. Polit. Sci.*, *29*, 183–96.

Robinson, D. B. 1970. *The 100 most important people in the world today*. New York: Putnam.

Robinson, J. P. 1971. The audience for national TV news programs. *Publ. Opin. Q.*, *35*, 403–5.

Roe, A. 1952. *The making of a scientist*. New York: Dodd, Mead.

Roe, A. 1965. Changes in scientific activities with age. *Science*, *150*, 113–18.

Roe, A. 1972. Patterns of productivity of scientists. *Science*, *176*, 940–41.

Roediger, H. L., III., & Crowder, R. G. 1976. A serial position effect in recall of United States presidents. *Bull. Psychonom. Soc.*, *8*, 275–78.

Rokeach, M. 1960. *The open and the closed mind*. New York: Basic Books.

Rokeach, M. 1970, April. Faith, hope, bigotry. *Psychol. Today*, 33–37, 58.

Rokeach, M. 1973. *The nature of human values*. New York: Free Press.

Root-Bernstein, R. S. 1989. *Discovering*. Cambridge, MA: Harvard University Press.

Rosenberg, S. W., Bohan, L., McCafferty, & Harris, K. 1986. The image and the vote: The effect of candidate presentation on voter preference. *Amer. J. Polit. Sci.*, *30*, 108–27.

Rosengren, K. E. 1985. Time and literary fame. *Poetics, 14,* 157–72.

Rosenstone, S. J. 1983. *Forecasting presidential elections.* New Haven, CT: Yale University Press.

Rosenthal, R. 1990. How are we doing in soft psychology? *Amer. Psychol., 45,* 775–77.

Rosnow, R. L. 1980. Psychology of rumor reconsidered. *Psychol. Bull., 87,* 578–91.

Rosnow, R. L. 1991. Inside rumor: A personal journey. *Amer. Psychol., 46,* 484–96.

Rosnow, R. L., & Fine, G. A. 1974, August. The media/inside rumors. *Human Behav., 64–* 68.

Ross, M., & Sicoly, F. 1979. Egocentric biases in availability and attribution. *J. Pers. Soc. Psychol., 37,* 322–36.

Rossetti, D. G. 1881. The house of life. In W. M. Rossetti, ed., *The collected works of Dante Gabriel Rossetti,* vol. 1. London: Ellis & Elvey, 1888.

Rothenberg, A. 1979. *The emerging goddess.* Chicago: University of Chicago Press.

Rothenberg, A. 1986. Artistic creation as stimulated by superimposed versus combined–composite visual images. *J. Pers. Soc. Psychol., 50,* 370–81.

Rothenberg, A. 1987. Einstein, Bohr, and creative thinking in science. *Hist. Sci., 25,* 147–66.

Rothenberg, A. 1990. *Creativity and madness.* Baltimore: Johns Hopkins University Press.

Rothman, A., & Lichter, S. R. 1980. Personality development and political dissent: A reassessment of the New Left. *J. Polit. Milit. Sociol., 8,* 191–204.

Rotton, J., & Frey, J. 1985. Air pollution, weather, and violent crime: Concomitant time-series analysis of archival data. *J. Pers. Soc. Psychol., 49,* 1207–20.

Rubenson, D. L. 1990. The accidental economist. *Creat. Res. J., 3,* 125–29.

Rubenson, D. L., & Runco, M. A. 1992. The psychoeconomic approach to creativity. *New Ideas Psychol., 10,* 131–147.

Rubin, D. C., & Kozin, M. 1984. Vivid memories. *Cognition, 16,* 81–95.

Rubin, E. 1960. The age factor in master chess. *Amer. Stat., 14,* 19–21.

Rubin, Z. 1970. The birth-order of birth-order researchers. *Dev. Psychol., 3,* 269–70.

Runyan, W. M. 1982. *Life histories and psychobiography.* New York: Oxford University Press.

Runyan, W. M. 1988a. Progress in psychobiography. *J. Pers., 56,* 295–326.

Runyan, W. M. 1988b. *Psychology and historical interpretation.* New York: Oxford University Press.

Rushton, J. P. 1988. Race differences in behaviour: A review and evolutionary analysis. *Pers. Indiv. Diff., 9,* 1009–24.

Rushton, J. P. 1990. Creativity, intelligence, and psychoticism. *Pers. Indiv. Diff., 11,* 1291–98.

Russett, B. M., ed. 1972. *Peace, war, and numbers.* Beverly Hills, CA: Sage.

Ryan, M. 1989, May 28. A hidden talent. *Parade Magazine,* 30–33.

Sagan, C. 1977. *The dragons of Eden.* New York: Random House.

Sales, S. M. 1972. Economic threat as a determinant of conversion rates in authoritarian and non-authoritarian churches. *J. Pers. Soc. Psychol., 23,* 420–28.

Sales, S. M. 1973. Threat as a factor in authoritarianism: An analysis of archival data. *J. Pers. Soc. Psychol., 28,* 44–57.

Samson, G. E., Graue, M. E., Weinstein, T., & Walberg, H. J. 1984. Academic and occupational performance: A quantitative synthesis. *Amer. Educ. Res. J., 21,* 311–21.

Scarr, S., & McCartney, K. 1983. How people make their own environments: A theory of genotype → environmental effects. *Child Dev., 54,* 424–35.

Schachter, S. 1963. Birth order, eminence, and higher education. *Amer. Sociol. Rev.*, *28*, 757–68.

Schaefer, C. E., & Anastasi, A. 1968. A biographical inventory for identifying creativity in adolescent boys. *J. Appl. Psychol.*, *58*, 42–48.

Schein, E. H., Schneier, I., & Barker, C. H. 1961. *Coercive persuasion.* New York: Norton.

Schlipp, P. A., ed. 1951. *Albert Einstein.* New York: Harper.

Schmookler, J. 1966. *Invention and economic growth.* Cambridge, MA: Harvard University Press.

Schneider, E. 1953. *Coleridge, opium, and Kubla Khan.* Chicago: University of Chicago Press.

Schofield, J. W., & Pavelchak, M. A. 1989. Fallout from *The Day After*: The impact of a TV film on attitudes related to nuclear war. *J. Appl. Soc. Psychol.*, *19*, 433–48.

Schroder, H. M., Driver, M. J., & Streufert, S. 1967. *Human information processing.* New York: Holt, Rinehart & Winston.

Schubert, D. S. P., Wagner, M. E., & Schubert, H. J. P. 1977. Family constellation and creativity: Firstborn predominance among classical music composers. *J. Psychol.*, *95*, 147–49.

Schubert, G. 1983. Aging, conservatism, and judicial behavior. *Micropolitics*, *3*, 135–79.

Schulz, R., & Bazerman, M. 1980. Ceremonial occasions and mortality: A second look. *Amer. Psychol.*, *35*, 253–61.

Schulz, R., & Curnow, C. 1988. Peak performance and age among super athletes: Track and field, swimming, baseball, tennis, and golf. *J. Gerontol.*, *43*, 113–20.

Schuman, H., & Rieger, C. 1992. Historical analogies, generational effects, and attitudes toward war. *Amer. Sociol. Rev.*, *57*, 315–26.

Schwartz, B., & Barsky, S. 1977. The home advantage. *Soc. Forces*, *55*, 641–61.

Schweidiman, G., Larson, K. S., & Cope, S. C. 1970. Authoritarian traits as predictors in 1968 United States presidential election. *Psychol. Rep.*, *27*, 629–30.

Sears, D. O., & McConahay, J. B. 1973. *The politics of violence.* Boston: Houghton Mifflin.

Seelig, C. 1958. *Albert Einstein*, M. Savill, trans. London: Staples Press.

Seligman, M. E. P., Nolen-Hoeksema, S., Thornton, N., & Thorton, K. M. 1990. Explanatory style as a mechanism of disappointing athletic performance. *Psychol. Sci.*, *1*, 143–46.

Seneca. circa 63–65 A.D. On tranquillity of mind. In *Moral essays*, J. W. Basore, trans., vol. 2, 203–85. Cambridge, MA: Harvard University Press, 1932.

Serebriakoff, V. 1985. *Mensa.* London: Constable.

Shakespeare, W. circa 1595–1611. The plays and sonnets, W. G. Clarke & W. A. Wright, eds. In R. M. Hutchins, ed., *Great books of the Western world*, vols. 26–27. Chicago: Encyclopaedia Britannica, 1952.

Shapiro, G. 1986. *A skeleton in the darkroom.* San Francisco: Harper & Row.

Shaw, G. B. 1903. *Man and superman.* New York: Brentano's.

Sheldon, J. C. 1979. Hierarchical cybernets: A model for the dynamics of high level learning and cultural change. *Cybernetics*, *22*, 179–202.

Sheldon, J. C. 1980. A cybernetic theory of physical science professions: The causes of periodic normal and revolutionary science between 1000 and 1870 AD. *Scientometrics*, *2*, 147–67.

Sherif, M. 1935. An experimental study of stereotypes. *J. Abnorm. Soc. Psychol.*, *29*, 371–75.

Shields, S. A. 1975. Functionalism, Darwinism, and the psychology of women: A study in social myth. *Amer. Psychol.*, *30*, 739–54.

Shin, K. E., & Putnam, R. H. 1982. Age and academic–professional honors. *J. Gerontol.*, 37, 200–29.

Shockley, W. 1957. On the statistics of individual variations of productivity in research laboratories. *Proc. Instit. Radio Engin.*, 45, 279–90.

Shrader, D. 1980. The evolutionary development of science. *Rev. Metaphysics*, 34, 273–96.

Shrager, J., & Langley, P., eds. 1990. *Computational models of scientific discovery and theory formation.* San Mateo, CA: Kaufmann.

Sigelman, L. 1979. Presidential popularity and presidential elections. *Publ. Opin. Q.*, 43, 532–34.

Sigelman, L., & Knight, K. 1983. Why does presidential popularity decline? A test of the expectation/disillusion theory. *Publ. Opin. Q.*, 47, 310–24.

Sigelman, L., & Knight, K. 1985a. Expectation/disillusion and presidential popularity: The Reagan experience. *Publ. Opin. Q.*, 49, 209–13.

Sigelman, L., & Knight, K. 1985b. Public opinion and presidential responsibility for the economy: Understanding personalization. *Polit. Behav.*, 7, 167–91.

Sigelman, L., & Sigelman, C. K. 1982. Sexism, racism, and ageism in voting behavior: An experimental analysis. *Soc. Psychol. Q.*, 45, 263–69.

Silverman, I. 1971. On the resolution and tolerance of cognitive inconsistency in a natural-occurring event: Attitudes and beliefs following the Senator Edward M. Kennedy incident. *J. Pers. Soc. Psychol.*, 17, 171–78.

Silverman, S. M. 1974. Parental loss and scientists. *Sci. Stud.*, 4, 259–64.

Silverstein, B., Perdue, L., Peterson, B., & Kelly, E. 1986. The role of the mass media in promoting a thin standard of bodily attractiveness for women. *Sex Roles*, 14, 519–32.

Simon, D. M., & Ostrom, C. W., Jr. 1989. The impact of televised speaches and foreign travel on presidential approval. *Publ. Opin. Q.*, 53, 58–82.

Simon, H. A. 1955. On a class of skew distribution functions. *Biometrika*, 42, 425–40.

Simon, H. A. 1973. Does scientific discovery have a logic? *Philos. Sci.*, 40, 471–80.

Simon, H. A. 1986. What we know about the creative process. In R. L. Kuhn, ed., *Frontiers in creative and innovative management*, 3–20. Cambridge, MA: Ballinger.

Simon, H. A., & Chase, W. G. 1973. Skill in chess. *Amer. Scient.*, 61, 394–403.

Simon, J. L., & Sullivan, R. J. 1989. Population size, knowledge stock, and other determinants of agricultural publication and patenting: England, 1541–1850. *Explor. Econ. Hist.*, 26, 21–44.

Simon, R. J. 1974. The work habits of eminent scientists. *Sociol. Work Occup.*, 1, 327–35.

Simonton, D. K. 1975a. Age and literary creativity: A cross-cultural and transhistorical survey. *J. Cross-Cult. Psychol.*, 6, 259–77.

Simonton, D. K. 1975b. Sociocultural context of individual creativity: A transhistorical time-series analysis. *J. Pers. Soc. Psychol.*, 32, 1119–33.

Simonton, D. K. 1976a. Biographical determinants of achieved eminence: A multivariate approach to the Cox data. *J. Pers. Soc. Psychol.*, 33, 218–26.

Simonton, D. K. 1976b. The causal relation between war and scientific discovery: An exploratory cross-national analysis. *J. Cross-Cult. Psychol.*, 7, 133–44.

Simonton, D. K. 1976c. Do Sorokin's data support his theory?: A study of generational fluctuations in philosophical beliefs. *J. Scient. Study Relig.*, 15, 187–98.

Simonton, D. K. 1976d. Ideological diversity and creativity: A re-evaluation of a hypothesis. *Soc. Behav. Pers.*, 4, 203–7.

Simonton, D. K. 1976e. Interdisciplinary and military determinants of scientific productivity: A cross-lagged correlation analysis. *J. Vocat. Behav.*, 9, 53–62.

Simonton, D. K. 1976f. Philosophical eminence, beliefs, and zeitgeist: An individual–generational analysis. *J. Pers. Soc. Psychol.*, 34, 630–40.

Simonton, D. K. 1976g. The sociopolitical context of philosophical beliefs: A transhistorical causal analysis. *Soc. Forces*, 54, 513–23.

Simonton, D. K. 1977a. Creative productivity, age, and stress: A biographical time-series analysis of 10 classical composers. *J. Pers. Soc. Psychol.*, 35, 791–804.

Simonton, D. K. 1977b. Eminence, creativity, and geographic marginality: A recursive structural equation model. *J. Pers. Soc. Psychol.*, 35, 805–16.

Simonton, D. K. 1977c. Women's fashions and war: A quantitative comment. *Soc. Behav. Pers.*, 5, 285–88.

Simonton, D. K. 1978a. Independent discovery in science and technology: A closer look at the Poisson distribution. *Soc. Stud. Sci.*, 8, 521–32.

Simonton, D. K. 1978b. Intergenerational stimulation, reaction, and polarization: A causal analysis of intellectual history. *Soc. Behav. Pers.*, 6, 247–51.

Simonton, D. K. 1979a. Multiple discovery and invention: Zeitgeist, genius, or chance? *J. Pers. Soc. Psychol.*, 37, 1603–16.

Simonton, D. K. 1979b. Was Napoleon a military genius? Score: Carlyle 1, Tolstoy 1. *Psychol. Rep.*, 44, 21–2.

Simonton, D. K. 1980a. Land battles, generals, and armies: Individual and situational determinants of victory and casualties. *J. Pers. Soc. Psychol.*, 38, 110–19.

Simonton, D. K. 1980b. Techno-scientific activity and war: A yearly time-series analysis, 1500–1903 A.D. *Scientometrics*, 2, 251–55.

Simonton, D. K. 1980c. Thematic fame and melodic originality in classical music: A multivariate computer-content analysis. *J. Pers.*, 48, 206–19.

Simonton, D. K. 1980d. Thematic fame, melodic originality, and musical zeitgeist: A biographical and transhistorical content analysis. *J. Pers. Soc. Psychol.*, 38, 972–83.

Simonton, D. K. 1981. Presidential greatness and performance: Can we predict leadership in the White House? *J. Pers.*, 49, 306–23.

Simonton, D. K. 1983a. Dramatic greatness and content: A quantitative study of eighty-one Athenian and Shakespearean plays. *Emp. Stud. Arts*, 1, 109–23.

Simonton, D. K. 1983b. Esthetics, biography, and history in musical creativity. In *Documentary report of the Ann Arbor Symposium*, Session 3, 41–48. Reston, VA: Music Educators National Conference.

Simonton, D. K. 1983c. Formal education, eminence, and dogmatism: The curvilinear relationship. *J. Creat. Behav.*, 17, 149–62.

Simonton, D. K. 1983d. Intergenerational transfer of individual differences in hereditary monarchs: Genes, role-modeling, cohort, or sociocultural effects? *J. Pers. Soc. Psychol.*, 44, 354–64.

Simonton, D. K. 1983e. Psychohistory. In R. Harré & R. Lamb, eds., *The encyclopedic dictionary of psychology*, 499–500. Oxford: Blackwell.

Simonton, D. K. 1984a. Artistic creativity and interpersonal relationships across and within generations. *J. Pers. Soc. Psychol.*, 46, 1273–86.

Simonton, D. K. 1984b. Creative productivity and age: A mathematical model based on a two-step cognitive process. *Dev. Rev.*, 4, 77–111.

Simonton, D. K. 1984c. Generational time-series analysis: A paradigm for studying socio-cultural influences. In K. Gergen & M. Gergen, eds., *Historical social psychology*, 141–55. Hillsdale, NJ: Erlbaum.

Simonton, D. K. 1984d. *Genius, creativity, and leadership*. Cambridge, MA.: Harvard University Press.

Simonton, D. K. 1984e. Is the marginality effect all that marginal? *Soc. Stud. Sci.*, *14*, 621–22.

Simonton, D. K. 1984f. Leader age and national condition: A longitudinal analysis of 25 European monarchs. *Soc. Behav. Pers.*, *12*, 111–14.

Simonton, D. K. 1984g. Leaders as eponyms: Individual and situational determinants of monarchal eminence. *J. Pers.*, *52*, 1–21.

Simonton, D. K. 1984h. Melodic structure and note transition probabilities: A content analysis of 15,618 classical themes. *Psychol. Music*, *12*, 3–16.

Simonton, D. K. 1984i. Scientific eminence historical and contemporary: A measurement assessment. *Scientometrics*, *6*, 169–82.

Simonton, D. K. 1985a. Intelligence and personal influence in groups: Four nonlinear models. *Psychol. Rev.*, *92*, 532–47.

Simonton, D. K. 1985b. Quality, quantity, and age: The careers of 10 distinguished psychologists. *Internat. J. Aging Human Dev.*, *21*, 241–54.

Simonton, D. K. 1985c. The vice-presidential succession effect: Individual or situational basis? *Polit. Behav.*, *7*, 79–99.

Simonton, D. K. 1986a. Aesthetic success in classical music: A computer analysis of 1935 compositions. *Emp. Stud. Arts*, *4*, 1–17.

Simonton, D. K. 1986b. Biographical typicality, eminence, and achievement style. *J. Creat. Behav.*, *20*, 14–22.

Simonton, D. K. 1986c. Dispositional attributions of (presidential) leadership: An experimental simulation of historiometric results. *J. Exp. Soc. Psychol.*, *22*, 389–418.

Simonton, D. K. 1986d. Multiple discovery: Some Monte Carlo simulations and Gedanken experiments. *Scientometrics*, *9*, 269–80.

Simonton, D. K. 1986e. Multiples, Poisson distributions, and chance: An analysis of the Brannigan–Wanner model. *Scientometrics*, *9*, 127–37.

Simonton, D. K. 1986f. Popularity, content, and context in 37 Shakespeare plays. *Poetics*, *15*, 493–510.

Simonton, D. K. 1986g. Presidential greatness: The historical consensus and its psychological significance. *Polit. Psychol.*, *7*, 259–83.

Simonton, D. K. 1986h. Presidential personality: Biographical use of the Gough Adjective Check List. *J. Pers. Soc. Psychol.*, *51*, 149–60.

Simonton, D. K. 1986i. Stochastic models of multiple discovery. *Czech. J. Physics*, *B 36*, 138–41.

Simonton, D. K. 1987a. Musical aesthetics and creativity in Beethoven: A computer analysis of 105 compositions. *Emp. Stud. Arts*, *5*, 87–104.

Simonton, D. K. 1987b. Developmental antecedents of achieved eminence. *Ann. Child Dev.*, *5*, 131–69.

Simonton, D. K. 1987c. Multiples, chance, genius, creativity, and zeitgeist. In D. N. Jackson & J. P. Rushton, eds., *Scientific excellence*, 98–128. Beverly Hills, CA: Sage.

Simonton, D. K. 1987d. Presidential inflexibility and veto behavior: Two individual-situational interactions. *J. Pers.*, *55*, 1–18.

Simonton, D. K. 1987e. *Why presidents succeed*. New Haven, CT: Yale University Press.

Simonton, D. K. 1988a. Aesthetic success in 36 Hungarian and American short stories: An American–Hungarian cross cultural study. In C. Martindale, ed., *Psychological approaches to the study of literary narrative*, 66–73. Hamburg: Buske.

Simonton, D. K. 1988b. Age and outstanding achievement: What do we know after a century of research? *Psychol. Bull.*, *104*, 251–67.

Simonton, D. K. 1988c. Galtonian genius, Kroeberian configurations, and emulation: A generational time-series analysis of Chinese civilization. *J. Pers. Soc. Psychol.*, *55*, 230–38.

Simonton, D. K. 1988d. Presidential style: Personality, biography, and performance. *J. Pers. Soc. Psychol.*, *55*, 928–36.

Simonton, D. K. 1988e. *Scientific genius*. Cambridge, England: Cambridge University Press.

Simonton, D. K. 1989a. Age and creative productivity: Nonlinear estimation of an information-processing model. *Internat. J. Aging Human Dev.*, 1989, *29*, 23–37.

Simonton, D. K. 1989b. Shakespeare's sonnets: A case of and for single-case historiometry. *J. Pers.*, *57*, 695–721.

Simonton, D. K. 1989c. The swan-song phenomenon: Last-works effects for 172 classical composers. *Psychol. Aging*, *4*, 42–47.

Simonton, D. K. 1990a. Creativity in the later years: Optimistic prospects for achievement. *Gerontologist*, *30*, 626–31.

Simonton, D. K. 1990b. Creativity and wisdom in aging. In J. E. Birren & K. W. Schaie, eds., *Handbook of the psychology of aging*, 3rd ed., 320–29. New York: Academic Press.

Simonton, D. K. 1990c. Lexical choices and aesthetic success: A computer content analysis of 154 Shakespeare sonnets. *Comput. Humanit.*, *24*, 251–64.

Simonton, D. K. 1990d. Political pathology and societal creativity. *Creat. Res. J.*, *3*, 85–99.

Simonton, D. K. 1990e. *Psychology, science, and history*. New Haven, CT: Yale University Press.

Simonton, D. K. 1991a. Career landmarks in science: Individual differences and interdisciplinary contrasts. *Dev. Psychol.*, *27*, 119–30.

Simonton, D. K. 1991b. Emergence and realization of genius: The lives and works of 120 classical composers. *J. Pers. Soc. Psychol.*, *61*, 829–40.

Simonton, D. K. 1991c. Genes and genius from Galton to Freud. *Behav. Brain Sci.*, *14*, 406–7.

Simonton, D. K. 1991d. Latent-variable models of posthumous reputation: A quest for Galton's *G*. *J. Pers. Soc. Psychol.*, *60*, 607–19.

Simonton, D. K. 1991e. Personality correlates of exceptional personal influence: A note on Thorndike's (1950) creators and leaders. *Creat. Res. J.*, *4*, 67–78.

Simonton, D. K. 1991f. Predicting presidential greatness: An alternative to the Kenney and Rice Contextual Index. *Presid. Stud. Q.*, *21*, 301–5.

Simonton, D. K. 1992a. Gender and genius in Japan: Feminine eminence in masculine culture. *Sex Roles*, *27*, 101–19.

Simonton, D. K. 1992b. Leaders of American psychology, 1879–1967: Career development, creative output, and professional achievement. *J. Pers. Soc. Psychol.*, *62*, 5–17.

Simonton, D. K. 1992c. The social context of career success and course for 2,026 scientists and inventors. *Pers. Soc. Psychol. Bull.*, *18*, 452–63.

Simonton, D. K. 1993a. Foresight in insight? A Darwinian answer. In R. J. Sternberg & J. E. Davidson, eds., *The nature of insight*. Cambridge, MA: MIT Press.

Simonton, D. K. 1993b. Genius and chance: A Darwinian perspective. In J. Brockman, ed., *Creativity*, 176–201. New York: Simon & Schuster.

Simonton, D. K. 1993c. *Presidents' wives and first ladies: Woman behind the man? Or reflected glory?* Unpublished manuscript.

Singer, J. D. 1981. Accounting for international war: The state of the discipline. *J. Peace Res.*, *18*, 1–18.

Sipes, R. G. 1973. War, sports and aggression: An empirical test of two rival theories. *Amer. Anthropol.*, *75*, 64–86.

Skinner, B. F. 1959. A case study in scientific method. In S. Koch, ed., *Psychology*, vol. 2, 359–79. New York: McGraw-Hill.

Skinner, B. F. 1972. *Cumulative record*, 3rd ed. New York: Appleton-Century-Crofts.

Skipper, J. K., Jr., & McCaghy, C. H. 1970. Strip-teasers: The anatomy and career contingencies of a deviant occupation. *Soc. Prob.*, *17*, 391–405.

Slater, E., & Meyer, A. 1959. Contributions to a pathography of the musician: 1. Robert Schumann. *Confinia. Psychiatrica*, *2*, 65–94.

Smart, J. C., & Bayer, A. E. 1986. Author collaboration and impact: A note on citation rates of single and multiple authored articles. *Scientometrics*, *10*, 297–305.

Snow, C. P. 1960. *The two cultures and the scientific revolution*. New York: Cambridge University Press.

Snow, C. P. 1969. Foreword. In G. H. Hardy, *A mathematician's apology*, 9–58. Cambridge, England: Cambridge University Press.

Sokolsky, E. 1964. *Our seven greatest presidents*. New York: Exposition Press.

Sorokin, P. A. 1925. Monarchs and rulers: A comparative statistical study. I. *Soc. Forces, 4*, 22–35.

Sorokin, P. A. 1926. Monarchs and rulers: A comparative statistical study. II. *Soc. Forces*, *4*, 523–33.

Sorokin, P. A. 1937–41. *Social and cultural dynamics*, 4 vols. New York: American Book.

Sorokin, P. A. 1947. *Society, culture, and personality*. New York: Cooper Square, 1969.

Sorokin, P. A. 1963. *A long journey*. New Haven, CT: College and University Press.

Sorokin, P. A., & Merton, R. K. 1935. The course of Arabian intellectual development, 700–1300 A.D. *Isis*, *22*, 516–24.

Spangler, W. D., & House, R. J. 1991. Presidential effectiveness and the leadership motive profile. *J. Pers. Soc. Psychol.*, *60*, 439–55.

Spellman, B. A., & Holyoak, K. J. 1992. If Saddam is Hitler then who is George Bush? Analogical mapping between systems of social roles. *J. Pers. Soc. Psychol.*, *62*, 913–33.

Spilka, B., Lacey, G., & Gelb, G. 1979–80. Sex discrimination after death: A replication, extension and a difference. *Omega*, *10*, 227–33.

Springer, S. P., & Deutsch, G. 1989. *Left brain, right brain*, 3rd ed. San Francisco: W. H. Freeman.

Sproul, K., ed. 1953. *The shorter Bartlett's familiar quotations*. Garden City, NY: Permabooks.

Stack, S. 1987a. Celebrities and suicide: A taxonomy and analysis, 1948–1983. *Amer. Sociol. Rev.*, *52*, 401–12.

Stack, S. 1987b. Publicized executions and homicide, 1950–1980. *Amer. Sociol. Rev.*, *52*, 532–40.

Stagner, R. 1988. *A history of psychological theories*. New York: Macmillan.

Stannard, D. E. 1980. *Shrinking history*. New York: Oxford University Press.

Stein, E., & Lipton, P. 1989. Where guesses come from: Evolutionary epistemology and the anomaly of guided vision. *Biol. Phil.*, *4*, 33–56.

Stent, G. S. 1972. Prematurity and uniqueness in scientific discovery. *Scient. Amer.*, *227*, 84–93.

Stern, N. 1978. Age and achievement in mathematics: A case-study in the sociology of science. *Soc. Stud. Sci.*, *8*, 127–40.

Sternberg, R. J. 1985. *Beyond IQ*. New York: Cambridge University Press.

Sternberg, R. J., & Lubart, T. I. 1991. An investment theory of creativity and its development. *Human Dev.*, *34*, 1–31.

Stewart, J. A. 1986. Drifting continents and colliding interests: A quantitative application of the interests perspective. *Soc. Stud. Sci.*, *16*, 261–79.

Stewart, L. H. 1977. Birth order and political leadership. In M. G. Hermann, ed., *The psychological examination of political leaders*, 205–36. New York: Free Press.

Stewart, L. H. 1991. The world cycle of leadership. *J. Analyt. Psychol.*, *36*, 449–59.

Stewart, N. 1947. AGCT scores of Army personnel grouped by occupations. *Occupations*, *26*, 5–41.

Stimson, J. A. 1976. Public support for American presidents: A cyclical model. *Publ. Opin. Q.*, *40*, 1–21.

Stoll, R. J. 1984. The guns of November: Presidential reelections and the use of force, 1947–1982. *J. Confl. Resolut.*, *28*, 231–46.

Stolzenberg, R. M. 1975. Occupations, labor markets, and the process of wage attainment. *Amer. Sociol. Rev.*, *40*, 645–65.

Stone, W. J., & Abramowitz, A. I. 1980. Winning may not be everything, but it's more than we thought: Presidential party activists in 1980. *Amer. Polit. Sci. Rev.*, *77*, 946–56.

Storfer, M. D. 1990. *Intelligence and giftedness*. San Francisco: Jossey-Bass.

Strouse, J. 1988. Alice James: A family romance. In W. M. Runyan, ed., *Psychology and historical interpretation*, 86–103. New York: Oxford University Press.

Suedfeld, P. 1980. Indices of world tension in the *Bulletin of the Atomic Scientists*. *Polit. Psychol.*, *2*, 114–23.

Suedfeld, P. 1985. APA presidential addresses: The relation of integrative complexity to historical, professional, and personal factors. *J. Pers. Soc. Psychol.*, *47*, 848–52.

Suedfeld, P. 1992. Bilateral relations between countries and the complexity of newspaper editorials. *Polit. Psychol.*, *13*, 601–11.

Suedfeld, P., & Bluck, S. 1988. Changes in integrative complexity prior to surprise attacks. *J. Confl. Resolut.*, *32*, 626–35.

Suedfeld, P., Bluck, S., Ballard, E. J., & Baker-Brown, G. 1990. Canadian federal elections: Motive profiles and integrative complexity in political speeches and popular media. *Canad. J. Behav. Sci.*, *22*, 26–36.

Suedfeld, P., Corteen, R. S., & McCormick, C. 1986. The role of integrative complexity in military leadership: Robert E. Lee and his opponents. *J. Appl. Soc. Psychol.*, *16*, 498–507.

Suedfeld, P., & Piedrahita, L. E. 1984. Intimations of mortality: Integrative simplification as a predictor of death. *J. Pers. Soc. Psychol.*, *47*, 848–52.

Suedfeld, P., & Rank, A. D. 1976. Revolutionary leaders: Long-term success as a function of changes in conceptual complexity. *J. Pers. Soc. Psychol.*, *34*, 169–78.

Suedfeld, P., & Tetlock, P. 1977. Integrative complexity of communications in international crises. *J. Confl. Resolut.*, *21*, 169–84.

Suedfeld, P., Tetlock, P. E., & Ramirez, C. 1977. War, peace, and integrative complexity. *J. Confl. Resolut.*, *21*, 427–42.

Suler, J. R. 1980. Primary process thinking and creativity. *Psychol. Bull.*, *88*, 144–65.

Sulloway, F. J. 1990. *Orthodoxy and innovation in science: The role of the family*. Unpublished manuscript, Harvard University.

Suls, J., & Fletcher, B. 1983. Social comparison in the social and physical sciences: An archival study. *J. Pers. Soc. Psychol.*, *44*, 575–80.

Sweeney, P. D., & Gruber, K. L. 1984. Selective exposure: Voter information preference and the Watergate affair. *J. Pers. Soc. Psychol.*, *46*, 1208–21.

Synodinos, N. E. 1986. Hindsight distortion: "I knew-it-all along and I was sure about it." *J. Appl. Soc. Psychol.*, *16*, 107–17.

Taylor, D. W. 1963. Variables related to creativity and productivity among men in two research laboratories. In C. W. Taylor & F. X. Barron, eds., *Scientific creativity*, 228–50. New York: Wiley.

Taylor, C. W., & Ellison, R. L. 1967. Biographical predictors of scientific performance. *Science*, *155*, 1075–80.

Taylor, C. W., Smith, W. R., & Ghiselin, B. 1963. The creative and other contributions of one sample of research scientists. In C. W. Taylor & F. X. Barron, eds., *Scientific creativity*, 53–76. New York: Wiley.

Taylor, M. S., Locke, E. A., Lee, C., & Gist, M. E. 1984. Type A behavior and faculty research productivity: What are the mechanisms? *Organ. Behav. Human Perform.*, *34*, 402–18.

Taylor, T. 1972. *The book of presidents*. New York: Arno Press.

Terman, L. M. 1917. The intelligence quotient of Francis Galton in childhood. *Amer. J. Psychol.*, *28*, 209–15.

Terman, L. M. 1925. *Genetic studies of genius: Vol. 1. Mental and physical traits of a thousand gifted children*. Stanford, CA: Stanford University Press.

Terman, L. M., & Oden, M. H. 1947. *Genetic studies of genius: Vol. 4. The gifted child grows up: Twenty-five years' follow-up of a superior group*. Stanford, CA: Stanford University Press.

Terman, L. M., & Oden, M. H. 1959. *Genetic studies of genius: Vol. 5. The gifted group at mid-life: Thirty-five years' follow-up of the superior child*. Stanford, CA: Stanford University Press.

Terry, W. S. 1989. Birth order and prominence in the history of psychology. *Psychol. Rec.*, *39*, 333–37.

Tetlock, P. E. 1979. Identifying victims of groupthink from public statements of decision makers. *J. Pers. Soc. Psychol.*, *37*, 1314–24.

Tetlock, P. E. 1981a. Personality and isolationism: Content analysis of senatorial speeches. *J. Pers. Soc. Psychol.*, *41*, 737–43.

Tetlock, P. E. 1981b. Pre- to postelection shifts in presidential rhetoric: Impression management or cognitive adjustment. *J. Pers. Soc. Psychol.*, *41*, 207–12.

Tetlock, P. E. 1983. Cognitive style and political ideology. *J. Pers. Soc. Psychol.*, *45*, 118–26.

Tetlock, P. E. 1984. Cognitive style and political belief systems in the British House of Commons. *J. Pers. Soc. Psychol.*, *46*, 365–75.

Tetlock, P. E. 1985. Integrative complexity of American and Soviet foreign policy rhetoric: A time-series analysis. *J. Pers. Soc. Psychol.*, *49*, 1565–85.

Tetlock, P. E., Bernzweig, J., & Gallant, J. L. 1985. Supreme Court decision making: Cognitive style as a predictor of ideological consistency of voting. *J. Pers. Soc. Psychol.*, *48*, 1227–39.

Tetlock, P. E., & Boettger, R. 1989. Cognitive and rhetorical styles of traditionalist and reformist Soviet politicians: A content analysis study. *Polit. Psychol.*, *10*, 209–32.

Tetlock, P. E., Hannum, K. A., & Micheletti, P. M. 1984. Stability and change in the complexity of senatorial debate: Testing the cognitive versus rhetorical style hypothesis. *J. Pers. Soc. Psychol.*, *46*, 979–90.

Tetlock, P. E., Peterson, R. S., McGuire, C., Chang, S., & Feld, P. 1992. Assessing political group dynamics: A test of the groupthink model. *J. Pers. Soc. Psychol.*, *63*, 403–25.

t'Hart, P. 1991. Irving L. Janis' victims of groupthink. *Polit. Psychol.*, *12*, 247–79.

Thigpen, C. H., & Cleckley, H. M. 1957. *The three faces of Eve*. New York: McGraw-Hill.

Thistlethwaite, D. L. 1963. The college environment as a determinant of research potentiality. In C. W. Taylor & F. X. Barron, eds., *Scientific creativity*, 265–78. New York: Wiley.

Thompson, C. P., & Cowan, T. 1986. Flashbulb memories: A nicer recollection of a Neisser recollection. *Cognition*, *22*, 199–200.

Thompson, J. L. P. 1989. Deprivation and political violence in Northern Ireland, 1922–1985. *J. Confl. Resolut.*, *33*, 676–99.

Thompson, W. F., & Robitaille, B. 1992. Can composers express emotions through music. *Emp. Stud. Arts*, *10*, 79–80.

Thoreau, H. D. 1854. *Walden*, G. H. Haight, ed. New York: Black, 1942.

Thorndike, E. L. 1936. The relation between intellect and morality in rulers. *Amer. J. Sociol.*, *42*, 321–34.

Thorndike, E. L. 1950. Traits of personality and their intercorrelations as shown in biography. *J. Educ. Psychol.*, *41*, 193–216.

Thucydides. circa 400 B.C. The history of the Peloponnesian war, R. Crawley, trans. In R. M. Hutchins, ed., *Great books of the Western world*, vol. 6, 347–593. Chicago: Encyclopedia Britannica, 1952.

Tolstoy, L. 1865–69. *War and peace*, L. Maude & A. Maude, trans. In R. M. Hutchins, ed., *Great books of the Western world*, vol. 51. Chicago: Encyclopedia Britannica, 1952.

Tomlinson-Keasey, C. 1990. The working lives of Terman's gifted women. In H. Y. Grossman & N. L. Chester, eds., *The experience and meaning of work in women's lives*, 213–39. Hillsdale, NJ: Erlbaum.

Tomlinson-Keasey, C., & Little, T. D. 1990. Predicting educational attainment, occupational achievement, intellectual skill, and personal adjustment among gifted men and women. *J. Educ. Psychol.*, *82*, 442–55.

Tomlinson-Keasey, C., Warren, L. W., & Elliott, J. E. 1986. Suicide among gifted women: A prospective study. *J. Abnorm. Psychol.*, *95*, 123–30.

Torrance, E. P. 1962. *Guiding creative talent*. Englewood Cliffs, NJ: Prentice-Hall.

Toynbee, A. J. 1946. *A study of history*, abridged by D. C. Somervell, 2 vols. New York: Oxford University Press.

Travis, C. B., & Yeager, C. P. 1991. Sexual selection, parental investment, and sexism. *J. Soc. Issues*, *47*, 117–29.

Triplet, N. 1898. The dynamogenic factors in pacemaking and competition. *Amer. J. Psychol.*, *9*, 507–33.

Tufte, E. R. 1978. *Political control of the economy*. Princeton, NJ: Princeton University Press.

Turner, S. P., & Chubin, D. E. 1976. Another appraisal of Ortega, the Coles, and science policy: The Ecclesiastes hypothesis. *Soc. Sci. Inform.*, *15*, 657–62.

Turner, S. P., & Chubin, D. E. 1979. Chance and eminence in science: Ecclesiastes II. *Soc. Sci. Inform.*, *18*, 437–49.

Turpin, W. H. 1988. Development of expert system applications using Personal Consultant™. In A. Gupta & B. E. Prasad, eds., *Microcomputer-based expert systems*, 285–89. New York: Institute of Electrical and Electronics Engineers.

Tweney, R. D. 1990. Five questions for computationalists. In J. Shrager & P. Langley, eds., *Computational models of scientific discovery and theory information*, 471–84. San Mateo, CA: Kaufmann.

Uhrbrock, S. R. 1973. Laterality in art. *J. Aesthet. Art Crit.*, *32*, 27–35.

Vaillant, G. E., & Vaillant, C. O. 1980. Determinants and consequences of creativity in a cohort of gifted women. *Psychol. Women Q.*, *14*, 607–16.

Vallone, R. P., Ross, L., & Lepper, M. R. 1985. The hostile media phenomenon: Biased perception and perceptions of media bias in coverage of the Beirut massacre. *J. Pers. Soc. Psychol.*, *49*, 577–85.

Van Lange, P. A. M. 1991. Being better but not smarter than others: The Muhammad Ali effect at work in interpersonal situations. *Pers. Soc. Psychol. Bull.*, *17*, 689–93.

Veblen, T. 1919. The intellectual preeminence of Jews in modern Europe. *Polit. Sci. Q.*, *34*, 33–42.

Veitch, R., DeWood, R., & Bosko, K. 1977. Radio news broadcasts: Their effects on interpersonal helping. *Sociometry*, *50*, 383–86.

Veitch, R., & Griffitt, W. 1976. Good news—bad news: Affective and interpersonal effects. *J. Appl. Soc. Psychol.*, *6*, 69–75.

Verplanken, B. 1989. Beliefs, attitudes, and intensions toward nuclear energy before and after Chernobyl in a longitudinal within-subjects design. *Environ. Behav.*, *21*, 371–92.

Visher, S. S. 1947. Starred scientists: A study of their ages. *Amer. Scient.*, *35*, 543, 570, 572, 574, 576, 578, 580.

Von Lang, J., & Sibyll, C., eds. 1983. *Eichmann interrogated*, R. Mannheim, trans. New York: Farrar, Straus & Giroux.

Wagner, M. E., & Schubert, H. J. P. 1977. Sibship variables and United States presidents. *J. Indiv. Psychol.*, *33*, 78–85.

Waite, R. G. L. 1990. Leadership pathologies: The Kaiser and the Führer and the decisions for war in 1914 and 1939. In B. Glad, ed., *Psychological dimensions of war*, 143–68. Newbury Park, CA: Sage.

Walberg, H. J. 1988. Creativity and talent as learning. In R. Sternberg, ed., *The nature of creativity*, 340–61. New York: Cambridge University Press.

Walberg, H. J., Rasher, S. P., & Parkerson, J. 1980. Childhood and eminence. *J. Creat. Behav.*, *13*, 225–31.

Waldrop, M. M. 1989. Humanity 2, computers 0. *Science*, *246*, 572–73.

Wallace, D. B., & Gruber, H. E., eds. 1989. *Creative people at work*. New York: Oxford University Press.

Wallace, M. D., & Suedfeld, P. 1988. Leadership performance in crisis: The longevity–complexity link. *Internat. Stud. Q.*, *32*, 439–51.

Wallach, M. A., & Kogan, N. 1965. *Modes of thinking in young children*. New York: Holt, Rinehart & Winston.

Wallas, G. 1926. *The art of thought*. New York: Harcourt, Brace.

Waller, N. G., Bouchard, T. J., Jr., Lykken, D. T., Tellegen, A., & Blacker, D. M. 1993. Creativity, heritability, familiality: Which word does not belong? *Psychol. Inquiry*, *1*, 235–37.

Waller, N. G., Kojetin, B. A., Bouchard, T. J., Jr., Lykken, D. T., & Tellegen, A. 1990. Genetic and environmental influences on religious interests, attitudes, and values: A study of twins reared apart and together. *Psychol. Sci.*, *1*, 138–42.

Walters, J., & Gardner, H. 1986. The crystallizing experience: Discovering an intellectual gift. In R. J. Sternberg & J. E. Davidson, eds., *Conceptions of giftedness*, 306–31. New York: Cambridge University Press.

Ward, C. H., & Eisler, R. M. 1987. Type A behavior, achievement striving, and a dysfunctional self-evaluation system. *J. Pers. Soc. Psychol.*, *53*, 318–26.

Warren Commission. 1964. *Report of the President's Commission on the Assassination of President John F. Kennedy*. Washington, DC: U.S. Government Printing Office.

Wasserman, I. M. 1983. Political business cycles, presidential elections and suicide and mortality patterns. *Amer. Sociol. Rev.*, *48*, 711–20.

Wasserman, I. M. 1984. Imitation and suicide: A reexamination of the Werther effect. *Amer. Sociol. Rev.*, *49*, 427–36.

Watson, R. I., Jr. 1973. Investigation into deindividuation using a cross-cultural survey technique. *J. Pers. Soc. Psychol.*, *25*, 342–45.

Weber, P. J. 1984. The birth order oddity in Supreme Court appointments. *Presid. Stud. Q.*, *14*, 561–68.

Weinstein, E. A. 1981. *Woodrow Wilson*. Princeton, NJ: Princeton University Press.

Weinstein, E. A., Anderson, J., & Link, A. 1978. Woodrow Wilson's political personality: A reappraisal. *Polit. Sci. Q.*, *93*, 585–98.

Weisberg, R. W. 1992. *Creativity*. New York: Freeman.

Weizmann, F., Wiener, N. I., Wiesenthal, D. L., & Ziegler, M. 1990. Differential *K* theory and racial hierarchies. *Canad. Psychol.*, *31*, 1–13.

Wendt, H. W., & Light, P. C. 1976. Measuring "greatness" in American presidents: Model case for international research on political leadership? *Eur. J. Soc. Psychol.*, *6*, 105–9.

Wendt, H. W., & Muncy, C. A. 1979. Studies of political character: Factor patterns of 24 U.S. vice-presidents. *J. Psychol.*, *102*, 125–31.

Wertheimer, M. 1945. *Productive thinking*, M. Wertheimer, ed. Chicago: University of Chicago Press, 1982.

West, D. M. 1984. Cheers and jeers: Candidate presentations and audience reactions in the 1980 presidential campaign. *Amer. Polit. Q.*, *12*, 23–50.

West, S. S. 1960. Sibling configurations of scientists. *Amer. J. Sociol.*, *66*, 268–74.

West, S. S. 1961. Class origin of scientists. *Sociometry*, *24*, 251–69.

Whaples, R. 1991. A quantitative history of the *Journal of Economic History* and the cliometric revolution. *J. Econ. Hist.*, *51*, 289–301.

White, L. 1949. *The science of culture*. New York: Farrar, Straus.

White, R. K. 1931. The versatility of genius. *J. Soc. Psychol.*, *2*, 460–89.

White, R. K. 1968. *Nobody wanted war*. Garden City, NY: Doubleday.

White, R. K. 1969. Three not-so-obvious contributions of psychology to peace. *J. Soc. Issues*, *25*(4), 23–39.

White, R. K. 1977. Misperception in the Arab–Israeli conflict. *J. Soc. Issues*, *33*(1), 190–221.

Whitehead, A. N. 1929. *Process and reality*, D. R. Griffin & D. W. Sherburne, eds. New York: Free Press, 1978.

Whiting, B., & Edwards, C. P. A. 1973. Cross-cultural analysis of sex differences in the behavior of children aged three through 11. *J. Soc. Psychol.*, *91*, 171–88.

Whitman, W. 1855. Song of myself. In *The selected poems of Walt Whitman*, 25–110. Roslyn, NY: Black, 1942.

Who said what when. 1991. New York: Hippocrene Books.

Wiener, N. 1953. *Ex-prodigy: My childhood and youth.* New York: Simon & Schuster.

Williams, C. D. 1963. Authoritarianism and student reaction to airplane hijacking. *J. Soc. Psychol., 60,* 289–91.

Winkler, J. D., & Taylor, S. E. 1979. Preference, expectations, and attributional bias: Two field studies. *J. Appl. Soc. Psychol., 9,* 183–97.

Winograd, E., & Killinger, W. A. 1983. Relating age at encoding in early childhood to adult recall: Development of flashbulb memories. *J. Exp. Psychol.: Gen., 112,* 413–22.

Winter, D. G. 1973. *The power motive.* New York: Free Press.

Winter, D. G. 1980. An exploratory study of the motives of southern African political leaders measured at a distance. *Polit. Psychol., 2,* 75–85.

Winter, D. G. 1982. Motivation and performance in presidential candidates. In A. J. Stewart, ed., *Motivation and society,* 244–73. San Francisco: Jossey-Bass.

Winter, D. G. 1987a. Enhancement of an enemy's power motivation as a dynamic of conflict escalation. *J. Pers. Soc. Psychol., 52,* 41–46.

Winter, D. G. 1987b. Leader appeal, leader performance, and the motive profiles of leaders and followers: A study of American presidents and elections. *J. Pers. Soc. Psychol., 52,* 196–202.

Winter, D. G. 1988a. The power motive in women—and men. *J. Pers. Soc. Psychol., 54,* 510–19.

Winter, D. G. 1988b, July–August. What makes Jesse run? *Psychol. Today, 20,* 22, 24.

Winter, D. G., & Carlson, D. G. 1988. Using motive scores in the psychobiographical study of an individual: The case of Richard Nixon. *J. Pers., 56,* 75–103.

Winter, D. G., Hermann, M. G., Weintraub, W., & Walker, S. G. 1991a. The personalities of Bush and Gorbachev at a distance: Procedures, portraits, and policies. *Polit. Psychol., 12,* 215–45.

Winter, D. G., Hermann, M. G., Weintraub, W., & Walker, S. G. 1991b. The personalities of Bush and Gorbachev at a distance: Follow-up on predictions. *Polit. Psychol., 12,* 457–64.

Winter, D. G., & Stewart, A. S. 1977. Content analysis as a technique for assessing political leaders. In M. G. Hermann, ed., *The psychological examination of political leaders,* 27–61. New York: Free Press.

Wispé, L. G. 1965. Some social and psychological correlates of eminence in psychology. *J. Hist. Behav. Sci., 7,* 88–98.

Witty, P. A., & Jenkins, M. D. 1935. The case of "B," a gifted Negro girl. *J. Soc. Psychol., 6,* 117–24.

Woods, F. A. 1906. *Mental and moral heredity in royalty.* New York: Holt.

Woods, F. A. 1909. A new name for a new science. *Science, 30,* 703–4.

Woods, F. A. 1911. Historiometry as an exact science. *Science, 33,* 568–74.

Woods, F. A. 1913. *The influence of monarchs.* New York: Macmillan.

Woodward, W. R. 1974. Scientific genius and loss of a parent. *Sci. Stud., 4,* 265–77.

Woody, E., & Claridge, G. 1977. Psychoticism and thinking. *Brit. J. Soc. Clin. Psychol., 16,* 241–48.

Woolf, V. 1929. *A room of one's own.* New York: Harcourt, Brace & World.

Wordsworth, W. 1807. My heart leaps up. In T. Hutchinson, ed., *The poetical works of Wordsworth*, 79. London: Oxford University Press, 1928.

Wrightsman, L. S. 1969. Wallace supporters and adherence to "law and order." *J. Pers. Soc. Psychol.*, *13*, 17–22.

Yarmey, A. D., & Bull, M. P., III. 1978. Where were you when President Kennedy was assassinated? *Bull. Psychonom. Soc.*, *11*, 133–35.

Young, E. 1725–28. Love of fame: The universal passion. In J. Nichols, ed., *The complete works: Poetry and prose*, vol. 1, 344–409. London: Tegg, 1854.

Youngblood, J. E. 1958. Style as information. *J. Music Theory*, *2*, 24–35.

Zajonc, R. B. 1986. The decline and rise of Scholastic Aptitude Test scores: A prediction derived from the confluence model. *Amer. Psychol.*, *41*, 862–67.

Zeidenstein, H. G. 1985. Presidents' popularity and their wins and losses on major issues in Congress: Does one have greater influence over the other? *Presid. Stud. Q.*, *15*, 287–300.

Zhao, H. 1984. An intelligence constant of scientific work. *Scientometrics*, *6*, 9–17.

Zhao, H., & Jiang, G. 1986. Life-span and precocity of scientists. *Scientometrics*, *9*, 27–36.

Zuckerman, H. 1977. *Scientific elite*. New York: Free Press.

Zuckerman, M. 1990. Some dubious premises in research and theory on racial differences: Scientific, social, and ethical issues. *Amer. Psychol.*, *45*, 1297–1303.

Zullow, H. M., Oettingen, G., Peterson, C., & Seligman, M. E. P. 1988. Pessimistic explanatory style in the historical record: CAVing LBJ, presidential candidates, and East versus West Berlin. *Amer. Psychol.*, *43*, 673–82.

Zullow, H. M., & Seligman, M. E. P. 1990. Pessimistic rumination predicts defeat of presidential candidates, 1900 to 1984. *Psychol. Inquiry*, *1*, 52–61.

Zusne, L. 1976. Age and achievement in psychology: The harmonic mean as a model. *Amer. Psychol.*, *31*, 805–7.

Zusne, L. 1986–87. Some factors affecting the birthday–deathday phenomenon. *Omega*, *17*, 9–26.

Zweigenhaft, R. L. 1975. Birth order, approval-seeking, and membership in Congress. *J. Indiv. Psychol.*, *31*, 205–10.

Subject Index